Writing Kit Carson

Writing Kit Carson

Fallen Heroes in a Changing West

Susan Lee Johnson

Published in

association with the

WILLIAM P. CLEMENTS CENTER

FOR SOUTHWEST STUDIES,

Southern Methodist University,

by the UNIVERSITY OF

NORTH CAROLINA PRESS

Chapel Hill

The publication of this book was supported in part by a generous gift from the Harry Reid Endowment for the History of the Intermountain West, College of Liberal Arts, University of Nevada, Las Vegas.

Designed by Richard Hendel
Set in Utopia and Antique No 6 types
by Tseng Information Systems, Inc.

Cover art: (foreground) Quantrille McClung and Donna Northrup at Rocky Mountain National Park, 1924, courtesy History Colorado—Denver; (background) *La Ciudad de Santa Fe*, by U.S. Army artist James William Abert, ca. 1846, courtesy of Wikimedia Commons. Artwork adapted by Robin Moore.

Library of Congress Cataloging-in-Publication Data
Names: Johnson, Susan Lee, author.
Title: Writing Kit Carson : fallen heroes in a changing West / Susan Lee Johnson.
Description: Chapel Hill : The University of North Carolina Press ; [Dallas, Tex.] : in association with the William P. Clements Center for Southwest Studies, Southern Methodist University, 2020. | Includes bibliographical references and index.
Identifiers: LCCN 2020022323 | ISBN 9781469658834 (cloth : alk. paper) | ISBN 9781469679310 (pbk. : alk. paper) | ISBN 9781469658841 (ebook)
Subjects: LCSH: Carson, Kit, 1809–1868—In literature. | McClung, Quantrille D., 1890– Carson-Bent-Boggs Genealogy. | Blackwelder, Bernice, Great westerner. | McClung, Quantrille D., 1890– | Blackwelder, Bernice. | Frontier and pioneer life—United States—Historiography. | Women authors, American—Biography.
Classification: LCC PS169.F7 J643 2020 | DDC 978/.02092 [B]—dc23
LC record available at https://lccn.loc.gov/2020022323

Portions of part 1 originally appeared as Susan Lee Johnson, "Writing Kit Carson in the Cold War: 'The Family,' 'the West,' and Their Chroniclers," in *On the Borders of Love and Power: Families and Kinship in the Intercultural American Southwest*, ed. David Wallace Adams and Crista DeLuzio (Berkeley: University of California Press, 2012), 278–318.

FOR HOWARD LAMAR

Contents

A section of illustrations begins on page 149

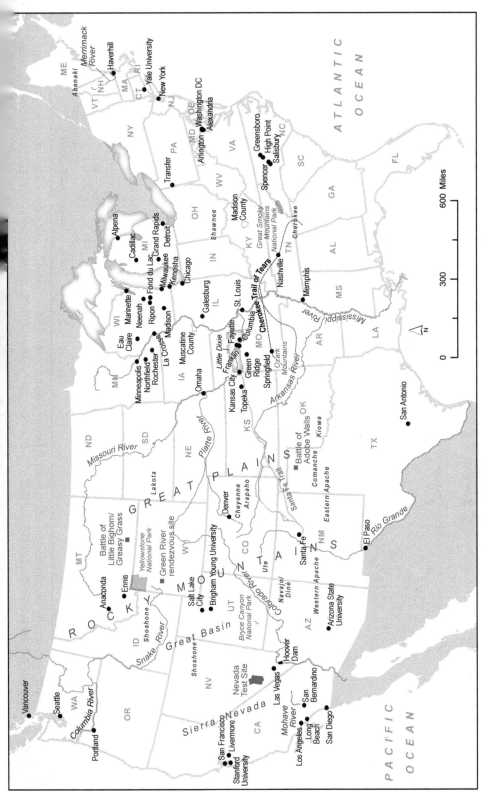

This wide-angle map references histories that spanned centuries. It locates places where twentieth-century historians Quantrille McClung and Bernice Fowler Blackwelder, as well as the subject of their work, nineteenth-century frontiersman Christopher "Kit" Carson, lived and died. Their lives or those of their forebears were caught up in the dispossession of American Indian peoples, so the map locates relevant Indigenous homelands as well. It also locates selected places in the life of the author. Courtesy of Cartography Lab, University of Wisconsin–Madison.

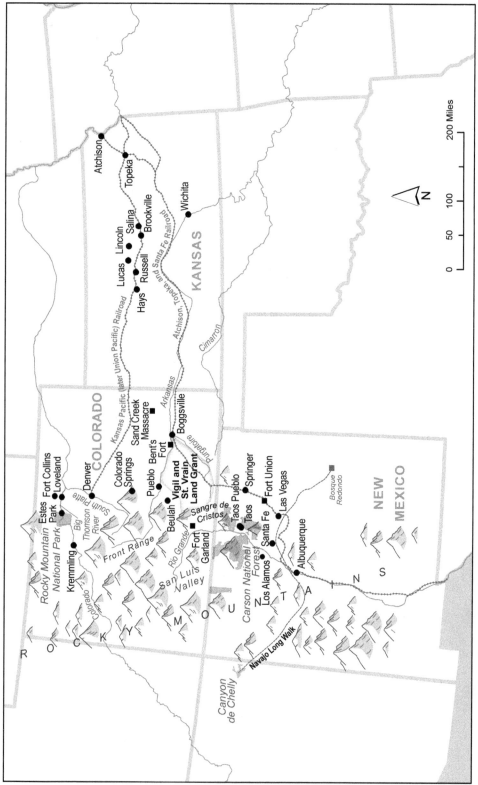

This close-up map also references histories that spanned centuries. It locates places in New Mexico, Colorado, and Kansas where the lives of historians Quantrille McClung and Bernice Fowler Blackwelder and that of frontiersman Christopher "Kit" Carson most overlapped. It also locates places central to the rethinking of Carson's legacy. Courtesy of Cartography Lab, University of Wisconsin–Madison.

Writing Kit Carson

Prologue

Grandmothers' Eyes

Curiosity is not trivial; it is the respect one life pays to another.

—JOAN NESTLE, "The Fem Question"

In Which We Meet

This is a book about two women I never met, although my life and theirs in this world overlapped in time and in space and in passion. I have met people who knew them, people who loved them. I have touched and turned, poked and pondered parts of their lives like pieces of a puzzle, a puzzle without a box for loose pieces, without borders when assembled. I have cruised their apartments and read their mail, considered their desires and visited their graves. I have stuck my nose in their business, from housekeeping habits to political predilections.

They were like me: white and Protestant in a world where race and religion mattered, though both mattered differently over time and across space. They were like me: captivated by the past, intrigued by the place we call the American West, drawn to the men who lived there. They were like me: working out ways to exist in relation to ideas about women and womanhood, men and manhood—ideas that often chafed. They were like me: dutiful and rebellious in turn.

They were not like me: in fact, they were more like my grandmothers, and poring over their lives helps me see the last century through my grandmothers' eyes. But they were not like my parents' mothers, either: they pushed past the domestic concerns that defined my grandmothers' lives, working for wages or for the love of it in libraries, radio stations, and government agencies. They were not like me: they were sure they were women; they did not think out loud about racial power and privilege; they lived intimate lives of discretion and quietude, making no issue of what my generation calls sexuality. They lived frugally, in urban apartments, and they studied history without advanced degrees and university affiliations, their dining tables often doubling as desks.

They were Quantrille McClung, a librarian and genealogist, and Bernice Fowler Blackwelder, first a singer on radio and the stage, then a CIA employee, and last a biographer who managed apartments. Few have heard of these women, and that matters. They both wrote history but did so in relative obscurity. Their work often centered on the famous frontiersman Christopher "Kit" Carson. In 1962, Blackwelder published *Great Westerner: The Story of Kit Carson*.[1] She spent the rest of her days trying to finish a biographical dictionary of westerners. McClung published the substantial *Carson-Bent-Boggs Genealogy* in 1962 and an even longer supplement a decade later.[2] McClung was born, lived, and died in Denver. She did not marry and she had no children. Blackwelder, born Bernice Fowler, hailed from small-town Kansas but lived much of her adult life in Chicago, with brief stints in other locales, including suburban Washington, D.C. She married singer Harold Blackwelder, a North Carolinian who once performed as Neil Fortune, Gentleman from the West, and who in later years sold southern barbecue and then filed traffic reports for Cook County. The Blackwelders did not have children. They died in Cadillac, Michigan, where they moved in old age to be near family. Quantrille McClung lived from 1890 to 1985. Twelve years younger than McClung, Bernice Fowler was born in 1902 and died as Bernice Blackwelder in 1986, eighteen months after McClung passed. Bernice outlived husband Harold by three years.

In order to make sense of Quantrille McClung's and Bernice Blackwelder's twentieth-century attachment to nineteenth-century western men like Kit Carson, this book braids lives together across generations and geographies. Mostly, it is a story of two white women, published but amateur historians, who made the life of a well-known western white man their own life's work. They published books about Carson in the early 1960s, when, in the context of the Cold War, men like him still seemed to most Americans the heroes of U.S. westward expansion, when popular culture still celebrated pioneers. They also published at a time when books about the West were as likely to be written by amateur as by academic historians, though most of the history buffs were white men, not women. They published just as the field of western history was professionalizing, so that shortly, academics would wrest control away from the amateurs. Blackwelder and McClung continued writing western history into the 1970s but under different conditions. Not only had the field professionalized, putting them at further disadvantage, but also, with the changes that social movements of the 1960s and '70s brought to politics and popular culture, western deities such as Carson were falling headlong from grace. Writing Carson across these tumultuous times brought McClung and Blackwelder together. It later drew me to them, too. Thus, another of the lives plaited into this book's tale is my own, including the part of it I lived with my late lover, who hailed from the western places Kit Carson came to call home and who died as I was finishing this book.

In telling the lives of Quantrille McClung and Bernice Blackwelder, in reflecting on how they identified and disidentified with people from the past, and in keeping my own identifications and disidentifications always in view, I fix on certain aspects of life stories more than others, paying attention to how people in those stories navigated realms of social and cultural power. For example, although they were both published authors, Blackwelder and McClung called themselves by names that shrunk their lives to gendered clichés: McClung referred to herself as an "old maid," while Blackwelder called herself a "housewife." "Old maid" and "housewife" masked loves and labors that lapped over those labels' limits; the terms were drops in buckets of life. In telling McClung's and Blackwelder's life stories, then, I hoist buckets into the air, refracting the light of history through hundreds of thousands of such drops, splashing opalescent arches across the page. Nonetheless, discerning patterns in rainbows and choosing which to highlight is a key challenge of life writing. That is among the reasons I focus on how these women practiced what I call a traffic in men. When McClung and Blackwelder set their sights on Carson, putting him at the center of their published work as well as the hundreds of letters they wrote to each another, they engaged in this practice. Men in general and Carson in particular became for them objects of barter and banter, valued objects that tied them together and linked them to a larger world of publishers, booksellers, librarians, readers, scholars, and history buffs.

A traffic in men is an imperfect, here barely conscious, there deeply ironic, and often doomed reversal of that more common and malign set of cultural practices called the "traffic in women," whereby actual women have been objects of exchange in social and cultural systems dominated by men.[3] A traffic in men, by contrast, is more symbolic than real. When women engage in it, it is best understood as a weapon of the weak, an often hidden transcript by which the disempowered ponder and manipulate and, on occasion, critique the powerful.[4] In some times and places and among some people, a traffic in men shades into a traffic in things male, whereby the female-bodied appropriate traits and trademarks of manhood, as those habits and styles have evolved historically and culturally. All such gender traffic is infused with power and desire, envy and artistry, longing and privilege, need and want, materiality and imagination. And just as different kinds of trade move along the same roads, so does a traffic in men and things male travel in tandem with racial negotiation, political deal-making, territorial swap, economic transaction, and the give-and-take of culture. I met Blackwelder and McClung along these crowded highways, where men and things male were objects of exchange and Carson was prized cargo.

I encountered these women but never actually set eyes on them, although I could have. When McClung died on the eve of Independence Day in 1985, I was about to drive across country from the West Coast to begin my doctoral program in the East, where I planned to study western and gender history. When Blackwelder died on Christmas Eve in 1986, I had finished my third semester of graduate school. But I had worked in western history for a while; already I had completed a master's degree at a western state university and published a scholarly article, and I attended my first Western History Association conference in 1979. So I could have crossed paths with Blackwelder and McClung. Other western historians knew them or knew of them, inside and outside the academy. No doubt I had seen the women's books on library shelves. Though born and raised in Wisconsin, I fell in love with the West when I first traveled there with my parents to visit my great-aunt in 1972. A couple of years later, I entered a Lutheran liberal arts college in my home state, took courses in American Indian and western history, and haunted the library stacks where materials on the West were shelved. There or elsewhere, I probably saw Blackwelder's name on the spine of a book, if not McClung's. Blackwelder had published her biography, *Great Westerner*, when I was six years old. McClung had published her original *Carson-Bent-Boggs Genealogy* the same year and its supplement when I was seventeen. Both of McClung's volumes graced library collections, though not as often as *Great Westerner*. In the 1970s and 1980s, these women and I swam in the same ocean on different shores.

If we overlapped in time, we also overlapped in space.[5] We lived together most clearly in a place that none of us could call home: the piñon-studded hills, cloud-mottled mountains, and sun-parched high plains of greater northern New Mexico, a region that spills north into southern Colorado and through which the Rio Grande runs south as life-giving artery—after a rain, a ribbon of bronze under an azure sky. We were each drawn there by research and travel and love in different measures. We were each outsiders to and guests in this place, which Indigenous and *hispano* peoples have called home for generations. We lived together in greater northern New Mexico through our mutual interest in the aforementioned historical figure: Kit Carson, himself an outsider who, like me, married an insider. We lived there together mostly in minds.

Blackwelder, McClung, and I lived together in other places, too. We crossed paths in Denver, McClung's lifelong home, one of Blackwelder's temporary residences, and, for me, the metropolis next door when I taught in Boulder, Colorado. My research for this book began in Denver. We nearly crossed paths in Michigan, where I also taught and where I returned years later to meet Blackwelder's living relatives. We crossed paths in Chicago, Blackwelder's home for decades and the nearest big city when I was growing up in Wisconsin and again when I moved back to my home state to teach after decades away. I did research in Chicago as well. And we crossed paths as travelers in any number of places, from Milwaukee to El Paso, from San Diego to New York. Ultimately, though, the space we most occupied together was the imagined space of the American West.

Time and space we shared, it is true, but nothing connected our lives so much as passion. It is with some trepidation that I acknowledge more directly than I already have the nature of that connection. But for Kit Carson, I would know nothing of Quantrille McClung and Bernice Black-welder. Blackwelder and McClung spent much of the later years of their lives researching and writing about Carson. I learned of the two women in the late 1990s as I embarked on what I thought would be my own Carson project. It was a project quite different from theirs, which were rooted in the concerns of the 1950s and '60s, but there were eerie parallels. And there was the passion itself.

Carson is a controversial historical figure, and one can say nothing about him without provoking various stakeholders in how the western past is represented: American Indian people and historians of American Indians, museum patrons and museum administrators, fur trade historians and mountain man reenactors, Carson kinfolk and the kin of his wives, military veterans and military historians, women and women's historians, *nuevomexicanos* and scholars of New Mexico's past, university-based historians and western history buffs, to name but a few (and these are overlapping categories, hardly mutually exclusive). Once celebrated by some as a hero, later denounced by others as a villain, and since the subject of waxing and waning debate among many, Carson was born in Kentucky in 1809 and raised among slaveholders in Missouri. In 1826, he followed the Santa Fe Trail to New Mexico and entered the western beaver pelt and buffalo hide trade during the era when the Southwest was still Mexico's northern frontier. His home base was often Taos. In the 1840s he served as guide for government expeditions into territory beyond the boundaries of the United States. In the 1850s and 1860s, after the U.S. conquest of the West, Carson served as an Indian agent for the federal government and as a military officer, fighting for the Union in the Civil War. When he died in 1868, he was superintendent for Indian affairs in Colorado Territory, having worked to negotiate a new treaty for the Utes. Carson is perhaps best known, especially among his detractors, as the soldier who helped to dispossess the Navajos by leading the military campaign in 1863–64 that sent them on a brutal forced march, known as the Long Walk, from their beloved Four Corners homeland to the bleak Bosque Redondo in eastern New Mexico. He is also known, though among far fewer, as a man who loved first a Northern Arapaho woman, then a Southern Cheyenne woman, and finally an *hispana* from Taos.

The nature of McClung's and Blackwelder's passion for Carson—for McClung, the exacting, patient passion of a genealogist and for Black-welder, the dramatic passion of a portraitist and storyteller—is at issue throughout this book and can only be explicated through an accumulation of incident and remark and context and reflection. Central to that passion, though, was their practice of trafficking in men and things male. Such traffic is, and long has been, common among female-bodied people, who have used it to engage and survive male supremacy and, less often, to challenge it; a traffic in men is not necessarily subversive. I see McClung and Blackwelder trafficking in men and things male in part because I do it myself. It is among my ways of being, part of a repertoire for negotiating my own "known world," a phrase novelist Edward P. Jones uses to describe the taken-for-granted oppositions and hierarchies that structure social life so fully that they seem natural (rather than human inventions created to benefit some over others).[6]

It matters, then, that while my passion for the West and its men is not the same as that of Blackwelder and McClung, neither is it wholly different. It would be easy to say that McClung and Blackwelder held an older view of Carson as hero, as pioneer paving the way for American civilization in the West, engaging in violence only so far as history demanded, befriending those nonwhite western residents willing to work, live, and love toward one nation, indivisible, with liberty and justice for all.[7] Not only would it be easy to say this, but it would be easy to demonstrate it using evidence Blackwelder and McClung themselves left behind. It would be equally easy to say that I, on the other hand, hold a newer view of Carson, newer still than those in the 1960s and '70s who reversed older assessments by branding Carson, in the words of one who deplores the trend, "an archvillain of the American frontier ... an unprincipled exploiter and murderer of Indians."[8] I could easily add that my perspective also differs from those turn-of-the-twenty-first-century writers who have worked to discredit the villain thesis and provide a more historicized Carson: flawed, human, a man of his times—but a good one, an essentially good one.[9] I could even say that my view diverges from that of one of Carson's more recent chroniclers, who works diligently to combine older and newer views and to see Carson from the perspective of long-term residents of the West, particularly Navajos, thereby characterizing Carson paradoxically as both "a dashing good Samaritan" and "a natural born killer."[10] My view, I might say, is more *complicated*, to invoke a popular adjective in the lexicon of western historians today. It would be especially easy to demonstrate these claims about my view, given that it would be largely a matter of self-representation.

As simple as it would be to make and support these statements, and as accurate as they are as far as they go, they do not go far enough. They do not tell enough truths. Because part of what made McClung and Blackwelder cleave to Carson is what drew me to him as well: the human connections that defined him and his place in the West. This is one of the stories I tell—not just of those ties but also of Blackwelder's, Mc-Clung's, and my own investment in them. Carson's human relationships took myriad forms, from shared blankets to trade ties, from the bonds of slavery to the cares of parenthood, from the enmity and alliances of war to the obligations of patronage, from the measured gestures of diplomacy to the blows and caresses of kinship. Blackwelder and McClung foregrounded these relationships—tangled knots, all of them, knots that drove both women to productive distraction and that bedevil me as well. In the end, though, as novel as McClung and Blackwelder's approach was, and as much as I have come to appreciate aspects of that approach, their very interest in Carson was predicated on the cultural work that had been producing a known and knowable historical figure for more than a century before the two women began to hold this man's story in their hands.

Westerner Sparks Story, Falls from Grace

There was little in Kit Carson's actual life worthy of fame. Countless early nineteenth-century white Americans pushed west from the old borderland of Kentucky to the fresh field of endeavor that was Missouri. A good many men then left Missouri for New Mexico or traveled back and forth between those places when the Santa Fe trade opened in 1821, a consequence of Mexico's independence from Spain and the new nation's enthusiasm for commerce with the United States. Plenty of Anglo Americans from the old states and territories entered the western fur trade from the 1820s through the 1840s, well before the United States laid claim to far western lands. These men's names did not become household words. Lots of former trappers and traders stayed in the West, and some found work guiding government explorers or white settlers across overland trails and through mountain passes to California or Oregon. After the late 1840s, still others served the U.S. military as it worked to turn a West that had become American in name into a truly American place, one overseen by a national state, fueled by an economy centered in the East, and ordered by a racial regime that, however contested, enshrined white supremacy. A good number of Anglo men also took their place in that nation-state's nascent bureaucratic structure, which in the nineteenth century was nowhere better developed than in the arena of Indian affairs. Carson did all of these things. In doing them, he was about as remarkable as buffalo grass on the high plains.

But Carson eventually entered a pantheon of white frontiersmen whose names did become household words, even if today few other than western history enthusiasts can place every one of those names in time and space and match them with actual deeds: Daniel Boone, Davy Crockett, and all the western Bills—Billy the Kid, Buffalo Bill, Wild Bill Hickok (only one of whom started out life as a William). Throughout the twentieth century and into the twenty-first, Kit Carson has almost always made the list, the offhand, unthinking enumeration of white men so imprinted by the imagined space of the American West as to seem synonymous with it, even though each lived out his life in radically different landscapes and moments, from Daniel Boone's late eighteenth-century trans-Appalachian frontier to Davy Crockett's early nineteenth-century Texas to Buffalo Bill's world-traveling, turn-of-the-twentieth-century Wild West show. These men followed different paths to fame: Daniel Boone as a long hunter and pathfinder and settler; Davy Crockett as a martyr for Texan independence; Wild Bill Hickok as a scout and scoundrel, lawman and gunman; Billy the Kid as a ranch hand and outlaw and hit man; and Buffalo Bill as a Pony Express rider and then self-promoting showman. With the exception of Buffalo Bill and his outdoor extravaganza, they all achieved fame through print media and in theaters—via ostensibly nonfiction reports in newspapers, biographies, and autobiographies and via fictional portraits in dime novels and stage plays. The men had precious few points of connection. Boone's family, like Carson's, migrated from Kentucky to Missouri, and after Daniel Boone's death, became distantly related to the Carsons by a granddaughter's marriage that produced a son who wed a niece of Carson's third wife. Buffalo Bill and Wild Bill met as young men when both worked in overland transport of mail and freight; later, Wild Bill performed in the Wild West show. Buffalo Bill named his son after Kit Carson. Otherwise, the deities of the western folk pantheon were as separate as stars in the night sky, any constellation, like all constellations, imagined.[11]

Like the others, Carson's particular path to fame came about initially through print media. It was when he served as a guide for U.S. government expeditions that a land-hungry nation first heard of him. John C. Frémont, an officer in the Army Corps of Topographical Engineers, met

Carson by chance in Missouri while Frémont was preparing for what would be the first of four far western explorations. Carson, who knew the West well from his time in the fur trade, signed on with Frémont in 1842 and would accompany two more of Frémont's expeditions within a few short years. Frémont, in turn, produced reports and maps of his travels that were printed by the federal government and reissued by commercial publishers. Those reports became best sellers, often serving as guidebooks for overland migrants to Oregon and California. Carson figured in the reports as a dashing, competent, and fearless frontiersman who was yet loyal and humble.[12]

But Frémont's reports were not his work alone. He had a silent coauthor, perhaps even a ghostwriter, in his wife, Jessie Benton Frémont, daughter of Senator Thomas Hart Benton, Democratic expansionist from Missouri. Jessie Benton Frémont had the brains to match John's ambition and derring-do. Though often lauded and constantly enlisted in nation-building schemes, John Frémont was not a consistently successful man—he was court-martialed for his role in the U.S. conquest of California; he failed in his bid as the first presidential candidate of the new Republican Party in 1856; he mismanaged investments in virtually every western venture, from mines to railroads; and he was forced to resign as Arizona's governor when he focused on recouping lost fortune over running the territory. As a result, Benton Frémont's writing career sometimes kept the couple afloat. Not only did she assist in work issued under her husband's name, she also published magazine articles and essay collections of her own. Her writing included tributes to Carson, whom she met in 1847 and came to love. Indeed, it is not too much to say that if Jessie Benton Frémont had not wielded her pen on his behalf, few today would know the name Kit Carson.[13] In her traffic in Carson, then, Benton Frémont had the jump on Blackwelder and McClung by a hundred years.

Benton Frémont not only wrote about Carson; she also came to his defense when others besmirched him. Shortly after he died, Carson rose from the grave in what to Benton Frémont seemed an unflattering poem, "Kit Carson's Ride," by the eccentric western writer Joaquin Miller (Miller affected a frontier style for the benefit of fawning British readers and played western by appropriating a name he heard among Mexicans in gold rush California, Joaquín, instead of using his own Roman moniker, Cincinnatus). In response to the poem, Benton Frémont worked alongside Edward F. Beale to restore Carson's good name. Beale was a naval lieutenant who had traveled with Carson under dangerous conditions during the U.S.-Mexico War and felt deeply in his debt. For her part, Benton Frémont wrote to Gen. William Tecumseh Sherman, of Civil War and frontier fame, imploring him to help keep Carson's name "as he kept it clean and honored." Meanwhile, Beale wrote a scathing newspaper critique of the poem (also under an ethnically appropriated pen name, El Mariposo), declaring Carson "a man cleanly of mind, body and speech."[14]

How had "Kit Carson's Ride" made the frontiersman seem dirty? Miller had placed Carson in flagrante delicto with a lover "won from an Indian town": "Her touch was as warm as the tinge of the clover / Burned brown as it reached to the kiss of the sun." This was strong stuff in the Victorian era, made stronger by the interracial and hence illicit embrace, even though the poet had them married according to the custom of the country. What was worse, when a prairie fire raised the temperature further, Miller's Carson abandoned that lover. Rather than rescuing his bride, he saved from the flames the horse that she had taken for him from her own father as a wedding gift. This was what upset Benton Frémont and Beale. Both no doubt knew of the real Carson's first marriage to a Northern Arapaho woman, if not his second to a Southern Cheyenne woman (the second was short-lived). And they certainly knew of his long third marriage to a New Mexican *hispana*. Carson did not abandon even one of these loves. But neither Benton Frémont nor Beale made a case for Carson by citing his more or less enduring tender ties. Instead, they vaguely denounced the poem's eroticism while vigorously defending Carson's chivalry—so vigorously that when Miller published his *Complete Poetical Works* later in life, he rewrote the poem's ending, allowing Carson to rescue his Indigenous damsel in distress.[15]

Champions such as Jessie Benton Frémont, John Frémont, and Edward Beale first created and nurtured Carson's national reputation. In doing so, they created a market for later installments of Carson's legacy in print, a legacy that, if recounted in full, would delay the start of the story I tell herein about two twentieth-century Carson enthusiasts. Happily, others have recounted that inheritance in detail and with devotion (many of them bigger fans than I am), which allows me to summarize. It was a U.S. Army surgeon named DeWitt Clinton Peters, a Taos acquaintance, who took down Carson's version of his own life up to that point and used it as the basis for the first biography, *The Life and Adventures of Kit Carson, the Nestor of the Rocky Mountains, from Facts Narrated by Himself*, published in 1858. That book served as source and model for many others into the early twentieth century. Then, in 1914, Edwin Sabin, a midwestern writer of western fiction, published a sprawling two-volume work of Carsoniana that was mostly biographical but also reprinted historical documents and relied as well on interviews with Carson associates then still living. Not long after, in 1926, the eastern-educated, Taos-based artist and author Blanche Grant followed suit by bringing the first edition of Carson's actual memoirs, as they had been dictated to Peters, into print (the original remains among the collections of Chicago's Newberry Library). Other editions followed, including the most scholarly, edited and annotated by historian Harvey Lewis Carter in *"Dear Old Kit": The Historical Kit Carson* and published in 1968. (Carter's title came from the verbal effusion of Edward Beale, who took such offense at Joaquin Miller's poem: "Dear old Kit! Not such as this poet painted you, do I recall the man I loved. . . . Oh, wise of counsel, strong of arm, brave of heart and gentle of nature, how bitterly have you been maligned.") The published memoirs, as well as manuscripts archived in libraries across the United States, have informed and generated even more biographies, which appear every few years with no sign of stopping.[16] The work of Quantrille McClung and Bernice Blackwelder, then, is part and parcel of Carson's patrimony in print.

But even all this does not exhaust that patrimony, because just as poet Joaquin Miller could craft a frontiersman that contemporaries did not recognize, there were fiction writers who manufactured a Kit Carson from whole cloth. Later, there would be filmmakers and television producers who did the same. Once again, other scholars have traced the evolution of fully fictional Carsons, sometimes with scorn, leaving me the easier task of recapping their insights without fully embracing their disdain, since my aim is not so much to insist on history's superior ways of knowing as it is to cast a quick eye over Carsoniana while holding at bay judgments about truth and falsehood (while I am a historian driven by the conviction that archival research gets us closer to determining what actually happened in the past, I am also mindful that the relationship between truth and the practice of history has long been a contested one).

Carson's slow rise to minor fame coincided with the rise of cheap fiction in the form of dime novels, which were especially popular among readers in the nineteenth century's emerging working class.[17] It was the dime novel that produced the most sensational Carson, though some of the earliest ones drew on the Frémonts' writings and the Peters biography and thus kept a loose hold on real events in Carson's life. All in all, though, as one historian puts it, Carson in dime novels "is repeatedly cast as the frontier's greatest guide, hunter, trapper, and Indian fighter. . . . unsurpassed in his knowledge of wilderness living. . . . a brave, noble, honest, and unassuming companion." He is *Kit Carson, King of Guides* or *King of the Scouts*; he is *The Fighting Trapper* or the dashing father figure of *Kit Carson's Boys*.[18] By the time the twentieth century produced the art and technology of big and little screens, then, Carson was known and knowable, capable of constant resurrection, from the 1940 film *Kit Carson*, featuring the handsome heartthrob Jon Hall, to the 1950s television series, *The Adventures of Kit Carson*, starring the more prosaic Bill Williams.[19]

All of this remained true until the social movements of the 1960s and '70s brought towering frontier figures like Carson to their narrative knees, cutting them down to size, drowning out their voices, and exposing the dark underbelly of U.S. empire as it unfolded not only in the nineteenth-century North American West but also in the twentieth century, as the United States strained for global power. So pivotal is this fall from grace to the story I tell that I hesitate to outline it here lest you, dear reader, settle for summary and turn the attention that I covet to other matters—your job, your lover, your daughter, your dog, climate change, world peace, local protest, evening prayer, a light lunch or a walk in the woods or a date with a different book. I do not ask you to neglect these urgencies for long, and what is more, I suspect that you will find what you read here relevant to matters of current concern. So stay with me for a bit, and I will take you to a time and place where stars tumble from the sky.

Historian Comes Clean, Stays Dirty

While we are talking about our relationship, let me introduce myself further by elaborating on aim and catalyst and muse for this tale of two women, one man, and a cast of many, a cast in which I sometimes figure. The women, Quantrille McClung and Bernice Blackwelder, were especially interested in Kit Carson's intimate bonds with long-term residents of the West. Decades later, so was I. I was interested in Carson's story not least because, in striking and unsettling ways, it reminded me of my own. Carson was short and white and he ventured into western places not his own, finding love among women for whom the West was home, eventually settling into a quarter-century marriage to a *nuevomexicana*, a daughter of the Mexican North turned U.S. West. I had done much the same, albeit in a wholly different historical context. More on that later.

When I first started to think about Carson's intimate life, I had already been, for twenty years, studying the place many call the American West. Just calling that place by that name presupposes the present-day boundaries of the continental United States, even though those boundaries are less than two centuries old. It only takes naming my field of inquiry, then, for me to cross contingency's threshold and conjure up for you set pieces of the West's bloody past: cowboys and Indians, forever at odds, and a U.S. cavalry that thunders in to settle the score; U.S. infantry storming Chapultepec, the fabled Halls of Montezuma, to secure territory hundreds of miles north for an expanding nation. I conjure up fighting men of dark and light complexion, and the light-skinned men are winning. I do not conjure up any women at all, no matter their color, though I inhabit a female body encased in white skin, a body from which I am often estranged. We do not get along, my bodily configuration and I, though my fair skin deals me worlds of unearned comfort. I have lived in precisely this tension for as long as I have studied the West. For that reason, in telling the tale of McClung and Blackwelder and their attachment to Carson, I tell parts of my own tale, too.

I do so because I want lovers of history to consider how we know what we know about the past and how that knowing is shaped by the conditions of our knowing. Of all my layered agenda, this one is bedrock. On the surface, this book weaves a story of lives intertwined across time and space. Underneath runs a current of questions about how we know what we know about history and how what we know is shaped by who we think we are, where and how we live, how we feel ourselves connected to the past, when and why we create knowledge, what we think are the benefits of knowing, whether we think knowing the past can help us or others, whether we think we deserve our lives or perhaps deserve better or worse, and why we think we live and love even as others have suffered and died, are suffering and dying still. I wrote this book to show by intimate, quotidian example what is at stake in questions such as these and also to press for answers.

When I started my research many years ago, I thought I might write a book about Carson's intimate ties to American Indian and Spanish Mexican women and about what those ties meant to a colonized West. It was the character and content of those relationships that I planned to study when I mapped out a project called "Marrying Power: The Intimate World of Kit Carson." Of concern to me were Carson's bonds with women whose ties to western places and peoples were different from and deeper than his own: Singing Grass, who was Northern Arapaho; Making Out Road, who was Southern Cheyenne; and Josefa Jaramillo, who descended from two *hispano* families of northern New Mexico, the Jaramillos and the Vigils. Each of these women was married to Carson according to the varied customs of the country—Singing Grass for several years in the 1830s; Making Out Road for several months in the 1840s; and Josefa Jaramillo for a quarter century after Carson renounced

Protestantism and was baptized a Catholic in 1843. And these were just three intimacies among many similar connections that crossed cultures in Carson's world, relationships in which newcomers in the West cast their lot with companions whose own peoples still held sway over their geographies of residence. Most who have written about Carson have acknowledged these kinds of bonds, even if they have neither perceived the habit as a matter of "marrying power" nor seen power as residing historically among Indian and *hispano* peoples.

When I conceived of my project, as far as I knew, no one had given these ties their narrative or analytical due, preferring instead to keep the historical spotlight on Carson himself—as hero, as villain, or as man of his times.[20] By focusing on these ties but also by situating them in the context of Carson's manifold relationships with fellow trappers and opponents in battle, *hispano* neighbors and Indigenous hunters, his mixed-race children and his "adopted" Indian servants, I aimed quite literally to put Carson in his place. I aimed to diffuse the light so that it fell instead on a broader social and cultural milieu that gave birth to the world that persists in the spaces Singing Grass, Making Out Road, and Josefa Jaramillo called home, a borderlands world that bleeds out across North America to touch many more peoples and places in our own time.[21]

Imagine my surprise, then, to learn that four decades earlier, at a time when there was little interest in Carson's intimate life, McClung and Blackwelder had wrestled with these very same relationships—and sometimes with each other over how best to present them. After uncovering evidence of a sexual bond in the Carson family circle that was forged without benefit of clergy, for instance, biographer Blackwelder wrote to genealogist McClung that she worried about "broadcasting anything" that would "smirch" the reputations of the couple involved. Blackwelder went on, "It is different for you to put all information you wish in a family history but not for me. Don't you agree?"[22] I saw similar evidence myself, and while I did not worry much about matters of reputation (having come of age at a time when protecting sexual reputations, for white people, anyway, seemed old-fashioned), I did worry about matters of representation.[23] What did it mean, I wondered, to write even one more word about a figure like Carson, even if my focus and purpose differed from those of enthusiasts who had celebrated or vilified or rehabilitated him in the past? The longer I wondered, the less I could separate my own project from those of earlier Carson specialists—and especially from the projects of Blackwelder and McClung. Separation could come only through pride of profession, the arrogance of relative youth (my youth was long gone, anyway), and the condescension of historical hindsight. As I thought through all of this and as I also reckoned with my own relationship to Carson and his intimate life, I realized that I had in my hands a very complicated story indeed.

This book tells that tale. It interweaves the lives of two minor historians, embracing and exploring their minor status, and it braids those lives together with the life of a so-called pioneer. Like a simple braid, the book starts by plaiting three strands: Quantrille McClung, Bernice Blackwelder, and Kit Carson. But Carson is not just a historical figure; he is also a character endlessly recreated in collective memory and popular culture. What is more, activists and historians fought over his legacy in the 1970s and they argue about him still. In other words, Carson has not only a life but a half-life, and that half-life is as much at issue here as the days he walked the earth. So, like a complex braid, the book ultimately interlaces more than three strands. As a text about the everyday conditions in which people produce knowledge about the past, it centers the stories of McClung and Blackwelder. It explains how their daily lives across the twentieth century brought them to love nineteenth-century history and what kind of history those lives made them love. Yet how I see those lives and the historical knowledge those lives produced is a product of my own life path, which makes me a strand in this braided story, too, not an absent, omniscient observer. I am present in the text for a purpose: to insist that when we interrogate the lives of others, we also ought to examine our own. Just so do we learn how we know what we know about the past and how that knowing is shaped by the conditions of our knowing.

More than anything, though, this is McClung and Blackwelder's book. The two women took hold of me and would not let me go. And they would not let me *not* acknowledge the cords that connected us. The book is about myriad issues that arise out of Blackwelder's and McClung's lives and work. I cannot pretend to enjoy distance from these issues as a historian or human being, so it is, episodically, about me as well. When it is about me, it is about me because historians are always present in the work they produce, and I think it better to acknowledge and explore that presence than to deny it by feigning a blinkered God's-eye view of the past (blinkered by the limited evidence that survives to us in the present). I err on the side of being too present for two reasons: First, I am more connected to McClung and Blackwelder in time, space, and passion than to any other subject about which I have written, and honesty and humility demand that I walk the paths between us. Second, I am dubious that the professional distance historians often put between themselves and their subject matter is altogether helpful—to historians, to readers of history, and to the larger project of social justice, which for me is linked to the project of history. I take seriously a late twentieth-century redefinition of the old ideal of historical objectivity as "an interactive relationship between an inquiring subject and an external object."[24] An inquiring subject, I make myself visible herein.

The issues around which I circle in this book include but are not limited to the set of practices I call a traffic in men and things male. Those practices are central here both because they make sense of key aspects of McClung's and Blackwelder's lives and work and because they make sense of my own. In deploying the notion of a traffic in men and things male, I am not referring to the contemporary idea of human trafficking that, in its United Nations definition, refers to "the recruitment, transportation, transfer, harbouring or receipt of persons, by means of threat or use of force or other means of coercion … or of the giving or receiving of payments or benefits to achieve the consent of a person having control over another person, for the purpose of exploitation." Trafficking by this definition encompasses historical and contemporary phenomena that have generated wellsprings of necessary resistance. Such resistance is best conceived when it does not reduce the idea of trafficking to the practice of prostitution and to the often related assumption that all sexual commerce is coerced in a simple, straightforward fashion.[25]

In this book, however, I am thinking about trafficking less literally, building on the incisive ways that feminists have thought about it in the past. From anarchist Emma Goldman to anthropologist Gayle Rubin, twentieth-century thinkers explicated the idea of a traffic in women, exposing how men, through marriage, prostitution, and heterosexual relations more broadly defined, have exchanged women in a manner that has served to consolidate bonds among men. Embedded in this idea is recognition that, historically, women's identity has been largely relational and that women often have lacked clear ownership in their own persons.[26]

In the twenty-first century, though, feminists talk much less about the traffic in women, except for those active in the fight against human trafficking, since the female-bodied are overrepresented among the targets of traffickers the world over. In part, the ebb of traffic-in-women talk reflects the positive changes feminism ushered in across the last century. But the category "women" also grew notoriously unstable by the end of that century, as feminist and queer theorists repudiated binary notions of gender that split humanity into two distinct, dichotomous, and self-evident classes, "women" and "men." As the categories came apart, ideas that depended on them, such as the traffic in women, started to seem old-school. So advancing the notion of a traffic in men, as I do here, is something of a throwback. But what it throws back to is an original feminist insight into how gender difference has been arranged not just as opposition but also as hierarchy. Social worlds have been organized as if the categories "women" and "men" are indeed real, discrete, and inevitably and hierarchically wed, as in "man and wife." In social worlds that take men and women for granted and that grant men more power than women, women have learned to cope. One of the ways they have done so, I argue, is by trafficking in men and things male. While progressive thinkers nowadays tend to frame discussions of masculinity as conversations about gender identity, I am interested in the broader ways that people called women have handled and made use of men and male gender. The idea of a traffic in men and things male, then, honors twentieth-century feminists even as it belongs to our century.

Notions of gender traffic underpin gender history scholarship, one of the fields to which this book is indebted. The idea of a traffic in women informed much early women's history as that subfield gained ground in the last quarter of the twentieth century. The work of women's historians has been written in part against the grain of this idea and the processes it describes, showing how women have both participated in and contested gender systems in ways that have allowed them to be not just objects in the lives of men but also subjects of their own lives. This intellectual project is ongoing, as it should be. Following in the wake of women's history, scholars started writing the history of men and maleness, turning their gaze on those heretofore unmarked categories, trading on men and things male in a manner that left both marked and denaturalized. Men were no longer normative human beings, and masculinities were no longer the natural consequence of human bodies configured male. Maleness had a history, and it traveled through time and across space, often heedless of bodily configuration.[27] Feminist work in this area, which I see as a kind of traffic in men, further unhinged gender hierarchies and, when it was done well, also unsettled interrelated systems of power based on other key historical constructions such as race.[28] Those engaged in this trade, however—and I was one of them—did not always remember that women have long trafficked in men and things male and have done so toward a variety of ends.

McClung and Blackwelder reminded me of this and helped me to see that their ends differed from, and yet were processually related to, those of feminist historians in my own era. Their traffic in men was not radical; it did not upend gender and racial hierarchies. But it did inch understandings of men like Carson along a path toward a wholesale reevaluation (which others would take up in years to come), and it does reveal the gender and racial hierarchies that defined these women's lives. Blackwelder and McClung reminded me of this through the twenty-five years of letters they wrote to each other from the 1950s to the 1980s, as they swapped research on and ideas about Carson specifically and western history broadly. McClung, the librarian, saved their correspondence and donated it to the Denver Public Library, her former workplace, when she died.[29] In those letters, men were symbolic objects of exchange, a kind of intellectual property—a patrimony, if you will—that they traded back and forth. And if McClung and Blackwelder saw value in men and things male, they often devalued women and things female, not least through their habit of identifying themselves, respectively, as an "old maid" and a "housewife."[30]

Reading their letters raised myriad questions for me: What drew these women to a male historical figure like Carson and, through him, to each other? What did it mean for Blackwelder and McClung to be amateur western historians at the very moment when male academics were belatedly professionalizing the field of western history? What sorts of relationships did the women develop with academic historians as well as other buffs, male and female? How did they confront the changes that transformed the discipline—and, by extension, the field of western history—as a result of the social upheaval of the 1960s? What was the relationship between their own twentieth-century patterns of residence—McClung, a lifelong urban westerner, and Blackwelder, a small-town Kansas girl who lived most of her adult life in the metropolitan Midwest and East—and their fascination with nineteenth-century western hinterlands? How did it matter to their lives and work that both spaces—the nineteenth-century frontier and the twentieth-century city—were sites of profound racial transformation? As I read their letters, I wondered if McClung and Blackwelder were obscure aberrants or if their traffic in western men in fact reflected crucial changes over time in gender and racial formation, geographical imagining, political economy, human intimacy, and disciplinary consolidation. In the end, I decided that they were both: aberrations (my favorite kind of folks) and exemplars of dramatic twentieth-century historical developments.

For example, Blackwelder's and McClung's work lends new insight into a moment in the history of history as a discipline. At first glance, this seems likely to matter more to some readers than others (historians love to think about the evolution of their craft; nonhistorians not so much). But the transformation of the discipline reflects broader cultural trends and has vital implications for the meaning of the West as it circulates in everyday life. So bear with me. Scholars identify World War II and its aftermath as an era when historians recuperated the ideal of objectivity and embraced a related valorization of facts and the 1960s as a period when objectivity and the status of facts came into question.[31] They have not, however, explored how this process worked itself out in the subfield of western history, which had only begun to professionalize, included a mix of academics and amateurs, and carried the burden of vexed ties to a popular-culture West that gripped the postwar public. McClung and Blackwelder traversed the divide between professionals and nonprofessionals in this milieu. The overdetermined relationship between things western and things male made it hard for them to navigate the terrain, but the related coziness between things western and things white helped them gain traction. Indeed, the foundational whiteness of the field of western history is another of my key concerns. To this day, the Western History Association (WHA), the professional organization established to foster scholarly study of the West, struggles with the legacy of those origins. And that organization was founded in 1962, the very year that Blackwelder and McClung first published.[32]

Also at issue is the peculiar relationship between professors and buffs who have studied the West. Outside the field of western history, scholars argue that women created a separate world of amateur history even as university men professionalized the discipline, infusing it with deeply masculine assumptions. At the same time, female amateur historians, as well as the small number of women who broke early into the professoriate, helped pave the way for the transformation of the discipline in later decades by focusing on social and cultural matters and by writing from the perspective of the disempowered.[33] In the twentieth-century field of western history, however, amateur historians were as often men as they were women, and male buffs nationally (and, later, internationally) organized themselves into a group called the Westerners.[34] The Westerners predated the WHA by almost twenty years and, in fact, influenced the development of the later professional association. McClung and Blackwelder were in the thick of all this as they rethought Carson.

Still, the Carson buffs at the center of this book are virtual unknowns; they are decidedly minor historians. Far from trying to recover Blackwelder and McClung as major figures unfairly swept into the dustbin of both history and historiography, I am concerned precisely with their minor status. Just as minor writers produce literature from a vantage point that provides a novel, critical view of the literary canon and the process by which it is constituted, so do minor historians produce work that brings into bold relief the hierarchies that attend the production of historical knowledge. Negative critical positions such as this are not inherently radical, and this is surely true for the U.S.-born white women whose fascination with Kit Carson I examine.[35] Nonetheless, by embracing their minor status, I encourage all of us to examine our assumptions about the work historians do, assumptions about where historical knowledge resides, who has access to it, how it is best communicated to a broader public, whose work ought to be taken seriously, and what sorts of rewards should be conferred on those who make which contributions to our collective understanding of the past.

In addition, this book foregrounds an aspect of history as knowledge production that is often neglected in historiographical analysis. Those who study the practice of history make sense of change over time in the discipline by examining the broader political, social, and economic circumstances in which historians do their work.[36] But few take that contextualization to its most intimate level by investigating the quotidian conditions that enable (or disable) the production of historical knowledge. Even though women's history as a subfield has long paid attention to the dailiness of women's lives, the small existing literature on women and historical practice shies away from viewing knowledge production as embedded in everyday life.[37] By focusing on women who not only published histories but also left behind a rich record of the conditions in which they did so, and by acknowledging that my own everyday life enables and disables and shapes the work I do as a historian (not to mention the rewards I receive for it and those that prove elusive), I seek to expand the study of the study of history, modeling more thoroughly contextualized stories about the production of historical knowledge.

Finally, because I tell the story of women whose lives spanned the twentieth century and whose work covered the nineteenth, this book also speaks more generally to our understanding of the last two hundred years of North American history. For instance, although Blackwelder and McClung did not see it this way, they were writing what we now call borderlands history. So I am in dialogue with borderlands historians, especially those whose work is set in the worlds of Carson and his Northern Arapaho, Southern Cheyenne, and *hispana* companions.[38] To cite a second example, McClung and Blackwelder recall a range of historical actors who lived the moments we commonly call the Cold War and the '60s but lived them in a manner few have had reason to highlight. They both embraced and rejected the containment culture of the 1950s by perpetuating the era's celebration of the American West and its white, masculine heroes, even as they subtly changed those heroes and even as their own lives broke with dominant cultural ideals for white women and "the family" in the postwar United States.[39] Meanwhile, the 1960s are viewed as an era of awakening for women, people of color, sexual minorities, and anticolonialists of various sorts and also as a breeding ground for conservative backlash. Less often, however, are the era's social movements seen from the perspective of people who—for reasons of age, residence, politics, and relative access to privilege, both economic and racial—lived on the fringes of social ferment and wondered at its meaning.[40] Blackwelder and McClung help us see the 1950s and '60s from unfamiliar vantage points, perspectives not necessarily highlighted even in scholarship on cultures of conservatism.[41]

In the end, this book wears bifocals, the better to see both close up and far away. Through one lens, it discerns granular detail; through another, it sweeps the historical horizon. So, for instance, it examines the practice of history in the context of everyday life and the spatial dimensions of twentieth-century relationships predicated on nineteenth-century regional pasts. It also surveys the seductions of gender in the context of racialized power—how and when and why U.S.-born white women have given gendered selfhood shelter, leaving their racial selves out in the wild, untended and too often malign. Yet the fine-grained texture of my sources forces me to situate McClung's and Blackwelder's historical work and their larger traffic in men in the midst of messy, even contradictory lives—that is, to explore not just practices of history but also discourses of family and womanhood as well as the material of amateur production, the edginess of race, the politics of social revolution, and the intimacy of collaboration.

Examples abound: McClung, the librarian who never married, began her career among free-spirited young women who loved to cross-dress, and she retained a bit of the bohemian into her old age. Nevertheless, as she aged, she was distressed by the countercultural youths she met on Denver's streets. And although McClung was a genealogist, she lacked what most people called "family ties," at least of the immediate sort. For her part, Blackwelder not only sang on the radio before she wrote history, she also worked for the CIA in the 1950s. She was a political conservative who, more than McClung, bemoaned the social upheavals of the 1960s as well as the influx of people of color into her Chicago neighborhood. At the same time, Blackwelder complained that her husband, whose musical career had collapsed, was the single biggest impediment to the intellectual work she longed to do. In griping about Harold, Bernice Blackwelder made of him one of those male objects of exchange that drew her and Quantrille McClung together. Meanwhile, both women were baffled by Kit Carson's fall from grace in the 1970s, when activists and academics demoted him from the status of western hero to that of "Indian killer." Was this the sort of man they had traded back and forth in their letters and then out to readers in their books? What was the world coming to?

I confront questions like these through a focused but contextualized method that reads deeply into the lives of two individuals, opening up questions about identity and subjectivity and about knowledge and politics more difficult to pose in traditional hyperopic histories.[42] If this method also opens up my own traffic in men and things male, my own attachment to the West, my own racial politics and racial privilege, my own '60s childhood an '70s coming-of-age, my own profession and the trappings of class and status that go with it, my own bond with a woman whose ties to western places and peoples were different from and deeper than my own, then so be it. I have shuffled the puzzle pieces of Blackwelder's and McClung's lives shamelessly; I ought not myself resist scrutiny. Those who cannot stand the heat have no business cooking in the kitchen.

Disorder Misrules

The pages that follow are all out of order. Initially, that may prove disconcerting. We are accustomed to novelists playing with time, narrating events that happened later before telling us what happened first. This kind of storytelling can arrest us, letting us meet characters at one moment and understand those characters in one way, leading us to grow fond or averse, to sympathize or to rage, only to reel us back in time and expose us to hidden pasts of longing and privation, dream and strife, tenderness and pain, cruelty and fortune that dislodge or cement our fondness or aversion or else conjure in us new registers of thought and feeling.[43] Something similar occurs in our daily lives as we come to know other humans through particular kinds of meetings—in a home, on the road, at war, in embrace, on the job, in struggle. If we choose and are able to continue knowing those humans, whether individuals or groups, we eventually learn a backstory that puts that initial knowing—that first glance, that first stroke, that first fist, that first offer of sustenance or recognition, that first demand for labor or obedience—in perspective, allowing us to reevaluate and recalibrate the connection or, if the tie is brutal and we can leave, to escape entirely. In these ways, we are familiar with reading lives backward, familiar with the delight and dismay, the urge to embrace or expel, that accompanies the disclosure of hidden pasts. But we are not used to historians playing with time in this manner.[44] To be sure, historians handle the past in myriad ways, not all of them chronological; some prefer a thematic approach that can account for change over time without making of history a linear telling of one damn thing after another. Still, most historians do not save the beginning for the end, or close to the end, as I do here.

I invite you, then, to meet the main characters of this book as I met them, when they were women in their fifties and sixties researching and writing western history at the very moment when western history as a field was professionalizing, when that field was still very white, when the Cold War was hot, and when the metropolitan world that both women inhabited was being transformed. Then, move forward as I did to the end of the 1960s and the dawn of the '70s, when Bernice Blackwelder and Quantrille McClung continued to write history, but under different conditions, in a field where the balance of power had tipped from amateur to academic historians and in a nation caught up in a costly foreign war while facing social, economic, and cultural upheaval at home. Wonder all the while about the backstory, but wait to know it in full as you would wait to know that of a new neighbor or a new love. When that backstory unfolds, see what it does to what you first understood of Quantrille Mc-Clung and Bernice Blackwelder, what you first thought of westering men like Kit Carson and western women like Singing Grass and Josefa Jara-millo, what you first suspected of me and my motivations for telling you tales of the West and the world, the city and the suburb, the underdog and the overlord, the passions of women and the traffic in men.

I met Blackwelder and McClung initially in their letters, more than three hundred of them spanning 1956 to 1982, and it is through that correspondence and their first published works that I introduce them to you here. But the letters prompted me to search for more sources that would help me make better sense of their lives and work. Finding such sources opened the way to a more spacious story. The letters alone told a tale of two white women in their middle and older years (McClung was sixty-six and Blackwelder fifty-four when they started to correspond, and they were ninety-two and eighty, respectively, when the letters ceased). In that tale, both women devoted much energy to producing western history; each had established a more or less coherent sense of self; both lived lives that had settled into predictable patterns, at least until their health faltered; each coped with aging and worried over the social and cultural changes of the 1960s and '70s.

Other sources, however, shed light on different parts of their lives and told different stories. There were McClung's scrapbooks and photograph albums from the 1910s and 1920s, when she was a youthful Denver librarian running in a brainy, rowdy circle of women similarly employed.[45] There was Blackwelder's diary from the late 1930s, when she was a young wife singing on the radio, intertwining her life with those of other Chicago musicians, and wishing that her husband would make it big as an entertainer, sometimes traveling with him to the East or West coast in search of a break.[46] All of the sudden, the work of Blackwelder's and McClung's middle and later years took on a new look: their traffic in men and things male had its own history; their response to racial revolution reflected racial formations decades in the making; their settled lives were both the product of youthful dreams and the denial of youthful desires; and their shock at radical social transformation belied lifetimes that saw little but change.

In letting disorder misrule, then, I seek to convey that all-of-the-suddenness to you, following on the laconic insight of a fictional frontiersman in a favorite novel of the North American West: "It is a sudden country," he opines.[47] For me, it is a country that humbles and sparks. It allows no easy answers to the past, only fragile reservoirs of pain and pluck. It provides no clear path to a future, but now and then, it offers a tourniquet to bind and a tonic to soothe. It is a country, actual and imagined, where, thus repaired, we can walk alongside one another, for one another, for as long as we stride on this earth. What is due from each of us and to each of us is not the same, because our histories are not the same, and so with each step, we listen.

The Lay of the Land

If you tend to skip chapter summaries except when you are preparing for a class or reading group or exam or book club, you can stop here and jump ahead. I sometimes skip chapter summaries myself because I love the adventure of a book. I love putting my mind in the hands of writers who love the tales they tell and who tell those tales for readers unversed in a book's subject matter. But giving oneself over to a writer can make readers nervous, especially if they have been led astray before by writers who pay uninitiated readers no heed, writers who care more for their own passions than all else. Then, too, you may indeed be preparing for class or reading group or exam or book club, and you may want me to cut to the chase. These next paragraphs are for you.

But these paragraphs do not quite amount to chapter summaries, because rather than chapters, this text is organized into three parts, bookended by a prologue and epilogue. Parts 1, 2, and 3, as well as the prologue and epilogue, are further broken into sections. The sections differ from chapters in that each section advances the narrative and analytical threads of the larger part in which it is situated rather than making a discrete argument. Part 1, "Crafting Kit Carson, 1950s–1960s: The West Is a Happy Vector," focuses on the late 1950s and early '60s, when Quantrille McClung and Bernice Blackwelder first published. Part 2, "Crafting Kit Carson, 1960s–1970s: Down on Wounded Knee," centers on the late 1960s and early '70s, when McClung published her second Kit Carson book and Blackwelder tried and failed to finish her next project. Part 3, "Creating Craftswomen, 1890s–1940s: The Past Is Another Place," constitutes the backstory to parts 1 and 2: it reveals the lives that birthed the historians Blackwelder and McClung became.

Part 1, then, details the two historians' midcentury reappraisal of Carson, chronicling Blackwelder's work on *Great Westerner* and McClung's on her *Carson-Bent-Boggs Genealogy*. It situates their work vis-à-vis amateur, academic, and popular-culture portrayals of the West created when history buffs and Hollywood moguls, not university-trained scholars, monopolized regional representations. To trace both macro- and microhistorical contexts for the production of knowledge about the past, part 1 also explores the daily lives of McClung in downtown Denver and Blackwelder in suburban Washington, D.C., and it shows how Cold War politics and racial change shaped their books. I argue that Blackwelder and McClung produced a new sort of Carson, fashioned in part out of their own experiences as white women living in a rapidly changing postwar present that embraced "the family" and "the West" as anchors to an imagined past. In a nation beset by Cold War fears and civil rights struggles, their Carson still stood tall, but he stood newly connected to the diverse peoples of a still decidedly American West.

Part 2 covers the late 1960s and early '70s, when McClung and Blackwelder produced knowledge about the West under dramatically different conditions. It explores McClung's 1973 *Carson-Bent-Boggs Genealogy Supplement* as well as Blackwelder's unfinished biographical dictionary of westerners. Part 2 forms the ballast of the book. Nestled in the middle of the text, it is also central analytically. I contend that by the 1970s, McClung and Blackwelder's collaboration—their exchange of research on Carson and his kind—had become a traffic in men. All the westerners Blackwelder planned to put in her biographical dictionary were men and virtually all were white. Meanwhile, McClung's genealogies traced the kin ties of Carson, the brothers Charles and William Bent and their friend Thomas Boggs, all Anglo American frontiersmen who married American Indian or Spanish Mexican women. Here, then, I examine most fully the practice of trafficking in men and things male, and I show

how Blackwelder and McClung deployed it. Men of the past were not the only ones who figured in their traffic. As western history professionalized and academics took the helm, the two women saw that the reception of their own work hinged on these men's assessment. So exchanging information about professors and scholarship became another market for their traffic in men. That exchange took an intimate turn, too, because Blackwelder saw her husband as the chief impediment to the progress she longed to make on her biographical dictionary. In frustration, she traded in his flaws and frailties with a vengeance.

All this transpired as the world these women had known turned upside down. Film and TV Westerns declined in number and popularity as the victory culture of the postwar years waned and the Cold War turned hot in Southeast Asia. On the home front, anti–Vietnam War protests and a host of concurrent social movements wreaked havoc. African American, American Indian, Latino, and Asian American activists worked to dismantle a racist social order, and women's and gay liberationists made gender and sexual hierarchies seem artificial and thus subject to change. Even Carson himself came under attack, and Blackwelder and McClung suddenly found that to some eyes, they were researching not frontier heroes but violent colonizers of the West.

By the end of part 2, you will know McClung and Blackwelder and the contexts of their late twentieth-century lives and work well, but you will know little of the pasts that informed their traffic in nineteenth-century western men. Part 3 tells that tale by looping back to the newly colonized, turn-of-the-twentieth-century West. It shows how that world begat the white, déclassé, history-obsessed women Blackwelder and McClung became. While parts 1 and 2 are based mostly on the work the two women published and the letters they exchanged from the 1950s to the 1970s, part 3 relies on a larger archive: McClung's scrapbooks from the 1910s and '20s, Blackwelder's diary from the 1930s, and both women's early photograph albums, for instance. It considers how their archives came into being and how these women shaped them and thus what could be said about their lives after they passed. It chronicles their growing-up years in big-city Denver and small-town Kansas, respectively, as well as their young adulthoods—McClung's as an urban librarian living with her parents and working and playing alongside other librarians and Blackwelder's as a college student in western Kansas, a voice teacher in Missouri, and an aspiring performer in Chicago who met her husband there. It follows them into the 1940s and '50s, tracing their paths from the era of the New Woman to that of Cold War containment, considering their divergent intimate lives, financial struggles, political leanings, and experiences as white women in changing ethnoracial landscapes.

Part 3 also traces these women's relationship to a western past through their family histories and through random encounters that turned them into researchers: for McClung, a chance appointment as a genealogy librarian, and for Blackwelder, a would-be affair with a country lawyer who loved Kit Carson and a stint at the CIA that boosted her appetite for investigation and planted her near the National Archives. It argues that the knowledge McClung and Blackwelder produced about Carson and men like him reflected not only the immediate historical contexts in which they did their work but also lives begun when railroads had only recently made a latticework of the West and linked it to the East. McClung hailed from Colorado's locomotive center, Denver, and Blackwelder from Brookville, a tiny Kansas railroad town. They came of age in those places with peculiar relationships to the West and at particular moments in the histories of women and men, of white people and people of color. They also came of age when human intimacies more and more fit prescribed categories, from a privileged heterosexual form to a disparaged but increasingly recognizable homosexual form. Their midcentury encounter with Carson and with each other, it turns out, had its own history.

McClung's and Blackwelder's lives ended in unfamiliar places. The epilogue time-travels forward to the late 1970s and early '80s, when both were elderly women still trying to write history but hobbled by slender means and failing health. Though McClung was older, decline hit Blackwelder harder. Blackwelder could not complete her biographical dictionary; she burned it before she died. And as Latinos filtered into their Logan Square neighborhood, Blackwelder and her husband felt stranded in their Chicago apartment. So here, I finish a story begun earlier about the Blackwelders' racial resentment—an emotion they held so tightly that they even tried relocating to Harold's home state of North Carolina. I relate Bernice's racial feeling to her lifelong embrace of family stories that saw her forebears as victimized by Indians. And I chronicle her final return to that family's embrace when the Blackwelders moved to live near relatives in Michigan. I explain that McClung stayed in her Denver apartment longer. The city now seemed strange to her, but she was disturbed by urban decay, not filled with racial fear. She continued her research and though retired, she parlayed her professional contacts into a modicum of success: 1979 saw the publication of her quirky *Memoirs of My Childhood and Youth in North Denver*, and in 1983, Colorado's governor declared her ninety-third birthday Quantrille McClung Recognition Day.[48]

Even as the epilogue ties up loose narrative ends and gives both women the dignity of death that eluded them in the 1980s, it also drives home the book's contentions about how we know what we know about the past and how that knowing is shaped by the conditions of our knowing. I come clean about my own relationship to the West and its chroniclers, to Kit Carson and Josefa Jaramillo, and to the idea of a traffic in men and things male. I mourn aloud the loss of my beloved. The epilogue deals in death, even as it keeps moving—forward and also back. It details how, as McClung and Blackwelder died, I started graduate school fueled by the fracturing of feminism. My work was shaped by that fracture: the critiques launched in anthologies such as *This Bridge Called My Back: Writings by Radical Women of Color*, for instance, and the arguments feminists had with each other about power and desire, about pleasure and danger—debates we called the sex wars.[49] By example, then, I ask readers to think about how our identifications and disidentifications shape the stories we tell and how, in turn, the stories we tell can advance an ethic of social justice, of reparation and reconciliation.

Part One

Crafting Kit Carson, 1950s–1960s

THE WEST IS A HAPPY VECTOR

She had some horses she loved.

She had some horses she hated.

These were the same horses.

—JOY HARJO, "She Had Some Horses"

Some Guys on Some Horses

In the years before I was born, on the first television my family owned, a buckskin-clad Kit Carson galloped across the West and through the decade of the 1880s. He rode with his Mexican pal El Toro, dueling with desperadoes. The black-and-white syndicated program, *The Adventures of Kit Carson*, aired in the early 1950s. My older sister and brother do not recall watching this particular TV Western in the ranch-style house my parents had built for their growing family in Wisconsin in 1952. But my brother reminds me that *The Adventures of Some-Guy-on-a-Horse* shows were a dime a dozen in those days. My lover and life partner, on the other hand, distinctly remembered the fringe on Carson's shirt and his jaunty stride. She watched the program with her brothers in northern New Mexico, in country that the real Carson once called home.[1]

The Adventures of Kit Carson must have irritated Bernice Blackwelder and Quantrille McClung as much as it captivated youngsters in the 1950s. It would have annoyed any viewer conversant with the actual history of western North America. It would have outraged most Diné, whose ancestors were the target of Col. Kit Carson's 1860s Navajo campaign, but only Diné city dwellers saw it, since reservation-based Navajos did not have access to television in the 1950s.[2] The show would have annoyed western history buffs because Kit Carson died in 1868, leaving little substance to fill a saddle two decades later. And El Toro never lived. Kit's closest Mexican companion was his wife Josefa Jaramillo. She was moldering in the grave by the end of 1868 as well. Had the couple been resurrected to ride again in the 1880s? After all, Kit had been born on Christmas Eve, and perhaps like Jesus he rose from the dead. And maybe, since the moral economy of the Western dictated that men rode with men, Josefa got a makeover, rolled back the stone, and charged out as El Toro, the bull.[3]

It was a bother, the West of the Western. When McClung saw another inaccurate portrayal of Carson, in a cameo appearance on the TV show *Death Valley Days*, she was peeved. She quickly telephoned Blackwelder and found her friend "in the same state and for the same reason." Then McClung wrote a letter of protest to the television network, CBS. Finally, she dashed off a note to Marion Estergreen, a Carson devotee in New Mexico, suggesting that Estergreen enlist the aid of the man who ran the Kit Carson Home and Museum in Taos. "I consider it unpardonable to present programs that so distort history," McClung declared.[4]

For Quantrille McClung and Bernice Blackwelder, the moment to set the record straight came in 1962. They had spent years working in libraries across the United States, and they had exchanged hundreds of letters with Carson descendants, Carson enthusiasts, and each other. The West of the Western and the West of history were due for a showdown. Blackwelder and McClung took aim and then fired. Early that year, an Idaho-based publishing house, Caxton Press, released Blackwelder's biography, *Great Westerner: The Story of Kit Carson*.[5] A few months later, the Denver Public Library published McClung's precisely titled *Carson-Bent-Boggs Genealogy: Line of William Carson, Ancestor of "Kit" Carson, Famous Scout and Pioneer of the Rocky Mountain Area, with the Western Branches of the Bent and Boggs Families, with Whom "Kit" Was Associated, and the Line of Samuel Carson, Supposed to be a Brother of William Carson*.[6] Yet even as the gun smoke cleared, another shot rang out, seemingly from the same end of the dusty street. Marion Estergreen, it turned out, was packing, too. Much to Blackwelder's dismay (she did not appreciate the competition), Estergreen published a rival biography before the end of 1962 called *Kit Carson: A Portrait in Courage*.[7] Whatever the differences in these women's work, they all pledged allegiance to an actual past. The West of history was winning.

But the West of history was also changing. So was the West of the Western. So was the wider national landscape in which western history enthusiasts as well as producers of film and television Westerns did their work. It was a landscape in which civil rights struggles, the Cold War, and the shifting contours of city life loomed large. McClung and Blackwelder lived this changing landscape. It touched everything from the tables where they typed their books to the paths their letters traced across the miles to the way they made sense of Kit Carson and the western past.

The year 1962 represents a particular moment in the lives of Bernice Blackwelder and Quantrille McClung, of western history as a field of inquiry, of the Western as a form of popular culture, and of the nation itself. Not only did McClung and Blackwelder publish their books that year, but academics and amateurs joined forces to establish the Western History Association, the first professional organization devoted to the West and its history. The founding of this association marked the beginning of the end of the reign of western history buffs—amateurs like Blackwelder and McClung—in the field. Meanwhile, film and television Westerns had barely begun to fade from their glory days, when they had dominated both big and little screens, providing a visual feast of western men and western landscapes to viewers nestled in theater seats and living room sofas across the country and around the world.[8]

In 1962, national events and trends pulled in different directions. On the one hand, the Cuban Missile Crisis evoked an older Cold War United States, in which frontier heroes like Carson were celebrated and "the family" was enshrined as a truly natural human collectivity that could be opposed to the unnatural collectivism promoted by communists. On the other hand, social movements evoked a nation on the edge of racial, gender, and sexual change, creating an atmosphere in which frontier heroes—and nuclear families—would fall from grace. At the same time, suburbanization was accelerating, stirring cities and their suburbs into a bubbling cauldron of political economy that left some metropolitan residents longing not just for a rural past but a past of unexplored frontiers and undetermined futures: in a word, for the West.[9]

In 1962, Quantrille McClung, who was seventy-two, lived a secure if spartan retirement from librarianship, dwelling in a downtown Denver apartment and working as an independent genealogist. Bernice Blackwelder, at sixty, lived a more insecure and inconstant—but, for now, comfortable—existence in suburban Washington, D.C., even owning a home there. She helped her husband, Harold, in his business ventures but carved out as much time as she could for her work as an independent historian. McClung and Blackwelder—and I, as a child of six—lived in a world that still mostly revered the Wild West, though storm clouds threatened those sunny skies. Out of that world, McClung and Blackwelder produced novel visions of Carson, visions based on hard historical research, to be sure, but also on their experiences as differently situated white women in a Cold War United States that vaunted "the family" and "the West" as ramparts against changing times. They remade Carson from a lone pioneer who helped win the frontier for white America to a family man, the head of an expansive household who, despite his small stature, threw a protective arm around kinfolk of color. In the process, they created a vision of the nation that served Cold War culture, itself a locus of contradiction, conflict, and change. As for me, I was no special fan of Westerns in childhood, but I nonetheless imbibed the same intoxicating cultural brew, endured the same soft visual blows, ending up punch-drunk on the Rifleman, television's tallest, leanest, most home-loving rancher, a widower on a horse in an impossibly white New Mexico, raising a winsome son and brandishing a Winchester in defense of that son, who called him "Pa," and of all that was fair and just on a nineteenth-century frontier that somehow faced the same dilemmas as the ones folks met day by day in the twentieth-century metropolitan United States.

Come, then, to the late 1950s and early '60s, when McClung and

Blackwelder plied their craft on behalf of a different man on a different horse in a different West. Meet these late-middle-aged women as I met them, through their published work and the letters they exchanged as they did that work, having introduced themselves by mail in 1956 when a fellow Carson buff told them of each other, and I having stumbled across their correspondence decades later. Encounter them first through the biography Blackwelder wrote and the genealogy McClung compiled. The Kit Carson who appeared on the pages of those books was something of a new man. He was, predictably, the "Great Westerner" of Blackwelder's title. And he was, in McClung's rendering, the "Famous Scout and Pioneer of the Rocky Mountain Area." But he was also, less predictably, a man intimately connected to a host of people with whom he had seemed more loosely associated in the past: New Mexican *hispanos*, Indigenous peoples of the plains and mountains, and, especially, women of many descriptions. McClung drew these connections in the stark, outline form of the genealogist, creating two hundred pages of charts that traced the "begats": the parents and the parents' parents, the children and the children's children, the cousins, the aunts, and the uncles of Kit Carson, Josefa Jaramillo, and scores of others related by birth and marriage. Blackwelder, in surprisingly stirring prose for a first-time author whose life had been filled with other pursuits, drew the connections through well-researched, if sometimes embellished, stories of meeting and parting, romance and estrangement, birth and death. Encounter these women through the man they crafted, a nineteenth-century fellow nonetheless caught up in twentieth-century concerns about "the family" at a moment of racial change.

Begotten, and Made

First, the begats: Quantrille McClung's *Carson-Bent-Boggs Genealogy* opens with a Carson family record that she received from one of Kit Carson and Josefa Jaramillo's grandsons. That record starts with an entry for William Carson, Kit's paternal grandfather, an eighteenth-century Scots Irish migrant to Pennsylvania and then the western Piedmont region of North Carolina. The rest of the volume is filled with the results of McClung's own genealogical research. But those results begin exactly where the family record began: with William Carson.[10] They follow fathers and their wives and children down through the decades and also across space, as the Carsons migrated from North Carolina to Kentucky to Missouri, and finally to the Mexican North in the heyday of the fur trade and the Santa Fe trade. Tracing male lines of descent more thoroughly than female lines was a habit among genealogists, following broader cultural and legal practices that identified men as heads of families and by which women routinely took their husbands' names at marriage. It would be much later, after years of feminist ferment, that some published guides started to focus explicitly on strategies for researching female lineages, or, as one genealogist put it, the "hidden half of the family."[11] Such resources did not exist when McClung was doing genealogical work, and she did it, for the most part, the old-fashioned way.[12] She was also doing it the old-fashioned way simply by being both a woman and a genealogist, since genealogy had not professionalized the way the discipline of history had—and the way the subfield of western history soon would—and thus provided an intellectual home for women with historical interests.[13]

As the title suggests, the *Carson-Bent-Boggs Genealogy* was not limited to the Carson family. McClung, back when she worked as a librarian, had helped to develop the Genealogy Division of the Denver Public Library, and her interest in Carson began, she recalled, when "a lady in North Carolina wrote asking my help in relating her Carson line to that of the 'Kit' Carson family." Realizing that no full genealogical record existed for Carson and his kin, McClung decided to compile one herself.[14] Over time, she found Carson's life had been so intertwined with the lives of the Bent brothers, especially Charles and William, and of Thomas Boggs that it would be useful to include their family lines in the genealogy, too.[15] The Bents, along with Céran St. Vrain, were the proprietors of Bent's Fort along the Santa Fe Trail, which, through the exchange of Mexican silver and mules for U.S. textiles and hardware, increasingly tied the northern territories of Mexico to the western territories of the United States starting in the 1820s and culminating in the U.S. conquest of the 1840s. Indeed, Charles Bent became the first American governor of New Mexico in 1846. Thomas Boggs was younger and came later to New Mexico, but like Carson and the Bents, he helped tighten the bonds that were slowly creating a U.S. Southwest.

What McClung's genealogy revealed more clearly than any earlier work, though, was that Carson, Boggs, and the Bents shared more than Missouri origins and adult lives spent on the borderlands of commerce and war between the United States and Mexico, a borderland overwhelmingly occupied by Indigenous peoples. McClung showed that each of these men had intimate relationships with either American Indian women or Spanish Mexican women or both during the years of the fur trade and Santa Fe trade; that the women with whom the men intermingled were often related to one another; and that these relationships produced a large number of mixed-race and ultimately bicultural children who lived out their lives all over the West but especially in southern Colorado and northern New Mexico.[16]

Or at least that is what I most noticed when I first scanned the *Carson-Bent-Boggs Genealogy* in the 1990s. When Bernice Blackwelder anticipated her friend's book in the 1950s, however, she wrote simply, "I am eager to see the completed work and know it will be a real contribution to information about a truly American pioneer family."[17] Unlike Blackwelder, McClung was not given to such verbal flourishes. Indeed, she eschewed narrative prose altogether in the published genealogy. For example, when McClung decided to include a brief sketch of "Kit Carson and Family" in her book, she asked Blackwelder to write it.[18] Although it was Blackwelder who called the subjects of McClung's forthcoming genealogy "a truly American pioneer family," given the two women's close collaboration, it may not be too much of a stretch to assume that McClung shared her friend's estimation of this group of people.

In what sense, then, might McClung and Blackwelder have seen the Carson, Bent, and Boggs kin network as "truly American"? The people who populate the *Carson-Bent-Boggs Genealogy* constitute a striking mix: Arapahos, Cheyennes, other Indigenous peoples, Spanish Mexicans (people of Spanish and often American Indian and even African descent, many of whom downplayed or even denied their non-European ancestry), Anglo Americans (here, mostly people of English and Scots Irish descent), as well as various and sundry human amalgamations. If this group of people was not just American but hyper-American, by what processes did they achieve their Americanness? With McClung's genealogy as guide, we might conclude that they gained this identity by meeting, by recognizing one another as different but also useful and desirable, by engaging with one another intimately and economically and making mutual accommodations appropriate to existing relations of power, and, ultimately, by losing markers of difference in a manner that created a singular place called the American West.

Except when they did not. So, for instance, in the genealogy, Josefa Jaramillo and Kit Carson meet. Kit converts to Roman Catholicism and finds himself called Cristobal. He marries Josefa, and she bears the children they conceive, children who answer, depending on circumstances, to names like Julián or William, Josefita or Josephine. Eventually, however, they become Carsons all, with no more Spanish given names or surnames to twist the tongues of "truly American" readers.[19] On the other hand, there is William Bent, who goes west and finds himself called Little White Man by Cheyennes and Lakotas. He meets and marries Owl

Woman, who is Cheyenne. Owl Woman bears the children they conceive, children with names like Mary and Robert and George and Julia. But Mary and Robert and George and Julia do not become Bents all; they do not blend into white America. Rather, they follow distinct paths through an ethnoculturally complex and constantly changing West, growing old on ranches and reservations alike. If the Carson family story, as one can divine it from McClung's genealogical charts, is the typical trail to a truly American identity, the routes taken by Owl Woman and her children reached the destination well enough to fit within the covers of the same book.[20]

If McClung and Blackwelder agreed that McClung was producing a genealogy of "a truly American pioneer family," there were subtle differences in their understanding of the phrase. McClung was not one to draw the curtain on a historical drama like the one played out by William Bent and Owl Woman, even as she might not give it center stage. (By contrast, after Blackwelder published *Great Westerner*, she worked on a biographical dictionary of western men from which she consciously excluded Indians.)[21] When Blackwelder told McClung that she thought the genealogy would be "a real contribution to information about a truly American pioneer family," McClung's book was not yet published. Blackwelder may not have realized how significant a place the Bent and Boggs family lines would occupy in the finished product. Thus the "truly American" clan in Blackwelder's mind may have been the Carson family more narrowly defined. It is, in fact, the Carson lineage that is the most elaborately traced in the *Carson-Bent-Boggs Genealogy*, but as even the title suggests, McClung's American family was a bit more expansive than Blackwelder's.[22]

One dimension of this family story, however, remains mostly hidden in the genealogy, and that is the frequency with which those represented on its pages lived alongside enslaved people, generally African Americans or American Indians. These Native and black people were bound to labor through one of two systems of slavery that pervaded North America into the nineteenth century—the enslavement of African-origin and African-descent people, rooted in the East, and the enslavement primarily (though not exclusively) of Indigenous people, which increasingly was localized in the West.[23] Scant traces of enslaved African Americans do appear in the *Carson-Bent-Boggs Genealogy*. For instance, McClung reproduces the military record of Lindsey Carson, Kit's father, who served in the American Revolution. The elder Carson was supposed to have received part of his compensation for service "in Negroes," though the record notes that he "rec'd. none." Lindsey's brother Andrew, Kit's uncle, wrote a will in North Carolina in 1836, which McClung also reproduces, bequeathing no fewer than ten enslaved black people to his children and grandchildren (a will he later revised so that the slaves would not be scattered geographically on his death but rather kept in close proximity).[24] Absent in the genealogy, however, is any indication that those Carsons who left the old southern backcountry for the lower Missouri River frontier in the early nineteenth century took slaves along with them—that is, any indication that Kit Carson himself grew up in Missouri alongside black children and among white slave owners.[25]

More completely obscured in the genealogy is a western system of slavery by which *hispanos* in New Mexico purchased Native people, often from rival Indian groups, incorporating the captives into their households as servants and often "adopting" them as family members, or *criados*, as they were called.[26] While sixteen-year-old Kit Carson did not take black slaves with him in 1826 when he ran off from Missouri and headed for New Mexico, he did, once he married Josefa Jaramillo in 1843, live in a household that "adopted" Indigenous people.[27] McClung probably understood little of this slave trade and the practices of bound labor it generated. Even if she encountered evidence of it in her research—such as baptismal records for the three Navajo *criados* raised in the Carson household—she might not have recognized its significance. She made no record of it. But this, too, was part and parcel of a "truly American" clan.

These are some of the ways that McClung saw and did not see the Americanness of her historical charges. But a more fundamental question remains: In what sense did she see the people of the *Carson-Bent-Boggs Genealogy* as constituting "a family"—with emphasis on both the indefinite article "a" and the vexing noun "family"? First, and most obvious, the phrase suggests a single entity: just one family. The very presence of three surnames in the genealogy's title, however, announces that multiple families populate the text. The table of contents pluralizes the problem. We might expect the chapters titled "Line of William Carson," "Kit Carson and Family," and "Bent and Boggs Families—Western Branches." But there are also chapters devoted to the "Wood Family," "Boone Carson Intermarriages," and "Jaramillo-Vigil Ancestry." Of course one always finds multiple surnames in a genealogy: people marry and names proliferate. But the three surnames of this book's title—Carson, Bent, and Boggs—were linked to one another in ways that, on the one hand, exceed conventional definitions of family ties and, on the other, bring to mind not fathers and husbands but mothers and wives and lovers and children.[28]

Before people named Carson, Bent, and Boggs settled in northern New Mexico and southern Colorado, there was but one family relation among them (as genealogists reckon such relations). Juliana Bent—a sister of Charles and William, who established Bent's Fort—had married Lilburn W. Boggs. Lilburn, years later, became Missouri's governor and, later still, went west to California. But Juliana was only nineteen when she died, after she bore two children. Then Lilburn Boggs married Panthea Boone, a granddaughter of frontiersman Daniel Boone. Panthea had ten children, most of whom ended up in California. One of them, Thomas Boggs, migrated first to California and then backtracked to New Mexico. It was Tom Boggs who became a close associate of Kit Carson's, thus earning the name Boggs a place in McClung's work.[29]

When Kit Carson, Tom Boggs, Charles Bent, and William Bent lived in Missouri, then, the only genealogically recognizable connection among them was this: Tom's father had been married to Charles and William's sister before she died. Tom Boggs's mother was not a Bent but a Boone. And Tom Boggs, in fact, was almost a generation younger than the other three men; he was a toddler when Kit Carson started down the Santa Fe Trail. What connected these men at first were patterns of residence and migration and the frontier economies that encouraged such men now to stay put, now to move on. It was what happened once the men came of age and headed farther west that made them kin.

What made them kin were intimate partnerships with women and an expansive sense of responsibility for children. It started around 1840, when Kit Carson, having lost his first wife, the Northern Arapaho woman Singing Grass, married the Southern Cheyenne woman Making Out Road. Making Out Road was kin to—perhaps a sister of—Owl Woman, who had married William Bent.[30] If the two women were sisters, then this would be the first kin relationship between a Carson and a Bent that a genealogist might recognize. McClung probably never suspected that Making Out Road and Owl Woman were related; if she had, she would have called attention to the tie. At any rate, Kit Carson and Making Out Road's marriage did not last, and within a couple of years Carson cast his lot with Josefa Jaramillo of Taos. Already, Charles Bent was living with Josefa's older sister, Ignacia Jaramillo. When Bent was killed in the 1847 uprising of *hispanos* and Pueblo Indians against U.S. rule in New Mexico, Kit and Josefa took Charles and Ignacia's daughter Teresina into their home. Later still, a now grown-up Tom Boggs married another of Ignacia's daughters, Rumalda. Then, when Josefa and Kit both died suddenly in 1868, Tom and Rumalda assumed responsibility for the seven Carson children.[31] It was women—Cheyenne and *hispana*—and the children they bore who made William Bent, Kit Carson, Charles Bent, and Tom Boggs kin.

Even though McClung worked within the confines of what was then normal genealogical practice—that is, tracing lineages of men more thoroughly than those of women—she nonetheless turned up evidence demonstrating that a "truly American pioneer family" was one created by the intimate relationships that newcomers like Kit Carson formed with regional residents like Making Out Road and Josefa Jaramillo. The form of a genealogy—schematic charts that list offspring in cascading lines of text, with the first male forebear flush left on top, followed by each subsequent generation indented further to the right, like a staircase descending across the page to the present—only alludes to a story and barely hints at the values that inform such kinship tales. But the traces of narrative and interpretation that haunt McClung's tidy charts, like echoes hardly heard, suggest a modestly inclusive notion of family, where white forefathers tend to tumble headlong into busy human hives that buzz of their own accord, quite heedless of husbands who would be lords.

Souls Lost in Purgatory

If Quantrille McClung the genealogist tells a spare tale of an expansive American family made kin through the daughters of the country, Bernice Blackwelder the biographer narrates an elaborate saga of a strange son of the frontier—small of stature, soft of voice, unlikely to be favored, but somehow still "the greatest Westerner of all."[32] Like the *Carson-Bent-Boggs Genealogy*, Blackwelder's *Great Westerner: The Story of Kit Carson* is a family tale.[33] It is also a romance. But for Blackwelder, both family and romance are perpetually deferred by the racial responsibilities of westering—by the struggle to move whiteness west—and the tragic end comes all too soon. Part of the difference between the two books is simply one of genre: genealogy resists narrative, and biography demands it; genealogy tracks connections, and biography trails the individual. The rest of the difference between the *Carson-Bent-Boggs Genealogy* and *Great Westerner* lies in the two women who spent years creating these texts. And there are crucial similarities alongside these distinctions, reflecting Blackwelder and McClung's long collaboration and the shared circumstances in which they wrote history.

Great Westerner is a work of narrative grace that grips the reader like a rousing patriotic song, rich with tales of adventure but always situating those adventures in meditations on Kit Carson's sterling character and his strong family ties. It opens flushed with sensuous anticipation: "Missouri's hardwoods were tingeing, bittersweet pulsed languorously in the underbrush, and September waited quietly, expectantly." Gazing out at this landscape from a saddler's bench is "a rather ordinary-looking youth, clothed like any border boy in nettle shirt and linsey-woolsey from his mother's loom, quiet and undersized, likely to be overlooked among his tall brothers." The boy, of course, is Kit Carson, and he watches as freight wagons assemble for their now-annual trek to northern Mexico. He faces west, "as all Carson men had since the first one left Dumfriesshire, Scotland, to find greater freedom in North Ireland."[34] From his mother's loom and his father's longing comes a slight border boy, all dressed down and ready to go.

Blackwelder establishes much of import in this opening, crafting as she does key characteristics for Carson and his life story that give coherence to all that follows. Kit's body and voice mark the improbability of his rise to fame: He is small and hushed. But he is also hardwired for westering, a trait passed down for generations from father to son, the reward for which is freedom. Blackwelder drives these points home again and again: Kit "stood only five-feet-six"; he was a "scrappy little leader." She also quotes contemporaries who remarked on Kit's stature: Englishman George Ruxton called him "last in height but first in every quality which constitutes excellence in a mountaineer," while U.S. Army officer William Tecumseh Sherman, on meeting Kit, declared that he was shocked to set eyes on such a "small stoop-shouldered man."[35] As for Kit's voice, Blackwelder describes it as "soft," "gentle," "high-pitched," and "almost feminine."[36] In other words, Kit's manhood was not secured by his body or his voice; it would have to be won. And destiny drew him to win it in the West. For Blackwelder, the relationship between Carson and western places is reciprocal; inheritance propelled him west, and "the West claimed him forever." Blackwelder also likens Carson to another famous fur trapper, Jim Bridger: "A demanding curiosity led them through seemingly impenetrable forests and over hitherto impassable mountains to break the westward path." Penetrate they did, and the prize was great: "Few men have reached such fullness of freedom."[37]

For all his freedom, though, Blackwelder's Carson is a family man—an ardent suitor, a devoted husband, and a father who delights in his children. Blackwelder was proud of this depiction. Years after *Great Westerner* appeared, while acknowledging that each book published on Carson "contributed something," she wrote that she believed hers showed "more of his personality and his home life than any other."[38] Carson called many places home: he lived in forts and towns and on farms and ranches; he slept in tents and tipis and cabins and adobes alongside any number of human companions, including fellow trappers like Joe Meek and famous explorers like John C. Frémont. But for Blackwelder, home-life connoted the presence of women. Children sweetened the deal.

In *Great Westerner*, then, Carson's homelife does not begin until he woos and wins the Northern Arapaho woman Singing Grass. In Black-welder's telling, it is a swashbuckling courtship in which the diminutive Carson stands his ground against a rival suitor, a burly French Canadian who hates all Americans. (Blackwelder and others call this man Shunar, though his name was probably Chouinard. She claims that Carson killed Shunar, while others say the man survived.) The scene of the fight is a fur trade rendezvous—the annual Rocky Mountain trade fair that drew trappers, traders, and Native people—and when Kit rides away from the gathering in the summer of 1835, Singing Grass is "beside him to be his companion in the wilderness, his wife, his warmth and comfort." Sing-ing Grass cures animal skins, gathers roots and greens, and gives birth to Adaline, the couple's daughter. The little family prospers in the moun-tains until the decline of the beaver pelt trade leads Carson to Bent's Fort out on the plains, where he works as a hunter. There, Singing Grass sud-denly takes ill and dies, ending for Kit what Blackwelder calls "a genuine happiness."[39]

Little Adaline lives, however, and Blackwelder says that the women of Bent's Fort assumed responsibility for her care. Blackwelder does not specify who those women were, but they probably included the Indige-nous and Métis wives of trappers and traders; some Mexican and other mixed-ancestry women (a domestic known as Chepita, for example, was said to have been of Mexican and French descent); and also Char-lotte Green, an enslaved African American woman owned and brought west by the Bent brothers.[40] They no doubt eventually included Kit's sec-ond wife, but Blackwelder was never convinced that Carson married the Cheyenne woman Making Out Road. Tucked in a footnote after the reference to Adaline's care is a cryptic remark about an earlier biogra-pher who claimed that Carson had "another Indian wife." Blackwelder dispatches this relationship by stating that it "was vigorously denied by Kit."[41] Carson's second marriage dismissed, Blackwelder then narrates the doting father's decision to take Adaline east to be educated among his Missouri relatives.[42]

Kit does seem to have told Teresina, Ignacia Jaramillo's child, that he had never been married to Making Out Road.[43] Teresina was Josefa and Kit's niece. More than one historian has surmised since *Great Westerner* appeared that Carson lied to his New Mexican kinswomen about Making

Out Road. A male relative, by contrast, confirmed the marriage.[44] Blackwelder probably did not know of this confirmation, and she trusted Teresina's report. But Blackwelder surely did know that a Cheyenne woman named Sitting in the Lodge had told naturalist, historian, and ethnographer George Bird Grinnell about Carson's union with Making Out Road in 1917 and that other elderly Cheyennes remembered it as well.[45] Blackwelder did not credit Cheyenne memories.

Carson's marriage to Making Out Road presented Blackwelder with problems of evidence, to be sure. It also presented problems of narrative. Put most simply, the thread of Blackwelder's story that follows Carson's intimate life is in part a tale of racial and material ascent by association, an ascent that helps fit Carson for the title "Great Westerner." The thread leads directly from Singing Grass to Josefa Jaramillo, and Making Out Road would have frayed it. Blackwelder does not minimize Carson's attachment to Singing Grass, whom she calls a "bronze-skinned beauty."[46] But Singing Grass is the love of Kit's younger, more primitive years. Josefa is the love of his later, more civilized years, and unlike Singing Grass, she is of propertied, European origins. According to Blackwelder, Kit and Josefa met in the home of Ignacia and Charles Bent:

> Doña Ignacia Bent was a handsome woman and her home one of the most attractive in Taos. Rich rugs of Eastern import and native bright-striped serapes brought color to the rough floors and heavy hand-hewn furnishings. Ornate religious articles and sconces of hammered tin reflected soft candlelight in an atmosphere of quite serenity. Here Kit Carson met and fell in love with Ignacia's sister Maria Josefa, a fourteen-year-old dark-eyed beauty. Kit, approaching thirty-three, was a man of some importance in the West and in spite of that fact that he had spent most of his years living in a very primitive manner, possessed a natural dignity that impressed young Josefa. Her family— the Castilian Jaramillos and Vigils—made no objection to Kit's suit though he had no fortune to offer and Josefa chose to accept the gentle man whose destiny of fame appeared certain.[47]

For Blackwelder, then, Carson marries into a family of means with Spanish, not Mexican, origins—that is, a white family, not one with mestizo, say nothing of *mulato*, ancestors, Josefa's dark eyes notwithstanding. And the family is not just Spanish in a generic sense but rather Castilian: identified with the old kingdom of Castile, which united with Aragon to create modern Spain and provided the Spanish state with its primary language.

The Jaramillo and Vigil families dated back to the 1690s in New

Mexico; their forebears were among those sent by colonial authorities to reestablish Spanish settlement there after the Pueblo Revolt of 1680 had expelled the first colonizers. Josefa's ancestors hailed from Mexico City and Zacatecas, respectively. Five generations in the north, and as many as five generations farther south in colonial Mexico, the Jaramillos, the Vigils, and all those families with whom they intermarried (Trujillo, Martín, Medina, Archuleta, Cárdenas, Márquez, Fernández, Torres, Sotomayor, Ávalos, Serrano, Montoya, Leyva, and the like) were long residents of the New World.[48] While Spanish Mexican families of some means struggled to preserve their *limpieza de sangre,* or purity of blood, sexual ties with Indigenous people, both coerced and consensual, went to the heart of the colonial project. Furthermore, slave traders brought some 200,000 Africans to Mexico during the colonial era. If every one of Josefa Jaramillo's forebears over two centuries succeeded in avoiding close contact with Indian and black people in New Spain, and if their pursuit of blood purity extended backward in time through Spain's complicated Mediterranean past, when Iberian Catholics lived alongside Muslims and Jews, then perhaps they earned the label "Castilian." But in the mid-to-late eighteenth century, some fifty years before Josefa was born, intermarriage in New Mexico was on the rise, such that by the end of the century, whole new peoples found themselves incorporated under the label *españoles.* Meanwhile, the Spanish crown began selling certificates that allowed people to "cleanse" themselves of "impure" ancestry (generally Indian or African), obscuring a past of racial mixing and creating a racial category associated with affluence. Just how Spanish the leading *hispano* families of New Mexico were (not to mention those of early modern Spain) remains an open question.[49]

But these insights depend on scholarship unavailable to Blackwelder in the mid-twentieth century. And her designation of the Jaramillos and Vigils as Castilian, at any rate, is largely a narrative device, no doubt abetted by the defensive response of some *nuevomexicanos* to the Anglo-American conquest that began with the arrival of men such as Carson in the nineteenth century and continued well into the twentieth: reinventing themselves as "Spanish Americans" to avoid the anti-Mexican racism of Anglo newcomers and the U.S. government alike.[50] The device ultimately serves Blackwelder's story of Carson himself, who, in spite of his recent rustic life, is destined for fame and, indeed, for greatness. And everyone around him, including Josefa and her parents, seems to know it. In this telling, then, as Carson matures, so do his desires, from the more primitive yearnings of youth to the more civilized longings of adulthood.

If Kit has a happy family life with Singing Grass in *Great Westerner*, his homelife with Josefa is exuberant, at least when he is home. He is not there often. Shortly after the 1843 wedding in Taos, Kit Carson and Charles Bent, Ignacia's husband, head east along the Santa Fe Trail to assist Céran St. Vrain, who has grounded a boatload of buffalo robes along the Arkansas River. At the ford, they run into U.S. troops escorting a wagon train owned by New Mexican governor Manuel Armijo down the U.S. portion of the trail (the Arkansas marked the boundary between Mexico and the United States). Armijo faces a difficult crossing back into Mexico because a band of marauders from the newly established Republic of Texas is out on the plains harassing Mexican travelers. The traders pay Kit to carry communications about the threat to Armijo's caravan back to the capital at Santa Fe. Carson dodges Ute warriors along the way and then stops in Taos, where Josefa and Ignacia are keeping house in the absence of their husbands. The unexpected visit prompts Josefa to realize "how unpredictable her life" is going to be. This is just the first of Kit's brief conjugal visits to the homes he shared with Josefa in northern New Mexico and southern Colorado over the next quarter century.[51]

Back on the north bank of the Arkansas, Kit learns that Armijo's wagons are safely on the trail to Santa Fe. But rather than return to Josefa, he sits tight at Bent's Fort awaiting word of John C. Frémont, who has embarked on his second western expedition. Just before he married Josefa, Kit had served as a paid guide for Frémont's first journey. When Kit learns that Frémont's entourage is just to the west at the foot of the Rockies, he puts "the spurs to his pony" and signs on.[52] For a full year, Frémont's men traverse the West, from the Columbia River in the north to the Mojave River in the south, and then back through the Great Basin and over the Rockies to the Arkansas. By then, Blackwelder says, Kit's thoughts are "all of Josefa," who awaits him at Bent's Fort, almost two hundred miles from her Taos home.[53]

Now Kit's plans are to build a ranch along the Little Cimarron, fifty miles from Taos, but after months of work, duty calls—again. It is Frémont—again. Frémont's third expedition is embarking at a perilous moment. The United States has annexed the former Republic of Texas, angering the Mexican government, which had refused to recognize the rogue republic that staged a revolution and broke off from Mexico a decade earlier. Kit hates to forgo "his dream of a home and a life of comparative tranquility for another long absence from Josefa." But he does it. This expedition puts him in the middle of conflicts that evolve into the U.S.-Mexico War and on the U.S. side of those conflicts, despite his residence in Mexican territory and his marriage to a Mexican citizen.[54]

While he is off helping win California for the United States, Josefa is at the Bent home in Taos. Soldiers have marched on New Mexico, too, raising the U.S. flag and establishing rule with none other than Charles Bent, Josefa's brother-in-law, as governor. When the main detachment of troops departs for the war's California front, northern New Mexico erupts in violent protest over the U.S. occupation. Pueblo Indians and *hispanos* alike descend on the Bent home, killing Charles Bent as well as Pablo Jaramillo, Josefa and Ignacia's brother, and one of their Vigil uncles. According to Blackwelder, the womenfolk use kitchen tools to dig through a thick adobe wall and then hide themselves in a neighbor's house disguised as Indian servants grinding corn. Local volunteers and U.S. troops chase the insurgents, who take refuge in the mission church at Taos Pueblo, until the soldiers lay siege to the adobe structure, killing at least 150 and subjecting the leaders to a makeshift trial presided over by Bent's closest associates. All the while, Kit is en route from California to Washington, D.C., carrying government dispatches, oblivious to the bloody events unfolding at Taos. But his travels take him through New Mexico, where he hears the news and rushes to Josefa's side. He stays a few days. Then, he is off again for the nation's capital.[55]

Much of *Great Westerner* reads like this, with Kit chasing around North America and Josefa living in Taos with relatives. Once, in 1849, Kit checks in on Adaline, his daughter by Singing Grass, who is attending a female seminary in Missouri. By then, Kit and Josefa have been married for six years, but they have spent less than six months together. That year, Josefa gives birth to their first child, who lives but a short time. After this loss, Josefa has a baby every two or three years, until there are seven young Carsons. Sometimes, Kit lives with his growing family, even for months at a time. They are together on a ranch near the spot where his last attempt at settled life had foundered, Kit having finally "established a home worthy of his aristocratic wife." He even brings Adaline, now an "attractive, well-schooled young woman with pale copper-tinted skin," to this ranch, though she soon marries and heads to California. The family is also together in Taos, where Kit works as a federal Indian agent to Pueblo, Ute, and Apache peoples. When the U.S. Civil War breaks out, however, Carson becomes an officer with the New Mexico Volunteers in support of the Union cause. For a time, he takes his family to the military headquarters in Albuquerque. There, Blackwelder says, he is a "most unsoldierly officer," who romps "on the floor with his children swarming over him, searching for candy in the pockets of his uniform." But then Kit is relocated to Fort Union, on the plains along the Santa Fe Trail, and Josefa and the children return to Taos. The rest of the war finds Carson dealing with Confederate incursions from Texas and, crucially, with Indian peoples as yet unaccustomed to U.S. rule.[56]

Carson's participation in the 1860s Navajo campaign would soon become the touchstone for a wholesale reevaluation of his legacy. Blackwelder could not have known this when she was writing in the 1950s, because criticism of Carson was muted then.[57] The campaign must have given her pause, though, since *Great Westerner* works to depict Carson as a man "devoted to achieving a lasting peace with the Indians and providing for their welfare," in general, and as an admirer of the Navajo Nation, in particular. The problem, as Blackwelder lays it out, is that Diné raiders plagued the villagers of the upper Rio Grande, both *hispanos* and Pueblo Indians. Navajos raided for livestock, especially sheep, but also for human captives, who could be used as servants, incorporated into families, or sold in the borderlands slave trade. What Blackwelder does not say, and may not have known, is that raiding was a two-way street: Pueblo Indians and *hispanos* alike also plagued Diné communities as part of a wider political economy of exchange and violence that had evolved and intensified over two centuries. The U.S. government, a newcomer on the scene, came down on the side of the villagers, and Col. Kit Carson, under the direction of Gen. James Carleton, was the officer in charge.[58]

It is their plan, as Blackwelder puts it, "to force the Navajos into submission by systematically destroying their crops and driving off their sheep." And Carleton wants to move the Navajos out of their homeland to the spot in eastern New Mexico known as the Bosque Redondo. In Blackwelder's telling, Carson proceeds with his grim duty, even destroying thousands of peach trees, some of them planted by Hopi Indians rather than Navajos, but "not without regret and admiration for the primitive farmer that had made them flourish in that arid land." In the end, Carson achieves "victory almost without bloodshed," and eight thousand Diné begin their Long Walk to the Bosque Redondo. Blackwelder admits that the Bosque experiment was disastrous for Navajo people. At the same time, she contends that it was "a great heartache" for Carson and Carleton.[59]

Still, it is heartache of another sort that prompts Kit first to request reassignment at a post where his family can be with him and then to try to resign his command. Worried that Plains Indians have not yet been subdued, officials do not accommodate him, so "in spite of his personal feeling," he stays with the army. A last campaign rounds out his military career, this one against Kiowas and Comanches on the plains. Then Kit receives his highest reward; he is brevetted brigadier general. Finally, in 1866, the army reassigns him to Ute country at Fort Garland, north of

Taos in the San Luis Valley of southern Colorado. There, Josefa joins him, as do the children, who run around the fort, in Blackwelder's words, "like a small tribe of untamed savages, completely adored by their father."[60]

This, then, is a final moment of family fare for Carson, for his health is slowly failing as the result of an old injury. But he has achieved the fullness of Blackwelder's title, *Great Westerner*. He is still, of course, a short fellow (Josefa is "slightly taller"), but now his body is "stout" and "solidly built."[61] His voice is still soft, but it commands "respect and attention," and with it he speaks English, Spanish, French, "and many Indian languages."[62] From a slight border boy—a provisional American, a provisional man—Kit has evolved into a brigadier general who bests even a Civil War officer as renowned as William Tecumseh Sherman. When Carson negotiates with the Utes alongside Sherman, the Union hero remarks, "Those redskins think Kit twice as big a man as me."[63] Carson also has evolved from a lad who loves a "bronze-skinned beauty" and sires a child with "pale copper-tinted skin" to a mature man who marries an "aristocratic," "Castilian" woman (even if she can, inexplicably, pass for an Indian servant when necessary). Granted, Kit and Josefa's children are boisterous—Blackwelder calls them "untamed savages," while Sherman says they are "as wild and untrained as a brood of Mexican mustangs."[64] These are clearly racialized references that might seem to disrupt the narrative of racial ascent that Blackwelder plots for Carson. But her use of them may draw loosely on an educational theory that had passed into popular thought by the mid-twentieth century. Recapitulation theory said that youngsters, and particularly boys, benefit from a wild youth, because a child's growth essentially must recapitulate the development of the "white race" from savagery to civilization. Children who act like "untamed savages" and "Mexican mustangs" can fully expect, given proper grooming, to learn the habits of civilization over time.[65] In this sense, then, the racialized references to Kit and Josefa's rowdy offspring fit Blackwelder's larger story.

The devil of that story, however, is in the human details. Blackwelder spares nothing in relating the denouement: Rather than remain at a remote post like Fort Garland, Josefa suggests that the family join her niece Rumalda, who is now married to Tom Boggs, in southeastern Colorado. The couple has settled on land Tom claimed for Rumalda as an heir to the Vigil and St. Vrain Grant, one of the last extravagant land grants of the Mexican era. The spot is not far from Carson's old haunt, Bent's Fort, on a tributary of the Arkansas River called the Purgatoire, known to Rumalda and Josefa as el Río de las Ánimas Pérdidas en Purgatorio (the River of Souls Lost in Purgatory). Meanwhile, Kit asks to be appointed superintendent of Indian affairs for Colorado, arguing that his new home on the Purgatoire will place him "in the midst of the Indians." The family moves to the settlement of Boggsville, and Kit learns that his appointment has been confirmed. Now, however, Ute leaders urge him to accompany them to Washington, D.C., where they will negotiate a new treaty. Though much of that journey could by then be taken by rail, the trip wearies Kit, who returns to Colorado unwell. Josefa meets his stage-coach heavy with child, and they return to Boggsville. Five days later, she gives birth to Josefita, their eighth baby. Ten days after that, Josefa, Kit's "beautiful beloved," is dead. Kit lives for a month, cared for by a doctor, his niece Teresina, and her husband, German-born Aloys Scheurich. One afternoon, Aloys cooks Kit a supper of buffalo and chile and gives him a pipe of tobacco. Kit relishes the fare, but then, suddenly, cries out his dying words, "Doctor, *Compadres, Adios!*"[66]

This closing episode makes sense of the epigraph Blackwelder chose for her biography, a quotation I found unsettling when I first cracked the cover of *Great Westerner*. The epigraph comes from the work of Blackwelder's fellow Kansan Eugene Fitch Ware, a nineteenth-century lawyer, politician, and poet:

> Time is pursued by a pitiless, cruel oblivion,
> Following fast and near.[67]

The words evoke a foreboding and fatalism that do not characterize *Great Westerner* until its final passage. There, Carson has become "the greatest Westerner of them all," which, if westering is a quintessentially American habit, means that he is among the greatest of Americans. He even consumes unique products of the Americas in the moment before his death: buffalo, chile, and tobacco.[68] What is more, each of these products is linked to one of the many peoples of the Americas: buffalo to Indian hunters, chile to Mexican farmers, and tobacco to African slaves. Kit Carson absorbs them all. But pitiless, cruel oblivion chases him down. He dies the father of a "truly American pioneer family" with whom he has never really lived.

Both Blackwelder and McClung spun tales about Carson that bespoke a family romance. But McClung, the genealogist, was more taken by the web of western connections that enveloped Carson in a variegated human frontier fixed in place by female moorings. Blackwelder, the biographer, was keen on creating a new American man, one who tried to resolve the tensions of an older, remembered empire through his own racial ascent by association but who also tried to balance newer, contemporary ideals for white, middle-class, heterosexual manhood—

competing Cold War ideals that cherished both breadwinning providers and engaged, affectionate husbands and fathers.[69] On the one hand, Blackwelder's melancholy conclusion reflects the obvious: the inevitability of death. On the other hand, it suggests that rhetorical equipoise could not answer the riddles of injustice, inequality, and imperialism. No wonder Blackwelder never wrote another book; cruel oblivion was following, fast and near.

Westerns, Westerners, and Western Historians

When Quantrille McClung and Bernice Blackwelder began researching Kit Carson in the 1950s, historians and purveyors of popular culture had distinct relationships to North America's frontier past. Popular culture found in the West a happy vector. Historians, however, forked into two branches: amateurs embraced the West, while professionals held it at arm's length. That would soon change, but Blackwelder and McClung initially did their work when amateur historians dominated the field. The two women paid attention to both popular culture and historical study. But historians mattered to them most, so the West's status among those who studied the past is the first point of reference in explaining McClung's and Blackwelder's historical practice.

They were, in fact, among thousands of history enthusiasts in this era who worked on western topics without the benefit of advanced degrees or academic affiliations. At the same time, there were perhaps hundreds of degreed western historians teaching at colleges and universities; working in libraries, museums, and historical societies; and managing historical sites. But as a senior scholar recalls, "in American academic circles," western history "was not considered mainline in the 1950s."[70] No professional organization of U.S. western historians existed. In the post–World War II era, then, the history of the American West was largely the domain of the amateurs. A majority of these western history buffs were men, and almost all were white. There were prominent exceptions, such as the well-published Mari Sandoz, daughter of Swiss immigrants to the Great Plains and author of books like the biography *Crazy Horse*. Earlier in the century, there was Delilah Beasley, African American clubwoman and author of *The Negro Trail Blazers of California*.[71] But the exceptions proved the rule: western history was a wide-open field for well-read amateurs who had the time and resources to devote to their hobby, and most such enthusiasts were white and male. It was in this milieu that Blackwelder and McClung embarked on their Carson projects.

These western history buffs were an organized bunch. It all started in Chicago, the city that had once served as the grand gateway between western resources and eastern markets.[72] There, in 1944, a small gathering of men established a group called the Westerners. The twenty-three founding members of this first chapter named themselves the Chicago Corral. Thinking back several years later on the Westerners' subsequent growth, founder Leland Case put it this way: "As we grew in vigor, we thought of men elsewhere who were also interested in lore of the West." So when Case's work as a journalist took him to Denver, he met with western history enthusiasts there, and soon the Colorado capital had its own Denver Posse. Most of the subsequent chapters that formed took on a "corral" or "posse" title, organizing by the late 1950s in cities such as St. Louis, New York, Tucson, Washington, D.C., Kansas City, and Spokane and also, on a statewide basis, in Wyoming and South Dakota. The association jumped the Atlantic when the English Westerners organized in 1954, followed by chapters in Sweden and Germany. Within a decade of the Chicago Corral's founding, Westerners from all over began to meet annually at the Inter-Posse Rendezvous.[73]

Most of the corrals and posses did not admit women. The New York Posse was the first to break the mold; the wives of two of the New York men as well as Mari Sandoz, who had by then published more than a half dozen books, were among the founders. As a Westerners chronicler wrote in 1957, "There were a lot of wranglers in the Corrals and Posses further west who damn near moved camp over this, but it wasn't too long before the men stopped airin' their lungs and the whole outfit ... is now bridle-wise. After all, one can't say 'No' to a Mari Sandoz!"[74] Nonetheless, the Westerners remained an overwhelmingly male group; early membership materials from chapters in Tucson, Los Angeles, Kansas City, Denver, and Santa Fe all indicate that men alone could become active members and attend regular gatherings. Women could join only as corresponding members, and they were not welcome at meetings.[75] As late as 1970, Leland Case said this: "The Westerners are bunches of males mostly, who meet monthly usually, to chomp and chat—then, after a speech on Western history to haze or praise the speaker."[76] White men, who were most of the members, gave most of the speeches. White men assumed virtually all chapter offices, serving in such capacities as sheriff, roundup foreman, tallyman, registrar of marks and brands, and wrangler.[77] (Privately, these men noted that their wives often did the clerical work required of them as officers.)[78] Newspaper coverage of the Chicago Westerners put it bluntly: "This is a stag outfit."[79]

Meanwhile, Chicago's corral was bursting; by 1947 there were seventy-five members. According to the *Chicago Tribune*, they included "lawyers, artists, doctors, anthropologists, geologists, bank presidents, industrialists, and advertising men." In other words, this was a middle-class and upper-middle-class organization. The members met monthly at the Merchants and Manufacturers Club in downtown Chicago's Merchandise Mart, finding "a happy escape from current problems by thumping a hairy-chested past."[80] Predictably, then, the Chicago Corral was not among the first to go coed. Even a designated Ladies Night in 1952 drew criticism from some members. The gathering featured a display of Native women's traditional clothing in a show dubbed "America's First Fashions." One man grumbled, "It's bad enough to have a ladies' night … but to have a dress parade is too much. What is this? A knitting society?"[81] Despite such grousing, annual Ladies Nights became standard fare not only in Chicago but for many corrals and posses. So did more sporadic coed gatherings: a Wyoming Westerners Roundup where men were asked to come in blue jeans and women in "A BIKINI BATHING SUIT," and a Chicago barbecue where "wranglers" and their "gals" could feast on "THE FINEST SIRLOIN DONE TO A TURN WITH THAT SAUCE THAT SMACKS OF THE WIDE OPEN SPACES WHERE MEN WERE MEN AND WOMEN WERE GLAD OF IT."[82] In the 1950s and '60s, the Westerners both reflected and perpetuated prevailing middle-class norms for relations between women and men, norms that would soon come under siege. Members anxiously associated those norms with an imagined western past IN ALL CAPS and did so in a manner that diminished women.

While almost all corrals and posses expressly excluded women, racial and ethnic exclusion was neither explicit nor uniform. Still, white men of non-Latino heritage constituted the overwhelming majority of participants. Scanning membership lists from the 1950s and '60s, for example, one must search long and hard to find a Spanish surname or a name clearly belonging to an Indigenous man, even though the Westerners claimed the history of the Spanish Southwest and especially that of Indian peoples as within their purview.[83] A fellow named A. E. "Rod" Rodríguez was a long-standing regular member of the Chicago Corral, but available records reveal little about his background.[84] Pawnee artist Brummett Echohawk of Oklahoma was a corresponding member of the same chapter. Echohawk did indeed correspond with the local group, and he even traveled to Chicago to address a Ladies Night gathering on the subject of Pawnee history.[85] North America's Indigenous past more generally was a staple for Westerners speakers, and even contemporary issues affecting Indians provoked lively debate, including the 1950s federal policy that sought to terminate tribal communities' unique relationship with the U.S. and state governments.[86] But one looks in vain for evidence that non-Anglo-American men regularly found a congenial home in the burgeoning corrals and posses of the Westerners.[87] This was a white man's playground.

When McClung and Blackwelder began their work on Carson in the 1950s, then, they faced a curious situation. They were amateur historians in a field where amateurs predominated, which could have worked to their advantage. They were also white in an arena that assumed whiteness as a ticket of admission. But the flip side of that ticket said that white men ought to be admitted first. In other words, they were white women in a world defined by almost parodic performances of white masculinity.[88] Well-educated, well-established white men would find themselves most at home on this range, where they offered one another a backslapping welcome to each chest-thumping roundup.

But change, of a sort, was on the horizon. In 1961, a small group of white men, mostly academics, met at the annual conference of the Mississippi Valley Historical Association, forerunner of the Organization of American Historians, now the leading professional group for U.S. historians. That year's conference was in Detroit, and the western historians who huddled there were promoting, as Robert Utley recalls, a "regional association of specialists, such as already existed for the South, the Midwest, and elsewhere."[89] Utley himself was strategically positioned in this effort, since he had begun but not finished his own PhD program, choosing instead a career with the National Park Service (he went on to publish widely in western history as well). Indeed, Utley remembers himself as always trying "to keep one foot in each of two worlds," though the distinctions between those two worlds may be clearer in hindsight than they were in 1961: "One was what has since come to be called 'public history,' the world of which the Park Service was a part but that also included state and local historical societies, museums, groups of 'buffs' such as the Westerners corrals, and freelance writers and 'grassroots' historians. All these people strove ... to communicate history to the reading and traveling public. The other was the scholarly world almost entirely centered in the nation's colleges and universities. Scholars in academia communicated mainly with their students and, in their publications, with one another."[90] Utley's ties to both professors and buffs proved an asset in establishing a new organization of western historians that drew on the strength of the Westerners but also appealed to degreed scholars working in academia. The men who met in Detroit in the spring of 1961 announced a fall gathering in Santa Fe, where the call for a new association would "spontaneously" arise.[91]

Organizers, including Utley, expected fewer than a hundred registrants at the First Conference on the History of Western America, held in October 1961. Three hundred showed up, filling the meeting spaces and guest rooms of La Fonda, the grand hotel on the plaza at the end of the Santa Fe Trail. The location of this gathering (in the midst of Pueblo Indian country and at the heart of the old Mexican North) and the conference program distributed to participants (the cover featured a "prairie schooner lady" complete with rifle) suggested that a newer day might dawn in western history. To twenty-first-century eyes, a "Southwestern Borderlands" session and ethnologist John Ewers's adaptation of the "marginal man" concept in his paper "Mothers of the Mixed-Bloods: The Marginal Woman in the History of the Upper Missouri" look promising. But of the twenty-five papers presented, none were by women or people of color, though one white woman chaired a session and another delivered a comment on two papers.[92]

Of more lasting impact than the sessions themselves, however, was an evening business meeting, which staged the call for a new organization. Apparently liquor lubricated the proceedings, and although Utley recalls that fur trade historian LeRoy Hafen questioned the antidemocratic "railroading" tactics at the gavel, a consensus about the proposed group emerged. (Hafen, a devout Mormon, was no doubt not among the drinkers.) A "quiet dinner" of organizers followed, with a mollified Hafen at table. All the men who dined, save Utley, had doctoral degrees and most were professors. Some, including both Utley and Hafen, were active in the Westerners. Ray Allen Billington, the era's best-known western historian, agreed to serve as the new group's first president.[93] The actual founding of the Western History Association (WHA) came a year later, in 1962, at the Second Conference on the History of Western America, held in Denver.[94] Reflecting the organization's commitment to bringing academics and buffs together, the first publication of the WHA was not a scholarly journal, dense with text and lacking in visual appeal, but a slick, illustrated magazine called the *American West*.[95] Over time, professional historians assumed greater control over the WHA and hence over the field of western history. But for now, a gentlemanly bargain kept the stags grazing more or less amiably in the same glen.

Unlike most early Westerners chapters, the WHA did not exclude women, though many of us who joined the WHA in later decades believe that a hot western sun of white male privilege bathed our organizational forebears in its glow.[96] The earth did not begin to turn until the 1970s, and the changed angle of light was not fully apparent until the 1980s.[97] In the meantime, as one white woman who worked in the field early on put it, "there were very few of us, and we were treated like morons by most male historians."[98] Still, the WHA's open membership policy mattered. Blackwelder, who lived in suburban Washington, D.C., could not have joined the Potomac Corral of the Westerners. She could, and did, become a charter member of the WHA.[99] McClung did not join, perhaps because her own work identity was less as a historian and more as a librarian and genealogist, and her chief organizational tie was to the Colorado Genealogical Society.[100]

WHA members or not, Blackwelder and McClung were marginal figures in the field. Indeed, they were minor historians, bit players whom the major actors barely noticed.[101] Blackwelder's book was reviewed sporadically and the reviews were mixed. Ray Allen Billington published a polite notice in the *Chicago Tribune*, concluding, "The author's readable style and her laudable dependence on fact rather than imagination have produced a book that can be recommended to the general reader interested in one of the nation's most dramatic eras," apparently not recognizing or else choosing not to mention the authorial license Blackwelder took in imputing motivation and emotion where little evidence existed. Otherwise, *Great Westerner* was reviewed in state and regional history journals as well as the *Denver Westerners' Roundup*. In *Arizona and the West*, fur trade historian John Sunder called attention to Blackwelder's photograph on the book's dust cover, noting that the book "was compiled by an attractive . . . former Professor of Voice at Central College, Fayette, Missouri," thereby undercutting an already irrelevant academic affiliation with the sort of comment on appearance that male scholars never made when they reviewed one another's books.[102] McClung's *Carson-Bent-Boggs Genealogy* was not the sort of text to be reviewed in either the popular press or history journals, but other Carson scholars knew of it and relied on it in their own research. Later in the decade, historian Harvey Carter would call McClung's genealogy "a most useful work of reference," praising "her happy inspiration to include the Bent and Boggs families as well." Likewise, Carter applauded Blackwelder's *Great Westerner* for its "original contributions on small points" as well as its "swiftly moving style," even as he criticized it for minor errors of fact.[103]

Given the modest recognition Blackwelder and McClung received for their work, they were vitally important to one another. Each took the other and her contributions seriously, and both thrived on their collaboration, an exchange of ideas and research conducted by mail. Yet Blackwelder, in particular, remained acutely aware of her status as a woman working in western history (and, like most white people, oblivious to the privilege afforded by race). The first time she sent her Carson biography out for consideration, an editor returned it, recommending that she rework it as a "youth book."[104] The suggestion irked her, so she revised the manuscript and sent it to Caxton Press instead.[105] "I know there is a good and authentic story there," she told McClung of her work, but, she went on, "perhaps it [is] too ladylike for a Wild West thriller."[106] Such protests notwithstanding, the psychic damage was done, and even though there is no indication in Blackwelder's letters that she originally intended her work for young readers, ever after that initial rejection and revision she clung to the notion that hers was "a story rather than a history book." She insisted in retrospect that she had always "had in mind the young adult" and claimed that she would be satisfied if the book found a place in "school libraries."[107] Feigning low expectations, Blackwelder inoculated herself against the disappointment that might follow any woman, even a married white woman of an appropriate class, who ventured into the gendered space of the American West.

Blackwelder's rivalry with the woman who published a competing book about Carson in 1962 opens a different window on these dynamics. In 1961, Blackwelder wrote to McClung that she had heard about "some woman in Taos" who was also writing a biography of Carson.[108] The woman was Marion Estergreen, and her *Kit Carson: A Portrait in Courage* was published by the University of Oklahoma Press just months after Blackwelder's book appeared.[109] Like Blackwelder, Estergreen was an amateur historian captivated by Carson. Unlike Blackwelder, Estergreen won a contract with a university press and published under a gender-ambiguous name, M. Morgan Estergreen.[110] Although Blackwelder referred vaguely to Estergreen as "some woman," the two were hardly strangers. They had met and even cooperated with each other on public commemorations of Carson, though they may not have known of one another's book projects. Blackwelder felt that her relationship with Estergreen had soured years earlier when Estergreen asked for comments on a short Carson piece she had written. "I answered her honestly and offended her I suppose," Blackwelder griped to McClung about Estergreen, "as she has been very cool to me ever since."[111] Estergreen and Blackwelder also disagreed over what constituted valid membership in a fledgling Kit Carson Memorial Association.[112] These earlier differences informed Blackwelder's reception of Estergreen's book.

Blackwelder's *Great Westerner* and Estergreen's *Kit Carson* share much: both are admiring biographies covering the full sweep of Carson's life, from his birth in Kentucky to his death in Colorado.[113] Estergreen relates more of Carson's family history, while Blackwelder chronicles the final years of Carson's life more completely. Blackwelder's book has greater narrative verve. Estergreen, by contrast, peoples her stories with the full cast of characters who accompanied Carson in his western adventures, and she maps those adventures assiduously. As a result, Estergreen's book is more thorough in places but also sometimes tedious to read. Neither author had scholarly training, but each researched both primary and secondary materials and worked to identify her sources. Though Blackwelder published with a nonacademic press, her documentation is easier to follow, since she uses a system of endnotes coupled with a bibliography of published sources, even if her endnotes are sometimes sketchy. Blackwelder also did archival research for *Great Westerner*, but her citation of such materials is often vague. Estergreen, notwithstanding the university press that published her work, does not use endnotes but rather a list of sources that inform each chapter, making it difficult to identify exactly which materials inform various aspects of her narrative. Estergreen's bibliography of published sources is similar to Blackwelder's, but Estergreen more carefully cites her archival collections. Estergreen also cites sources held in private possession—sets of letters and such that have not found their way into archival repositories—making it impossible to retrace all the steps she took in her research.[114] In sum, Blackwelder's and Estergreen's books have similarities of tone and content, but they differ in strengths and weaknesses.

Blackwelder herself revealed a difference between the two texts when she reviewed Estergreen's book in *Arizona and the West* (a journal that almost became an official WHA publication but for the refusal of the publication's sponsoring institution, the University of Arizona).[115] Blackwelder applauded Estergreen's "earnest adherence to fact" and "admirable restraint of sentimentality" but warned that the book's readers might "bog down in the plethora of minute detail." And Blackwelder specified the sort of detail that bothered her: "The names of the commissioners who drew up the treaty at the Council of the Plains Indians and those who signed the Ute treaty in Washington are more important for the record than lists of obscure bondsmen."[116] In other words, she thought Estergreen should have named the officials who presided over the treaties the U.S. government negotiated with Plains peoples and Ute bands in the 1860s and not the polyglot and often unfree laborers who worked alongside white frontiersmen, accompanied U.S. government expeditions, or found themselves captured and traded among the Native, Mexican, and Anglo populations of the borderlands. Indeed, Estergreen, more often than Blackwelder, took pains to identify the enslaved and free blacks, the French voyageurs, the Mexican and Indigenous captives, and the Delaware Indian hunters who crossed paths with Carson.[117] For Blackwelder, such characters played inconsequential roles in the saga of the West.

Estergreen never got the chance to return Blackwelder's fire in a print review, but she had the last laugh.[118] Perhaps because it was published by a university press, *Kit Carson* garnered more attention than *Great Westerner* did, at least in history journals. And Estergreen—while she was, like Blackwelder, a minor historian—was the more recognized and well connected of the two authors. In addition to her book, Estergreen published magazine articles as well as tourist tracts that circulated in northern New Mexico, and she was loosely tied to the long-standing creative arts community in Taos.[119] Blackwelder had no such ties or texts to her credit.

The breach between Blackwelder and Estergreen began before they both published in 1962, fueled by disagreements about Carson and, no doubt, by jealousy. When their books appeared, the gulf widened. Indeed, Blackwelder wrote to McClung that she "wondered what Kit was thinking about the old hens fighting over his memory."[120] Blackwelder held that Estergreen got details of Carson's life wrong.[121] But it was also clear that try as she might to be fair to Estergreen, Blackwelder did not like her rival. "She has worked so hard on every Carson project and is a very pleasant and attractive person," Blackwelder wrote of Estergreen and then turned the knife: "The last time I saw her, she said she expected to be married to a very wealthy man who was travelling in Europe. . . . I think she has a vivid imagination."[122] (Estergreen, who grew up in Albuquerque, had once been married to a man who worked for the U.S. Forest Service in the Southwest, but he was long since out of the picture.)[123]

In calling her struggle with Estergreen a hen fight, Blackwelder abased not only Estergreen but also herself, trivializing not just their differences but the very intellectual work that animated both women. In suggesting that Estergreen's romance with an affluent, worldly man was a flight of fancy, Blackwelder hurled among the sharpest insults one white, aspiring middle-class, heterosexual woman could fling at another. Both aspersions bespoke a cultural conservatism about women and their worth, a language so pervasive in this era that many women themselves were experts in its grammar. But Blackwelder's resentment may have stemmed, too, from an unconscious root of bitterness about how that language circumscribed her own life chances, especially as a woman working in western history.[124] When Estergreen published under a gender-ambiguous given name like Morgan and with a university press renowned for its western history list, she increased the chances that the very people who were gaining ground in the field—white male professors—would stand up and take notice. And indeed, Estergreen's *Kit Carson* was available in a handsome paperback edition for over four decades, displayed at western historical sites and visible to western historians in the University of Oklahoma Press catalog.[125] Blackwelder's *Great Westerner* went out of print in just eight years.[126] Estergreen won the hen fight in part by passing as a rooster.

Nonetheless, there was one thing on which all creatures great and small—amateurs and professionals, lowly hens and high-stepping roosters—could agree: historians told the truth about the western past.[127] In this, historians set their West, the West of history, in opposition to the West of the Western. This habit of opposition developed in part because the field of western history had lagged in the mid-twentieth century at the same moment that film and television Westerns—oaters, as they were called—reached the height of their popularity.[128] Western history lagged because decades of criticism had battered the field's founding argument, the famous frontier thesis. Frederick Jackson Turner had written in 1893, "Up to our own day American history has been in large degree the history of the colonization of the Great West. The existence of an area of free land, its continuous recession, and the advance of American settlement westward, explain American development." Turner's thesis fell on hard times, especially during the Great Depression, when the agony of many Americans seemed better explained historically by such forces as urbanization and industrialization.[129]

Meanwhile, in the mines of myth and memory, the West maintained its luster, and purveyors of popular culture tapped that bright vein with a vengeance. Between 1935 and 1959, the percentage of Westerns as a proportion of all Hollywood feature films produced annually never dipped below 20 percent. The peak came after World War II, from 1946 to 1956, when at least a quarter of feature films made yearly were Westerns. In 1950 alone, Westerns constituted more than a third of movies produced, and by 1956, the proportion was approaching half.[130] No other single film genre could match these proportions. The new medium of television followed suit, though the peak came later, in 1959, when the largest number of Western TV series was on the air—forty-eight in all.[131] Westerns were not just plentiful; they were popular. In 1958, seven of the top ten Nielsen-rated series were oaters. As one scholar argues, "No television program genre, not even the situation comedy, ever became so dominant at any given moment in time as the Western during the late 1950s and early 1960s."[132]

Raw numbers and relative proportions, however, do not reveal the changes taking place within the Western genre in this era. Some film

Westerns, for example, began to take a darker, more complicated view of the frontier. The most famous of these anti-Westerns was *High Noon* (1952), which, through Gary Cooper's character, critiqued not only the "civilizing" projects of the Old West but also the conformist, anticommunist politics of the Cold War.[133] Two years later, *Johnny Guitar* did likewise, this time with a butch-looking Joan Crawford getting the gun. The year I was born, 1956, saw the release of *Giant*, a Texas epic in which neither Rock Hudson as venerable cattle king nor James Dean as upstart oil baron hold a sustainable vision of the West's riches. In a striking critique of regional racism, *Giant* ends with a new take on the wealth and promise of Texas: a scene of two handsome toddlers in a playpen—cousins—one a tow-headed Anglo and the other a dark-eyed mestizo. Television Westerns changed as well. The early 1950s saw a preponderance of morally simple, action-packed shows like *The Adventures of Kit Carson* and *The Lone Ranger*, which appealed to youngsters. The late 1950s and the '60s witnessed the birth of series like *Gunsmoke* and *Bonanza*, dramas capable of moral complexity and geared toward adult audiences.[134]

The Western evolved aesthetically but also in accord with Cold War politics, a central concern of which was to reconcile the workings of democracy with the exercise of power, whether the external power of a United States emboldened by its status in the postwar world or the internal power of those accustomed to domestic rule, who were mostly white, male, heterosexual, and comfortably situated in a corporate, consumer economy. Both externally and internally, though, power was disputed, and democratic values dictated that disputation could not be dismissed out of hand. This was true if the contest took shape in the anticolonial demands of so-called Third World countries or it if it took the form of social justice claims among minoritized peoples in the United States. And even the World War II triumph of the United States and its allies had come at a terrifying cost; the threat of nuclear war and the global spread of communism produced what one thinker calls "triumphalist despair" and a concomitant "nightmarish search for enemies" that became the "defining, even obsessive domestic act of the Cold War." It is in this context that the dark turn of some Westerns makes sense, where a brooding hero like Gary Cooper's Will Kane saves a town unworthy of salvation—unworthy because the evil of the outlaws who threaten it is matched by the complacency and cowardice of the townsfolk. It is in this context, too, that a morally compromised woman like Joan Crawford's Vienna wields a weapon on behalf of her business and in the interests of a band of male ruffians, confronting a morally bankrupt cattle baron, played by Mercedes McCambridge, and her despicable male compatriots. And it is in this context as well that Texas is cut down to toddler size—in WarnerColor hues, no less, not monochromatic whiteness.[135]

Still, as multiple and mutable as Westerns were, they had weak links to an actual western past. They were overwhelmingly set in a late nineteenth-century West, somewhere on the arid plains or in edge landscapes between the prairies and mountains, and they focused on the passing of the frontier, on contests between "civilization" and "savagery," on appropriate and inappropriate uses of violence, and on competing styles of manhood. Westerns resolved those conflicts variously, but they did not overly concern themselves with history as it happened, as people had lived it. It was those tenuous ties to a real past that bothered the historically minded, who, for better and worse, saw themselves engaged not in acts of representation but in acts of recuperation. In the view of most historians, producers of popular culture created stylized images of the past; historians recreated what really transpired. It would be decades before historians would start to recognize that their own practices were at least in part representational. In the meantime, historians saw themselves as rescuing the West from the Westerns.[136] For instance, the academic Ray Allen Billington sniffed, "To a generation of Americans bred on television and cinema 'westerns' ... the West is to be enjoyed rather than understood." Enjoyment was kid stuff.[137] For their part, members of the Westerners, not unfairly, boasted that they had preserved the field of western history at a time when even academics had shied away and before movie and TV Westerns exploded in the 1950s. Leland Case, a founder of the Chicago Corral, states, "In those early forties, there was no subculture or public of Western buffs. The dime novel era was over, steel-eyed William S. Hart's fans were of Boy Scout age, and college catalogs attest that Western history was scantily accepted by academics. TV's 'oaters' were yet to be, and the Western History Association was almost two decades in the future."[138] The resurgence of western history, first among buffs and then among academics, would wean the Boy Scouts from their oaters for a manly meal of meat and potatoes—and no skipping the vegetables.

McClung and Blackwelder ate at a table nearby, even if the men of the Westerners who gathered to "chomp and chat" in Chicago and the WHA organizers who sat down to a "quiet dinner" in Santa Fe rarely glanced their way. So identified were these two women with the larger recuperative project of the historian—the sober reconstitution of a lost world that little resembled the formulaic West of the Western—that they barely realized the singular contribution their work had made in 1962. Seeing themselves as engaged in a broader contest between the truth of history and the sham of popular culture, they did not recognize that their achievements were partly in the realm of representation. They succeeded in domesticating a key icon of the western past, in tying Kit Carson tightly to the people who populated his everyday world—and not just the mountain men, explorers, warriors, and soldiers featured in earlier accounts but also the wives, lovers, children, nieces, and brothers-in-law who in fact anchored Carson in the borderlands and kept him coming back, and back, and back again, until he finally spoke his dying words in Spanish to a German-born kinsman who understood him, as they rested not far from the old traders' fort where Kit had once held an Arapaho and then a Cheyenne woman in his arms, the same arms that shouldered a gun trained on Navajo people. No one at an Inter-Posse Rendezvous, no one at the Santa Fe conference, and no Saturday matinee Western had done that.

Cold War, Color Line, and Cul-de-sac

In 1958, Bernice Blackwelder had finished her Carson manuscript and was waiting to learn its fate. She was living in Alexandria, Virginia, where she and her husband, Harold, had just purchased a house—a one-story brick rambler financed with a government-guaranteed loan. Harold was running an eatery called Blackwelder's Barbeque. Meanwhile, Bernice spent time in Washington at the Library of Congress and the National Archives.[139] But one day in March, she went to see Gore Vidal's *Visit to a Small Planet*. In this satire, an earth-curious space alien lands in Manassas, Virginia (not far from Alexandria), and "goes native," provoking war between the United States and the Soviet Union in the process. Whether or not Bernice fully appreciated Vidal's send-up of the era's anticommunist paranoia, the play did provoke her. She wrote to Quantrille McClung that it made her "wonder what good it really is to dig into the past and unearth little nobodies when it is now a possibility that we may all be blown to nothing."[140] Quantrille, sitting at the typewriter in her Denver apartment, wrote back, "Yes, in view of the possibilities of world destruction, genealogical research seems silly." But Quantrille carried on with her work by day and attended meetings and concerts by night, declaring, "I shall enjoy my life and try to accomplish something."[141]

Their mobility through metropolitan space and their exchange of postwar angst bespoke the milieu in which Bernice and Quantrille lived. Cold War culture, political and otherwise, influenced them and their work, and so did the rapidly changing relationship between cities and suburbs that was fueled by the post–World War II boom. The postwar standoff between the capitalist United States and the communist U.S.S.R. fostered multiple cultural by-products. For McClung's and Blackwelder's work, two of these were especially relevant: the promotion of the heterosexual, nuclear family as a locus of and metaphor for national security, and the idealization of the West and its past as a sort of savings bank where American character might be safely deposited to earn interest against attempts at assassination, foreign or domestic. Just as important, civil rights movements among minoritized populations in the United States both appropriated and challenged Cold War dogma, leavening lumpish notions of "the family" and "the West" and creating conditions for social change—and for conservative resistance to change. These dynamics, as well as the twinned process of suburban growth and urban decay, with all of its racial impetus and consequence, did not just shape Blackwelder's and McClung's work casually, the way a cloudy day affects one's mood. The climate of the Cold War rained down on these women and saturated their daily lives, providing both the elements for a good creative yield and the storms that left crops waterlogged.

Conspicuously absent in the way they represented themselves and their daily lives to each other, however, was any explicit discussion of how race helped to create those lives and those selves. McClung and Blackwelder would not openly address racial matters in their letters until the late 1960s. Such conversations came when both began to live in closer proximity to people of color and when movements for racial justice fully penetrated their consciousness, forcing them to foreground views and experiences they had left in the background before. For the time being, they maintained a racial silence, reflecting one of the key consequences of segregation and the chief benefits of whiteness: lives lived behind a shield that makes racial privilege all but invisible and with it the effects of that privilege on racialized others. Their silence makes it hard to write about some, but not all, of the ways racial hierarchies shaped their lives and work using their own words, which means that I address issues such as the homogeneity of their neighborhoods using other sorts of sources. But silence is its own kind of evidence.

As their 1958 exchange about "the possibilities of world destruction" suggests, McClung and Blackwelder did speak aloud about the geopolitical climate of the Cold War, a climate that bolstered interest in all things western and so helped nurture a market not only for Hollywood's West but also for the work that western historians were producing.[142] When *Great Westerner* was released in 1962, for example, no less a Cold War figure than former president Dwight D. Eisenhower sent Blackwelder his congratulations. Blackwelder—a Republican, fellow Kansan, and trained singer—had connections to Eisenhower's administration and had even performed at a party for his 1953 inauguration. The note he sent was in part political payback. But Eisenhower loved the frontier, and so the focus of *Great Westerner* mattered.[143]

Just as postwar politics laid out a welcome mat for work on the West, so, too, did it place limits on where and when that work could proceed. In May 1958, McClung received an invitation to a Carson family reunion in Kansas, where she might have gleaned new information for her genealogy. But, she told Blackwelder, "I did not feel like spending my own money to go and I did not want to be on the road at such a dangerous time."[144] Lack of financial resources was a perennial theme in both women's letters, but the danger McClung felt that May was particular. She did not spell out her fear, but she may have been referencing nuclear test blasts conducted by the Department of Defense and the Atomic Energy Commission in the South Pacific. Or she may have been alluding to heightened international tensions created by the ongoing Cuban Revolution and, most immediately, by Vice President Richard Nixon's ill-fated tour of Latin America, where violent anti-U.S. protests prompted Eisenhower to send troops to Caribbean bases.[145] These tensions would intensify when the 1960s dawned, as John F. Kennedy assumed the presidency and as McClung and Blackwelder finished their book manuscripts, culminating in the autumn of 1962 with the Cuban Missile Crisis, which brought the United States and the U.S.S.R. to the brink of nuclear war.[146]

Blackwelder's and McClung's responses to this brinkmanship are lost to the historical record because of a hiatus in their correspondence between the summer of 1962 and the fall of 1965 (of which, more anon). Regardless, the clearest indication of their broader engagement with the Cold War cultural milieu in which they did their historical work lies in their representation of Kit Carson as a family man. And their subtle disagreements about what fit in a family story remind us that in this era, the idea of "family" was a flash point for debate as much as it was a cultural fund for the discipline of nonconformists. Blackwelder and McClung's crisis of representation started in 1957, when they heard rumor of murder and mayhem among Kit Carson and Josefa Jaramillo's offspring. One story had Kit and Josefa's son Cristobal shooting his in-laws, the parents of his wife, Lupe. After the shooting, Cristobal was said to have run away to escape authorities. While he was gone, Lupe was said to have had a baby that could not have been her husband's, though the child came to be called Kit Carson III.[147] A second story had Kit and Josefa's son Julián killing his wife Pasqualita's father.[148] McClung and Blackwelder found plausible the story of Lupe's parents' murder as well as the related tale of Kit III's illegitimacy. They dismissed the tale of Julián shooting his father-in-law. But they stopped short of working to confirm or discredit these stories.[149] Blackwelder was blunt: as for "the family scandal," she wrote, "I believe we should keep the closet doors tightly shut." McClung was equivocal: "Accounts of the supposed Carson homicides just show how incorrect stories get around and how hard it is to clarify them."[150] Given how diligently they worked to clarify other aspects of Carson family history, however, their decision to maintain a public silence about these tales is notable. Not all stories had a place in the family room; some belonged in the closet.

It was not just murder that counted as scandal, as Kit Carson III's alleged illegitimacy suggests.[151] In years to come, Blackwelder and McClung's crisis would only grow, as they began to see more evidence of sexual relationships outside of marriage in the Carson family circle. This information was just starting to surface as they finished their books in the 1950s. The main case in point was what McClung called the "mystery of the Rumaldas."[152] Recall that Tom Boggs married a woman named Rumalda, the daughter of Ignacia Jaramillo, Josefa's sister. Rumalda was Ignacia's child from her first marriage, to a man called Rafael Luna, before she took up with Charles Bent. This Rumalda was born about 1831. Yet early on, Blackwelder and McClung ran across references to another daughter of Ignacia's named Rumalda. Bent descendants told McClung that this Rumalda was the child of Ignacia and Charles, born in the summer of 1847. But in one Bent family bible McClung consulted, all of the marriage records had been erased, and a second family bible listed this Rumalda's year of birth as 1850. If Rumalda the younger was indeed born in 1850, she could not have been Charles Bent's daughter, because he had been murdered in the January 1847 uprising against U.S. rule in New Mexico. A birth date of 1850 would have given the second Rumalda an amazingly long gestation, so long as Charles was considered her father.[153] In 1958, McClung wrote confidently to Blackwelder that she thought she would be able "to clear up the mystery of the Rumaldas in the Bent and Boggs families."[154]

In fact, when McClung published her genealogy in 1962, the mystery was only half-solved. In an entry for the Bent family, McClung repeats the contention of some family members that Rumalda the younger was born six months after the death of her father, Charles, in the Taos rebellion, as the 1847 uprising came to be called. But McClung also spells out the inconsistencies in Bent family bibles that point to an 1850 birth date for this Rumalda and thus a different father.[155] In an appendix, McClung quotes from an 1865 court decree that not only listed just three children of Charles Bent, none of them named Rumalda, but also explained that these three were "the *natural* son and daughters of … Charles Bent … by him begotten upon and conceived and born of Ignacia Jaramillo."[156] In other words, Ignacia and Charles themselves might never have married. This and other related plots would thicken after the publication of the *Carson-Bent-Boggs Genealogy* and *Great Westerner*, as more information came to light and as attitudes about sexuality changed, until even the tale of Carson's three marriages would no longer seem the whole story of his intimate life. By 1969, Blackwelder would write to McClung in defense of the man she had portrayed in *Great Westerner*: "There is nothing gained by passing on 'gossip' of Kit's amorous associations. … To me he was a devoted family man and a great humanitarian."[157] Meanwhile, Mc-Clung went about her genealogical business, quietly hinting at how complicated nineteenth-century domestic life in the borderlands could be.

For both women, in different ways, the Cold War love affair with the family permeated their work. After all, this was the era in which the fight against communism and the search for security in idealized heterosexual homes intertwined to produce a dominant discourse of "domestic containment," which, of course, obscured the actual complexity and diversity of both politics and intimate life in the United States.[158] It was hard to write a family history when so much of what swirled around folks like the Carsons also gusted up against conventional definitions of family. Such definitions were informed by prescriptions for sexual intimacy: it should happen in the context of marriage.[159] They were also informed by assumptions about nurturance and affection: these were the natural currency of family relations. Tales of murder and nonmarital sex alike gave pause. Regardless, Blackwelder, deliberately, and McClung, ambivalently, made of Kit Carson a family man who fought for America, a fellow any Cold Warrior could love.

All of this was not a little ironic, since neither Bernice Blackwelder nor Quantrille McClung themselves lived in idealized Cold War family forms. Bernice came closest, with her marriage of many years to Harold Blackwelder, but the couple had no children. Apparently, they had wanted to conceive, and Bernice keenly felt their inability as well as her apparent difference from the women she encountered in everyday life. According to her favorite niece, Doris Lance, whenever Bernice walked her dog, she wished she could "hang a sign on herself that read, '*We tried.*'" That way, "people wouldn't keep remarking that she should be pushing a baby carriage instead of walking a dog."[160] Bernice may have joked about it, but her neighbors' comments reflect the pressure childless couples in general, and women in particular, felt in the era of "compulsory parenthood."[161] Quantrille, by contrast, spoke no regret about her own solitary situation. Most of her life, she lived alone in a downtown apartment near the Denver Public Library, which had been her workplace and where she later did research. Quantrille's health had forced her into an early retirement, and, as she told another genealogy enthusiast, a woman in an abusive marriage, "Thank God, I never had to cope with a husband! Life has been difficult without that complication!"[162]

Of course, neither Quantrille nor Bernice were of the generation toward which Cold War prescriptions about the primacy of the family and women's place in it were directed; in the 1950s, Quantrille was in her sixties and Bernice in her fifties.[163] They came of age under different expectations for white, middle-class women—expectations that arguably allowed them to envision more independent lives.[164] Nonetheless, while they were not among the principal targets of Cold War precepts, they imbibed enough of postwar cultural conversations to produce a Kit Carson for the era. The subtle differences in the family man each crafted no doubt reflected her own desires, politics, and access to privilege, both sexual and racial.

For example, while the Blackwelders did not raise a family, their lives when Bernice was working on *Great Westerner* reflected the political economy of the postwar United States in key ways. They lived outside Washington, D.C., where they took advantage of the governmental largesse that helped re-create the white middle class and secure the white working class, moving both to the booming suburbs that circled the cities.[165] The Blackwelders did not profit from that largesse as richly as some, though. Their first suburban home was one side of a duplex in a modest Arlington subdivision, Columbia Heights. The duplex went up during the postwar housing boom, sandwiched in a tiny lot on a cul-de-sac in a residential neighborhood.[166] Bernice and Harold took out a mortgage on their four-room home in 1952 and then sold it in 1958—for less than they had paid for it.[167] They took a loss, then, on the first dwelling they ever owned.

Despite the loss, Bernice was thrilled when they secured a mortgage on a new, single-family home on a quarter-acre lot in nearby Alexandria. After living in cramped quarters for a half dozen years, Bernice told Quantrille in 1957 that she finally would have space for her notes and books: "Will be wonderful to spread out a little more as now I will ... have a room for assembling all this material." The new house, then, gave this writing woman the proverbial room of her own.[168] It must have felt like a mansion, with its living room, dining room, kitchen, three bedrooms, and even an extra half bath, not just the lone bathroom Harold and Bernice were accustomed to sharing. There was space for guests, and Quantrille probably slept there when she visited Bernice in 1962.[169] A cloistered garden of redbrick ramblers in a honeycomb of broad, curving lanes with no easy outlet to a major thoroughfare, the Blackwelders' neighborhood exuded suburbia's tamed and contained state of nature: the subdivision itself was called Parklawn, and streets bore the names of U.S. national forests and parks. As a western historian, it must have tickled Bernice to live on Yellowstone Drive and to stroll with her dog along the sidewalks of Teton Place, Tahoe Court, and Olympic Way. Thus planted, Bernice finished *Great Westerner* and sent letters to the *Washington Post* calling attention to Carson's memory.[170]

Like other postwar white married couples, Harold and Bernice Blackwelder benefited from federal housing policy, which underwrote mortgages for single-family, suburban homes on generous terms. Such loans went hand in hand with systematic racial discrimination by both the Federal Housing Administration and the Veterans Administration, which endorsed racially segregated neighborhood patterns. This left poor people and people of color, often living in rentals, overrepresented in the cities and more prosperous white people, most of them homeowners, overrepresented in the suburbs—though the relative prosperity of suburban whites was itself often the product of federal policy, since the mortgages guaranteed by the government often went to buyers in working-class housing developments.[171] It was a vicious cycle of suburban development and urban decline, since suburbs boasted property owners who created a strong tax base, while the urban tax base lagged, leaving city dwellers hurting for services and amenities that the more comfortable took as their due.[172] In the years that they lived in Arlington and Alexandria, the Blackwelders were in the thick of all this.

But they were not secure in this world. And Bernice herself was ambivalent about her neighborhood, an enclave of revolving residents in the shadow of the nation's capital. She told Quantrille, "I do not have many neighbors with my particular interests though they could not be more pleasant folks—mostly military and many soon move on." At least, she noted, perhaps comparing Washington's suburbs to those of other cities, "this world-wide wave of changing populace does give insight into much beyond our own back yards."[173] It was probably as much her husband's changing fortunes as it was the transience of Parklawn homeowners, though, that gave Bernice a sense of impermanence. When they lived in Arlington and when they first moved to Alexandria, Harold ran

Blackwelder's Barbeque. But in 1960, he and Bernice opened a more elaborate, southern-themed restaurant called Blackwelder's Country House, featuring multiple dining rooms (such as the equine Blue Grass Room), an electric kitchen (the "only one in Virginia," Bernice boasted), wood paneling ("synthetic but pretty"), a stone fireplace, red-and-white-checked tablecloths, and waitresses with "aprons to match." Once this restaurant was up and running, Harold took over day-to-day operations, and Bernice told Quantrille, "I am now free to pursue my own interests."[174] But less than two years later, Harold abandoned the Country House and opened a barbecue carryout in an Arlington shopping center, where Bernice was responsible for making "the pastries, pecan tarts, brownies, pralines, and three kinds of cake: German's Sweet Chocolate, pineapple [and] banana."[175] This new business must have failed, because within months Bernice worried that they might have to sell their house. She wrote to Quantrille in the summer of 1962 that she hoped she and Harold would still be in Alexandria in the fall: "Expect to be as I will not be too easily moved from this home." Though Quantrille visited shortly thereafter, this was the last letter Bernice posted from the East.[176] Within months, she and Harold put the house up for sale.[177] Suburban dreams could die hard.

Quantrille McClung never had those dreams, or, if she did, she did not have the resources to pursue them. In the 1950s, she did not discuss her finances in letters, but years later she told Bernice that her "modest affairs" were in a bank trust that allowed her "a small sum each month." Quantrille also reported then that she enjoyed a "small pension from the City" and that she kept a savings account for emergencies.[178] She seemed more or less content to live in the city of her birth, renting a one-bedroom apartment that allowed her to walk to the library, the state historical society, and other downtown attractions such as museums, theaters, and Colorado's capitol building (indeed, her neighborhood was and is known as Capitol Hill). In 1962, she moved to a new apartment, but it was just five blocks from where she lived in the 1950s and in a similar brick building that housed a number of units.[179]

In this period, Denver was a segregated city, and it remained so because of restrictive real estate covenants and, after legal challenges to such covenants, because of discriminatory practices by banks, realtors, and white property owners. In 1950, for example, almost 90 percent of African Americans lived in the Five Points area, a neighborhood over a dozen blocks northeast of Quantrille's apartment. By 1960, the black population had grown, and more prosperous families had begun to move east toward the Park Hill area, but this was even farther from Quantrille's residence. Denver's ethnic Mexican population, which included *hispanos* with roots in northern New Mexico as well as Mexican immigrants and their descendants, similarly lived in separate districts, especially to the north and west and along the South Platte River.[180] One exception to the rule of racial segregation involved American Indians, who came to Denver from reservation communities under the auspices of federal relocation programs after 1952. For the most part, Indigenous people did not congregate in particular Denver neighborhoods. But Capitol Hill, because of its central location, often did serve as an initial destination for migrants, who later moved to outlying areas.[181] If Quantrille encountered any of her new Native neighbors, she did not reflect on it in her letters. Still, in this period, Quantrille was more likely to encounter people of color from time to time in downtown Denver than Bernice was in suburban Arlington and Alexandria.

Both women could not have been unaware that racial change was brewing, even though they did not discuss it in their letters. They had lived through the upswing of racial resistance that followed World War II among virtually all racialized minority peoples in the United States, including American Indians, Asian Americans, African Americans, and Latinos. Denver, with its substantial ethnic Mexican population, was home to active chapters of the American GI Forum and the League of United Latin American Citizens. Meanwhile, the White Buffalo Council of American Indians saw to the needs of Denver's burgeoning Native population and played host to other intertribal organizations.[182] But no movement was more visible to white Americans nationally than that of black civil rights activists, whose attack on the legal basis for discrimination and segregation, exemplified most famously in the 1954 U.S. Supreme Court decision in *Brown v. Board of Education*, had turned toward direct action of the sort associated with the Montgomery bus boycott of 1955–56 and the student sit-ins in the years that followed. And Virginia, where Bernice and Harold lived, participated in the "massive resistance" that southern states mounted to black civil rights.[183]

Quantrille and Bernice were silent about all this in their correspondence, probably because they were just getting to know each other. They met by letter in 1956, and by 1962, when their books were published, they had seen one another face-to-face just twice, once when Bernice passed through Denver and once when Quantrille visited the Blackwelders in Alexandria.[184] Most of their letters in these years were filled with exchanges of research information; only later would their relationship become more intimate and would their correspondence range widely over many more aspects of their lives. For white women who collaborated on historical projects and were not yet terribly close, it was likely white racial etiquette, itself an aspect of racial privilege, that dictated their silence about the changes that were wrenching the U.S. social order.[185]

As their depiction of Kit Carson demonstrates, though, there was no aspect of that social order that did not pervade their thinking. The *Carson-Bent-Boggs Genealogy* and *Great Westerner* told tales about race as much as they told family stories, and they no doubt told different tales than they would have if they had been written before the postwar civil rights movements flourished. Indeed, the books themselves constitute the strongest evidence McClung and Blackwelder left behind of their encounter with racial change in the late 1950s and early 1960s. The evidence suggests that the two women met the challenge of civil rights in both similar and different ways. Neither of them, for instance, obscured Carson's marriages to Singing Grass or Josefa Jaramillo, but both neglected his connections to enslaved people, both black people in Missouri and Indigenous people in New Mexico. These decisions were neither innocent nor wholly individual but rather reflected at once prevailing and countervailing political winds, the scaffoldings of power that structured the Cold War nation, and the two women's own personal proclivities.

McClung and Blackwelder detailed Carson's interethnic, interracial marriages at a very specific historical moment: civil rights groups had been campaigning against miscegenation laws for decades, even if the U.S. Supreme Court would not declare those laws unconstitutional until five years after Blackwelder and McClung published their books.[186] The message of these campaigns seems to have reached both women but in unequal measure. McClung was little fazed by Carson's mixed marriages, while Blackwelder arranged those nuptials along a continuum of ascending whiteness.[187] Indeed, Blackwelder, a married white woman who wanted but could not have children and whose politics tended toward the conservative, was the most taken with the idea of Carson as a loving husband and father, and she wove together what she clearly recognized as his masculine responsibilities with a less articulated, but no less powerful, sense of his racial obligations. Meanwhile McClung, a contentedly single woman whose closest ties had always been to other white women (and who rarely revealed her own political views), remained curious about the intimacies represented by Carson's relationship with Josefa Jaramillo and William Bent's with Owl Woman. She seemed less determined to depict those bonds as ill-conceived detours on the path toward a white West, even as she kept men like Carson and Bent at the center of her genealogical story.

Carson's ties to enslaved people, however, must have been disconcerting for both women. By 1962, slavery was an embarrassment to many white Americans, better forgotten, pushed far back in time, or imagined to have existed only in particular (southern) places—the easier, perhaps, to dismiss the persistent demands made by the descendants of slaves in the present.[188] Accordingly, Blackwelder erased those ties altogether, while McClung documented only the slaveholding of Carson's distant forebears. Like western historians of all stripes, they situated stories of bondage long ago and far away, misremembering the frontier as a time and space of freedom for all.[189]

While Blackwelder's and McClung's focus on the family, the era's bulwark against foreign communists and domestic deviants, was not identical, it displayed, shall we say, a certain kinship. That congruity arose from their collaboration, from the historical moment they lived in common, and from their respective positions in a world structured by shifting hierarchies of race, of gender, and of nation. Nothing served Cold War culture better, though, than their refurbishing of an old western hero into a white man who stood above all those around him but now stood connected to them, too.

At Home with the Rifleman

I did not read *Great Westerner* when I was growing up, though I would have loved it. And I had no idea what a genealogy was, or even what might fall from a family tree; my parents were both only children, and there were not many relatives to trace. I did not live in a suburb, but only because I grew up in a small city—Madison, Wisconsin—that did not yet have them. I did live with my parents and two siblings in a newly built ranch-style house that must have been financed by a federally guaranteed loan. I do not know for sure how the mortgage worked because my businessman father, who had served in the Pacific theater during World War II, died over two decades ago, and he managed that aspect of family finances. That left my mother, who did not work outside the home, to concern herself with child-rearing and household consumption—reading us endless stories; walking us to the lakefront beach in the summer and dealing with our snow gear in the winter; purchasing and preparing our meals; outfitting us with clothes, some of which she sewed; and decorating three bedrooms, living room with dining area, kitchen, bathroom, and screened porch. My parents both hailed from smaller Wisconsin towns. They were churchgoing Lutherans and moderate Republicans, though dad sometimes shook a bemused head at mom and muttered, "You think like a Democrat." Everyone in our neighborhood was white and no one was poor. We did, in fact, live in the Cold War's idealized family form, and it was in folks like us that the era's prescriptions took root and grew like a hothouse flower. I do not think any of us realized, and certainly none of us admitted, how much of our comfort was subsidized by governmental largesse, corporate profits, and an enduring cultural apparatus of white supremacy.

Unlike some of our neighbors, my family did not go to Western movies, though my folks watched television oaters like *Bonanza*. I did not much care for TV Westerns—save one: I loved *The Rifleman*. *The Rifleman* aired from 1958 to 1963, and it featured a tall white guy with a very big gun.[190] The show was set somewhere in a mostly white New Mexico, and the man with the gun was a widower raising a son on his own. I adored that boy. I wanted to be him. I wanted to live in that place with those people and learn from that father, who was taller than my own (though I adored him, too). I could imagine riding my horse through a white western world, where no women would boss me around, telling me to lower my voice and check my stride. It did not occur to me that I might not have a thing to eat or wear in such a world.

Had I found it in my school library, I would have devoured Bernice Blackwelder's *Great Westerner*, for I was becoming a voracious reader. It would have taught me much about a West where people besides white men and boys lived, even as it would have reinforced other assumptions that needed no reinforcement in the world of my childhood. Still, in some ways, I would grow up to have more in common with Quantrille McClung—except, of course, I do not share her aversion to narrative, at least not now. Back then, when the 1960s dawned, we all lived behind the color line in the Cold War cul-de-sac, a street with no outlet, only a distant view of a western past.[191]

Part Two
Crafting Kit Carson, 1960s–1970s

DOWN ON WOUNDED KNEE

*The statue of Kit Carson on horseback, down
in the Square, pointed Westward; but there
was no West, in that sense, any more.*
—WILLA CATHER, *One of Ours*

By 1973, I had seen the West with my own wide eyes. This was the year that Quantrille McClung, still living alone in Denver, published a doorstop of a supplement to her *Carson-Bent-Boggs Genealogy*. Her previous volume had run a scant two hundred pages. The *Carson-Bent-Boggs Genealogy Supplement*, despite its soft cover, weighed in at three pounds and filled over six hundred pages.[1] Meanwhile, Bernice Blackwelder, now living with her husband in Chicago, toiled away on her second, mammoth book project, a biographical dictionary of westerners. We all had big-sky imaginations.

Mine was sparked by a 1972 western road trip with my parents. It was just the three of us, since my sister and brother were now out on their own. I was fifteen when I first slept in a motel on the line of semiaridity near Fargo, North Dakota.[2] Past that line, fewer than twenty inches of rain fall each year, marking an eastern boundary for western North America. Presumably, when I crossed it, I was a girl—almost a woman—in the American West. But the West for me was about boys and men, not girls and women, so the farther west I went, the less female I felt. The following day, I passed through Bismarck, over the Missouri River, and across the line of sixteen inches of annual rainfall—ever more western but ever less womanly. After a few hours, I entered Montana, leaving behind North Dakota, familiar to me in its plethora of Lutheran churches and names like Johnson and Swenson and Bjornson but foreign in its sunflower crops and oil rigs and treeless stretches of grass. The next day, after a night in a western-theme motel in Billings, I caught sight of the Rockies. My father liked to recall that moment, when I peered out the front windshield from my perch in the back seat and debated whether the white patches on the horizon were merely clouds or really snow-capped mountains. This was all about the West to me, not a bit about womanhood—and that felt just fine to one approaching the latter with all the enthusiasm of a death marcher.

I was on my way to the summer home of my great-aunt near Ennis, Montana. My aunt and late uncle were not westerners by birth or even permanent residence. He was a Wisconsin boy named Harold Prebensen, the only sibling of my maternal grandmother, Effie; everyone called him Preb. He had alienated his family by committing a trinity of sins: he married not just a non-Lutheran but a Christian Scientist, made a small fortune as an engineer in air conditioning, and moved to the Chicago suburbs. It was no accident that we did not visit Preb's Montana getaway until after both he and Effie died: aside from financial constraints on family travel, there were familial constraints on fraternizing with those strange relatives for whom Wisconsin, the middle class, and the Lutheran church were not good enough. My great-aunt Kay, who outlived my great-uncle, embodied an inimitable combination of wealth, privilege, generosity, duplicity, female independence, white racism, and affected western style. When she drove west from her Illinois home to what she called her "ranch"—she owned no livestock, just a two-bedroom house on a small plot of land—she kept the gas pedal of her Cadillac near the floor. Once, when stopped by a patrolman, she forced tears to her eyes and claimed that her ranch foreman had urged her to rush to Montana, that all her cattle were sick and dying. The officer waved her on: "You drive safely, ma'am." It was this woman, by opening her mountain retreat to my family, who introduced me to the West.

But the West was a male place to me, as it still was in the broader culture. It was rugged and hand hewn. It was where the Rifleman and his son made their home and made their way in a world without women, mostly.[3] Good relations traded on a handshake, bad relations on a gunshot. Now and then, but only now and then, a woman appeared. If the men found her beautiful, she assumed a small place in this world, and she made the men act befuddled, like their stomachs felt funny. A woman like this made my stomach feel funny, too. If the men did not find her beautiful, she did not belong there and she just made them mad. A woman like that made me mad, too: she made it seem like this was not a good world where the men were living. She invariably returned to the East, where she did belong.

So the West was a mostly male place, and suddenly, in the summer of 1972, I had *arrived*. I arrived courtesy of Aunt Kay, who was the right kind of woman. Her youthful beauty had evolved into an impish old age, brimming with vigor and vinegar. When she got to Montana, she garaged the Cadillac and set aside her suburban attire. She donned cowboy boots, western shirts, and blue jeans and hoisted her small frame into a yellow GMC Jimmy. She spent summers alone far up a gravel road in Jack Creek Canyon. Her nearest and only neighbors were beyond shouting distance, since they owned ample land—two rich families and another that kept a dude ranch. The road ended not far past these human habitations, and a national forest lay beyond.[4] I could walk to the campsite where the gravel ended and up a Forest Service trail that followed Jack Creek from there. I rode a horse at the dude ranch, read *Gone with the*

Wind, watched through binoculars as mountain sheep traversed terrain above the tree line, and bumped down the gravel road in the back seat of "Jimmy" to visit Ennis (there was a Dairy Queen there) and to eat steak at a real ranch on the Madison River (my aunt knew the rancher). I was in a hormone-fueled fog of adolescent angst, but as long as I was left alone with a book, the binoculars, and my imagination, there was peace in Jack Creek Canyon.

This was good, because in the early 1970s, there was little peace anywhere else, and the West of my dreams existed mostly in small pockets such as Aunt Kay's retreat, protected by affluence, whiteness, federal funds, and rough roads. By 1973, when the Denver Public Library released McClung's *Carson-Bent-Boggs Genealogy Supplement*, the world she and Blackwelder had known when their first books were published in 1962 had been turned upside down, and the West and its meanings followed the beat of new drums. Film and television Westerns had declined in numbers and popularity as the victory culture of the immediate post-World War II era faded and the United States faced failure abroad.[5] The evolving Cold War had found its hottest expression in Southeast Asia, where U.S. involvement in the Vietnam War escalated in the 1960s but did not prevent the communist take-over of South Vietnam. The conflict provoked an antiwar movement that shook the domestic political landscape and helped shape the march toward a cease-fire in 1973, though not before U.S. invasions of Cambodia and Laos and final, massive bombings of North Vietnam.[6]

On the home front, fault lines created by antiwar protests and a host of concurrent social movements left a fractured body politic. What in blinkered hindsight looked like the decorous years of civil rights had given way to fist-clenched demands for Black Power. Meanwhile, other racialized peoples rose up with their own demands for social, cultural, and economic justice: American Indians, Mexican Americans and Puerto Ricans, and Asian Americans. A multifaceted women's movement laid bare the male dominance inherent in most aspects of American life, and gay men and lesbians began to engineer the means of their own liberation. An energy crisis lent fuel, so to speak, to a burgeoning environmental movement. Young people, even those with little taste for activism, reshaped the cultural terrain of everyday life with new styles of clothing, music, and dance; flamboyant expressions of desire; and open indulgence in mind-altering drugs. Finally, the shadow of Watergate—the scandal that began with a 1972 break-in at the headquarters of the Democratic Party and ended with the 1974 resignation of Republican president Richard Nixon—cast a pall over Washington, D.C., nurturing nationwide disdain for governmental officials. The Vietnam War was ending, but domestic battle lines were etched across the United States of America.[7]

Quantrille McClung and Bernice Blackwelder saw the lines clearly, and by 1973, having forged a friendship for over fifteen years, they traced these fissures more openly in their letters, trading tales about war, race, protest, rock and roll, feminism, and party politics. Blackwelder was especially outspoken, in part because she was more troubled by the era's social upheaval and in part because she was the more politically engaged of the two women. Nowhere were the battle lines of these years drawn more closely to McClung and Blackwelder's intellectual home, though, than they were across the person of Kit Carson. In 1973, both Colorado College, in Colorado Springs, and the town of Taos, New Mexico, grappled with Carson controversies.[8] At Colorado College, a new Native faculty member protested an exhibit featuring photographs of Carson. In Taos, the argument centered on Kit Carson Memorial State Park, where Carson and Josefa Jaramillo were buried. Local *hispano* and Indigenous activists launched a protest, demanding that the space be renamed in honor of a Taos Pueblo man who died in a Japanese prison camp during World War II. Disputes like this made both Blackwelder and McClung articulate their attachment to Carson and, by extension, to the place they imagined as the American West.

They did this in letters to each other even as they continued to use their correspondence for sharing research materials and interpretive insights in their ongoing effort to contribute to the field of western history. Carson still tied Blackwelder and McClung to one another in the decade after they first published, but the web that connected them grew more complex the longer they collaborated. By 1973, both women had broken free from a focus defined by Carson and his world, though in different ways. McClung's second book, the *Carson-Bent-Boggs Genealogy Supplement*, was ostensibly just that: a work of "additions and corrections" to the genealogies compiled in her first. But the supplement provided little new information about Carson himself and not much more about Tom Boggs and the Bent brothers. Instead, it traced a mind-numbing network of genealogical links that followed from McClung's earlier research on the Carson, Bent, and Boggs families. In some cases, this meant following lines of kinship back further in time, but often it meant tracing family ties both forward into the twentieth century and more widely to include those with only distant connections to the Carson, Bent, and Boggs clans. McClung, then, produced a western history ever more removed from founding fathers like Carson but nonetheless relentlessly tied to a conception of family defined by a reproductive logic—even though, as we shall see, family thus conceived provided precious little comfort in McClung's own daily life.

Meanwhile, Blackwelder's unfinished biographical dictionary of westerners, while it included men named Carson, Bent, and Boggs, was as expansive as the West itself—or at least as expansive as a western drama in which people like Kit Carson played the crucial roles. As Blackwelder explained to McClung, the project covered "men who contributed to the development" of the West, such as "painters, scientists, military men, traders," as well as those who "wrote about it." Despite her own interest in politics, Blackwelder added that she included "few politicians per se," perhaps because biographical dictionaries such as *The Dictionary of American Biography* (first proposed in the 1920s by Frederick Jackson Turner) as well as the federal government's *Biographical Directory of the United States Congress* surveyed that ground.[9] Still, unlike McClung, Blackwelder worked to produce a western history with a plentitude of patriarchs, even if they were not the father figures identified with the nation's founding—not political leaders like Washington and Jefferson but rather explorers, soldiers, and merchants, as well as writers and painters. "My men," Blackwelder called these agents and artists of empire, even as she described her own husband as too often "underfoot."[10]

Indeed, by 1973, McClung and Blackwelder's exchange of research on Carson and his world had evolved into the set of habits that I call a traffic in men and things male.[11] Historically, most traffic in men has been symbolic, at least when compared with such traffic in human beings as slavery in its myriad forms or with the practices that have been called a traffic in women (prostitution and some forms of marriage, for example). When men have trafficked in women, actual women have often been objects of exchange.[12] At the very least, significant aspects of a woman's person have been on the market—her sexual or labor power, for instance, which might be one and the same. When people have been enslaved, the enslaved have been seized or bought and then bound, body and soul. Those who have engaged in a traffic in men, by contrast, unless they have enslaved actual men or otherwise harnessed their labor, have exchanged words, gestures, opinions, and information about men, generally out of the purview of men. Such exchange historically has taken place in contexts of unequal power, and through it, women have worked to survey, survive, affirm, manage, negotiate, contain, circumvent, criticize, or even subvert male dominance. Women have said things to one another about men—through a bit of gossip or a roll of the eyes—that they would not have said in the presence of men. Women have also said things about men to men, things that men have wanted to hear about themselves or their forebears and for which men have offered approval, gratitude, praise, or compensation. And sometimes women have risked saying things to men that men have *not* wanted to hear, and men have listened or not, absorbed the hard message or else withheld, rejected, punished, abused.

A corollary to a traffic in men is a traffic in things male. When a woman has trafficked in things male, she has assumed for herself a privilege or a posture or a vocation or an avocation or an attire or an attitude of manhood, however manhood has been defined in a particular circumstance.[13] When female-bodied people have done these things, they have, at best, courted social disapproval. At worst, they have courted loss of livelihood, loss of loved ones, and even loss of life. (Sometimes they also have courted actual women, but the practice I call a traffic in things male cannot be narrowed to the cross-gender behavior of some seemingly same-sex lovers, which I see as just one instance of a broader set of practices common among a wide range of women.)

Trafficking in men and things male is hardly universal. It is a historically specific set of habits that has reflected configurations of power in distinct cultural and economic contexts. It has often been circumscribed by the relative disempowerment of some actual men by other actual men (and their womenfolk), which has also restricted the extent to which actual women have engaged it.[14] That is to say that when the men whom women have embraced as brothers or friends or fathers or lovers have themselves been subjected to routine humiliation or violence or exploitation, limiting or even eliminating the ability of those men to enact male dominance, or when men themselves have rejected the terms of male dominance, then the traffic in men and things male has taken on different forms and meanings or even ceased to be a needful, efficacious set of practices.

In the lives of McClung and Blackwelder, however, a traffic in men and things male was necessary and effective and they took it up with a vengeance. Carson, his compadres, and western men generally remained the chief objects of trade in this traffic, and it was Blackwelder's and McClung's work on these mostly white men that gave the women whatever stature they enjoyed as chroniclers of the western past. Had they centered their research instead, say, on Josefa Jaramillo, her sister Ignacia, and Ignacia's daughter Rumalda or on any of Josefa's relatives, male or female, who did not intermarry with Anglo Americans, it is doubtful that their work would have gained much notice. It may not have been published. Simply put, white men were the heroes of the frontier story, and trading on the imaginative overidentification of things western and things white and male brought rewards.[15]

Still, as amateur women historians working in a male-dominated field, McClung and Blackwelder had long faced barriers, and those barriers shaped another aspect of their traffic. Indeed, the late 1960s and early '70s brought new challenges. The gentlemanly bargain between western history buffs and academic western historians was showing signs of strain. That bargain had allowed the happy coexistence of the Westerners and the Western History Association as well as overlapping membership rolls in the two organizations. But as professional historians achieved new prominence and the nationally based Western History Association began to overshadow the local, more loosely organized corrals and posses of the Westerners, amateurs lost status. McClung and Blackwelder, although they had never been members of the fraternity of western history buffs, had at least benefited from the predominance of amateurs in the field. In the early 1960s, it was common for nonacademics to publish western histories, and so *Great Westerner* and the *Carson-Bent-Boggs Genealogy* found themselves in good company on shelves tended by librarians, booksellers, home collectors, and professors alike. A decade later, amateurs still published, but in academia, their work began to be eclipsed by that of professionals. As academic scholars gained stature, Blackwelder and McClung realized that reception of their own work now hinged on the assessment of professionals, most of whom were white men. Trading tidbits about professors and their scholarship became another market for McClung's and Blackwelder's traffic in men.

Their traffic also took on an intimate dimension. Unbeknownst to him, Bernice Blackwelder's husband, Harold, joined the male historical figures, history buffs, and history professors in the symbolic auction house that was the two women's correspondence. Bernice traded in Harold's moods and manners, faults and foibles, with a marked lack of reverence. Harold, she intimated to her friend Quantrille, was in the way. He stood between Bernice and the full realization of her potential as a researcher and writer. It was not that Bernice did not love Harold, but she did wish that he would take up less of her time and energy and that the western men who were the subject of her biographical dictionary would take up more. Harold, like Bernice, had once been a singer, and part of his repertoire had included performing as the character Neil Fortune, Gentleman from the West. Neil Fortune had sung western ballads in a dreamy bass voice. By 1973, that tall, dapper youth—who had been born a southerner, not a westerner—had become a county file clerk of a certain age. For Bernice, fortune now lay down a different trail, and she did not hesitate to finger Harold as the stone in her path.

In 1973, Bernice Blackwelder, Quantrille McClung, and I occupied different spaces; from them, we conjured different lands but called them all the West. My parents' Buick backed down the driveway from a new family home not yet eight years old—a white southern colonial in a snowy northern clime—and headed west, to my promised land. From the car window, I glimpsed the past, where the West had lived. I faced back from the future and found solace in an imagined frontier. Blackwelder struggled to write the West in the dark Chicago apartment she shared with her husband, venturing out by bus and commuter rail to the libraries of a city that owed its nineteenth-century growth to the Great West and now was caught up in the midst of twentieth-century change.[16] But Blackwelder remained tied to that dim dwelling by wifely obligations, dwindling resources, and racial fears. She glimpsed the future, where the West she loved was dying. She faced forward from the past and saw betrayal. McClung, too, toiled away in a city apartment, though she lived alone. Her building was in a Denver neighborhood that had been transformed, like Blackwelder's in Chicago, by human migrations and capital flows.[17] McClung traversed that neighborhood as she walked to the public library. She shared some of her friend's dismay over the shifting meanings of the western past and the changing realties of the urban present, but McClung came closest to unsentimental conjurings of place and time. McClung's own western history haunted her every step, living as she did not far from the place of her birth, childhood, and youth. Back and forth from apartment to library, back and forth from past to future: here and now embodied neither promise nor betrayal—or perhaps both in equal measure. Frontier nostalgia found precious little foothold in this walking world. The West was home—no more, no less.[18]

Founding Families

The begats that shaped Quantrille McClung's 1962 *Carson-Bent-Boggs Genealogy* reproduced themselves queerly in the supplement she prepared over the following decade. McClung had long employed a more elastic notion of family in her work than did her friend Bernice Blackwelder, but the *Carson-Bent-Boggs Genealogy Supplement* stretched it even further. There were limits to McClung's definitional flexibility; she was a genealogist and so the reproductive consequences of heterosexual intercourse remained paramount. But by tracing the Carson, Bent, and Boggs lineages more widely and further forward in time, McClung moved further and further away from founding fathers and ever deeper into family not always defined by legal marriage, into child-rearing that produced tragically troubled offspring, and into ancestry that defied the norms of racial exclusivity.

Documenting McClung's increasingly expansive impulses involves delving into sample minutiae to show how her elastic notion of family played out on the genealogical page. It was hard work. After toiling away on the supplement for years, McClung worried about her slow progress. "So much needs … to be redone," she told Blackwelder. This was because new information kept materializing that allowed her to solve genealogical problems left unsolved in the original volume. "For instance," she instructed her friend in a letter, "find Bento and Guadalupe Long in the first book."[19] In fact, if Blackwelder looked, she would have found that in the original genealogy, Guadalupe's surname was absent. The volume specified only that "a woman known as Guadalupe" married Alfredo Bent. Alfredo was the son of Ignacia Jaramillo and Charles Bent, born before Governor Bent met his fate in the 1847 Taos uprising against U.S. rule in New Mexico. In the *Carson-Bent-Boggs Genealogy*, Bento Long does not seem to be related to Guadalupe. He is simply listed as someone who married into the family of Alfredo's sister Rumalda, once assumed to be another child of Ignacia Jaramillo and Charles Bent. Whoever her father really was, Rumalda went on to marry twice, and Bento Long, it appeared, married one of her granddaughters by her second husband.[20]

In 1969, McClung triumphantly told Blackwelder that she had determined the shared parentage of Bento and Guadalupe Long. They had the same Anglo father, a man named Long from Missouri, but different *hispana* mothers and thus were separated by a twenty-two-year age gap. Both married descendants of Ignacia Jaramillo—Guadalupe married Ignacia's oldest son, Alfredo, and Bento, it now seemed certain, married a daughter, rather than a granddaughter, of Ignacia's youngest daughter, Rumalda—and those descendants were at least a generation apart. This made sense once McClung worked out all the details. First, Guadalupe, though she was Bento's half sister, was old enough to have been his mother. Second, Rumalda was fourteen years younger than her probable half brother Alfredo. Since *nuevomexicanas* often wed in their early teens, Bento easily could have married a daughter, if probably not a granddaughter, of his half sister's husband's half sister.[21]

But this was just background for what McClung was keen to tell her friend. What most thrilled McClung is that finding the shared parentage of Guadalupe and Bento Long and their respective marriages to descendants of Ignacia Jaramillo allowed her to see the U.S. census with a new eye. This is what she saw: When Guadalupe's first husband, Alfredo Bent, died, she married Missouri immigrant George Thompson. The 1880 census showed that Guadalupe and George's home sheltered not only their offspring but also Guadalupe's children from her marriage to Alfredo as well as her younger half siblings, including Bento. Or as McClung exclaimed to Blackwelder, "Guadalupe's 2nd husband not only took care of the children of her first husband … but … her half brothers and sisters as well."[22] McClung found the detective work involved in dredging up such details "electrifying."[23]

If you, dear reader, find these matters less than electrifying, then imagine working out scores of such genealogical puzzles and preparing six hundred pages of similar minutiae for publication. It took her a decade, but McClung did just that. She knew it was a strange obsession. When she encountered an odd character in a novel by Anthony Trollope, McClung felt that she was looking in a mirror. Trollope describes a "small, elegantly made old woman" whose "favorite insanity was genealogy." In the same letter where McClung revealed to Blackwelder her discoveries about Guadalupe and Bento Long, McClung confessed, "It seems to be mine also."[24] McClung indulged the insanity of genealogy with precision and persistence. She checked and rechecked the *Carson-Bent-Boggs Genealogy*, expanding her findings and bringing them into line with information gleaned from correspondence with Carson, Bent, and Boggs descendants; from western history scholarship; and from new research, conducted largely by mail but also by visits, for example, to a Catholic church in Trinidad, Colorado, and to the New Mexico state archives in Santa Fe.[25]

With regard to Kit Carson and Josefa Jaramillo, their descendants, and their ancestors, McClung corrected little. She had never used Spanish-language sources available in New Mexico. Indeed, she does not seem to have been fluent in Spanish (let alone the colonial Spanish used in early New Mexican records), and she paid for what research travel she did out of a fixed and limited retirement income.[26] Oddly, she seems not to have used the work with which those interested in *hispano* family history have usually begun ever since it was first published in 1954: Fray Angélico Chávez's *Origins of New Mexico Families*, which outlines the earliest presence of Josefa's ancestors—especially the Jaramillos and Vigils—in New Mexico.[27] All of this limited what McClung could document about the *hispano* side of the Jaramillo-Carson kin network.

As for the Carson branches of the family tree, McClung had already sketched them in her first genealogy with reasonable accuracy. She had worked backward in time to find the family's roots in Missouri, Kentucky, the British Atlantic colonies, and northern Ireland, and she had worked forward, tracing Kit Carson and Josefa Jaramillo's descendants down to those born in the 1950s. These included great-grandson John Michael Carson, who, as an adult, would portray his famous ancestor in historical reenactments and who is said to resemble Kit more closely than any of his relatives.[28] In the 1973 *Carson-Bent-Boggs Genealogy Supplement*, then, McClung merely filled in blanks that she had been unable to fill in her earlier volume, adding, for example, further information about Kit's half brother Moses, his half sister Sarah, his brother Lindsey, and his niece Susan. For each of these relatives and many others, McClung traced kin ties by birth and marriage both backward and forward as far as she could.[29] In doing so, she often found that descendants of Josefa and Kit, who were themselves bicultural, intermarried with other *hispano* or bicultural residents of northern New Mexico and southern Colorado and that they did so for generations. In other words, McClung discovered that the descendants did not, in fact, become Carsons all. More than one, for instance, became a Martínez.[30]

The newest revelations about Carson himself came with respect to his second marriage, to the Southern Cheyenne woman Making Out Road. In the *Carson-Bent-Boggs Genealogy*, McClung had documented Carson's first marriage, to the Northern Arapaho woman Singing Grass.[31] By contrast, McClung's references in that volume to Making Out Road were cryptic: "Carson [married circa] 1840 'Making Out Road' a South Cheyenne Indian woman of a different nature than the first wife. Her baby died and she left Carson by the winter of 1841/2."[32] In her 1973 supplement, however, McClung explored this marriage further, drawing on the work of historian Harvey Lewis Carter, the foremost Carson scholar of the period, as well as on correspondence with Carson enthusiast Walter Nathaniel Bate. McClung offered no conclusions of her own but instead laid out more evidence for Carson's union with Making Out Road—a union she had already confirmed in the first genealogy, even as Bernice Blackwelder denied it in *Great Westerner*.[33] In this, McClung elaborated on the relatively expansive view of North American frontier families that she established in her 1962 genealogy.

Further elaboration came in McClung's reworking of the Bent and Boggs family lines. Already in the *Carson-Bent-Boggs Genealogy*, McClung had documented William Bent's marriages to Owl Woman, who was Cheyenne, and, after Owl Woman's death, to her sister Yellow Woman. McClung had also noted the offspring of these unions: Mary, Robert, George, and Julia were Owl Woman's children, and Charles was Yellow Woman's son.[34] The supplement extended the lines of William

Bent, Owl Woman, and Yellow Woman, relying on a wider variety of sources, including reports of the U.S. commissioner of Indian affairs and the newly published *Life of George Bent*, based on letters author George Hyde exchanged with Owl Woman's son George. In doing this, McClung traced some of the descendants into the fourth and fifth generations, including the children and grandchildren of William Henry Bent, son of George Bent and the Cheyenne woman Magpie. William Henry married a Lakota woman and they in turn had a daughter, Lucille, also known as Red Deer Woman. They lived in Oklahoma. By 1954, Lucille was raising her own child, Roberta, also called Brave Woman.[35] All this led McClung across an increasingly complex ethnocultural West, more deeply into the twentieth century, and further away from the men — Kit Carson, Charles and William Bent, and Thomas Boggs — whose family ties had first transfixed her.

But no genealogical puzzle intrigued McClung more than the one she now called "the riddle of the Rumaldas."[36] Already in the *Carson-Bent-Boggs Genealogy* she had determined that Ignacia Jaramillo had two daughters named Rumalda: one by first husband Rafael Luna (Rumalda Luna would marry Tom Boggs) and another almost twenty years later. It was Rumalda the younger who continued to create confusion for the meticulous McClung. In the 1950s, descendants had told McClung that this Rumalda was Charles Bent's daughter, conceived just before Bent died in the Taos uprising of 1847. But McClung also had evidence that the younger Rumalda was born in 1850. The 1962 genealogy did not resolve these conflicting accounts but did reveal that Ignacia and Charles might never have married — say nothing of having conceived Rumalda either in or out of wedlock.[37] In the 1973 *Supplement*, McClung took a stronger stand: "It [has] long been a matter of debate as to whether this Rumalda was entitled to the surname of Bent. The descendants are sharply divided on the question, some adhering to the belief that she was Gov. Charles Bent's daughter.... Others believe her to have been the Maria Rumalda Jaramillo, baptized in Taos, 10-9-1850. An 1870 Census record gives her age as 20 years, so the latter date seem[s] most likely." McClung followed this rare prose passage with a transcription of Rumalda's 1850 baptismal record, signed by the New Mexico state archivist and notarized. The record called this Rumalda the "natural daughter" of Ignacia Jaramillo.[38] McClung received the record from one of Rumalda's descendants, Mary Neugent, who was among those convinced that Charles Bent was not their forebear. Neugent and her grandmother — María Celia Martínez, daughter of Rumalda by her second husband — came forward in Denver in 1966, declaring that this Rumalda's father was not Charles Bent but rather Céran St. Vrain. St. Vrain had been Bent's partner in Bent, St. Vrain, and Company, the firm that established Bent's Fort on the Arkansas River in 1833. These descendants were sure that St. Vrain had taken up with Ignacia Jaramillo after Bent's death and that he, not Bent, was their ancestor.[39]

This tale unfolded only gradually, and it was a frequent subject in letters McClung exchanged with Blackwelder. In 1967, Blackwelder exclaimed to McClung, "I think you have a 'scoop' for I have never seen anything faintly suggestive about Ceran and Ignacia."[40] The two women debated about how to use the information. Blackwelder was working on her biographical dictionary, so she had reason to care about the "scoop" as well. In the end, Blackwelder came down on the side of silence: "What is the use of broadcasting anything that would smirch St. Vrain or Ignacia???"[41] McClung responded, "I believe I will just say that a descendant of Ignacia has given me several items ... that lead to interesting speculation. Anyone who wishes to follow it up may do so and I will not have made any definite statement."[42] But by reproducing Rumalda's baptismal certificate as well as other evidence that pointed to the possibility that Céran St. Vrain was her father, McClung's statement in 1973 proved more definite than she had intended when she wrote about it to Blackwelder in 1967.[43] In the long run, Blackwelder, a married woman, was more reticent about revealing nonmarital intimacies than was McClung, who never wed. Blackwelder persisted in calling the story of Ignacia Jaramillo and Céran St. Vrain a "scandal," while McClung's chief concern was "not to offend the family"—that is, the descendants—even though it was descendants who first claimed Ignacia and Céran as their forebears.[44]

The "riddle of the Rumaldas" was just one of the mysteries Blackwelder and McClung tried to sort out in their letters. Soon enough, largely through the research of others, they discovered that Céran St. Vrain had enjoyed a series of sexual relationships with women to whom he was not married, including one with María de la Cruz Padilla, widow of Charles Bent's brother George (Blackwelder wryly observed of St. Vrain, "He sure was taking care of the widows!").[45] At one point, McClung and Blackwelder learned from Harvey Carter's work that sometime after his marriage to Singing Grass and before he wed Josefa Jaramillo, Kit Carson himself had lived with Antonia Luna, an *hispana* who might also have been involved with the famed black fur trader Jim Beckwourth. McClung saw this reference and wrote to Blackwelder: "I have never, in all my research ever come across such a statement—not that I am disturbed but I wonder where [Carter] got it." Characteristically, Blackwelder took a stand against revealing such bonds, calling evidence of Carson's "amorous associations" mere "gossip." Also characteristically, McClung took a practical approach, though one guided by the genealogist's concern with procreative sex: "I do not intend to pay any attention to [the relationship between Carson and Luna] since no descendants are involved."[46] The affair found no place in the *Carson-Bent-Boggs Genealogy Supplement*.

There were limits, then, to McClung's increasingly elastic notion of family in the 1970s, influenced as that notion may have been by the era's sexual revolution and by her own lifelong status as an unmarried woman.[47] Still, compared to Blackwelder, McClung was more apt to take changing values in stride, whether sexual values or the cultural value that inhered in frontiersmen themselves. For instance, when McClung first told Blackwelder that Ignacia Jaramillo might have had a relationship with Céran St. Vrain, Blackwelder was startled, especially, she told her friend, because she had always thought of St. Vrain as a "knight in shining armor."[48] McClung did not use such language to describe the men at the center of her work. Where Blackwelder's first book had christened Kit Carson the "great westerner," McClung's dialed back the hyperbole to call Carson merely a "famous scout and pioneer." For McClung, then, Carson and his compadres did not have so far to fall from grace, and the varieties of intimacies they pursued, while sometimes surprising, seemed to come with the genealogical territory.

Likewise the sad fates of two daughters of Josefa Jaramillo and Kit Carson. In the 1962 *Carson-Bent-Boggs Genealogy*, McClung had acknowledged that Rebecca Carson, born four years before both her parents died, committed suicide as a young woman.[49] In the 1973 *Supplement*, McClung went further, quoting an 1885 newspaper article which noted that a week before her twenty-first birthday, Rebecca had taken "morphine in a Springer restaurant . . . and died."[50] Springer was in northern New Mexico along the Santa Fe Trail, which first brought Kit Carson to the borderlands as a youth. The supplement also revealed that Rebecca's sister Josefita, born two weeks before her mother Josefa passed in 1868, died when she was about thirty in New Mexico's territorial insane asylum at Las Vegas.[51] By then, Las Vegas, once a stop along the Santa Fe Trail, boasted a depot for the Atchison, Topeka, and Santa Fe Railway, which had replaced the trail as the chief thoroughfare connecting New Mexico to points east. McClung may have blinked before committing such tales to paper, but commit them she did, hinting that the roads traveled by the famous scout and pioneer could leave tracks of death and derangement, even among those he held most dear. No other Carson scholar, before or since, has bothered to tell these tales.[52]

For McClung, the 1960s and early '70s brought a subtle, gradual change in her perception of the men at the center of her work. And that center barely held, snarled as it was in the human web that enveloped it. As a genealogist, McClung felt obligated to investigate the intimate consequences of the presence of men like Kit Carson, the Bent brothers, and Tom Boggs in the West. She may have started from the premise that they were pioneers, an identity that had long held wholly positive meanings in the minds of most white people in the United States and even some people of color, especially those whose ancestors' dispossession had not come about by white westward migration (but rather by other means, such as disfranchisement, exploitation, enslavement, or exclusion). But that premise did not entirely preclude thoughtful reexamination in light of new evidence nor did it preclude diligent research in pursuit of such evidence. The *Carson-Bent-Boggs Genealogy Supplement* was what it is: a gargantuan supplement to a genealogy of white men and their families, men who trespassed on places already occupied by others. What made it supplemental, however, was also what made it gargantuan: it more fully considered a West that outlived the frontier; it more frequently recognized westerners who were neither white nor male; it more frankly acknowledged that pioneers could beget troubled progeny; and it more openly admitted that desire and its expression often spill over the cultural and legal dams designed to contain them.

Plentitude of Patriarchs

Quantrille McClung's friend Bernice Blackwelder, on the other hand, pursued interests in the 1960s and early '70s that were more of a piece with the work she had done since the '50s, when she began her research on Kit Carson. Carson was no longer the central actor in the drama, but pioneers as a category continued to command the stage. All of the pioneers were men and almost all were white. Some of these men moved in the same worlds as Carson, so Blackwelder had encountered them before: Ewing Young, a fellow trapper and trader; Lafayette Head, a fellow Indian agent; and John Prowers, an associate of Carson's and the Bents'. Prowers, like William Bent, married a Cheyenne woman and, like Carson, settled in the multiracial community of Boggsville in the 1860s (though Prowers outlived Carson and became a successful rancher, merchant, and politician).[53] Even for these men, Blackwelder had to track down details that had not concerned her in *Great Westerner*. As she told McClung, "You can't write a brief account of anyone without finding out all about him. So that makes for scratching out, adding . . . & rewriting if it is to be of any value."[54] There were also men whose careers were further afield from Carson's: various Mormon leaders who fascinated Blackwelder; French Creoles who oversaw an earlier fur trade empire from St. Louis, such as the Chouteaus; U.S. Army officers; and frontier doctors, a group dear to Blackwelder's heart because her own father had been a physician in Kansas.[55] By 1967, Blackwelder had determined what sort of finished product this research would produce: "At first I intended only to make it a listing," she told McClung, "and now I have more of a biographical dictionary." And what a dictionary it was: that same year, she announced that she had already compiled information on 242 men whose names started with the letters *a*, *b*, and *c* alone.[56]

Blackwelder never finished this volume, and none of her drafts or notes have survived. So its content can only be divined from what she reported to McClung. Fortunately, Blackwelder told McClung a great deal about her daily work on the project, and she repeatedly enlisted McClung's aid on specific westerners. In this, the two women were true collaborators. Neither could afford a good home library of western Americana, and neither, as apartment dwellers, had space for many books. But both lived near first-rate research repositories. McClung did work at the Denver Public Library (DPL), where she had once been employed. DPL housed the Western History Department, which held fine resources for the study of the West broadly and Colorado specifically, as well as the Genealogical Division, which McClung herself had helped develop.[57] She also worked at the nearby Colorado Historical Society. Meanwhile, Blackwelder had access to the Chicago Public Library and its branches and, crucially, to the Newberry Library, a private institution open to the public that housed the Everett Graff and Edward Ayer collections of American Indian and western materials as well as good genealogical resources.[58] And Blackwelder could fall back on research she had done in the National Archives and the Library of Congress when she lived near Washington, D.C. The two women's correspondence, then—filled as it is with accounts of progress and exchanges of information—provides a good guide to the biographical dictionary that Blackwelder was struggling to produce.

Blackwelder's labors on this project were every bit as exacting and exhausting as McClung's on her genealogy supplement. As early as 1966, overwhelmed by the work, Blackwelder contemplated enlisting a coauthor. In correspondence with western historian John Porter Bloom, Blackwelder learned that the well-published railroad expert David Myrick was thinking of producing a "Who Was Who" of the West. So she sent Myrick "a feeler" to see if he might want to collaborate. "It would be fine for me if someone would do the writing while I do the research," she told McClung. When Myrick passed through Chicago, he telephoned Blackwelder and they had what she called "a spirited conversation." But she decided that his "knowledge of Western History" was "limited." She wrote to McClung, "[He] is probably not the assistant I need."[59]

A few years later, when McClung's second book was in production, Blackwelder thought again about seeking assistance, this time from an active participant in both the Westerners and the Western History Association, Samuel P. Arnold. A restaurateur, Sam Arnold so loved the world of Carson and the Bents that he built The Fort, a restaurant replica of the original Bent's Fort. Bent's Fort, of course, had been located in the nineteenth century on the plains along the Arkansas River in southeastern Colorado. Arnold, a savvy twentieth-century businessman, nestled his replica up against the Rockies near Denver and its suburbs. There, he served pricey signature dishes such as Rocky Mountain Oysters and Moose Nose, as well as one called the Bowl of the Wife of Kit Carson, a take on *caldo tlalpeño*, a chicken soup with chile, rice, and garbanzos. Blackwelder and McClung had known Arnold for years, and in 1972 Blackwelder wrote, "I was thinking of writing to Sam to ask him if [he] would like to take a half interest in my Directory of Westerners as we are both amateur historians & both have published material." It was not just Arnold's passion for history that interested Blackwelder but also his business acumen. "He could prepare the material for publication," she told McClung, and "contribute what he wished." McClung advised against this partnership, warning that Arnold had "so many irons in the fire" that he might "not be reliable."[60] More than once, then, the burden of her project prompted Blackwelder to consider sharing responsibility with a male history buff. But when it came to contemplating actual co-authors, she demoted the first, David Myrick, to the status of "assistant" and then dismissed him, and she allowed McClung to brand the second, Sam Arnold, as unreliable.

So Blackwelder was on her own with her biographical dictionary. Her progress reports to McClung sounded like variations on a theme: too many men, too little time. As Blackwelder put it in 1968, she was finding "good biographical material on now almost-forgotten men," but in typing completed records, she had barely "finished with the 'A's.'" Six months later, she reported, "My trouble is that I have over-extended myself with too many names." The following year, when she thanked McClung for checking references at DPL, Blackwelder wrote, "You see how much I have to do to get the dates for these men." In 1972, she sent a sample entry—for Albert Gallatin Boone, grandson of Daniel Boone and brother of Panthea Boone, who married into the Boggs family—hoping for McClung's comments. Blackwelder noted that she had "several hundred" of such entries "nearly complete," while many others were still "up in the air." By then, she had decided that she would add "no more names" and concentrate instead on "consolidating" the "mountain of material" she had collected.[61]

Nonetheless, the project seemed endless, and Blackwelder worried that she might not "live long enough to see it finished." As years passed, she grew discouraged, though she was determined to keep her spirits up. In 1973, when McClung's supplement had been published, Blackwelder spoke of nearly pitching her own work "into a bonfire." Still, Blackwelder kept at it, thinking that at the very least she might turn it all over to a "bright young student" who would finish it. In 1974 she declared, "Have been working constantly on my 'men' and feel I am making some headway." Meanwhile, she told McClung that her husband, while patient, wondered why she did "not have 'enough for a big book.'" Blackwelder's wifely retort was that she "was hoping to write a 'good' book not a 'big' book." A few months later she declared, "This work of mine may never get out of my kitchen but it has been good for me."[62] More and more, Blackwelder voiced the pleasure she took in the project more than the progress she was making toward completing it. She began to turn that corner as early as 1970, when she wrote to McClung, "I do not suppose I will ever finish [the volume] but should leave it in shape for someone to take it over—I vowed I would never again work as hard as I did on Carson as I want to enjoy the search." Still, there is little evidence that Blackwelder worked any less diligently in the 1960s and '70s than she had in the '50s, when Carson was her main man.[63]

As she studied a wider array of western men, a discriminating passion continued to mark Blackwelder's work. She complained to McClung, "Many of my friends cannot seem to appreciate the excitement I find in historical research." McClung did appreciate the thrill of discovery, and Blackwelder repaid her friend's enthusiasm with tales from the research trenches. After a winter's day session at the Chicago Public Library in 1973, for example, Blackwelder announced, "I found several of my men in the *Biog[raphical] Dict[ionary] of the Am[erican] Congress*." The following summer—after Blackwelder, her husband, and their dog had all suffered health crises—she reported, "I am hoping to get back to work on my 'men' after two months of neglect." Blackwelder described "her men" as "interesting character[s] who should be remembered." She held a fondness for those whose paths had crossed with Carson's, including, for instance, the artist Charles Stobie, who had worked as a scout and a buffalo hunter and who had both lived with and painted Ute Indians. Blackwelder even took such objects of interest to bed with her: "Often," she told McClung, "I lie awake thinking of some of my *men*." Perhaps after rereading those words and seeing a double entendre, Blackwelder added parenthetically that when she spoke of "my *men*," she was referring to "characters in my research."[64]

Not all male westerners earned entry into Blackwelder's boudoir. Among the scores of men she mentioned to McClung as candidates for inclusion in her biographical dictionary, only one—mountain man Jim Beckwourth—was not white. James Pierson Beckwourth was the son of an enslaved black woman and a white male slaveholder. Manumitted in Missouri, Beckwourth joined the Rocky Mountain fur trade and formed intimate relationships with both Indigenous women and *nuevomexicanas*. Beckwourth was too much a figure in the West of trappers and traders—and the geographical and conjugal trajectories of his life too much resembled those of men like Carson—to justify his exclusion. If thoughts of the handsome Beckwourth kept Blackwelder up at night, however, she did not commit them to paper.[65]

While Blackwelder did not disclose why she put Beckwourth in her book, she said explicitly that she would *not* include Indigenous men. In 1969, McClung wrote to Blackwelder about the newly published multivolume *Biographical and Historical Index of American Indians and Persons Involved in Indian Affairs*, offering, "If you want me to look [up] any of the names in which you are interested I will be glad to do so." Blackwelder did not reply. In a subsequent letter, McClung told Blackwelder of an article she had read about the Eastern Shoshone leader Washakie, offering to send her friend a copy. This time, Blackwelder responded, "As for the article on 'Washakie' do not send as I am not including any Indians in my list." She explained that she was interested only in men who contributed to the West's "development."[66] Adding even more interpretive insult to Indians' historical injuries, Blackwelder later told McClung that she *was* interested in the families of white people "who were k[illed] or captured by the Cheyennes." In this, Blackwelder likely was referring to the 1864 conflicts between white settlers and Cheyenne and Arapaho bands in Colorado Territory, which culminated in the horrific Sand Creek Massacre. At Sand Creek, Col. John M. Chivington and his volunteer regiment slaughtered and then mutilated the bodies of more than a hundred Indian people who believed they had reached a peace agreement with U.S. officials. (One of William Bent and Owl Woman's sons was in the Cheyenne and Arapaho camp when troops attacked at dawn, while another was forced to guide the soldiers to the tipi village where his relatives slept.) Even in the face of the most egregious colonial violence—no less than a U.S. congressional committee condemned Chivington's actions—Blackwelder stuck to her guns: White men developed the West. Indian men were, at best, obstacles to development. McClung responded to Blackwelder's stated interests with rare sarcasm: "If you want to include John M. Chivington, I have all you need on him. He was the 'hero' of the Sand Creek Massacre, you know."[67]

Blackwelder and McClung, then, could differ over which westerners were worthy of remembrance. Both began their inquiries with those whose roles in the history of the West had already been legitimated by generations of scholars, writers, and purveyors of popular culture. Carson epitomized such characters. But Blackwelder generally ended her inquiries there, too. McClung, by contrast, was more apt to track the networks that linked men like Carson to a host of westerners who had been ignored, infantilized, dismissed, or demonized by earlier chroniclers: adventurous lovers and white frontierswomen; Indian peoples and ethnic Mexicans, male and female alike; and the many hybrid children that agents of empire and the native-born together begot. Blackwelder and McClung engaged in a traffic in men that shared a point of departure, and the historical person they met there was the archetypal pioneer. But the roads the two women followed sometimes diverged so that the histories they produced, or tried to produce, portrayed different Wests. In Blackwelder's West, the pioneer developed a wilderness whose previous residents were of little consequence. In McClung's West, the pioneer entered a landscape that he meant to change but by which he, too, was transformed and into which he all but vanished.

Bankrupt for Heroes

However the Wests of Quantrille McClung and Bernice Blackwelder differed, both women were taken aback when Kit Carson himself tumbled from his pedestal and fell into the hands of critics who identified less with pioneers and more with people whose life chances had been diminished by the privileges those pioneers had embraced in nineteenth-century North America. Carson's fall from grace was symptomatic of the cultural and political revolution that swept the United States in the 1960s and '70s, in which critics of Cold War ideas and practices met increasingly receptive audiences for their positions (and a backlash from those who held older views dear). The basic trajectory of such a fall, then, is familiar to students of the era's social movements, even as the particular physics of Carson's fate evinced specificities of time and place.

The decline in Carson's reputation was a century in the making, but the effects of political gravity that pulled him down to earth became most evident in the 1970s. It was the Navajo Nation that had the gravest historical grievance against Carson, given his role in the brutal 1863–64 Navajo campaign conducted by the U.S. Army. Mescalero Apaches and neighboring Comanches and Kiowas could indict Carson as well. The Navajo campaign ended when eight thousand Diné were forced on the Long Walk that removed them from their beloved homeland and imprisoned them three hundred miles away in eastern New Mexico Territory. At the Bosque Redondo, they joined Mescalero Apaches (with whom Navajos were not on friendly terms) driven there by an earlier army campaign under Carson's command. The bosque was not alien country for the Mescaleros in the same way it was for the Diné, because these Apaches had gathered there along the Pecos River in summers past. Still, the mobile Mescaleros had no interest in becoming sedentary farmers, which is what the army intended for them, and relations between the captive Apaches and Navajos were tense. Scarce government supplies, failed crops, disease, and Comanche raids made the bosque as much death camp as relocation camp. Then, just after the Navajo campaign, late in 1864, Carson received orders to embark on what would be his last military venture, an expedition against Comanches and Kiowas on the Southern Plains. Accompanied by Ute and Apache scouts, Carson and his volunteer troops engaged Kiowa and Comanche warriors at a site in the Texas panhandle known as Adobe Walls, a crumbling fort built and then abandoned by the Bents. Scholars disagree over whether Carson won or lost the fight at Adobe Walls—he had to retreat, but many more Comanches and Kiowas died in the battle than did New Mexico Volunteers and their Native allies. Victories or not, it was these military aggressions against Navajos, Apaches, Comanches, and Kiowas that supplied Carson's detractors with the most ammunition across the generations. A century later, the armory of resentment exploded.[68]

The outcry against Carson that garnered the most attention, however, could not be traced directly to the Navajo Nation. (The Diné reclaimed their homeland by treaty with the United States in 1868, and in 1968 they commemorated the centennial with ceremonies, publications, and cultural events that stressed a hundred years of Navajo progress; indeed, it was after the centennial that the tribal council renamed the tribe the Navajo Nation.)[69] Nor did the protest against Carson hagiographics emanate directly from Kiowa, Comanche, or Apache critics. Tribal activists in this era often concerned themselves with pressing, present-day issues of self-determination, and as in the case of the Diné, tribal governments, themselves created in response to federal mandates, were apt to emphasize contemporary achievements over past violence and starvation.[70] So instead of emerging from the Native peoples most intimately affected by Carson's military campaigns, the outcry against him arose along a corridor that he had known well, stretching from the Front Range of the Rocky Mountains in Colorado south into the Sangre de Cristos in New Mexico. Colorado Springs and Taos became centers of controversy, and then the argument migrated north to the heart of the urban interior West in greater Denver.

Sparks ignited within months of each other at Colorado College in Colorado Springs and at Kit Carson Memorial State Park in Taos, though only the Taos controversy was widely publicized. At Colorado College, in a display near the gymnasium, the campus Reserve Officers' Training Corps (ROTC) had mounted two photographs of Kit Carson, one labeled as such and the other with no identifying caption. In the fall of 1972, the captioned photo caught the eye of a new faculty member, Shirley Hill Witt. Witt, a member of the Akwesasne Mohawk Nation, had earned her PhD in anthropology at the University of New Mexico in 1969. She also helped found the National Indian Youth Council, a pan-tribal association of younger Indians who organized in 1961 to pursue self-determination for Indigenous peoples more aggressively than the National Congress of American Indians—the era's most established Native political group—had done, though with similar goals. Witt, then, was an experienced activist when she embarked on her academic career. So when the Colorado College display of Carson's image offended her political sensibilities, she demanded its removal. She may not have known at first that her new academic home was also the institution that employed the Carson scholar Harvey Carter, since the two were rostered in different departments, Carter in history (where he had taught since 1945) and Witt in anthropology, and since Carter was away on research leave when the fall term began.[71]

According to Carter, when he returned to campus in November 1972, he learned that "a new associate professor of anthropology had raised such a fuss about a picture of Kit Carson displayed by the R.O.T.C. that, under pressure from the Dean of Colorado College, it had been taken down."[72] Carter also learned that the student newspaper had approvingly noted the photograph's removal and quoted Witt's argument against it: "I find it perfectly offensive to have a terrorist and a killer displayed with honor," she said, adding, "Southwest America must be very bankrupt for heroes, if it has to enshrine the likes of Kit Carson."[73] Carter was the author of *"Dear Old Kit,"* which combined an annotated edition of Carson's memoirs with new writing that chronicled Carson's later years, assessed his treatment in scholarship and popular culture, and positively appraised his place in western history.[74] Carter was deeply wounded by what had transpired at the college in his absence, and he quickly penned a response, which he published in the *Denver Westerners Brand Book*. His 1973 essay, "The Curious Case of the Slandered Scout, the Aggressive Anthropologist, the Delinquent Dean and the Acquiescent Army," appeared shortly after Carter retired.[75]

Carter's essay responded to questions that he thought were implicit in Witt's critique: Was Carson racist? Were his actions genocidal? Carter noted that the word "racist" was "of popular current usage" but not yet listed in most dictionaries, and so he provided his own definition: racists assumed their own racial superiority and advocated racial separatism.[76] Carter concluded that Carson was "the opposite of all that the term 'racist' implies." He did so by citing Carson's marriages to two Indigenous and one Mexican woman, his advocacy on behalf of the Utes when he worked as their agent, his friendship with individual Delaware and Iroquois Indians, and his adoption of the Navajo boy Juan. Carter also argued that Carson did not engage in genocide: First, Carson fought Indians only when they attacked or stole from him or others; second, when Carson was in the military, he resisted unreasonable orders to kill Native people and retreated when continued fighting would have led to unnecessary bloodshed. More particularly, Carter noted that during the Navajo campaign, Carson resisted Gen. James Carleton's orders to kill all Diné men of fighting age and to capture women and children (instead, Carson destroyed Navajos' means of subsistence and thus forced their surrender). Carter also contrasted Carson's retreat at Adobe Walls with Chivington's almost simultaneous slaughter of Indian people at Sand Creek and likewise opposed Carson to George Armstrong Custer, who led his troops into assured destruction by Lakota, Cheyenne, and Arapaho warriors at the 1876 Battle of the Little Bighorn.[77]

But Carter bookended this sober, if debatable, historical logic between biting critiques of Shirley Hill Witt (primarily) and Colorado College and the ROTC (secondarily).[78] Of Witt he noted that he easily *could* have adopted *her* manner "by saying 'Colorado College must be very bankrupt for anthropologists, if it has to employ the likes of Shirley Hill Witt,'" but then he claimed, once he had used them, to "repudiate such language and tactics." Carter accused his dean of betraying the principles of academic freedom. He blamed his faculty colleagues for their silence, especially because some among them had been vocal "in defense of nudity on the stage, spit upon the flag, and homosexuality on the campus." Carter let the ROTC off with a lesser charge, though one sure to hurt a soldier's heart: mere cowardice. The officers involved were cowards because even though they shared Carter's positive view of Carson, they bowed to the college dean's request. They were not worse than cowards because they silently permitted the second, uncaptioned photograph of Carson—which Witt had not recognized as his likeness—to remain in the display that Witt had first noticed in 1972.[79]

The Carson controversy at Colorado College gained attention mostly around the campus and then, once Carter published "The Curious Case of the Slandered Scout" in the *Denver Westerners Brand Book*, within the Denver Posse of the Westerners.[80] By contrast, the storm in Taos sounded its thunder across a wider landscape. The first clouds gathered in the Taos chapter of the American GI Forum, a Mexican American civil rights group that organized first in Texas after World War II and then spread to other parts of the Southwest. The Taos chapter, however, was only months old in the summer of 1973, and members had engaged in just a couple of initiatives—they had called for the resignation of President Richard Nixon and lodged complaints against Mountain Bell for discrimination against Spanish-speaking telephone customers.[81]

On the Fourth of July, the group took out a quarter-page notice in the *Taos News*, featuring two photographs, one of Kit Carson and the other of Santiago "Jimmy" Lujan, a Taos Pueblo man who had served in the U.S. Army during World War II. (Taos Pueblo was the more-than-five-hundred-year-old Indigenous village next to which the *hispano* town of Don Fernando de Taos—or simply Taos—was eventually established.) Across the top of the notice was a banner that read, "TAOSENOS, AWAKEN TO THE NEEDED CHANGES IN TAOS!" The author called Taoseños to meet about changing the name of Kit Carson Memorial State Park to Santiago (Jimmy) Lujan Memorial State Park. The notice condemned the naming of area establishments after Carson, including the park, a utility company, and a national forest (as if to amplify the notice, directly adjacent was an advertisement for Kit Carson Drive-In Theatre). According to the author, much of the lure of Taos for outsiders was "due to the Indian, his dwelling, and his culture." And yet Carson had been "a threat to the very existence of the Indian in New Mexico." Sgt. Lujan, on the other hand, was one of "the true heroes of Taos," having enlisted with the 200th Coast Artillery, Battery H, "an outfit composed of Indians and Chicanos." Lujan had been sent to the Pacific theater, captured in the Battle of Bataan, forced on the Bataan Death March, and then transferred to a Fukuoka prison camp in Japan, where he died.[82] The notice concluded, "The contributions of people like Sgt. Lujan are ones that should be recognized rather than the selfish and exploitative actions of people such as Kit Carson."[83]

At least seventy people—by some reports, as many as two hundred—attended the GI Forum meeting, in what the *Taos News* called "the first shot in ... a war of 'symbols'" that "took dead aim at Taos' most famous historical figure."[84] It was hardly a shot heard around the world, but it did ring more loudly than the gunplay at Colorado College. United Press International (UPI) took up the Taos tale and, in New Mexico alone, newspapers from Albuquerque, Santa Fe, Clovis, and Las Cruces all ran stories within days.[85] On July 8, the *New York Times* published its own brief account, quoting Taos GI Forum leader Philip Vargas: "Kit Carson has been peddled off as a folk hero frontiersman and patron saint when in reality he was a tramp and renegade who was responsible for the deaths of a large number of Indians."[86] Meanwhile, the longer article in the *Taos News* noted that Vargas, a graduate of the University of New Mexico and Harvard Law School, had told those at the GI Forum meeting that the drive to rename the park was meant to foster the "mutual respect and dignity and health of Indians, Anglos, and Chicanos."[87]

When Vargas spoke of Indians, Chicanos, and Anglos, he echoed, in updated form, a vision of New Mexico that, like Carson's fall, was a hundred years in the making. In the wake of the mid-nineteenth-century U.S. conquest, and especially following the more thorough economic conquest that came with the railroads' arrival in the 1880s, Anglo newcomers and elite *hispanos* worked to create an image of tricultural harmony in New Mexico that nonetheless emphasized the separateness of the three cultures as well as the European origins of Anglos and *hispanos* alike. In the process, ethnic Mexicans became "Spanish Americans," which in turn helped end New Mexico's prolonged territorial status, since no longer would statehood mean admitting large numbers of Mexicans to full U.S. citizenship rights (New Mexico achieved statehood in 1912).[88] Vargas's version of triculturalism turned Spanish Americans into Chicanos, thereby laying claim to a heritage of race mixture—a *mestizaje*—that embraced Indianness.[89] Vargas stepped down as head of the Taos GI Forum in the middle of the park name controversy (to study for the New Mexico bar examination), but his successor, David Fernández, continued to invoke tricultural rhetoric. Fernández, an activist and *Taos News* columnist, remarked after a late-July rally promoting the name change, "It is the first time Indians, Chicanos, and Anglos have gotten together in a spirit of brotherhood."[90]

This long-standing tricultural vision, now revised, allowed the local GI Forum to take up an issue that might at first glance appear to belong more to American Indian than Mexican American activists—that is, the struggle over Carson's legacy vis-à-vis Indian people. But the line between Indians and *hispanos* in and around Taos came in and out of focus depending on who was, or was not, looking for it. Chicano activists, simply by identifying as such, made implicit claims to their own Indigenous ancestry, however those claims were received by Indian people. And Fernández maintained that the Taos GI Forum included both Chicano and Indian members.[91] Newspaper accounts did not specify how many Indigenous people joined the group when it organized, but it is clear that GI Forum members reached out to Native communities, especially Taos Pueblo. The first meeting about the renaming of Kit Carson Memorial State Park included pueblo residents, some of them relatives of the late Jimmy Lujan, as well as a Navajo tribal government representative. Nonetheless, a reporter noted that Philip Vargas, then still head of the GI Forum chapter, "seemed at times to have difficulty getting the more than 30 Pueblo residents who attended ... to voice their participation."[92] Tricultural rhetoric did not always translate into tricultural, or even bicultural, unanimity.

Indeed, Taos Pueblo residents had historical reasons to consider overtures from the GI Forum carefully before taking a stand. For centuries they had sometimes allied themselves with their *hispano* neighbors, especially in moments of multivalent conflict, as they did in the face of raids on pueblo and *hispano* villagers alike by mobile bands of Navajos, Apaches, and other equestrian Indians, and as they did in the 1847 Taos rebellion, when pueblo and *hispano* forces opposed U.S. rule in New Mexico.[93] And Taos Indians, unlike Navajos, Mescalero Apaches, Kiowas, or Comanches, had no special tribal history of enmity against Carson but rather a more generalized antagonism toward men of his ilk given their role in the U.S. conquest. In fact, from 1854 to 1861, Carson had served as Indian agent for Taos Pueblo as well as for Muache Utes and Jicarilla Apaches. Carson's dealings with the Taos Pueblo—a self-sufficient, horticultural village—were largely uneventful, at least when compared with his constant struggles to negotiate the turbulent relations among Utes, Apaches, *hispanos*, and Anglo newcomers. Then, too, individual Taos Indians had served as scouts and soldiers in Spanish, Mexican, and then U.S. campaigns against their nomadic Native neighbors, which is hardly surprising given the vexed and violent history of raiding and trading between sedentary, farming peoples and mobile, hunting peoples in the region's ongoing colonial past.[94]

But Taos Pueblo's relationship to Carson's legacy was even more complicated than this, given the proximity of Carson National Forest. In 1970, Taos Pueblo residents had won a decades-long fight against the U.S. government by which they took back 48,000 acres of mountainous terrain to the east and north that, in 1906, had been declared U.S. Forest Service land. Within those acres lay Blue Lake, which fed the Rio Pueblo de Taos, the main source of water for Taos Indian people. Blue Lake was (and is) a sacred site, the destination of an annual religious trek for pueblo residents, and it served other spiritual purposes as well. Until it was restored to the pueblo during the Nixon presidential administration, Blue Lake was part of Carson National Forest.[95] So even if it was not a specific historical animosity toward Carson the person that prompted some Taos Indians to respond to the GI Forum's solicitations, the Carson name must have raised hackles. Surely Taos Pueblo shared—and, through the Blue Lake fight, helped to foster—the common, contemporary Indigenous commitment to sovereignty. Indeed, pueblo residents participated in the pan-Indian consciousness that had grown over the twentieth century, reaching new heights in the 1970s, by which Carson, the enemy of Navajos, became the more generic Indian killer of activists' estimation.[96] All of these factors must have influenced Taos Pueblo residents' views on the renaming of Kit Carson Memorial State Park.

Finally, there was a very immediate rift within Taos Pueblo itself. Just months before the Carson Park controversy, a group of pueblo residents, calling themselves the Taos Pueblo People's Committee, had presented the tribal governor with a list of grievances regarding the administration of federal programs on tribal lands. Complaining that they received no response, the group circulated a petition that they planned to forward to federal officials, hoping that U.S. government intervention would bring about changes in the way land management, law enforcement, and access to housing and electricity proceeded at the pueblo. These issues were unresolved when the drive to change the name of Carson Park began. By the end of July, the Taos Pueblo People's Committee officially endorsed the GI Forum's cause.[97]

This helped pave the way for a rally that the local GI Forum planned in conjunction with the town's annual Fiestas de Taos, a summer celebration honoring the two patron saints of Taos, Santa Ana and Santiago. The event, then and now, has served to highlight New Mexico's tricultural vision but also has traded in symbols of Spanish conquest, including a royal court of almost always Spanish-surnamed young women who serve as *reina* and her *princesas*.[98] In 1973, the GI Forum, along with some Taos Pueblo residents, entered its own float in the Fiestas parade, boasting images of Jimmy Lujan as well as signs that read, "Why, Kit Carson? Why not, Santiago Jimmy Lujan Memorial Park?" The parade's announcer, however, failed to identify the float's sponsors from the reviewing stand, in a perceived snub reported not only in the *Taos News* and *Albuquerque Journal* but in the *New York Times* as well. The subsequent rally was also a disappointment. The GI Forum had wanted to hold it in Taos's central plaza, but the town council refused to issue a permit. So the activists gathered in Kit Carson Memorial State Park. A smaller crowd attended than expected (one reporter counted fifty people and another over a hundred). Furthermore, the organizers had invited representatives from the American Indian Movement, the era's most visible pan-Indian organization; celebrity Anthony Quinn, an actor identified with Native causes; and various regional politicians, but few such guests materialized.[99] The park dispute continued in and around Taos, but after the Fiestas fiasco, it faded from national view.[100]

Slow to react to contemporary controversy, historians took up the fight eight months later. In March 1974, restaurateur Sam Arnold, who had established The Fort in suburban Denver, sent out letters on behalf of a group called the Green River Scalping and Joy Society, encouraging recipients to attend a dinner and debate "on the present public pressure to change the name of Kit Carson State Park to Santiago 'Jimmy' Lujan State Park." Arnold had invited David Fernández from the Taos GI Forum and Carson scholar Harvey Carter to present the opposing viewpoints after a dinner of roast buffalo. Arnold called himself the "head haar-lifter" of the Green River Scalping and Joy Society, which sponsored such dinner seminars with an admonishment that purported to reflect the ambience of the western fur trade and the patois of mountain men: "Keep yer haar on!"[101] As the *Santa Fe New Mexican* noted of the debate, "The subject matter, which is being treated tongue-in-cheek in faraway Denver, has been a matter of considerable controversy in Taos."[102]

The April debate received little press, and no transcripts have survived. But the *New Mexican* briefly covered it, calling it an "amicable draw." According to the newspaper's Taos bureau, Fernández conceded that he had "gained respect for the opposite opinion" in the debate, while Carter admitted there were "two sides to the story."[103] The head haar-lifter saw it differently. Arnold felt Carter had prevailed, while Fernández came across as a "nice guy who didn't know anything," someone who could only talk in lofty terms about "love and brotherhood."[104] For historians, then, Carson's specific engagements with various Indian peoples—which arguably *were* less lethal than those of frontier soldiers like Chivington or Custer and arguably *did* include moments of advocacy and friendship as well as incidents of appropriation and violence—were more important than the ways in which Carson's life course both mirrored and participated in U.S. conquest, by which older residents of the Southwest were dispossessed.

Blackwelder and McClung followed what they could of this controversy. Blackwelder learned of the Taos affair from a newspaper clipping sent by a friend.[105] McClung, for her part, received an anguished telephone call from Kit Carson and Josefa Jaramillo's granddaughter Leona Wood. McClung was the first to broach the subject of Carson's fall in a letter to Blackwelder. A week after the April 1974 debate at The Fort, McClung reported that Wood, daughter of Estella Carson and Tom Wood, had called just before the event, "greatly disturbed and so angry at Sam [Arnold] that she was incoherent." Wood had received an invitation, and she was livid that her grandfather could even be the subject of debate. (Arnold remembered years later that despite her anger, Wood attended and ended up mollified because Kit Carson's reputation had been enhanced rather than stained by the debate.) McClung explained the background: "You see, there is a plan to change the name of the Kit Carson Park at Taos to Lujan to honor a young Chicano k[illed] in WW II. . . . The terms used re[garding] Carson are 'a tramp,' 'Indian killer,' 'brutal Anglo soldier carrying out the Brutal policies of the U.S. Govt.'" McClung concluded by stating her view: "It seems to me that only evil can come from using such terms & nothing can be gained by the Chicano." This was her first and last observation.[106]

Blackwelder, on the other hand, addressed the Carson controversy several times. After receiving McClung's letter about the debate at The Fort, Blackwelder reported that she had been "shocked" when she first heard about the drive to change the park's name. She added that she had considered contacting Jack Boyer, director of the Kit Carson Memorial Foundation, which operated the Kit Carson Home and Museum in Taos, telling him to "take precautions" but then "decided not to get into it." Blackwelder surmised that author Dee Brown was "at the bottom of the whole fracas." Brown was the non-Native author of *Bury My Heart at Wounded Knee: An Indian History of the American West*, the wildly popular 1970 book that indicted U.S. Indian policy and lamented the fate of Indigenous peoples.[107] Blackwelder had no evidence that Brown was involved in the Taos protest except that he had, more generally, "taken up the cause of the neglected Indians." Nonetheless, she complained that Brown "(should be) enough of a historian to evaluate Kit Carson's great accomplishments," since, as she put it, "Carson was a friend of the Indian." Blackwelder concluded, "I think it would be very proper to recognize young Lujan, but why all this anti-Carson fervor?"[108]

Two weeks after sending this letter, Blackwelder wrote again to McClung and reported that she had just received from "Professor Harvey" a reprint of his article "The Curious Case of the Slandered Scout." This was the first that Blackwelder had heard of the earlier Colorado College controversy over the display of Carson photographs. Of Shirley Hill Witt's protest Blackwelder wrote, "This is frightening to me for the so-called Intellectuals are helping to stir up trouble by supporting these 'causes.'" (Her fright notwithstanding, Blackwelder was pleased that in his article about the college affray, Harvey Carter approvingly mentioned her biography, *Great Westerner*.) Blackwelder reiterated her worry that activists might attack the Carson museum, just a few blocks from the park at the center of the naming dispute. She concluded that she could not "see how the Indian will be helped in any way" by all the upheaval.[109]

Neither Blackwelder nor McClung, then, believed that good could come to contemporary minoritized communities from activist denunciations of a historical figure like Carson, even if McClung was confused about which community would be represented if Carson Park were renamed—ethnic Mexican or American Indian (this because Spanish surnames like Lujan were ubiquitous among Pueblo Indians). That both self-identified Chicanos and Indians participated in the protest no doubt increased her confusion. Of course in arguing that Chicanos had nothing to gain or that Indians would not be helped by activism that highlighted the perfidy of white pioneers toward people of color in the western past, McClung and Blackwelder tacitly acknowledged that many Indigenous people and many Mexican Americans in fact lived in need—that is, they inhabited communities plagued by profound social, political, and economic deficits, deficits that had a history in which white Americans were complicit. Blackwelder was convinced that her Kit Carson, the great westerner, played no part in creating such crises, that he had been "a friend of the Indian." McClung, by contrast, offered no impassioned defense of Carson, even as she maintained that attacks on his legacy were ineffective tools for promoting change in the U.S. racial order.

A remark Blackwelder made back in 1970 in response to what she called the "Hippie Invasion" of Taos—an influx of mostly white countercultural youths—further illuminates the subtle difference in how the two women thought about the connections between their own contemporary work as historians and the lives of the western men their work highlighted. Blackwelder had bemoaned the changes that she thought the

"Hippie Invasion" signified, including rampant drug use and increased crime. She wrote to McClung, "Glad we can keep our interest in Western History as a sort of antidote."[110] As this remark suggests, Blackwelder preferred to distance herself from present-day problems by studying the western past, which she idealized as a time when giants like Carson walked the earth. McClung, on the other hand, seemed more open to the idea that stories of giants were in part tall tales. Indeed, even as she continued to research the Goliaths of the West—the Carson men, the Bent men, the Boggs men—she stood them alongside their kith and kin until the breadth and depth of their collective relations were just as visible as the stature of the men themselves. At the same time, McClung diligently collected newspaper clippings on the proverbial Davids of the West and their environs; she categorized the clippings as pertaining to "Hispano-Americans," "Mass Transportation," "the Negro question," and "Ecology."[111] McClung, it seems, was not so sure that western history could serve as an escape from current affairs, even as she remained convinced that the remembrance of things past ought not be a battleground for settling old colonial scores and redressing their painful present legacies.

Making It with the Professionals

Even as Quantrille McClung and Bernice Blackwelder grappled with Kit Carson's fall from grace in the arena of popular opinion, they also fought on other fronts, positioning themselves in relation to a quieter struggle whose principals were fellow historians, both amateur and academic. Back when the two women started their work on Carson, they were nonprofessional historians working in a field full of nonprofessionals, especially those affiliated with the Westerners. That changed in the 1960s and '70s, thanks in large part to the growth of the Western History Association (WHA), its annual conferences, and its new scholarly journal, the *Western Historical Quarterly*, founded in 1970.[112] Both women noted these developments—indeed, Blackwelder was a charter member of the WHA—and paid attention to how often and in what manner their books were cited by university-based scholars.[113] In the mid-1960s, they began to write to each other about their relationship to the professionalizing field of western history.

Blackwelder, a WHA member, attended more closely to the organization and its publications, but both women followed developments in the field. Neither attended annual WHA meetings, although Blackwelder noted when she received conference programs in the mail. When the

1976 meeting convened in Denver, for instance, Blackwelder was living in Chicago. Reflecting the material constraints both women faced, she wrote to McClung, "Wish I could attend but not at such prices!!"[114] Blackwelder reported that she kept up with the field by reading the *American West*, the WHA's magazine, and, later, the *Western Historical Quarterly*, too.[115] Both women felt overwhelmed by the outpouring of scholarship. Blackwelder told McClung in 1969 that each issue of the *American West* listed new books, some of which, she griped, "contradict each other!"[116] Likewise, McClung remarked in 1972, "It seems to me that the more books I consult the more discrepancies I find and the more 'confuseder' I get!"[117]

For both women, history was first and foremost a matter of getting the facts right—of resolving contradictions and sorting out discrepancies—and only less consciously one of creating value-laden interpretations of the past.[118] At first glance, this distinction might seem characteristic of a divide between nonprofessional and professional historians, especially by the late 1960s, when many U.S. history scholars began to retreat from an earlier recuperation of the ideal of objectivity and the related notion that facts spoke for themselves, which had defined the World War II and early Cold War era.[119] But Blackwelder and McClung's conception of history was not wholly at odds with scholarly ideas and practice more specific to the field of western history during this period. Even as some scholars called for a more analytical and interpretive—as opposed to descriptive and narrative—history of the West, there was a way in which professional western historians had to embrace factualism in order to maintain credibility with nonprofessionals who were so active in the field.[120] Western history buffs—like Civil War buffs—often boasted an encyclopedic knowledge of the minutiae of the past, and woe to the university-based western historian, for example, who publicly confused an early Hawken rifle with a later Winchester model. So even as the field of western history felt the drift away from objectivism that characterized the profession as a whole, there was a countervailing pull back toward the ennobling of facts that originated in part with well-read western history buffs.

This tug-of-war played itself out in the pages of the newly launched scholarly journal, the *Western Historical Quarterly*, the very existence of which marked the professionalization of the field.[121] In the 1970 inaugural issue, Ray Allen Billington, the first president of the WHA, published an invited article in which he chronicled his own intellectual path as a frontier historian. He ended the essay with an academic call to arms, charging western historians with three lines of attack. First, echoing

Frederick Jackson Turner, who had trained one of Billington's own mentors, Frederick Merk, Billington urged western historians to convince their readers and students that "knowledge of the nation's pioneer past is essential to an understanding of today's social order." Second, he urged his colleagues to "pay less attention to the distant past and more to the usable near-present." It was Billington's third call that rankled western history buffs: that scholars "must abandon description for analysis and narration for interpretation." He went on to provide examples, imploring historians to

> appraise the economic results of the fur trade rather than repeat the tale of [trapper] Hugh Glass and the grizzly bear, ... relegate the glamorous history of overland stagecoaching to a brief mention and dwell instead on the impact of the railroads on regional development, ... pay less attention to prospectors and more to the eastern capitalists who elevated mining to an important role in the national economy,... focus on the business activities of ranch owners rather than on the adventures of cowboys, ... concentrate on the unromantic farmer who ... transplanted civilization to the successive frontiers and not on the outcasts who preceded them in the march across the continent, ... compare urbanization in the West with city growth in the East and explain any differences detected.

As if to further tarnish the reputation of buffs and burnish that of academics, Billington added an indictment of provincialism, antiquarianism, localism—all associated with amateur historians—and went on to list fifteen degreed scholars who were producing the sort of cutting-edge work he thought the field needed in order to thrive.[122]

One year later, a history buff wrote an aggrieved response to this and other calls for the professionalization of the field. Dale Schoenberger, who worked on such iconic topics as gunfighters and Custer's Last Stand, published a short piece in the *Western Historical Quarterly* decrying what he called the "new trend" in western history.[123] His subtitle—"Academics versus Buffs"—drew the battle lines more clearly than Billington had. Schoenberger argued that the new trend sought to "dehumanize" nineteenth-century western history, that its practitioners lived "in fear of glamorizing the West, lest it be classified by others as 'cowboy and Indian.'" Then he elaborated: "This trend is the interpretation of Western history by scholars for scholars, specialized interpretations on the American West for professional scholars and their captive classroom audiences. It features scholars seeking to up-grade the field of Western history from the former trend of mere narration and reporting, but it pooh-poohs a biography of a gunfighter or a mountain man as adolescent and beneath the standards of their profession." Schoenberger concluded by calling for "mutual respect" between "professional historians and buffs."[124] The peaceful coexistence between amateurs and academics that had characterized the field in the 1950s and '60s was giving way to conflicts such as these, and western history buffs were the ones losing ground.

Still, the struggle between professional and nonprofessional western historians was for the most part a comradely contest among white men. Despite their differences, history buffs attended the annual WHA meeting alongside history professors, and the Westerners hosted a breakfast there each year that drew hundreds, amateur and academic alike.[125] Historian Robert Utley—who was a bridge between the professors and the buffs, given his unfinished PhD, his work for the National Park Service, and his impressive publication record—served as WHA president in 1967–68.[126] Many Westerners chapters maintained their men-only membership policies into the 1970s, while the WHA had been coed since its founding in 1962. But in practice both organizations served a field notable for both its gender exclusivity and racial homogeneity.[127] In this context, then, the divide between amateurs and academics was no Grand Canyon.

What is more, western historians bonded across that divide when Kit Carson came under attack. The debate at The Fort featured a professor and an activist arguing during a buffalo dinner prepared under the direction of a restaurateur who was among the most prominent western history buffs in the nation. The event followed quickly after Harvey Carter published "The Curious Case of the Slandered Scout," and Carter distributed his article widely, bringing copies to the debate and sending others to an army of western history enthusiasts. Each of the responses Carter saved applauded his stance, especially his retort to Shirley Hill Witt. Lawrence Kelly, a scholar of federal Indian policy, wrote that he, too, was "mystified at the intolerance and shoddy thinking which some members of our profession manifest."[128] John Wickman, director of the Eisenhower Presidential Library, quipped, "If I ever find myself locked in mortal combat with a Grizzly Bar [sic], I shall call, not for my guns, but Harvey's sharp and rapid fire pen, and thus flay the monster right down to his yellow toe nails."[129] The illustrious Ray Billington's response evoked the history of colonial violence and enacted verbal violence against women for good measure, as if it were all a colossal joke: "If I were Mrs. Shirley Hill Witt I would quietly fold my tepee and put as much space between myself and the Colorado College campus as the globe allowed. You have done a superior scalping job on her—far more brutal, I suspect, than Kit Carson ever performed on an Indian. And a hell of a lot more deserved."[130] But it took a South Dakota prison inmate, a fur trade buff with whom Carter exchanged letters, to put into words what some western historians felt as the subjects of their work fell from grace. Dennis Ottoson wrote that although he was "not quite as sympathetic" toward Carson as Carter was, he did "dislike the rhetoric indulged in by Dr. Hill." Ottoson reported that he heard "similar noises from the local [American Indian Movement] boys" and then got to the point: "It is just not fashionable right now to be other than black, Indian, homosexual or female. You and I are just not with it."[131] It was as if the practitioners who had dominated western history felt themselves under attack along with their research subjects, and they responded, regardless of their status in the field, by circling the wagons.

Indeed, the dynamics between amateurs and academics in western history during this period had some peculiar characteristics. In other subfields and during other eras, women were disproportionately represented among amateur historians, while men dominated the professional terrain. This created a gendered hierarchy in the production of knowledge that generally worked to the benefit of men.[132] In western history, however, white men toiled on both sides of the amateur/academic divide. Thus, in the 1960s and early '70s, the gendered struggle among historians was not so much one between women and men as it was a contest over which male intellectual style would garner the most respect in the academic venues where western history was on display: WHA conferences, the *Western Historical Quarterly*, and the myriad books being published in the field.[133] Over time, western historians reached a kind of gentlemanly bargain. Academics asserted more control over the field, but they did so in part by incorporating amateurs' proclivity for description and detail, their sartorial styles (hence the cowboy boots and bolo ties sported at WHA conferences), and their penchant for invented western traditions—most notably, the mountain man toast raised annually by Sam Arnold at the WHA meeting banquet: "Here's to the child's what's come afore 'an here's to the pilgrims what comes arter. May yer trails be free of grizz, yer packs filled with plews and fat buffler in your pot! Waugh!"[134] With enemies like this, buffs hardly needed friends. So, in spite of the conflicts that arose, there was no exodus of nonprofessionals from the field, even as western history professionalized in ways that now and then gave amateurs cause to harrumph.

Blackwelder and McClung drifted in this ebb and flow and got caught on the shoals, but they ultimately realized that the recognition of professional scholars would keep them and their work afloat. This is not to say that they ignored western historians working outside of academia. Sam Arnold was a frequent topic of conversation in their letters.[135] They also discussed other members of the Denver Posse of the Westerners, including Fred Rosenstock, a dealer in books and art of the West and founder of the Old West Publishing Company, and Nolie Mumey, a doctor who was also a prolific author, a collector of things western, and a would-be *santero* (that is, he carved cottonwood figures of Catholic saints as *nuevomexicanos* had for centuries).[136] McClung and Blackwelder did not always approve of these buffs. As fond as they were of Arnold, they were appalled when he appropriated Céran St. Vrain's headstone from a grave in northern New Mexico's Mora Valley and moved it to The Fort (McClung coached Mora County resident Carlos López from the sidelines about how to get the tombstone back without causing embarrassment, as she put it, "either to Mr. Arnold or to myself").[137] Similarly, McClung must have regaled Blackwelder with an unflattering story about Rosenstock, because Blackwelder wrote back calling him "rude" and "mean" and wishing him "his come-uppance."[138] As for Mumey, McClung acknowledged that he was the person who first put her in touch with Carson enthusiast John McCurdy of Kansas, who in turn introduced her to Blackwelder. McClung also contacted Mumey for assistance in getting her work published (though she scrawled "no reply" across the copy she kept of her letter). McClung summed up her opinion of Mumey in a letter, calling him "a semi-professional writer on western subjects [who] needs an editor badly!"[139] Blackwelder and McClung paid attention to fellow history buffs but hardly fawned over them.

Far more often, the two women focused on professional historians, trading information about how their own work had been received by such scholars. The two academics whose opinions most mattered to McClung and Blackwelder were LeRoy Hafen and Harvey Carter. Hafen served as Colorado's state historian from the 1920s to the 1950s, and by the 1970s, he was a professor at Brigham Young University. He was well published; his most recent claim to fame was his edited biographical collection, *The Mountain Men and the Fur Trade of the Far West*, a ten-volume work published between 1965 and 1972.[140] Carter, in addition to *"Dear Old Kit,"* had published a biographical sketch of Carson in Hafen's multivolume work.[141] McClung and Blackwelder pored over these texts and were gratified to see their own books cited favorably therein. When Blackwelder found her work referenced in one of Hafen's volumes, she told McClung, "I felt like I had been struck by lightning!" In the same letter Blackwelder added, "It was a thrill for me to think a scholar like Hafen would read and use my book." In another she wrote, "I am glad that Mr. Carter respects us."[142] Blackwelder seems to have cared more about such recognition than did McClung, but McClung could take pleasure in being noticed as well. When she found herself included in the index of Hafen's collection, she exclaimed, "I have finally made it with the professionals!"[143]

Blackwelder and McClung were fortunate that Hafen and Carter were the academics whose scholarship was closest to their interests. It was true that Hafen had belonged to one of the earliest, all-male Westerners groups, the Denver Posse (Carter belonged to the Pikes Peak Posse, which formed later and admitted women members).[144] But both men encouraged the work of white women historians. Indeed, Hafen often collaborated with his first wife, Ann Woodbury Hafen, and unlike some male historians of his generation, he acknowledged that collaboration by sharing authorship or editorship on several books, including *Handcarts to Zion*, about the Mormon handcart migration to Utah in the 1850s.[145] Furthermore, Janet Lecompte, a nonprofessional historian who in the 1970s and '80s published on the history of northern New Mexico and southern Colorado, singled LeRoy Hafen out as uniquely supportive. It was Lecompte who said so bluntly that women who worked early on in western history "were treated like morons by most male historians." But she hastened to add that she had been "very kindly treated by LeRoy Hafen."[146] Likewise, Carter nominated Norma Peterson, a historian who taught at nearby Adams State College, as well as Lecompte for honorary doctorates at Colorado College, which they received in 1978 and 1979, respectively.[147] And by 1980, Carter would accept Thelma Guild's proposal to coauthor a biography of Carson based on the work that Carter did in the hybrid text *"Dear Old Kit."* Guild, like Blackwelder and McClung, was a nonprofessional historian captivated by Carson and his world.[148]

So, McClung and Blackwelder found receptive readers in Hafen and Carter, and both women also found a willing correspondent in Carter. McClung's letters to Carter did not start out on a happy note, though. When she found the *Carson-Bent-Boggs Genealogy* cited in a biographical essay on Moses Carson (Kit Carson's half brother) that Carter published in one of Hafen's volumes, McClung noticed that Carter had not listed her as the genealogy's compiler. So she wrote to Carter, telling him that while she was "gratified" that he had used her book, she would have been "more gratified" had he used her name. Carter replied apologetically, thus establishing a correspondence that endured for a half dozen years.[149] McClung and Carter shared information gleaned from their research and congratulated each other when their respective books were published.[150] Blackwelder waited to contact Carter until *"Dear Old Kit"* was released and then sent him a letter with a check enclosed, requesting a signed copy. The book arrived with a "gracious signature," and Blackwelder and Carter corresponded thereafter.[151] Both women, meanwhile, wrote about the letters each of them received from Carter, calling him "most cordial," "open-minded," and an "approachable scholar."[152] Whatever the complex relations between white women and white men and between professors and buffs in western history, a shared passion for that history—and, no doubt, an unexamined racial affinity—could allow for mutually respectful and beneficial ties like those that Carter, McClung, and Blackwelder shared.

During the period of their lives when Blackwelder and McClung immersed themselves in western history, then, they were swimming for the most part alongside a diverse assortment of white men. In the early years, those men were as likely to be amateur as academic historians. But as the 1960s unfolded, professional historians gained new stature in the field, even as they continued to negotiate on friendly terms with history buffs. McClung and Blackwelder maintained relationships with male historians on either side of the divide. They recognized more and more, though, that having "made it with the professionals" gave their own work legitimacy, and so they filled their letters with discussions of university-based scholars and scholarship.

There were a few degreed or soon-to-be-degreed white women active in the field by the 1970s, scholars such as Mary Lee Spence (the first woman elected president of the WHA, in 1981), Joan Jensen, Glenda Riley, Sandra Myres, and Iris Engstrand.[153] And there were other nondegreed women publishing in western history as well; of special relevance to Blackwelder and McClung was Janet Lecompte's work.[154] Indeed, the full representation of women scholars in the WHA, according to Spence, "did not come without a great deal of effort on women's part and perhaps some guilty consciences on the part of men."[155] Other than a brief letter or two between McClung and Lecompte preserved in McClung's papers, however, there is no evidence that these pathbreaking female historians made much of an impression on Blackwelder and McClung.[156] Their preferred medium of intellectual exchange was the white male scholar, someone like Harvey Carter or LeRoy Hafen, whose approval contributed to McClung's and Blackwelder's sense of self-worth. This dynamic—whereby the women traded stories about men and used those stories to establish truths about themselves—was one of the ways that Blackwelder and McClung steered a course through the shifting currents of social power in this period; it was part of their traffic in men. But each woman also navigated turbulent waters even closer to her home port.

Invasion of the Malcontents

One lovely Sunday in June 1967, Bernice Blackwelder sat down in her Chicago apartment and wrote to Quantrille McClung. It was a newsy letter with only two paragraphs of nine devoted to research matters. The rest was filled with talk about the mild weather, an impending visit from Bernice's niece, husband Harold's search for work that would still allow him to accept singing jobs, and plans that fell through for a rendezvous with an old colleague from Bernice's time in Washington, D.C. The letter also lamented Quantrille's ill health and praised her choice of heirloom china as a wedding gift for young relatives. Bernice said that she planned to go to the Chicago Public Library the next day and explained that she did not frequent the Chicago Historical Society in part because it, unlike the city library, was not near the downtown stores. Bernice liked to shop, if not to buy, though she added that she would be unlikely to "buy much of what is offered now-a-days" even if finances allowed. She went on, "I wonder what the world is coming to with the revolution in music, art, styles, literature and drama. I must be getting on in age but it really shocks me." Then she signed off, "Must close now and get something on the table for a hungry man."[157]

This missive bespoke the changes that, by the late 1960s, gripped Bernice's life and her friendship with Quantrille. Both women recognized the upheaval. Quantrille replied to Bernice, "Seems I feel just as you do about the revolution in every aspect of our life and I am certain it is for the worse." In this exchange, the two stressed aesthetics: fashion and the arts concerned Bernice, while Quantrille bemoaned architectural styles, noting, "I would like to dynamite nearly all of the new buildings."[158] Soon, though, they would reflect, too, on the revolution in race and gender relations, the rise in counterculturalism, the activist movements that called into question long-standing social hierarchies, the deterioration of local urban environments, and the economic and demographic forces that transformed their neighborhoods. Their friendship had grown to where they spoke openly of such matters as well as about the challenge of living on limited incomes and the somatic and sensory experience of aging. They also wrote about the burdens and blessings of family ties. And Bernice, for her part, spoke candidly about her husband

and her frustration over having to keep house when what she wanted to do was write history. In covering this new ground, Quantrille and Bernice's relationship now encompassed more than the terrain of western manhood that had brought them together. Their traffic in men did not cease, though, even as the landscape of their daily lives came into sharp relief. And those daily lives continued to shape their historical practice.

When Bernice and Harold Blackwelder left the East Coast in 1962, just after the release of *Great Westerner*, they became a couple in motion. Their precise movements are difficult to trace, in part because the letters Quantrille saved from Bernice stop abruptly in August 1962, starting up again in September 1965.[159] But a trail of evidence tracks a westward migration for Bernice and Harold in 1962, followed by a 1965 return to Chicago, where they had met, married, and lived in the 1930s and '40s. It seems likely that Harold's aspirations as a restaurateur prompted the move west, and it may have been his desire to return to the world of music that drew them back east.

Bernice and Harold left the Washington, D.C., suburbs for Omaha, Nebraska, late in 1962, and they had set up an apartment there by New Year's Day.[160] They stayed in Omaha only a few months, however, before moving on to Colorado. They considered, but decided against, buying a restaurant in Loveland, north of Denver.[161] Instead, by 1964, Harold was running a business called the Dixie Pit Bar-B-Q in North Denver.[162] By 1965, they were living in Arvada, just northwest of the city, probably renting an apartment there.[163] This put Bernice in proximity to Quantrille—less than a half hour by car—for the only time during the women's acquaintance, a quarter-century friendship conducted otherwise almost entirely by mail. Before the Blackwelders' move, the two women had met one time in Denver, and Quantrille had once visited Bernice in Virginia.

Without letters between Bernice and Quantrille in these years, it is hard to reconstruct the Blackwelders' daily life during their brief stint in Omaha and their longer residence in greater Denver. But Quantrille reported to others about the time she spent with Bernice in Colorado: the two worked side by side at the Denver Public Library (DPL); they went together to visit history buff Sam Arnold at his restaurant, The Fort; and, however busy Harold was with his eatery, he found time to take Bernice and Quantrille to Estes Park, sixty miles away, to meet with a Carson descendant.[164] Bernice reflected on this period in later letters, where she revealed that the Dixie Pit had not been Harold's venture alone. Just as she had baked for her husband's businesses in Virginia, so did she lend a hand in Colorado. When she moved to Chicago, Bernice reported that her apartment there had "a lovely two oven stove that surely would have been a boon … in Arvada." Still, the Dixie Pit must not have thrived. As Bernice later wrote, she and Harold knew "something about the ups and downs of the restaurant business."[165]

Their western adventure came to naught, and by fall 1965, Bernice and Harold were in Chicago, living in the apartment with the two-oven stove. It was three flights up from the street and a block or so from Wrigley Field, home of the Chicago Cubs and, at the time, the Chicago Bears as well—"not a prime neighborhood," Bernice opined.[166] She was sixty-two and looking for a job. Harold was sixty, and he performed intermittently at clubs and conventions, hauling his bass fiddle up the stairs. He also did work for the (at first) segregated white Chicago local of the American Federation of Musicians (AFM); it merged with the black local in 1966.[167] Bernice also contemplated a return to music, practicing voice with an old friend and working up confidence to start teaching. "It seems like the curtain is going up again," she told Quantrille. The curtain soon fell. In less than three months Bernice confessed, "I feel like I am building a road to nowhere as I don't expect to sing anywhere." Meanwhile, she applied for jobs at the Field Museum, then called the Chicago Museum of Natural History, as well as the Chicago Historical Society and a publishing company, insisting that she was "not counting" on the outcome. As she wrote to Quantrille, "I know at my advanced age, I am a terrible hazard!" Bernice received no job offers. It was a tense few months, easier when Harold had work and Bernice could concentrate on her research and harder when Harold's income diminished and his daily demands kept Bernice on edge. Bernice described their financial situation as one in which they were "making ends meet."[168]

They could not make ends meet, though, and in 1966, less than a year after relocating to Chicago, the Blackwelders moved to what Bernice, putting a positive spin on it, described as a "better section of the city," the Logan Square neighborhood. "Harold will manage an apartment house for a good reduction in rent," Bernice announced. Although their own unit was smaller than the one they had rented near Wrigley Field, it was on the first floor, which benefited bass player Harold as well as their dog, Elsa. Public transportation was also less convenient from Logan Square, but car owner Bernice told Quantrille that the "Kennedy Express[way] is in the next block."[169] What Bernice did not tell Quantrille is what she meant by "the next block." The apartment building was U-shaped, with a courtyard in the middle. When Bernice walked out of her unit and through the narrow courtyard toward the street, Logan Boulevard, she saw nothing but that street and the elevated, concrete expressway just beyond, with cars and trucks hurtling back and forth from downtown

Chicago to O'Hare Airport and the northwest suburbs.[170] Logan Boulevard was one of the grand thoroughfares built in response to Daniel Burnham and Edward Bennett's 1909 *Plan of Chicago*, which envisioned a city and its suburbs linked by radial and concentric streets.[171] Bernice noted that the boulevard was once known as "Millionaire's Row," and it did indeed boast gracious gray-stone mansions alongside homes that had been converted into apartments and sturdy brick buildings such as the one where the Blackwelders lived.[172]

But Logan Square had long since become a working-class neighborhood; an early 1960s study found that 60 percent of residents were craftsmen or skilled factory workers. A majority were of Polish ancestry, while others descended from German, Russian Jewish, Scandinavian, Belgian, and Italian immigrants. The previous decade had seen an exodus, especially of young people, that coincided with the construction of the Kennedy Expressway, finished in 1960. As a result, the percentage of residents over sixty-five doubled.[173] In 1963, a reporter characterized Logan Square as a community in decline, the business district peppered with "for rent" and "going out of business" signs as well as boarded windows.[174] The Blackwelders moved there less than three years later.

Bernice lived in the brick apartment building in the shadow of the Kennedy Expressway for fifteen years. Although she reported to Quantrille that her husband would serve as apartment manager, most of the managerial work fell on Bernice's shoulders. Quantrille predicted as much when she wrote to Bernice after the move, "I trust you may not find that you have taken on too much responsibility as I assume Harold will continue with his music."[175] For four years, until she gave up the job and moved with Harold into a different unit in the same building, Bernice was responsible for answering inquiries about rentals, showing apartments to prospective tenants, and giving keys to workers who came for repairs. Sometimes the tasks tied her down when she wanted to escape to one of Chicago's libraries, and other times the duties disturbed her when she was working at home.[176] When she resigned in 1970, she confessed that even though it was "not a difficult job," it did "not pay for all the interruptions ... and crises that keep me here day after day." The new apartment, next door to the old one, promised "a little more room and much more privacy."[177] And indeed, once settled there, Bernice reported that she was "relieved of a lot of irritation."[178] Still, according to Bernice's niece, the unit where the Blackwelders lived for another decade was "old," "small," "dark," and "dingy."[179]

Managing rentals was not Bernice's only source of irritation, though it was in supervising the building that she first recognized Logan Square's changing racial composition, which displeased her. At first, Bernice reported to Quantrille that her neighbors were all "upper middle class, a fine clientele."[180] But the building was not filled with the professionals and businesspeople who constituted an upper-middle class in the mid-twentieth century. One tenant had been a telephone operator, for example, while another worked as a waitress.[181] When Bernice described her neighbors in class terms, those terms may have in part been encryptions for race. Because what kept the Logan Boulevard apartments exclusive were explicit restrictions imposed by the owner: "No children, no pets, no single young women or men, no dark-skinned, two-year lease, security deposit."[182] Bernice's letters suggest that only the rules about race, employment, and children were enforced, since she mentions both young, unmarried tenants and tenants with pets.[183] In spite of these restrictions, Bernice worried about the prospect of African American applicants because she was the person who would have to turn them away. When a black woman came to the building in 1968, Bernice wrote nervously to Quantrille, "I hope I do not have any trouble." This woman lacked funds for a deposit, so refusing her was easy. But soon more black people as well as Puerto Ricans sought to rent on Logan Boulevard, signaling the demographic shift under way in the area.[184]

Bernice's response to this shift was complicated. She often fixated on a perceived influx of African Americans, even though the actual growth in the black population around her was minimal, perhaps because landlords like her boss kept black people out. Her concern about Latino tenants emerged more slowly, in reaction to a real, dramatic increase in Logan Square's Latino population. First Cubans and then Puerto Ricans and ethnic Mexicans moved to the area in the 1960s and '70s, with Puerto Ricans in the majority.[185] In a 1968 letter, Bernice expressed her concern in an odd succession of sentences. Speaking of a vacant apartment she wrote, "I have ... experience with all kinds of applicants." Then she added, maybe to clarify, "There are so many Puerto Ricans moving into Chicago and the Negroes are pushing in all directions." Without explaining the connection, she went on, "In our advertising, I give only my phone number and make appointments to show the apartment so I am not bothered as much as before." (Perhaps she meant that she was no longer bothered by people like the black woman who stopped a few months earlier.) Then Bernice concluded, "I would not object to either if they were desirable tenants."[186] She may have assumed that Quantrille would follow her racial logic without further elaboration: A unit was vacant. Various types of people had applied for vacancies in the past, including Puerto Ricans and African Americans, who Bernice preferred would not knock on her door—and she had taken steps to achieve that end. Her final sentence, then, was an obligatory white denial of racism in the age of civil rights: Bernice would not object to black or Latino tenants if only they were suitable. What went unsaid was how unlikely she thought it was that suitable tenants of color would materialize.

As the 1970s unfolded, at the same time that she was up in arms over criticism of Kit Carson, Bernice became more outspoken about Logan Square's transformation. Despite her worries in the late 1960s about prospective tenants, she continued to maintain in the early '70s that her neighborhood was an oasis in an urban desert plagued by racial change and rampant violence. As late as 1973 she told Quantrille, "We live quietly and not too disturbed by the problems of the city."[187] In a couple of months, though, Bernice explained that she and Harold never went out at night, in part because Harold fell asleep on the couch after dinner but also because it was "getting too dangerous." The next year she complained that she did not go to the movies because "good films" showed only in the suburbs, while "the downtown theaters show nothing but violence, sex and dope to feed the young blacks who are causing the crime rate to rise." A month later, musing about what was causing Quantrille night pains and lost sleep, Bernice surmised that "constant bad news, nationally and locally," was in part to blame: "It is not very healthful, mentally, to be afraid to walk around the block or to the store without fear of attack. All the time creeping closer to this nice neighborhood." Even in addressing Quantrille's woes in Denver, then, Bernice remained distracted by her own surroundings. By 1974, Bernice was convinced that "the Latin gangs" were "the problem," causing many people to "flee to live in condominiums in the suburbs, leaving vacancies soon filled by Latinos."[188] She would repeat this refrain in years to come.[189]

Bernice's grousing about imagined black and actual Latino neighbors reflected a wider white response to political, economic, and demographic change. Urban landscapes had been battlegrounds for decades. South and west of Logan Square, the Chicago neighborhoods collectively known as the West Side had seen protracted struggles in which some white residents (descendants of European immigrants who, like those of Logan Square, over time came to think of themselves as white) fought first to improve aging area infrastructure. But then activists merged those struggles with attempts to exclude African Americans from their midst. When such efforts failed, whites departed one block at a time, pushed by "block-busting" tactics of real estate brokers who stoked fear of declining property values in cities and pulled by the governmental largesse that subsidized white home ownership in the suburbs. White people sold their property at depressed prices to brokers who resold the homes to black people at a profit. African Americans could not obtain regular mortgage loans in part because the Federal Housing Administration would not insure loans made in "redlined" areas—those where blacks lived. So they purchased overpriced homes on contract, often from broker-owners who threatened repossession after even one missed payment, encouraging black homeowners, if they did not lose their property outright, to take in more tenants and neglect costly maintenance, which in turn contributed to overcrowding and blight.[190] Bernice and Harold, in fact, had lived in a West Side residential area in the 1940s that, by the 1960s, was undergoing this shift, though they left for the East Coast before the change occurred.[191] When they returned to Chicago, then, they settled in a neighborhood embarking on its own transformation—not from white to black but rather from mostly Anglo to an area where Latinos held a slim majority.[192]

In the late 1960s and early '70s, however, the political and economic milieu in which such shifts occurred was changing. The postwar economic boom and the optimism it spawned were grinding to a halt, culminating in a full-blown recession in 1974–75. Steep inflation, sluggish economic growth, lackluster productivity, stagnant wages, and high unemployment—stagflation, pundits called it—left many Americans worried about their daily lives and frightened for the future. Rising interest rates, caused by a decline in the value of the U.S. dollar, further dimmed the hopes of would-be home buyers as well as of homeowners who wanted to upgrade. All this, along with the long-term process of deindustrialization and the declining power of labor unions, hit working-class communities hard.[193] So an economic slump was one part of the context in which Logan Square changed and in which Bernice and Harold Blackwelder lost whatever tenuous hold they ever had on the middle class.

The politics of race constituted another. The postwar era's black civil rights movement had borne fruit in court decisions and federal laws that dismantled much of the legal basis for segregation and discrimination. And in the 1960s, direct action campaigns challenged institutions, businesses, and municipalities that continued to exclude and disadvantage African Americans. Massive white resistance to the liberal gains of civil rights and to the federal government's slow but steady response to the movement, however, prompted some black activists to press beyond integrationist goals. They focused instead on community empowerment and the protean notion of Black Power, which in turn drew on anticolonial thought and rhetoric. Black Power, with its focus on self-determination, also inspired parallel movements among other racialized minority peoples, including the Latinos who were moving into Logan Square. The struggles of Puerto Ricans and ethnic Mexicans in this era were distinct, rooted as they were in different histories of U.S. colonialism. Puerto Rico was a self-governing U.S. commonwealth, which allowed its residents to migrate freely to the mainland but did not save them from ill will and hard use once they arrived—nor did it offer those who stayed behind full national citizenship. Puerto Rican activists fought not only for rights and opportunities on the mainland but also for self-rule on their Caribbean island home, which for some meant arguing for statehood but for others meant advocating independence from the United States. Ethnic Mexicans, including those with roots in the old Mexican North (now the U.S. Southwest) as well as recent immigrants from Mexico, recalled a history of both expropriated land and exploited labor. In the 1970s, activists increasingly saw the fates of older residents and newer immigrants tied together, and they fashioned a Chicano movement that, like other insurgencies in this era, emphasized self-determination. Add to this mosaic the struggles of both reservation-based and urban Indigenous people for redress and sovereignty, and the picture that emerges is one to which Bernice responded in this way: "There is so much publicity now given to the minorities. There are many Indians living in poor areas of Chicago who need help but will not help themselves. Also Chicanos and Puerto Ricans and Blacks—all feeling discrimination—with whites fleeing to the suburbs—a real powder keg."[194]

Not all of these dynamics were visible to Bernice in a daily way: neither African Americans nor Native people lived in large numbers in Logan Square, so her conjectures about blacks and Indians, and perhaps even about white flight, came from news media, white neighbors, and forays into other parts of Chicago.[195] But the presence of Latino neighbors was palpable, and newspaper reports, while seldom as disapproving as Bernice was in her letters, track both the demographic shift and Logan Square residents' responses. And the change was not only racial; local activists could not and did not separate the influx of Latinos from the urban politics of class and property ownership.

Those politics played out differently in Logan Square than they had, for example, on Chicago's West Side, when areas shifted, block by block, from white to black. In 1963, the Logan Square Neighborhood Association (LSNA) and another local group, The Organization of Palmer Square (TOPS), formed to address infrastructural decline. Both addressed housing and zoning violations and urged absentee landlords to keep their properties in good repair.[196] If these organizations had followed in the footsteps of many postwar neighborhood associations, Logan

Square might have gone the way of other urban communities across the nation—first "defended" as a white-only area and then abandoned to poorer people of color and discriminatory real estate practices.[197]

By the early 1970s, though, new activist groups, churches, and social service agencies set different agendas, which were sometimes compatible and sometimes in competition with those of LSNA and TOPS. Casa Central, for instance, a citywide clearinghouse for Latino social services, moved to Logan Square in 1971, offering legal and medical clinics, tutoring and day care, English-language and high school equivalency training, welfare counseling, employment assistance, and meeting space for Latino groups. And although most Latinos attended Roman Catholic churches like the parish a block from the Blackwelders' apartment, Logan Square's First Spanish United Church of Christ set up a fund that would make loans to would-be home buyers, while the Episcopal Church of the Advent got a "new lease in life" when the priest inaugurated Spanish-language services. Meanwhile, in 1972, LSNA established an economic development arm and began buying and rehabilitating abandoned houses and then reselling them, assisted by an interest-free state loan and in cooperation with local lenders. The support of savings and loan associations and banks was key, because lenders, following decades-old practices, had balked at offering conventional mortgages in redlined areas, which included those seen as racially transitional. Some neighbors argued that LSNA's rehabilitation and reselling program benefited not current residents but more affluent Anglo newcomers, especially young married couples who were willing to take a chance on a new area. Critics worried that this would lead to gentrification.[198]

But the tide continued to turn. In 1974, a new group, Logan Concerned Citizens, took a more aggressive approach than LSNA, aligning itself with an interracial organization from Chicago's South Side, the Citizens Action Program. Logan Concerned Citizens promoted a "greenlining" campaign, asking local savings and loan associations to pledge mortgage funding within the neighborhood and then instructing residents to remove their savings from institutions that refused to invest in Logan Square.[199] At the same time, all community groups addressed the problem of neighborhood crime and violence, advocating various remedies. By the late 1970s, even the local district commander for the police took a more accommodating stance than LSNA on gang activity, arguing that "gang members have to live in the district too, and only a few of them actually commit crimes."[200] Racial and class tensions could run high in Logan Square, but frequent accommodation of those tensions by residents and activists as well as the eagerness of some to maintain a racially mixed and economically diverse neighborhood meant that no wholesale transition took place. Change was incremental, contested, and multivalent.

Unlike what happened on the West Side, then, white flight from Logan Square was selective rather than pervasive. And unlike what transpired in nearby areas like Lincoln Park, where upscale residents did indeed displace working people, neither did gentrification become the rule in Logan Square (though gentrified pockets surely emerged).[201] Into this milieu, Cubans, Puerto Ricans, and ethnic Mexicans arrived, establishing effective organizations and joining churches that worked to accommodate their presence. Some young Latinos also joined gangs to defend their turf. But as one white homeowner, a truck driver named Mel Hoff, put it in 1977, "I see a lotta people fixin' up their places: Paintin' the porches, plantin' the grass. They decided to stay.... Oh, it was rough about three years ago. Puerto Ricans were moving in and you had the fights between the Spanish and the Polish. But . . . people got used to one another, things settled down quite a bit.... The only thing is that the Puerto Ricans don't know how to drive in the winter time.... But other than that, hey, it's beautiful. My kids and they get along fine. They're friends. Live and let live, right?"[202] If the worst stereotype a white, working-class man could muster about his Puerto Rican neighbors was that they could not yet drive well on snow, then racial change in 1970s Logan Square proceeded with less hate and harm—not to mention less scaremongering and scamming—than it had earlier in other areas. Perhaps this was in part because the newcomers were Latino rather than African American; black people surely bore the heaviest burden of white racism in Chicago. But perhaps the activism of communities of color across the nation since World War II, which transformed attitudes as well as laws, also explains the nature of change in Logan Square, even if Bernice Blackwelder, for her part, was less hopeful and more fearful about it all than her neighbor Mel Hoff.

Then, too, Bernice Blackwelder probably had less control over the conditions of her daily life than Mel Hoff did. Bernice certainly felt that her husband Harold's demands took precedence over her own desires, and her racial complaints about Logan Square were often linked to a general sense of entrapment in a life not sufficiently of her own making. This is not to say that her racial complaints were encoded criticisms of a male-dominated culture. It is to say that for Bernice, a quotidian lack of control lent fuel to the fire of all manner of anxiety—about tenants and neighbors, about family finances, and about urban violence. Bernice felt trapped because Harold's plans for securing work that kept him happy and paid the bills had long determined where and how the couple lived, and she had to fit her own aspirations around his. Even when Harold finally abandoned the schemes he had pursued for decades and accepted a nine-to-five job at Chicago's City Hall and County Building, his schedule still ruled household rhythms and dictated, on any given day, whether Bernice could pursue her dream of writing history—or at least that is how Bernice saw her plight.

After the Blackwelders moved back to Chicago in 1965, Harold tried to revive a musical career that he had not followed full-time for years. First in Arlington and Alexandria, and then in Omaha and Denver, he had managed restaurants and takeouts, with help from Bernice. These businesses failed. Chicago was the last place where Harold had found regular jobs singing and playing bass, and he still had contacts there in the music world and in one or more performers' unions—the AFM and perhaps also the American Federation of Television and Radio Artists. Harold renewed these contacts as soon as he and Bernice took up residence near Wrigley Field. He worked off and on for Chicago's white AFM local and felt gratified when his friend Barney Richards was reelected to the local's presidency in 1965 (it was during Richards's presidency that Chicago's black and white AFM locals merged, though Richards tried at first to circumvent the merger).[203] These ties also brought gigs at country clubs, holiday parties, veterans' hospitals, ethnic organizations, industrial picnics, business conventions, and even, as Harold put it, for the "big boys" of Chicago's Merchants and Manufacturers Club. But the work was intermittent and unpredictable and so was the income it produced.

For Bernice, who could not land a job and was trying to complete her biographical dictionary, all of this was unsettling at best. When Harold had work, Bernice described herself as "relaxed" and "optimistic."[204] When he did not, she complained that his appetite, his love of sports, and the lure of Lake Michigan intruded upon her days, as she did in summer 1966: "Harold is home most of this week and I find it almost impossible to get much done as he loves for us to spend hours at the lake which I enjoy . . . but begrudge the time I would like to spend on my 'stuff.' "[205] When Harold finally gave up on music and took a full-time job the next fall, Bernice first expressed relief: "Now our biggest worries are over." But she also was blunt about what Harold's daily absence meant for her as a historian: "I hope to get down to hard work on my project now that Harold is 'out of the way.' That may sound cruel but I just could not accomplish a thing with the ball game competition and the hungry mouth."[206]

Harold, the hungry mouth that distracted Bernice from her work and worried her when she carried a light pocketbook down three flights of stairs en route to the grocery store, decided after the couple moved to Logan Square and began managing apartments there that even the rent reduction would not keep them afloat. So at the age of sixty-two, in fall 1967, he accepted a job with Cook County searching and filing court records. The steady, if limited, income helped—"good for the nervous system," Bernice noted—but now apartment supervision fell even more exclusively to her. In fact, Harold's new job with the county coincided with more management tasks for Bernice. As Bernice put it, "We will have another reduction in rent with a little more responsibility for me."[207]

And Bernice still found her days punctuated by Harold's needs. There were good days, as when Bernice told Quantrille, "Now that the apartments are all filled here and [Harold] is 'gainfully employed,' I feel like I am released from prison."[208] But there were bad days, too. Between looking after her life with Harold and managing apartments, Bernice often found little time to write history. On a typical day, she made Harold breakfast and drove him to the L, Chicago's rapid transit, at 8 A.M. Then, she might call a repairman to fix an appliance, order nameplates for mailboxes, supervise a unit's painting, bring in mail for a vacationing tenant, answer phone calls about vacancies, drive a neighbor to the store, shop for groceries, water her plants, and walk the dog. She might also sew on a dress she was making, both because it saved money and because she was too tall for the ready-to-wear clothing she found in stores. When such tasks went well, she hauled out her notes and books and typewriter and put them on the dining table for a few hours of work. On a rare day, she might take public transportation to the Chicago Public Library or the Newberry Library (complaining that the bus to the Newberry required two transfers). She needed to start dinner for Harold by 3 or 4 P.M., which also meant packing up her research materials and moving them off the table. She usually picked Harold up from the L at 4:30.[209] But his work hours could vary. Bernice had to be available if he got off early, which, she griped to Quantrille, "chops up my day."[210]

Bernice summed up the effect of all this on her biographical dictionary: "I still try to work at it several hours a day but I have many interruptions and after all, I am a housewife and have work to do."[211] Her definition of "work" was slippery and changeable: depending on the day, her real work could be labor in her own household, her tasks as apartment manager, or the progress she made on "her stuff." She felt her energies divided and often sapped, and she attributed this sensation to her status as a wife of a man whose needs came first.

By contrast, Quantrille McClung, though she did her own cooking and cleaning and sewed for herself, too, never complained of household labor interfering with the genealogical tasks that so enthralled her. In fact, she thought housework blended nicely with history. In a 1966 letter, for example, Quantrille puzzled over the incomplete record she had included in the *Carson-Bent-Boggs Genealogy* for Alexander Carson, Kit Carson's cousin, a record she was trying to correct in the supplement. She typed up the current state of her work on Alexander and then concluded, "I will be mulling it over as I do my ironing & laundry." The mulling must have helped, because when she returned to finish her letter the next afternoon (announcing that she was about to take a rest and then make dinner), she closed by promising Bernice not to "bombard" her "so often with letters now that I have Alexander under control! . . . Next I must get after Moses."[212] (The letters did not let up, and Quantrille reworked records for both Moses Carson, Kit's half brother, and Alexander in the *Carson-Bent-Boggs Genealogy Supplement*.)[213] Like Bernice, Quantrille did much of her historical work on the same table where she ate, but the dual use only occasionally presented problems, such as the time she spilled a bottle of ink and was saved only by her habit of keeping "an old plastic tablecloth over the good one."[214] Moving easily from a multipurpose kitchen table to the laundry to an ironing board to her bed (where she took many rests), Quantrille sensed little division of time or space or energy or task.

Indeed, Quantrille organized her life with a marked singleness of purpose. She set up her Capitol Hill apartment as both workplace and home, and, when she felt well, she could easily walk from her building to DPL and CHS.[215] Fellow genealogists who visited Quantrille in the 1970s remember her apartment as small, with just a living room, kitchenette, bedroom, and bathroom. The living room was lined with bookcases, cardboard file boxes, and a metal filing cabinet. Guests also recall a "little old typewriter," which Quantrille's letters reveal was a Corona portable that she kept in working order by lugging it to a fix-it man a few blocks away.[216] Her apartment building, however, was not well maintained, and Quantrille complained of ceiling leaks, a faulty radiator, and broken cabinetry. In 1970, the leaks forced her to haul research materials from room to room to avoid water damage. Then, she reported with sarcasm, during repairs, her "fine manager" (who, she assured building supervisor Bernice, was a man) "went to the hospital and died."[217] Such vexations notwithstanding, Quantrille's living quarters helped more than hampered her historical labors.

The proximity of the public library and historical society did not always permit easy passage, however, because Quantrille suffered chronic poor health. In fact, she often walked to DPL but then fell ill there, and staff had to call a taxi to take her just a few blocks back to her apartment.[218] The etiology of her illness is unclear, but the symptoms—headaches, blackouts, dizziness, as well as intermittent confusion and memory problems—were long-standing. In fact, Quantrille described herself as suffering from a "life-long disability." In letters, she mentioned cerebrovascular insufficiency, or blockage in the blood supply to the brain, as well as "Dr. Mieries Disease," by which she probably meant Ménière's syndrome, an inner-ear disorder that impairs balance. Elsewhere, she explained that she had contracted meningitis when she was sixteen, which left her with the vascular problems that caused headaches and blackouts. Whatever produced her symptoms, she experienced them as periodically debilitating. It was her illness that had prompted her to retire when she was just fifty-eight.[219] By 1968, she described herself as "swinging between days of hellish pain and days of recovery." In 1972, she saw a new, young doctor who—though she looked to Quantrille like a teenager and insisted on a tiring battery of diagnostic tests—hit on treatment that brought some relief. Quantrille endured the hospital visits, just as she had endured sixty years of disability, with dark humor: "Since I am condemned to go on living I must make one more effort on my own behalf."[220] The effort paid off. Before 1972, her letters are peppered with reports of collapse—at home, at the library, at restaurants and the bank. After 1972, such reports cease. But by then she was eighty-two, and other, age-related infirmities had set in.[221]

Quantrille faced other aggravations, too. Chief among them was her relationship to the library. As a retired DPL employee and an accomplished Colorado genealogist, Quantrille felt that she deserved not only deference but also professional courtesy and assistance. Library staff—including head librarians John Eastlick (1951–69) and Henry Shearouse (1969–84)—were often happy to oblige. DPL published both the 1962 *Carson-Bent-Boggs Genealogy* and its 1973 *Supplement*, providing labor in the form of typing and proofreading and materials in the form of paper, filing aids, and typewriter ribbons. Once sales had covered publication costs, DPL split the (very modest) profits evenly with Quantrille. Librarians also granted her stack privileges; wrote letters of introduction for her when she visited other repositories; and arranged to transport materials (and sometimes Quantrille herself) between DPL and her apartment.[222]

But Quantrille had complaints. In 1967, when she was preparing a talk for the Colorado Genealogical Society on DPL's genealogy resources, city librarian Eastlick insulted her by sending a letter in which he reprimanded her for calling the Genealogy Division a "department." Reflecting tensions between the library's Genealogy Division (often used by

amateurs researching family histories) and its more prestigious Western History Department (often used by professional scholars), he also
corrected her apparent assumption that the lofty department had commissioned her to write a history of the lowly division.[223] Quantrille told
Bernice, "This letter made me sick & I was ill for several days. After all
I have done for the Library!"[224] Meanwhile, Quantrille felt slighted and
ignored at library gatherings, and she was furious that when she first
offered DPL her research files from an earlier project on Colorado's governors, a librarian had "tittered" and told her, "I don't know what I'd do
with 'em if I had 'em."[225]

Her relationship with DPL improved when Henry Shearouse became
head librarian in 1969.[226] For example, Quantrille told the woman who
was typing the *Carson-Bent-Boggs Genealogy Supplement* that she had
been treated poorly in the Western History Department: "I went to West.
Hist. where I was carefully ignored which was tantamount to a refusal of
service." The typist, who worked for DPL, reported this to the library's
public information officer, who relayed it to the new city librarian. Shearouse, in turn, sat down with Quantrille and asked if there was any DPL
department where she "was not satisfied with the service." She reluctantly told him, and he promised to take action.[227] Meanwhile, Shearouse and his staff kept meticulous records of the library's work on the
supplement, and they quietly accommodated Quantrille and her health
challenges, even admitting her to the library early before it opened and
offering her "all courtesy of a staff member" while she was there on book
production errands.[228] She was never at ease in the rarefied atmosphere
of the Western History Department (where, she said, she was always
in "hot water"), but under Shearouse's direction, DPL seemed a more
welcoming place.[229] Even when he had to deny her requests—she had
hoped, for example, that the library would publish yet another supplement to the *Carson-Bent-Boggs Genealogy* even after the 1973 volume was
issued—Shearouse did so respectfully and offered alternative solutions,
thus smoothing Quantrille's ruffled feathers.[230]

Quantrille may have loved genealogy, but her own family was her
other major aggravation. She held no illusions about the nature of kin
ties. Her parents had both died just before she retired in the 1940s, and
she had only one sibling, a younger brother named Denzel. Denzel was
a banker in the small town of Kremmling, a hundred miles north of Denver and west across the Front Range along the upper Colorado River.[231]
He and his wife, May, had raised two sons. In the letters from Quantrille to Bernice that survive, Quantrille spoke little of Denzel, though
she must have mentioned him from time to time, because once in 1967,

Bernice remarked, "It is a shame that your brother and his wife could not have brought you a little warmth and affection."[232] It is not clear what sort of reunion inspired Bernice's comment, but it is clear that Quantrille's relationship with Denzel and May was tense.

Then, in December 1970, Quantrille received the shocking news that Denzel "was suddenly desperately ill, cancer, the brain affected and no hope at all." The news came not from Denzel or May or their sons but from May's niece. On hearing it, Quantrille collapsed.[233] At first, she received no updates on her brother's condition, and she told Bernice that did not dare inquire, for fear of what more bad news would do to her.[234] Quantrille did not save copies of letters she wrote to Bernice in the coming months, perhaps because of the family drama they revealed. But she did save notes she exchanged with May and Denzel that show the strain of their tie, the root of which, for Quantrille, might have been May's constant resort to an overbearing, distancing religiosity that left little room for sharing fear and anticipatory grief. For instance, in the only letter May sent Quantrille that discussed Denzel's horrific pain and shocking decline, May emphasized that "the Lord Jesus Christ" had pulled her through. She added that when neighbors remarked on her calm during the crisis, she thought, "They don't know Jesus Christ as well as I do."[235] Her husband was suffering, but May boasted about her special bond with Jesus. Denzel died just six months after Quantrille learned of the cancer that stalked his brain. Afterward, Quantrille reported to Bernice, "My brother's widow phoned me to tell me of his death & to practically tell me she did not want me at the interment."[236]

Denzel's passing at the age of seventy-four hardly ended the family feud. Much of what Quantrille wrote to Bernice about her sister-in-law is now lost, but the tenor of those chronicles is evident from Bernice's epistolary replies. Bernice called May a "'Holier than thou' hypocrite," adding, for good measure, that Denzel's widow was "anything but Christian" and urging Quantrille, "Break away from her!"[237] In one letter that survives (from a year after Denzel died), Quantrille reported that May and a friend had shown up at her apartment door unannounced, without ringing the buzzer at the building entrance. Quantrille answered their knock and did not even recognize her sister-in-law until she introduced herself, "her appearance had changed so greatly." (Quantrille added, "She could easily have been entered in a fashion show.") May stepped over the threshold, so Quantrille had no choice but to let her in. May saw Quantrille's work spread out on a table and asked, "Are you writing another book?" Provoked, Quantrille corrected her, "I do not write, I compile." Then Quantrille nearly fainted, and as she slumped, she added darkly,

"You should not have come here." The visitors helped her to her bed and called the building manager. "I will see you in Heaven," May declared as she left. "God forbid" was Quantrille's unspoken reply.[238]

After this incident, Quantrille spoke rarely of Denzel's clan, except to worry over threatened visits from the sons and to wonder if she should revise her will to "stipulate that if that family ceases to harass me, anything that is left could be divided between the nephews." Otherwise, she speculated, she might split her estate "between the Nuns who took care of my parents [before they died] & my church."[239] This musing said more about Quantrille's family than it did about her finances—there was precious little of monetary value for her to bequeath.[240]

Quantrille was on better terms with other relatives, but they were more distant kin and did not live in Colorado. The Denver McClungs she had known when she was young had all died, and on her mother's side, only one cousin remained, the son of her mother's sister. That cousin maintained a grudge nurtured first by his mother, Quantrille's aunt, who was outraged when Quantrille placed her aging parents, who were Protestant, in a Catholic nursing home. Quantrille and her cousin attended the same Methodist church in Denver, but he refused to speak to her. As Quantrille told Bernice, "The relatives who are closest to me in affection all live in Calif."[241] In the 1960s, Quantrille visited the California cousins, but by the 70s, she contented herself to see them when they passed through Denver.[242] The most memorable visit came when her cousin's son and his new wife spent a day with her (a couple of weeks earlier, she had shipped the young couple heirloom china as a wedding gift). Quantrille took the newlyweds to the Denver Art Museum and the Civic Center, concluding that the groom was "all that a young man should be and ... the bride all a young woman should be—she does not PAINT and she does not SMOKE!" Quantrille was thrilled by the brief reunion, remarking to Bernice, "To think they would stop off on their cross country bridal journey to see an old maid!"[243] Years later, other young relatives moved to Denver and maintained a relationship with Quantrille, and she also flew to visit cousins in Memphis. Such exceptions aside, Quantrille's kin provided cold comfort, at best.[244]

All these daily dilemmas—institutional indifference, chronic illness, and icy family ties—unfolded for Quantrille across a city landscape that was changing as much as the one Bernice was navigating in Chicago. Just as Quantrille's assessment of Kit Carson's world both resembled and departed from Bernice's, Quantrille experienced urban change in both similar and different ways. The Denver metropolitan area boomed in the postwar era, but that growth enriched the suburbs at the expense of the city itself, a familiar pattern in much of the urban United States. Denver's population peaked in 1970 and then dropped off, while the surrounding counties—Arapahoe, Jefferson, Boulder, and Adams—continued to grow. But Denver maintained its dominance as a regional economic and political hub, even if aviation, petroleum, and technology overtook the old mainstays of mining, ranching, and railroads.[245]

Living in Denver's Capitol Hill area—as its name suggests, in the shadow of Colorado's state capitol building—Quantrille was in a good position to watch the changes. Like Bernice's Logan Square neighborhood, Capitol Hill had once been home to an urban elite—bankers and merchants and mining magnates. The elite and their heirs had long since moved on, first to streetcar suburbs that were later incorporated into the city and then, with the explosion of automobile ownership and road building in the twentieth century, to adjacent suburban counties. Capitol Hill, meanwhile, evolved into a diverse, densely populated neighborhood of homes, apartment buildings, and commercial properties, though it was far closer to Denver's center than Logan Square was to the heart of Chicago. This was why Quantrille, when she felt well, could walk to DPL, while Bernice had to rely on public transport to visit Chicago libraries.[246]

But the walk from Quantrille's apartment to DPL was not what it had been in 1963 when she moved to Clarkson Street from a Capitol Hill apartment five blocks away. Quantrille lived at the corner of Clarkson and Thirteenth Avenue for twenty years, and it was eight blocks down that avenue to DPL. In 1969, Quantrille reported to Bernice, "The filth on 13th Ave. between here and the Library is so disgusting I go out of my way to avoid it."[247] In this letter, Quantrille did not attribute the "filth" to anyone in particular, but a couple of years later, she fingered urban developers, implicitly, and countercultural youths, explicitly, for the changes she saw. She started with the developers: "This area is fast becoming one big parking lot. I fear I shall waken some morning to find the building is coming down about my ears." Then she described the exodus of small businesses: "So many of the small shops, a restaurant for the old folk; a high class meat market; the variety store where one could get all sorts of small items without going downtown; a decent barber shop; an excellent shoe repair shop and so on, have all gone out of business." The reason? Quantrille was convinced that these establishments "could not brave the onslaught of the 'hippies.'" What was left was a chain grocery store, Safeway, where the police were on duty "all the time."[248] The decline of small business and the triumph of supermarkets, of course, could not be blamed on bell-bottomed, befringed young people. It reflected an economic restructuring that favored large corporations and the commercial landscape of the suburbs over mom-and-pop stores in struggling city neighborhoods.[249] But from Quantrille's street-level perspective, when the hippies showed up, small shops were shuttered. Little wonder, then, that she praised the bride of her cousin's son as someone who neither painted nor smoked; these were hippie habits that signaled for Quantrille all manner of urban decline.[250]

Indeed, where her friend Bernice blamed Chicago neighborhood change on Latinos and African Americans, Quantrille was apt to attribute Denver's transformation to countercultural youths, to city planners and developers, and more generally, to people with poor taste. This was not because racial politics in the metropolitan mountain West were less fraught than those in Great Lakes cities. Quantrille's awareness of events that unfolded on the fringes of her neighborhood suggests which sorts of changes worried her and which escaped her concern. In the late 1960s, for instance, she made a point of criticizing plans to redesign Denver's Civic Center. She especially loathed the proposed new Denver Art Museum, a fortress-like building completed in 1971, which she termed an "eyesore."[251] Brutalist architecture and ill-conceived city planning made her mad. But even closer to her home, near Capitol Hill on Downing Street, was the very visible headquarters of Denver's most prominent Chicano movement organization, the Crusade for Justice. Quantrille never mentioned this Denver landmark or the momentous events that unfolded there in 1973.

The Crusade for Justice was the brainchild of Rudolfo "Corky" Gonzales. Gonzales founded the organization after a 1966 Civic Center rally protesting his dismissal as head of Denver's local War on Poverty, the umbrella term for the economic reform agenda enacted under President Lyndon B. Johnson. (Gonzales had been accused of showing favoritism to Chicana/os in the Neighborhood Youth Corps, an employment program.) In 1968, the Crusade bought Denver's Calvary Baptist Church building on Downing Street for its operations and then, in 1972, an adjacent apartment complex, where some members lived. The group pursued a multifaceted activist agenda from Downing Street, holding dances, running a school, editing a newspaper, and organizing protests against discrimination by the city police, in local schools, and at public parks and pools (members even protested DPL for hosting an insufficiently community-based "Viva Mejicano" program).[252]

The Crusade for Justice center was a half dozen blocks northeast of Quantrille's apartment. Since she walked east less often than she walked west (the library and downtown were to the west), she may have been unaware, at first, of the church-turned-movement-headquarters less than a mile away. But the night before St. Patrick's Day in 1973, police were patrolling the area, apparently monitoring a party under way at the Downing Street apartments. Around midnight, a dispute arose between the police and young people gathered there, and the argument quickly escalated into a gunfight that left one Chicano activist dead and sixteen others, including a dozen police officers, injured. Then, an explosion rocked the apartments, tearing through a wall. Police accounts of the gunfire and the blast differed radically from testimony provided by Crusade for Justice members. Officers claimed to have found an arsenal in the complex; they insisted that the shots exchanged between police and activists had inadvertently set off explosives hidden there. Party-goers contended that most of the weapons at Downing Street were either hunting rifles or else props used by the dance troupe Ballet Chicano de Aztlán, and they blamed the explosion on an intentionally launched police grenade. It is conceivable that Quantrille knew little of the Crusade for Justice headquarters before this infamous St. Patrick's Day incident, but she could not have remained unaware in the aftermath, when local media blanketed the city with arrest and trial coverage.[253] Nonetheless, she wrote nothing about the racial violence that unfolded six blocks from her home. She was more concerned about the proliferation of parking lots, ugly buildings, and scruffy youth.

Quantrille's relative lack of concern about racial change, compared with her friend Bernice's fixation on the same — like their distinct assessments of Kit Carson's world — probably resulted from an amalgam of differences in the two women's surroundings and a divergence in their attitudes. Unlike Logan Square, Capitol Hill was not in the midst of such a rapid, dramatic transformation in racial demographics. Change in Quantrille's Denver neighborhood was under way, but it was more gradual and less remarkable. Census takers in 1960 found Capitol Hill's population overwhelmingly white: more than 16,000 Anglos lived alongside just over 300 Latinos, most of them U.S.-born ethnic Mexicans. There were fewer than 200 people of any other race, and of these, only 6 were African American, reflecting the long legacy of segregation and antiblack racism in Denver. Twenty years later, Capitol Hill's population had increased modestly and census takers now reported that a smaller proportion was white — 84 percent (compared to 98 percent in 1960). But the U.S. census practice of insisting that Latinos "may be of any race" suggests that the Anglo percentage of that "white" population was lower, since now almost 1,500 residents, or 9 percent, were Latino (and many of these undoubtedly had been classified as "white"). Meanwhile, 8 percent of residents were identified as black, and the remaining 3 percent were divided evenly between Indigenous peoples and those of Asian and Pacific Island origin and descent.[254] When Quantrille was completing the *Carson-Bent-Boggs Genealogy Supplement*, then, Capitol Hill was becoming less white but was still a majority-white neighborhood.

If racial change was less pronounced in Quantrille's Denver than in Bernice's Chicago, it was not absent in Capitol Hill, and it was not the only demographic shift under way. Quantrille likely noticed that she saw people of color on the street more often as the 1960s and '70s unfolded. Still, she was more apt to remark on the young people she encountered, without identifying them by race, and on what she saw as their sloppy appearance. Although she was not referring to hippies in her own neighborhood, her remarks about students at the University of Colorado in nearby Boulder best exemplify her response to countercultural youths. The campus, she reported to Bernice, was beautiful. "But the students!" she wrote. How could the professors, who had to teach these misfits, "retain their breakfasts"? McClung had lunch at the university, in a spot that forbade bare feet and required men to wear shirts. "Imagine having to insist," she exclaimed to Bernice.[255]

There were reasons beyond the proverbial generation gap that hippies preoccupied Quantrille. Capitol Hill had become a destination for young people—so much so that the proportion of the neighborhood made up of young adults increased 17 percent between 1960 and 1970, until almost half of the residents were between the ages of eighteen and thirty-four. Meanwhile, older people like Quantrille were also overrepresented; they had constituted 20 percent of the population in 1960, and that proportion had declined only slightly by 1970. Capitol Hill, then, was at once strikingly youthful and notably elderly, with far fewer children and middle-aged people than other areas of Denver.[256] Accordingly, matters of age provoked more comment from Quantrille than did matters of race.

Still, what little Quantrille did report suggests that, when it caught her attention, racial change both frightened and inspired her. Like Bernice, Quantrille worried about urban violence, and since Quantrille was a walker, street assaults especially troubled her. But she only sometimes viewed sidewalk crime through a racial lens. In January 1968, for example, she told Bernice that three elderly women from her church had been out canvassing when they "were knocked down & their purses snatched."[257] Quantrille said nothing about the race of the attackers. Three months later, though, after the assassination of Martin Luther King Jr. and the uprisings that followed, she did comment on race and violence in the city. She told Bernice that it had been relatively calm in Denver but then mused, "There is a lot happening that does not get into the papers in the hope that perhaps it will help to keep things quiet."[258]

By way of example, Quantrille explained that she had heard about an attack on "the Potentate of the Shrine" (the highest ranking of the local Shriners, the fraternal organization whose Denver headquarters was near Quantrille's church). The Shriner had been "set upon by 2 men, slashed, beaten into insensibility & left for dead." Quantrille added, "Considering the connection in which I was told this I assume the assailants were colored."[259] Then she cited other assaults, concluding, "Isn't it sad when one is on the street to need to wonder if the person coming toward you will strike you?" Just when it seemed as if Quantrille was telling a familiar white tale about black violence in what was becoming the age of Black Power, her narrative veered in the opposite direction. "Yet," she reported, "while in the laundry at the traffic rush hour" one morning, she had glanced out the window, only to witness a very different kind of racial interaction: "When a car stalled in the middle of the street, a well dressed young negro got off his handsome motorcycle and came to the rescue of the young woman driver. They were joined by a young white man, but neither could do anything with the car, so together, they managed ... to push it into the cathedral parking lot. The young woman got on the back seat of the motor cycle and the man evidently was taking her to work." In the same letter, Quantrille referred to the murder of the nation's most famous civil rights leader as "the King tragedy" and noted how it, along with her own poor health and illness among her friends, brought her spirits to "a new low."[260] Racial change was woven into the texture of Quantrille's life, and the new fabric of her days predictably chafed at her own white skin, with all its taken-for-granted privileges. But it could also, less predictably, warm the red blood that coursed toward her own human heart.

Quantrille's and Bernice's distinctive responses to racial change were also linked to differences in political consciousness. In short, Bernice was both more conservative and more politically engaged than Quantrille. Bernice worked for local election campaigns in Chicago and was more open about her views of both activist and party politics.[261] For example, where Quantrille was silent about the Chicano movement events that transpired just blocks from her home, Bernice expounded on (admittedly larger) conflicts that unfolded in Chicago farther away from hers—especially the clash between police and anti–Vietnam War protesters outside the 1968 Democratic National Convention (held in the Loop, a half dozen miles from Logan Square). "It was quite a terrifying time ... with the invasion of the malcontents—hippies, yippies and anarchists," Bernice wrote.[262] She criticized Hollywood figures on the left, too. When Quantrille recommended the musical *Camelot*, Bernice replied that she hoped to see the film, even though she considered the star, Vanessa Redgrave, a "fly in the ointment." Bernice, who had once been a stage performer, thought Redgrave "a fine actress" but added, "She has not made friends here because of her 'pink' leanings."[263]

Meanwhile, Bernice warmed to those with leanings more like her own. In November 1968, she applauded Richard Nixon's election to the presidency, remarking, "The Nixons are an attractive family." She continued to support Nixon well into the Watergate affair that followed on the heels of his reelection in 1972. Bernice was keenly interested in the Senate Watergate hearings because she had known some of the men involved when she was employed by the CIA and because the Watergate complex stood on the site of the building where she had worked in the 1950s. But her prophetic powers proved weak; she thought that Nixon would "ride right through" the Watergate crisis.[264] If Bernice was deeply engaged by politics, Quantrille was not only disengaged but also disaffected. Quantrille's one statement about the 1972 electoral process was "I won't comment on the election—I am so tired of politics and politicians."[265]

Back in 1967, when Quantrille had decried "the revolution in every aspect of our life," neither she nor Bernice could have envisioned how far that revolution would reach, from the streets they traversed in their neighborhoods to the city centers of Denver and Chicago to their nation's capital and, by extension, to old outposts of European empire like Vietnam—and then back again. By 1973, when Quantrille published the supplement to her Carson genealogy, the world had tilted on its axis. As older white women living on limited incomes in urban apartments, Quantrille and Bernice sometimes responded to racial transformation, generational strife, and economic upheaval in similar ways. But just as their historical assessment of frontiersmen displayed subtle differences, so, too, did their encounter with the changes that the 1960s bequeathed to the 1970s.

Old Maid and Housewife

Despite their differences, by the late 1960s and early '70s, Bernice Blackwelder and Quantrille McClung had built an enduring friendship. At first, their relationship traced a single trail: a shared passion for Kit Carson connected them. Now, a labyrinth of paths tied the two women together across the distance, the divergent attitudes, and the disparate life choices that otherwise kept them apart. When they started to correspond in the 1950s, they used formal salutations: "Dear Miss McClung" and "Dear Mrs. Blackwelder." But by the 70s, "My Dearest Quantrille" and "Dear, Dear Bernice" graced the top of most missives.[266] In these letters, they poured out both hearts and minds to each other, supporting and affirming each other in turn. Bernice said it best when she contrasted her own unpunctuated allegiance to Quantrille with the pinchfisted reception her friend sometimes faced at the Denver Public Library: "I'm for you all the way," adding, "All the time & anywhere always." Quantrille returned Bernice's longhand love by locking the shift key of her Corona: "WHAT A COMFORT YOU ARE TO ME!"[267]

No longer was Carson their sole coin of exchange; their friendship had deepened. The two years Bernice spent in Colorado, after she and Harold left Virginia and before they moved to Illinois, surely played a role. Once she was gone, Bernice often harked back to her time in Denver, telling Quantrille how she missed their trips to the library as well as the telephone conversations they could have without running up a long-distance bill, which neither of them could afford (they rarely spoke on the phone when they lived in different states).[268] But something else must have happened while Bernice was in Colorado that further cemented her relationship with Quantrille, something all but lost to the historical record. From Chicago, Bernice looked back at those years and confessed to Quantrille, "You really saved my life when I was at a point of desperation."[269] It is unclear what Bernice meant when she wrote of the despair she had felt in Denver. She might have been referring to the dislocation of a cross-country move or to anxiety about her next historical project. She might have been referring to troubles with Harold. Restaurateur Sam Arnold believed Bernice was separated from her husband in Denver, though Bernice's niece doubted that the Blackwelders ever parted company during their five decades of marriage.[270] Bernice might have been referring to Harold's businesses, which, in Colorado as in Virginia, did not thrive, leaving the couple in dire financial straits. With diplomacy and feeling, Quantrille responded to Bernice's confession, "I would never have known that you were 'desperate' while you were here altho I was certain you were worried."[271] Whatever happened in Denver that left Bernice despondent, she was sure that Quantrille had helped her survive.

Out of this troubled time emerged an impassioned relationship that at times shaded into a romance, one not entirely, though still most notably, cerebral. Bernice emphasized the life of the mind when she wrote to Quantrille in 1965, "It seems the right time now to tell you of the inspiration you have given me. . . . I believe kindred spirits do find each other." A dozen years later, she declared her great fortune in having chosen her particular research topics: "I have been . . . luckiest . . . because through it all, you became my dear friend. . . . I needed the stimulation you give."[272] Quantrille was the less effusive of the two, but even she could burst forth with gratitude for intellectual camaraderie. After typing a two-page, single-spaced letter to Bernice in 1969, with all but one scant inch devoted to things Carson, Quantrille closed, "What would I do without you?" And Quantrille ended a similar missive three years later, "Dear girl—you can't know what a comfort you are to me."[273] Sometimes, though, the two women's expressions of intimacy had little to do with historical research. In 1971, for instance, Quantrille wrote to Bernice, "You may not believe it, but I watch for your letters as a girl might watch for a letter from her boy-friend!" A few months later, when Bernice received the gift of an apron that Quantrille had sewn for her by hand, Bernice wrote back that she would "wear it with complete joy as tho your arms were around me."[274] As such declarations took wing from Chicago to Denver and back again, hearts skipped beats.

What tied those hearts together now went well beyond Carson and his chroniclers, both amateur and academic. Nineteenth-century hinterland heroes and their historians still loomed large in Bernice and Quantrille's relationship, but so, too, did the day-to-day changes that shaped their twentieth-century city lives. The tales Quantrille and Bernice told each other about kinfolk drew them closer, too. In Quantrille's case, those stories were more often gloomy than gladsome. Bernice, by contrast, was apt to relate cheery anecdotes about her beloved niece Doris (who visited from northern Michigan and shared Bernice's love of the arts) as well as Doris's brood of smart, well-mannered children.[275]

Quantrille and Bernice also bonded over key components of their very persons. For instance, whiteness—that is, a racial identity as people of European descent who, historically, have enjoyed unearned privileges— linked them to one another, though not always in consistent or predictable ways. Their respective self-identities as both female and elderly were more in accord, at a moment when new possibilities for women and the aged rose on the cultural and political horizon. And they shared an ambiguous class standing: both came from arguably middle-class backgrounds, but both struggled mightily as adults, living more like working-class people than their parents ever did, even as their own individual labor histories bespoke a higher status. Status did not pay the bills, however, so trading stories about making ends meet was another way for Bernice and Quantrille to connect. Self-identities—of class, race, age, and gender—are unstable, intertwined, and intersectional; people are not simply lower-middle class or simply white or simply old or simply women. Rather, people richly occupy multiple, mutable, and entangled categories of identity and rebel against them, too.[276] But Bernice and Quantrille, like other humans, could cordon those categories off from one another rhetorically, holding them separate in order to build and maintain a friendship.

Take, for example, the sentiments they shared about growing old. As Quantrille and Bernice exchanged impressions of aging, the politics and the very language of old age were in flux: the older lobbying organization, the American Association of Retired Persons, exploded in membership in the 1970s, while activists on the left founded a more radical advocacy group, the Gray Panthers, in 1972. As for language, even though the term "senior citizen" was not new in this era—it dated from the 1930s—its use now surged.[277] Bernice lived through her sixties in this context and then, in 1972, she entered her seventies. By then, Quantrille was already eighty-two. Bernice loved the language of senior citizenship, though she often employed it tongue in cheek. In 1968, she began a letter, "Well, I might as well let you in on a little secret. I have discovered I must be getting senile! I just got out the ironing board instead of the typewriter!! I guess it happens to everyone called a 'senior citizen.'"[278] When Quantrille replied, she noted that she had mislaid Bernice's letter for quite some time. But, she added, "I find that not all of the folk who are absent minded are 'senior' citizens," blaming forgetfulness instead on the distractions of modern life. Just a few months later, though, as a torrid summer ended, Quantrille confessed that she had discovered in her basement storage locker a "big air cooler" that she purchased years earlier but "forgot all about." Quantrille was dismayed, declaring, "I need a guardian!"[279] Both the experience of aging and the meanings Bernice and Quantrille attached to it—as a cause for health concerns, of course, but mostly as a bountiful font of humor—bound the two women together.

Quantrille, more than Bernice, spoke of age and gender in the same breath, identifying herself specifically as an older woman rather than generically as a senior citizen. She did so when she quipped that she needed a guardian and then, as she considered the demographics of nursing homes, quickly retracted her declaration: "I can't bear to think of being shut up with a lot of old women! That would surely drive me to suicide!"[280] Likewise, when Quantrille and three elderly friends shared Christmas dinner, Quantrille was amused by the hostess's remark, "Now, ladies, let us not talk about our ailments." "Old girl," Quantrille thought to herself, "you have your work cut out for you."[281] And when telling

Bernice about altering a dress that had cap sleeves, Quantrille opined, "I feel old ladies should cover up their ugly arms."[282] Quantrille considered herself an old woman, but her assessment of the category to which she felt she belonged was often unflattering. Meanwhile, Bernice was aging alongside her husband, Harold, which may explain why her remarks about growing old more often employed the gender-neutral vocabulary of senior citizenship.[283] Thus, there were mostly similarities but also subtle differences in the way Quantrille and Bernice saw themselves as older people.

The same was true for their sense of themselves as women. As Quantrille's disparaging remarks about "old ladies" suggest, the old Cold War cultural conservatism about women and their worth was alive and well in the letters these two friends exchanged, and it shaped their lives. That conservatism, back in 1962, had inspired Bernice to depict her rivalry with another female Carson buff as a "hen fight."[284] Now, it prompted Quantrille to refer to herself as an "old maid" and Bernice to call herself—no matter the range of tasks that filled her days—a "housewife."[285] Both women, then, represented themselves by calling attention to marital status, however marginally important that status was to their collaboration. In such representations, the contours of womanhood and the nature of its constraints depended on relationships with men. "Old maid" was an identity that encompassed not only social distance from men but also a negative evaluation of that distance; it was a diminished sort of self, a self not fully realized. Quantrille indicated as much when she told Bernice about a dinner she had attended at her minister's home. Also invited, according to Quantrille, was "another leftover female," a term she immediately followed with a sarcastic parenthetical correction, "(or should I say unappropriated blessing)."[286] Euphemized or not, a woman without a man was a woman without a man—a recognizable cultural category, to be sure, but not a happy one. "Housewife," on the other hand, was a normative identity for white women who at least aspired to the middle class. It was not so fully realized as "housewife *and* mother," but it was still within striking distance of the natural order of things. These familiar categories were the ones Bernice and Quantrille used most frequently with each other—which is not to say how deeply the women internalized them or how they reconciled those categories with incongruous life experiences.

The humor with which Quantrille and Bernice traded both self-appraisals and opinions of other women suggests that they lived on the edge of a critical gender consciousness. But as often as not, the demands of daily life militated against sustained cultural critique and incited instead a deprecation of actual women that cut dangerously close to the bone—hence their response to the resurgence of feminism in the 1960s and '70s.[287] Bernice first took notice of the women's movement in 1972, when she received mail that addressed her as "Ms." She relayed this event to Quantrille with hilarity: "I have been 'liberated,'" Bernice wrote, "I am now Ms. Blackwelder. How I did laugh!" Quantrille's response, though facetious, was telling: "So you have been liberated! Liberation will never come to me, I am just an old maid!"[288] The new feminisms of this era challenged the structures of domination that had shaped both women's lives. But Bernice and Quantrille were so accustomed to those structures, so habituated to maneuvering within them, that the women's movement seemed like a joke. Why tear out a wall or bust down a door when one has more or less profitably spent a lifetime looking out windows and knocking before entering?

Quantrille and Bernice had their own tactics for navigating what for them was still a man's world. They were so adept at these navigations that the borders of the world felt less like fixed walls and more like the portable partitions that emerged in this era's corporate offices — graceless, perhaps, but moveable. Key among the tactics the two women used was a traffic in men. And in keeping with their growing closeness, they no longer limited that traffic to western heroes and western historians. Bernice, for her part, traded in her husband as well. She often put it bluntly: "Hard to get much done with a man around the house," she griped, or "Most of my time has been spent in such menial tasks as housecleaning, shopping ... and waiting on Harold." Once, Bernice had to nurse Harold and a sick pet at the same time, and she reported to Quantrille that Harold "was more trouble than the dog."[289] Others who knew Bernice confirm that Harold, while he loved Bernice dearly, was an exacting spouse. Bernice's niece Doris recalled that "he loved to be waited on at home." An unmarried friend was more frank; to her, Harold was "a baby" and Bernice was "a patsy" for putting up with him. But Bernice was conscious of the dynamic that kept her at his beck and call, and she did not hesitate, in exchanges with other women, to diminish him behind his back. As Doris explained, Bernice "enjoyed making him happy, even though she would wink at me as she served him."[290] When Bernice wrote in a letter, then, that Harold was "under foot" or, on a good day, that he was "out of the way," she was not just reporting his whereabouts. She was distancing herself from his quotidian claims and cleaving instead to Quantrille and all that Quantrille, as intellectual collaborator and commiserating friend, had come to represent for her.[291] In this,

Harold became one of those objects of barter and banter that tied the two women together.

Thus bound to each other, Bernice and Quantrille shared a litany of verbal embraces. Still, Harold was not the main object of trade in this traffic in men, nor was same-sex romance a chief purpose: this was an economy of power. One locus of that power was the academic historian, here always white and male, who became a key figure in Bernice and Quantrille's letters. But the power bartered through this traffic in men still inhered most centrally in Kit Carson himself, linked as he was to origin stories of the American nation. In those tales, a holy trinity of white men once walked the West and made it their own, thus our own—Daniel Boone, the father; Davy Crockett, the son (if we remember the Alamo, then we recall that he sacrificed himself for us); and Kit Carson, the westward-leading holy ghost. It was Carson who tied the two women together. He also gave them access to a wider world. That world of publishers, libraries, and readers paid attention to these women because their stock-in-trade was a man who had moved with the defining vector of the nation. On the one hand, Quantrille's and Bernice's identification with this man affirmed the structures of power that created both racial comfort and gendered constraint in their own lives. On the other hand, by the 1960s, that man had become something new because of the way these women had passed him back and forth and then out to a broader public. Carson had been domesticated, never again so freely to roam a mythic western past. Then, in the 1970s, a new cast of actors surged onto the stage, insisting that domestication was not enough: it was time to discipline Carson. In an age when the empire struck back, the power that Quantrille McClung and Bernice Blackwelder had harnessed in Kit Carson came back to haunt them.[292]

When the Empire Struck Back

I was haunted, too, though not yet by Kit Carson, who meant nothing to me. I was haunted by dissonance. I was haunted by all I saw and heard that gave the lie to the safe, ordered world of my childhood. My northern family had moved across town to a southern colonial home. It was half again bigger than the ranch house into which I was born, though it seemed to me that we had moved mostly because five people fought too much sharing one bathroom. *Southern Living* magazine came by mail to the southern colonial, apparently to supply décor ideas.[293] But the word "southern" for me was now less apt to inspire images of gracious living and more apt to evoke pictures of police dogs lunging at black people. And the word "colonial" was starting to sound less quaint in a global era of decolonization and amid local invocations of anticolonial rhetoric.

I heard such rhetoric expressed most vociferously in the Vietnam War protests that erupted three miles from that new house, on and around the University of Wisconsin–Madison campus.[294] I was in my early teens then, and my parents forbade me from taking the bus downtown to the scene of the demonstrations. But news came readily over the radio, on television, and by word of mouth. It also came from my older sister and brother, when they were home; both had left for college by 1970. The news often turned the family dinner table into a battleground between my right-leaning parents and my left-leaning siblings. Sometimes the vehemence reflected in their respective positions took brick-and-mortar form, as it did in 1970 when antiwar activists set off a bomb meant to destroy the Army Math Research Center at the university, killing one researcher, causing massive damage to the building that housed the center, and blowing out a stained-glass window at my parents' church two blocks away.[295]

That bombing occurred just days before I began my freshman year of high school, where, for the first time in my life, I had not one or two classmates of color but scores of new African American peers, many of them bussed from Madison's south side after Central High School closed its doors.[296] Their presence, reminding me as it did of earlier civil rights struggles against segregation in the schools, told me that the South was not a long-ago and faraway place but a location here and now, right across town, tied to me by public transportation. Other contests for rights, redress, and self-determination seemed more distant but nonetheless ubiquitous in the news: ethnic Mexican farmworkers organizing in California, for instance, and American Indians occupying Wounded Knee in South Dakota. Similar contests broke out closer to home, as when migrant workers from central Wisconsin marched on the state capitol in Madison and formed a union, Obreros Unidos, or when Menominees in the northeastern part of the state fought the federal government's termination policies.[297] However far or near, such struggles told me that the relative ease of my daily life was not the norm in the United States of America, let alone elsewhere.

Already I had learned that my physical comforts, while not as great as those enjoyed by some neighbors, nonetheless exceeded those of others. My father worked in middle management for Ray-O-Vac, the battery and flashlight manufacturer, while other fathers were firemen and carpenters, on the one hand, or doctors and lawyers, on the other. Most mothers in the neighborhood did not work outside the home, at least when their children were small.[298] As a nine-year-old, my sharpest recognition of class gradations came when we moved into our new house in the mid-1960s and a classmate, who lived in a smaller home, asked me, "Are you rich?" I was quite sure my family was not wealthy; we had two cars, for example, but one was always so rusted out that it was destined soon for the dump. So I answered no. Then the girl asked, "Are you poor?" I was certain we were nowhere near impoverished, so again I answered no. Ever after, the term "middle class" took on new clarity for me. By the late 1960s, so did the word "white."

It was in the heat of all this that I first saw the West with my own eyes. That road trip to Montana in 1972 seemed to take me far away from it all—except when it did not. By then, I might conjure the Rifleman's West for a moment, but the Indigenous homelands across which we drove never fully receded from my view. And I was too old to imagine myself as the Rifleman's son anymore. An early bloomer, I was well past puberty, and I collected and discarded boyfriends as readily as I acquired and then wore out bell-bottom pants; both were equally necessary to my teenage self and both equally disposable. There was nothing unusual about that; the same could be said for many of my friends. Even so, I suspected that there was something unusual, even strange, about me. I was haunted by my younger self, the one who so identified with the Rifleman's son, and I could not for the life of me understand how I had grown into my body and all that it seemed to require of me. I wanted to take a step back, start over, see if it might all turn out differently. That seemed most possible in the place that I imagined as the West.

But there was no West, in that sense, anymore. The West was down on wounded knee, brought low by the heirs of those who first called that place home. Quantrille McClung, Bernice Blackwelder, and I would face that reality for the rest of our lives.

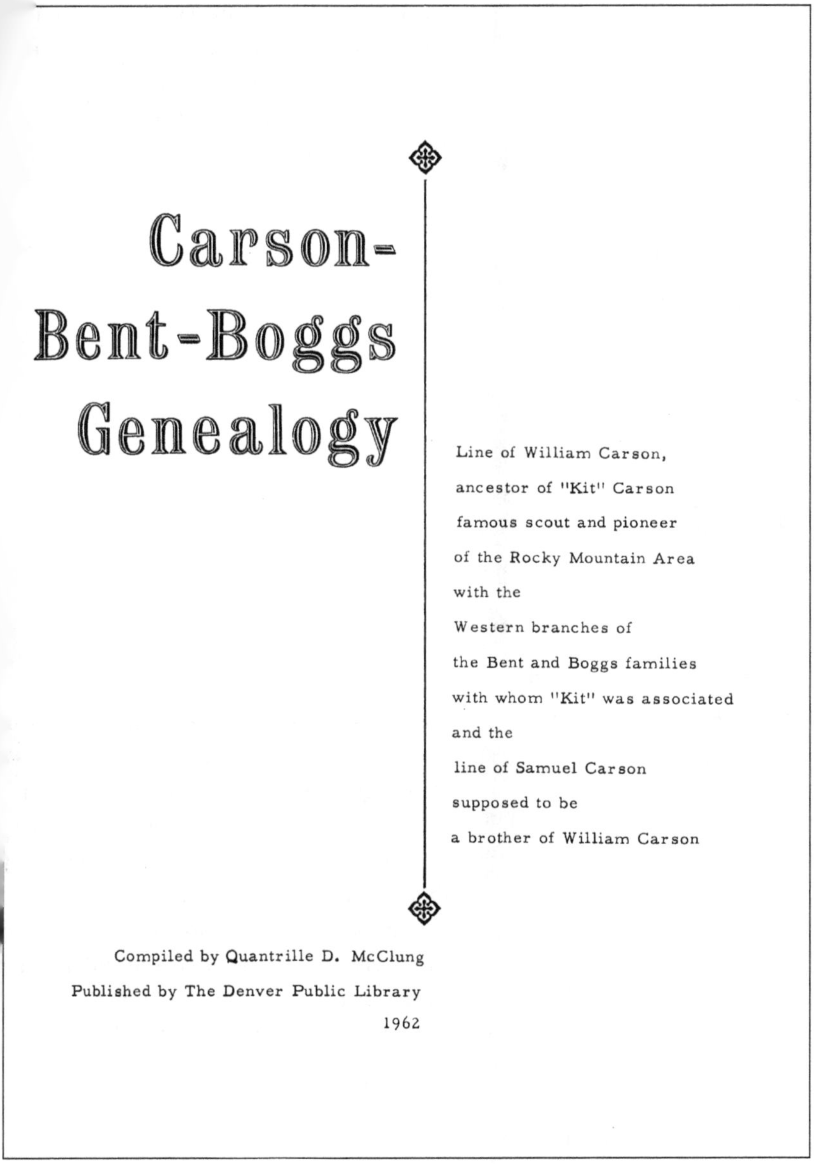

Carson-
Bent-Boggs
Genealogy

Line of William Carson,
ancestor of "Kit" Carson
famous scout and pioneer
of the Rocky Mountain Area
with the
Western branches of
the Bent and Boggs families
with whom "Kit" was associated
and the
line of Samuel Carson
supposed to be
a brother of William Carson

Compiled by Quantrille D. McClung
Published by The Denver Public Library
1962

Figure 1.1. *Carson-Bent-Boggs Genealogy*, 1962. The Denver Public Library published this 214-page book, Quantrille McClung's first foray into the interlinked genealogies of the Carson, Bent, and Boggs families. Eleven years later she published the 607-page *Carson-Bent-Boggs Genealogy Supplement*, which looked much the same. In the late 1970s and early '80s, she researched and began compiling, but did not complete, a second supplement. Courtesy of Denver Public Library, Western History Collection.

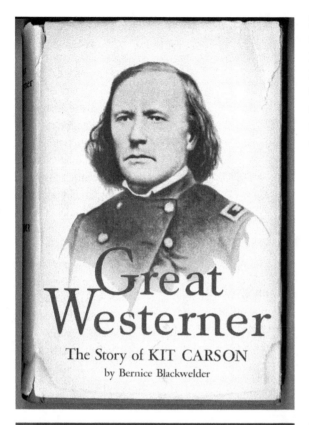

Figure 1.2. *Great Westerner: The Story of Kit Carson*, 1962. Caxton Printers of Caldwell, Idaho, published this biography, Bernice Blackwelder's only book. From the 1960s to the early '80s, she researched and compiled a biographical dictionary of western men that she did not complete. Courtesy of Caxton Printers.

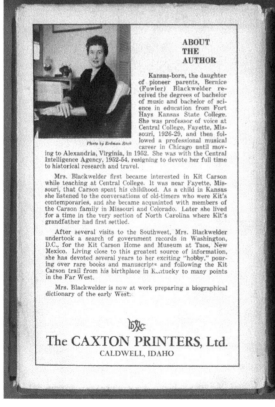

Figure 1.3. *Great Westerner*, back cover. Bernice Blackwelder's author blurb identified her as the daughter of pioneers and explained her Kit Carson "hobby" as a consequence of her brief residence in Missouri, supplemented by time spent in Colorado, North Carolina, the Southwest, and Washington, D.C. Her portrait was likely taken in the home she and husband Harold owned in Alexandria, Virginia, from 1958 to 1962. Courtesy of Caxton Printers.

Figure 1.4. Christopher "Kit" Carson, 1809–68. This portrait's date is unknown, but historian Harvey Carter thought it was from the 1850s, when Carson was in his forties and had been married to Josefa Jaramillo for about a decade. Carson's face is fuller in this portrait than in many others. Notably, given his work as a fur trapper and trader in the 1820s and '30s, he is wearing a beaver hat. Contemporaries described him as a small, soft-spoken man who did not turn heads. In addition to English, he spoke Spanish and Indigenous languages but could not read or write. Courtesy of Southwest Research Center, University of New Mexico–Taos.

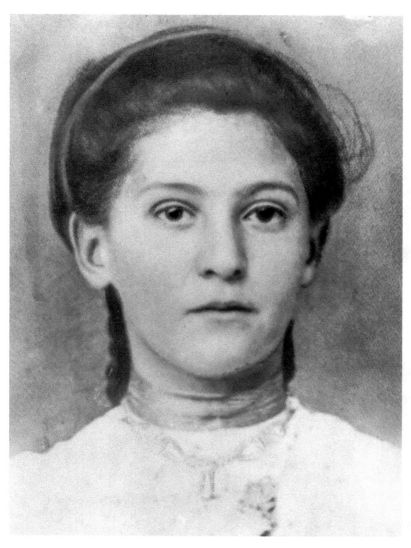

Figure 1.5. (Long believ[...] Josefa Jaramillo, 1828-6[...] fifty years, this and one [...] photograph have circul[...] images of María Josefa J[...] of Taos. The sitter for th[...] appears to be about the [...] in her midteens, when J[...] Jaramillo married Kit Ca[...] and the picture matches [...] contemporary descriptic[...] her well enough. Unlike [...] unprepossessing husban[...] Josefa did turn heads. He[...] Teresina Bent remembere[...] her as "rather dark, very [...] hair, large big bright eyes[...] well built, graceful in ever[...] way, quite handsome." An[...] described her as well. Tra[...] Lewis Garrard called her b[...] the "haughty, heart-break[...] kind—such as would lead [...] with the glance of an eye, [...] his life for one smile." Men[...] Marian Russell recalled "a [...] Mexican girl with heavy br[...] of dark hair. Her demure li[...] face was round and brown [...] and her great dark eyes we[...] usually cast down." Also un[...]

Kit, Josefa was literate. She descended from the Jaramillo and Vigil families, whose roots in New Mexico went back to the late seventeenth century. Josefa had eight children, seven of whom lived to adulthood. But this aln[...] certainly is not an image of her, nor is the other frequently reproduced picture. Both appear to be photograph[...] prints on paper, and yet the images are said to be from an era (the 1840s and '50s) when this technology was ei[...] completely or largely unavailable and certainly unavailable in remote northern New Mexico. To be pictures of [...] young Josefa, this and perhaps the other oft-copied image would need to have been daguerreotypes, the preva[...] photographic technology of the antebellum era. Both images came to the Kit Carson Home and Museum in 19[...] 70, but their provenance is dubious. Quantrille McClung and Bernice Blackwelder learned of the photo discove[...] from the museum's newsletter, *Las Noticias Alegres de la Casa Kit Carson*, and they wrote to each other about [...] the finds. Of the first image that materialized (just months before the second), Blackwelder penned, "I hope it i[...] authentic." That first image is reproduced here (the second image has similar problems and also does not matc[...] contemporary descriptions of Josefa). Efforts to determine the identity of the sitters for both images are ongoin[...] Courtesy of Southwest Research Center, University of New Mexico–Taos.

Figure 1.6. Bernice and Harold Blackwelder house, Alexandria, Virginia, 1958–62. This is the only single-family home that the Blackwelders ever owned, though they purchased half of a duplex in nearby Arlington in 1952 (and sold it at a loss in 1958). The Alexandria home was in the Parklawn subdivision on Yellowstone Drive; other neighborhood streets were also named for national parks and forests. This image is from a 1962 real estate listing. The Blackwelders sold the house then and moved west, first, briefly, to Omaha and then, until 1965, to the Denver metropolitan area, where Bernice lived near Quantrille McClung for the only time in their nearly thirty-year friendship. Bernice Fowler Blackwelder Papers.

Figure 1.7. Blackwelder's Country House place mat, circa 1960. Like his father in North Carolina, Harold Blackwelder ran barbecue restaurants and takeouts, especially in the 1950s and '60s. None of the restaurants was successful for long. Bernice Blackwelder produced baked goods for Harold's eateries. The Country House may have been the most elaborate of these enterprises; it had multiple dining rooms featuring red-and-white-checked tablecloths as well as a fully electric kitchen, and it served barbecue, chicken, steak, and prime rib. By 1962, it had closed and the Blackwelders had moved west. The last eatery Harold ran was the Dixie Pit Bar-B-Q in North Denver in 1964. In 1965, the Blackwelders moved back to Chicago, where they had met, married, and lived through the 1940s. Bernice Fowler Blackwelder Papers.

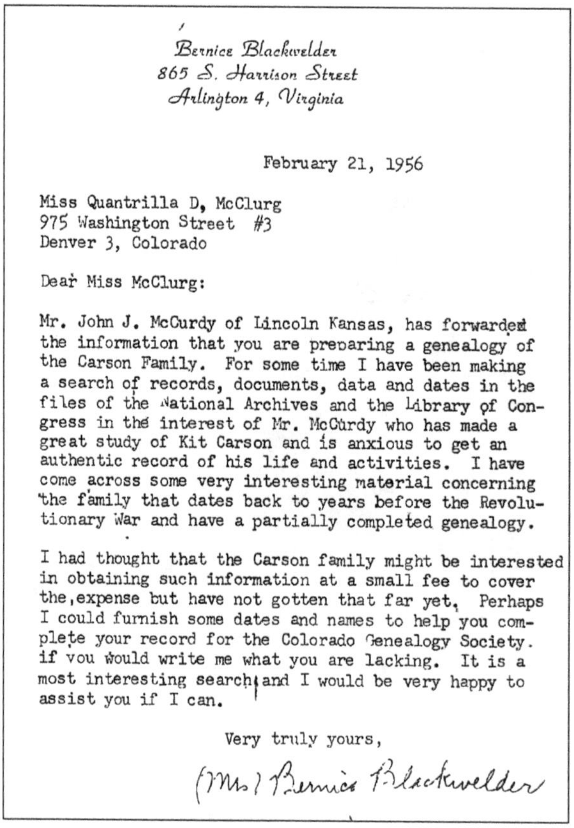

February 21, 1956

Miss Quantrilla D. McClurg
975 Washington Street #3
Denver 3, Colorado

Dear Miss McClurg:

Mr. John J. McCurdy of Lincoln Kansas, has forwarded
the information that you are preparing a genealogy of
the Carson Family. For some time I have been making
a search of records, documents, data and dates in the
files of the National Archives and the Library of Congress in the interest of Mr. McCurdy who has made a
great study of Kit Carson and is anxious to get an
authentic record of his life and activities. I have
come across some very interesting material concerning
the family that dates back to years before the Revolutionary War and have a partially completed genealogy.

I had thought that the Carson family might be interested
in obtaining such information at a small fee to cover
the expense but have not gotten that far yet. Perhaps
I could furnish some dates and names to help you complete your record for the Colorado Genealogy Society.
if you would write me what you are lacking. It is a
most interesting search and I would be very happy to
assist you if I can.

Very truly yours,

(Mrs.) Bernice Blackwelder

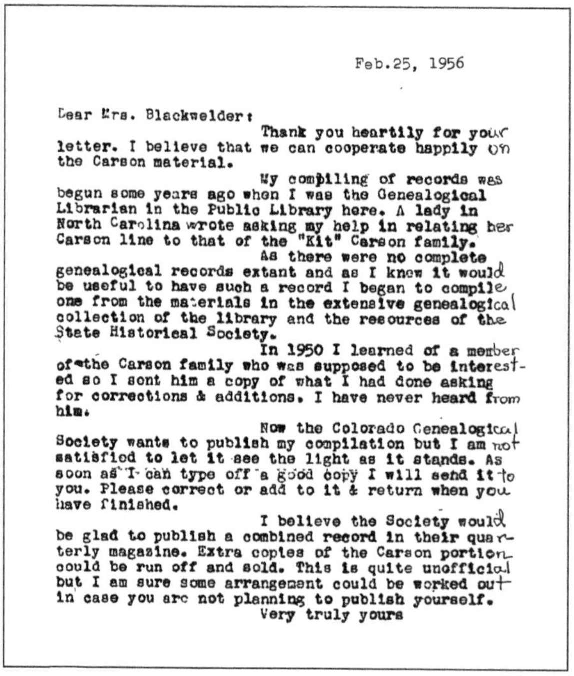

Feb. 25, 1956

Dear Mrs. Blackwelder:
                    Thank you heartily for your
letter. I believe that we can cooperate happily on
the Carson material.
                    My compiling of records was
begun some years ago when I was the Genealogical
Librarian in the Public Library here. A lady in
North Carolina wrote asking my help in relating her
Carson line to that of the "Kit" Carson family.
                    As there were no complete
genealogical records extant and as I knew it would
be useful to have such a record I began to compile
one from the materials in the extensive genealogical
collection of the library and the resources of the
State Historical Society.
                    In 1950 I learned of a member
of the Carson family who was supposed to be interested so I sent him a copy of what I had done asking
for corrections & additions. I have never heard from
him.
                    Now the Colorado Genealogical
Society wants to publish my compilation but I am not
satisfied to let it see the light as it stands. As
soon as I can type off a good copy I will send it to
you. Please correct or add to it & return when you
have finished.
                    I believe the Society would
be glad to publish a combined record in their quarterly magazine. Extra copies of the Carson portion
could be run off and sold. This is quite unofficial
but I am sure some arrangement could be worked out
in case you are not planning to publish yourself.
                    Very truly yours

Figure 1.8. First letters Bernice Blackwelder
and Quantrille McClung exchanged, February
1956. Bernice was living in Arlington and
Quantrille in Denver. They learned of each
other's work through Kit Carson enthusiast Jo
McCurdy, a Kansas lawyer. By the time their
correspondence ended in the 1980s, Quantrille
and Bernice had exchanged over three hundre
letters. While their early letters were formal an
concerned only with historical research, their
friendship deepened over the years, and later
letters ranged over all aspects of their daily live
Quantrille donated the correspondence to the
Denver Public Library along with the rest of he
research materials. Courtesy of Denver Public
Library, Western History Collection. WH1057.

Figure 2.1. Bernice and Harold Blackwelder and dog Elsa, 1970s. This picture was taken outside the Blackwelders' apartment on Logan Boulevard in Chicago's Logan Square neighborhood. The Blackwelders lived in the same building for fifteen years, sometimes serving as building managers. Behind the Blackwelders is an embankment for the Kennedy Expressway, connecting downtown with northwestern suburbs and O'Hare Airport. Logan Square was once an affluent area but had long since become a working-class neighborhood populated by Polish immigrants and their descendants as well as people of Russian Jewish, Italian, Belgian, and Scandinavian origin and descent. The 1960s and '70s saw a massive influx of Puerto Ricans and ethnic Mexicans. Bernice and Harold responded negatively to this demographic shift. Courtesy of Denver Public Library, Western History Collection. WH1057.

Figure 2.2. Quantrille McClung, 1972. Quantrille was eighty-two years old when this picture was taken on a spring day in downtown Denver. She would publish the massive *Carson-Bent-Boggs Genealogy Supplement* the next year. She lived in an apartment in Denver's Capitol Hill neighborhood, and she could easily walk from her building to the Denver Public Library and the Colorado Historical Society, at least when her health allowed. In the 1970s, she bemoaned the changes that closed small businesses along her pedestrian route and filled the sidewalks with hippies. She was no fan of high-rise buildings like the one behind her, either. Courtesy of Barbara L. Osiek.

Figure 2.3. Quantrille McClung, 1976. The Colorado Genealogical Society honored Quantrille for her services in 1976. She had joined the organization in the 1930s and by 1940 served as its president. At a monthly meeting, she received a plaque and a corsage. Later, the *Colorado Genealogist* published notice of the recognition along with this picture. When Quantrille reported the honor in a letter to Bernice Blackwelder, Bernice replied, "About time you were getting some recognition." Courtesy of Denver Public Library, Western History Collection. WH1057.

THE SLANDERED SCOUT

THE CURIOUS CASE OF THE SLANDERED SCOUT THE AGGRESSIVE ANTHROPOLOGIST, THE DELINQUENT DEAN AND THE ACQUIESCENT ARMY

By Harvey L. Carter, C.M.

The student newspaper at The Colorado College, known as *The Catalyst*, in its issue of Sept. 28, 1972, reported on the addition of several new faculty members. Among these was Mrs. Shirley Hill Witt, Associate Professor of Anthropology, B.A. Michigan, 1965; M.A., 1966; Ph.D., New Mexico, 1969. Concerning her *The Catalyst* stated, "The power of Dr. Hill's sensitivity has been felt in more than one department already this year. Upon arriving at the school, she immediately persuaded the campus R.O.T.C. office to remove the Kit Carson exhibit from the foyer of Cossitt Gym." "I find it perfectly offensive to have a terrorist and a killer displayed with honor," she said bitterly, recalling Carson's slaughter of Indians and wild animals. "Southwest America must be very bankrupt for heroes, if it has to enshrine the likes of Kit Carson."

95

Figure 2.4. Harvey Carter's "The Curious Case of the Slandered Scout." In response to a controversy in which a new Colorado College faculty colleague, anthropologist Shirley Hill Witt (Mohawk), protested the display of a Carson photograph in an ROTC exhibit on campus, historian Carter penned "The Curious Case of the Slandered Scout, the Aggressive Anthropologist, the Delinquent Dean, and the Acquiescent Army," which the *Denver Westerners Brand Book* published in 1973. Witt—academic, activist, and cofounder of the National Indian Youth Council—had maintained that the "Southwest . . . must be very bankrupt for heroes, if it has to enshrine the like of Kit Carson." Carter was author of *"Dear Old Kit": The Historical Kit Carson* and would soon coauthor, with Thelma Guild, *Kit Carson: A Pattern for Heroes*. Courtesy of the Denver Posse of the Westerners.

Figure 2.5. Western History Department, Denver Public Library. The Western History Department at the central library opened in the 1930s under the direction of librarian Malcolm Wyer. It continues to hold one of the premier collections of western history sources in the United States. It has occupied different spaces in different buildings over the decades; this is in the Burnham Hoyt building completed in 1955. In 1995, when the library moved into its current Michael Graves building, the Western History Department finally merged with the Genealogy Division to become the Western History/Genealogy Department. But in the years when Quantrille McClung worked at the library, first as an employee and then as an independent researcher, Western History enjoyed a higher status than Genealogy. Quantrille never felt fully at home in Western History, where, she told Bernice Blackwelder, she often found herself in "hot water." Courtesy of Denver Public Library, Western History Collection. DPL Archives.

Figure 2.6. Genealogy Division, Denver Public Library. In the 1930s, when Quantrille McClung became the Denver Public Library's genealogical librarian, the genealogy resources there were reputed to constitute one of the five largest collections in public libraries nationwide. By midcentury, when this photograph was taken, Genealogy constituted a library "division" rather than a "department," making it lower in status than Western History. Courtesy of Denver Public Library, Western History Collection. DPL Archives.

Figure 3.1. (*top left*) Quantrille Day McClung (1890–1985) childhood portrait. Quantrille was the older of two child' born to Henrietta Gutzman McClung and Benjamin Fran McClung. Henrietta's parents where Prussian immigrant farmers in eastern Kansas, while Benjamin hailed from a white farm family that had migrated from the mid-Atlant to the Midwest, where he was born and raised. The McCl' lived in North Denver. Benjamin worked for a Denver who and later, after a period of unemployment, for the U.S. Mi Henrietta took in boarders. Courtesy of History Colorado. Accession no. 30003448.

Figure 3.2. (*bottom left*) Quantrille McClung's mother, Her Gutzman McClung. This is almost certainly an early twent century picture of Quantrille's mother at her daily chores outside the McClungs' Goss (now Tejon) Street house in N Denver. Quantrille identified with both of her parents and visited her maternal Gutzman relatives in Kansas when sh was growing up. Courtesy of History Colorado. Accession no. 30003426.

Figure 3.3. (*below*) Quantrille McClung outside the McClur home in North Denver. The McClungs moved to this home Goss (now Tejon) Street in 1903, when Quantrille was thirte from a more modest house on Bell (now Osage) Street. In t' 1910s, the wholesale business that employed her father clos' and while he was out of work, Quantrille's labor as a libraria and her mother's taking in boarders allowed the family to k' the house. Quantrille lived in the Tejon Street home until th' 1940s, when she could no longer care for her aging parents there. Then, she sold the house and moved her Methodist parents to a Catholic nursing home. Courtesy of History Colorado. Accession no. 30003440.

Figure 3.4. Bernice Fowler Blackwelder's father, Wilbur Fowler. Trained as a physician at Chicago's Rush Medical College, Wilbur was born in Minnesota and raised in Indiana and Missouri. He wed twice, first to Hattie Knapp, who died young, and then to Hattie's sister Mabel, who was born in Illinois but raised in Missouri. Wilbur lived with these wives and the children they bore along the Union Pacific line in Kansas, settling in Brookville, a town founded by the railroad. Brookville lost population in the years before Mabel had Bernice in 1900. Bernice had an older sister and a younger brother. Their father began his career as a doctor for the railroad, and by 1910 he also ran a drugstore. In 1930, a census taker listed Mabel as the store's proprietor, suggesting that both parents played a role in the business. Bernice identified more deeply with her father than her mother. Bernice Fowler Blackwelder Papers.

Figure 3.5. Perry Street in Brookville, Kansas. This 1920s photograph shows a street scene in tiny Brookville, where Bernice Fowler Blackwelder grew up (population 292 in 1900, when she was born, though the larger area that included Brookville, called Spring Creek Township, boasted 729 souls). Her father's office, and perhaps the drugstore that he and Bernice's mother ran, is at right. In 1920, Bernice left Brookville for college in Hays, Kansas, ninety miles west along the Union Pacific line. Both of her parents died in the early 1930s, when she was living in Chicago. Courtesy of the Smoky Hill Museum, Salina, Kansas.

Figure 3.6. Fowler plot outside Brookville, Kansas, in Spring Creek Township. This early twentieth-century photograph likely captures Bernice Fowler Blackwelder's uncle Arthur Fowler (her father's brother), her aunt Lottie Fowler, and one of their three children standing with their animals on the Fowler plot, which both Spring Creek and the Union Pacific line bisected. The Fowler land changed hands between the two brothers over the decades, though Arthur and Lottie likely resided there much of the time. Bernice may or may not have lived on the eighty-acre plot, but even if she lived mostly in town, she certainly spent time on her aunt and uncle's farm. Bernice Fowler Blackwelder Papers.

Figure 3.7. Denver Public Library apprentice class, 1911. These ten white women passed a test that allowed them to enroll in the first-ever apprentice class for new librarians at the brand new Denver Public Library building in what would evolve into the Civic Center. Nine of the women, including Quantrille McClung, third from right, completed the training. Quantrille was twenty-one years old when she entered the class. Like Quantrille, most of these women did not marry. Courtesy of History Colorado. Accession no. 30003442.

Figure 3.8. Denver Public Library. This Greek revival building, completed in 1910, was located in what was then becoming Civic Center Park in downtown Denver. It was the library's first location. The Colorado State Capitol stands in the background. The library building was financed in part by a grant from philanthropist Andrew Carnegie. It continued to serve as the city's main library until 1955, through all of the years when Quantrille McClung was employed there (1911–48). Courtesy of Denver Public Library, Western History Collection. DPL Archives.

Figure 3.9. Denver Public Library station, Globeville. In addition to its main and branch libraries, the Denver Public Library also ran temporary depots, called library stations, in poor, working-class, and immigrant neighborhoods such as Globeville and Elyria, where smelter and packinghouse workers lived. Quantrille saved a 1912 library pamphlet which noted that three library stations had reading rooms, while the others were "for distribution only"; these included stations in Globeville and Elyria, as well as those at the municipal bathhouse, the Jewish Settlement House, and the Neighborhood House (which probably referred to a facility on the north side that served Italians, though there was also one on the west side that served Germans, Irish, and Scandinavians). Quantrille worked at Elyria, in the Italian district on the north side, and at the municipal bathhouse. At the bathhouse station, she became acquainted with the Look family, prominent in Denver's emerging Chinese American community. Courtesy of Denver Public Library, Western History Collection. DPL Archives.

Figure 3.10. Quantrille McClung and friends at a "Bohemian Party," circa 1913. This is a page from one of three photograph albums Quantrille compiled in the 1910s, '20s, and '30s. Quantrille is in front. The pictures were taken at the home of Anna Hillkowitz, an established librarian ten years older than Quantrille. Anna likely shared this rented house with her brother Philip, a doctor, and her sister Ella. In the upper right corner of both photographs is an image of Anna's late father, Rabbi Elias Hillkowitz. Elias and Rebecca Hindelson Hillkowitz and their children emigrated from Lithuania in 1881, settling first in Cincinnati and then in Denver, where the family helped establish the Jewish Consumptives' Relief Society, which, along with National Jewish Hospital, was one of two Jewish tuberculosis sanatoria in the city. Courtesy of History Colorado. Accession no. 10031896.

Figure 3.11. More McClung and friends at a "Bohemian Party," circa 1913. This page from one of Quantrille's albums features photographs from the same party at the Hillkowitz home. In the picture on the left, Quantrille is on the far left. In the one on the right, she is on the far right. Courtesy of History Colorado. Accession no. 10031897.

Figure 3.12. Quantrille McClung and friends in female attire, 1910s. Some of the same librarians pictured here likely also appear in the "Bohemian Party" photographs. Quantrille is seated at left with her arm around her librarian friend Martha Levy. Behind Martha Levy, standing, is Ina Aulls, who went on the manage the Western History Department at the Denver Public Library. Ina Aulls never married, and I have found no evidence that Martha Levy did either. Courtesy of History Colorado. Accession no. 30003409.

Figure 3.13. Quantrille McClung and friends outdoors, 1910s. Here, librarian friends picnic in the mountains i... or near Denver. Quantrille, with come-hither look, lounges in front of the others. Ina Aulls may be the second from the right. Courtesy of History Colorado. Accession no. 30003410.

Figure 3.14. Quantrille McClung scrapbook title page. Between 1911 and 1931, Quantrille compiled nine scrapbooks, repurposing discarded books she saved from the trash at the Denver Public Library. She replaced the book pages with pages of her own, pasting memorabilia on them and keeping a written record of her comings and goings. As shown here, she also created title pages for the volumes. She apparently misnumbered this one and later corrected herself. Volume 5 covered her activities from 1921 to 1923. Courtesy of History Colorado. Accession no. 30003422.

Figure 3.15. Halloween party invitation, 1921. This is one page of an elaborate invitation to a librarians' party put together in booklet form. Quantrille McClung pasted the invitation into one of her scrapbooks and also copied out her own RSVP, which read, "Dear Kitty Anonymous—We accept with alacrity (if you know what that means—the way a cat goes up a tree) and think you are perfectly cataleptic to ask us. Your invitation is quite the cleverest thing in the catalog and we know the party will be just like it. Do have a bit of catnip or catalufa for us when we arrive in our catafalque from the catacombs. Catachismically yours, The White Cat." Courtesy of History Colorado. Accession no. 30003424.

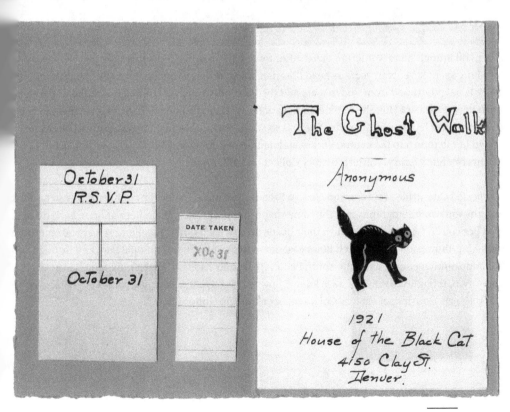

Figure 3.16. Park Hill Branch Library interior, 1920s. After four years working in the main library downtown, Quantrille McClung spent seventeen years as head librarian of two different branch libraries, the Warren Branch in the Cole neighborhood from 1915 to 1920, and the Park Hill Branch in the neighborhood of the same name from 1920 to 1932. At Park Hill, she initiated innovations, including a poetry circle for girls and a women's club that helped organize lectures and forums. She was so successful at this that in 1932, the head librarian downtown called her to return to the central library and named her director of library clubs for the city. Courtesy of Denver Public Library, Western History Collection. DPL Archives.

Figure 3.17. (*opposite*) Quantrille McClung and George Prendergast, 1924. Quantrille composed this scrapbook page, cropping the top two photographs into the same shape and positioning them in relation to each other so that she and her cousin George seem to turn their heads toward each other. The pictures were taken during a drive along the Big Thompson River, which flows east out of Rocky Mountain National Park and through Loveland, Colorado, until it empties into the South Platte. Quantrille also had herself photographed at the wheel of George's car, though she may not have known how to drive. Quantrille and George kept company from 1922 to about 1928. Courtesy of History Colorado. Accession no. 30003421.

QDMcC

George
Prendergast

in George's Ford

Figure 3.18. Donna Northrup, Donr
parents, and Quantrille McClung, ▮
Quantrille did not label this photog
when she pasted it into an album, ▮
almost certainly a picture taken wh▮
accompanied the Northrups on a tr▮
Rocky Mountain National Park. Qua
kept company with Donna from 192▮
about 1927. Donna's father died in t▮
1920s, and Donna is difficult to track
1940, when a census taker found her
with her mother, who had remarried
in West Palm Beach, Florida. Five ye▮
later, Donna was living alone in West
Palm Beach, and she died there in 19▮
She never married. Courtesy of Histo▮
Colorado. Accession no. 30003413.

Figure 3.19. Quantrille McClung and Donna Northrup, 1924. The two young women seated are
Quantrille and Donna. This is the same trip to Rocky Mountain National Park pictured in the previous
photograph. Donna's parents are immediately to her right. The travelers likely had reached a lower
elevation and found a sunny spot to rest, since they have opened their heavy coats and, with the
exception of Donna, removed their hats. Courtesy of History Colorado. Accession no. 30003415.

Figure 3.20. More Quantrille McClung and Donna Northrup, 1924. Here, on the same trip to Rocky Mountain National Park, Donna (*left*) and Quantrille (*right*) take delight in something the camera lens did not capture, perhaps a mountain bird. Courtesy of History Colorado. Accession no. 30003416.

July 12th

In the evening Donna and I took a moonlight walk then sat down on these rocks under these trees and she sang to me.

July 13th

Home via Lewiston Hotel— Stanley Hotel — Devil's Gulch

Big Thompson Canon

Figure 3.21. Quantrille McClung scrapbook page, July 12 and 13, 1924. For July 12, Quantrille wrote, "In the evening Donna and I took a moonlight walk then sat down on these rocks under these trees and she sang to me." For July 13, she recorded the route of their journey back to Denver. Courtesy of History Colorado. Accession no. 30003432.

Figure 3.22. Quantrille and Denzel McClung, sister and brother. This picture was probably taken in the late 1910s or early '20s. Denzel was a half dozen years younger than Quantrille. They were close until Denzel married May Shore, who grew up in a northern Colorado ranch family. Sometime thereafter, the siblings suffered a rift in their relationship. May Shore McClung remained the bane of Quantrille's existence for decades, even as Denzel was dying of cancer in 1971. Courtesy of History Colorado. Accession no. 30003427.

ENVER CHINESE BOY TO GRADUATE FROM SCHOOL OF MINES

FRANK LOOK.

Frank Look, one of Denver Chinatown's brightest sons, is graduating with high honor at the Colorado School of Mines at Golden next Friday afternoon.

Center fielder on the Colorado School of Mines baseball team, he is an athlete as well as a scholar. He has mastered the mysteries of baseball along with the secrets of oil shale, in which he has specialized during his four years at Mines. He spent a year at the University of Colorado after completing his Denver high school studies.

Quiet, unassuming, Frank Look has put in the four school years in Golden profitably, and he will leave his alma mater as one of the leaders of the senior class. He will go to the Massachusetts Institute of Technology in the fall to continue his studies in oil shale, which he intends to make his life work. He is the son of Mrs. Lily Look of 2057 Market street and the grandson of Chin Lou Son, father of Willie and Jimmy Chin, and the first Chinaman in Denver. He is 23 years old and has won his letters in several major sports at Mines in addition to holding unusually high averages in class work.

The
Golden Bough

THE SHOP UNIQUE!
GENUINE CHINESE GOODS

IMPORTED TEAS

DRIED MUSHROOMS

GINGER AND SWEETS

TEA ROOM OPEN FROM
4 TO 6 P. M.

SPECIAL
CHINESE DINNERS
BY APPOINTMENT

MISS GUM GEE
PHONE MAIN 3499
207-209 FIFTEENTH STREET

Gum Gee — Golden Bough

Pearl Pang

Figure 3.23. Quantrille McClung scrapbook page, 1927. Quantrille fondly followed the activities of the Look family in Denver. Quantrille first met Pearl Look at the municipal bathhouse library station in the 1910s. Pearl was the daughter of Lily Chin Look, said to be the first ethnic Chinese born in Colorado. At nineteen, Pearl married Harry Pang. While Pearl was married to Harry (he died young and she then married Franklin Chin), Quantrille ran into Pearl at the Golden Bough, a Chinese shop and restaurant in downtown Denver, and saved a memento from that meeting. When Pearl's younger brother Frank graduated with high honors from the Colorado School of Mines in 1927, Quantrille clipped a notice from the newspaper and pasted it in her scrapbook. Courtesy of History Colorado. Accession no. 30003437.

Figure 3.24. Quantrille McClung and at Lake Yellowstone, 1935. Quantrille a health crisis in 1935 that forced her take a leave of absence from the Den Public Library. She recuperated for n and then took a road trip to Yellowstc National Park before embarking on a coursework at the University of Denv library school, which earned her a lib science diploma. When she returned to the library's employ, she was name genealogical librarian. During the 193 Yellowstone jaunt, she sent postcards her parents in Denver assuring them t despite her recent illness, she was "sta the trip fine." Courtesy of History Colo Accession no. 30003447.

Figure 3.25. Denver Public Library meeting, 1946. Attendees heard a report that recommended an overhaul of library procedures for classifying employees, which in turn, the following year, led to a new personnel system and higher salaries. This and a retirement bill passed by the city council, which included disability benefits for Denver workers, made it possible for Quantrille McClung, who was in frequent poor health, to retire on disabi in 1948. Quantrille is seated in the third row, fourth from left in a dark hat. Other women she had known since the 1910s were at the meeting, including a mentor, Helen Ingersoll (*first row, fourth from left*), and Ina Aulls (*second row, fifth from left*). Head librarian Malcolm Wyer (*first row, sixth from left*) and future head librarian John Eastlick (*fourth row, second from left*) were also there. In the sixth row, in the center between the first two pillars, is a lone African American woman. She was Pauline Robinson, the first black librarian in Denver. She attended the University of Denver's library school and went on to staff branch libraries. She was instrumental i acquiring African American materials for the library. In 1996, the Pauline Robinson Branch Library was named in her honor. Courtesy of Denver Public Library, Western History Collection. DPL Archives.

Figure 3.26. Bernice Fowler Blackwelder (1900–1986), college portrait. This picture was likely taken in Hays, where Bernice Fowler attended Fort Hays Kansas Normal College (now Fort Hays State University), 1920–24, though she was wearing a borrowed University of Kansas letter sweater. Bernice Fowler Blackwelder Papers.

Figure 3.27. Bernice Fowler and friends, early 1920s. Here Bernice and two college friends pose in front of a sign advertising the virtues of their college town, Hays, billed as "The Educational Center of a Farming Community." Bernice is standing on the right. The young women are notably modern in their knickerbockers. Bernice Fowler Blackwelder Papers.

Figure 3.28. Bernice Fowler and friends at a train, early 1920s. Although the Fowler family owned the first automobile in Brookville, where Bernice grew up, both Brookville and her college town of Hays were still defined by the railroad. The Union Pacific line connected the two towns. Bernice, a budding musician, carries an instrument case. Bernice Fowler Blackwelder Papers.

3.29. Bernice Fowler and friends in drag, early 1920s. Here Bernice and her college friends clown in depicting various American types: workingman with a corncob pipe, top-hatted gentleman, soldier hite girl in white dress with immense white hair bow, Indian woman in braids and blanket. Bernice he workingman. Bernice Fowler Blackwelder Papers.

Figure 3.30. Bernice Fowler and friends, mid-1920s. After finishing college, Bernice left Kansas for good, pursuing further musical training at Columbia School of Music in Chicago (not the precursor of today's Columbia College Chicago, which began as a school of oratory). Claire Osborne Reed, who also campaigned on behalf of women's municipal suffrage, established Columbia School of Music in 1901. Bernice spent 1924 to 1926 there. She did not identify any of these Chicago friends when she pasted the photograph in an album. Bernice is the taller of the two women. Bernice Fowler Blackwelder Papers.

Figure 3.31. Bernice and Duane Fowler, sister and brother. This photograph of Bernice and Duane was likely taken during Bernice's first residence in Chicago, from 1924 to 1926. Duane was a couple of years younger than Bernice. It was during this time period that he married Jessie Granger. Both Duane and Jessie had attended Fort Hays Kansas Normal College with Bernice, though only Jessie graduated. Duane joined the J. C. Penney Company, working first in Salina, Kansas, and then, for the rest of his life, in Cadillac, Michigan. Duane often played rescuer for his sister Bernice, helping her financially after she married Harold Blackwelder in 1930 and, decades later, moving the couple to Cadillac as they aged. Bernice Fowler Blackwelder Papers.

Figure 3.32. Bernice Fowler and Charlotte Phillips, Central College, late 1920s. After two years in Chicago, Bernice moved to Fayette, Missouri, where she taught voice at Central College, a Methodist school that had merged with a women's college specializing in music education (Central College is now Central Methodist University). In this photograph, Bernice grips the knee of college orchestra conductor Charlotte Phillips. Bernice taught at Central College for three years. The college was in the Missouri region known as Little Dixie because of the southern roots of its white residents and their history of owning black slaves. Fayette was a dozen miles from Kit Carson's hometown of Franklin. Bernice Fowler Blackwelder Papers.

Figure 3.33. Central College Glee Club, late 1920s. In addition to teaching voice at Central College, Bernice Fowler directed the women's glee club, which sang on campus and toured the state of Missouri. Here, club members prepare to board their tour bus. Bernice is likely the person hanging on to the railing just to the right of the bus. Bernice Fowler Blackwelder Papers.

Figure 3.34. Bernice Fowler, circa 1929. Bernice inscribed this portrait for her new beau Harold Blackwelder in 1930, sometime after the two met while auditioning for the Chicago Civic Opera's season of light opera. By the end of the year, they had married. This print was produced in Chicago, but the photograph was likely taken before Bernice left Central College in Missouri, since writing on the back directs delivery to a campus address. Bernice Fowler Blackwelder Papers.

Figure 3.35. Harold Blackwelder with the Wanderers, circa 1930. Harold had just moved to Chicago from his home state of North Carolina when he met Bernice Fowler during auditions for Chicago Civic Opera's light opera season. His audition was successful, but he decided instead to join the Wanderers, a quartet that performed both live and on the radio. Harold, who sang bass, is on the far right. His collaborators, from left to right, were Sam Thompson, Phil Culkin, and Irwin Dillon. Sam was best man at Harold and Bernice's wedding in 1930. When the American Federation of Radio Artists formed in 1937, both Sam and Phil served leadership roles. Harold and Bernice drifted in and out of the union. Bernice Fowler Blackwelder Papers.

The Civic Theatre
WACKER DRIVE at WASHINGTON Street

A Season of

LIGHT OPERA
In English

April 21 to June 21
1930

Presented by the

Chicago Civic Opera Company

NIGHTS (except Sunday)   MATINEE (Saturday Only)
at 8:15   at 2:15

Saturday Matinee, May 31, at 2:15

The Gondoliers

Book by Sir William Gilbert
Music by Sir Arthur Sullivan

The Duke of Plaza Toro (a Grandee of Old Spain) . . . . . William
Luiz (his Attendant) . . . . Bar
Don Alhambra del Bolero (the Grand Inquisitor) . . . . Mark
Marco Palmieri   Charles K
Giuseppe Palmieri   Bertram R
Antonio   } Venetian Gondoliers . . . . Carroll van A
Francesco   William
Giorgio   Guido
The Duchess of Plaza Toro . . . . Constance E
Casilda (her Daughter) . . . . Margery M
Gianetta   Lois Jo
Tessa   Lorna Doone J
Fiametta   } Contadine . . . . Alice F
Vittoria   Bernice F
Giulia   Ruth R
Inez (the King's Foster-Mother) . . . . Helen C

Chorus of Gondoliers and Contadine, Men-at-Arms, Heralds and Pages.

Incidental Dances by Marion Finholt, Naomi Smith, Lee Foley and Boris
Meroff, assisted by Misses Chapman, Corrigan, Davis, Nugent, Vaughn and
Warren and Messrs. Abbott and Strechneff.

Conductor . . . . Franco Autori
Stage Director . . . . Charles Jones

Members of the Chorus: Sopranos—Virginia Beckquist, Ruth Bellinger, Harriet
ham, Helen Brundage, Betty Dando, Josephine Haynes, Anne Kanter, Alice Phi
Edith Trewartha, Ruth Racette, Lucille Wachtel. Contraltos—Ruth Black, A
Brandt, Bernice Fowler, Helen Golden, Doris Moore, Helen Snyder, Erma W
Wilson. Tenors—Earl Alexander, Arnold Isolany, Earl Johnson, Arthur Lind
John Monti, William Ross, James Scott, Robert Dunville, Peter Maltese, Haw
Nelson. Baritones—Walter Hardwick, Claude Martin, John McDonald, Hea
Skoog, Solon West. Basses—Guido Guidi, David Radoff, Carroll van Buskirk,
Weiskoff, Robert Phillips.

SYNOPSIS OF SCENES
Time: 1750
ACT I—The Piazzetta, Venice.
ACT II—Pavilion in the Palace of Barataria.
(An interval of three months is supposed to elapse between
Acts I and II)

WEEK BEGINNING JUNE 2
The Yeomen of the Guard
SEATS AT THE BOX OFFICE NOW

BALDWIN PIANOS USED EXCLUSIVELY

Figure 3.36. Chicago Civic Opera, Season of Light Opera program, 1930. In addition to choosing principal performers, the opera company auditioned hundreds of singers for the chorus, selecting just forty of them. Bernice Fowler was one of the forty. Her favorite performance was of Gilbert and Sullivan's *The Gondoliers*, because in addition to singing in the chorus, she had a small named part and was listed among the principals. On this program, she underlined her name in both places. Among the baritones in the chorus was Walter Hardwick, who would later marry Bernice's friend Grace Diebold, one of three intimate friends Bernice had named Grace. Bernice Fowler Blackwelder Papers.

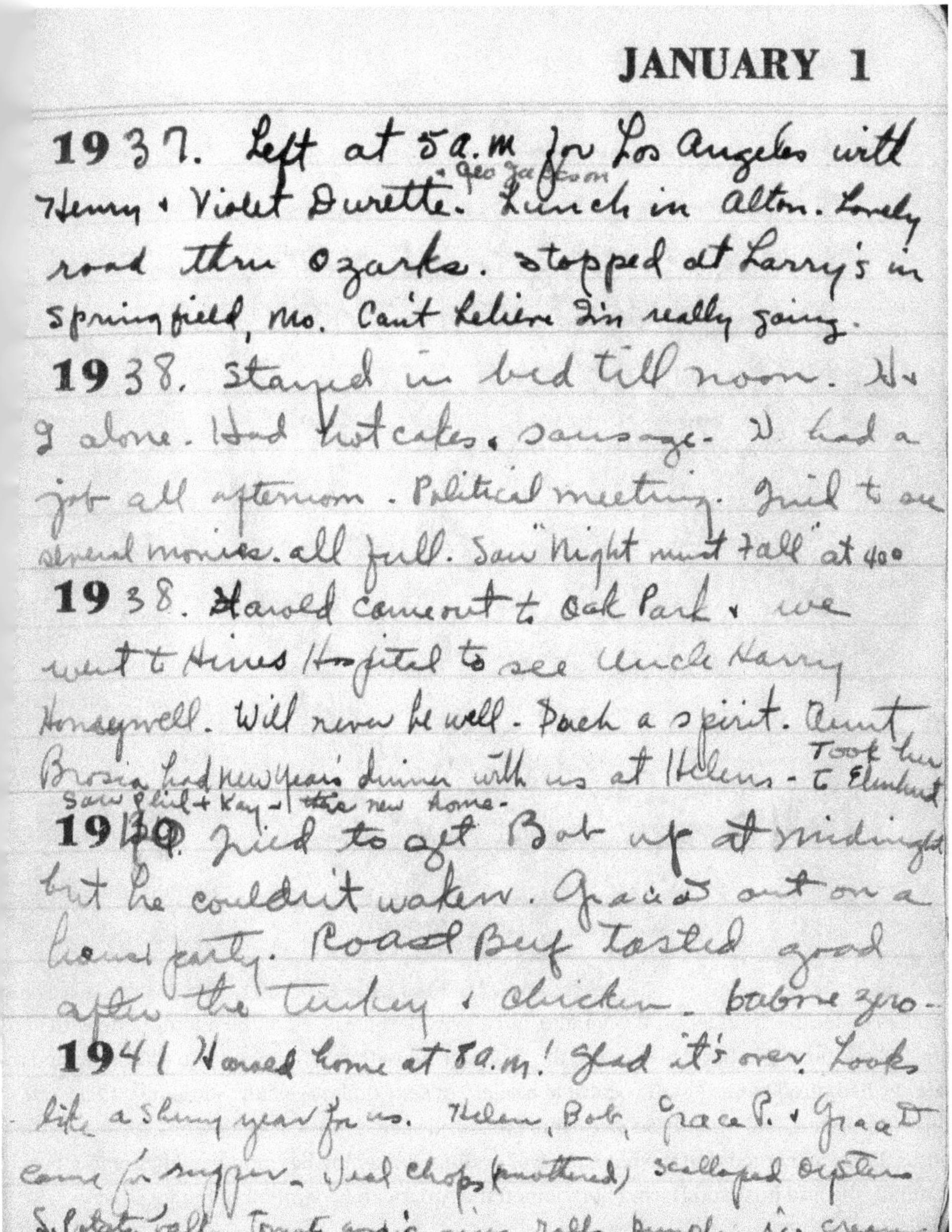

1937. Left at 5 a.m for Los Angeles with Henry & Violet Durette. *Geo Jackson.* Lunch in Alton. Lonely road thru Ozarks. Stopped at Larry's in Springfield, Mo. Can't believe I'm really going.

1938. Stayed in bed till noon. H & I alone. Had hot cakes, sausage. H had a job all afternoon. Political meeting. Tried to see several movies. All full. Saw "Night must fall" at 40¢

1938. Harold came out to Oak Park & we went to Hines Hospital to see Uncle Harry Honeywell. Will never be well. Such a spirit. Aunt Brosia had new year's dinner with us at Helens. *Took her to Elmhurst. Saw Phil & Kay - their new home.*

19¾9. Tried to get Bob up at midnight but he couldn't waken. Grace was out on a house party. Roast Beef tasted good after the turkey & chicken. below zero.

1941 Harold home at 8 a.m! Glad it's over. Looks like a shiny year for us. Helen, Bob, Grace P. & Grace D came for supper. Veal chops (smothered,) scalloped oysters S. Potato balls, tomato aspic ring, rolls. pumpkin ice cream & cookies.

Figure 3.37. Bernice Fowler Blackwelder diary page. In 1937, Bernice started a five-year diary. It was organized so that the same day of each year appeared on the same page. On January 1, 1937, Bernice was driving to the West Coast to join her husband, Harold. In 1938, she was back in Chicago and stayed in bed with Harold until noon. In 1939, she and Harold visited an uncle in the hospital and had dinner at her sister Helen's in Oak Park, a Chicago suburb. In 1940, Bernice was living in Oak Park with Helen, Helen's son Bob, and Helen's sister-in-law Grace Dunn. In 1941, Bernice and Harold had their own apartment in Austin, a neighborhood on Chicago's West Side, and Helen, Bob, and two of Bernice's friends named Grace came for supper. Bernice Fowler Blackwelder Papers.

Figure 3.38. Bernice Fowler Blackwelder on WGN radio, circa 1937. Bernice is left of the microphone with WGN call letters. In February 1937, Bernice received the welcome news that WGN, the radio station owned by the *Chicago Tribune*, had hired her as a staff vocalist at a salary of sixty dollars weekly. She sang on *Pageant of Melody*, a concert program, and *Midday Service*, which featured sacred music and religious speakers. After only seven months, Bernice learned that the noon job was ending, darkening her mood and lightening her pocketbook. That fall, she and husband Harold both joined the American Federation of Radio Artists. Bernice Fowler Blackwelder Papers.

Figure 3.39. Harold Blackwelder as Neil Fortune, Gentleman from the West, circa 1938. Harold performed in many capacities over the course of his musical career, but Neil Fortune was his most memorable persona and most independent venture. In this guise, Harold toured the Midwest and interior West, and then his agent took him to New York. Bernice gave up her job at WGN to join her husband there, but the East Coast debut never materialized. The Blackwelders turned to Harold's father in North Carolina to bail them out. In frustration, Harold found a new booking manager who lined up jobs for him on the West Coast, where Neil Fortune found more enthusiastic audiences, from Vancouver in the north to Los Angeles in the south. The Blackwelders thought they might make new lives for themselves in California, but neither Harold nor Bernice found work in Hollywood, and the Blackwelders limped back to Chicago after begging help again from Harold's father and now from Bernice's brother, Duane, too. Bernice Fowler Blackwelder Papers.

Figure 3.40. Harold Blackwelder's interview pass to Paramount Pictures, 1939. The pass appears to have been signed by Eugene Zukor, son of Paramount founder Adolph Zukor. Aaron Fox, brother of William Fox, who founded Fox Film Corporation (but lost control of it in the Depression), took Harold to the Paramount studios and Selznick International Pictures hoping for an entrée into the film industry, but the two found no takers for Neil Fortune. Aaron Fox may have befriended the Blackwelders in part because he needed a place to live and they had a spare room. Of Fox and the rest of Hollywood, Bernice reflected, "Why must everyone we meet here have to be a heel?" Bernice Fowler Blackwelder Papers.

To Harold & Bernice - with sincere affection - Weaver Bros & "Elviry"

Figure 3.41. Bernice and Harold Blackwelder with the Weaver Brothers and Elviry, 1939. Harold is in the back row on the left, and Bernice is in the second row, third from left of those seated on the bench. To the left of Bernice is her friend Grace Prince. To the right is June Petrie Weaver, who performed as Elviry. The Weaver Brothers, Leon as Abner and Frank as Cicero, sit on the floor on either side of Elviry. The Weaver Brothers and Elviry were vaudeville performers who caricatured the white southern culture that birthed the brothers in the Missouri Ozarks. June married and divorced Leon and then married Frank. This 1939 tour was one of the only times that Bernice and Harold performed together. Bernice felt that a "petty undercurrent of intrigue" poisoned the engagement, though she enjoyed seeing the sights in Oklahoma and Texas. Bernice Fowler Blackwelder Papers.

Figure 3.42. Bernice Fowler Blackwelder with the Vocaliers, circa 1946. Bernice told her brother that the Vocaliers' engagement at a private party in 1947 might be her "swan song." The group also performed for ladies' auxiliaries of fraternal organizations. Bernice is in the middle, with Paula Dohrn to the left and Grace Prince to the right. Grace had lived with Bernice and her husband in the 1930s and earned Bernice's wrath when she moved to Chicago's South Side. The two made up and performed together off and on, including in the 1939 Weaver Brothers and Elviry tour. Bernice Fowler Blackwelder Papers.

Figure 3.43. Harold Blackwelder with the Gentlemen of Note, 1942. This was one of Harold's later ensembles. He is in the middle on bass, with Paul Fay on guitar and Joe Costa on accordion. They are performing for WDSU radio in New Orleans, which operated out of the De Soto Hotel near the French Quarter. A clipping Bernice Blackwelder saved described her husband's group as "in heavy demand for hotel jobs" and "one of the strongest in the cocktail field." Bernice Fowler Blackwelder Papers.

Figure 3.44. Harold Blackwelder with the Gentlemen of Note at Camp Shenango, 1940s. The Gentlemen of Note perform here during World War II at what may have been a United Service Organization show. The venue was Camp Shenango, a personnel replacement depot with impressive leisure facilities, from which African Americans in the segregated military were mostly restricted. In July 1943, tension over these and other indignities sparked a racial conflagration that killed and maimed black soldiers. It is not clear whether the Gentlemen of Note appeared at Camp Shenango before or after the race riot, but it is certain that the presence of performers in blackface contributed to white supremacist attitudes and practices at the depot. Bernice Fowler Blackwelder Papers.

Figure E.1. Quantrille McClu[ng]
and Henry Shearouse, Denve[r]
Public Library, 1983. This pict[ure]
of Quantrille with head libra[rian]
Shearouse was taken the day [of]
her ninety-third birthday, wh[en]
Colorado governor Dick Lam[m,]
by executive order, proclaime[d]
Quantrille McClung Recognit[ion]
The library held a tea for her, [and]
current and former employee[s]
as Denver mayor Bill McNich[ols]
her birthday, the *Denver Post* [ran]
a photo of Quantrille, caption[ed]
"A History Unto Herself." In he[r]
thank-you note to the library,
Quantrille called the day "the
apogee" of her career, adding t[hat]
it "was a natural result when th[e]
Head Person has the fine quali[ties]
of our City Librarian," generou[sly]
granting Shearouse a genderles[s]
title in a profession where wom[en]
predominated in numbers but [not]
in power and prestige. Courtesy
Denver Public Library, Western
History Collection. DPL Archive[s]

Figure E.2. Sudie Mai Hodnette, 1920s. This friend of Quantri[lle]
McClung's is a riddle in the archive Quantrille produced
and divided up, leaving personal materials to the Colorado
Historical Society (now History Colorado) and research files
to the Denver Public Library. In the scrapbooks Quantrille
left to the historical society, Sudie Mai appears in this photo,
which Quantrille captioned "Sudie Mai Hodnette in costume[,]
and also in comic notes from the 1920s in which Sudie Mai
identifies as "Hen Pecked Harry." In the work materials
Quantrille left to the library, Sudie Mai appears in a single 198[1]
letter congratulating Quantrille on the publication of *Memoir[s]*
of My Childhood and Youth in North Denver, a letter that reca[lls]
the bohemian milieu of the 1910s via reference to the 1981 mov[ie]
Reds. In the 1930s, Sudie Mai left Denver for Omaha and then
the San Francisco Bay area, where she worked as a bookkeepe[r]
and was active in hiking clubs. She never married. Courtesy of
History Colorado. Accession no. 30003445.

Part Three

Creating Craftswomen, 1890s–1940s

THE PAST IS ANOTHER PLACE

In the beginning of the century the Indian smoke still mingled with ours. The frontier of the whites was violent, already injured by vast seizures and massacres. The winter nightmares of fear poisoned the plains nights with psychic airs of theft and utopia.

—MERIDEL LE SUEUR, "The Ancient People
  and the Newly Come"

Here the problem wasn't that nothing lasted, but that nothing disappeared.

—KIRSTIN VALDEZ QUADE, "Canute Commands the Tides"

Q uantrille McClung and Bernice Blackwelder first learned of each other's work in the 1950s from a mutual friend, John McCurdy. McCurdy, a lawyer from Lincoln, Kansas, was so enthralled with Kit Carson that, as he aged, he made arrangements to be buried alongside his hero in New Mexico. Carson and his wife Josefa Jaramillo had died in Colorado, and initially they were buried there. But their bodies were soon moved to Taos, where to this day they remain interred in the cemetery that is part of Kit Carson Memorial State Park. McCurdy's wish was granted; he is buried there, too, his headstone engraved, "I am at rest for eternity near my idol Kit Carson."[1]

Bernice and Quantrille were shocked when John died in 1958. He was elderly but not ailing and he died without warning. Only two years earlier, he had introduced the two women. As Bernice wrote in her first letter to Quantrille: "Mr. John J. McCurdy ... has forwarded the information that you are preparing a genealogy of the Carson Family. For some time I have been making a search of records, documents, data and dates in the files of the National Archives and the Library of Congress in the interest of Mr. McCurdy who has made a great study of Kit Carson & is anxious to get an authentic record of his life and activities." Quantrille responded, "I believe that we can cooperate happily on the Carson material."[2] McCurdy never wrote a word about Carson, but he encouraged and even subsidized those who did. He financed some of Bernice's research, and before he died, he told Quantrille that he would cover the cost of a typist to ready her genealogy for publication. His death saddened both women, and it threw Quantrille into turmoil about how to pay for manuscript preparation (eventually, his secretary sent the money her boss had promised). John remained a lodestone for Quantrille and Bernice, and Bernice rarely mentioned him without recalling fondly that he was the person who had brought Quantrille into her life.[3]

It was not until 1972, however, after the two women had been friends for over fifteen years, that Bernice revealed a secret about her relationship with John. The secret was that John, a friend of Bernice's father's, had courted Bernice before she met and married Harold and changed her surname from Fowler to Blackwelder. Bernice Fowler saw John McCurdy now and then when she was growing up in Kansas, but she did not spend time with him as an adult until 1928. That year, she accompanied two other Kansas friends, Bess and Fred Heine, on a trip to John's summer cabin near Beulah, Colorado, and then the four drove to Taos, where they spent a night in a hotel. Bernice was single and twenty-six. John was fifty-three and estranged from his wife. "We were together only one full day," Bernice told Quantrille, though she recalled that John "was in seventh Heaven." Thereafter, John pressed his case with Bernice in a flood of letters, but Bernice refused him. "He seemed to me like an old man of 50," Bernice wrote, with some irony, when she was seventy. In the margin of her letter to Quantrille, Bernice scribbled that she had worn a red dress on the 1928 trip to Taos and that from then on, John called her Red Wing. Quantrille had little direct response to these tales of failed romance, but soon, she began to send Bernice missives addressed to Red Wing. Bernice, on seeing this endearment, reported that she "nearly swooned."[4] Once again, a man became a medium of exchange for the two women, allowing them to create a language of ardor that became their own.

It is possible that this language was not an entirely new tongue for Quantrille. It is also possible that her closeness with Bernice was novel and singular or that the affection they shared resembled the myriad garden-variety female friendships that such women formed over the course of their lives. It is hard to know, because where Bernice waited a decade and a half to tell Quantrille the story of her flirtation with John but then unburdened herself, Quantrille stayed silent about her own younger years. She kept her own council about her past and preserved that quietude for a lifetime. Never once, in the letters from Quantrille to Bernice that have survived, did Quantrille make reference to past intimacies, to roads left untraveled.

Quantrille donated copies of those letters along with research materials from her major genealogical projects—on the Carson, Bent, and Boggs kin and on the families of Colorado governors—to the Denver Public Library (DPL) when she died.[5] Curiously, she donated a batch of older, more personal materials to the Colorado Historical Society (CHS), then located two blocks from the library.[6] There is no way to know why Quantrille left her postretirement research files to her former place of employment, while leaving youthful scrapbooks and photograph albums to the nearby historical society. But the separation of her work papers from her personal papers seems telling. The research files did include her correspondence with Bernice, but those letters maintained Quantrille's customary silence about the intimate aspects of her life. The personal papers she donated to CHS, by contrast, speak more openly, if not always more clearly, about the bonds that linked Quantrille to those around her. In addition, Quantrille—in a rare fit of prose—wrote a memoir of her childhood in North Denver, which the Colorado Genealogical Society published.[7] In other words, Quantrille left behind a puzzle and put various pieces of it in different places for others to find. Consciously and strategically, she created her own archive.[8]

Bernice shaped her own archive, too, but her method was less systematic and purposeful. On occasion, it was also more dramatic. In one theatrical act, she obscured for all time a key part of what might have been a more extensive paper trail: according to her niece Doris Lance, Bernice set fire to her unfinished biographical dictionary of westerners before she died.[9] Bernice's one fleeting claim to minor fame, then, was her book, *Great Westerner*; though it stayed in print less than a decade, it remains on library shelves. And yet, even as she destroyed evidence of her incomplete second book project, Bernice saved memorabilia from the years she spent performing on stage and radio as well as a diary from the same period. Her niece kept these materials and, in turn, gave them to me. Bernice held tightly to her younger years as a performer, and she had no wish to part with the head shots, newspaper clippings, and stage bills that brought it all back. She probably did not expect anyone besides her relations to take interest in her music career after she was gone; the collection she created was a family archive.[10]

Bernice exercised less control over the records her life produced than Quantrille exercised over hers. Bernice likely was unaware that Quantrille had made copies of her own letters and saved Bernice's, intending to add the correspondence to research materials that ended up at DPL. Likewise, Bernice could not have known that an audiotape made in 1953—when she, John McCurdy, and Bess and Fred Heine reunited and retraced the steps of their 1928 trip—would resurface in the 1970s and that it, too, would be included in one of Quantrille's donated collections. On that tape, both Bernice and John referred wistfully to the one magic day they shared in Taos; indeed, Bernice's words were elegiac.[11]

These materials, archived intentionally and unintentionally, point to a complex past that informed the work Quantrille McClung and Bernice Blackwelder did to preserve—in fact, to create—memory of Kit Carson and other male westerners. Their historical practice and the knowledge they produced reflected more than the social, cultural, intellectual, economic, and political contexts of the 1950s, '60s, and '70s. Long lives animated the work these women did in the middle and later years of those lives.

For example, Bernice's own disappointments in love and labor goaded her as she made sense of Kit Carson's life with Josefa Jaramillo and his career in the West.[12] And as the child of a father who was a Union Pacific physician and of a mother who sang in a railroad town's church choir, Bernice thought in particular ways about place and time, about performance and the modern—even as those thoughts shaped her determination to quit Kansas and seek out the spotlight that a singing career in Chicago seemed to promise. Marriage to Harold, a fellow performer from North Carolina, at first nurtured that career, as did their decision to live in unconventional households with other musicians. But when new venues for entertainers together with Harold's latest scheme for making a living dashed Bernice's dreams, she rolled with the punches, moving farther east and taking a job with the CIA. By the time she began her work on Carson, then, Bernice's life as a transplanted white woman from the Great Plains who had wed a transplanted white man from the Upper South, as well as all the constrained choices in work and romance and residence she had made over the years, informed her traffic in western men.

As for Quantrille, what appeared to be her lifelong status as a single woman masked a young adulthood of uncertain, queered couplings and, more generally and more like Bernice, dewy years of spark and desire.[13] For Quantrille, these years were complicated by chronic illness and responsibility for her aging parents. She found a suitable job for a woman of her many conditions: she became a librarian. In her spare time, she did church work, especially work devoted to foreign missions. But the status of librarian and mission enthusiast masks as much as the status of single woman: Quantrille saved memorabilia from library parties, for instance, that hardly bespoke the hushed voices and reverent tones one might expect from a bookish Methodist dedicated to fostering literacy at home and spreading the gospel abroad. Gin with beer chasers, tipsy couples cavorting, jealous threesomes shooting daggers—all figure in that memorabilia, as do handsome women got up in male attire. In Quantrille's scrapbooks, a white gentleman friend appears at her side, hovers briefly, and then seems to disappear; so, too, does a white woman friend. Other female friends endure, along with their calling cards and love notes, their photographs and poems—but at a similar distance. Meanwhile, Quantrille lived for ninety-five years in the diverse urban center of the interior West, but she also kept in view what she inherited from her parents, who came to Denver from the rural Middle West. All of this shaped the woman who became, as she aged, Carson's spry genealogist.

Here, too, historical contexts matter, stretching from 1890, when Quantrille was born (Bernice entered the world twelve years later, in 1902), through the 1950s, when John McCurdy introduced the two women and their collaboration as western historians began.[14] The West itself, where both women were born and raised, was an end product of a process of incorporation. By that process, long-inhabited western places violently changed hands and eventually landed, and then remained, in those of the United States. Western places came to be linked to one another and to eastern urban centers by economic and cultural ties clearly reflected in both a major metropolis such as Denver, where Quantrille lived, and a beleaguered Kansas railroad town such as Brookville, Bernice's home. White women like Bernice and Quantrille, too, were emblematic of changes under way among U.S. women, changes that offered new opportunities for education and employment, new possibilities for political participation, new models for intimate relationships, and new avenues for self-expression. Their whiteness itself—"white" was a newly reconsolidated racial category that insisted on its own normativity and superiority—set them apart from nonwhite residents and former residents of the places they called home. But that separation and its associated privileges played out differently in small-town Kansas than in Denver's dense human geography. And Bernice was not long for Brookville; she left for college ninety miles west in 1920. Thereafter, work and residence took her all over the country—that is, everywhere and anywhere but Kansas.

Place, gender, and race all shaped Quantrille's and Bernice's life choices and chances, but nothing drew the contours of their daily lives more than the economic ebb and flow of the twentieth century. Both of these women came of age in arguably middle-class families but families that were less secure in that class position than they might have wished. Bernice's relatives recalled that there were not enough funds for all the Fowler children to attend college, for example, though the Fowlers were likely better situated than the McClungs. The McClungs took in boarders to make ends meet, while the Fowlers enjoyed the services of a live-in housekeeper. Quantrille's father was unemployed for a time when she was a young woman, and Quantrille ended up living with her parents until they died, contributing to the family economy through her earnings as a librarian. Both the Fowlers and the McClungs owned their houses. When the Great Depression struck in the 1930s, Quantrille and her reemployed father maintained their incomes and held on to their home. Meanwhile, Bernice had just married Harold Blackwelder in Chicago, and the two commenced their peripatetic lives as singers in an ever-changing world of entertainment. Radio, stage, and other live performance work continued through the 1930s and '40s. Ever so briefly, their labor found protection through union membership; both joined the American Federation of Radio Artists when it formed in 1937. After World War II, however, when television became the medium of choice for entertainers and audiences alike, Harold and Bernice could no longer support themselves. That is when they left Chicago and moved to Washington, D.C. Harold opened a barbecue joint, and Bernice took a job with the CIA, dabbling in history during her spare time. A few years later, John McCurdy told Bernice Blackwelder of a former librarian who was compiling records about Kit Carson's kin. That Denver librarian had retired on disability, and her city pension as well as the proceeds from the sale of her parents' home allowed Quantrille McClung to pursue her passion for genealogy.

I lived through none of the times when these two women came of age and embarked on their life's work, nor did my forebears dwell in western places. I may have learned to walk in a ranch house designed in keeping with the postwar nation's westward tilt—from popular culture's fascination with the frontier to modern migrations that swelled western cities to suburban home styles that beat to the drum of the new Sunbelt.[15] But Blackwelder and McClung were heirs of an actual West. As they wrestled with Carson, they wrestled with that inheritance, as moderately rich as it was for them and theirs, as decidedly poor as it was for many westerners, as convertible as it was across a century that made all things new again. And again. And again.

Inheriting the Old West

The town where Bernice Harriet Fowler grew up has seen better days—but not for a long time. The home where she spent her childhood is either going or gone, depending on which Brookville resident one asks. Just west of town, another house she must have frequented and where she may have lived has left no trace on the land. In late summer, the place where that home stood is a study in grass and grasshoppers, singing in the morning sun.[16] Nearby, cottonwoods lean over Spring Creek, which bisects the old eighty-acre Fowler plot (in public-land survey terms, half of a quarter section). But the creek flows with scant conviction. Stagnant pools stand in spots; so, too, do canted slabs of concrete, remnants of some hopeful human scheme, now forgotten. If the creek is a sorry excuse for a waterway, there are other, more imposing features on this lot: A railroad runs through it. So does a highway. The railroad gave Wilbur Fowler, Bernice's father, a living, and in 1920 it took Bernice away for good. The highway brought her back as an adult, but she did not linger; like many who travel the Great Plains, she was just passing through. By 1972 she could write, "Strange how I keep tied to Kansas, tho there is no one left there of my kin. I really would rather not ever go back there."[17] She never did.

How different the cityscapes where Quantrille Day McClung came of age. She lived in several houses growing up, but two were more permanent residences, and until recently, both still stood in North Denver—the area northwest of the South Platte River, which flows out of the Rocky Mountains and through the city.[18] Quantrille was born in a tiny frame house a mile from downtown. The "shanty," as her parents called it, perched on a sparsely populated hill where unclaimed lots sported wildflowers and prairie grasses; in the draw, cattails grew. When she was three, her parents replaced the shanty with a small but sturdy brick house, which a century later still reflected the modest means and domestic aspirations of its first occupants. Those aspirations took the McClungs, when Quantrille was thirteen, ten blocks north and west to a Dutch colonial revival house (with its distinctive barnlike roof line). Quantrille lived in that home and helped to maintain its stolid respectability for more than four decades. The street names where she dwelled have changed—from Bell to Osage, and from Goss to Tejon. They now sound more western than they ever did in her youth, echoing as they do Indigenous and Spanish pasts. But the Tejon house remains, a steadfast marker of the dreams that built an urban West at the corner of commerce and desire. Quantrille never left Denver.

These, then, were the Wests that Bernice and Quantrille inherited. As for Bernice, she did not "keep tied" only to Kansas; she linked herself to a longer family history, and the bond she formed was one that braided pioneer pride, the thrill of borderland adventure, and a deep identification with her father. The whole frontier experience of the Fowlers, her father's family, and the Knapps, her mother's, enthralled her. On the Knapp side, Bernice traced her ancestry to New England and especially to Hannah Dustin of Haverhill, Massachusetts, taken captive by Abenaki Indians in the late seventeenth century. Dustin famously slew her captors and paddled home down the Merrimack River in a canoe.[19] On the Fowler side, Bernice followed her forebears to colonial Virginia, especially those with the surname Donelson (or Donalson); Rachel Donelson married future president Andrew Jackson, who advanced the U.S. policy by which Indigenous peoples of eastern North America were removed to the West in the 1830s.[20] A closer relative, Israel Donalson (Bernice's great-great-grandfather and, apparently, Rachel's uncle), was one of many male branches of the family tree who spent part of their work lives surveying western lands. In the late eighteenth century, Shawnees seized Israel as he marked out territory in Ohio. Like Hannah, Israel escaped. Remarking on her forebears' captivities, Bernice told Quantrille, "The Indians were after us on all sides."[21] These words reflected such a common ideological inversion of the history of white westward movement that Bernice did not recognize their deep irony.[22] Little wonder, then, that she went to her grave believing that invasion and conquest were necessary and inevitable and that Indigenous people were obstacles to those processes.

And yet, Bernice simultaneously held views incompatible with a frontier history imagined as white people besieged by Indians. When she and Harold took a vacation in 1975, driving from Chicago to North Carolina through Great Smoky Mountains National Park and the adjacent lands of the Eastern Band of the Cherokee Nation, Bernice told Quantrille that it made her "almost ill to realize" that Cherokees "had been forced to move to Ark[ansas] and Oklahoma" (the Cherokee people Bernice saw in North Carolina, of course, descended from those who avoided removal). The next day, Bernice and Harold visited the Hermitage, the Nashville-area retreat of Andrew Jackson and Bernice's distant relative Rachel Donelson Jackson, a federal-style brick structure that Jackson remodeled into a Greek revival mansion. Bernice did not remark on the connection between that "elegant" house and the diminished presence of Cherokee people nearby (nor that between the house and the hundreds of black slaves Jackson owned).[23] Like many twentieth-century white Americans who grew up in a nation that had relocated and then segregated Native peoples through the reservations established in the nineteenth century, Bernice could separate sad stories of Indian removal from happy stories of white people and their imposing white houses, as if the two tales were not inextricably bound.[24]

More often, though, when Bernice discussed her frontier heritage, she spoke of her parents' lives and especially her father's. She credited her interest in history to her father, whom she saw as a "knowledgeable man in a historically interesting location."[25] That location was along the route of the Kansas Pacific Railroad, which, by the 1880s when Wilbur Fowler came into the country, had consolidated with the Union Pacific. Builders conceived of the east–west route, which followed the old Smoky Hill Trail that had taken would-be miners to the Colorado goldfields, as one that would provide access to Rocky Mountain resources via Denver. The Kansas prairie through which the railroad passed was not foremost in the builders' minds, and all told, the Union Pacific founded only four towns along the route constructed across the western two-thirds of the state; Brookville, where Bernice was born, was one of these towns.[26]

Wilbur Fowler, born in Minnesota but raised in rural Indiana and Missouri, did his schooling at the University of Michigan and Rush Medical College in Chicago before returning to practice medicine briefly in Missouri and then moving on to Kansas.[27] He was a country boy who took part in the postbellum surge of professionalization that, together with urbanization and an increasingly corporate capitalism, remade the U.S. middle class. The consolidation of the Kansas Pacific and Union Pacific and Brookville's ties to cities east and west were part of that transformation. But Wilbur ended up back in the country, practicing his profession as one of the few big fish in a small-town pond. His ties to the new urban middle class were attenuated.[28] First employed as a physician for the Union Pacific west of Brookville at Russell, Wilbur and his young wife Hattie Knapp Fowler soon relocated to Spring Creek Township.[29] They arrived in the agricultural boom of the 1880s, and they must have envisioned a bright future along Spring Creek just beyond Brookville's town center, where Wilbur and brother Arthur purchased the eighty acres that both creek and railroad crossed. By the 1890s, the boom busted and western Kansas (Brookville sat near the eastern edge of western Kansas) became the depressed landscape depicted in the 1900 novel *The Wonderful Wizard of Oz*.[30] To make matters worse, Hattie died in 1896 after bearing two sons (one perished as a toddler and the other died of tuberculosis as a young man).[31] So Wilbur traveled east to Green Ridge, Missouri, Hattie's home, and married her younger sister Mabel. Mabel returned to Kansas with Wilbur, and there they raised three children, Helen, Bernice, and Duane. The children excelled in music, taking after their mother, who sang in the church choir.[32]

Brookville never amounted to much. In 1889, when new technologies allowed trains to travel longer distances between service stops, the Union Pacific closed facilities at Brookville that had prompted its growth.[33] Between 1890 and 1900, Spring Creek Township lost population.[34] By 1910, Wilbur was running a drugstore in town alongside his medical practice. But Mabel worked in the store, too; a census taker in 1930 listed her as proprietor. The Fowlers must have made a decent living, because their household, when the children were small, included a domestic servant. And, according to Bernice, her parents owned the first automobile in Brookville, a red Cadillac.[35] Still, Bernice's most vivid memory growing up was of the family's large yard, where, as she put it, "my father raised, besides his three offspring, guinea pigs, bantam roosters, pigeons and other off-beat animals."[36] The creatures must have provided endless amusement for the Fowler children, but none of those youngsters stayed in Kansas as adults.

Nonetheless, Bernice remained enchanted by her father's memory.

When she saw a copy of *Pioneer History of Kansas* by Adolph Roenigk, she devoured it, connecting her father's experience at Russell in the 1880s to that of Roenigk, who worked there under very different circumstances in the 1860s, when Cheyennes, black and white cavalrymen, and buffalo all frequented the newly laid Kansas Pacific tracks at what was then called Fossil Creek Station.[37] That time was long past when Wilbur Fowler cared for railroad crews at Russell and then Brookville, but Bernice thrilled to find names of older men she had known as a child, "who were fighting Indians when they were young settlers."[38] Her father, Bernice told Quantrille, "really loved that country and was proud to have been a part of the pioneering."[39] These kinds of tales excited her more than those she recalled about her mother. In 1971, Bernice and Harold visited her mother's birthplace in Galesburg, Illinois, and then drove southwest along the route that the Knapp family had traveled by covered wagon to Green Ridge, Missouri, where her parents met. That trip did give Bernice "a warm and sweet feeling."[40] But it was her father's life that generally informed her attachment to the past: "Just working on history seems to bring him closer to me—more so than my mother, although she was unselfish and played a devoted role."[41] Having had to play that role herself too often, Bernice identified more with her father and his self-satisfaction at having played a manful role in the frontier's last gasp.[42] All this would later inform Bernice's encounter with Kit Carson, her great westerner.

Quantrille McClung had a less romantic relationship to her own western history, and she did not embrace the past embodied in her father any more or less than she held her mother's heritage dear. This was true even though the daily division of household labor, both material and emotional, was probably similar in the Fowler and McClung families. And although she was a genealogist who was as keen on her own ancestry as she was on that of men like Carson, when she wrote to Bernice, Quantrille seldom referred to the deep history of her people's westward march and never to forebears who fought with Indians. Quantrille's father, Benjamin Franklin McClung, descended from white folks who had migrated from the mid-Atlantic through Ohio and Illinois, where Benjamin was born, and then to Iowa, where he was raised on a Muscatine County farm. Her mother, Henrietta Gutzman McClung, called Hattie, was born to Prussian farmers who settled near Atchison, Kansas, a German stronghold.[43]

Quantrille remained tied to her mother's German-immigrant and Kansas-farm heritage. Hattie's sisters visited from Kansas; Quantrille went there as a child to see relatives; and every year when autumn filled the air, her family received a barrel from the Gutzman farm that would outfit them for the holidays. Quantrille recalled that the barrel "contained a dressed turkey for Thanksgiving, a goose for Christmas and a chicken for New Year's. There would also be a large lump of butter securely wrapped in cheese cloth. There would be potatoes, onions, apples and possibly a few pears." It was not only farm-raised food that linked her to the immigrant homestead; Quantrille also learned to speak the language of her maternal kin when her parents sent her to Sunday school at a German church (rather than at the family's English-language Methodist parish). And, while Quantrille entered the world in 1890 with the assistance of a physician—Dr. Edward Day, from whom Quantrille's parents took her middle name, Day—when brother Denzel was born six years later, Hattie McClung hired a German midwife.[44] Even Quantrille's unusual first name came from her mother's family. Many assumed that her given name had some relation to the guerrilla fighter William Quantrill, whose Confederate raiders sacked the antislavery stronghold of Lawrence, Kansas, during the U.S. Civil War. But Hattie named her first child Quantrille at the suggestion of her sister, who came to Denver for the birth and convinced Hattie to name the baby after Quantrille Sallee, a woman from St. Joseph, Missouri (just across the Missouri River from the Gutzman farm), someone Hattie's sister admired.[45]

Quantrille's father may not have been so taken with his sister-in-law's suggestion. When Quantrille started school, a teacher questioned her about her first name, and Quantrille replied that her father "had always called her 'John.'"[46] Indeed, Quantrille was convinced that when her mother conceived, her father hoped that their first child would be a boy. Quantrille even wondered if some of her passions could be attributed to her father's dreams. Railroads thrilled her, for instance, and she mused, "I don't know whether I acquired my interest naturally or whether my father deliberately taught me to love trains because of his disappointment that I was not a boy."[47] Whatever Benjamin McClung's gender preference for his offspring, he did take an active role in Quantrille's upbringing. He taught her to read and write before she started school, using newspapers and the Bible. So closely did she associate literacy with her father that when she learned to write a new letter of the alphabet, she would wait for him to come home from work and rush with pencil in hand to meet him. On one such occasion, Quantrille fell pell-mell and drove the pencil into her forehead. The injury was minor. In years to come, as she recalled, it was hard for her father to keep her supplied with reading material. In addition, because he was employed by a Denver wholesale dealer, Struby-Estabrook Mercantile, Benjamin satisfied her equally endless desire for novel ephemera by bringing home advertising cards and other consumer premiums.[48] Quantrille/John got on well with her/his father, and this bond, so deeply internalized, shaped the bookish, independent, but also filial career woman that Quantrille became.

Benjamin and Hattie McClung introduced young Quantrille to a wider world in Denver, a railroad hub of over 106,000 residents (and expanding), than Bernice could access as a child in Brookville, a town of about 250 (and contracting) served by a single rail line.[49] At a remove of eighty years, Quantrille described that wider world in the memoir she wrote about her childhood. In it, she narrates "going over town," that is, walking from her North Denver home to the city center past a kaleidoscope of urban enterprise, spirituality, and sociability. The homes of neighbors—folks of German, Italian, Irish, and Anglo American origin and descent—quickly gave way to larger establishments. One of the first was Mother Francesca Cabrini's school and orphanage, established when the local priest called Cabrini to minister to the burgeoning community of Italian immigrant workers in North Denver (Mother Cabrini was later canonized; she is considered the patron saint of immigrants). After the school came a drugstore; a general store; a car line that ran out to the smelter complex at Argo; a meat market; a blacksmith's shop; a firehouse; the bridge that crossed the South Platte; a soap factory; a potter's shop; River Front Park, with its castle-like Exposition Building; the wholesale house of Struby-Estabrook, where Quantrille's father worked; Union Station and its beloved trains; a private mint; a Chinese folk temple; and, finally, the shopping district at Larimer Street, with its dry goods, stationery, souvenir, cigar, and other specialty stores. Quantrille explained that her parents hurried her past Market Street, where, in addition to perusing wholesale produce, men could purchase pleasure at brothels and saloons—though the McClungs did stop in to see the Chinese laundry there. In the heart of the city, they might encounter American Indians, African Americans, or even, as Quantrille put it, "a group of persons from the Middle East in their national costume."[50]

Quantrille reacted to this pulsing heart of commerce, industry, and migration in both predictable and surprising ways, though it is hard to sort her responses as a child from those she called to memory when writing about her experiences at the nether end of the century. Quantrille lived for ninety-five years and witnessed a nation's grappling with the legacies of colonialism and imperialism, slavery and emancipation, dispossession and diaspora, urbanization and industrialization. All of this shaped her adult understanding of the scenes she saw as a child. So, too, did the consumer revolution, which many of those scenes embodied. Nonetheless, something of a child's wonder and warmth creeps through descriptions that are otherwise couched in parental and community admonitions about who and what belonged where in a turn-of-the-twentieth-century city graded by human hierarchies. Likewise, wonder and warmth creep through Quantrille's own late twentieth-century mindset, informed (even disciplined) as it was by post–World War II struggles that challenged such hierarchies.

Quantrille spent much of her childhood, for instance, near the heart of Denver's Little Italy. At a time when Italians, like other newcomers from southern and eastern Europe, were finding their way in a racialized order that positioned them as provisionally white industrial workers beholden to their so-called social betters, Quantrille recognized the medium-range distance her parents kept from their immigrant neighbors. Recalling the family story of an Italian man who tried to court Hattie McClung's sister when she visited from Kansas, Quantrille declared, "Needless to say, he had no luck." Similarly, Quantrille remembered the Cafaretta family, which consisted of a "very respectable saloon keeper" and his "beautifully dressed" wife and daughter, who attended school with Quantrille. "My mother's sort spoke to them, and that was all," Quantrille wrote, "and I was not allowed to play with my schoolmate." Quantrille, however, quietly distinguished herself from her "mother's sort" by devoting many pages to Italian neighbors and their churches, their black calico dresses, their white lace bed linens, their swaddled babies, their noisy nighttime altercations, their beautiful truck gardens, their outdoor ovens, their pasta factories, their fragrant tomato paste drying in the autumn sun, and their flavorful dandelion wine. As a final rebuke to her "mother's sort," Quantrille noted that years later, as a young librarian, she was assigned to Little Italy's library station, adding, "It was a great satisfaction to think that I could serve the community in which I had been born and where I had spent my childhood."[51]

Quantrille's respectful recollections of North Denver's Little Italy might reflect the process by which Italian immigrants became ever more securely white in the twentieth century, as understandings of whiteness in the United States expanded to incorporate recent arrivals from southern and eastern Europe, to the benefit of Italians, Greeks, and Russian Jews and to the detriment of those whose descendants would be called African Americans, American Indians, Asian Americans, and Latinos.[52] Some of her references to black, Chinese, and Native people suggest that this was the case. But others suggest that while Quantrille was no stranger to notions of racial difference and hierarchy, she sometimes struggled with those notions and experimented with revising them.

Her childhood experiences with Indigenous people were weighed down by a recent history that Quantrille probably glimpsed only darkly. Actual Indian people walking down the street, cigar-store wooden Indians, Indian encampments set up as displays in City Park—all seemed to affect her similarly, as if Native people were less human residents of Denver than relics of a time gone by.[53] Indeed, of all the racialized people Quantrille wrote about in her memoirs, Indians, some of whom had called the South Platte drainage home just decades earlier, seemed most misplaced in Denver, reflecting the white habit of divorcing Indigenous people from the urban lives that so many of them actually lived.[54] Apparently out of place in what often was, in fact, their own backyard, Indians in the city proved endlessly interesting to Quantrille.

Meanwhile, Quantrille's discussions of African Americans in Denver were rare, reflecting the small black population there, the racism that maintained distance between blacks and whites, and the city's racial geography; black neighborhoods emerged northeast of the city center, while Quantrille grew up to the northwest. But she vividly recalled a porter named Ellick who worked with her father at Struby-Estabrook. Ellick "made a great fuss" over Quantrille, who, when she thought back on it, reflected, "It must have been strange to see the small golden-haired child in her white dress trimmed in hand-crocheted lace in the arms of the big black man in his dirty overalls." Heightening the difference between them by emphasizing her clean dress and the porter's dingy pants, and freighting what was as much a contrast of class, age, and gender with the baggage of race and respectability, Quantrille nonetheless recalled her connection to Ellick as a "lesson in good race relations." And she followed this story with another about a black man she met when out walking with her parents. During the promenade, she was distracted by children who beckoned from a window. Excited, she cried, "Look!" and grabbed the hand of the nearest adult. When she glanced up, she recalled, she was "holding hands with a good looking, nicely dressed negro gentleman." All the adults present, black and white, smiled at the confused child, who later remembered herself as "embarrassed, not that I had been holding the hand of a colored person but that I had made a mistake." She concluded, "I always carried a pleasant memory of this gentleman," adding, "He may have had a little girl too."[55] Quantrille probably did not know much about African American struggles in early twentieth-century Colorado; though more affluent than their counterparts in many eastern cities, Denver blacks faced discrimination and white racism when they stepped outside their own communities.[56] But in her memoir, Quantrille not only retraced the heavy horizontal lines that divided her from and placed her above African Americans; she also sketched the tenuous human ties that linked her to the tenderhearted fathers of black Denver.

Likewise, Quantrille's encounters with Chinese immigrants in Denver prompted, when she wrote about them later in life, both predictable racializations (Chinese men sporting "pigtails") and thoughtful reflection on cultural practices that she realized she only dimly understood. She described a McClung family visit to a local cemetery, for instance, during which she happened upon a Chinese burial. When the mourners departed, she saw that they had left a table with "food placed upon a neatly spread cloth" along with "joss sticks and paper flowers." The scene moved her, and she noted, "Not one of us touched anything." Similarly, she visited a Chinese temple, which white people called a "joss house," and was pleased that "it was always impressed upon me that this was a kind of church and I must show the greatest respect." Some of what Quantrille came to know about Denver's Chinese community she learned from a business associate of her father's, a tobacco salesman for Chinatown. This man, whom the McClungs called Sam (he did not enjoy the dignity of a full name in family memory), took Quantrille and her brother on tours of temples, courtyards, private altars, opium houses, and Chinese groceries. Her account of those tours was replete with descriptions of difference—"strange Chinese coins" and "lugubrious" stringed instruments—but also with expressions of gratitude: "I hope Mr. Sam understood how wonderful all this had been for us."[57] Full of wonder, Quantrille the child spoke to and through the adult she became, an adult who displayed curiosity about the West and its many peoples—sometimes in spite and sometimes because of her own white selfhood and the racial privilege that brought that self into being.

If Hattie and Benjamin McClung introduced Quantrille to the wide world that converged in central Denver, they also moved her farther away from that preternatural node as she grew up. From the modest house on Bell Street, the McClungs moved west and north in stages, finally settling in the Dutch colonial revival house on Goss Street in 1903. Or as Quantrille put it, "We gradually worked our way up the hill."[58] This phrasing did not just reflect the increased elevation of each successive dwelling. It also reflected a rise in class status and proximity to more well-to-do neighbors. Along the way, the McClungs likewise transitioned from an outhouse to running water and a flush toilet and then to what Quantrille called a "really modern bathroom" on Goss Street, a consequence of both changing technologies and growing financial ease.[59] The new neighborhood still had a rural flavor; the McClungs raised chickens, and another family grew corn and raised livestock (the McClungs bought milk from them, and one of their children, Jack Smith, later in life helped prepare Quantrille's memoirs for publication).[60] All of this brought new social interactions: "When we were living on Goss Street, we seemed to know more about the neighbors than we had ever known before. This was partly due to the type of neighbors we had and partly to the fact that I was getting older and could know people better and appreciate them."[61] Those people included the Seerie family, Scottish immigrants whose menfolk were contractors who built the Colorado State Capitol and myriad other local structures. The Seeries also owned property in Platte Canyon that became the site of the family's mountain retreat. Quantrille visited there often. The urban meanderings of Quantrille's childhood gave way to rural getaways such as this, where she enjoyed amenities financed by others, far from the dense human tapestry that had once fascinated her in Denver.[62]

Quantrille must have appreciated such gratis creature comforts in her teens and twenties, when affliction visited the McClungs. First, in 1906, when Quantrille was sixteen, she contracted meningitis, which forced her to drop out of school and left her with headaches and other debilitating symptoms that continued for the rest of her life. A kinetic and voracious learner, Quantrille was loath to leave the classroom. Within a few years, though, in 1911, she felt well enough to start a training course, the first ever offered, for employment at the new Denver Public Library. Her family could not have been more fortunate, because a couple of years later, Struby-Estabrook, where Benjamin McClung had long worked, without warning closed its doors. In her memoir, Quantrille wrote little about these two calamities, referring to the onset of her illness only as the moment when "the blow fell" and noting sarcastically and cryptically Benjamin's response to sudden unemployment: "My father felt this a good time to take a vacation so he went to California to visit relatives." Quantrille's childhood was over.[63] Hattie McClung did, in 1896, bear the son that Quantrille was sure her father had wanted in 1890, but in the 1910s, it was Quantrille, not her brother, Denzel, whose breadwinning helped sustain the family.

A dozen years separated Quantrille McClung's birth from that of Bernice Fowler, so their childhoods spanned different decades. Quantrille embarked on the training that would prepare her for her life's work in 1911, while Bernice did not leave Brookville for college until 1920. And while both women grew up in western places, those places were as different as land and water. But like land and water, Denver and Brookville met; they were linked, quite literally, by the train tracks that passed through the Fowler lot west of Brookville and extended to the railyard that so transfixed Quantrille as a child. Both youngsters grew up in a world that railroads made, even as they were connected to a frontier past that moved at a different pace, one set by horse hooves and wagon wheels. The places Bernice and Quantrille inhabited were defined by dissimilar demographics, and so each child met up with different kinds of people in her daily life. Bernice's Brookville was far more homogenous than Quantrille's Denver; the Cheyenne raiders and black cavalrymen who once frequented the Kansas Pacific line were gone, and traces of the colonial violence that had brought them there in the 1860s were now figments of white men's memories. Denver, by contrast, bore the visible traces of past and present migrations and of the commerce and industry that gave those migrations birth. By 1903, Quantrille's parents had the means to move a bit farther away from that maelstrom but only by a matter of blocks. Bernice's parents enjoyed the professional status that Dr. Fowler's medical practice and drugstore provided, even as Brookville drifted in a steady decline. As both women came of age, the West they inherited from the past continued to shape them, even as the West continued to change.

New Woman in a New West

Her long hair pulled back beneath a bowler hat, but with golden wisps framing her neatly mustached face, Quantrille McClung mugs for the camera in dark trousers and jacket, a floppy men's tie at the neck.[64] She sits cross-legged on what might be a Navajo rug, a cigarette in the left hand and a German beer stein in the right. Quantrille is twenty-three, and she looks hale and hearty alongside her three female friends, who are similarly posed and attired. Behind them on the wall is a framed picture of the late Rabbi Elias Hillkowitz, father of Anna Hillkowitz, one of Quantrille's fellow librarians.[65] This scene—which someone captured in two paired photographs—likely unfolded in the rented home Anna shared with her brother Philip, a Denver physician, and her sister Ella.[66] Anna was ten years older than Quantrille and was already working at the Denver Public Library (DPL) when Quantrille began her own career in 1911. In late 1913 or early 1914, Anna hosted a group of costumed librarians in what they called a "Bohemian Party." Quantrille pasted the snapshots from the party on a black page of a photograph album and, in the dark space between them, she used a white pencil to caption the scene "In Gay Bohemia."

Bernice Fowler did something similar, probably a decade later, affixing seven photographs in the same sort of album.[67] In those pictures, Bernice wears an overcoat, slouch hat, trousers, and boots, and in some shots she grips a pipe or a whiskey bottle. She stands and she kneels, she hoists a wooden wheelbarrow and she sits in an old buggy with feet propped up on the door. She and her female friends pose near a ragged fence and a rough-hewn outbuilding. The friends appear in a variety of getups, from a soldier's tunic and garrison cap to an Indian blanket, headband, and braids and from the tuxedo and top hat of affluent manhood to the Edwardian dresses and frighteningly large hair bows of respectable girlhood. Bernice's moustache is not as artful as Quantrille's, but her varied postures suggest that she has studied men who labor out of doors and recline in women's arms. In one photo, Bernice, on bended knee, looks up at a friend, one of only two pictured who wear conventional womanly garb. She is seated, and workingman Bernice has placed folded hands beseechingly on her lap, as if to pray for her attentions. The soldier boy drapes an arm possessively around the same female prize, even as the Edwardian girls lavish him with affection. No captions grace these pictures, but they were probably taken in the town of Hays, ninety miles west of Brookville, where Bernice attended Fort Hays Kansas Normal College.[68] These were her classmates.

Denver librarians in the 1910s and Kansas college students in the 1920s, then, staged not dissimilar scenes; Quantrille figured in one and Bernice in the other. Specifics of time and place for both sets of images matter, however, and they point to different moments and divergent milieux. Among the transformations that separated those images historically was the Great War—the global conflict that erupted in 1914 and later became known as World War I—as well as the changes that war bequeathed to those who survived it. What separated the images spatially was not just the 350 miles between Denver and Hays but also the urban tapestry captured in Quantrille's album and the raw Great Plains college town captured in Bernice's. And while both sets of images depict early twentieth-century white women of some means kicking around in contemporary conventions of gender in ways that their mothers had not attempted and upon which their fathers might have frowned, every term of that equation varies according to the image: the decade, the whiteness, the women, the means, the conventions, the quality of the kick, and the mothers and fathers themselves. Accordingly, photos of Quantrille and Bernice in drag foreground the journeys the women took through young adulthoods that spanned the early years of what would come to be called the American Century. The photos also prefigure their later traffic in men and things male.

Quantrille's journey started first. At twenty-one, having seen to her own education since meningitis had forced her to leave school, Quantrille entered the first apprentice class organized in a brand new DPL building. The library was young when Quantrille began her training. It dated from 1899, when an older, exclusive Mercantile Library, directed by the conservative Charles Dudley and located in the city's chamber of commerce building, consolidated with a newer, more progressive public library housed in East Denver High School. But there was precedent for the training Quantrille received in 1911. The library at the high school, under the leadership of innovator John Cotton Dana, had sponsored classes for librarians; Anna Hillkowitz as well as Helen Ingersoll, another of Quantrille's mentors, attended them. According to Ingersoll, she and Hillkowitz were two of three young women who passed the entrance exam for the training course of 1898. Ingersoll chose this career route after the Panic of 1893 left her family in financial straits, dashing her hopes of attending the University of Denver.[69] When DPL settled into an impressive Greek revival building financed by the city as well as industrialist Andrew Carnegie a dozen years later, ten young women with like aspirations and perhaps similarly limited resources passed an entrance exam and began their studies. Quantrille was among them, having responded with ease to test questions that included U.S. history ("In what foreign wars has the United States been engaged since the year 1800?"), current affairs ("What reasons have been given for the mobilization of United States troops in Texas?"), state economy ("Tell the different sources of Colorado's wealth"), civic improvements ("How would the proposed Moffat tunnel affect Denver?"), historical figures ("For what were the following persons noted? Abraham Lincoln; Daniel Webster; Napoleon; Bismarck; Dante"), and literature ("Who wrote the following? Answer ten only. David Copperfield. Kenilworth. Virginians. Sketch Book. Scarlet Letter. Evangeline. Marmion. Princess. Adam Bede. Canterbury Tales. Biglow Papers. Sordello. Aurora Leigh. Walden.").[70]

The women who passed this exam had answered a newspaper notice soliciting applicants for a ten-month apprentice class that would give "scientific instruction in the various branches of library work" each morning followed by afternoon labor "as pay for the instruction received." Men were eligible, but new head librarian Chalmers Hadley said that he did not "dare hope that any but women" would apply. His lack of hope was not misplaced. Ten women began the training course. Nine completed it and entered the library's employ, with more established professionals like Hillkowitz and Ingersoll, as well as apprentice instructor Rena Reese, to guide them. Several of the trainees, as well as these more mature librarians, also became Quantrille's friends, as did other women from later apprentice classes.[71]

The trainees were fortunate that women like Ingersoll and Hillkowitz had paved the way for them. In an era when opportunities for women's paid employment outside the home were increasing, especially among U.S.-born white women (nonwhite and immigrant women had long worked as either waged or enslaved laborers), and as more such women pursued postsecondary education, certain fields became feminized— that is, women came to be overrepresented in them. For those who hailed from or aspired to the middle class, the jobs included teaching, nursing, and librarianship. Then, too, in each of these professions, the percentage of women, already large, rose over the decade when Quantrille entered the labor force (between 1910 and 1920, the proportion of women in teaching increased from 80 to 85 percent; in nursing, from 93 to 96 percent; and in library work, from 79 to 88 percent). The feminization of any occupation entailed downward pressure on compensation and status, and female-intensive work often took on the demeaning designation of "semiprofessional."[72] But women thus employed were not without recourse, and early Denver librarians tapped female networks to ameliorate, if not transform, their own situation and that of younger women who followed them to the shelves, card catalogs, and charging desks that structured their workscape.[73]

Of her first years at DPL Helen Ingersoll wrote, "I cannot tell how unhappy we all were."[74] When Ingersoll joined the staff, the library was still housed in the high school, and then it moved twice before settling into the new building, located in what was becoming Denver's Civic Center.[75] These moves created commotion and confusion, and one interim location was plagued by bedbugs and bats. But young librarians like Ingersoll and Hillkowitz had other complaints, too. They traced those complaints to librarian Charles Dudley, who had headed the Mercantile Library and was chosen in 1899 to manage the newly consolidated DPL. During the twentieth century, all of the head librarians were men, but to the women who worked beneath them, these men were not created equal. Dudley especially came up short. Ingersoll recalled a salary of twenty dollars monthly when the library was in the high school, for example, earnings that dropped to fifteen dollars when Dudley hired her into the consolidated city library. "When I think of those days," Ingersoll wrote, "I grind my teeth."[76] The staff entered the new building in 1910, and then Ingersoll's salary jumped to sixty-five dollars (she thought that Hillkowitz, as children's librarian, earned as much as seventy-five dollars monthly). But the women were convinced that "the men folks on the staff" had higher salaries and that "Dudley showed favoritism to the men ... even when they did not bother to wait on the public at all." The city librarian also scoffed at library school and "gave no recognition" to those who went. Nonetheless, when Ingersoll inherited some money, she enrolled in the library program at Boston's Simmons College. When she returned to Denver, Dudley rehired her at a lower salary than she had earned before.[77]

Ingersoll and Hillkowitz did not take such debasement and discrimination lying down. They took their complaints to a female member of the city's library commission, Anne Evans, a reformer, arts enthusiast, women's club activist, and daughter of a former Colorado territorial governor.[78] At a meeting in the Ingersoll home (Ingersoll was unmarried and lived with her parents), librarians convinced Evans that Dudley had to go. Dudley went. Evans and another woman on the commission traveled to the American Library Association headquarters in Chicago and chose a replacement, Chalmers Hadley, whose tenure proved happier for Ingersoll, Hillkowitz, and their coworkers. Hadley instituted the new training course; he shared funds with staff so that they could attend American Library Association meetings; and he oversaw the building of branch libraries and then tapped women like Ingersoll and McClung to manage those branches.[79]

Times were good at DPL, then, as Quantrille embarked on her career, and she thrived there. She recalled that she and her peers received a "wide variety of experience in practically all departments of the library" as well as "a great deal of liberty" to use their "own initiative." Although not an official part of the library's curriculum, members of her apprentice class also sought out a private teacher who provided "lessons in story telling, book reviewing, play reading, public speaking and so on."[80] They used that training when they went out once a week to library stations in poor, working-class, and immigrant neighborhoods. These stations were not branch libraries but temporary depots set up in community buildings. It was a library station assignment that took Quantrille back near her childhood home on Bell Street, an area that by the 1910s was mostly Italian. Another depot was at the municipal bathhouse; Quantrille worked there once a week. Years later, she wrote of this station that she remembered "only one patron, a lovely young girl, Pearl Look." Pearl Look was the daughter of Lily Look, often cited as the first ethnic Chinese born in Colorado; Lily's father was known as unofficial mayor of Denver's Chinese community, and Lily, who married a merchant, was called the "Queen of Chinatown." Quantrille also traveled to the neighborhood house in Elyria, once a smelter and packinghouse town, now annexed to the city and filled with Eastern Europeans. At Elyria, Quantrille recalled that the young people wanted to dance rather than read, so when there she set aside her books and played the piano instead.[81]

Librarians like Quantrille came mostly from U.S.-born, Protestant families of Western European descent and they represented middle-class interests, so in work such as this, they followed Progressive Era impulses to Americanize immigrants, defuse class tensions, and rescue the poor through cultural uplift.[82] But DPL also employed Jewish women and others who were either immigrants or daughters of immigrants: Anna Hillkowitz's family had come from Lithuania, for instance, as had the parents of Quantrille's classmate Martha Levy. And at least two of the women in Quantrille's training course lived in households that had lost a male breadwinner: Gladys Charles resided with her mother, a dress-maker, and Lucile Jaeger's German-born father was absent from the home she kept with her U.S.-born mother. Thus the grip some of these librarians had on the middle class was weak.[83] And whatever the intentions of those who trundled off to library stations in working-class districts, as Quantrille found in Elyria, residents negotiated with these outsiders to set the terms of cross-class, cross-ethnic interaction. Not only did immigrant youths dance (not read) the day away; they induced a librarian to provide the music. And at the public bathhouse, just blocks from Chinatown, librarians encountered the daughters of queens.[84]

After these early years at the central library, with weekly forays to library stations, Quantrille entered a new phase of her career: she became head librarian at two different branch libraries. The first was the Warren Branch in the Cole neighborhood, where Quantrille took over in 1915, and the second was the branch at Park Hill. Both were impressive structures designed by noted Denver architects, funded by Andrew Carnegie, and situated in residential areas on the city's east side. Park Hill was more prosperous, and by the time Quantrille took over there in 1920, she was a seasoned community librarian.[85] Her experience and Park Hill's affluence prompted her to initiate innovations there, including a poetry circle for girls. As she said to peers at a 1924 Colorado Library Association meeting, "We librarians have little reason to expect hours of leisure.... We shall probably work on to the end of our days until we literally fall to pieces[;] why not do the thing in our libraries which we really want to do?"[86] In explaining why she took on such tasks, Quantrille voiced the pleasure she took in reading poems with girls, a delight akin to borrowing leisure from a lifetime of labor.

Soon, though, Quantrille would link the work she did at branch libraries to less individual and more ideological goals. Those goals mixed echoes of an older, Victorian women's culture with a modern impulse toward differentiating highbrow from lowbrow culture and defending access, for those of the middle class, to loftier cultural forms.[87] Accordingly, Quantrille convened a group of Park Hill women who cooperated with the library to arrange lectures, book discussions, play readings, and forums for art and music appreciation. A reporter saw the library club's purpose as suggesting "to busy people the best and higher types of reading."[88] Quantrille later recalled that she had created the club out of her belief that "there existed among the women of the United States a kind of articulate mass movement toward culture" and that libraries ought to tap it. She added that she had tried to make of the group "a woman's community movement." (To speak of "woman" in the singular form, as Quantrille did when she recounted these efforts, evoked erstwhile notions of women's presumed domestic attachments and about how those attachments could translate into commitments outside the home. Such commitments—temperance, benevolence, or suffrage, for instance—promised to improve women's status as well as the worlds where women lived.) Even though she wanted the club to be a "woman's community movement," Quantrille had difficulty getting others to preside over events. In time she realized that she herself was the singular "woman" referenced, the one who must "take her proper place as the guiding and motivating spirit." Thereafter, she not only attended but also orchestrated every gathering. She also spoke on a Denver radio station about the group's work. These middlebrow activities—middlebrow in the way that they made cultural forms often deemed highbrow accessible to a middling sort of public—were a great success. They were so popular that, in 1932, city librarian Malcom Wyer (who had replaced Chalmers Hadley in 1924) called Quantrille to return to the central library on Civic Plaza and named her director of library clubs for all of Denver.[89]

Quantrille was riding high in her career, then, as the Great Depression descended. When Wyer brought her back to DPL's main building, he did so as part of a national initiative to make public libraries vital institutions in advancing adult education. Doing so would address the needs of patrons who had fallen on hard times, to be sure, but would also shore up municipal support for institutions oft seen as nonessential and hence less deserving of dwindling city resources.[90] The kinds of programs Quantrille had developed in Park Hill would spread throughout Denver, spearheaded by the sort of women's clubs she had already successfully nurtured. As Quantrille put it, "Sharing the church and social interests of those about them, cognizant of the undercurrents as well as the more obvious aspects of their neighborhood life, these women were able to bring us valuable reflections that the librarians, however wide-awake they might be, were often unable to secure." In turn, the women became advocates for the embattled library. Thus, deep in the heart of the Depression, Quantrille oversaw diverse programs on literature, music, art, philosophy, economics, archeology, utopias, French language, and southwestern Indians.[91] Just as her career took flight, however, Quantrille fell to pieces. As she put it, "In 1935 a serious illness made it necessary for me to relinquish this fascinating occupation." The library granted her a leave of absence.[92] It would not be the last time that ailments derailed her work.

Quantrille was sick for months, but as she recuperated, she decided to take advantage of the situation. She asked the library to extend her leave so that she could pursue further training at the University of Denver. Her boss, city librarian Wyer, had founded the school of librarianship there and also served as its dean, so he was happy to grant her request. After a year of classes, in 1936, Quantrille received a library science diploma. When she returned to DPL, Wyer offered her a new assignment as genealogical librarian, a position that opened up when the woman who had held it moved. Quantrille recalled her quick retort to Wyer's offer: "I know nothing of the subject!" Wyer replied that her predecessor had learned and so would Quantrille.[93]

It was an odd situation; Quantrille had just spent a year gaining advanced library training and then found that nothing she learned "had the slightest value" in her new job.[94] Nonetheless, she embraced the opportunity. The appointment coincided with an upgrade of the library's genealogical section, which had formerly been part of the Reference Department. Now Genealogy was independent (a reform that, Quantrille noted, also gave the genealogical librarian "the dignity of a desk").[95] By the mid-1930s, then, the new Genealogy Department stood alongside the new Western History Department, which Wyer had established at the urging of author Willa Cather and with the support of library commissioner Anne Evans.[96] A city newspaper noted that DPL had one of the five largest genealogical collections in public libraries nationwide. Quantrille took charge of it all, a decision that shaped the rest of her life.[97] She also joined the Colorado Genealogical Society (CGS), which formed in 1924 and ever after remained interested in DPL's genealogical materials and interlinked with library resources and personnel. By 1939, Quantrille was vice president of the society, and in 1940, she became president.[98] Thus, despite the setback that illness had spelled for her, Quantrille carved out a new professional niche, one that, like the niche she had occupied as director of library clubs, connected her to habitats outside the library walls.

In the first three decades of her career, Quantrille served a wide range of Denver's diverse population, from the U.S.-born, white, middle-class adult learners of Park Hill to the young, working-class, and often immigrant patrons of Elyria, Little Italy, and Chinatown. As director of library clubs, she served, from a greater remove, an even wider swath of the city, and she did so especially through the medium of Denver's middle-class married women, those whose husbands' earnings allowed them to stay out of the paid labor force and hence available for the sorts of clubs that Quantrille had first created in Park Hill. Still, her contacts retained some of their older catholicism.

For instance, when Denver's NBC radio station heard about the library clubs, Quantrille recalled, "we were the means of introducing [the station] to the Housewives League which began, by request, a series of radio programs that proved so popular that they were continued for several years."[99] The Denver Housewives League, like similar groups across the nation, had been founded during the Progressive Era after passage of the 1906 Pure Food and Drug Act to push for its enforcement. The groups went on to protest rising food prices in the 1910s and again in the 1930s, when they organized boycotts that sometimes crossed lines of class and race and ideology, joining in a larger consumer movement that politicized the role of women as consumers.[100] In coordinating library clubs, then, Quantrille connected herself to emerging critiques of the U.S. political economy. Still, she was never any kind of radical, even at times during her life—in the 1930s and 1960s—when radical rebukes of inequity and injustice thundered all around her. And her work as genealogical librarian must have taken her even further from leftist and laborite critiques of the social order, because, in this era, genealogy was most accessible to those who considered themselves well born and their family trees worthy of study.[101]

But Quantrille stumbled into genealogy by chance, not because she embraced the field's conservative impulses. And earlier, even as she spearheaded middlebrow cultural forums, she and her librarian friends also flirted with a broader range of cultural possibilities and often took an ironic view of highbrow/lowbrow distinctions. They exchanged among themselves, for example, an arch text delineating what constituted "highbrow," "low highbrow," "high lowbrow," and "lowbrow" persons, passions, and pursuits, one in which even the lowbrow must have seemed familiar, if comfortably beneath what the librarians perceived as their own station. In that delineation, President Woodrow Wilson, the beverage lemon phosphate, the field of anthropology, the idea of uplift, and the card game of duplicate whist sat safely in the highbrow category. Things low highbrow included President Theodore Roosevelt, the gin rickey, socialism, grand opera, and bridge. Down the cultural (and class) scale, in the high lowbrow category, were poet and New Thought proponent Ella Wheeler Wilcox, whiskey, moving pictures, musical comedy, baseball, and euchre. And relegated to the lowbrow were ward bosses like Chicago's "Bathhouse John" Coughlin, dime novelist Laura Jean Libbey (who wrote romances devoured by young workingwomen), beer, the malapropism "meller drammer" (and its stage and film referents), and card games like pitch. In circulating this text, Quantrille and her friends could easily locate themselves—as aspiring middle-class women conversant with persons, passions, and pursuits ranging from the highbrow proper down into the high end of the lowly—even as they mocked the pretensions of the highest and distanced themselves from the lowest of brows. They might as readily appreciate anthropology, talk socialism or New Thought, watch movies or hear opera, but lemon phosphate was a silly drink when gin was at hand, and no self-respecting librarian liked out loud a working girl's romance.[102] Just as Quantrille's youth had traversed a span of Denver's class worlds, excluding only the richest and poorest denizens, so did her life as librarian wander across many, though not all, social boundaries in the Mile High City.

The same can be said for Quantrille's life outside DPL, though her days and nights were so tied up with fellow librarians that it is hard to say where her work life ended and the rest of her life began. For two decades, from the time she finished her training until she was named director of library clubs, Quantrille compiled meticulously organized scrapbooks—nine volumes in all—in which she kept a handwritten record of, as well as copious memorabilia from, her life outside the library. In keeping with her profession, Quantrille used discarded books for this purpose, replacing the original pages with pages of her own, binding her fondest memories into volumes such as *Nobody* by mystery writer Joseph Louis Vance, *The Healer* by literary realist Robert Herrick, and *Letters to a Friend* by naturalist John Muir.[103] She retitled the books "My Memoirs" and gave each a volume number. In addition, she pasted photographs into albums that extended even further into the 1930s. She also kept travel scrapbooks and tourist ephemera, primarily from Colorado and Wyoming, some from the 1930s and some from later decades.[104] These materials document countless hours Quantrille spent in the company of two circles of women—librarians and Methodists—as well as time spent with family in Colorado, Kansas, and California. They also document close relationships with both women and men, some of which may have been romantic.[105]

Quantrille's friends were more often than not fellow librarians, those who went through training with her as well as older women already employed by DPL and others who entered the library's employ later. Only when these women married did they retreat from the social circle, and most of them never wed at all.[106] Of the more established librarians, Anna Hillkowitz alone married. Helen Ingersoll and Rena Reese did not; Reese often lived with a female companion, while Ingersoll lived with her parents.[107] Among Quantrille's eight classmates who completed the 1911 library course, none were married when the training began, though one was older and widowed.[108] Of the other seven women, just one definitely wed later.[109] Most, like Quantrille, lived with family members. Martha Levy, for instance, one of Quantrille's most constant friends, lived with a brother who worked for a radio station; a sister, a salesperson for Frigidaire; their mother; and their father, who taught at a synagogue.[110] Among Quantrille's other close mates were librarians who trained later, and most of them were also unmarried. Ina Aulls never wed, for example, and in 1920 she lived with her parents, while Florence Briber, whom friends called Flossie, lived on her own by 1930; both figure prominently in Quantrille's memorabilia.[111] Census takers invariably enumerated all these women as "single," and legally, of course, they were. But they also swept through a social whirlwind powered by intellectual, artistic, and personal passions and propelled as well by ample stagecraft of their own.

Luncheons, concerts, parties, mountain getaways, movies, picnics, lectures, art exhibits, sleepovers, hikes, teas, readings, recitals, and country drives: Quantrille and her friends engaged in a constant round of these activities, in pairs and in groups. They also traveled to professional conferences, especially Colorado Library Association meetings held in different parts of the state. Theirs was both an indoor and an outdoor world, enabled by the distinctive technologies, land uses, and cultural forms of the early twentieth century—streetcars and automobiles, city parks and national parks, movie houses and performance halls, restaurants and grand hotels. It was a social world also enabled by the increasingly common practice whereby some unmarried women professionals lived apart from their parents.[112]

That practice allowed Quantrille and her friends in 1913 or 1914 to stage their "Bohemian Party" at the home that Anna Hillkowitz, as yet unmarried, shared with her siblings. Rabbi Hillkowitz may have watched over the party from his portrait on the wall, but neither he nor Anna's mother, Rebecca Hillkowitz, was physically present to pass judgment on the young women's antics.[113] Quantrille saved more photos from this affair and other costume parties than from any other kind of gathering. She captioned the party pictures not with her friends' given names but with the dress-up names they assumed for the festivities or else with tongue-in-cheek references to the festivities themselves ("In Gay Bohemia," "A Jolly Bunch," "A 'Tacky' Crowd"). Their costumes were so elaborate and skillfully made that it is hard, from a century's remove, to match each individual in the pictures with other photos of the women in different settings, but it is evident that the same circle of friends appears in both, especially the younger women of the bunch.[114]

One affair was a Valentine's Day party, where the librarians spoofed writers and historical figures as well as characters from literature, legend, folklore, and opera. So, for instance, Barnyard Kindling in top hat and tails proposes on bended knee to Empress Josephine (though in life author Rudyard Kipling and Marie Josèphe Rose Tascher de La Pagerie, who married Napoléon Bonaparte, did not share historical and geographical coordinates). Other famous couples similarly pose together: Helen and Paris, Ivanhoe and Rowena, Cinderella and Prince Charming, Madame Butterfly and Lieutenant Pinkerton, Valentine and Sylvia. Only Saint Valentine (not to be confused with Shakespeare's Valentine) appears solo.[115] In time-honored fashion, these young women celebrated male-female romance, but with nary a man present, and they captured the moment in photos.

The bohemian party at the Hillkowitz home and a Halloween gathering that the young women organized in 1913 were much like the Valentine bash. Some came once more as literary figures—Barnyard Kindling showed up again, this time along with Shernard Baw and his wife (even if socialist playwright George Bernard Shaw and his actual spouse, Charlotte Payne-Townshend, did not enjoy the most ardent of marriages). Vaudeville character Sis Hopkins, a comic country bumpkin, made an appearance, too. Others came as various male types: a cowboy, an artist, and a worker clad in rough overalls (this was Quantrille's costume). Still others arrived in women's attire but far racier than the clothing they wore in their day-to-day lives. In photos, a handsome woman appears in an off-one-shoulder floral gown, for example, while another looks the chorus girl. One shot pictures the show girl lying on the rug in front of her mates with a stocking-clad leg kicked up behind her, and in a second, she is seated, gazing up at a top-hatted gent while another fellow sits on the floor, cradling her calf and a foot sheathed in a high-heeled shoe.[116] The party photos boast these women's familiarity not only with literature and popular culture but also with legible forms of love and desire.

Men were usually, but not always, absent from these gatherings. When men were present, sometimes they were managers or other high-ranking coworkers at DPL. Other times they were younger men, often the women's siblings or else youths who were just passing through the library's employ on their way toward different careers. Quantrille's friend Lucile Jaeger hosted a coed party in 1912, for instance, where all five women present were librarians. Five men came as well; two of them worked at DPL, and one of these would soon marry Lucile. But three of the men were relatives of female librarians: two were younger brothers and one was the son of a middle-aged widow. On average, the female partygoers were three years older than the men. Since, in this era, men tended to marry women who averaged three years younger, it is not surprising that parties like this fostered few male-female romances, Lucile and her beau notwithstanding.[117]

Quantrille and her friends attended larger mixed gatherings, too, events they memorialized in both photo and verse. Quantrille, Anna Hillkowitz, and another librarian composed a poem, "The Lay of the Last Spree," that recounted one such party. It begins:

Once upon a time
I'll tell it in rhyme
Twill make you laugh
For it's about the staff
Of the Denver Public Libaree
On a bright autumn day
They were all led astray
In a very supercilious way.

As the stanzas unfold, Alma Menig steals a pfennig, prompting Mr. Cree to propose a spree. Then Miss Jaeger orders lager; Miss Barnes tells yarns; Rebecca Strasser drinks from a saucer; dear Dolly gets jolly (and dances with Kenneth Colley); Miss Crippen finds her gin rippin'; Miss Jerome drinks all the foam (and cannot make it home); Miss Sims sings hymns; Miss McIntyre kicks higher and higher (until her friends must tie her, and then send her off in a hack with Miss Black); Miss Greene slips behind a screen, where Dexter Keezer tries to squeeze her; and Bonny Jean gets lean saving Miss Aulls from falls. Not every librarian appreciates the merriment: cries the modest Miss Ingersoll, "This [will] never do at all," and declares the abstemious Miss Hall, "I really never indulge at all," adding, "My only drink is at the 'kitchen sink.'" But many imbibe with abandon, and Miss Hillkowitz, in a skirt of slits, dances on the table with little Mable. Others, young and unattached, play out the dramas of vernal desire, one moment budding with romance and the next, turned green with envy:

> Cried Wendell Stocks,
>   "Love laughs at locks!"
> "I get you Steevie,"
>   said Miss Levy.
> Then Miss McClung
>   felt badly stung
> And vowed she'd see
>   her rival hung
> To a telephone pole
>   near the Libaree.

Apparently, it was the senior staff who quashed the party: instructor Rena Reese called the police; chief engineer Robert Stanley acted manly; and head librarian Chalmers Hadley, though he felt badly, watched the patrol remove every last drunken soul from the Denver Public Library.[118]

We may wonder if Quantrille and her coworkers actually caroused with as much gusto as "The Lay of the Last Spree" intimates they did. And we may question whether or not the reprimanding elders—Helen Ingersoll, Agnes Hall, Rena Reese, Robert Stanley, and Chalmers Hadley— were even present to blow the whistle on the festivities, say nothing of summoning the police. But the younger librarians (along with the older but adventurous Anna Hillkowitz) certainly relished the image of themselves gone wild, just as they reveled in revealing what drew them one to another, as hands reached, feet danced, and hearts raced. Or to be more precise, they reveled in half revealing, but also half concealing, the contours of their polymorphous desires. The poem's subjects drank deeply, but they courted more coyly: What happened when Miss McIntyre and Miss Black headed home in a hack? Did Mr. Keezer succeed behind the screen with Miss Greene? When Mr. Colley took a turn with Dolly, did their dance steps end in embrace? When Miss Hillkowitz, in a skirt of slits, shook a leg, what showed and who looked? Did little Mable leer? Did the manly Mr. Stanley? At whose locks did Wendell Stocks laugh? If Miss Levy got Steevie, what sort of person did she get? Who was Miss McClung's rival? After whom did both lust? Nothing in Quantrille's scrapbooks answers these questions directly. But there are hints.

It is hard to trace the intimacies among Quantrille's coworkers and friends, since so few married and since nonmarital romances left such faint traces in a historical record that routinely recognized only male-female courtship and legal marriage. But Quantrille left behind evidence of her own entanglements, even if it is often translucent and sometimes opaque. The evidence suggests that Quantrille flirted with a range of tender ties. Her most frequent companions were fellow librarians as well as women she met through Methodist church groups. Helen Ingersoll, who was as much mentor as friend, appears constantly in Quantrille's scrapbooks and photo albums, and among those Quantrille's age, Martha Levy and Flossie Briber are equally prominent.[119] None of these women ever married, but nothing suggests that Quantrille's relationships with them were romantic. A few other people occupy a more ambiguous status in Quantrille's memorabilia. They appear more frequently than her casual friends, and Quantrille's references to them bespeak closer ties. Or they appear more fleetingly, through mementos that imply brief, intense encounters. It is evidence of these relationships that sketches the contours of Quantrille's desires.

Quantrille's more ephemeral connections take concrete form in her scrapbooks and photo albums through items she saved or notations she made, which suggest that now and then, male suitors came and went. In the 1910s, she kept company with a man a half dozen years her junior, Hubert Eldridge, who later married another woman. Quantrille noted a few outings with "H.E." in her scrapbooks, and she saved World War I–era photographs of him, when he was single and a soldier, as well as World War II–era newspaper clippings, when he was a married officer and prisoner of war.[120] Likewise, during the Great War, she stepped out a few times with a painter, Benjamin Silbert, who soon registered for the draft. Silbert was a Russian Jewish immigrant whose work would be exhibited at the Chicago Art Institute. In 1918, he sent Quantrille four signed photos of himself at Camp MacArthur in Texas, politely addressed to "Miss McClung," one of which she has captioned, "Ben Silbert went to Paris to live and became one of the important young artists."[121] There is no hint of romance in any of this, but both Hubert and Benjamin felt enough attached to send Quantrille photos of themselves in uniform, and she was sufficiently fond to save the pictures.

By contrast, Quantrille saved a 1926 note from a mystery woman that is drenched in sentiment. The letter is signed "With love—Iris," but Quantrille kept no other record of knowing an Iris, so this must have been a fleeting connection. The missive begins, "Like a warm sweet kiss was your thought yesterday—so refreshing—so fragrant was every dear word. It is good to know one's feeling of another is returned so fully." The note reveals no context for the two women's exchange; it is all fervor and devotion. Perhaps they crossed paths at the Park Hill Branch Library or through a church group. Iris expressed the kind of regard that might arise in such a setting: "I always feel stimulated when I think of you, Quantrille. It seems that you give the world the best you have."[122] If Quantrille gave the world the best she had, did she also give her heart to H.E. or to Ben or to Iris? Or did such admirers pine for her and then drift away, their affections unrequited? Or were they dear friends who gave passion little thought? We cannot know for sure.

In addition to short-lived encounters, Quantrille also maintained longer-lasting relationships, especially when she was in her thirties. In the 1920s, she spent more time with two people than with she did with others: Donna Northrup and George Prendergast. Both ties tightened simultaneously. Quantrille kept company with George for at least a half dozen years, starting in 1922. George did not live in Denver but in Larimer County, sixty miles north. So Quantrille saw him only intermittently, when he traveled to Denver or she ventured north. George owned an automobile, so many of their outings involved mountain drives up into the Front Range of the Rockies, from Fort Collins south to Colorado Springs, or along the high country rivers that careened down canyons to the plains below. Alone, with friends, or with Quantrille's mother, they explored Colorado's most stunning vistas in George's Model T Ford. When George came to Denver, the two shared meals and went to movies, and they also attended concerts (Anna Case and Lawrence Tibbet, both of Metropolitan Opera fame), plays (Broadway musicals such as *Little Jesse James*, *Peter Pan*, and *Rose-Marie*), and modern dance events (the pioneering Denishawn Dancers). When Quantrille met George in Larimer County, they hiked in the mountains, attended church in Loveland, or dined in Fort Collins. In 1924, George came to Denver for Christmas, and on Christmas Eve they hung stockings at the fireplace of the home Quantrille shared with her parents, while an artist friend of George's played the family piano. All of this Quantrille noted in her scrapbooks, sometimes pasting in a theater program or a photograph of George aside his car.[123]

How close was Quantrille's relationship with George? The only letters from him that she saved (perhaps the only ones she received in the 1920s) were three notes he penned while on a road trip to Iowa. He signed one "Love, George," but nothing in them hints at romance. Likewise, Christmas Eve by the fire sounds cozy, but George's friend, the artist Harold

Skene, was at the piano, and Quantrille's parents may have been home as well. More to the point, George was Quantrille's cousin, and she was eight years older than him. George's mother, Leticia McClung Prendergast, was Quantrille's father's sister.[124] Neither the family connection nor the age difference precludes a deeply felt, even intimate, bond, but both make an explicit and mutually acknowledged romance less likely, given that women in this era tended to choose male partners who were slightly older and given cultural (and, in some states, legal) proscriptions against cousin marriage.

If an acknowledged intimate relationship between Quantrille and George was unlikely, if not impossible, then what to make of their tender tie and especially of the way Quantrille made it visible in her scrapbooks? In those volumes, she twice artfully arranged adjacent photographs of George and herself. One set of paired photos, from 1923, captures each of them posed alone in hiking gear and perched on a boulder in Big Thompson Canyon. Quantrille has placed her own image overlapping that of George; he looks out directly at the camera, while she turns her head in his direction. A second set of photos finds George and Quantrille on a 1924 trip along the Big Thompson River, this time by car. Both stand, separately, near a stone wall. Again, Quantrille has positioned the photos side by side, so that the two seem to be turning their heads toward each other, though each holds a downcast gaze. George is in suit and tie, his hairline receding and his kindly eyes bespectacled. Quantrille wears a string of beads and a dress she probably made for herself, a loose-fitting gown with flared sleeves, looking more 1910s bohemian than 1920s modern.[125] Without even one photo of the two in the same frame, these intentionally juxtaposed images suggest that Quantrille labored to create a legible sort of connection with George on the pages of her scrapbook.

And yet, a handwritten passage from 1927 in those pages alludes to an actual night of magic in Denver: "George came down and we went moon-gazing—shall I ever forget it?" The two spent this August night at three City Beautiful haunts: Cheesman Park, City Park, and the Civic Center's Pioneer Monument. The monument features a white miner and a white mother—the mother holds a baby in one arm and a rifle in another—with these figures overshadowed by Kit Carson on horseback mounted, quite literally, on a pedestal above them.[126] There is a dreaminess to Quantrille's words that is easy to read as tender remembrance of nocturnal ardor. Ironically, Carson presided over the moment, as did a mother with a gun. Whatever passed between the cousins in that moment—a touch, a heartfelt conversation, shared wonder at urban landmarks bathed in moonlight—is lost to the historical record. All things considered, it is almost as if, in the scrapbook record she created of the company she kept with cousin George, Quantrille was working out for herself, and whoever else might see the record, the potential of an intimate bond with a person who lived full-time in men's clothing.

If that record is ambiguous, it is also little different from the one she crafted of her relationship with Donna Northrup. Donna came into Quantrille's life in 1922 as well, probably after Quantrille began to attend functions at Trinity Methodist Episcopal Church, a few blocks from the main library. Quantrille may have met Donna at a meeting of Trinity's Young Woman's Home Missionary Society (YWHMS), a group Quantrille joined in 1920.[127] A year or so later, Quantrille noted meetings that she attended with Donna; afterward, the two would spend the night together. Donna lived with her parents three blocks from the Park Hill Branch Library, where Quantrille worked, so it must have been convenient for Quantrille to stay with the Northrups rather than traipsing back to North Denver.[128] Later, the Northrups moved a mile or two west, so that their home was halfway between the branch library and downtown Denver, and Quantrille continued to spend the night with them after she and Donna attended cultural events.[129]

Quantrille and Donna's relationship may have begun in a mission society meeting, but they spent most of their time together at concerts, plays, and movies. They also shared literary and outdoor interests. The two women went to some of the same kinds of events that Quantrille attended with George, but they especially enjoyed Civic Symphony concerts, after which they often spent the night together. They talked about books and attended lectures. They went to City Park and watched birds.[130] In July 1924, Quantrille accompanied Donna and her parents on vacation to the newly established Rocky Mountain National Park. There, the two women hiked among the lakes and valleys and hotels that dotted the high country. They viewed a collection of western paintings, many by Taos Society of Artists founders, and other attractions in the village of Estes Park.[131] A set of photographs chronicles this trip. It must have been cold in the mountains, because the photos picture Quantrille and another young woman, perhaps Donna, and an older couple, perhaps Donna's parents, all dressed warmly, touring Estes Park and Big Thompson Canyon in a roadster. The woman who might be Donna is at the wheel. One striking photo of Quantrille and this woman captures them standing on rough terrain, silhouetted by the sun, with Quantrille leaning back toward her friend and pointing up into the distance, perhaps at a mountain bird that caught her eye.[132] Quantrille recorded these outings in her scrapbooks and pasted the photos in a separate, undated album, where she provided place-name captions but did not identify the people.

Was the relationship between Quantrille and Donna more or less or differently intimate than the one between Quantrille and George? It is hard to tell. Just as she saved only three notes from George, Quantrille saved four letters and a card from Donna. Donna wrote the letters in July 1924, after Quantrille returned to Denver from her mountain sojourn with the Northrups (Donna stayed there longer). The letters were newsier and more effusive than George's notes, but then Donna was vacationing rather than driving across country as George was. Donna addressed Quantrille as "My dear little Quantrille dushka," "Chére Amie," and "Chére Enfant" and closed the letters "Love" or "Much love" (once signing herself as "Doughnut"). The letters ranged across topics, from distinctive birds and lovely vistas to annoying bugs and irritating tourists (including a "soulless" woman, the sort "who drops in irrelevant remarks about acquaintances she considers important, with their initials tacked on to them, as [in] ... 'I told Mrs. P.D.Q. Bumpty-Ump'"). Donna also wrote about what she was reading, offering literary analysis of a passage from Joseph Conrad's novel *Victory*, which she compared to a line from Ralph Waldo Emerson. Talk of Emerson perhaps recalled earlier exchanges; a few months before, Donna had given Quantrille a hand-painted Easter card on which she copied two Emerson quotes, one about forfeiting the little "to gain the great" and the other indicting the rich for their "want of thought." Quantrille and Donna's relationship, then, involved a meeting of the minds and a shared affinity for the land.[133]

At least one of Quantrille's scrapbook references to Donna suggests a more ardent bond, especially if one compares it to the record Quantrille created of moon gazing with George.[134] When Quantrille was vacationing with the Northrups, the night before she returned to Denver, she and Donna shared a memorable night under the stars. It was so memorable that Quantrille saved a daylight photograph of the spot where the two women had lingered. The photo shows a mountain meadow studded with rock outcroppings and shaded by pines. Next to the picture, Quantrille has written, "In the evening Donna and I took a moonlight walk then sat down on these rocks under these trees and she sang to me." The human absence in the photo is striking. It is almost as if the intimacy Quantrille and Donna shared that night could not be, and yet somehow had to be, represented. It was not any rocks upon which the women sat; it was "these rocks." It was not any trees under which Donna sang to Quantrille; it was "these trees." In her scrapbook, Quantrille did not work to make her relationship with Donna legible the way she did hers with George; there are no juxtaposed photos orienting bodies in relation to each other. There are only rocks and trees and a bodily absence that, called to mind by adjacent words, haunts the picture. And there is a voice, lilting in the moonlight, that no one else will ever hear.[135]

Quantrille's moonlight idylls with both Donna and George are echoed in a sensuous essay she wrote in the same decade, when she was Park Hill branch librarian. Her intended audience is unclear, though on the first of three typed pages, Quantrille listed her work address and provided a word count, suggesting that she intended to publish it or enter it in a contest. She called the piece "Moon Madness." It begins, "When I opened my eyes this morning I saw in a tiny vase beside my bed, sweet flowers . . . perishable reminders of a never-to-be-forgotten night." Recalling a line from British poet John Drinkwater, she continues, "Last night I kept tryst with the moon." She recounts a midnight ramble under a lunar orb, figured as female, who warns her, "Tonight I shall make you mad." Under the "dusky blue arch of the sky," Quantrille trips through a park rich with aromatic conifers, graceful maples, and stately elms. She greets a blossoming hawthorn, "How soon will you let down your tiny delicious apples for my pleasure?" Down a path, over a bridge, and through a garden, she navigates a hybrid landscape, both built and natural, until she lingers in an arbor that defines the park's edge. Finally, she crosses that border, holding in her hand purloined flowers: "A half-opened rose, red as heart's blood, a white star of fragrant nicotina, and the soft sobriety of heliotrope." She returns home to her room, where she "part[s] the curtain and fling[s] open the windows." She drifts off, moonlight flooding her bed.[136]

Near the end of "Moon Madness," now safe in her room, Quantrille notes that she has hidden her telltale shoes, "lest one should ask, inquisitively, 'Where in the world have you been?'"[137] This, of course, is the question one asks Quantrille of all her midnight trysts: What landscapes of love and longing did you visit and what did you do while you lingered there? Quantrille does not answer, but neither does she scrub away the loam that clings to her shoes; she reveals what she has concealed. "Moon Madness" surely signals Quantrille's fondness for the natural-and-built world of urban parks and her lust for moonlight. Set alongside her record of midnight moments with human companions, it might also be read as a displacement of desire. Or not. She has ensured that it is hard for us to know. Were the pine needles and maple leaves and rose petals in lunar shadow enough to set her heart ablaze, to make her body quiver?

Certainly Quantrille enjoyed her own company, perhaps best of all. When she was much older, she reflected back on her youth and recalled,

One of my favorite waking dreams as a child was to be able to take over City Park for myself. The large pavilion would become my home. A high wall was to be built around the park and all the gentle animals, like the deer, would be allowed to run free. My idea was that all the people should become invisible, life would go on but I would not need to cope with persons. When I wanted or needed anything I could get on the visible street car, go down town and carefully select, without bothering about the price, whatever was needed, then go home again.[138]

She did, in fact, create a life that limited her "need to cope with persons." Both George and Donna disappear from Quantrille's scrapbooks in the late 1920s, and the scrapbooks themselves end not long thereafter.[139] The record Quantrille kept of her daily life in the 1910s and '20s drops off in the 1930s. By then, her brother, Denzel, had married and Quantrille lived alone with her aging parents. In 1940, a census taker listed Quantrille, not her father, as head of the McClung household and sole breadwinner. By 1946, both Benjamin and Henrietta McClung were dead, and Quantrille was on her own.[140]

Quantrille's young adulthood unfolded across a transitional era in women's lived experience of intimacy and in ideas about it as well. The burgeoning field of sexology detected new relational patterns and, most often, diagnosed them as deviant. Meanwhile, the flowering of bohemian social worlds both reflected and fostered political and cultural ferment. When the United States entered the Great War in 1917, however, young men enlisted, disrupting these milieux. And war-era repression of radicalism shot fear through communities that had experimented with new ways of relating. Then, two constitutional amendments ratified in 1919 and 1920, respectively—the Eighteenth, which, along with the Volstead Act, inaugurated the Prohibition era, and the Nineteenth, which gave women the franchise—signaled further upheaval. All of this informed Quantrille's life choices.

The late nineteenth and early twentieth centuries saw the production of new knowledge about human intimacy.[141] While same-sex desire and its expression have taken myriad forms over time and across cultures, by the early twentieth century in the United States, urbanization, industrialization, and labor migration fostered an economic independence and anonymity that allowed more people opportunity to pursue such desires beyond the watchful eyes of families and small communities. Sexologists recognized this, and worked to explain—and, generally, to pathologize— such behavior. In the process, they created new taxonomies for those who engaged in it. At first, they focused on "inverts," or those whose gender attributes ran counter to their assumed biological sex. Then sexologists started to identify "homosexuals," or those who desired same-sex partners. "Homosexual" is the category that would stake its claim most boldly to the twentieth century, though always haunted by the figure of the "invert"—this because of a failure of imagination (if sexual desire depended on a male-female dyad, then same-sex intimacy entailed one partner's gender inversion, or so the story went) and because of actual gender nonconformity among some who pursued same-sex desires. This process in turn led to the birth of "heterosexual" as the category against which the "homosexual" would be defined and measured—and found wanting. On the one hand, the emergence of this hierarchically arranged taxonomy, with heterosexuality taken as normative and homosexuality as deviant, opened a constricted and policed space within which "homosexuals" could find one another and create community (eventually, this would lead to whole new political movements based on sex and gender alterity). On the other hand, the new categories eclipsed, prohibited, and disciplined a range of human relationships that had been differently intelligible in the past.

The knowledge sexologists produced did not circulate widely in the early twentieth century, and it passed only gradually into popular thought. But librarians would have been among the first outside the medical profession exposed to it. Quantrille left no record of her encounter with sexology, but it strains credulity to imagine that the encounter did not happen. Once she met the doctors or their popularizers, then, how did she come to think about the freewheeling library parties in the 1910s that she so carefully documented? About Donna Northrup's well-preserved endearments or her moonlight serenade in the 1920s? Quantrille might well have subsumed her intimate relationship with Donna under a category that historians, looking back at this era, would later call "romantic friendship," a pattern of intensely emotional ties between women that predated the birth of the homosexual. Some of these relationships no doubt involved sexual congress; many did not. Since, in the nineteenth century, white middle-class women were presumed to be purer and less passionate than their menfolk (another failure of imagination), all manner of intimacy between female friends might pass unremarked, even when couples set up housekeeping with one another, as they did in so-called Boston marriages. These were precisely the kinds of relationships, however, that came under new scrutiny in the twentieth century.[142] Perhaps displaying some defiance, Quantrille saved record of her tender ties with women and of the happy, albeit temporary, inversions in which she and her friends routinely indulged.[143] Perhaps displaying some reticence, she kept that record ambiguous. What is more, she kept it away from the knowledge emporium that was Denver Public Library; she left her scrapbooks and photo albums not to her former place of employment but rather to the Colorado Historical Society, where she and her friends would not share shelf space with sexologists. Reuniting the personal materials she left to CHS with the research materials she left to DPL reveals the deep and desiring past of Quantrille's lifelong traffic in men and things male.

But the evolution of thought about queer relationships and gender nonconformity does not provide a full context for Quantrille's desires, because the company she kept with men as well as women calls to mind bohemian impulses that linked social worlds from as far away as New York City's Greenwich Village to as near as Taos, New Mexico. In these worlds, expectations for relations between women and men evolved. The bohemias of New York and New Mexico involved small numbers of people, but denizens were self-promoters who produced art, literature, and journalism that gained widespread attention. As the most eloquent chronicler of New York's scene puts it, "The bohemians were terrific self-dramatizers ... adept at creating themselves as a cast of fascinating characters: not only exuberant artists but plucky New Women, idealistic New Men, brilliant immigrant Jews, smoldering revolutionaries, and farsighted workers, all vaunting their renovations of artistic endeavor, politics, and sociability. They made Greenwich Village into a beacon of American possibility in a new age."[144] This milieu proved fertile soil for a new word—"feminism"—to take root, and feminists worked to enact sexual equality and reciprocity. Doing so meant supporting causes like birth control and women's suffrage. But it also meant experimenting with intimate partnerships that, ideally, allowed women economic independence and sexual pleasure and that, also ideally, created an ethos of shared political, intellectual, and artistic passions—however unevenly realized in practice.[145] Then, when a central figure in this enclave, Mabel Dodge, decamped for Taos in 1917, she established an outpost in northern New Mexico and drew other artists and writers to her flame. Through interaction with the local cultures of *hispanos* and Pueblo Indians (made flesh in Dodge's marriage to Tony Lujan from Taos Pueblo) as well as Taos Society of Artists members, Dodge's home became the center of a new bohemia, where novel intimacies continued apace.[146]

Denver did not develop a comparable milieu, but the proximity of Taos made such sensibilities more accessible to Denver residents like Quantrille and her friends. What is more, at least one of those friends,

Anna Hillkowitz, had ties to Eastern European Jews in New York, some of whom would go on to infuse Greenwich Village with all manner of socialist, anarchist, and free-love ideas. In 1906—at a moment when talk of the first Russian revolution inflamed passions among Jewish immigrants—Hillkowitz took a leave of absence from DPL to work as a fundraiser for the Jewish Consumptives' Relief Society (JCRS). The JCRS, established by Russian Jews, ran a Denver tuberculosis sanatorium that was open to all but designed especially to serve recent immigrants (in this, the JCRS set itself apart from Denver's more exclusive National Jewish Hospital, founded by German Jews). Hillkowitz's rabbi father had been a founder of the JCRS, and her brother, a doctor, was president. As a traveling fundraiser, Hillkowitz visited New York.[147] Then she returned to her work at DPL, which is where Quantrille met her in 1910. Three or four years later, Anna hosted the "Bohemian Party" where Quantrille and her friends so exuberantly cross-dressed.[148]

To be sure, Quantrille, Anna, and the rest were probably playing bohemian more than they were living bohemian lives.[149] But the connections to Taos and Greenwich Village gave them access to a sense of possibility that encompassed new egalitarian aspirations for male-female partnerships, aspirations reflected in the way Quantrille represented her relationship with George Prendergast. There is little in that representation of the male suitor eager to possess, protect, and provide for a potential wife; instead, there are two accomplished adults, companions and equals, dressed for a strenuous hike or stepping from the car to strike a cerebral pose. As if to amplify this modern allusion, beneath the paired photos of the two in street clothes, Quantrille placed another of herself at the wheel of George's Model T.[150] And even as both Greenwich Village and Taos, as bohemian referents, invigorated and hence helped to invent heterosexuality, both also encompassed the potential for same-sex intimacy.[151] In New York, for instance, the club for "unorthodox women" called Heterodoxy included both those who lived with other women and those forging egalitarian partnerships with men.[152] Meanwhile, in the creative arts community of Taos, intimate relationships between men were hardly unknown.[153] Quantrille and her friends may only have flirted with bohemianism, but the object of their social desire was multiple and mutable, and thus open to endless engagements.

Thus, when Quantrille attached the label "In Gay Bohemia" to a pair of 1910s photos of herself and female friends in drag, what she meant by "bohemia" is clearer than what she meant by "gay." Depending on when she wrote the caption, she may or may not have known that "gay" was a code word used among men who sought sex with men; perhaps more likely, she was invoking the term's older association with flamboyance or illicit pleasure. But "bohemia": now *there* was a word with rich, precise referents, readily available to a librarian. Quantrille captioned other photos from the same party—of costumed female couples, each with one partner dressed in men's clothing and the other in women's garb—"A night in Bohemia" and "Comrades." In doing so, she named the male-female relational egalitarianism and the revolutionary panache of Greenwich Village. But she hung both banners over photos of her female friends.[154]

Then came the Great War. The United States did not join the global conflict until 1917, after three years of unremitting bloodshed in Europe. For Quantrille and her friends in Denver, the U.S. entry took away siblings, coworkers, and companions. Quantrille's brother, Denzel, served in the marine corps. Ralph Munn, a DPL assistant, joined the army and wrote to his coworkers from a transport ship and from "somewhere-in-France."[155] "H.E." (Hubert Eldridge) and Ben Silbert departed and sent Quantrille their photographs. When the fighting ended on the western front in November 1918, Quantrille and her friends took pictures of themselves on a snow-covered street holding a newspaper with the bold headline "PEACE!"[156] But the war had not only interrupted women's ties to men in the military, relationships that might be restored with those fortunate enough to return. It also interrupted a heady sense of possibility that had seeped into stolid, workaday cities like Denver from fonts of modernism in fabulous places like Greenwich Village and Taos. The breach came with the crackdown on antiwar opposition, and ultimately all manner of radical politics, that accompanied U.S. entry into the war, exemplified by the Espionage Act in 1917 and the Sedition Act in 1918. Indeed, World War I itself sent disillusioned modernists such as Mabel Dodge running from the brutal urbanism of New York to the adobe village of Taos. As Dodge's best chronicler puts it, "If skyscrapers were twinned with machine guns," then bohemians wanted no more of this kind of modernity.[157] The remoteness of northern New Mexico shielded some displaced city dwellers from the Red Scare's worst fallout, but nationally, the damage was done: with a frenzy only intensified by the Bolshevik Revolution in Russia, U.S. radicals were beaten, jailed, and deported.[158]

In the wake of the Great War and the Red Scare, Quantrille's scrapbooks record a subdued sociability, with less evidence of riotous parties replete with copious alcohol and conspicuous cross-dressing.[159] By then,

Quantrille was in her late twenties and no longer a new librarian learning her craft. Her more sober social life might reflect her age as well as the responsibilities of her job and its bourgeois expectations of respectability. It might also reflect the broader institutionalization of feminist goals, signified nationally in 1920 by the Nineteenth Amendment to the U.S. Constitution, and a paradoxical cultural retreat from the most revolutionary implications of those goals. (Women in Colorado had long since gained the franchise, ever since a state constitutional amendment in 1893). But Quantrille's flirtation with bohemianism lingered in the way she represented her relationship with George Prendergast, in the style of dresses she sewed for herself, and in the persistence of her intimate ties to women, especially Donna Northrup.

The literal sobriety of Quantrille's life in the 1920s—or at least the appearance thereof—suggests as well a different sort of triumph by female activists, who had long argued that alcohol was at the root of myriad social problems, not least the abuse of wives by drunken, domineering husbands. The Woman's Christian Temperance Union (WCTU) could not claim responsibility for passage of the Eighteenth Amendment and the Volstead Act, which together enacted a national ban on making, moving, and marketing alcohol. But neither was the Prohibition era (1920–33) imaginable without a half century of WCTU agitation. Colorado went dry even sooner, in 1916. Illicit spirits still flowed, lubricating the decade of the 1920s through the good offices of bootleggers and basement brewers. But for an aspiring middle-class professional who lived with her Methodist parents, openly flouting liquor laws was a bridge too far. And it was alcohol that had fueled the wildest of library parties, where a suit and tie gave a girl license to love up the ladies in their gowns. For Quantrille, the '20s did not roar.

Instead, Quantrille devoted herself to activities organized in and through the Methodist Episcopal church. She had always been a church member, attending Asbury Methodist in North Denver. She learned to love music there, taking piano lessons from the church's pianist ("the prettiest woman I ever knew"); enjoying the pipe organ that Asbury had purchased from Denver's first Jewish congregation, Temple Emanuel, when it built a new synagogue; and thrilling to the visits of Welsh workers who came down from the mines to sing at the church. She attended Junior League meetings, where, as she recalled, "I learned to preside over a meeting, speak before an audience, and in general how to conduct myself in public." She was active in the Standard Bearers, a youth missionary society that taught her "something of foreign lands." When she got older, she taught Sunday school.[160] But her most intense engage-ments in Methodism came in the 1920s, when she was in her thirties, working as a branch librarian and spending time with Donna Northrup and George Prendergast.

Now Quantrille's attentions shifted away from her parents' congrega-tion and toward Trinity Methodist Church downtown. In 1920, just be-fore she took over the Park Hill Branch Library, she attended a meeting of the YWHMS at Trinity (where she may have met Donna). The YWHMS occupied Quantrille for several years and drew her into Trinity Method-ist's orbit.[161] By 1923, she was involved in another Trinity group called San Grael, a Sunday school class and service organization designed for young women new to the church.[162] Through these affiliations, Quantrille also joined theatrical troupes that performed religious-themed plays written by a local woman. They staged shows in area churches; for missionary and uplift groups, including the local WCTU; and at an army hospital, where convalescents preferred "wet" to "dry" monologues (even if tem-perance was among the plays' themes).[163]

Central to these activities was Quantrille's interest in mission work. Despite her membership in the YWHMS, the name of which indicates a concern with "home" mission work (that is, within the United States), Quantrille was most captivated by missions abroad. She attended lec-tures by and benefits for women who served as missionaries in China, Burma, and Korea. Usually these were U.S.-born white women, but Quan-trille also heard Shi Meiyu from Jiangxi Province, the Chinese Methodist who studied medicine at the University of Michigan and then returned to China, establishing hospitals there and becoming the first president of China's WCTU. In her scrapbooks, Quantrille pasted missionary photos from China and Africa that depicted both the white women who served there and the local people to whom they ministered.[164] At a pivotal mo-ment, then, when Quantrille's work and social life were framed by a nar-rower focus, her spiritual life provided an expansive view of a global canvas.

Thus for Quantrille, three changes coincided in the 1920s. First, the geography of her employment contracted to branch libraries, first in the Cole neighborhood and then in more affluent Park Hill. Her work as a branch librarian took her away from the Denver's working-class and im-migrant districts, where she had once staffed library stations, and from the downtown crossroads of the Civic Center. Second, her social life began to take on a more proper bearing—albeit still populated by a com-peting cast of characters, especially in the persons of Donna and George, with whom she illumined the night. Third, her religious commitments put her in front of local audiences eager for tales of industry, sobriety, and rectitude (with the exception of the army hospital crowd), even as those commitments kept her mindful of a wider world.

In this, Quantrille partook of the era's Christian internationalism that infused U.S. women's missionary work. Methodist Episcopal participants insisted on the equality of all baptized Christians and so granted increasing authority to converts in their own homelands. They had long since changed the name of their chief publication, the *Heathen Woman's Friend*, to the more enlightened *Woman's Missionary Friend*, and in 1920, they linked their support for the Nineteenth Amendment to an antimilitarist stance—all of this at a time when the science of race and the politics of empire pushed in different directions.[165] Yet mission work, even when it challenged racisms, nationalisms, and imperialisms in a belligerent age of races and nations and empires, was predicated on enduring aspects of white Protestant women's power, rooted as it was in beliefs about the superiority of specific domestic arrangements, in assumptions about racial hierarchy, and in an evangelical ethos that denied the worth of both non-Protestant forms of Christianity and non-Christian religions.[166] Quantrille's interest in missions abroad gave her a global vision at a time when the rest of her life unfolded in restricted social and spatial borders, but that vision also reflected a fantasy of rescue to which white Protestant women had long been prone.[167]

Missionaries both within the United States and around the world assumed that evangelism began with the promotion of Christian homes—idealized domestic spaces where men's breadwinning, women's household labor, and children's moral development proceeded under the tutelage of the one Lord and Savior. But historians have demonstrated that mission women themselves often occupied different kinds of homes, ones where unmarried women lived apart from men and children (save, perhaps, the children to whom the women ministered or those they adopted).[168] Just as the missionaries Quantrille supported lived in households that departed from such ideals, so, too, did her family life little resemble the norm. Her father lost his job not long after she finished her library training, and he retreated to stay with relatives in California, leaving Quantrille and her mother to fend for themselves while Denzel was still in school. Henrietta McClung boarded a former teacher of Quantrille's, and the household managed on a librarian's salary and the rent the teacher paid. Quantrille's father finally found work at the U.S. Mint in Denver and retired with a pension in the 1930s. But at a crucial moment in the family's history, when Quantrille was in her twenties, her income, along with what her mother earned taking in a boarder, kept the McClungs afloat. Even after Benjamin McClung got a new job, Henrietta continued to board a single worker, this time a young electrician. When her father retired, Quantrille became sole breadwinner, though her father's pension must have remained a key source of livelihood. Benjamin's turn-of-the-century earnings as a wholesale company employee had allowed the McClungs to climb "up the hill" to the Dutch colonial revival on Tejon Street, but it took Quantrille's and Henrietta's labors to keep the family rooted in Denver's white middle class.[169]

If the McClungs defied bourgeois expectations of gender and generation, they also belied ideals of familial harmony and happiness. It was in these years that Quantrille's relationship with her brother deteriorated. They had once been close companions, going to movies, rowing in the park, or just "gadding" about town together, and she had fondly noted his comings and goings in her scrapbooks. According to the memoir she wrote much later, after his World War I service, Denzel tried ranching in Middle Park, the high basin amid the mountains of north-central Colorado. There, he met a local woman, May Shore, and in 1924 married her. In her memoir, Quantrille quickly dispatched the rest of Denzel's life: "As ranching did not prove successful, he tried politics and proved such a good County Treasurer that on leaving that office he went into the Bank at Kremmling, Colorado, where he remained until his death in 1972."[170]

But Denzel followed a more complicated life course, and somewhere along the way he and Quantrille parted company not just geographically but emotionally as well. Quantrille made no note of attending her brother's wedding. Still, the summer after Denzel and May married, Quantrille and her mother visited the Shore family ranch in Middle Park, a trip Quantrille relished for the chance it gave her to hike and ride the high country on horseback. In the fall, ten months after May and Denzel wed, their first child was born, a baby named after Henrietta McClung and called Hattie. Thereafter, Denzel, May, and Hattie disappear from Quantrille's scrapbooks. The couple did not, in fact, always live in north-central Colorado. In 1930, they were living in Denver with two children, Hattie and an infant named after his father, and Denzel was working as a deliveryman. By 1940, the younger McClungs had moved back to Middle Park and the family circle had expanded to include a third child, another boy. But young Hattie McClung, her grandmother's namesake, died eight years later when she was only twenty-two. She is buried alongside her McClung grandparents and her aunt Quantrille. The only record Quantrille kept of what happened to her niece indicates a deep rift and a heartbreaking loss.[171] In 1971, when Denzel was dying, a family friend wrote to Quantrille about her brother and the drama of his household. Thinking back to Hattie's death in 1948, the friend told a confusing tale that nonetheless hints at the tenor of the tension: "The day Denzel & May's daughter died I went to the house.... May was at Beauty Parlor— Denzel home alone—I had been to house to see May—but she didn't let me see daughter—talked of Book of Revelation—so I never went back. She did tell [me] she had told girl she was a very sick girl & had she asked for forgiveness for her sins?—That upset me—at funeral Rev. Tausig repeated that, also said what a good girl she was."[172] Other than this letter, Quantrille did not document what befell her niece or, indeed, what ended the closeness she once enjoyed with her brother, a rupture so complete that May McClung did not even call her when Denzel was diagnosed with cancer in 1970.

Whatever heartbreak Quantrille faced in her relationship with her brother, it must have intensified when their parents' health failed in the 1940s. Quantrille preserved virtually nothing from this period, but it was clearly a trying time filled with difficult decisions. As both parents entered their eighties, Quantrille could no longer take care of them. So she sold the house on Tejon Street, took a room for herself until she could find an apartment, and moved her mother and father to a nursing home. The home had been founded by a North Denver grain miller, John Kernan Mullen, an Irish immigrant who became a Catholic philanthropist. Quantrille never forgot the kind aid her folks received from the Little Sisters of the Poor, the nuns who ran the Mullen Home. When sister-in-law May was harassing her after Denzel's death in the 1970s, Quantrille told Bernice that she might cut the nephews out of her will and divide all between Trinity Methodist and the Catholic sisters who had cared for her father and mother. Her parents did not live long at the nursing home; Benjamin died in 1945, just before the end of World War II, and Henrietta lived for one more year. But the decision Quantrille made to put her parents in a Catholic institution provoked lasting family strife; some of Henrietta's Methodist relations shunned Quantrille for the rest of her life.[173]

If broken kin ties, her parents' aging, and the Great Depression were not enough in the 1930s and '40s, Quantrille also faced her own bodily crisis. It was in 1935 that illness forced her to take a leave from DPL. As she recuperated, she snuck in a road trip with three women friends to Yellowstone National Park, sending her parents postcards to assure them that she was feeling fine.[174] But even after she returned to work, Quantrille rarely enjoyed robust health. There were good days and bad days. In

1943, the library granted her more sick leave but also took away her job as head of Genealogy. When her symptoms subsided, she went back to the library and staffed various departments. In the meantime, she found an apartment on Capitol Hill, one that she would occupy for almost twenty years. In 1947, a friend from CGS noted in her diary that she had telephoned Quantrille and found the librarian's voice "a whisper."[175] Finally, in 1948, Quantrille retired on disability; she was just fifty-eight years old. But her timing could not have been better. By 1947, DPL had overhauled its personnel system, reclassifying employees and boosting salaries. In addition, the city council passed a retirement bill that included disability benefits for Denver workers (which, in Quantrille's case, came to a hundred dollars per month).[176] It all came not a moment too soon.

And yet, there was something unvanquished about Quantrille McClung. She lost her job as genealogical librarian but returned to the library for as long as she could, working in other capacities. She continued her midlife passion for genealogy as a member of CGS, and she embarked on two major research projects—one on the families of Colorado governors and the other on the Carson, Bent, and Boggs clans.[177] Her life had narrowed spatially and socially, but when she was able, she still explored the mountain West with women friends. She was a lifelong Methodist but used that affiliation to educate herself about a wider world, even as she sustained friendships with Jewish women and ignored devout kin who censured her for entrusting her elderly parents to Catholic nuns. Despite her professional retreat from Denver's working-class and immigrant neighborhoods, she kept track of the connections she had made there. For example, she followed the fortunes of Chinatown's Look family: she was delighted to meet up with her "old friend Pearl Look Pang" when she lunched at the Golden Bough, a Chinese shop near the Civic Center, and she proudly pasted in her scrapbook a newspaper notice of Pearl's brother, Frank Look, when he graduated with high honors from the Colorado School of Mines.[178] And even as her flirtation with bohemianism came to an end after World War I, she maintained a keen interest in public figures who critiqued the structures of power that diminished the lives of so many Americans; she went to a lecture writer Mary Austin delivered in Denver in 1927, for instance, and four years later, she attended a concert featuring singer and activist Paul Robeson.[179] Quantrille lost her family, her home, and her job. Somewhere along the way, she may have lost a sweetheart or two as well. But she moved forward with open eyes and carved the second half of her life out of reversal and grief.

Pageant of Melody, Straw in the Wind

It was in the second half of that life that Quantrille McClung met Bernice Fowler Blackwelder, who likewise had transformed herself over the years. Unlike Quantrille, Bernice left behind scant written record of her young adulthood. Instead, she collected photographs, starting with her college years in the early 1920s and continuing with her music career, which spanned the 1920s to 40s. She also saved playbills and news clippings from her own performances and, after she married Harold Blackwelder in 1930, from his as well. Then, for five years when she was in her late thirties, Bernice abandoned this preference for the visual over the verbal; she kept a daily diary. Together, these sources document a life far less rooted than that of Quantrille, who lived in the same house and had the same employer for over thirty years.[180] By contrast, from the 1920s to the 40s, Bernice called as many as twenty different addresses home; she moved from Kansas to Illinois to Missouri and back to Illinois; she resided briefly on both the West and East Coasts; and, except for a couple of years teaching voice at a small college, she lived a performer's life, stringing together short- and long-term engagements on the stage, at clubs and county fairs, and on the radio. In one way, though, Bernice and Quantrille were alike: During World War II and the early Cold War, both women generated a less voluminous personal archive. Their scrapbooks, photo albums, and journals ceased, making their lives in the 1940s and '50s more difficult to document.

In 1920, Bernice Fowler enrolled at Fort Hays Kansas Normal College, founded in 1901 on the site of a frontier army post. The school was in Hays, ninety miles west of Brookville, on the same Union Pacific tracks that ran through the Fowler homestead along Spring Creek. When Bernice arrived, she was one of just under 250 students taught by 40 faculty members (in a town of over 3,000 souls, three or four times larger than Brookville).[181] In 1923, Bernice earned a bachelor of music degree and, in 1924, a bachelor of science degree in geology.[182] In college, she was a joiner. She sang in the festival chorus. She played violin in the orchestra and French horn in the concert band. She also performed as both singer and violinist in smaller ensembles, including a Ladies' Quartette. And she appeared on the stage in shows like Gilbert and Sullivan's *H.M.S. Pinafore*. In addition, Bernice served as cabinet member of the college YWCA, chairing committees on music and public service. She shared some of these activities with a classmate named Gertrude Winkler; they would both later move to Chicago and remain friends for the rest of their lives. In 1923, Bernice enjoyed another distinction when she was voted among the "Favorites" in the college yearbook under the category "Beauty."[183]

In addition to sharing activities with her friend Gertrude, Bernice had family ties at the college. Her sister, Helen, and brother, Duane, both attended Fort Hays. The Fowlers were a musical bunch, perhaps emulating their mother, who sang in Brookville's church choir. Bernice, Helen, and Duane were joined at Fort Hays by a young woman named Jessie Granger, who played tuba and violin and quickly caught Duane's eye. Jessie earned a music degree, while Duane played in the band with Bernice but did not finish college. Helen did not graduate either. Still, family stories recall that Helen used up the funds that would have allowed Duane to finish college, creating a rift so deep that Duane's children grew up thinking that he had only one sister, Bernice. Those children, who have now died, did not know why Helen, and not Bernice, was deemed at fault for Duane's reduced prospects, but Bernice and Duane stayed close, while both had strained relationships with Helen. Even though Helen was older than Bernice, it was Bernice who stole the show at Fort Hays; perhaps this provoked jealousy that fed familial ill will. As for Duane, he went on to lifetime employment with J. C. Penney Company. He married Jessie Granger when he was promoted from the store in Salina, Kansas, to a management position in Cadillac, Michigan, where the couple raised their children.[184]

The visual record Bernice kept of her college years includes the photos of Bernice and her female friends in costume, some of them in men's attire. At first glance, these pictures resemble those of Quantrille and her librarian friends in drag. Both capture women in the guise of white manhood alongside other women in the guise of white womanhood—or, in the case of Bernice's friends who donned Edwardian frocks, white girlhood. Both capture women representing heterosexual ties by positioning those in female attire entwined with those in male clothing—hands on knees, arms slipped through elbows or draped across shoulders. Both, then, instantiate male-female difference and desire, even as they hint at the mutability of conventional gender and sexual arrangements by making it clear that female-bodied people play all the roles in these photographic dramas.[185] But the two women's pictures also differ. Quantrille's interior photos, taken at night in a Denver dwelling where only young adults lived, reflect a cosmopolitan urban milieu and a bohemian historical moment. Bernice's exterior photos—anyone passing by would have seen these students capering about in full daylight—recall the rural roots of those pictured and the small-town setting of Fort Hays Normal College. The young women pose in a yard marked off by a shed and rough fencing, with the implements of outdoor work at hand. Their outfits lack the wide-ranging literary and historical derivation of the Denver women's; the librarians' costumes have international referents that favor Europe and North America but also include East Asia. Bernice and her classmates, by contrast, appear as customary American types—a working man with a corncob pipe (this was Bernice), a top-hatted gentleman, a soldier boy, white girls in white dresses, and an Indian woman in braids and blanket (patterned stockings and oxford pumps peeking out below). These young women, hailing from Kansas towns and farms and crossroads, reference a nation changed by a world war, hence the fellow in military garb caressed by coeds clad in the styles of their own girlhood. But they also reference a nation that held the past and its necessary oppositions dear—male and female, Indian and white, rich man and poor man.[186]

What is more strikingly different about Bernice's and Quantrille's photos, however, is their number and what surrounds them in the albums where they are affixed. Quantrille saved many more pictures like this of herself and her friends, pictures taken on more than one occasion, and she juxtaposed them most often with others of the same women in conventional female attire. Bernice saved just a half dozen drag photos, all taken in one day. The rest of her album is filled with a range of collegiate images: the family with whom she lodged; dapper college men in cardigans and ties; all manner of students playing all manner of musical instruments; graduates in their commencement gowns; a startling array of coeds wielding pistols and rifles and sporting wry smiles; Bernice and her women friends in straight-waist dresses or letter sweaters or knickers paired with sailor blouses; a joint YWCA/YMCA ceremony with young folks in classical garb posed against a backdrop depicting the old army post of Fort Hays; men and women alike on a school trip to Colorado, lounging in Denver's Civic Center, standing by a mountain stream, and tossing snowballs in the high country. Bernice's pictures of herself and female friends in costume, then, are subsumed among assorted images reflecting the high-spirited, coeducational world of college students in the 1920s, made geographically specific by references to a violent frontier past of guns and forts and vanquished foes.[187]

Quantrille's and Bernice's photographs differ for reasons of time and place but also of life course and inclination. Quantrille did not attend college, even though she entered her late teens—the typical age of beginning students—at a time when enrollments nationwide rose by 50 percent and when women's attendance was approaching an all-time high (from 1910 to 1920, enrollments increased from 40 to 47 percent female).[188] Quantrille's health and her family's fortunes limited her to training in librarianship. The absence of a college degree hardly signaled a lack of education, however, as her command of literature and history indicated. Working as a librarian not only served Quantrille's bookish bent, but it also kept her by day in a largely single-sex workplace, one that spilled over by night into a frequently all-female world of leisure. That world, nonetheless, offered the common pleasures of gender. All of this suited Quantrille well.

Bernice came of age a dozen years later than Quantrille, at a time when college enrollments had risen further—though when Bernice began at Fort Hays, it was still only 7 percent of U.S. young people who had access to higher education. Between 1920 and 1930, the proportion of women students actually declined (from 47 to 44 percent), placing Bernice in a small and privileged minority.[189] But her photo album reflects virtually nothing of the academic world she inhabited. Instead, it reveals an intensely social, coeducational milieu of clubs, outings, and performances. It also features local excursions in a western Kansas dominated by agriculture and transitioning from trains to automobiles: students feasting on watermelons or perching on the rails or posing by a pumpkin patch; coeds flanking a mile marker on the brand new Victory Highway (it was 1,400 miles east to New York and 1,700 west to San Francisco); barbed wire surrounding bison, perhaps at the agricultural experiment station that shared the old Fort Hays site with the college; young women beside a billboard declaring that "It Pays to Live in Hays, The Educational Center of a Farming Community."[190] Like coeds everywhere in the 1920s, Bernice and her friends produced a peer culture that reveled in modern freedoms even as it socialized participants for a middle-class future of marriage, financial comfort, and conventional family life. For Bernice, however, the future would not unfold in Kansas. And because she followed a life path into an urban world of amusements that was itself changing, her grip on the middle class and its conventions would prove weak.

Bernice finished college in 1924, and then she left Kansas for Chicago. Her first move to the big city by the great lake is barely documented in the materials she left behind, but later in life Bernice told the publisher of *Great Westerner* that she had pursued graduate study at the Columbia School of Music.[191] Columbia had been established in 1901 by Clare Osborne Reed, a musician who was also an activist on behalf of women's municipal suffrage.[192] While studying there, Bernice saved far fewer photos than when she was an undergraduate at Fort Hays. Just a handful of grainy images remain: the lakefront near Michigan Avenue, autos clogging downtown streets, Great Lakes steamers approaching the harbor, and brick buildings so tall that the camera's lens could not contain them—the sorts of scenes that reminded Bernice she was not in Kansas anymore. There are only a few images of the people she knew in Chicago, perhaps other students. The men are bundled in woolen outerwear and each sports a fedora or trilby or flatcap; the women wear fur or fur-trimmed coats and stand crowned by the era's ubiquitous cloche hat. Everyone smiles, but no one clowns for the camera; these are not college students but rather young adults on a mission to establish themselves in the world of music. In some of the pictures, Bernice stands with a tall, handsome man who may have been a suitor, but his identity is lost to the historical record.[193] She would not meet Harold Blackwelder for a few more years.

In the meantime, Bernice left Chicago and headed to central Missouri, where she taught voice at Central College in the town of Fayette. Central College was affiliated with the Methodist Episcopal Church South, the denomination that had split off from other white Methodists in the past century over the issue of slavery. The institution as Bernice found it resulted from a 1923 merger of a nominally coeducational Central College and Howard-Payne Female College, which excelled in music education. When Bernice started teaching there in 1926, the reconfigured college was completing a new conservatory, using funds from a Kansas City banker, Edward Swinney, whose great-uncle, a tobacco farmer and the county's largest slave owner, had donated the land for the school's first building in the nineteenth century. No doubt Bernice was present for, and perhaps performed in, the 1927 dedication of the Swinney Conservatory, which featured a composition by its director, N. Louise Wright, titled "Negro Suite." Wright's stepmother was Edward Swinney's sister. From the moment she set foot on the Central College campus, then, Bernice stepped into Missouri's vexed racial history, as white residents understood that history.[194]

She also stepped into the geography that had nurtured Kit Carson a century before. Fayette was a dozen miles from Franklin, where Carson was raised (though the Franklin that Bernice saw was in a different place than Carson's Franklin; Missouri River flooding forced most residents to relocate to nearby New Franklin in 1828). Franklin had once been the Howard County seat; now Fayette enjoyed that distinction. Howard was one of seven Missouri counties known collectively as Little Dixie, named for the southern roots of its residents and its history of slaveholding; in 1850, Howard County had the largest enslaved black population in the state.[195] Like the Swinney family, the Carsons owned slaves. Franklin was also the point of departure for the first trade wagons that headed southwest along the Santa Fe Trail. Deeply indebted denizen William Becknell organized that expedition in 1821 and was fortunate (given his debts) to arrive in a territory that had just become part of the new nation of Mexico, which abolished the Spanish colonial ban on trade with the United States. Carson departed along the same route in 1826. A hundred years later, in 1926, Bernice Fowler made her way to Howard County.

There, in Little Dixie, Bernice had a full-time job for three years—one of only two periods in her life when she worked for a single employer (it would be a quarter century before she had another steady job with a regular salary).[196] She not only taught voice but also directed the women's glee club, which performed on campus and around the state; she and a faculty accompanist performed their own solos on the road, too. In addition, Swinney Conservatory offered the services of faculty members for concerts, and contralto Bernice was among those whose talents were advertised, as was director N. Louise Wright. Bernice saved many images of her time at Central College, including photos from her own camera, portraits that students must have given her, and pictures of faculty clipped from college publications. In her own photos, Bernice appears with her grinning glee club members—once, in front of the "Fayette Co-op Elevator" sign—or with her faculty coworkers, all young and middle-aged white women. Bernice stands most often alongside—indeed, entwined with—the college orchestra's director, an ethereal beauty named Charlotte Phillips, who must have been a special friend.[197] For a time, then, even though she worked at a newly coeducational college, Bernice spent her days mostly in the company of other music-minded women.

When Bernice published *Great Westerner* in the 1960s, the book jacket told readers, "Mrs. Blackwelder first became interested in Kit Carson while teaching at Central College."[198] But in the 1970s, Bernice told Quantrille a different story about her historical consciousness in the 1920s. The two had been corresponding about Arrow Rock, a Missouri River town that grew as Santa Fe Trail traffic increased. The town was near both Fayette and Franklin, though on the opposite side of the river (traders often crossed on the Arrow Rock ferry). Quantrille's side of the exchange has not survived, but it seems likely that she had written to Bernice about Taos artist Ernest Blumenschein's mural *Meeting of Washington Irving and Kit Carson at Arrow Rock Tavern*, which graces a corridor at the Missouri State Capitol. The mention of Arrow Rock prompted a stream of loosely connected recollections from Bernice: "I remember Arrow Rock near Fayette, Mo., where I taught. I knew several Carsons. The tavern there is, I believe, still operating. Strange that I did not absorb more history while I was there for three years!" She concluded, "Music was my life!"[199]

Music was Bernice's life at Central College, and it would continue to be her central passion and chief source of income for two more decades. But there was another encounter during her Missouri years that drew her into Carson's orbit, one that proved more significant to her later work than her residence near Carson's hometown. In 1928, Bernice traveled to Kansas and visited her friends Bess and Fred Heine at their ranch near Lucas, halfway between Brookville and Hays but north of the railroad and highway that connected those two towns. Bess had attended the Columbia School of Music with Bernice, and Fred, when he was young, had served as an interpreter for John McCurdy when the local attorney worked with German-speaking clients. McCurdy, in turn, had known Bernice's father. Now Bernice was grown and John was all but divorced from his wife. John lived twenty miles west of Bess and Fred in Lincoln, but he also had a cabin in the mountains near Pueblo, Colorado, and the Heines drove with Bernice to visit him there. They had planned to motor north to Cheyenne, Wyoming, for the annual Frontier Days festival, but John talked them into driving south instead to Taos, New Mexico, where the foursome checked into Hotel Don Fernando on the town's plaza, renting three separate rooms for their stay. On that trip, John took Bernice to visit the graves of Kit Carson and Josefa Jaramillo in the cemetery that would be incorporated into Kit Carson Memorial State Park more than two decades later.[200] John would assist in efforts to create the park, and he would enlist Bernice in his search for records documenting Carson's life, too.

John fell in love with Bernice on this trip. Bernice's feelings are less clear, but the connection between the two was undoubtedly intense. They took most of what transpired between them that night on the Taos plaza to their graves. Nonetheless, for years, Fred Heine teased them about what might or might not have happened. Fred, Bess, Bernice, and John reunited in 1953 and retraced the steps of their 1928 journey (this more than twenty years after Bernice married Harold, who stayed behind in Arlington). During that reunion, John made a tape of the time the foursome spent together, and the tape caught Fred badgering Bernice and John about the 1928 trip to Taos: "Just between us four, and the deep secrets of this world, I shall now, having studied a little law, go ahead and … question this great criminal attorney and said Bernice Fowler: Are you two guilty or not?" Fred recalled that he had found Bernice's hotel room open and empty and that he had gone to find her, only to see her down a hallway, deep in conversation with John. Fred claimed to have halted their tête-à-tête sternly: "Far enough! Bernice, you are a virgin, you're an innocent girl. Go back to your room, where your pocketbook is open, where your suitcase is open, and ... leave this great attorney to himself." John insisted that Fred was "dwelling wholly in his imagination," recalling that the following morning in Taos, Fred had asked, "Where were you there for about an hour last night?" "Well," John recalled that he had replied, "where do you think I was?" In 1953, John bantered that Fred "couldn't think how to ask me where I was, for I wouldn't have admitted it if he had," adding, "I enjoyed my visit to Taos."[201]

Bernice, for her part, also asserted that whatever Fred thought he saw "was just in [his] head" and that the hallway conversation he had witnessed was about her career: "I was a very ambitious young singer and I had dreams of being a great concert artist, and my newly found and very dear friend had promised to buy me a lovely Indian costume if I would accept it, and we were down there taking measurements to see if it would fit." At any rate, John cut short Fred's interrogation by addressing Bernice directly, borrowing from poet John Greenleaf Whittier, "Of all sad thoughts of pen or tongue, the saddest are these, it might have been."[202] Did Bernice share John's regret? It is hard to tell. In 1972, she told Quantrille, "It was a lot of fun—that was it as far as I was concerned, but [John] started writing to me and never stopped until the day he died."[203]

After Bernice returned to Fayette, John tried telephoning and sending gifts. When he was a couple of hours away in Kansas City, for instance, he called, wanting to see her. Bernice told him that "the book was closed and not to come." She was seeing "a young doctor" at the time, and, she later remembered, by comparison John seemed old to her.[204] John recalled this period, too: "I often thought about her, and I tried to phone her a couple of times, down at Lafayette or some other damn place down there in Missouri, but she intimated that it wasn't proper for anyone to be phoning to the girls' college."[205] John also sent her the "Indian costume" that he had promised, a transfer facilitated by Taos Pueblo artist Albert Looking Elk, who had traced Bernice's foot when John took her to the pueblo during the Taos trip (this following the measurements the two made at the Don Fernando).[206] Once John retrieved the outfit—a green cloth dress, a woven sash, and what Bernice called "squaw boots"—he mailed it to her in Fayette.[207] Neither the gift nor the calls changed her mind. She later confided to Quantrille, "[John] wanted to marry me in 1928 but I told him he had a living wife and was such a strict Catholic that it was impossible," even though he had assured Bernice that "he could get a special dispensation." When Bernice finally saw John again in the 1950s, she told him how lucky he was that she had refused him, insisting, "I would never have been happy not to follow a music career."[208] Regardless, Bernice's connection to John continued, and through him, she pursued research on Carson and found common ground with Quantrille.

For now, Bernice followed her music career. She stayed at Central College only a year after the Taos trip, returning to Chicago's North Side in 1929. She moved into a brick courtyard apartment building in the Lakeview neighborhood, which she shared with her college friend Gertrude Winkler and another musician.[209] Bernice had performed before, both in college and while teaching in Missouri, and she had worked in the music industry during her first stint in Chicago—serving as an usher at the city's sumptuous Auditorium Building, for example, and thus hearing gratis pianist Sergei Rachmaninoff and violinist Fritz Kreisler.[210] On her return, though, Bernice got her big break. In 1930, perhaps in need of revenue after the stock market crash of 1929, Chicago's Civic Opera Company announced a season of light opera to be staged at the Civic Theater, a smaller venue within the Civic Opera Building, home also to the grand Opera House. It was a bold venture designed to lure a paying audience, and it found supporters in the music columns of the *Chicago Tribune* and the *Chicagoan* (Chicago's short-lived answer to the *New Yorker*). In addition to the principal performers, the company auditioned hundreds of singers for the chorus, choosing just forty for the season.[211] Among those tapped were contralto Bernice Fowler and a young bass from North Carolina named Harold Blackwelder. Harold declined the offer, opting instead to join a radio quartet called the Wanderers. Bernice accepted and began rehearsing in March 1930.[212]

In the months that followed, Bernice's and Harold's careers took flight, and the two began to keep company as well. Bernice's nine-week season in light opera opened in April with seven weekly performances of Balfe's *The Bohemian Girl*.[213] She appeared as well in three productions that followed: the French operetta known in English as *The Chimes of Normandy*, Gilbert and Sullivan's *The Gondoliers*, and then their *The Yeomen of the Guard*. *The Gondoliers* was always her favorite, she told Quantrille decades later, "probably because I had a small solo part with my name in the program."[214] Audiences and critics alike received the season warmly, with the first works earning polite reviews and the later productions garnering more lavish praise. Bernice saved all of the notices, underlining remarks that reflected her own work on stage, including *Tribune* music critic Edward Moore's opinion that "one of the reasons for going to this season of light opera is ... the chorus. The group numbers forty, they are young, they are ambitious, they are good looking almost without exception, and without any exception at all they have heavenly voices."[215]

Meanwhile, Harold had just arrived in Chicago the year before, in 1929, but he was finding his footing. His all-male quartet, the Wanderers, landed a regular spot on the radio station WGN, sang on other radio programs, and performed live.[216] The Wanderers' tenor, Sam Thompson, had attended Central College, where Bernice taught, and along with Bernice he had enjoyed a successful audition for the Civic Opera's season of light fare. Like Harold, Sam chose the radio quartet instead. The *Tribune* grandly styled Harold, Sam, and the rest of the Wanderers as former "vaudeville stars." In truth, the four young white men were quite new to the music world.[217] They also had more than music on their minds, or at least Harold did. Neither Harold nor Bernice left record of their whirlwind courtship in 1930, save a photo of Bernice that she signed for him between the time they met, in early spring, and when they married, in late fall. The eight-by-ten head shot likely had been taken before Bernice left Missouri, perhaps in preparation for what she hoped would be her professional debut, and she inscribed it, "To Harold, the dearest sweetheart in the world, with love forever, Bernice." On Halloween, the two wed in the small Episcopal chapel that is part of the magnificent St. James Cathedral in downtown Chicago. Sam Thompson was best man, and Bernice's roommate Gertrude Winkler was maid of honor. Bernice remembered years later that she and Harold did not take a wedding trip, but she called the first dwelling they shared in Lincoln Park, south of her old Lakeview apartment, their "Honeymoon House."[218]

From their honeymoon house, Bernice and Harold ventured forth as performers into a world of public amusements that survived in spite of the Depression that descended in the 1930s. Bernice often used her own family name professionally (though she took her husband's name legally and used it frequently), and as Bernice Fowler, she took jobs on the stage and in radio. She performed, for instance, at the opulent Chicago Theatre in the Loop, a French baroque edifice with an exterior vertical sign that stretched six stories high. Theater entrepreneurs built it in the 1920s, when mammoth movie palaces that doubled as live performance venues were all the rage.[219] She appeared as well in a stage production of *A Midsummer Night's Dream*, directed by Max Reinhardt and starring an eleven-year-old Mickey Rooney and an eighteen-year-old Olivia de Havilland (both appeared in Reinhardt's 1935 film version, too). Bernice played a court lady and also sang with the fairy chorus when the touring play opened at the landmark Auditorium Theatre. The production earned rave reviews.[220]

Likewise, Bernice performed at the Apollo, a variety theater that, in 1933, featured a revival of the Duncan Sisters' *Topsy and Eva*, a comic takeoff on Harriet Beecher Stowe's antislavery novel *Uncle Tom's Cabin*. Bernice sang in a chorus for the show, which had premiered a decade earlier in San Francisco only to be reinvented on stage and screen for thirty years. In the Chicago revival, Vivian Duncan reprised her role as Little Eva, the angelic white mistress, and Rosetta Duncan did the same in blackface as Topsy, Eva's mischievous slave counterpart.[221] The sisters wrote new songs for this performance, ones that captured the musical idiom of a new decade, providing "fresh fodder," as a reviewer put it, for "the jazz band and the radio warblers."[222]

The Apollo's *Topsy and Eva* was a vaudeville minstrel act updated for a time when vaudeville—the vehicle that carried the nineteenth-century practice of minstrelsy into the twentieth—was starting to fall from favor, shadowed and eventually eclipsed by moving pictures. But vaudeville was not dead yet and neither was blackface. Blacking up had once been a special province of white male actors whose performances were consumed with gusto by white working-class men who loved to mock—and mocked from envy of—black men, whose imagined liberties they both disdained and desired.[223] Rosetta Duncan was one of a smaller number of white women who blacked up, and she created an anarchic character in Topsy, a slave girl whose sly humor and physical comedy lampooned all that was proper. Not incidentally, Topsy also nurtured in Little Eva a longing for similar license—and perhaps a longing for Topsy herself.[224] For all her racist appropriation of blackness, Rosetta inhabited her role "manfully," according to a reviewer. And given her reported offstage entanglements with women, she also embodied the era's shifting practice of locating alterity first in gender nonconformity and then in sexual object choice, a shift that birthed the century's homosexual/heterosexual binary. This transition reflected and joined itself to a simultaneous hardening of black/white racial categories across the same era.[225] Rosetta Duncan capered on stage and off where these two changes beat with a single heart. Bernice Fowler sang along.

Aside from arranging photos, playbills, and reviews in a scrapbook, Bernice kept no record of her musical labors or of her life with Harold for most of the 1930s, or at least none that has survived. But on New Year's Day in 1937, she started keeping a journal. The leather-bound book in which she wrote was a five-year diary, set up so that each page collected entries for a single date across the years—the first page, for instance, included records for New Year's Day in 1937, '38, '39, '40, and '41. Those entries give a feel for the diary's structure as well as a sense of how Bernice's life unfolded in this period. January 1, 1937, found Bernice on the road with two musicians and a stagehand headed for Los Angeles, where Harold was performing. The next year Bernice and Harold were back in the Windy City and they slept until noon; on New Year's Eve, Harold had sung at the Trianon Ballroom on the South Side—a segregated white dance palace not far from the heart of black Chicago. In 1939, after another late night, Harold joined Bernice at her sister Helen's place in Oak Park, a suburb just west of Chicago, where they shared a New Year's meal with a maternal aunt whose husband was hospitalized nearby. Helen Fowler, now called Helen Dunn, had moved to greater Chicago. She taught music and was raising a son on her own. Bernice and Helen's relationship could be stormy, but they still spent time together, and Bernice doted on her nephew Bob Dunn. In fact, New Year's 1940 found Bernice and Harold living with Helen, little Bob, and Helen's sister-in-law Grace. Mr. Dunn, Grace's brother and presumably Helen's husband, was out of the picture, and Grace was divorced. By 1941, the diary's last year, Bernice and Harold were on their own again, living in an apartment in Austin, a neighborhood adjacent to Oak Park. Both had singing jobs on New Year's Eve, and even though Bernice did not make it home until the wee hours of the morning and Harold trailed in after daybreak, they had Helen, Bob, Grace, and another friend, Grace Prince, for a holiday feast of smothered veal chops and scalloped oysters.[226]

How Bernice spent these five holidays says much about how she spent the half decade she recorded in her diary. She found work as a singer but also set aside her dreams to follow Harold's, even trailing after him to either coast in his search for a big break. Harold never turned down a job so that Bernice could work. And Bernice sometimes stayed behind while he toured the country or slept alone while he played late-night venues in town. Just once, they went on tour together. The caprice of performers' work lives, amplified by the privations of the Depression, meant not only that Bernice and Harold were often separated but also that they moved their belongings from one rented space to another with exhausting frequency. They struggled to make ends meet. Whether Harold was home or not, Bernice passed many hours in the company of women, often other musicians. She maintained ties—sometimes troubled ones—to family, especially to her sister. And she poured out affection on other women's children, often wishing she had one of her own. Through it all, Bernice's choices were shaped by the life chances afforded in this era to white, married women of modest means.

Bernice started her music career with only her own prospects to consider, but by the late 1930s, the decisions she made about work were tied to those of her husband. Her aspirations often took a back seat to Harold's, even as the income she earned was essential to the couple's well-being. Harold, more often than Bernice, took his show on the road, as Bernice's 1937 New Year's diary entry reveals. When Bernice set out for the West Coast that day, she was headed for Los Angeles to visit Harold, who was performing with the Weaver Brothers and Elviry, a vaudeville act rooted in a caricature of the white southern culture that birthed the brothers Weaver in the Missouri Ozarks: Leon, whose stage name was Abner, and Frank, whose stage name was Cicero. Elviry was the stage name of June Petrie, Chicago born but Missouri raised, who married first Leon and later, after divorcing him, brother Frank. The Weaver Brothers and Elviry were part of a broader southern diaspora that included not only migrations of both black and white southerners north and west but also a diffusion of southern cultural forms across the United States, with different consequences for the social fortunes of white and black people. Harold, a transplanted white southerner, embraced the Weavers' hillbilly act.[227]

But even when he performed with the Weavers, Harold's solos had more western than southern themes. In tunes that allowed his "high class voice to get low down," according to one reviewer, he sang about wagon wheels and overland trails.[228] Soon, Harold would leave the Weavers and reinvent himself as a wholly cowboy character, Neil Fortune, Gentleman from the West. It would be his most memorable persona, and Bernice's relationship to that persona was complex, full of pride and pique and desire, augmenting and reflecting, no doubt, her lifelong romance with western manhood. As Neil Fortune, Harold intoned mostly cow-country tunes to reviews that found him "a grand singer with a big bass voice."[229] In this, he followed a broader musical trend, as southern "hillbilly" music, itself a blend of Anglo-Celtic and African American folk styles, morphed into "country" and then "country western" music, the latter by incorporating songs of the range and other regional tunes, not to mention a western sartorial aesthetic that bore scant resemblance to the clothing actual cowboys wore.[230]

The Neil Fortune act took Harold from Grand Rapids, Michigan, to Rochester, Minnesota, and then even farther afield—he toured from Kansas City, Missouri, to San Antonio, Texas, where he told Bernice that he was "stopping the show." In this guise, Harold worked with an agent, Marvin Welt, and he sang with Benny Meroff and His Orchestra, a popular stage and dance band.[231] Bernice stayed in Chicago, wondering if she should join Harold on the road. "I'm just a straw in the wind," she lamented. Welt became so enthused about Neil Fortune's prospects that after the successful western tour, the agent decided his vocalist was ready for the East Coast. In January 1938, Bernice noted, she "met . . . the agent who says he will put my Haroldy on Broadway." Welt helped the cowboy singer break in his boots in the Midwest and West first, and then, in July, Bernice wrote triumphantly, "Harold and Marvin left for New York."[232]

By then, Bernice had given notice that she would be leaving the steadiest job she held in the 1930s, as a WGN staff vocalist. She gave it up to join Harold, and it was no small sacrifice. The engagement was not her first at WGN, the radio station owned by the *Chicago Tribune*, but when she got word of the new position in February 1937, she wrote in her diary, "What marvelous news. I am a member of the WGN staff at sixty dollars a week. I am so thrilled!" The next day, she wired the news to Harold, who was on the West Coast with the Weavers, and returned to her diary, noting, "How this can change the world for us." On WGN, Bernice sang for *Pageant of Melody*, a concert program, as well as *Midday Service*, which featured sacred music as well as religious and educational speakers (on her first day, Rabbi George Fox of Chicago's South Shore Temple spoke).[233] Once a staff vocalist, Bernice proudly kept track of her paydays and trips to the bank ("Got my check and it warms my heart!" "Cashed my check and I feel rich."), even as she also noted more occasional contributions Harold made to family coffers ("Nice contrib[ution] from Harold. Makes him feel better to be more reg[ular].").[234] Still, this was the Depression, and good employment often did not last. Seven months after Bernice began singing on *Midday Service*, she wrote, "Bombshell exploded at rehearsal when we learned that our noon job was not going on." She kept working at the station, but the tone of her diary entries darkened: "Pepless bunch at W.G.N. Wish we had more to do," she wrote one day, and the following, "H[arold] and I are getting restless."[235] By then, Harold had been back from his western tour for six months and had been piecing together singing jobs at weddings, funerals, festivals, hotels, country clubs, and political meetings in Chicago, the suburbs, and regional cities and resorts— from nearby Glen Ellyn and Medinah to Delavan Lake in Wisconsin and Cincinnati in Ohio.[236] His work as Neil Fortune had not yet begun.

Given the vagaries of entertainment work, it is not surprising that when radio performers first unionized in fall 1937, both Bernice and Harold signed up with the fledgling American Federation of Radio Artists (AFRA). "H and I have joined the Radio singers union," Bernice wrote. "Hope it's a success." Two more times that autumn she noted that she attended a union meeting, but the tenor of her diary entries otherwise did not change. Rainy fall days were "bad for blue kids." Worried for his future, Harold was "all torn up inside." Small sums of invested money vanished, leaving Bernice to exclaim, "Our stocks are tumbling!" All in all, she pined, "Wish we could start out in quest of adventure."[237] Meanwhile, friends and fellow musicians worked to build AFRA's Chicago local; Sam Thompson, Harold's best man and first tenor in the Wanderers, was on the executive board, and so was the group's baritone, Phil Culkin.[238] But Bernice and Harold drifted away from the union, no doubt in part because they always envisioned themselves in some better place, some more congenial employ, untethered by connections and commitments to others caught in like conditions.

Those who founded AFRA imagined a happier work life in the dark days of the Depression, too, but were convinced that collective effort was more likely to bring their individual dreams to fruition. Commercial broadcast radio was not yet two decades old in 1937, but it was booming. Employment practices favored broadcasters, especially as stations both proliferated and consolidated and as competition between them made pay rates for singers, actors, and announcers erratic and drove them down as well—all this on top of radio work's unpredictability and irregularity. Artists might not earn a dime for rehearsal time, and shows could be canceled at will, as Bernice learned when her work with WGN's *Midday Service* came to a sudden end. Radio artists wanted better and standardized rates; they wanted to be paid for rehearsals; and, most of all, they wanted an organization to represent them as they negotiated the terms of their employment.[239]

They got that and more, aided by the 1935 passage of the National Labor Relations Act, or Wagner Act, a key component of President Franklin Delano Roosevelt and congressional Democrats' Second New Deal. The Wagner Act guaranteed workers the right to organize their own unions and bargain collectively. Working people of all stripes embraced these rights, broadening a social movement that had found more limited success during the First New Deal, when a wave of strikes met either partial victory or bitter defeat, when conservatives attacked what they saw as government meddling in the affairs of business, and ultimately, when the Supreme Court declared earlier prolabor legislation, the National Industrial Recovery Act, unconstitutional. The Wagner Act helped to revivify the labor movement, especially among the diverse workers in mass production industries and those who organized under the auspices of what became the Congress of Industrial Organizations (CIO).[240]

But unions formed under the auspices of the American Federation of Labor (AFL)—such as AFRA—also saw growth. While scholars sometimes see this era as one in which an expansive, inclusive industrial unionism gained ground at the expense of the more exclusive, hidebound craft unions, in fact, between 1937, when AFRA began, and 1945, when World War II ended, AFL unions recruited twice as many workers as CIO unions did. The AFL was a loose and relatively weak federation that afforded its affiliates autonomy, and those affiliates exhibited a range of structures and commitments as well as a variety of responses to the technological and workforce developments that constituted industrial change in the early twentieth century. AFL unions grew especially outside of manu-facturing—in construction, transport, and service industries—and, of relevance to radio workers, in communications. AFRA's founding, then, evinced a new participatory culture in which working people sought to lift themselves, together, out of the depths of the Depression and into a more democratic and just social order. Bernice and Harold considered what that culture and its organizations had to offer but ultimately chose to follow individual rather than collective paths forward.[241]

The Blackwelders' tepid embrace of the union also reflected their poli-tics. They were Republicans, though they likely adhered to the more lib-eral wing of that party, which in this era was not altogether hostile to the statism of the New Deal order but rather to that order's perceived ex-cesses and feared drift toward socialism, especially given the muscle of the labor movement. Neither were liberal Republicans altogether hostile to unions, even as they sought to curb union power and routinize collec-tive bargaining to the benefit of business. So Bernice and Harold's brief foray into union membership is not surprising. Still, they probably kept their political sympathies quiet in a city like Chicago, where the Demo-crats took hold in the 1930s and did not let go for the rest of the century. It was only privately, in her diary, that Bernice recorded her convictions, especially during the 1940 presidential election, when liberal Republi-can Wendell Willkie faced off against two-term incumbent FDR. When Willkie won the Republican primary, Bernice was pleased, and when the Democrats again nominated Roosevelt, she wrote, "Hope Willkie pins his ears back." When Harold performed for a political gathering in Octo-ber, she noted that because those attending were Democrats, "he sang flat." And when Willkie lost the general election in November, she pined, "Feel like going into mourning."[242]

If these were their sentiments in 1940, then Bernice and Harold probably felt few qualms about severing their union ties in 1938 and fleeing the Democratic stronghold that was Chicago for the bright lights of New York. Harold left first, driving with agent Marvin Welt in a car that Harold's father had helped finance. Harold's first dispatch from New York was "glowing." He told Bernice, "Marvin knows everyone." Bernice followed by train a week later and found Harold "a-beaming at the station."[243] An engagement at the palatial Roxy Theatre was soon in the offing. The Roxy seated almost six thousand and had multiple balconies, not to mention "live music . . . provided by a 110-person symphony orchestra, four conductors, [and] an organ so mammoth it required three organists to play it." The venue was any performer's dream. Paul Ash, who directed the house band, assured Harold that Neil Fortune was "all set for the Roxy" and destined to "be a star." But the show ultimately went on without the cowboy crooner, and Welt retreated to Chicago. Ash's consolation promise of club dates for Harold did not bear fruit, either. Harold pursued the bandleader, but Ash made himself so scarce that Bernice referred to him in her diary as "a *low rat*." Harold auditioned for the radio station WOR and sang for a Columbia Pictures agent, but nothing panned out.[244]

Meanwhile, Bernice and Harold's cash reserves dwindled and she wondered what they could do, as she put it, to "Keep the Wolf From the Door." They waited for a check that was due Bernice, sold a bond at a loss, split five dollars with generous but similarly strapped musician friends, and watched as their near-empty purse shrank from three dollars to fifteen cents. Finally, they sent an "S.O.S. to Dad Black," Harold's father. Dad Black came through, but the cash only bought groceries, some theater tickets, and enough gasoline for a drive in the country. Welt soon wired Harold and Bernice to return to Chicago and set them up in an apartment there.[245] Harold's East Coast debut never happened. Without Dad Black's contributions—first a car down payment and then emergency funds—the trip itself would have been nearly impossible. (Harold's father owned a café in the railroad town of Spencer, North Carolina.)[246] Less than two months after they left Chicago, Harold and Bernice were back home and broke.

But not for long. Living in the shadow of an agent who had failed to promote Neil Fortune in the East proved too much; as Bernice put it, "Wish Marvin had never come in our lives." The Blackwelders found a new apartment across the street from their 1930 "Honeymoon House" and Harold found a new booking manager. In the meantime, Bernice tried to assemble a trio and Harold hustled singing jobs, but Bernice earned no income and Harold's work was episodic. A chance for another tour with the Weaver Brothers and Elviry fell through, and Harold botched an audition at the radio station WLS. So when the new booking manager landed jobs in the West starting in January 1939, the Blackwelders jumped at the chance to take Neil Fortune on the road again. After spending New Year's with Bernice's sister, Helen, the couple went home and packed (Bernice wrote, "Can hardly wait to hit the trail!"). They began the drive west on January 3, even though Harold was not due to open in Seattle until the end of the month. He had lined up a job en route at the Varsity Theater in Columbia, Missouri — "an awful place," Bernice complained. At least the stop gave them some travel funds.[247]

Then they drove on to Bernice's old haunts in Kansas. Her parents had both died in the early 1930s, but her aunt and uncle were still in Brookville. The Blackwelders also called on Bess and Fred Heine in Lucas, saw oil fields near Wichita, toured the Fort Hays college campus, and performed in intimate, local settings, including on a Brookville stage between the acts of a community play and on KSAL radio in Salina. The couple did not make much money during their brief Kansas sojourn, but the Heines bought them car insurance and they ate and slept free, which meant that the travelers got a good start for the rest of their trip. Harold's West Coast opening had been postponed to February, so they did not hurry. A five-day drive through Colorado, Wyoming, Idaho, Oregon, and Washington, some of it tracing the route of the Oregon Trail, took them to Seattle, where they settled into a steam-heated cabin at a tourist camp.[248]

The West Coast proved more hospitable to Neil Fortune. Harold opened first at Seattle's Palomar, a combination movie-and-vaudeville theater, alongside a ventriloquist, a dance team, two clowns, and some bicycle-riding comedians. The clowns were the vaudeville headliners, but they were overshadowed, in both billing and reviews, by the motion picture that filled the Palomar's screen, *The Little Tough Guys in Society*, a film about New York street kids. Still, Neil Fortune earned good notice: "'The Gentleman from the West' was well received in a musical number in which he released a strong bass voice on 'Home on the Range' and 'Old Faithful.'" Soon Bernice reported of the other performers, "They call me Mrs. Cowboy."[249] From Seattle, Neil Fortune and Mrs. Cowboy drove north to British Columbia, where Harold opened at the Beacon Theatre in Vancouver, with comedian Maude Hilton as the headliner. Then they turned south again, passing through Portland and on to San Francisco, where they moved into a "Spanish cabin" at an auto court and, in a fit of optimism, got a new license plate — a field of blue sporting yellow digits and letters, with "California World's Fair 39" at the top.[250]

Bernice wanted to put down roots in the Golden State. She thought San Francisco might be her "favorite city," especially since it was "all dressed for the fair," though Harold found the Golden Gate Theatre a "hard house to play." He enjoyed the Roosevelt in Oakland, where Maude Hilton again had top billing. And the couple did get to see the World's Fair on Treasure Island.[251] But in the end it was Southern California that beckoned them. Hilton followed the same path, so when the Blackwelders found a Hollywood apartment in April, she asked to move in with them and they agreed. Bernice told her diary, "This is the place to live." Harold had doubts, but Bernice pushed him to stay and "get planted."[252]

Thus began three months of Hollywood drama, replete with dashed hopes for roles in film and radio and on the stage, hopes nourished by new acquaintances, many of whom turned out to be, in Bernice's estimation, "leeches and four flushers." Maude Hilton was an exception. Bernice relished the comedian's company, remarking, "She is so much fun and such a regular guy." The women played rummy and shopped for slacks, leaving Bernice feeling "glamorous." And Bernice was happy to keep house while Maude and Harold "fared forth and did the agents," calling them the "kids" and the "breadwinners" as they ventured out.[253]

But they lived in a vortex of underemployed performers and overconfident agents. All were on the make and some were publicly vexed by affairs of the heart. Not only was Hilton's husband conspicuously absent as she and her female fellow comedians came and went (they found more work than Harold did), but the Blackwelders also lived next door to a romantically challenged booking agent, Ann Dempster. Dempster took Harold to Republic Pictures, which produced B Westerns. No contract materialized. Though she did book a job for Harold in San Bernardino, the Blackwelders felt themselves mostly an audience for her troubles with men, one named Harry, who drank too much, and another named Howard, who Bernice thought was "too much gypsy for a husband." Next, the Blackwelders met Aaron Fox, who took Harold to Selznick International Pictures and the Paramount studios and then told the singing cowboy to wait by a telephone that never rang. (Aaron Fox was the brother of William Fox, who established Fox Film Corporation but then lost control of it after the 1929 stock market crash.) Meanwhile, with Hilton headlining out of town, Fox proposed moving in with Harold and Bernice—indeed, Fox's housing needs may have been one reason he befriended the couple. Hilton tracked Fox down and told him off, and Bernice was disgusted, too, reflecting, "Why must everyone we meet here have to be a heel?" The Blackwelders did find a friend in Henry Sanders, who kept a women's clothing store on Hollywood Boulevard. Sanders was the son of Jewish immigrant parents; he grew up in Los Angeles, where he learned the tailoring business at his father's elbow. Bernice described the clothier as a "genuine note in a discord of acquaintances." But dissonance was the rule.[254]

All this drama produced little income. Harold played the Orpheum Theatre in Los Angeles alongside Hilton, but the job lasted only a week. He also played the Strand in Long Beach, for just ten days. Harold and Bernice alike endured auditions that went nowhere; both sang for the Paul Taylor Chorus on NBC radio, and Bernice tried out for a light opera troupe as well as the Hollywood Bowl Opera Company. She practiced at a Hollywood spot—Goodman's Studio—run by an old acquaintance, and she learned of potential jobs there, but nothing materialized: "Sang awhile at Goodman's. I really could sing if I had a chance. I know it."[255] She did not get a chance. Less than two months after the Blackwelders arrived in Hollywood, Harold wrote to his father, asking for help again. Two weeks later, Bernice wrote in her diary, "Dad Black came thru so we ate." Even that assistance was not enough. So Bernice turned to her brother, Duane, who was now with J. C. Penney in Cadillac, Michigan. It was, she noted, the "first favor I ever asked."[256]

Duane Fowler sent a check that came just as Bernice and Harold were leaving Los Angeles, heading to a show at the Capitol Theatre in Portland. They departed July 5, detouring east to see Las Vegas, the newly completed Hoover Dam, Bryce Canyon, and Salt Lake City, where they heard the Mormon Tabernacle Choir. From there they turned north toward the Snake River, which seemed "like an old friend," and then on to the Columbia River Highway, the first planned scenic road in the nation. They arrived in Portland, settled into a "nice modern cabin," and a few days later, Neil Fortune opened at the Capitol. For once, he had top billing. When Bernice saw him, she beamed, "Neil really is stopping them. Best I ever heard him do." It would be the last she ever heard him do, too. When the Capitol show closed and other western jobs fell through, Neil Fortune hung up his hat. He and Mrs. Cowboy drove back east, lingering briefly in Denver. Bernice had not been there since her college days. "How different things look after you've been around," she wrote. They made a quick stop in Lucas, Kansas, to see Bess and Fred Heine, who bought the Blackwelders a new tire to replace one that had blown en route, and paused in Brookville to see Bernice's aunt and uncle. Then they drove on to Chicago, where they bunked with friends until they could move in with Bernice's sister, Helen, in Oak Park. They were home, but Bernice confided to her diary, "Memories of the West surge up and choke us."[257]

Never again would Bernice and Harold reach so far and grasp so little, and never again would Bernice subordinate her work so thoroughly to

Harold's. The couple could not afford the illusion that a husband was a breadwinner and a wife a homemaker. That illusion had always been out of reach for the vast majority of immigrants, people of color, and poor whites in the United States, but among white middle-class and prosperous working-class families, a male provider ethic had held sway. During the Depression, though, many men lost their jobs and could not secure new ones, while women were more apt to find work and keep it, in part because they earned less than men and the kinds of service jobs women held better survived the downturn.[258] In abandoning the breadwinner ideal, then, Bernice and Harold were in good, or at least ample, company in the 1930s.

Working in live entertainment also buffered the blow. Since the late nineteenth century, women in theater, and especially vaudeville, had helped to advance new norms of womanhood by creating spectacles of themselves both on stage and off, norms that eventually dovetailed with political activists' assertions of female power and women's equality. As the twentieth century unfolded, male theater entrepreneurs found ways to harness such spectacle into the standardized "chorus girls" of the Broadway revue, which in turn prompted a spate of motion pictures that explored, through the figure of the chorus girl, the social anxieties prompted by an industrialized nation run amok. But none of what happened to female performers and their representation in the early twentieth century could alter this: Bernice and Harold alike inherited live theater's embrace of female autonomy, of a woman's capacity for independent selfhood.[259] However disappointed they were that life as Neil Fortune and Mrs. Cowboy did not continue, they were better prepared to roll with the Depression's economic punches than those in other marriages, where a husband expected to carry the weight of the couple on his working back.

When the Blackwelders got back to Chicago in August 1939, however, it was not clear that Harold's income would prove insufficient or that Bernice would abandon housewifery. Harold landed one-day jobs right away and then a longer engagement at the Ivanhoe, a restaurant and performance venue modeled on a medieval castle. Bernice stayed home, working with her sister, Helen (who also taught music), to cook, clean, sew, can produce, and wash and iron clothes. "I'm a housewife," Bernice told her diary. A few days later, though, a telegram arrived from June Weaver calling for "a trio and Boy" to join the Weaver Brothers and Elviry—that is, for three vocalists and Harold. Bernice organized a trio, enlisting her friend Grace Prince and a third singer. Meanwhile, Bernice and Helen rushed to sew the costumes, all "hair ribbons and prints," leaving Bernice feeling "twelve and Brookvillish." In ten days, the four performers were on the road for the Weaver home in Missouri, where, Bernice noted, "all we do is eat and rehearse a bit and eat some more." They soon opened at the Electric Theatre in Springfield, where, she declared, "I have arrived. I am a Hill Billy." Then the troupe toured Oklahoma and Texas. As in the past, Bernice loved seeing the sights, especially the Alamo, and the paycheck was welcome. But a "petty undercurrent of intrigue" poisoned the engagement with the Weavers, leaving Harold "so unhappy" that Bernice wished she and her husband had never joined the show. When the Weavers cut them loose in December, the Blackwelders took a bus back to Springfield, retrieved their car, and drove to North Carolina, where they visited Harold's relatives and marveled over how Dad Black ran his new barbecue place in High Point, forty miles northeast of Spencer. Thereafter, whenever singing jobs were scarce, Harold dreamed of running his own.[260]

Jobs were often scarce for both Harold and Bernice. They returned to Chicago in time for Christmas in 1939, which they spent with sister Helen, nephew Bob, and Helen's sister-in-law Grace Dunn in the Oak Park household they all shared. Harold went out after New Year's "to get the ball rolling," but even though he learned to play bass and formed one and then another trio—both failed—he did not work again until February. Bernice had no paid jobs at all. By the end of the month she wrote, "Our bank roll is getting too thin." Then, after Bernice fought with sister Helen, the Blackwelders left Oak Park. In March, they borrowed money again from Bernice's brother, and Harold joined a quartet. They found a tiny apartment in Montrose Beach—so small that Bernice had to stay in the Murphy bed while it was down "or camp in the bathroom." In April, Harold's new group, the Four Royalists, found late-night work at the Old Hickory Inn (this is why the bed stayed down; Harold got home just before dawn and the couple ate breakfast well after noon). Meanwhile, Bernice, alarmed by war news of Germany's gains in Europe, volunteered with the Red Cross, even as she sought out and then secured a berth in an outfit called the Master Singers. After weeks of rehearsals, the Master Singers embarked on a grand tour of late summer events in Iowa, Wisconsin, Minnesota, North Dakota, Oklahoma, and Michigan. While Bernice was still rehearsing, Harold got a call from an old vaudevillian, Bobby Kuhn, offering a seven-week tour in Canada. Harold quit his quartet and departed before Bernice did, and Bernice moved back in with Helen until Iowa called. By the time Bernice returned to Chicago in September, Harold was back in town and had moved them in with musician friends, perhaps in Rogers Park.[261]

The search for work continued. The Master Singers attracted no new jobs, so when choral director Frank Bennett invited Bernice to join a stage pageant for the upcoming Chicago Automobile Show, she said yes.[262] The show, the largest in North America, was four decades old when Bernice signed on in 1940. It cost fifty-five cents to attend. One could wander exhibits of cars, trucks, and military vehicles spread over two floors and both wings of Chicago's International Amphitheater, adjacent to the Union Stock Yards. One could also witness the twice-daily pageant produced on what promoters claimed was the biggest stage, with the most expansive curtain, ever constructed in the United States. It had to be huge to accommodate not only automobiles but also the cast of the revue, called *Non-Stop America*: actors, an orchestra, a ballet troupe, the Bennett Singers, and twenty "community queens" (young women chosen for their beauty to represent Chicago's neighborhoods and suburbs) who together dramatized "the history of cars in two acts." The *Chicago Tribune* termed *Non-Stop America* a "music and girl number."[263] Bernice, now thirty-seven, was part of the music, not one of the girls; she sang with seven other women and eight men. Three weeks of rehearsals preceded the nine-day show, and when it was all over, Bernice relished payday. When Harold came to see the revue, the two wandered among the cars and Bernice noted, "[We] decided Buick is the tops. Now for a job so we can have one."[264] Chicago had changed from the nineteenth century, when livestock and people moved by rail, to a twentieth century of truck transport and car trips. But the women, younger and older, hired to celebrate the nation's new automotive culture could not afford to buy the goods their bodies and voices promoted.

In the midst of all this, the Blackwelders' perennial uncertainty and anxiety began to give way to a semblance of security and stability. While Bernice was busy with the auto show, Harold sang at a country club, a machinists' gathering, and the Swedish Club. Then, however, "a blow fell"; they learned that they would have to move again. They went house hunting, found a three-flat brick building in the Austin neighborhood with a unit vacant, and hauled their worldly goods to the new spot, all while Bernice was singing at the stockyards and Harold was working here and there across the city.[265] The Austin apartment was a step up; they were no longer in a shared residence where someone else held the lease, as they had been when they lived with sister Helen or with friends, and they did not have to contend with cramped quarters as they had in Montrose Beach. They also lived across the street from a large park.[266] It was fortunate, then, that within a month of the move, Harold joined a new quartet, the Four Bards, under contract at the Ivanhoe. The show there was a far cry from the Weavers' hillbilly revue or Neil Fortune's cowboy act. Under a cartoon captioned "A Café in Sherwood Forest?"— depicting four musicians in feather-adorned felt caps performing for nightclubbers in a wooded glen—the *Daily News* described the scene: "Looking like a quartet of Robin Hood's men, the Four Bards entertain in the woodland spaces of Ivanhoe, picturesque old English café." The work paid well; Bernice estimated that Harold was bringing home ninety dollars a week, almost three times more than most manufacturing workers earned. Suddenly, the couple could afford a new car—a Chevrolet rather than a Buick. They named their maroon coupe Ivan Hope for, as Bernice put it, "Ivanhoe that made it possible." Then they bought a puppy, a Staffordshire bull terrier. The residential milieu and the park made it easy to keep little Duke active, and the dog brought them joy. As Bernice put it in December of 1940, "We are dreaming dreams again."[267]

Even with all this hope, the Blackwelders' struggles endured. Bernice still performed with the Bennett Singers and sang at banquets, clubs, and churches, but the work was irregular and the wages insufficient. As she told her diary, "I'm getting fed up with the B's. Wish I could get in a legitimate job." She auditioned for the operetta *The Student Prince*, staged at Cohan's Grand Opera House, and got the part of a court lady. Though the pay was meager, she took the part, reasoning, "Might as well be busy while H. is gone every nite." The show ran for three weeks. Meanwhile, Harold's work at the Ivanhoe was hardly permanent; the job lasted less than six months.[268]

So the dream Harold began to dream was of opening a barbecue place. The Four Bards stayed together after they closed at the Ivanhoe, working in nightclubs and hotel lounges. But when he was not performing, Harold led Bernice on a wild-goose chase for a location where he could sell slow-cooked meats and all the fixings to Chicagoans hungry for southern fare. His earnings from the Ivanhoe would cover the initial rent, equipment, and start-up costs. In 1941, Bernice reported, Harold was "talking nothing but barbeque." They considered a spot for rent at Harlem and Addison, on Chicago's northwest side. Then, with both Harold and Bernice shuttling in and out of town for work, Bernice went to see another location at Cicero and North, on the edge of Austin. Harold, from afar, told her to take it, but the rent was too steep. Later they drove north on the Skokie Highway and finally northwest to Des Plaines. On December 7, 1941, they visited a spot there called The Point. "Would be a good place," Bernice wrote in her diary, a sentence she followed with one more consequential: "Japs raided Pearl Harbor and declared war on us." It turned out that The Point was for sale, not for rent, and the price,

Harold learned when he went to see it again just before Christmas, put it far out of reach. Harold came home with a Philco combination radio-phonograph instead. They owned no records yet, but the couple could listen to the medium that had helped launch their musical careers. All in all, Bernice thought it a "very serious Christmas."[269]

The serious matter of a world at war had long been among Bernice's concerns, as her Red Cross work in spring 1940 showed. She followed the progress of the hostilities starting in December 1937, when Japanese forces that had invaded Nanjing attacked a U.S. gunboat and Standard Oil tankers evacuating U.S. citizens and company employees from the besieged Chinese city. "Japs sank one of our ships. Hope it doesn't mean war," Bernice wrote.[270] From then on, though, Bernice paid no attention to the conflict unfolding in the Pacific until October 1941, just before Pearl Harbor, when she noted, "Japanese situation grows more tense. . . . Looks like we are on the brink." Instead, she chronicled combat in Europe in over fifty diary entries (compared with just three on Asia). Indeed, by extracting Bernice's diary entries on the war from their contexts and assembling them in order, a headline-like chronology of the European conflict emerges: Hitler and Mussolini go on the offensive. Britain appeases Germany. Hitler takes Czechoslovakia. Nazis invade Poland. England, then France, declares war on the Germans. Russians attack Finland, then make peace. Germany invades Denmark and Norway, then Holland and Belgium. Nazis bomb and then march on Paris. Italy declares war. Hitler orders air raids on London. The United States approves support for Great Britain. War erupts in Bulgaria, Yugoslavia, and the Balkans. Germany attacks the Soviet Union, and the United States allies itself with the leader Bernice calls Bloody Joe Stalin.[271] Her chronicle reflects a common U.S. consciousness of the war, one focused on Europe, not Asia. It also reflects a moral trajectory that some Americans followed in the late 1930s and early '40s, from fervent isolationism to increasing revulsion against Nazism, growing fear of Axis power, and mounting recognition that the United States would and should enter the war. Her chronicle suggests as well the intimate anxieties the deepening conflict could evoke for women like Bernice. When Britain and France declared war on Germany in 1939, Bernice expressed her greatest fear: "Keep thinking that it might take my lover."[272]

War did not take Harold away, and thus Bernice's diary chiefly bespeaks a burgeoning international consciousness focused resolutely on Europe. Unlike her future friend Quantrille, Bernice was young when World War I broke out, so the coming of World War II was Bernice's introduction to global conflict. Her newfound consciousness may have been shaped not only by war news but also by encounters with expansive geo-political views at a critical moment. In 1939, when she and Harold were staying in a Seattle tourist cabin and he was preparing to open at the Palomar, Bernice exposed herself to two new intellectual currents. First, she read Louis Adamic's *My America*, which promoted, like the rest of the Slovene immigrant writer's corpus, a plebian cultural pluralism and a social order that embraced the dignity and diversity of working people. Bernice found *My America* "intensely interesting," calling it "the kind of book for me."[273] While she was finishing Adamic, she went to hear British Marxist Harold Laski speak at the University of Washington. Laski had been invited to teach a course there, one that found students crowd-ing the aisles and applauding his lectures. He also gave evening talks that were open to the public. Bernice attended one of these and then re-turned to her diary to describe Laski as a "fine orator" and herself as "edi-fied."[274] Adamic's text and Laski's talk seem to have had an effect. While Bernice had mentioned European tensions in her diary before this—especially in fall 1938 when Britain and France tried to appease Germany and when she first heard Hitler, who struck her as a "maniac"—it was only after reading Adamic and listening to Laski that she began to write faithfully about the unfolding conflict.[275] The two thinkers opened up a wider world to her, one stateside that must have resonated with her own foray into the labor movement and her perennial struggle to make ends meet, and another across the Atlantic, where political theorists like Laski saw fascism as a threat to working-class internationalism. Bernice would not entertain the most progressive implications of these worldly visions for long, but that she considered them at all evinces a historical moment in the late 1930s that had not yet banished radicalism from U.S. popular thought.

Bernice's new expansiveness, for all its internationalism, was mostly limited to European affairs—at least until the attack on Pearl Harbor de-manded a more global perspective. This identification with things Euro-pean also shaped Bernice's experience of the racial and ethnic land-scapes she traversed and peoples she encountered before World War II, though the coming of the war allowed her to distinguish between and among things European as well. By the 1930s, dominant understand-ings of race in the United States incorporated many of the new immi-grants from the late nineteenth and early twentieth century into a circle of whiteness. Southern and eastern European newcomers and their off-spring, who had once been able to make more provisional claims to the preferred and privileged U.S. racial category, found themselves em-braced as white. But at the same time, both liberal and more radical versions of cultural pluralism cut against the consolidation of whiteness by emphasizing—in the case of liberal versions, to the point of reifying—the cultural specificity, the "cultural gifts," as some put it, of various immigrant and resident populations in the United States.[276] In the everyday lives of many white Americans, these various strands of racialist and antiracist ideologies, which were conceptually and politically distinct, could weave themselves together in unpredictable ways, allowing for both new associations and old exclusions.

Accordingly, both Bernice and Harold, who descended from older-stock European Americans, developed close ties with Jewish friends and coworkers who were, or whose parents were, immigrants—witness Bernice's fondness for Hollywood clothier Henry Sanders and both Blackwelders' longtime association with vaudevillians Sylvia Clark Kuhn and Bobby Kuhn.[277] Bobby Kuhn's ancestry is hard to trace. He and his brothers, who performed in the 1910s and '20s as the Three White Kuhns (a racial, and racist, play on words), may or may not have been Jewish. But Sylvia Clark was a Syrian Jew born in Palestine; later in life, she and her husband converted to Christian Science.[278] Bernice and Harold stayed close to Sylvia and Bobby Kuhn for the rest of their lives. In 1965, Bernice described the couple to Quantrille as "old and very dear friends" and Sylvia as "a headliner in vaudeville as a comedienne, very handsome small Jewish woman, now a Christian Science practitioner who does not inflict her views upon anyone."[279] Likewise, Bernice was taken with Slovene American Louis Adamic's cultural pluralist vision of the United States. All of this reflected new ways of seeing race and ethnicity in the 1930s.

For Bernice, these new ways required adjustment. For example, her close friend from Fort Hays Kansas Normal College, Gertrude Winkler, married a Greek immigrant, Tony Koplos. Bernice shared an apartment with Gertrude in Chicago before the Blackwelders exchanged vows and Gertrude served as maid of honor at their wedding. The friendship endured, but Gert's marriage to Tony challenged Bernice's embrace of pluralism. While Harold was on tour with the Weavers in 1937, Bernice noted that she "went Greek" with Gert and Tony, dining at the Athenian Café and enjoying "some Greek nite life." But the next day she wrote that Gert was "helping the Greek-American cause," adding, "How can she?"[280] It is not clear what provoked Bernice to question Gertrude's work for her husband's ethnic community in Chicago, home to the largest Greek population in the United States (and so sometimes called Chicagopolis). Nor is it clear what sort of work Gertrude did. Long subject to divisions that reflected changing regimes in the homeland as well as struggles over belonging among co-ethnics in an often hostile United States, Greek American politics in the 1930s were complicated further by the rise to power of Prime Minister Ioannis Metaxas, a royalist and anticommunist who assumed dictatorial powers in Greece that some likened to those seized by Mussolini in fascist Italy. The Metaxas regime courted Greek Americans, and Greek Americans responded variously.[281] If Gert Koplos was working on behalf of those who supported Metaxas, then Bernice's disapproval may have been more antifascist than anti-Greek. Bernice criticized the Koplos family again after Gert bore a child, lending some credence to this suggestion. When she visited the newborn, Bernice noted that there had been a "big argument over the baby's name," adding smugly, "Glad my man's an American." Nonetheless, Bernice witnessed the child's christening as Barbara Vasiliki and stayed for Greek food and dance afterward. Vasiliki is a given name that connotes royalty. If Gert and Tony chose the middle name for this reason, then perhaps Gert had been working with Greek Americans who supported royalist Metaxas.[282] Or maybe the parents named their daughter after a relative or thought that she would henceforth rule their lives. Whichever was the case, a few days later, Bernice met Gert downtown for a show and reflected afterward, "Our lives have taken such different turns since Hays days."[283]

In the long run, those different turns made only so much difference to Bernice. For a time, the Koplos family lived in Wisconsin, where Tony worked at restaurants in La Crosse and Eau Claire. When the Master Singers took Bernice to Eau Claire in 1940, she visited with Gert and Tony, and they in turn came to see Bernice's show. "Nice to see them so well settled and happy," Bernice wrote in her diary. The Koploses returned to Chicago and opened a restaurant there in 1941, and Bernice went to try it. She worried, though, that her friends' travels and travails were wearing on them: "Tony so thin, Gert looks older."[284] Meanwhile, Bernice and Harold alike found work singing at Greek American festivals, churches, and funerals, and Harold sang regularly with the Byzantine Ensemble, a chorus organized "to interpret the ancient music of Greece and Byzantium." Harold was part of the non-Greek minority in that group.[285] And three decades after Bernice criticized Gert for assisting the "Greek-American cause," the Blackwelders were still entertaining the Koploses, inviting them for a meal of barbecued chicken in 1967: "Tony is Greek and a food expert," Bernice told Quantrille, "so I was happy to see him enjoying a real Southern dinner."[286] A sense of difference still inflected Bernice's thoughts about Gertrude's marriage but perhaps no longer a sense of her own superiority.

Bernice's encounters with other immigrant communities were fewer and more fleeting than those she had with Jews and Greeks. Passing contact came, for instance, when she patronized Chicago ethnic restaurants. These culinary adventures were possible after Harold's father bought the couple a car in 1937. Then, they could drive south to Chinatown or southwest to Little Italy from their Near North Side apartment. In Chinatown, they joined white friends and relatives in the rage for North American–style Chinese food at restaurants like Mei Hung, Nankin, and Hoe Sai Gai. The trips were notable enough to earn a diary mention—nothing more. The Blackwelders ventured out for Italian fare as well, to the neighborhood Bernice alternately called "Dagotown" and "Woptown."[287] Both Chinese and Italian enclaves offered Bernice a taste of exoticism in her own urban backyard. At the same time, restaurants there offered scant opportunity for sustained interaction with Chinese and Italian people, so Bernice had little incentive to rethink common prejudices or to inquire into the conditions that produced and sustained insular ethnic communities in Chicago.[288] Notably, she saved slurs for an Italian neighborhood. Perhaps she associated it with fascist Italy, merging an unexamined anti-immigrant sentiment with a more considered antifascism.[289] Meanwhile, residents of Chicago's Chinatown had engaged in anti-Japanese activism ever since Japan invaded Manchuria in 1931, which might help explain the neutral terms Bernice used to refer to the neighborhood that satisfied her craving for chop suey.[290] Although by now Italian Americans were considered white, while Chinese Americans remained racialized as nonwhite, the global upheaval of the 1930s and perceptions of that upheaval in the United States could alter older-stock European Americans' assessments of their neighbors, even as their power to make and act on such assessments continued.[291]

Nowhere was that power greater than in white people's relationship to African Americans. Bernice exercised such privilege most fully when, as an adult, she began to live in proximity to black people. She likely grew up knowing no African Americans in Brookville. When she was born in 1902, one black couple lived in town—an aging Union veteran of the Civil War named Joseph Clark, originally from Virginia, and his Missouri-born spouse, Harriet Clark. Joseph died in 1903, however, when Bernice was still an infant. Harriet lived until Bernice was five years old. But after she lost her husband, Harriet moved to nearby Salina, so Bernice may never have seen her among the 250 white souls who walked the streets of Brookville.[292] Once Bernice moved to Missouri and even more when she relocated to Chicago, the white world of her youth—itself the product of Indian dispossession—gave way to different racial landscapes. Black

Missouri was as old as white Missouri; the state had entered the union permitting slavery in 1820, thereby overwriting an older mingling of Indigenous peoples and migrants from French, Spanish, British, and then U.S. empires, often at first on largely Indian terms.[293] Bernice entered the enduring legacy of those shifts when she moved to Little Dixie in 1926, living among descendants of slaveholders and teaching alongside the white composer of a "Negro Suite."[294] But if black Missouri was over a century old when Bernice lived there in the 1920s, black Chicago was a new sort of place, a product of the Great Migration, still under way, of six million African Americans from the South to the North and West after 1910. No word better describes Bernice's activity in that place, which she began to visit in 1937, than the one she used herself: "slumming." The physical distance between Bernice and Harold's Near North Side apartment and the burgeoning South Side Bronzeville neighborhood that they visited was not so great as the racial distance Bernice felt they traveled when they drove there in their new car. As Bernice put it in 1937, "Harold and I went slumming to the Ghetto."[295]

When she adopted the language of slumming, Bernice tapped a deep vein of white supremacist thought, one that also informed the practice of blackface in shows such as *Topsy and Eva*. In slumming as in blackface, that vein was shot through with white desire for the greater social license assumed at work among black people: it was a vein that reified racial hierarchy even as it granted white people the privilege to cross racial boundaries. While historians have stressed the sexual dimensions of the license white slummers sought in their forays into black districts like Bronzeville, Bernice, traveling there with her husband, sought a different sort of pleasure. What most attracted the couple was a hot dog joint called Sadie's, which, Bernice seemed surprised to note, made hot dogs "as good as anywhere."[296] It was being in Bronzeville at all that constituted slumming.

Just as the South Side sold good hot dogs, so did black people more generally sell the kind of entertainment that white people in the urban North could newly enjoy without upending a racial system that positioned white over black. The black selling was not primarily aimed at white buyers but rather at an African American marketplace of goods and ideas that ultimately birthed a black metropolis and a black modernity.[297] Bernice, like most white people, was oblivious to this and sought only its ancillary products—an array of novel consumer experiences predicated on the lure of difference. So, as a musician whose husband loved sport, Bernice eagerly consumed African American artistry and athleticism. She heard "colored contralto" Marian Anderson in 1937 and praised her "luscious voice," for instance, and attended a "negro Mikado" in 1938, noting, "they really swing it." With Harold, she went to a "negro ball game" in 1940.[298] Bernice consumed without understanding—or needing to understand—the racial assumptions and structures that made it seem odd to her to find a tasty hot dog in a black neighborhood, that created a sensation out of an accomplished black vocalist like Marian Anderson, and that established separate venues for black ballplayers and black singers in light opera.

When Bernice left Chicago for points west, she again traveled across landscapes of human difference that captured her attention without challenging, or at least not much, the preconceptions she brought to each place. In El Paso, for example, she looked across the Rio Grande and saw what she expected: "Mexicans, colored potteries, & big hats." In New Mexico and Arizona, she glimpsed "desert & adobe houses, cactus & red peppers, Indians & teepees" (probably tourist tipis, since Indians in the Southwest mostly did not live in them and certainly did not do so in the 1930s). Olvera Street in Los Angeles, which she thought would be a "Mexican market," confounded her expectations a bit, with its "Chinese and Mexicans all mixed up." She would not have been so surprised had she known that Olvera Street's development as a tourist attraction atop the crumbling center of the old Mexican pueblo of Los Angeles coincided with the building of adjacent Union Station, which displaced the city's Chinatown (Olvera Street opened in 1930; Bernice visited in 1937; Union Station opened in 1939). Seattle offered Bernice its annual Potlatch celebration, a deeply non-Indian festival that, as its best interpreter puts it, nonetheless "appropriated Native imagery to create a regional vision of civic development." Across the border in Canada, Vancouver was disconcerting, with its unfamiliar mix of South Asian and East Asian migrants, or as Bernice put it, "Hindus and Chinese." But San Antonio reassured, with "Mexicans everywhere" safely overshadowed by the Alamo. "I ... could almost feel the spirits of its heroes," Bernice wrote of the iconic site where Anglo Texans lost a key battle but, collectively, went on in 1836 to win the Texas Revolution, creating a republic independent of Mexico, which in turn led to U.S. annexation a decade later. In all this, a North American West of staggering diversity created and divided by a complex history of empire and nation, of labor and capital, became a quaint, consumable tableau vivant.[299]

The legacies of conquest and colonialism and the consequences of the global migration of workers, both enslaved and free, weighed on Bernice as she probed the boundaries of her own personal pluralism. When it came to relationships with people of Southern and Eastern European (and even Syrian) descent, Bernice rolled up her sleeves and turned to the task of learning, however awkwardly and incompletely, to embrace the gifts those relationships had to offer. This was true unless the connection was fleeting—a drive to Little Italy for "real spaghetti"—and perhaps clouded by assumptions about ethnic communities' fascist sympathies.[300] Bernice was in good company in a United States where a still contested civic nationalism was slowly but steadily moving away from the exclusionary impulses of the 1920s, exemplified in immigration laws that limited the influx of Southern and Eastern Europeans (and that barred Asian immigration entirely), and toward a more inclusive nationalism that would become essential to the war effort in the 1940s. But like the pluralisms that pulsed through U.S. culture more generally, Bernice's knew profound limits when it came face-to-face with persistently racialized peoples, including African Americans, ethnic Mexicans, Asian Americans, and American Indians, whose communities, at best, constituted a colorful background or novel playground for white adventure. In such encounters, an older racialized nationalism prevailed; the terrain of whiteness had expanded, but borders remained.[301]

Even though Bernice spent time in the racial borderlands, she lived most of her life within a circle of whiteness. In addition to her coworkers on the stage and in radio, virtually all her intimate contacts lived in that circle as well—her husband, housemates, relatives, and friends. Calling these intimate contacts by different names, however, as if they constituted separate categories for Bernice, runs counter to how she experienced them, because as often as not, Bernice counted all as family. There was no set formula for these family relations, but a present or past of co-residence often tightened the bonds in ways that made them difficult to break, even as households came together and fell apart. Ties created by birth and marriage flowed into and out of these domiciles but did not determine them. What determined who lived where and for how long were emotional bonds, financial need, shared responsibility for children, and the vagaries of musical employment. In addition, a racial structure barely visible to most white people—an institutional racism—shaped these households and the family ties they helped cement, ensuring that all who lit up when Bernice walked in the room were white.

Bernice chronicled these relations from 1937 to 1941, though most started before she started keeping a journal and continued after she stopped. When she began her diary, Bernice was on a westward jaunt while Harold toured with the Weavers. She felt herself a "backstage wife" on the trip and noted that this was a "new experience" for her.[302] But the couple soon returned to Chicago, where they lived with fellow singer

Grace Prince, who also played piano. Sharing an apartment allowed all three performers to come and go as work required, since invariably someone was home to hold down the fort. Later, Grace—Bernice often called her Princie—would join Bernice and Harold on another Weavers tour. But the household that Bernice, Harold, and Princie shared was not simply one of convenience: Bernice cooked for Grace. They sewed with each other. Grace bought Bernice a dress. Bernice knitted Grace a sweater. Grace did Bernice's hair. They attended concerts and learned to swim together. When Harold was in town, the threesome might take a drive or go out for a chicken dinner. When Grace took a vacation and then returned, Bernice wrote in her diary, "Nice to have our family together again." And when Grace moved out, Bernice was crushed. She expressed her pique over Grace's choice of residence: "Grace left to live on the South Side. Sorry to see her go to such a place." The South Side, more and more, was a black place, and Grace moved to a white pocket of Bronzeville near the edge of a black neighborhood. Bernice said nothing explicit about Grace's decampment from the circle of whiteness, but she did not like it: "Drove out to see Grace's new apartment. I think it's terribly depressing for a person with so much talent. She does so little about it and criticizes others."[303] Bernice eventually got over her pique and repaired her relationship with Grace; it was after Grace moved out that she joined Bernice and Harold on tour with the Weavers.[304] But even at the center of the circle, racial meanings quietly structured family ties.

Princie was just one of three women in Bernice's life named Grace. The proliferation of Graces was such that one day in 1937 began with Grace Diebold waking up in the household of Bernice, Harold, and Grace Prince and ended with Grace Dunn coming to dinner with Bernice's sister, Helen, and nephew Bob. As Bernice put it in her diary, "We do have a Grace complex."[305] She might also have noted her Gertrude compulsion. Two of her closest friends were named Gertrude—Gertrude Koplos and Gertrude Miller. Following the connections that proceeded from the Graces and the Gertrudes gives a good sense of the networks Bernice navigated and how indistinguishable those networks were from any narrow definition of family.

While Bernice and Harold were living with Princie, for example, Bernice's friend Grace Diebold married a fellow musician named Walter Hardwick. Already this Grace was woven into the fabric of Bernice's life, and marriage did nothing to change that. Once, when newlywed Grace spent the night, Bernice noted, "She is such a sweet friend." Bernice and Harold started to spend more time with Grace and Walter even as Bernice and Grace maintained their bond. When the Hardwicks wondered if Grace might be pregnant, the Blackwelders loaned them their car so that Grace could see a doctor. That pregnancy either was a false alarm or else ended in miscarriage, but when Grace finally carried to full term, Bernice shopped with her for maternity clothes and reflected on the bodily experience of gestation: "Must be a queer feeling." Once little Herbie was born, the child entered Bernice's life as well. When Herbie was two and he accompanied Bernice and his mother on errands, Bernice wrote, "I'm one of the family."[306]

Bernice's relationships with the Gertrudes were similar. Gertrude Winkler's marriage to Tony Koplos forced Bernice to broaden her ethnic horizons, and the friendship endured. Meanwhile, Gertrude Miller, a fellow radio performer who married a fellow named Ralph, was another of Bernice's companions. The two women shopped and dined and attended movies, concerts, and stage shows together. Bernice and Harold also spent time with Gert and Ralph. When this Gert miscarried, Bernice worried for her and was pleased when Gert learned to take "her sorrow with the right philosophy." And when Bernice and Harold returned from their West Coast sojourn in 1939, they stayed with Gert and Ralph until they decided to move in with Bernice's sister, Helen.[307] The Gertrudes, like the Graces, were family.

The third Grace in Bernice's life further complicated any distinction Bernice might have made between family and friends. Grace Dunn was sister-in-law to Bernice's sister, Helen, who married Grace's brother Elmer Dunn. Elmer was out of the picture by the time Bernice started her diary in 1937, but he left Helen with a son, Bob. Grace Dunn was also separated from a husband; indeed, Bernice served as a witness when the case came up in divorce court.[308] Grace lived with Helen and Bob, and Bernice and Harold moved into and out of this household four times between 1938 and 1940, when the couple left for good and moved to Austin. Bernice liked Grace Dunn from the moment they met. But just as Bernice could be critical of Grace Prince, Bernice found fault with Grace Dunn, especially when she, like Princie before her, threatened to break up a household. When Grace Dunn considered moving, Bernice griped bitterly, "She is a queer combination of inhibitions and nerves and desires." Grace Dunn was also a singer who had performed in radio, but she later took an office job. Bernice drove Grace back and forth from work, and the two women spent time together both in the house and out on the town. They also cared for their nephew Bob at home and took him on outings, traipsing through the woods and going to movies, prompting

Bernice to note, "Bob has double aunt trouble." The child had, in effect, three mothers. (Harold was no father figure, though; Bernice thought that her husband was jealous of the boy, who was the apple of her eye.) When Bernice cooked for this domicile, she remarked that she was preparing "family dinner." And when she reflected on the comings and goings of its members, she wrote, "Such a queer household."[309]

The word "queer" had capacious meanings in 1938 when Bernice used it. It did not refer, in any transparent sense, to the same-sex desire and gender alterity that it would come to signal a half century later among activists and academics who sought to reclaim a term that had long been used to disparage inverts, homosexuals, and other sex and gender out-landers. Bernice used the term to refer to mannerisms and experiences that seemed strange and peculiar. But her decision to so label a household that fell outside expected patterns of familial co-residence—where non-kin who dwelled in family homes were generally paying boarders or paid help—shaded into a queerer kind of queerness, and Bernice well knew that the home she shared with Harold, Grace, Helen, and Bob was not the norm. It was a household run by three women, intimately tied to one another, who together cared for a child, and from which a lone man came and went. For all that, it was not entirely beyond the pale: family ties based on blood and marriage surely were present, and shared racial identity eased the routines of daily life.

Of the ties based on blood and marriage, none were more important to Bernice than those with her sister, Helen, and her husband, Harold. Both were complicated bonds, though Bernice and Helen had the stormiest relationship. Before they lived together, the sisters spent time with each other but also had run-ins that could last weeks or months. Bernice did not record the nature of her disagreements with Helen, but she clearly worried about her sister. In her diary, Bernice wrote that she wished Helen could get "straightened out" and "settled." Helen must not have appreciated her sister's wishes or the way Bernice communicated them. One especially icy period lasted for most of 1937, until Helen sent Bernice a plant for her birthday in December, leading Bernice to hope that a thaw might ensue: "Do white flowers mean a truce?" It took until Helen's birthday in the spring for the sisters to reach what Bernice called "an understanding." By May, with Harold away, Bernice had moved in with Helen, Bob, and Grace Dunn, and Bernice noted, "Helen and I are much happier." In 1939, when the Blackwelders were in California, Bernice worried if too much time passed without a letter from Helen, and when one came, it left Bernice "homesick." When Bernice returned to

Chicago, she and Harold moved back in with Helen. The sisters' relationship continued to ebb and flow: one day, they might do the family washing and can tomatoes side by side, but another day could produce between them "a reckoning," leaving Bernice's "nerves shot."[310]

Even after the Blackwelders left Oak Park, Bernice gave Helen rides, sewed her a coat, and even considered opening a catering business with her. Bernice still took care of Bob and continued to worry about Helen. Bernice was thrilled when her sister learned of an army job, which fell through, and again when Helen found work with the Works Progress Administration. But strife persisted, and the sisters' decision not to live together in 1940 left Bernice "all torn up." Shared birthdays and holidays continued, but eventually a deeper rift emerged, and Helen and Bernice's relationship remained distant and episodic for the rest of their lives. Three decades later, when Helen was remarried and residing in California, she was diagnosed with an aggressive cancer. When Bernice found out, she told Quantrille, "I am torn in spirit." But all Bernice could do was watch from a distance as her sister died.[311]

Unlike her relationship with Helen, Bernice's marriage to Harold endured for more than a half century, even if their work in the early years kept them apart for weeks at a time. In the 1930s, theirs was still a young romance, one that had not yet settled into the routines of later years, save one—an already established pattern in which Harold embarked on new ventures with the highest of hopes, only to meet disappointment, which then plunged him into what Bernice called a "black mood." In fall 1937, for example, after he returned from his first tour with the Weavers, joined the radio performers' union, and yet found work scarce, Harold worried over his prospects and settled into such a "dark mood" that Bernice griped, "He acts like a spoiled brat." Still, Bernice soon noted, "We are more like sweethearts than ever." A couple of months later, with job prospects opening for Harold in his new guise as Neil Fortune, he was ecstatic, his "head awhirl," as Bernice put it, adding with caution, "Hope he doesn't crack-up!" Head awhirl followed by crack-up became Harold's well-worn groove, one that Bernice would navigate for a lifetime. Five years later, when the Four Bards learned that their act would not reopen at the Ivanhoe, Bernice knew what was coming. "Bang go all the plans," she wrote, and a few days later, "H. is so blue." Bernice began to realize that when a blue mood hit, she need only wait it out. "Wish H. would snap out of it," she penned with little sympathy when Harold had trouble finding work in California. When one of his Chicago quartets, the Royalists, landed few engagements, Bernice noted that Harold was "a little low but that is rarely fatal." That was when Harold turned to the scheme of opening a barbecue joint, initiating a new round of dreams and despair.[312]

Despite all, there was an exquisite tenderness to Bernice and Harold's bond, sometimes intensified rather than diminished by their frequent separations. They fought like any couple, both face-to-face and by mail. "Had a squabble. I was to blame," Bernice wrote one day when they took a drive together north of the city. When Harold was touring with the Weavers, she noted, "Two letters from H. Says I wrote him a bad letter. I'm sorry." But she was not sorry, adding bitterly, "I'm so tired of being alone." And even this early in their marriage, Bernice could mock Harold's masculine pretensions, noting in her diary that she was awaiting the "return of the master," her tongue firmly in cheek. Still, their reunions could be blissful. When Harold returned from Neil Fortune shows in Texas and found Bernice at home with Helen and Grace, the couple absented themselves from the rest of the family, and as Bernice put it, it was "Romeo and Juliet upstairs." Three years later, at a time when Harold was often out of town, Bernice remarked, "Our days are so sweet they almost terrify me."[313] There was between them, then, a desire that burned through all the arguments and absences and through Harold's husbandly excesses as well. That passion, paradoxically, courted terror: in the most tender moments, the whisper of an end.

A fear of death, not the boon of life: Bernice and Harold's desire did not produce children. It became clear in the 1930s that the Blackwelders would not, probably could not, conceive. Childlessness was a source of sorrow for Bernice, sorrow that intensified as women around her gave birth. As late as 1937, Bernice held out hope that she might become pregnant, noting, "[I] started renovating my old duds so that I can blossom forth." "Blossoming" was the word she used to describe the pregnancies of Grace Hardwick and Gertrude Koplos, so Bernice likely anticipated the same for herself. Thereafter, though, Bernice's every musing about childbirth and motherhood was a lament. She visited a friend's new baby and wrote, "I wish I had one." She sewed a dress for her niece Doris, child of brother Duane, and repined, "Wish I had a little girl." She saw a friend's son and moaned, "I wish I had one like him." She shopped for other women's children and complained, "Best I can do is buy baby clothes for somebody else." Perhaps because of this, Bernice cleaved to her nephew Bob. But the unpredictability of the relationship with her sister meant that she sometimes lost access to Bob altogether. Once, when estranged from Helen, Bernice saw Bob from a distance on the street. "Breaks my heart," she wrote in her diary.[314] For all of Bernice's expansiveness and inventiveness when it came to family, friends, and household, there remained for her a hole that could not be filled completely by any other relation.

Her expansiveness and inventiveness may also have diminished over time. After Bernice and Harold moved into their Austin apartment and got a dog, they seem never again to have lived with others as they had in the 1930s. It is difficult to know for sure because Bernice stopped keeping a journal when her five-year diary ended shortly after the 1941 Pearl Harbor attack. But telephone directories find Harold at the same West Potomac Avenue address well into the 1940s (it was customary in that era for directories to list a husband's name without listing that of his wife).[315] More generally, Bernice and Harold are hard to track during and after the war because, in addition to not keeping a diary, Bernice all but stopped saving materials that documented her daily life. That decision itself is revealing, but what it reveals is not clear. Did the gravity of a world at war (first hot, then cold) make quotidian matters seem less crucial to recall? Or did both Bernice's and Harold's reduced prospects and, hence, expectations for their musical careers prompt Bernice to stop collecting memorabilia that would have evinced disappointment? Did disappointment and the material struggles that accompanied it so take their toll on Bernice and perhaps on her relationship with Harold that forgetting was less painful than remembering? Whatever was the case, the slim archive for the 1940s and early '50s makes it impossible to determine when and why and how Bernice made the decisions to give up singing and, ultimately, to relocate with Harold to Washington, D.C., to take up work at the CIA, and to begin research on frontiersman Kit Carson. But make these decisions she did.

By the late 1940s, it must have been clear to Bernice and Harold that their lives in Chicago could not be sustained. Both had found some work over the decade, and each had joined at least one new group—Bernice sang in the Vocaliers, and Harold performed with the Gentlemen of Note as well as with Tony Carsello and his Commodores.[316] Harold also appeared in what was probably a United Service Organization (USO) show and in doing so passed through a site of war-era racial violence. Formed in 1941, the USO worked with the Department of Defense to entertain troops. A single photograph and a USO pin that Bernice saved document whatever relationship Harold had with the organization. The photo shows the Gentlemen of Note trio playing for soldiers at Camp Shenango in Transfer, Pennsylvania. The camera looks from behind an audience of young white servicemen. Harold plays bass, while the others play guitar and accordion; all three are caught in song. Seated behind them on the stage are other performers—middle-aged white men in black tie, younger white men in uniform, and a half dozen white men in blackface, wearing flashy suits and flouncy ties. This was not Harold's first brush with minstrelsy; he had performed in blackface himself in the 1930s. But the setting this time was inauspicious. Camp Shenango had been thrown up quickly as a personnel replacement depot, and it had an impressive array of theaters, gymnasiums, and libraries. African Americans in the segregated military, however, were restricted from using most of the leisure facilities. In July 1943, tension over these and other indignities sparked a racial conflagration between whites and blacks that left black (but not white) soldiers dead. Since the photo of Harold singing at the base is undated, it is not clear whether the performance happened before or after the Camp Shenango race riot.[317] But surely the exclusion of African Americans from such shows coupled with rumors of whites cavorting in blackface contributed to black troops' complaints. For Harold, though, Camp Shenango was just another job. And jobs grew even scarcer in the postwar years, especially when the new medium of television eclipsed radio and the stage.[318]

Somewhere in the midst of this transition, Bernice and Harold left Chicago. They did not move immediately to Washington, though. They went first to Harold's home state of North Carolina, where he hoped to open a business. His father still had a barbecue restaurant in High Point, and Harold wanted a place either there or in the university town of Greensboro. The Blackwelders failed to find their dream. In 1949, Harold was a grocery store clerk in Greensboro and Bernice worked at a small restaurant, the Pickwick, a favorite of students, writers, and musicians. By 1950, they had left.[319] It is not clear what drew them to the nation's capital, but Bernice's sister and nephew had moved to nearby Alexandria, where Helen may have continued in federal employment. Perhaps Bernice heard of government jobs through her sister. By 1952, Bernice was working for the CIA and living in a duplex on a cul-de-sac in Arlington.[320]

Bernice's CIA job is hard to reconstruct. The agency will neither confirm nor deny her employment. But she told Caxton Press, publisher of *Great Westerner*, that she worked for the CIA from 1952 to 1954. And in the 1960s and '70s, she mentioned her job in four letters to Quantrille—twice when prompted by planned visits with an old CIA coworker, Nancy Elliott, and twice by national events that reminded her of her time with the agency. In 1972, when President Richard Nixon made his unprecedented trip to the People's Republic of China, Bernice wrote to Quantrille, "I was at CIA 1953–1954 and every day I read the *Hong Kong News* and anything else that came in about China looking for strategic materials, trade & transportation etc.—but nothing political as that was in another area." And the next year, when the Watergate hearings were under way in the Senate, Bernice explained that she was listening with interest, because, as she put it, "I worked at CIA at the same time some of these men were there." These were Bernice's only mentions of the CIA, and even her relatives did not know what her job entailed, only that she worked "for the government."[321]

Fortunately, Nancy Elliott—who was two decades younger than Bernice and who outlived her by the same number of years—was willing to speak about what she did for the agency, which in turn sheds light on what Bernice did there. Elliott, who hailed from Massachusetts and had worked for a time in California, heard in the early 1950s that the Department of the Navy was hiring and applied for a job. She got it but found the work boring. People told her that she should try the CIA instead. She recalled, "I had no idea what CIA was. I thought it was a labor union." She soon learned that it was not a union, and the job intrigued her. She worried about the required background check because, as she put it, she had lived "kind of a checkered life in California." But she survived the prying and went on to work for a CIA "reading panel." Each day she and her coworkers received information "in various forms, some letters, some documents, some newspapers," read the materials, and then directed them "to parts of the agency that could act on them." The information they sought about various countries, including the Soviet Union, Elliott remembered, was economic—"about the crops, if the crops were doing well," for example. Some of the materials she read were in English, while others were in Russian, though the readers were trained to look for specific words rather than understand what they read in depth. Elliott recalled that she worked mostly with other women, including several African Americans, but she also remembered that black women did different work than white women (she could not recall the nature of the difference) and that one of her white coworkers, who had grown up on a southern tobacco farm, behaved badly toward the black women. Bernice and Nancy labored in adjacent offices and performed similar tasks, at least until Nancy was transferred to another unit that focused on maps. By then, Bernice must have begun her research on Kit Carson. Her friendship with Nancy continued after Bernice left the CIA in 1954. Indeed, Nancy remembered typing Bernice's book manuscript for her.[322]

In working for the CIA and living first in an Arlington duplex and then in an Alexandria home, Bernice and Harold became part of what one historian calls Northern Virginia's emerging "landscape of denial"—that is, a place where the covert dimensions of U.S. imperialism, on the one hand, and lives lived in postwar suburbs, on the other, reinforced one another.[323] The CIA, established by the National Security Act of 1947, did not yet occupy the Langley headquarters that would be completed in 1961, and so Bernice toiled instead in one of Washington's awful temporary buildings, known as Tempos, that dated from World War I and were vulnerable to bugs and bad weather.[324] But Allen Dulles, whose vision Langley was, had ascended to the agency's helm after Dwight Eisenhower's election to the presidency in 1952. (Of Dulles, Nancy Elliott irreverently opined, "He was like a little teddy bear. Cute little thing, and he'd waddle down the aisle and talk to everybody.")[325] Dulles had already enjoyed a long career in diplomacy and intelligence, and as the first civilian director of the CIA, he oversaw the agency's growth, the building of its lasting physical imprint in Virginia, and the expansion of its concerns from containing communism in the Eastern Bloc to managing decolonization efforts in what was becoming known as the Third World (the vast, underprivileged portions of the globe not aligned with either the U.S.S.R. or the U.S.). By the early 1960s, the Langley CIA headquarters and the Defense Department's Pentagon, built in the 1940s, stood as the physical structures that anchored what Eisenhower warned was a "military-industrial complex," with its pernicious cultural and economic influence on the nation. If the Pentagon contributed to this complex overtly, the CIA contributed covertly. But the agency's open secret circulated freely in the domestic space of suburbs like Arlington and Alexandria, where most employees, including Bernice, lived.

While CIA chroniclers have focused on high-level male agents and officers and on the "close reading" those men imported from academia into agency practice, it was women like Bernice and Nancy—members of reading panels—who served as ground troops in CIA efforts to survey, surveil, and manipulate the world order for the benefit of U.S. capitalist democracy. And while chroniclers have also revealed how the racially homogeneous and gender-normative Northern Virginia suburbs incubated empire by providing a comfortable cover for the exportation of U.S. cultural values around the globe, those suburbs have been remembered more as a home for white men's aspirations than as a place where a couple like Bernice and Harold lived—a couple whose most reliable income came from a white woman's low-level work on behalf of U.S. empire.

How very far that woman had come. Bernice Fowler had once lived a fluid, urban domestic life alongside fellow musicians and had entertained a comparatively expansive political vision that incorporated union membership and cultural pluralism and that even flirted with

Marxist internationalism. Now, Bernice Blackwelder inhabited the privatized suburban landscape that nurtured the clandestine workings of U.S. global power. Soon, she would begin her research on Kit Carson, fashioning him into a domesticated hero suitable for a nation waging a Cold War.

A Place That's Known to God Alone

When Bernice Blackwelder and Quantrille McClung embarked on their Carson research in the 1950s, I had not yet been born. When they began to correspond in 1956, I had just been conceived (once, under the effects of medication for minor surgery, my otherwise very proper mother told me that she recalled the circumstances of my conception, but I did not encourage her to elaborate).[326] Quantrille and Bernice were contemporaries of my grandparents. When Quantrille entered the world in 1890, just one of my four grandparents had been born; my father's father was a year old. But by the time Bernice was born in 1902, my mother's father was already ten, and my two grandmothers were each five years old. All my grandparents were the children or grandchildren of immigrants, and all grew up in the Middle West. Their forebears came from Denmark, from Norway, and like Quantrille's maternal grandparents, from Germany. Quantrille's father's family and all of Bernice's people were of older European American stock, white folks who moved west across the generations. My kin left the Atlantic world in one great leap, crossing over in the late nineteenth century and rooting themselves midcontinent.[327]

Because my father was raised in Neenah, Wisconsin, and my mother's parents and grandparents had lived there as well, I grew up thinking that Neenah — a town built on the ancestral lands of Ho-Chunk people, on the labor of paper mill workers, and on the fortunes of mill owners — was Eden, the place where life began.[328] Neenah was not, of course, Eden, but it was where my forebears became middle class. My maternal grandmother's Danish-origin family, the Prebensens, had faltered financially when her father's alcoholism destroyed his Neenah photography business; he turned to house painting and my great-grandmother took in boarders. But my grandmother Effie Prebensen married well, considering; my grandfather Bernard Stecker was a Lutheran minister who got his start as a field missionary, founding new churches in and near Wisconsin's Fox River Valley and then spending the rest of his career shepherding one of those congregations, south of Neenah in Fond du Lac, where my mother was born and raised. Pastor Stecker's German-descent father had been a cheese maker and then a carpenter who moved from a nearby rural crossroads to Neenah, where the family contracting business thrived as the town grew.

My father's people came from farther afield to settle in Neenah. My maternal grandmother, Sarah Bjoraker, whose forebears were Norwegian, had been raised in the agricultural center of Northfield, Minnesota, until her father, a salesman, died young. Then her mother moved the family to Minneapolis and took in boarders, while the four daughters went to work to help support the household and to put their brother through college. But this grandmother married well, too; my grandfather Arthur Johnson, of Danish extraction, had trained as an osteopathic physician.[329] The two met in great-grandfather Johnson's butcher shop after the older Johnson family moved from Marinette, Wisconsin, to Minneapolis. After they married, the younger Johnsons settled in Neenah, where my father was born and raised. My father's folks were more prosperous than my mother's. As my father once said, crossly, when I put one too many demands on her, "Your mother wasn't born with a silver spoon in her mouth." But both families had ample flatware and plenty of food, even if Pastor Stecker's household was subsidized by clergy discounts at Fond du Lac stores and nourished by a fulsome fruit and vegetable garden out back of the parsonage.

All of this allowed my mother to become the first woman in my family to finish college, and it was while she was in school that she met my father. She also married well. When she first saw him playing basketball (she liked his legs and vowed that she would marry him), my father was not enrolled as a regular student at Ripon College, as she was; he was in the Army Specialized Training Program on campus. But after he was deployed to the Pacific theater during World War II, having survived Okinawa, he returned for a year of classes at Ripon while my mother finished her English degree. Then they married and moved to Madison, where he studied economics at the University of Wisconsin. When he graduated in 1950, he had an opportunity to pursue an advanced degree at Princeton University, but he was already the father of one, my sister. Instead he began a business career closer to home. He started (like his grandfather-in-law) in Wisconsin's cheese industry and then found employment with Ray-O-Vac, the battery-manufacturing firm. While my father was finishing school, my mother had a secretarial job with the same company, Dairyland Products, that later launched his career. But once he graduated, she never again worked outside the home. In 1952, they became parents of a second child, my brother. I came along, unplanned, four years later. By then they were living in the ranch-style house that was my first home.

My earliest memories in that home find me in my mother's arms and her in a wooden rocking chair that creaked lazily with each to and fro. She is singing to me the lullaby that always soothed my soul:

> With someone like you, a pal good and true
> I'd like to leave it all behind and go and find
> A place that's known to God alone
> Just a spot to call our own
> We'll find perfect peace where joys never cease
> Somewhere beneath a kindly sky
> We'll build a sweet little nest somewhere in the West
> And let the rest of the world go by.[330]

If I might echo Theodore Roosevelt's famous formulation, it was here that the romance of my life began.[331] That romance obscured the links that tied the West to the rest of the world, and it hid the human costs of the nests that newcomers built there—in Kit Carson's day, in the era of my youth, and in the lives and times of Quantrille McClung and Bernice Blackwelder.

Epilogue
Where Our Fathers Died

There is no forgiveness without stories. There is no dignity.

There is no way to speak in other tongues but that.

—KAREN FISHER, *A Sudden Country*

In Which We Part

When Quantrille McClung and Bernice Blackwelder were exchanging their last letters in the early 1980s, I was working in a building called Serra House, erected in 1923 as a retirement home for Stanford University chancellor David Starr Jordan. By the time I spent my days there, the Spanish eclectic structure had not been a private residence for decades; instead, it housed Stanford's Center for Research on Women, the Feminist Studies Program, and the editorial offices of *Signs: Journal of Women in Culture and Society.*[1] I worked for *Signs.* The many women and few men I encountered at Serra House never spoke of the building's namesake, Father Junípero Serra, the Franciscan friar who founded nine coastal missions among the Indigenous peoples of Alta California in the late eighteenth century. I did not speak of him either. Serra House and the architectural style that informed it—red tile roof, stucco walls, balconies, rounded archways, and wrought-iron grillwork—reflected California's romance with what is often called the "Spanish fantasy heritage," an uncritical embrace of colonial aesthetics bled white of colonial violence. There, in a house that trafficked in a man who was being canonized by the Roman Catholic Church and castigated by the ancestors of Mission Indians, I proofread and edited and corresponded with the first generation of women's studies scholars, a heady task for a midwestern Lutheran liberal arts college graduate still finishing a master's degree from a western state university.[2]

Until I started working at Stanford, I barely realized that there was a hierarchy of educational institutions, nor did I recognize that I had spent a half dozen years on the middle rungs of that ladder before I got there. Now there were daily reminders of academic power, privilege, and prestige, all in a gorgeously groomed, palm-studded setting that blended Richardson Romanesque and mission revival styles.[3] My access to that power, privilege, and prestige was limited by the nature of my job; I was neither student nor faculty but rather a staff member earning a low salary that barely covered a modest cost of living. So I did not feel as if I belonged there, at least not usually. Each day, though, I rubbed shoulders with high-powered professors, quick-witted undergraduates, and razor-sharp graduate students, who opened up new worlds to me. At first those worlds were cerebral and political. But in time Stanford boosted me up the very institutional ladder that had come into view from Serra

House, landing me, in 1985, across the continent in a doctoral program at Yale University, where I threw myself into the study of U.S. western and gender history.

That is one story about how I came to sit in an ergonomically designed chair in Madison, Wisconsin, where I pore over letters Bernice Black-welder wrote to Quantrille McClung in their last years (McClung's letters from this period have not survived). Another story unfolds thirty-five miles north of Stanford in San Francisco, where I spent much of my time when I was not at work. The two narratives are no more distinct than Stanford and San Francisco are unattached places; both Interstate 280 and U.S. Route 101 connect the campus and The City, and I drove those roads constantly. Likewise, my work and play life joined on a shifting terrain of left politics and gay revelry, an unfamiliar but endlessly enticing landscape for the child of churchgoing, moderate Republicans who did not color outside the lines. Still, the university story is one of intellectual growth and institutional mobility viewed from my Serra House desk, where I sat still for hours. The urban story, by contrast, is one of a body in motion: traversing city sidewalks in search of the brightest mural or the best burrito, milling at parades and marching in protests, making the rounds at the queerest of bars, raising dawn with whoever accompanied me home. In the political world I inhabited, it was a time when radical women of color and feminist sex warriors pulled the notion of a stable self—even of woman as the subject of feminism—off the shelf and dashed it to the ground.[4] As a result, whether sitting still or walking out, I returned to questions I had evaded for over a dozen years, questions about my own traffic in men and things male and the connection of that traffic to a West bleached of color and drained of blood. City grit and groomed campus alike grounded my reverie.

I was young and on fire and time seemed to stretch out endlessly before me; Quantrille and Bernice were aging and anxious about the narrowness of now. Would their work continue? Would it be recognized by others? Would their minds stay focused? Would their bodies meet the demands of daily life? Would they have enough money? Would their sidewalks be safe? Would the people they met there seem familiar or strange? Would they live longer than their loved ones? Or would their friends and relatives outlive them? Both women faced these questions, but they had individual concerns as well. Bernice wondered whether her husband, Harold, would be content to remain in Chicago and whether the two of them would be sufficient for each other's care as they grew old. Quantrille wondered if she would be able to sustain herself alone in her Denver apartment. Each wondered how and where and when she would die, who would attend that dying, how she would be remembered and by whom, and what would become of her worldly goods and the intellectual products she left behind, both finished and unfinished.

In the end, the two women made different choices about their legacies. Bernice did not save record of her historical work—except, of course, her published book, which lived on in libraries—but she did spare evidence of her college years and the time she and Harold spent in the music world. Quantrille not only left behind more published work but also preserved a range of materials her life had generated, including scrapbooks and photograph albums from her young adulthood; notes and correspondence from her genealogical labor on the Carson, Bent, and Boggs families and those of Colorado's governors; most of the letters she exchanged with Bernice; and even telltale proof of Bernice's connection to Carson enthusiast John McCurdy, the flickering old flame that had never fully flared. What Quantrille did not save was anything that attested definitively to the nature of the intimate ties she shared with other people or, alternately, any definitive statement that she had eschewed such ties altogether. Both women shaped the stories others could tell about them after they died.

I lived to tell those tales. Truth be told, of late I have sometimes lived only to tell those tales. I had been telling them slowly, haltingly, painstakingly for over a decade when I bore witness, in short order, to the deaths of the two people I loved most in the world: the predictable, inevitable, yet grievous and disorienting death of my aging mother (my father had long since passed) and, twenty-two months later, the shocking, calamitous, untimely, and utterly unhinging death of my beloved. Since then, the prospect of telling tales has, more than once, kept me alive, given me aim and velocity. So here, in the narrowness of now, I bring all the stories to an end. My chest feels heavy, inhaling a chore. But if there is, most certainly, no forgiveness without stories, it is also true that there is no life without stories, no breath, no heartbeat, no peal of laughter, no flash of anger, no caress, no pain. As my beloved put it seventy-nine hours before she died, "I believe our lives are stories with beginnings and endings." But also, "I believe our stories endure and unfold endlessly in space-time."[5] Stories endure also in their recounting. And people endure in part by telling tales.

Housewife

ernice Blackwelder continued telling tales of western men for a good long time. As she advanced in age and grew in fear of urban violence, however, she all but stopped visiting Chicago's major libraries. One of the last times she told Quantrille Mc-Clung of such a trip, Bernice was seventy-one. It was winter and she took the bus to the Newberry Library, making two transfers en route, which forced her to wait three times at windy street corners. When she arrived, she found a sign at the entrance announcing that the library was closed in honor of "the PEACE." It was January 27, 1973—the day of the Paris Peace Accords, which ended direct U.S. combat in Vietnam. Bernice griped, "I am glad we finally are peaceful but I felt like fighting!" Nonetheless, she braved the gales to return to the bus stop and thence to the Chicago Public Library, where she consulted the *Biographical Directory of the American Congress*. At day's end, when she went back out into the cold, she forgot her notes and so had to traipse back to the library to retrieve them. Tired and chilled to the bone, she opted to take the L home, calling husband Harold to pick her up at the Logan Square station.[6] Little wonder that thereafter, Bernice rarely made a library outing.

Fortunately, her biographical dictionary of westerners was far enough along that extensive research was no longer necessary; much of the work remaining involved assembling what she had gathered, writing the entries, and typing them up. After the 1973 trip to the Chicago Public Library, she kept at it, with interruptions, until 1981, just before she turned seventy-nine. In deference to the now clearer division between professionals and nonprofessionals in western history, Bernice held modest goals. She told Quantrille, "I think it should be something of value and interest to amateur historians, especially."[7] Modest goals did not diminish the demands Bernice placed on herself to get things right and make her work useful. And circumstances often conspired against her. Harold's comings and goings continued to dictate how much time she could devote to the project—and to corresponding with Quantrille about it. Penning a letter in 1976, Bernice wrote, "It is now 6:15 A.M. I have finished packing a lunch for Harold who—Here he comes!! Early! I wish he would stay in [bed] for another hour! Typical day!" As she had for years, she groused about Harold being "under foot."[8] Another obstacle was the constant need to type and retype entries. Bernice did much of this labor but she hired a typist as well, a hapless former tenant who faced near-constant health crises: foot surgery, a gallbladder operation, breast cancer, a stroke. The typist also had two other jobs that limited her availability: she worked nights at a hospital, and after she left the Logan Square apartment, she and her husband managed their own rentals on Chicago's South Side.[9] In spite of it all, in 1980 Bernice wrote of the alphabetized entries, "I am now in the 'W's," adding, "And there are so many of them!!"[10] It was not just that there were a lot of western men whose last names started with the letter *W*. The whole project overwhelmed, and Bernice wondered if she would ever finish it. As early as 1973, she had told Quantrille that she considered tossing her work into the fire but decided she should at least "get it into shape so that it could pass on to someone else."[11] Through it all, Bernice thought about her legacy. "There can be no better way to be remembered," she said to Quantrille of the book she hoped to publish. Bernice added that this way of thinking came from their friendship: "That is one thing I have learned from my ... association with you."[12]

What propelled Bernice to make a last push to finish was the vacation she took with Harold in 1975, when they went to Harold's home state of North Carolina (this was the trip that took them through the Cherokees' eastern lands and to Andrew Jackson's Hermitage).[13] Ever after, they dreamed of retiring there. Harold especially wanted to go. Bernice wanted to stay put at least until she was done with the book. It was not that Harold did not support Bernice; even after he began to lobby for the move, he set up shelves for her work materials in their apartment. And Bernice acknowledged, "He is very good to allow me to keep plugging away at my notes and making a little progress."[14] That was the rub. Harold's labor took precedence; Bernice's proceeded at his sufferance. Even if the Depression had taught them to be careful about subordinating her pursuits to his, ever since the postwar years, Harold's work had taken the wheel and Bernice's the back seat. When Bernice did remunerative labor, reading foreign newspapers at the CIA or managing apartments in Chicago, she did so in large part so that Harold could pursue his dreams— selling barbecue in the 1950s or making music in the 1960s.

After Harold found employment at the county clerk's office in 1967, the demands of his work and the paycheck it provided ruled the household and determined its future. So the plans for a move to North Carolina ebbed and flowed according to how ready Harold felt to leave his job. The couple started preparations not long after the 1975 vacation, taking another trip south to scout locations in 1976. But then Harold learned that if he kept working past his next birthday, he would be eligible for Social Security income along with his regular pay. They decided they did not have enough money for him to retire without the extra boost. Then they determined that they did not have enough money even with it. This disappointed Harold more than it did Bernice, who was working feverishly with an often-ill typist to finish her biographical dictionary. Bernice told Quantrille, "[Harold] is eager to leave Chicago and get to N.C. but I refuse to budge until I have this weight off my back." Two years later, they still had not left, the book still was not done, and Bernice's refrain continued; the slow progress on her project was "very discouraging since Harold is so eager to move down to No. Carolina."[15]

Harold's eagerness eventually prevailed. In fall 1978, they decided to move, though not until spring because that would allow them to meet the terms of their lease and avoid paying rent for an apartment they had vacated. Harold discovered that he could take a leave of absence from his job (in case things did not work out in North Carolina), thereby also continuing the health insurance they both enjoyed. But Bernice predicted that Harold "would never want to see Chicago again." Meanwhile, Bernice kept plugging away on the biographical dictionary until the movers came in April.[16] Then the couple piled their clothes and valuables into the car and drove south to Salisbury, North Carolina. Harold had grown up in a rural township nearby and had cousins in Salisbury. The couple found a two-bedroom unit in a new subdivision "right against the tall pines" for the same price they had paid for their Logan Square apartment right against the Kennedy Expressway. Even though the movers had not yet arrived and she had fallen in a motel bathtub before settling in the new place, Bernice was full of enthusiasm when she wrote to Quantrille. The second bedroom would be her study, and her typist even planned a trip there.[17] As with so many of their schemes over the years, though, this one fell apart. In less than two months, the couple received notice that a new company would be managing their apartment building and the rent would be raised by fifty-five dollars monthly. That was more than the Blackwelders could afford. So they rented a cheaper apartment across the street from Harold's cousin.[18] Whatever happened next is lost to the historical record, but by Christmas Bernice and Harold were back in Chicago. Their North Carolina retirement lasted six months.

However brief the move, it signaled something more than nostalgia for Harold's homeplace and a longing to escape Chicago winters. This move was motivated by racial change. The demographic dynamics in and around Logan Square that had left Bernice complaining to Quantrille by the early 1970s only increased as the decade went on.[19] Although Bernice had worried aloud about the prospect of African American neighbors, it was the influx of Puerto Ricans and ethnic Mexicans that transformed Logan Square. Between 1960 and 1970, the area's Latino population had risen from about 600 to about 16,000. Between 1970 and 1980, the numbers nearly tripled, from about 16,000 to about 44,000 Latino residents, over half Puerto Rican and more than a third ethnic Mexican.[20]

Bernice and Harold responded viscerally, linking all manner of mayhem to their Puerto Rican neighbors. When, in the space of a week, the Blackwelders' car battery was stolen and someone tried to pick the lock on their back door, Bernice told Quantrille, "All of this makes [North] Carolina seem more like heaven," adding that "most of the trouble" had arisen "since the influx of the Puerto Ricans," though Bernice did not know who had vandalized the car or the door. She concluded, "I wish the U.S. would give [Puerto Ricans] that country and send all of them back there," adding, "I have always tried not to [be] prejudiced but this is almost too much." Soon, she blamed a fire at a once Polish immigrant church on racial change as well: "It seems to be part of a plan by the incoming PRs (Puerto Ricans & Blacks) to burn all that is in the way of taking over a neighborhood." At times, Bernice attributed anti–Puerto Rican racism to Harold rather than owning it herself, as she did when she told Quantrille that three-quarters of the tenants in their apartment building were "'Spanish'—some of them very black and that is hard for Harold, a Southerner, to accept." But it was hard for Bernice, a northerner, too. Her complaints ranged from the gravest—blaming violence on Puerto Ricans—to mere annoyance. As for more trivial matters, she acknowledged that most "Spanish-speaking tenants" in her building did "not make much trouble," except, she told Quantrille, for "being noisy." She cited an example: "Instead of ringing the doorbell, someone will yell out to the third floor, 'José!! José!!'" Then, Bernice added, Harold would compound the problem by making even "more noise telling him to shut up!" The "constant Spanish music" also irritated Bernice, despite her own love of song; she found Latin rhythm "loud with drum beats that knock me out."[21]

Events that coincided with Chicago's annual Puerto Rican festival and parade further provoked Bernice's racial ire and fueled her hope that she and Harold could leave the city for good. On the day of the parade in 1977, a bomb rocked the County Building, where Harold worked. Because it was Saturday, no one was injured. The radical Puerto Rican independence group Fuerzas Armadas de Liberación Nacional claimed responsibility for the blast.[22] Later that day, revelers gathered in Humboldt Park, the oasis at the edge of the largely Puerto Rican neighborhood of the same name. In the evening, police intervened in an apparent dispute between rival gang members there, a dispute that observers said had escalated into gunfire. Bystanders watched as officers made arrests and then attacked the police for what seemed to them an overreaction, igniting a long-standing complaint among Puerto Ricans against police for racial profiling and brutality. The clash between police and revelers spiraled out of control, and in the melee that followed, officers shot and killed two young Puerto Ricans, Rafael Cruz and Julio Osorio. The uprising continued the next day, with violence spilling into adjacent streets. Later, a third victim, retired factory worker Domingo Torres, was found dead in an apartment that burned when a grocery store below was set ablaze. There was no coordination between the County Building bombing and the Humboldt Park uprising, though the police commissioner acknowledged that for his officers, the bomb blast set the "tone for the day" in the park.[23]

For Bernice, the events seemed linked, too, as she revealed in a stream-of-consciousness rant to Quantrille written ten days later. The rant must have bewildered Quantrille, who had not seen Chicago news coverage. First, Bernice bemoaned another stolen car battery. Then she decried the "hotbed of trouble with P.R.s," implying, without saying it, that the battery had been lifted by a Puerto Rican. Bernice did not take a writerly breath before adding that someone rang their doorbell at "2:00 A.M. the morning of the riot at Humboldt Park." The same happened to neighbors, leading Bernice to conclude, "I think it is a plan to aggravate until forced to move." Veering back to the uprising, she recalled that in years past, she and Harold took their dog to Humboldt Park, a couple of miles south of their Logan Square apartment, where Elsa loved to swim in the lagoon. Now, they were afraid even to drive through the park. Bernice wondered, "Why O why must these things happen?" Then, without prefatory explanation of the County Building blast, she penned, "The bomb exploded at the office of Harold's boss! Luckily closed for Puerto Rican Day. . . . Wish they had given them their independence long ago, but if we did they would not leave."[24] The confusion of referents was instructive; the "they" who Bernice wished had given Puerto Ricans their independence was the U.S. government, but that "they" suddenly became "we" when opposed to the "they" that was Chicago's Puerto Rican community. Although Puerto Ricans were U.S. citizens whose migration to the mainland was lawful, to Bernice they were perpetual aliens, permanent others; they were "them," not "us."

Bernice saw herself as victimized by Puerto Ricans in much the way she saw her ancestors as persecuted by American Indians in centuries past. Recalling Hannah Dustin's capture by Abenakis in the seventeenth century and Israel Donalson's seizure by Shawnees in the eighteenth, Bernice had once told Quantrille, "The Indians were after us on all sides."[25]

Now, in the twentieth century, Bernice thought that Puerto Ricans were trying to "burn all that is in the way of taking over a neighborhood" to "aggravate" white people until they felt "forced to move."[26] The colonial contexts for each set of events were far from Bernice's mind. There was the less-than-effectual colonialism of British imperial and U.S. national forces in the seventeenth and eighteenth centuries, respectively, which displaced Indian peoples but incompletely, leaving them room to assert power by taking white settlers and surveyors captive, incorporating them into Indian communities or holding them for ransom. And there was the more effective twentieth-century U.S. colonialism in Puerto Rico, which produced profits for U.S. businesses and poverty for many Puerto Ricans, prompting migration to the mainland.[27] In Bernice's view, white people were the victims, then and now. And the only way to avoid victimization was to flee to a place where whites remained in the majority and retained their racial power.

This, then, is part of what Bernice meant when she told Quantrille, "I believe we would enjoy a smaller southern town."[28] Maybe Bernice and Harold had in mind the rural North Carolina of Harold's youth, ruled by the dictates of Jim Crow, or else the fictional community depicted in television's hit series from the 1960s, *The Andy Griffith Show*: Mayberry, a tiny North Carolina town almost devoid of black people and certainly devoid of racial conflict. Salisbury, the place where Bernice and Harold landed in 1978, had a last-enumerated population of 22,515, over two-thirds of which was white. Few nonblack people of color lived there, so the rest of the population was mostly African American.[29] Mayberry it was not, but as sizeable as Salisbury's black community was, white power in North Carolina had barely diminished. The state had just ended an era in which it boasted a greater Ku Klux Klan presence than all other southern states combined, a presence that was itself a grassroots reaction to the state's acquiescence to federal civil rights initiatives. The North Carolina Klan went into decline in the late 1960s, but now, in the 70s, white people in Harold's home state were making the same political transition as their southern neighbors, the transition by which the white South broke its historical bond with the Democratic Party and pledged allegiance to a Republican brand of conservatism.[30] This was a place where Harold could feel right at home—could feel comfortably white at home—and perhaps Bernice could, too.

But Bernice and Harold could not make a go of it in Salisbury. They not only returned to Chicago; they went back to the very Logan Square apartment building they had left, where Puerto Rican neighbors enjoyed the rhythms of conga and called up merrily to friends from the street. And Harold returned to his job at the County Building. It was as if they had never left. Perhaps resigned to a coexistence that she probably still found distasteful, Bernice said no more about the Latino residents of Logan Square or nearby Humboldt Park, except obliquely when she told Quantrille, "[Harold] does all the shopping and with all the crime on the streets I would rather not venture out alone."[31] But by the time they returned to Chicago, other worries consumed Bernice, and her thoughts turned inward. Chief among those worries were her health and her biographical dictionary of westerners.

Even before Bernice and Harold's North Carolina sojourn, Bernice felt her body failing. At first her concerns were modest, and Harold's health problems seemed greater. Harold had been hospitalized for an ulcer as early as 1973, while Bernice had been diagnosed with diverticulitis, which did not require emergency care, only a change in the food she ate. Both Bernice and Harold altered their diets, sometimes drastically—at one point, Bernice was subsisting on baby food—and the restrictions made it hard for them to travel.[32] But both kept on working, Harold for the county and Bernice on her book project. In 1977, Harold went to the hospital again, this time for a nosebleed related to high blood pressure, while Bernice developed painful sciatica that limited her mobility and increased her fatigue. Once an avid consumer of art and music and history, Bernice confessed to Quantrille in 1978 that she might not be able to climb the stairs at Chicago's Field Museum of Natural History, where she wanted to see an exhibit of pre-Columbian golden treasures from Peru.[33]

But it was in the fall of that year, as she and Harold were planning their southern move, that more serious troubles started to stalk Bernice. On Halloween—coincidentally, the forty-eighth anniversary of her marriage to Harold—Bernice entered the hospital. She never named her illness to Quantrille, and, years later, even Bernice's living niece did not know what ailed her aunt. Whatever befell Bernice was grave enough that she had two surgeries and was hospitalized for a month. The first letter she wrote to Quantrille after she got home revealed a close brush with death, a long recovery, and mind-altering drugs. Bernice reported her surgeon's remark that "someone upstairs" had been looking out for her. What is more, under the influence of medication, Bernice imagined that Quantrille (who was then ninety) had made an overseas trip; "My last news of you," she wrote in error to her friend, "was a beautiful report of your visit to England." Quantrille had made no such trip. Given Bernice's condition, it was fortunate that Harold, as she put it, became her "wonderful nurse [and] housekeeper." For once, her needs came first: "[Harold] has anticipated my every wish and want, plans such tasty meals and always with the slow dry wit that is so lovable."[34] Bernice had not written of her husband with such tenderness in a long while. Remarkably, however, the couple did not rethink their planned move to North Carolina. They departed less than six months after Bernice's hospitalization—indeed, she attributed her bathtub fall in a Salisbury motel to postsurgical unsteadiness.

And still, Bernice did not give up on her biographical dictionary.[35] Her typist never made the planned trip to North Carolina, probably because the Blackwelders were there so briefly. Once back in Chicago, Bernice found that the typist had broken her ankle, so she started typing herself. "At least I am accomplishing something while waiting," Bernice wrote. A year later, with her typist now recovering from a stroke, Bernice announced, "I work every moment I can on my 'Westerners' and can almost see the finish." At the end of 1981, however, in weak handwriting on a Christmas card, Bernice reported, "I have been in and out of the hospital. It has been rather rough all the way around," adding, "I think I am gaining but get discouraged easily."[36] By then, the Blackwelders had left Chicago for good, this time going north rather than south.

It was their last long-distance move. Bernice was seventy-eight and Harold was seventy-five. Doris Lance, Bernice's niece, recalled that her father, Bernice's brother, Duane, worried about the couple. Duane Fowler lived in Cadillac, Michigan, but he had visited his sister in Chicago, as had his children and grandchildren, including Doris and her family. Duane was a businessman, a Rotarian, and a straight arrow who never understood his sister's peripatetic life and never approved of her husband, Harold. Duane saw in Harold a lack of ambition and a surfeit of needs, needs that Bernice had to meet. Duane's opinion only hardened over time, especially as his sister began to fail. Doris remembered, "He was disquieted about their living conditions, Hal not working and Bernice becoming stooped over but still trying to please her demanding husband." Duane did not think his sister could keep the household as clean as he thought it should be kept. So he became, as his daughter Doris put it, Bernice and Harold's "rescuer." He cajoled them to move to Cadillac and found them an apartment. In addition to family support, the couple no doubt had Social Security income as well as Harold's county pension (which must have been small given how late in life he started his desk job). Doris's brother Steve Fowler also lived in Cadillac and he helped the Blackwelders settle in. Steve kept a hair salon and he did Bernice's hair, helping her in from the car each time she came, because, as he recalled, she was "very weak, very frail, just lost her strength." For her part, Doris was two hours away in Alpena. She had lost her husband and was running a trailer park on her own, so she did not get to Cadillac as much as she would have liked. She had disagreed with her father about moving Bernice and Harold: "I thought it was not his place to disrupt their home." But Doris allowed that the apartment in Cadillac was "bright and cheery" and that her aunt and uncle "seemed more content."[37]

They had left behind a great deal—work, friends, and memories of old times in Chicago. The couple had spent holidays with Bernice's college friend and onetime roommate Gertrude, her husband Tony, and their family, for instance. Bernice and Gert, who once studied music together, attended concerts with each other and reminisced about the past. The Koplos family was more secure financially: they hosted the holiday meals; they traveled to Tony's native Greece and to Gert and Bernice's home state of Kansas; and they often bought the tickets when Gert and Bernice went to a show.[38] The Blackwelders' move to Michigan brought all this to an end. Likewise, Harold gave up the last remnant of his music career. For years, he had performed at Christmas with a group of male vocalists at a Chicago bank. One of the last times he sang carols with them, he brought home three hundred dollars and, with tears in his eyes, laid it in Bernice's lap. He was remembering, she told Quantrille, "when they passed the hat during Depression years."[39] Now all that was over.

So, too, were Bernice's efforts to finish her biographical dictionary of westerners. In September 1982, just before she turned eighty, she wrote a last letter to the fellow Kit Carson enthusiast who had become her friend and confidant.[40] In an unsteady hand, Bernice addressed her "dearest Quantrille," opening with the words "it has been so long since I have written you or heard from you!" Bernice reported that she and Harold had arrived in Cadillac a year before, noting that the move was arranged by her brother "so that the families could be together." She conceded that it had been "in many ways a good idea" but said it was "a little strange to make the inevitable change." Then she confessed, "I did not try to collect all my Western History records," adding, "The thought of another book has left my mind completely." She did not tell Quantrille what she told her niece Doris—that she had struck a match to the reams of paper that constituted her westerners dictionary.[41] Instead, Bernice told Quantrille, "Maybe it was time for me to get on a new track!" What that new track might be, she did not say, writing, "I have been quite ill and walk with a cane." Then, she brought her final missive to a close:

Looking forward to hearing from you and hoping soon to see each other. We will have much to discuss! I have thought of you many times.

My dear love
always—
Bernice

Nine months later, Harold died. He had spoken with a stammer; only when he sang did his diction flow. Now stuttering speech and mellifluous bass ceased, and all nights were silent.[42]

Once Harold was gone, Bernice's relatives did not think she could live on her own. So they helped her move into an adult foster care home. She spent three years there. The only record she left of that time is a small notebook in which she practiced a memory exercise, writing out women's names that began with the same letter of the alphabet, trying not to repeat herself: "Heidi, Holly, Hannah, Hazel, Hattie, Hannah, Hope." It was Christmas Eve in 1986, on Kit Carson's birthday, when Bernice Fowler Blackwelder took her last breath.[43]

Bernice's loved ones would not like for me to end her story there, though those who knew her best have themselves passed on. Niece Doris and nephew Steve visited her during the years she lived in adult foster care, and they agreed that "her showmanship came through right up until the end." Steve called her "the life of the party." Doris remembered her aunt as "quick witted and smiling" and told a tale that she thought best epitomized Bernice. The tale is set firmly in space but vaguely in time. Apparently, the *Queen Mary*, the famous British ocean liner, was once docking at the wharf in New York City, and Bernice took a taxi down to see it. She found the crowds so great, though, that she could not get out of the cab. She voiced her dismay to the driver, who, in response, rolled forward. He told her to look out the window. "You have a front row seat," he said. "See that moving wall? That's the Queen Mary." The story's lesson, Bernice told Doris, was this: "When you are living right, good things happen to you."[44]

I might end Bernice's story by turning to the last words about Kit Carson in *Great Westerner*. They are not Bernice's words but rather ones she borrows from Jessie Benton Frémont, whose husband, John C. Frémont, had employed Carson as a scout in his western travels. Benton Frémont, in turn, took the words from nineteenth-century romantic poet Sir Walter Scott. When notice of Carson's death reached the eastern United States, reported first in western newsprint and then "flashed east by telegraph," Bernice writes, "Jessie Fremont, hearing the long-expected last news ... opened her journal." Then, according to Bernice, Benton Frémont penned the lines that end *Great Westerner*, lines dipped in the carnage and misgivings of empire:

> Fleet foot in the forest
> Sage head in the cumber
> Red hand in the foray
> How sound is thy slumber?[45]

In Scott's poem, recollected imperfectly by Jessie Benton Frémont and again by Bernice Fowler Blackwelder, a killer's bloody hand recalls an unnamed death. In Bernice's imagining, a printer's ink, the tap of telegraph key, and a pen on paper record the named killer's death. In a broader world of academics and amateurs and consumers of culture, that death is trafficked, and dignified, over and over again, in archives and histories and museums and misquoted poems. Then, in 1986, there is another death, the barely remembered death of a teller of tales, a singer of songs, a lover of men, a housewife.

* *

There is no life without stories. There should be no death without names, without poetry, without pageant of melody.

Old Maid

When Bernice Blackwelder died in Cadillac at the age of eighty-four, Quantrille McClung was already gone, though it seems doubtful that Bernice knew of her fellow Carson buff's distant death in Denver. Quantrille, who had said in 1966 that she did not know just when she would "shuffle off this mortal coil" and who expected to do so sooner rather than later, lived until 1985, dying just eighteen months before her friend.[46] She was ninety-five years old.

Like Bernice, Quantrille told tales for as long as she could, though hers were mostly the elliptical tales of birth and death and marriage that genealogy tells. Like genealogy's spare, fragmented stories, any story of Quantrille's last years must at times be oblique. This is because Quantrille stopped saving copies of the letters she wrote to Bernice in 1975, though she kept those that Bernice sent her. The letters had been a venue for Quantrille to narrate daily life. Without her side of the correspondence, it is hard to capture how Quantrille experienced her last ten years. Yet even after 1975 Quantrille corresponded with the staff of the Denver

Public Library (DPL), despite the institution's proximity to her home. Those letters survive. She wrote in part because she could not always walk the eight blocks between her apartment and the library or even traverse it by bus. She also wrote to create a record of her negotiations about what she hoped would be more work published by DPL. In this, she would be disappointed, but her library correspondence, along with other letters, random scraps of paper, and acquaintances' recollections, tells of Quantrille's life in her late eighties and early nineties.

Even as DPL prepared to release the 1973 *Carson-Bent-Boggs Genealogy Supplement*, Quantrille wrestled with mountains of material that correspondents kept sending about branches of the Carson, Bent, and Boggs family trees. The constant additions stalled the *Supplement*'s publication because, as the library's public information officer Betty Jo Rule reported to city librarian Henry Shearouse, "Miss McClung continues to receive new material and she feels obliged to try to work said material into the book. This ... delays her in reviewing ... material which [the typist] has prepared."[47] Staff members like Rule indulged Quantrille's penchant for inclusion as well as the maladies that slowed her down and limited her mobility. But they finally drew the line on additions. After consulting with Rule, Shearouse wrote to Quantrille: "I understand that you have already collected a sizable amount of other material which has come in since our agreement on a deadline. . . . I expect that additional material will be forthcoming as a result of the publication of the Supplement. If you wish to consider a second supplement at a later time and have received enough material for such a supplement, we would, of course, be glad to talk with you concerning the future publication of this."[48] That second supplement never came to fruition. In 1980, Shearouse told Quantrille that he could not publish another volume after all, given that the library still had on hand, unsold, nearly a quarter of the *Carson-Bent-Boggs Genealogy*'s original print run and almost two-thirds of the *Supplement*'s. Quantrille fired back, "This has been a great shock to me. But that is little compared to the embarrassment of having to tell all those folk who have been sending me records ... that there will be no publication." She reminded Shearouse that he had promised at the very least to hire a typist to put the new material into a readable form that could be deposited at DPL. She added ruefully that this fallback agreement had been made "in conversation," leaving her with "no proof." Shearouse assured her by return mail that he would find a typist, which soothed Quantrille and restored her "faith in the Denver Public Library."[49]

Staff at the institution that had employed Quantrille for more than three decades alternately accommodated and evaded her many requests. When she complained that her old typewriter had given up the ghost in 1983, an employee found "a green one in good condition" and had it delivered to her apartment. "I knew the library would help me," she told a staff member over the phone.[50] When she acquired from a Kansas acquaintance the 1950s tape recordings of Bernice Blackwelder, John McCurdy, and Bess and Fred Heine—tapes that revealed Bernice and John's might-have-been love affair—Quantrille hoped DPL would transcribe them for her. Shearouse reluctantly agreed but warned her, "I do not feel that we can continue to do this type of work for you in the future."[51] And when Quantrille pulled together notes toward what would become her *Memoirs of My Childhood and Youth in North Denver*, she sent them to the city librarian, who replied diplomatically, praising the content but counseling Quantrille to "take a good bit of time and effort" putting the material into "publishable form." Shearouse suggested that the *Denver Post*'s weekly magazine might consider running a story based on her reminiscences and offered to contact a reporter on her behalf. He did not offer to publish the work, but he said that the library could archive it. In the end, the Colorado Genealogical Society (CGS) published the memoirs, and Quantrille donated a copy to DPL. A librarian wrote to thank her and told her that it would be cataloged in the Genealogy Division. Quantrille called him to say that she intended it to be cataloged in the higher-status Western History Department. He told her he would "see to the transfer."[52]

Quantrille got help preparing her memoirs for publication, but the help came from CGS rather than DPL (though the society's membership and the library's employee roster overlapped). Quantrille had once been president of CGS, and her work on the governors' families had appeared in its *Colorado Genealogist*. So when Henry Shearouse told her to revise her memoirs, she sought aid from the organization she knew best. Bonnie Garramone, then a member of the society's publication committee, remembers going with committee chair Kay Merrill to Quantrille's apartment to look at the manuscript. The three sat on the floor, and Quantrille went over the material, telling Merrill "what she would like to have done." Merrill wanted to take the material home, but that worried Quantrille. Once Quantrille was convinced that Merrill and Garramone knew what they were doing, she relented. Their work involved rearranging an already cut-and-pasted text into a more logical order and then typing a draft. When the work was done, Quantrille was pleased with it. "That's just what it needed," she told Merrill.[53]

Then they turned the project over to another CGS member, Jack

Smith, who had grown up near the McClungs in North Denver. Smith was younger than Quantrille; his grandmother and Quantrille's mother had been friends. He had retired early from a corporate career with Texaco and was spending his retirement traveling, working with CGS, and volunteering for the Colorado Historical Society. Quantrille's memoirs became one of his tasks, and through them he got to know her. The family connection helped, as did their mutual interest in history and genealogy. It also helped that Smith was, as he put it, "a bachelor," while Quantrille was, as he saw it, "the personification of a spinster." The two worked side by side, pulling together a manuscript that Smith thought was still too "disorganized" for publication. He was pleased that CGS was able to deliver a finished copy of the memoirs to Quantrille on her ninetieth birthday.[54]

It is characteristic of Quantrille that collaborators had to convince her to let a manuscript out of her sight for a few days and that she told her former workplace to catalogue her published memoirs in the more prestigious Western History Department instead of the more plebian Genealogy Division. The questions of status, reputation, and credit for their contributions that had long dogged both Quantrille and Bernice continued into old age. Restaurateur Sam Arnold once opined that Bernice was always "hoping for better recognition from the historic community."[55] Likewise, Jack Smith thought that Quantrille "craved recognition."[56] Compared with Bernice, though, Quantrille had stronger institutional and organizational ties—to DPL and CGS, respectively. So Quantrille did less hoping and more asking and, when necessary, more insisting. According to Smith, Quantrille had "a sense of her importance" and "wasn't overly modest about her accomplishments." But she clearly felt that if she did not demand her due, she was likely to be overlooked or underestimated or even exploited. When Quantrille hesitated to let a CGS member take her manuscript home, it was probably because she had once given it to the Colorado Historical Society for review and then had to "protest strongly to get it back." Smith said that the historical society found the memoirs "too gossipy" for publication, but Quantrille was sure that staff there "had decided that it belonged to them."[57] She was also adamant that the memoirs recorded "her memories only" and no one else's— especially not her once-estranged and now-dead brother's. This is *"my book,"* she declared.[58] And while Smith thought that DPL staff members "humored" Quantrille, others say that librarians who worked with her during her long retirement actually "revered her."[59]

No doubt various people responded variously to Quantrille's continued historical work and to the demands she made, but all agree that she made her presence felt, whether in the flesh, over the phone, or on the page. A younger librarian, Philip Panum, recalls that although she was of small stature, she always wore shoes with a "slight heel" that made a "distinctive sound." Speaking of a time when Quantrille could still make her way to the library, he says, "I was aware of her quick pace walk and knew it was her without looking up." Then, when her health started to fail, he recalls that older librarians would send him, "the kid," as he puts it, "up the hill to deliver books at her request." He would knock on her door and she would invite him in, saying, "Sit down, Phil," while she went to retrieve items she wanted to return.[60] In the last letter to Bernice that she copied and saved, Quantrille remarked on solicitous young men like Phil Panum, who, she said, were "most kind and even sweet." She acknowledged that "sweet" was not an adjective "usually applied" to men but added, "It is the only word that expresses the kind of attention I usually get."[61] She got that attention because, for some, her reputation commanded it. From others, her demands extracted a serviceable approximation of respect.

Likewise, as Quantrille's infirmities increased and her resources dwindled, she sought and received personal assistance from the younger and better heeled, especially from well-situated men and sometimes from their wives. In years past, Sam Arnold had hosted Quantrille at his Bent's Fort–replica restaurant tucked among the red rocks west of Denver, where she could dine on buffalo and mountain trout and the green chile stew called the Bowl of the Wife of Kit Carson. Now, in the late 1970s, Arnold brought groceries to her apartment.[62] Jack Smith did not deliver food, but he recalled bringing gallon jugs of port, which she used "as an assistance in sleeping." She could not lift a gallon on her own, though, so she would ask Smith to decant it into smaller bottles. He teased her that he was her "rumrunner." And he recalled that the wine was always a gift because, as he put it delicately, "she was living in rather modest circumstances in her later life."[63] That Smith could joke with Quantrille about his deliveries suggests that she felt little shame in wringing favors and free provisions from younger men.

Sometimes her acquaintances were of even higher status than Sam Arnold and Jack Smith (who, unlike Quantrille, did not live in "modest circumstances"). Because she had published genealogies of Colorado's governors, Quantrille got to know some of the state's chief executives and their wives. She liked to tell the story of a time when she had lunch with Dottie Lamm at the governor's mansion. Dottie Lamm was married to Governor Richard "Dick" Lamm, a Democrat who served from 1975 to 1987. After lunch, the governor's wife arranged for Quantrille to be taken home by the governor's driver. On the short trip to her apartment, Quantrille told the driver, "I have a stop I'd like you to make." He complied with the request, but the delay meant that a voice over the car radio kept saying, "Where's the governor's car? The governor is waiting!" According to Jack Smith, Quantrille thought this tale was "hilarious." Similarly, Ann Love, married to Republican governor John Love, who was in office from 1963 to 1973, once exclaimed to Quantrille, "I wish there was something we could do for you." As Quantrille told it, she replied, "You could give me a hundred dollars." Smith recalled, "I rather got the impression that she got the hundred dollars in the process."[64]

Still, there were not enough well-heeled men or spouses of governors to meet Quantrille's needs on a regular basis, and for the most part she fended for herself, sometimes with help from social services or distant relatives. For example, among her papers is a January 1984 menu for a meals-on-wheels program that provided shut-ins one full meal each day Monday to Friday.[65] Since she ate twenty-one meals a week, this left Quantrille with five fewer to prepare for herself.

Never before had Quantrille, the self-proclaimed old maid, felt so acutely the hazards of the identity she had assumed decades before. One Sunday in 1979, when she was eighty-nine and still fairly mobile, she attended Sunday services at Trinity United Methodist Church, her home congregation. After the opening hymn, those gathered joined in a call to worship. The minister began, "Who comes to worship God?" The congregation responded, "Husbands and wives, brothers and sisters, widows and widowers, we come." In the printed order of service that she brought home, Quantrille penciled in those with whom she most identified—"old maids," she wrote—right between "brothers and sisters" and "widows and widowers."[66] The paired gender categories that seemed natural to most churchgoers meant little to her—she had never married, and her only brother was dead and gone. By this time, Quantrille had stopped keeping copies of the letters she wrote to Bernice, and no other reflection on the amended church bulletin survives. But the bulletin does. In fact, though she went to church regularly for nine decades, it is one of only a half dozen orders of service Quantrille saved: the act of archiving is meditation enough. Setting this thought alongside one she articulated years before to Bernice indicates the attenuated sense of belonging Quantrille felt at the church as well as her need. In 1972, after a hard week filled with frightening health problems, Quantrille lamented that her neighbors ignored her and her nearest friend was too busy caring for an invalid husband to help. Then she added, "If I had money & a legacy ... someone from the church would be here pronto! The minister loves to tell how wonderful the church has been to various persons but it is always someone with money or a family with position."[67] It was never an old maid of modest means.

Sometimes Quantrille could turn to family members for help. She still detested her brother's widow, and even relations with her brother's sons were distant and tense.[68] But her cousin George Prendergast, once one of the dearest people in her life, was now a minor benefactor. He lived in San Diego, having retired as rector of an Episcopal parish there. In 1940, George had married Jane Tucker Warren, granddaughter of President Woodrow Wilson's advisor Edward M. House. George married money. Accordingly, now and then, George and Jane sent Quantrille a check to help out—fifty dollars here, twenty-five dollars there.[69]

There were also younger cousins who provided care and cheer. One set lived in Memphis, and they hosted Quantrille at Christmastime. When she was first invited there, she worried about flying alone. She worried even more about coping with one of her ailments in a strange place; she suffered from excessive perspiration that caused her to soak sleepwear and bedding. It must have worked out, because she made the trip a few times at least through 1980, when she was ninety years old. It is not clear who financed the travel—Quantrille or her cousins—but comments in Bernice's letters about Quantrille's holiday trips suggest that the Memphis relatives lived in ease.[70] Another set of cousins moved to Colorado from California, where Quantrille had not only paternal relatives, such as George, but also maternal kin. Sharon Morgans was the daughter of maternal relatives there. Once they settled in the Denver area, Sharon and her husband raised children and worked in the growing technology sector along the Front Range. They invited Quantrille for meals and lived close enough to check on her. They sometimes ferried her to medical appointments, at least when she informed them of her needs. She seemed hesitant to do so, perhaps because she did not know them well and they had demanding lives of their own. After Quantrille told Bernice the story of an ordeal at a laboratory, Bernice urged her, "By all means tell your cousins. You are fortunate that they live near and care."[71] Sharon Morgans would be the only relative who attended Quantrille's burial ten years later.

Through all this, Quantrille tried to focus on the work she loved, on her legacy, and on the world that was changing around her. In addition to her efforts to extend the Carson, Bent, and Boggs family trees, her work involved organizing the papers that she hoped to leave to DPL. She had considered doing this ever since she published the first *Carson-Bent-Boggs Genealogy*. Most of her papers related to these families and to those of Colorado's governors—that is, to the work she had done since retirement. She had long since given the scrapbooks and photograph albums she compiled as a younger adult to the Colorado Historical Society. Now, in a good hand, she printed out for DPL the contents of the file drawers and cardboard boxes that filled her apartment as well as the dimensions of each drawer or box. Years before, she had proposed that these papers be called the McClung Collection of Carsoniana. But the scope of her work had since expanded, and she also saved newspaper clippings on city, state, and regional topics. So by the 1970s, she no longer suggested a name for the collection. She did not even express a preference about whether the materials would end up in the Genealogy Division or the Western History Department, likely because while she realized that Western History had greater prestige, she also knew that Genealogy had staff who could help patrons make sense of her charts and notes.[72] She never told anyone at DPL that among her papers were the letters she had been exchanging with Bernice since the 1950s. But they were there.

There as well were some items that fit awkwardly with the rest of the materials, though they ended up in what became, after her death, the Quantrille McClung Papers. The miscellany includes the edited church bulletin and the meals-on-wheels menu, items that point, poignantly, to key aspects of Quantrille's last years—her invisibility as an older, unmarried woman in her church and her want for sustenance as resources dwindled and mobility declined. Other incongruous items include campaign literature for an embattled Democratic congressman; a newspaper clipping about a Methodist bishop who appointed an openly gay minister to a local church; and a valentine from a historic preservationist whose grandfather had served as building contractor for the Jewish Consumptives' Relief Society (JCRS), the sanatorium that the family of her old librarian friend Anna Hillkowitz had helped to found. Each of these pieces is anomalous, unlike other materials Quantrille saved. But she was mindful in organizing her papers, so the items provide clues to her allegiances and sympathies and attachments.

Consider, for instance, the 1970 campaign letter she saved from the Committee to Re-elect Rogers. Byron Rogers was the incumbent U.S. congressman from Quantrille's district. He had held office for twenty years but faced a more liberal challenger in the Democratic primary, one who favored racial integration in Denver's schools and an end to the Vietnam War. The challenger won the primary but was later defeated in the general election by Republican Mike McKevitt (who in turn lost two years later to Democrat Pat Schroeder). In the past, Rogers had served in the state legislature, as U.S. attorney for Colorado, and as the state's attorney general. During the Depression, he also worked in Washington, D.C., for two New Deal agencies. Perhaps Quantrille favored the reelection of this old-school Democrat and that is why she saved the letter. It is hard to know. She eschewed politics when writing to her Republican friend Bernice, and she kept her views to herself as she researched the genealogies of Colorado governors and their wives, since they hailed in roughly equal numbers from the two major parties and she needed the families' cooperation to do her work.[73] But in the privacy of the voting booth, Quantrille might have been a Democrat.

Likewise, she might have had a soft spot in her heart for the gay community in late twentieth-century Colorado. She may even have felt some connection to it. She saved a 1983 *Denver Post* article about opposition in the United Methodist Church to Bishop Melvin Wheatley Jr., who supported the inclusion of gay men and lesbians as members. Wheatley, whose son was gay, had opposed antigay positions taken at denominational meetings in the 1970s. As bishop for the Methodist Rocky Mountain Conference, which included Colorado, he had also reassigned an openly gay minister, Julian Rush, from a Boulder parish to one in Denver when some in Boulder objected to his presence. Quantrille saved an article about the bishop written by the *Post*'s religion editor Virginia Culver, who, Wheatley recalled, ran stories about the controversy "whenever there was the slightest new twist" to justify it. The article covered Wheatley's censure and a call for his resignation by the First Methodist Church of Colorado Springs, which Culver said was the largest Methodist church in the West.[74] It was the only article about Methodists Quantrille saved that was not about her own congregation. Given her marginality in that church (which was not the one where Wheatley reassigned Rush), it seems doubtful that she saved this clipping because she thought Wheatley should go. It seems possible that she identified with the sense of otherness that gay people and their allies so often experienced in late twentieth-century mainline Protestant churches. If this was the case, perhaps she also recalled the catholic desires of her own youth, when she flirted with bohemianism in matters of the heart.[75] Quantrille likely did not think of herself in the terms the *Post* used to describe Reverend Rush—"an avowed, practicing homosexual"—but she may have felt that she had come of age in a house that history had turned to glass, from which it would be unthinkable to throw stones.

Memories of her bohemian phase likely also percolated when she received a handcrafted valentine from her friend E. James "Jim" Judd, a historically minded builder committed to the preservation of places that bespoke Denver's past. The valentine is an elaborate, multipage exercise in graphic design that features doilies and hearts and cupids along with clip art, sketches, and calligraphy, all arranged in a style reminiscent of the homemade greetings that Quantrille exchanged with her librarian friends back in the 1910s and '20s.[76] It begins, "The custom's one of great ubiquity and extreme antiquity—Be My Valentine." Then it addresses Quantrille directly, noting the "soft life" she leads while recuperating from an unnamed ailment. There is talk of books and bookstores, of art and artists, and a vow to Quantrille that as soon as she recovers, "we'll have to have a Coming Out Party—just an informal group of friends for cocktails." Then comes a pen-and-ink sketch of three naked younger women of varied physiques, one gripping a cocktail glass; a wizened older woman wearing what might be a nun's habit (this may be Quantrille); and a portly middle-aged man clad in a loincloth (this may be Jim Judd). Female breasts and genitalia abound in the valentine, while male genitalia are covered by leaf or cloth, save one image of a cherubic cupid boasting a British bobby's hat and what may be the tiniest penis known to humankind.[77]

What sort of person sent a greeting like this to a retired librarian close to ninety years old? Jim Judd came from a long line of builders, starting with his grandfather Abraham Judelowitz, a Russian Jewish immigrant who moved to Denver in the 1880s. As a contractor, Judelowitz built Denver's first synagogue as well as the permanent structures that supplemented the original tents of the JCRS. He served on the board of trustees for that organization alongside Philip Hillkowitz, son of Rabbi Elias Hillkowitz and brother of librarian Anna Hillkowitz, Quantrille's friend and mentor. It was Anna who hosted the bohemian party featured in Quantrille's 1910s photographs and who, in the poem she and Quantrille wrote about another library frolic, wears a "skirt of slits" and cavorts on the table with Mabel. Abraham Judelowitz's son and Jim Judd's father, Samuel Judd, an engineer, worked on Colorado River projects for the federal Bureau of Reclamation and served as Denver's building inspector. (By Samuel's generation, the family had changed its name to the less Jewish-sounding Judd.) Jim Judd organized the Judd Construction Company in 1949 and, in 1970, founded Historic Denver, a nonprofit whose first project was to preserve and restore the Margaret "Molly" Brown house, once home to the "unsinkable" Titanic survivor, and to turn it into a museum.[78] Jim Judd was Quantrille's friend. He was also a conduit to her own personal historic Denver, a lost landscape of laughter and longing once observed in silence by a portrait of Rabbi Hillkowitz on the wall.

Because Quantrille stayed rooted in Denver, where she knew so many and so many knew her, even as she aged, she had constant reminders of youthful frolics. Indeed, as trying as the last chapter of her life was, it compared favorably to Bernice's final act. Bernice did have a wage-earning, companionable husband who tolerated her love of history and stepped in to help when she was ill. But Harold's preferences so took precedence that Bernice had limited control over her daily life and the arc of her future. Bernice also had a brother who cared for her, though the force of his opinions—about the cleanliness of her household, the worthiness of her husband, even about where she should grow old and die—must have grated. Quantrille had men in her life, too, but they did not run it. And while she lacked quotidian companionship, Quantrille created a life that revolved around her passion for genealogy, and that passion brought with it not only human contact but also deference and recognition. She did not get bored, either. Bernice, by contrast, wrote of the sameness of her days. She began one letter, "I have a very empty feeling that I will not be able to fill the page as my life is so uneventful."[79] For a woman who had once gloried in the highs and lows of a life shared with a fellow performer, who had once stood singing on a stage and savoring the applause, who had once felt herself a part, if a small part, of a national Cold War crusade, days spent writing a dictionary and waiting on a husband were dull. There seemed no end to it, no reward, no purpose. So Bernice threw her work away.

Quantrille, on the other hand, got her recompense. She did not live to publish another *Carson-Bent-Boggs Genealogy* supplement. (I am thankful for that on your behalf, dear reader.) But she did get into print her *Memoirs of My Childhood and Youth in North Denver*. And she earned commendation for her work. First, in 1976, CGS honored her at a meeting, where she got a plaque recognizing her "many fine services" as well as a "lovely floral corsage." She had been named an honorary life member of CGS in years past, so this was a sort of "thanks again." Then the society printed a notice in the *Colorado Genealogist* along with a picture of Quantrille standing, beaming, and wearing her best dress and the corsage. The note recalled the conferral of her honorary life membership in 1953, when she was working on the Colorado governors' families; it acknowledged the Carson, Bent, and Boggs genealogies; and it quoted Quantrille, who said of the honor, "It was a most gratifying experience as this was the first time public recognition of my work had ever been given me in Denver."[80]

It was not the last time. A year or so after CGS published her *Memoirs*, the *Denver Post* ran excerpts from it along with an article about her ongoing work, work so demanding that she told the newspaperman,

"I don't lie down in the afternoon anymore. I can't afford the time." The article detailed Quantrille's genealogical contributions and noted her regret over "the lack of recognition of her efforts by the Colorado Historical Society" (thus giving her the last word in her feud with the state institution that housed the scrapbooks of her young adulthood but refused to publish her memoirs). Apparently, the reporter who interviewed her remarked on her unmarried state and perhaps asked if there had been suitors, because he wrote, "Miss McClung never married, but carried on a trans-Atlantic friendship with an Englishman for 44 years. He died in 1975. They met for the first time 20 years after they began corresponding. He never married either. 'He was a little man, about my size, sweet, kind, gentle and thoughtful,' she said, turning back to her boxes, folders and cabinets of research." The content of those boxes, folders, and cabinets—eleven linear feet of materials—became the McClung Papers at DPL. There is no evidence in these papers or in the more personal documents she gave to the state historical society of this friend: no letters, no photos, no mementos. Quantrille did sail to England twice, in 1953 and 1955, when she was flush after the sale of her parents' house, and she might have visited the little man there. But the transatlantic friendship was likely more notable to the *Denver Post* writer than it was to Quantrille, who saved evidence of other tender ties but not even a scrap of paper reflecting this one. The story the *Post* told made Quantrille a legible character—an American spinster with an English gentleman friend. She played along but then cut the fellow down to size and turned back to her work.[81]

Final recognition came in 1983, when Governor Dick Lamm, by executive order, declared her ninety-third birthday Quantrille McClung Recognition Day in Colorado. Now she was fêted in grand style. The day before her birthday, on March 2, DPL held a tea for her, inviting not only current and retired employees but also Mayor Bill McNichols, brother of former governor Stephen McNichols and thus a public official whose family Quantrille had researched. The tea featured a formal proclamation from the governor's office, a certificate of appreciation from DPL conferred by city librarian Henry Shearouse, and a book-shaped cake. Quantrille's old neighbor and collaborator Jack Smith wrote an article about the event for the *Colorado Genealogist*, "An Honor for One of Ours," and noted that Mayor McNichols "presented a pin of gold and enamel, spoke of the great service Quantrille has rendered in preserving the history of the city and state and commented that her research may have contributed more to Colorado than some of the persons whose genealogy she has traced."[82] The next day, on her birthday, the *Denver Post* ran a large photograph of Quantrille, captioning it, "A History Unto Herself." There was Quantrille in the same dress she wore seven years earlier, with a similar corsage, but instead of wearing a jaunty beret as she had in 1976, her wispy hair a halo beneath it, now whatever hair she had left was drawn up in a head-scarf knotted Rosie the Riveter style. She was seated, a walking cane at her side. But again, she was beaming.[83] Smith recalled, "Everybody was hovering over her and, oh, she loved it, she loved it!"[84] She painstakingly handwrote a letter of thanks to Shearouse, telling him, "The Denver Public Library has made March 2nd the apogee of my career. I had never expected or even dreamed that such an event could ever occur." She added that it "was a natural result when the Head Person has the fine quality of our City Librarian," offering Shearouse the generosity of a genderless title in a profession where women predominated in numbers but not in power and prestige. Then she closed, "Your wonderful celebration has made me so happy and I shall never forget it."[85]

She would remember it for a couple more years. All this recognition and achievement reached backward into her past, because when friends who had left Denver learned of Quantrille's triumphs, they wrote to congratulate her. For example, after *Memoirs of My Childhood and Youth in North Denver* appeared, one of Quantrille's old cross-dressing pals wrote to her from the San Francisco Bay Area. Sudie Mai Hodnette had moved to Omaha decades before and then to the Bay Area, where she worked as a bookkeeper and was active in hiking clubs. Like Quantrille, she had never married and was now retired. The two women had corresponded before, but the 1982 letter is the only one Quantrille saved. In it, Sudie Mai praised Quantrille's memoir, musing that it would "delight" anyone familiar with North Denver. But what most excited Sudie Mai was a tiny detail in the book, where Quantrille described the brick house her parents built to replace the wood-frame structure that was their first dwelling. The new home had a root cellar. One reached the cellar via steps, Quantrille wrote, that "were covered by double doors sloping downward from the house wall." She recalled that "children liked to slide down such doors despite the damage to clothing," which in turn brought to mind a song she and her playmates had sung: "I won't let you come to my house, / I don't like you anymore, / Tra-la-la, la-la-la-la-la! / Sliding down my cellar door!" Quantrille closed this passage wondering if anyone still living "could fill in the third line" (that is, the line she turned into a "tra-la-la"). Sudie Mai eagerly reported that while she did not at first recall the lyric, she then heard the song in the film *Reds*, Warren Beatty's epic about the radical left in the United States during the Russian Revolution. The 1981 movie dramatized the free-love romance between journalists John Reed, author of *Ten Days That Shook the World* and once a lover of Mabel Dodge Luhan's, and Louise Bryant, author of *Six Red Months in Russia* and once a lover of playwright Eugene O'Neill's. In the film, Bryant, played by Diane Keaton, sings a strangely seductive version of the childhood ditty, which in turn supplied Sudie Mai with the line Quantrille had omitted: "You'll be sorry when you see me."[86] A letter like this from a friend with whom Quantrille had shared the era depicted in the film must have prompted a flood of memories—not just of high-spirited children sliding down cellar doors but also of lusty young women negotiating an alluring terrain of temptations under a bright bohemian sky before the cloud of Bolshevism threw shade on all manner of U.S. radicalism. With praise for Quantrille's accomplishments, then, came recollection of lost worlds.

Likewise, letters from an old library colleague named Julia both congratulated Quantrille on the accolades she received late in life and reminisced about times past. Julia, who had moved from Colorado to Arizona, learned from a mutual acquaintance about Quantrille McClung Recognition Day. She wrote to tell Quantrille how "thrilled" she was and pledged to pass the news on to old friends. Julia lamented of DPL's early twentieth-century cohort, "There are so few of our contemporaries left."[87] One of the few was a younger but also retired and unmarried librarian named Marguerite Barrett who still lived in Denver. It was Marguerite who kept Julia abreast of Quantrille's news. In the next (and last) letter from Julia, written in 1985, Julia again remarked on the passing of DPL's "Old Guard" and noted as well how much the library had gained from Quantrille's work. This time, though, Julia said she had heard from Marguerite that Quantrille was "considering moving" and added, "Or was it Marguerite that was considering it for you?"[88] Whether it was her own idea or that of a younger friend such as Marguerite, Quantrille had indeed decided to move from the Capitol Hill apartment where she had lived for over two decades. Her new residence was a nursing home.

I have not found anyone who knows how Quantrille came to live at Valley Hi Nursing Home in Denver, a few miles southeast of Capitol Hill and a couple of miles from the University of Denver, where Quantrille received her library science diploma in 1936. Jack Smith, her collaborator, was in Europe when she relocated and only learned of the move when he got home. James Kroll, recent manager of what is now DPL's Western History/Genealogy Department (the two units having finally merged), similarly does not know how Quantrille "was convinced to move into a nursing home," only that "she couldn't live on her own anymore." Kroll was a young librarian then and remembers her well, though he is not sure he met her more than once, at the tea celebrating Quantrille Mc-

Clung Recognition Day. Still, he says, "I have more images of her in my head than just that one time and I don't know why." Quantrille left an outsize impression. Kroll does recall that she was at Valley Hi only for "a short period of time" and that "what came back [to DPL] was that she was very unhappy." Smith, who visited her at the nursing home when he returned from Europe, concurred: "I really felt that her spirit was broken. She wasn't the same zesty Quantrille that I had known." It is true that she had always been, by necessity, resourceful and independent, and perhaps requiring constant care and supervision was soul-crushing. Jim Kroll—trained, like me, as a western historian—gives her quick decline a regional spin, characterizing her as the quintessential westerner: "Gets fenced in and dies." She was also ninety-five years old. Her heart beat last on the eve of Independence Day, July 3, 1985.[89]

Trinity Methodist Church held no funeral for Quantrille McClung. Perhaps she did not want one or did not want one at a church that she felt favored folks "with money or a family with position." Perhaps her estate lacked funds to pay for a funeral. Whatever the explanation, there was instead a graveside service attended by a dozen people—Jack Smith, Bonnie Garramone, Jim Kroll, and cousin Sharon Morgans among them. Quantrille was laid to rest alongside her parents, Henrietta Gutzman McClung, who was called Hattie, and Benjamin Franklin McClung, and with her brother Denzel's first child, Hattie Ellen McClung, namesake of Henrietta, who had died mysteriously when she was just twenty-two. Denzel was buried nearby. Although Quantrille was a half dozen years older than him, she had outlived her brother by a quarter century. She had also outlived her troublesome sister-in-law, May McClung, who was buried with Denzel. A few days after Quantrille's death, both the *Denver Post* and the *Rocky Mountain News* ran substantial obituaries. The *Colorado Genealogist* followed suit the next month.[90] Quantrille Day McClung had finally shuffled off her mortal coil.

* *

Not long ago, on a bright blue spring day, I laid a red rose on her grave.

The chair where I sit now is not ergonomically designed and my back hurts. I wrote most of this epilogue at my former home in Madison, Wisconsin, where I sacrificed style for comfort, since I spend more hours at my desk than anywhere else in the world. Now, I am at a different desk, a mission-style number from Pier 1 Imports that caught my eye when my beloved and I outfitted a condominium we bought in Santa Fe, New Mexico, many years ago. That real estate transaction was part of a relationship deal we made when we both joined the faculty at the University of Wisconsin: if we were going to take up residence in my home state, we agreed, we would find a way to spend time in hers as well—hence, the Santa Fe dwelling that we christened the "Casita" to distinguish it from the Madison house we called "Home Sweet Home." I was taken by the chair that matched the mission desk I got at Pier 1. It is profoundly uncomfortable, but it looks terrific and very western.

I was not supposed to be in Nuevo México alone. This was my beloved's place; these were her people. Like Kit Carson, I had married in. Nothing I had done before in the West or in relation to the West—not traveling or living or working here, not watching *The Rifleman*, not teaching or reading or writing western history—gave me a relationship to this place and connected me to people here the way that loving a *manita*, and loving her madly, did.[91] I had loved western women in the past, daughters of different nations and peoples, different struggles and strivings that all converged on California's shores. But I was older when I met Camille Guérin-Gonzales and ready to love with abandon. She was a daughter of the mountains they call the Blood of Christ, the Sangre de Cristo. Born in the Santa Fe Trail town of Las Vegas, New Mexico, which boomed again when the Atchison, Topeka, and Santa Fe Railway pushed through in 1879, she had Indigenous forebears as well as ancestors from Spain, France, Germany, Britain and, as revealed in a genetic test she took weeks before she died, likely from many other European, Central Asian, South Asian, Middle Eastern, West African, Southeast African, and Pacific Island places, too. She did not live to see the results of that test or to hear me say "I told you so." Long before the analysis of her saliva expanded what I knew of her ancestry, I often sang to her an altered version of "We Are the World," the 1985 USA for Africa benefit tune: "You are the world, you are the children." She always laughed. I could always make her laugh.

Camille was a child of the twentieth century.[92] Her paternal grandparents, on the side of the family where *hispanas* intermingled with new-comers, had once lived comfortable lives in Las Vegas, owning the first home there with indoor plumbing. But the Guerins lost their savings in the 1929 bank crash, sending her grandmother back to work as a hairdresser for the rest of her life. Her grandfather, a teamster, drove his pickup truck to retrieve the mail that arrived daily by train and delivered it to the post office. Her maternal grandparents, on the side of the family where there was little intermarriage, were ranching folk who had moved to town, where grandmother Gonzales—Camille called her Nenita—taught school. Some of the Guerins looked down on the Gonzales family, who had darker skin and had once been less prosperous (though one cousin on that side, James Almanzar, became an actor and played Indian and Mexican parts on TV Westerns like *High Chaparral* and *Gunsmoke*).[93] The Depression had leveled the financial disparities between the Guerin and Gonzales families, but racial hierarchies died hard.

Camille was raised as much by her grandparents as by her parents, who divorced while she and her younger brothers were small, but she sometimes lived with her mother and father and later with her father and stepmother. Her mother, who had worked as a teacher, a waitress, and a secretary, died in her forties of cirrhosis of the liver. (Nenita prayed for Camille's mother to St. Jude, the patron saint of lost causes—as did we for those afflicted with the alcoholism that stalks both sides of the family.) Camille's stepmother, a member of the Church of Jesus Christ of Latter-Day Saints, was a nurse. (It was good that when Camille's father remarried, he wed a Mormon, because that marriage curtailed his drinking.) Her father, after teaching school and running a record store, worked for Sandia Corporation, which contracted with the U.S. government to produce nuclear weapons. When Camille lived with her father, she lived in a radioactive West: in Los Alamos, New Mexico, where the atomic bomb was developed; in Henderson, Nevada, near the nuclear test grounds; and in Livermore, California, home of what was then the Lawrence Radiation Laboratory. Her father died of cancer at the age of seventy-five, after a remission of several years, and Camille died of cancer at the age of sixty-nine. Her cancer was relentless, and despite treatment, she lived just fourteen months after her diagnosis, with no remission at all. She left behind three adult children, their partners, seven grandchildren, one great-grandchild (and a second since she passed), loving friends, dear cousins, cherished students, and me.

That is how I ended up sitting in a torturous desk chair in the too-quiet Casita, writing about traffics in men and things male and about how they travel with the travails of colonialism and imperialism, nation building and border crossing, racial formation and civil rights resistance, industrialization and deindustrialization, political might and group disempowerment, academic professionalization and the pushback of amateurs, progressive social change and persistent social inequity, self-fashioning and collective identification. But there is more to say about why I see gender traffic so clearly in such disparate circumstances and why the traffic in Kit Carson so intrigues me. That traffic is legible to me and I relate it to so much else because it runs through the stories I tell myself about myself and about my relationship to those around me. What made that traffic and its correlates visible to me was the fracturing of feminism and its presumed subject in the 1980s.[94]

That visibility was predicated on what I witnessed the two decades before: the rise of Black Power, Brown Power, Red Power, and Yellow Power and the force of those movements' shared critique of U.S. global power. I also saw a new kind of feminism ferment. I listened, too, for the rumblings of gay liberation, sounds that were muffled by my constrained choice about which college to attend. The choice was constrained because my maternal grandfather, once a Lutheran field missionary, had received an honorary doctorate from a Wisconsin Lutheran college, and my parents had hoped that one of their children would go to school there. My older siblings had no interest, so it fell to me. Although gay and lesbian insurgence was well under way in 1974 when I enrolled at Carthage College in Kenosha, there was no sign of it there. I did, however, see intermittent signals of movements for racial and gender justice as well as their academic expressions. Indeed, I cannot imagine my openness to the fractures of the 1980s without the education I got in the 70s, in and out of the classroom.

In college, I did not gravitate to the study of history right away. First I thought I might major in biology. Then I drifted toward the field of education. Meanwhile I took history classes—most memorably, courses on American Indian history and the history of the American West, plus a well-taught U.S. history survey. I was getting hooked, though I still thought I would pursue just a history minor alongside my major in education. In my study of pedagogy, I found myself using what I had learned in history courses to devise related projects for the elementary grades. I created a board game called Arrowhead, for instance, that taught students about tribal histories in their regional contexts. And I designed a lesson plan based on Stevie Wonder's then-popular song "Black Man," which features Harlem children shouting out the historical contributions of assorted Americans—Bruce Lee, Sacagawea, César Chávez, Harriet

Tubman.[95] Because I was studying education in Kenosha, when I thought about using these projects in the schools, I thought about local children, who were racially and ethnically diverse and mostly working class. Kenosha had fallen on hard times—production at American Motors, the largest employer, had declined since the 1960s, and manufacturers such as the Simmons Bedding Company had left entirely. So I was studying education in a deindustrializing Rust Belt town, home to working-class African Americans and Mexican Americans and to southeastern Wisconsin's blend of white ethnics, including the descendants of Italian and Polish immigrants.[96] As a middle-class Lutheran of Danish, Norwegian, and German descent, I was in the majority population at Carthage but not in Kenosha at large.

That experience turned my world upside down. It provoked an intellectual and political crisis that defines me still. The crisis intensified when I worked as a teacher's aide in Kenosha's public schools and even more when I became a student teacher in a fourth-grade class with a mix of black, white, and brown children. Half the class was working below grade level, a quarter well below. Students of color, especially the boys, were overrepresented among those who had fallen behind. Some of the children were poor. Others came from the kind of secure working-class families that the U.S. labor movement had helped produce. None of them came from the world of my own youth in Madison. In the years that have passed since I worked in the Kenosha schools, I have often worked as hard and as passionately as I did there. But I have never worked harder or more passionately. I have never cared more than I did about those children. Even at a remove of many decades, I recall their struggles: the student working below grade level whose family traveled the migrant circuit from fields in rural Texas to fields in rural Wisconsin to service work in Kenosha; the child who, when he made it to school, came clad in unlaundered clothing accessorized with a fabulous feather boa (he worked at grade level and could channel Diana Ross like nobody's business); the student whose frustration over his difficulty in learning to read only eased when he got a chance to put on headphones and follow along with an audiotape I had made of a male friend reading textbook stories aloud. This was my new world.

I wanted to understand how this world came to be. I wanted to know why these children were growing up without the privileges and opportunities that I took for granted. In the end, I decided that history could best explain the inequities I saw in the schools. So I hurried, in my senior year, to turn my history minor into a major, which was possible because I had finished the requirements for my education major. By now, the courses I was taking were not big lecture classes but small seminars that entailed research. One was a western history seminar, where I first encountered primary sources; I wrote a paper on the nineteenth-century Rocky Mountain fur trade. I had to complete a second research project in order to qualify for honors in the major, so I enrolled in what was the first women's history course ever offered at Carthage; I did so mostly because it required a substantial final paper. It was an evening class designed for local teachers. One of my white male professors (there were only white male professors in the history department, but this one, a Europeanist, also taught African American history and served as faculty advisor to the Black Student Union) team-taught the course with his spouse, a white woman who was finishing her own PhD and teaching part-time.[97] The whole idea of women's history was a revelation. I devoured the common readings, savored the discussions, and could not fathom why I had never thought of women as historical subjects before. As I cast about for a research topic in that class, I briefly considered writing a paper on what I then conceived as "past attitudes toward homosexuals in newspapers." I had never heard of gay history and neither had anyone else at the college. That topic raised faculty eyebrows (though it brought no condemnation), so I settled instead on exploring why Wyoming in 1869 became the first U.S. state or territory to grant women the right to vote (to attract white women settlers, I argued).

I wish I could say that my passion for history was always as high-minded, clear-sighted, and rooted in a concern for social justice as I have intimated here. It was not. My interest in the West, especially, remained rooted in the frontier myths I had imbibed as a child of the Cold War, and my attachment to the region still encompassed that old sense that it was a male place, though outwardly I now disavowed that sense as inimical to feminist politics. In the midst of all this, during the summer of 1976, I traveled by train to Montana with three of my best female friends, college classmates. We stayed with my Aunt Kay near Ennis and with the aunt of one of my travel companions in Anaconda, and we spent a couple of nights in a rustic cabin in Yellowstone National Park. The four of us imbibed countless shots of the fabled Old West with chasers of Rainier beer, a now-defunct Seattle brew no better than any Milwaukee beer but somehow tastier because western-made. What I did not know until later was that two of my travel companions had fallen in love and were seizing every opportunity to be alone. What I did know was that I was in unrequited love with the third, who had the most soulful eyes I had ever seen. This was nothing new; I had spent most of high school attached to a boyfriend but secretly in love with my best (girl)friend.

Now, as I approached my twentieth year, I was just beginning to name this pattern in my own mind. It made me deeply unhappy. I thought a lot about death.

Nonetheless, in the summers after my junior and senior years, I returned to Yellowstone on my own to work for the concession company that ran the lodges, curio shops, and restaurants there. I learned much at Yellowstone—not least a greater lust for western landscapes. I did not yet understand the process by which Indigenous peoples had been removed from such landscapes, the better to preserve them for the benefit of non-Indians. If I had known this history, I might have connected it to a marginalization going on right before my eyes. In addition to the white college students who worked summers at Yellowstone, the concession company also recruited young people from the Navajo Nation. But the Diné who worked there got jobs that kept them out of sight. They washed dishes or cleaned rooms; they did not bus tables or work at a cash register, as I did. The person who drew this to my attention was an artist friend from the Bay Area who had grown up hearing that her family tree included an Indigenous branch. (Later that branch was described to her as Jewish, and much later my friend determined that rather than Native or Jewish ancestry, she probably had African American forebears. At least one relative had preferred to be vaguely Indian or kind of Semitic than to be even a little bit black.) This friend sketched cowboys, played guitar, and sang a deliciously mournful version of Bob Dylan's "Buckets of Rain." I was in unrequited love with her, too.

The West was becoming a more and more complicated place for me. When I finished my first summer at Yellowstone, I went back to Carthage for my senior year, told myself that I was as queer as a three-dollar bill, broke up with the dearest of boyfriends, declared my history major, agreed to edit the student literary journal, and set about finding a girlfriend who would love me back—and who could write. It took most of the school year, but I did it; I met a philosophy major who submitted work to the literary journal and who was as queerly curious as I was. We penned each other poems and argued about whether philosophy was prior to history or history to philosophy.

It was the next summer, after I graduated, when I started to connect my new gayness to my old love for the West. I went back to Yellowstone, bluffing confidence in what I now called my sexuality, to good effect. When my summer work ended, I went in search of an even queerer frontier. I had no job lined up for the fall, so when the first snow fell on Yellowstone in late August, I piled into a car with some gay men and drove to

San Francisco. We met up with other gay men when we got there, friends of one of my travel companions. San Francisco was everything I hoped it would be. When the boys wanted to ditch me so that they could go to the men's bars and baths, one of them called directory assistance and asked for the address of a women's bar he had heard about. The male operator quickly code-switched into gayspeak, exclaiming, "Oh, *honey*—that's a *girls'* bar!" My friend explained that he was asking for me, so he got the address for a club called A Little More. The boys drove me there and very nearly forgot to pick me up when it closed in the wee hours of the morning (I was petrified as I waited, never having been out alone in a big city before). In the daylight hours, we walked together through the Castro. There we saw street-level organizing against a California ballot initiative that would have denied gay people the right to work in public schools. A key opponent of that initiative was Harvey Milk, the first openly gay city supervisor in San Francisco. Little did we know that within three months, Harvey Milk and his ally Mayor George Moscone would be shot dead by a twisted opponent of queer visibility. By then, I was back in Wisconsin, working from sundown to sunrise at a funky twenty-four-hour counseling center, not far from my alma mater but worlds apart, talking down distraught and drug-addled folks on a crisis hotline. Whenever the phone fell silent, I watched San Francisco's grief on television. I also wrote graduate school applications. I was coming to see the West as a place every bit as embattled as Wisconsin's own stretch of the Rust Belt. I wanted to understand how it got that way.

I spent the next few years working toward that understanding *in* the West, first as a master's student at Arizona State University in Tempe and then as an editorial staff member for *Signs* at Stanford. At Arizona State, I took more western and women's history, studying the way that social power followed lines of racial difference and sexual alterity, which I had come to see as products of history. On the side, I did coursework in editing and publishing procedures. I started but did not finish a master's thesis on women's households and relationships in central Arizona's gold and silver boomtowns before I began my work at *Signs*.[98] That meant that I finished the thesis in the intellectual, political, and social milieu of Stanford and the Bay Area.

What a milieu it was. There were graduate students in Chicano history who helped me make better sense of the differences I saw between Anglo and Mexican women's relational lives in Arizona mining towns. There was a faculty member affiliated with *Signs*, Estelle Freedman, who had not only heard of gay history but helped to invent it as well as the history of sexuality, of which it was a subset. There were members of a women's history dissertation group who kindly invited me to participate, even though I was only writing a master's thesis and from a different, less prestigious institution. There was the publication of *This Bridge Called My Back: Writings by Radical Women of Color* and local talks by its Chicana lesbian editors, Cherríe Moraga and the late Gloria Anzaldúa. In the next couple of years, there was the publication and constant discussion of *Home Girls: A Black Feminist Anthology*, edited by Barbara Smith, and *Nice Jewish Girls: A Lesbian Anthology*, edited by Evelyn Torton Beck.[99] There was a brilliant graduate student in anthropology from Chicago's working class who challenged assumptions that even my time in Kenosha schools had not forced me to interrogate fully. There were unlearning racism Workshops in Berkeley. There were the bars in San Francisco. A Little More was no more, but Amelia's in the Mission District was going strong, and I went there most weekends. And there were the Sex Wars.

For many, the struggles that came to be called the Sex Wars were about arguments between antipornography feminists and the feminists who called themselves sex radicals. Working for the journal *Signs*, I heard these arguments and even saw some of the disputants wander through our offices when they visited Stanford. *Signs* also sent me on assignment, so to speak, to academic conferences in order to survey the field of women's studies and encourage practitioners to submit work to the journal. So at meetings of the National Women's Studies Association and the Berkshire Conference of Women Historians, I heard scholars debate sexual matters as well. I did not attend the famous (famous among feminists, anyway) "Towards a Politics of Sexuality" conference at Barnard College in 1982, where the discord broke out into rhetorical warfare, but news of the Barnard conference winged its way back to the West Coast.[100]

For me, though, the sex wars were less about pornography than about queer desire. Sex radicals, with whom I came to identify, reserved judgment about pornography, calling for mindful consideration of its content and the conditions of its production and consumption; some called, too, for a new feminist pornography. But sex radicals also embraced gendered relationships between female-bodied people (butch/femme) and the sexual exploration of power and pain (sadomasochism, or S/M) as legitimate, even bravely daring variants of lesbian sexuality, which, they argued, had too long been limited by feminist prescriptions for sweetly reciprocal encounters between partners who renounced gender identification as a tool of patriarchy. Butch/femme bonds, argued some sex radicals, especially the ones I talked to day to day, were common in working-class communities and among women of color, two overlapping constituencies, so the insistence on reciprocity and genderless re-lationships was a white, middle-class cultural imposition as well.

Even as these conversations were swirling around me, *Signs* was producing a special themed "Lesbian Issue." As befit the nonhierarchical ethos we tried to create in an academic setting that was anything but nonhierarchical—an ethos I credit not only to feminist practice but also, especially, to my coworker and friend Clare Novak—I got to coedit that special issue along with two faculty members, Estelle Freedman and *Signs* editor Barbara Gelpi, and then PhD candidate Kath Weston, the anthropologist from whom I had already learned so much. We solicited articles and agreed on who would serve as peer reviewers and then decided what to publish. My happiest solicitation was of a piece based on a conference presentation I had heard, Lourdes Arguelles and B. Ruby Rich's "Homosexuality, Homophobia, and Revolution: Notes toward an Understanding of the Cuban Lesbian and Gay Male Experience."[101] Once the articles were accepted, the rest of the labor fell to the in-house editors; I was one of these.

We chose as the lead essay anthropologist Esther Newton's "The Mythic, Mannish Lesbian: Radclyffe Hall and the New Woman," and amazingly, I got to work on it. The work we did with articles involved content editing, line editing, copy editing, and later, proofreading—the whole deal, from raw manuscript to published article. So when one of us was assigned an essay, we lived with it intimately for a good long time. I lived with "The Mythic, Mannish Lesbian" in just this way. I can still see the view out the window from my desk in Serra House as I tinkered with the prose and the footnotes. I can almost recite some passages: "Because the proposition that lesbianism is an intensified form of female bonding has become a belief, thinking, acting, or looking like a man contradicts lesbian feminism's first principle: the lesbian is a 'woman-identified woman.' What to do, then, with that figure referred to, in various times and circumstances, as the 'mannish lesbian,' the 'true invert,' the 'bull dagger,' or the 'butch'?"[102] What to do indeed? Newton takes the British writer Radclyffe Hall as a central figure in these debates, specifically through Hall's creation of the mannish character Stephen Gordon in the 1928 novel *The Well of Loneliness*: "As the Bowery bum represents all that is most feared and despised about drunkenness, the mannish lesbian, of whom Stephen Gordon is the most famous prototype, has symbolized the stigma of lesbianism and so continues to move a broad range of lesbians. A second reason for *The Well*'s continuing impact . . . is that Stephen Gordon articulated a gender orientation with which an important minority of lesbians still identify."[103] I gazed out the window more often than usual as I edited this essay, mental gears shifting into place and my mind starting to hum.

Suddenly, there was sound where there had been silence. I squared my shoulders and sat up straight. I remembered *The Rifleman*. I pondered the soulful eyes, the mournful song, the unrequited love. I recalled a recent winter day when I had stared at a young man on campus wearing perfectly fitted gray flannel pants. I looked at him long and hard, so long and hard that it had surprised me. Now I thought, "I didn't want to *have* that fellow; I wanted to *be* him." Sort of. I wanted the eyes, the song, the love; I wanted them to be meant for me, walking around looking like him. I wanted it in a way that I was not getting. I aimed to have it.[104]

I have not lived outside that moment since. It has shaped my love life, to be sure. The jitter and wonder I had felt in proximity to women who embraced aspects of conventional femininity gave way to unfettered desire. None of these women embraced the whole package, of course — they were feminists. They knew well the ways in which conventional gender arrangements disciplined the female-bodied and benefited men over women. Theirs was a selective, conscious, even ironic adoption of the feminine in allure and inclination, in adornment and coiffure, in fragrance and flirtation. More than one of these women has told me that she took her cues as much from effeminate gay men and drag queens as from conventionally gendered heterosexual women. Others have cited female sex workers as muses. (There is nothing queerer than queer gender arrangements.)

But the era of the sex wars and the moment of editing Esther Newton's essay have shaped more than my love life. They have influenced my work as a historian. So where my master's thesis centered on diverse women, their households, and their intimate relationships in Arizona mining towns, I decided that my doctoral dissertation on the California gold rush could focus as much on diverse men as men as it did on diverse women as women and yet still reflect and advance feminist, antiracist, and decolonial principles.[105] In making this decision, I realized that I had, all my life, been a student of manhood and womanhood, so uncomfortable in the skin of my assigned gender that it became an itch I could not help but scratch.[106] I had taken stock of how various kinds of men enacted and insisted upon their masculinity as well as how various kinds of women affirmed or disparaged, welcomed or walked away from that enactment, that insistence. No surprise, then, when I stumbled upon a twenty-five-year correspondence between two twentieth-century white women who were transfixed by a nineteenth-century white westering man, that I wanted to make sense of the dynamic that drew those women to that man and thus to one another, and I wanted to understand how this dynamic was nestled within their quotidian lives.

Quantrille McClung and Bernice Blackwelder were not drawn to just any nineteenth-century white man. They were drawn to Kit Carson, short in stature and fair of hair. They were drawn to a white man who felt pulled ever westward across North America. They were drawn to a white man who loved western women—first, daughters of the Central Plains peoples, Arapaho and Cheyenne, who lived at the crossroads of trade and migration in the beating heart of a changing continent. Then he loved a daughter of the mountains they call the Blood of Christ, the Sangre de Cristo. She was *hispana*, tall in stature and dark of eyes. He was culpable, capable of extreme, unthinking violence against people who had long called the West home. He was complicated, consumed by efforts to navigate North American places that were changing hands and North American economies that were burning themselves out— the trade in beaver pelts and buffalo hides, for example—even as they were tying peoples both closer together and closer apart. I could not help identifying with this white man, short as I am, naturally fair-haired as I once was, chemically fair-haired as I now am, drawn as I have been to all things western, in hopeless love as I was with a daughter of *la sierra* elegantly tall in stature and dancingly dark of eyes, culpable and complicated as I am, as all humans are, but culpable and complicated in my own particular ways. I do not take pride in this identification. I feel real racial shame in it. But I cannot disavow it as antithetical to a politics of social justice, of reparation and reconciliation. I can think critically about but cannot destroy my manly muses, the histories they compel me to write, the loves they bring my way, and the losses they help me endure.

* *

None of us reside in the land where our fathers died, even if we dwell in the selfsame place. We live in another country. We imprint that place daily with the traces of our hands, petroglyphs on walls that will crumble to dust. The traces we find and the traces we leave kindle recognition. They can spark repair.

Acknowledgments

I thank no one more than the two central figures in this book, Quantrille McClung and Bernice Fowler Blackwelder. Their intellectual work, which left such a light imprint on both history and historiography, as well as their struggles to navigate a world of capricious power that alternately privileged and diminished them, has transfixed me for two decades, even as it has also forced me to reckon with my own exemption from liabilities that others cannot escape, as well as the routine dismissal and derision I have encountered as I have walked through life. I do not know what each of them would think or how each of them would feel if they could read this book. I suspect it would astonish and please them in places and enrage and baffle them in others. In all, I aim to honor their memory even as I see them as fully human. I could not be more grateful to them for doing their work and living their lives with such passion and precision.

Indeed, passion and precision are among my guiding lights, and together they explain much about the long gestation of this book. But there is more: the need to refashion myself, a nineteenth-century historian, to research and write about the twentieth century; the limited funding available for a project featuring unknown, amateur, western, women historians; and the priority I place on (and satisfaction I take in) mentoring younger scholars. All of these factors pale, however, in light of the quotidian tasks and psychic resources it took to travel alongside the two people I loved most in the world as they journeyed through life toward death: my late mother, Janet Stecker Johnson, who passed in 2013 after a long decline, and my late spouse, Camille Guérin-Gonzales, who died less than two years later, in 2015, having lived for fourteen months after a cancer diagnosis. They are everywhere in this book and they are with me in each breath I take. No one believed in me and this book more than they did.

But others believed, too. Among them are those who read all or part of the book in manuscript form, listed here in order from those who were burdened with all to those who were burdened with part: Richard White, Katrina Jagodinsky, Honor Sachs, Regina Kunzel, Camille Guérin-Gonzales, Beryl Satter, Anne Hyde, Howard Lamar, and Alice Echols. In addition to these individuals, supportive groups of scholars at two institutions where I enjoyed fellowships read one or more parts of the book. As Lloyd Lewis Fellow in American History at the Newberry Library in 2007, I had the privilege of sharing the first writing I did (what became part 1) with a group of scholars, curators, and librarians that included Kathleen Neils Conzen, Laura Edwards, David Karmon, Doug Knox, Lucy Murphy, Barbara Naddeo, Dylan Penningroth, the late Helen Hornbeck Tanner (who gave me her mock buffalo skull, "Old Joe," from her days with the Westerners; it still hangs near my desk), and Richard Wistreich. As Bill and Rita Clements Research Fellow at the Clements Center for Southwest Studies, Southern Methodist University, in 2011, I shared even more of my writing (prologue, part 1, part 2, and a bit of part 3) in a manuscript workshop that featured not only the assessments of Anne Hyde and Beryl Satter but also feedback from Sherry L. Smith, Andrew Graybill, Crista DeLuzio, David Doyle, Katrina Jagodinsky, Megan Prins, Andrea Boardman, Matthew Alexander, Margaret Neubauer, and Jennifer Seman. In addition, I have benefited from the comments and questions of audiences at Brigham Young University, Whitman College, Carthage College, Yale University, Notre Dame University, University of Michigan, University of Virginia, Northwestern University, the Colorado Historical Society (now History Colorado), and Western History Association meetings.

A special group of scholars weighed in on what became part 1 of this book when I had the pleasure of joining the 2009-10 symposium "On the Borders of Love and Power: Families and Kinship in the Intercultural American West," cosponsored by the Clements Center for Southwest Studies at Southern Methodist University, the Institute for the Study of the American West at the Autry National Center, and the Center for the Southwest at the University of New Mexico. I am grateful to the conveners, David Wallace Adams and Crista DeLuzio, and to my esteemed coparticipants: Tracy Brown, Cathleen Cahill, Ramón Gutiérrez, Anne Hyde, Margaret Jacobs, Katrina Jagodinsky, Pablo Mitchell, Joaquín Rivaya-Martínez, Monica Perales, Erika Pérez, and Donna Schuele. A condensed version of part 1, "Writing Kit Carson in the Cold War: 'The Family,' 'the West,' and Their Chroniclers," was published in the volume that resulted from this symposium, *On the Borders of Love and Power: Families and Kinship in the Intercultural American Southwest*, edited by David Wallace Adams and Crista DeLuzio (Berkeley: University of California Press, 2012).

I spent most of the years researching and writing this book at the University of Wisconsin–Madison. There, I enjoyed support from the Wisconsin Alumni Research Foundation as well as a Vilas Lifecycle Professorship, an innovative program administered by the Women in Science and Engineering Leadership Institute that provides funds to faculty "who are at critical junctures in their professional careers and whose research productivity has been directly affected by personal life events." In addition, I was fortunate to secure two semesters of research leave, one through the Women's Studies Research Center as a Feminist Scholars' Fellow and the other through the Institute for Research in the Humanities as a Resident Fellow. Staff in the history department helped me manage all of this as well as the rest of my career, among them Leslie Abadie, Todd Anderson, Scott Burkhardt, Mike Burmeister, Isaac Lee (now a graduate student), Sophie Olson, Jim Schlender (now general counsel for Lac Courte Oreilles Ojibwe College), and Jana Valeo. Department chairs came and went while I was at Wisconsin and I appreciated the aid of all, but none more than David McDonald. David (in his civilian role) was also among the colleagues who provided insight, advice, or support at key moments as this project developed; others include Florence Bernault, Ashley Brown, Cindy Cheng, Bill Cronon, Suzanne Desan, John Hall, April Haynes, Pernille Ipsen, Steve Kantrowitz, and Jennifer Ratner-Rosenhagen. And I am grateful for help from outside Wisconsin: from the Charles Redd Center for Western Studies at Brigham Young University, the Huntington Library, the Beinecke Library at Yale University, the Newberry Library, and the Clements Center or Southwest Studies at Southern Methodist University (special thanks to staff Andrea Boardman and Ruth Ann Elmore).

I am especially grateful for such funding because this project often failed to attract support. My family stepped in to fill the breach. Toward the end of her life (not knowing that the end would come so soon), as I had nearly finished the book, Camille Guérin-Gonzales took on more household tasks to free me to write. Likewise, while I was on fellowship in Dallas, my mother helped with my rent so that I could live on a bus line to Southern Methodist University, and she bought me a new laptop computer. I did much of the research for this book at the Denver Public Library (DPL) and History Colorado in Denver, and Camille's son Mike Lester and our daughter-in-law Caryn Lester hosted me countless times in their basement guest room (Mike, a carpenter, finished the basement himself). They fed me after long days in the archives, while grandchildren Mason, Courtney, and Kelcey made me laugh. Son Ron Lester and daughter-in-law Sally Lester live in Southern California, where I had no research to do. But they cheered me on from afar and visited me in New Mexico even after Ron lost his mom. Camille's daughter, Kerrie Lester, is a Southern Californian, too, and her texts brought me comfort in the midst of grief. Ron's son, my grandson Casey, grew to adulthood alongside this book and during that time brought three precious new people into my life—granddaughter-in-law Michelle and great-grandsons Aiden and Fallon. Meanwhile, Grandma Camille got to see Casey's brother Michael one last time before she died and he moved to Michigan. And gaining daughter-in-law Sally also won me two new grandkids, Blake and Emma, making seven grandchildren and two great-grandchildren in all (and counting). This is a blessing, because my side of the family mostly refuses to reproduce. Nonetheless, my sister, Lynne Johnson, brother and sister-in-law Scott Johnson and Marlisa Monroe, and niece Michelle Ribeiro buoyed me up through the toughest times in my life. More recently, Phyllis and Bob Sachs welcomed me into a new family circle.

The tough times are a blur of hospitals and drugs and medical procedures I cannot believe I learned to perform. But they are also times when I saw Camille clawing her way back into life again and again, making herself vital and present to those who loved her. She was, in fact, my main support even as I was her sole caregiver. Main but not only: a host of family and friends and other helpers, too numerous to list fully, stepped in to carry me even as I carried her. I am thankful for the support and kindness of University of Wisconsin–Madison Associate Dean for Arts and Humanities Susan Zaeske, who assisted me in navigating the maze of FMLA and sick leave–funded time away from the classroom. In addition to family members mentioned above, I especially want to thank Camille's cousin Joan Carlson as well as my neighbors Sandy and Sharon Kampen and Jessie Lindner and Harry Harrison and my mom's best friend, Barb Ryder. And then there are all the friends, household helpers, personal care providers, spiritual and financial advisors, and medical, mental health, and legal professionals who assisted me right up to, through, and long past the day of Camille's funeral: Oswaldo Alvarez, Héctor Amézquita, Lisa Barroilhet, Cindy Cheng, Chuck Cohen, Dana Corbett, Erin Costanzo, Grace Peña Delgado, Sally Deutsch, Denise Fassbender, Sandy

Gehler, Jane Gogan, Deena González, Kori Graves, David Gutiérrez, Jennifer Hannon, Carol Harvey, Reeve Huston, Anne Hyde, Betsy Jameson, Steve Kantrowitz, Howard Lerner, Kären Schultz Maleske, Mary Mendoza, Erika Pérez, Amy Quartuccio, Estevan Rael-Gálvez, Kat Rajski, Jesus Ramírez, Frances Ríos, Juan Ríos, Chris Schindler, Franklin Wilson, David Winter, Marcia Yonemoto, and Sue Zaeske (as friend rather than dean), as well as my peerless Nineteenth Nervous Breakdown Committee: Florence Bernault, Bill Cronon, Suzanne Desan, Barbara Forrest, Yvette Huginnie, Reg Kunzel, Clare Novak, Abby Stewart, and Alice Wexler. You all know what you did for me. I will never forget.

This book began as an article I wrote in 2002 but never published. I did not publish it in part because of good questions people posed as I presented portions of it in public settings but also because of helpful readings of the article draft that made me realize there was much more to the story than I first recognized. The late Jeanne Boydston, Howard Lamar, and Abby Stewart all read that draft and together sent me back to the library and back to my sources. I also benefited from early conversations about specific aspects of the project with Ned Blackhawk, Peter Blodgett, Finn Enke, Nan Enstad, Karl Jacoby, Brian Klopotek, David Salmanson, Jeremi Suri, and Sharon Ullman (Brian put me in touch with folks familiar with the work of anthropologist Shirley Hill Witt, one of the first Indigenous women to earn a PhD and an activist who challenged the lionization of Kit Carson: Kathleen Chamberlain, Sterling Fluharty, Eric Johnson, Thomas Kavanagh, Jamie Ryan Lockman, Helen Hornbeck Tanner, and Michael Welsh). During the same period, I corresponded with historians, genealogists, and librarians who knew Quantrille McClung or Bernice Blackwelder or both (or knew their work) and received helpful replies from John Porter Bloom, the late Joanne Classen, the late Janet Lecompte, Donna Porter, and Mary Lee Spence. I also spoke with Cherry Carter Kinney, daughter of the late Harvey Carter.

One person played an outsize role in helping me see that I belonged in this text alongside the historical actors at its center. She likely has no idea that she played this role, so I am thrilled to be able to acknowledge it here. A decade and a half ago, I met up with Diana Selig at a conference. We had known each other since she was an undergraduate and I a graduate student at Yale University; I was her teaching assistant in a western history course. Over coffee, I described to her the book project I envisioned, but because of our long acquaintance, I also explained the deep connections I felt to the tales it would tell. She urged me to write about those connections, to become a character in the book. She said it all with such clarity, conviction, and compassion that I was convinced. She also told me about her forthcoming book, which kept me watching for it after we parted. That book, *Americans All*, later helped me make sense of how Bernice Blackwelder navigated racial and ethnic landscapes in the 1930s. Thank you, Diana.

As my abandoned article morphed into a book manuscript, I relied on the research assistance of a number of University of Wisconsin–Madison PhD students, some of whom have since become professors or found other innovative ways to use their historical training: Dustin Cohan, Brendon George, Michel Hogue, Jennifer Holland, Jillian Jacklin, Stacey Smith, and Maia Surdam. Other

PhD students enjoyed different sources of funding but nonetheless shaped my work and made my life in Wisconsin better, among them Ikuko Asaka, Kellen Backer, Meggan Bilotte, Jerome Dotson, Mark Goldberg, Sergio González, Kori Graves, Brenna Greer, Chris Hommerding, Jennifer Hull, Doug Kiel, Jennifer Martin, Chong Moua, Haley Pollack, Bree Romero, Cori Simon, Megan Stanton, Tyina Steptoe, Libby Tronnes, the late Skott Vigil, and Leah Webb-Halpern. Since joining the faculty at the University of Nevada, Las Vegas, I have benefited from the research assistance of Jenni Tifft-Ochoa and Maggie Bukowski, who recently earned her MA.

I was also extraordinarily fortunate to find people who knew Quantrille McClung or Bernice Blackwelder and were willing to talk. The late Sam Arnold, proprietor of The Fort Restaurant near Denver, knew both women but especially McClung, and he told me what he knew in two telephone conversations. The late Jack Smith grew up near the McClung family and worked on genealogical projects with Quantrille; he provided a delightful interview and a free lunch at his retirement community before he passed. James Kroll, former head of the Western History/Genealogy Department at DPL, introduced me to Jack Smith and then later consented to his own interview along with Bonnie Garramone of the Colorado Genealogical Society. Jim Kroll's assistance went far beyond the interview; he was amazingly generous to me in this project for all the many years that I worked on it. As for those who knew Bernice Blackwelder, I met both family and friends who wanted to talk. The late Nancy Elliott worked alongside Bernice at the CIA in the 1950s. Since the CIA will neither confirm nor deny that it employed Bernice, Nancy Elliott was my only source of information about that episode in Bernice's life other than a few random mentions in Bernice's letters. Even Bernice's relatives knew little about her CIA years; they knew only that she worked for the federal government. But the late Doris Lance, Bernice's niece, and the late Stephen Fowler, her nephew, told me much else about their aunt. And Doris Lance did more than talk; indeed, she not only corresponded with me for years, but she also hosted me when I traveled to her home in Alpena, Michigan, and she eventually turned over to me all of her aunt's papers, including scrapbooks, photo albums, and a diary, which together allowed me to piece together the backstory of Kit Carson's biographer. I had always envisioned flying back up to Alpena and placing this book in Doris's hands and was saddened to learn of her recent passing from her daughter Leslie Lance. Doris had her aunt Bernice's musical talents and zest for adventure; she was choreographer for the Alpena Civic Theatre and later danced with a group called the Hot Flashes. She produced beautiful paintings, led exercise classes at the Alpena Senior Center, and was a volunteer massage therapist for Hospice of Northeast Michigan. I am proud to have known her.

Librarians, archivists, and other keepers of historical records provided spectacular support. This project started at DPL, in Western History/Genealogy, where I perused the unprocessed Quantrille McClung Papers looking for references to primary sources that might illuminate Kit Carson's relationships with American Indian and Spanish Mexican women back when I thought I would continue writing nineteenth-century history. Instead, I stumbled upon the letters of McClung and Blackwelder stuffed in unmarked envelopes that no one had opened since McClung's death. From that time on, I benefited from the help not only of Jim Kroll but of many others at DPL, including Barbara Walton, James Jeffrey, Philip Panum, and Coi Drummond-Gehrig. When I discovered that Mc-Clung had left more materials to the Stephen Hart Research Center at the Colorado Historical Society, which was then across the street from DPL, I rushed over and found assistance with the Quantrille Day McClung Collection from Rebecca Lintz. The historical society moved twice in the years that followed, first to a temporary location and then to the new History Colorado Center. During the transition, Keith Schrum was exceptionally accommodating, allowing me to research in off-hours and make my own photocopies. When it came time to finalize my History Colorado photo order, Jori Johnson stepped in to help. Meanwhile, over many years and many visits, Nita Murphy assisted me with the Kit Carson Files in what were once the collections of the Taos Historic Museums and are now the holdings of the Southwest Research Center at the University of New Mexico–Taos.

Other repositories that provided support include the Newberry Library; the Research Center at the Chicago History Museum; the Virginia Room of Arlington Public Library; the Virginia Room of the City of Fairfax Regional Library; Special Collections at Colorado College's Tutt Library; the Beck Archives of Rocky Mountain Jewish History in Special Collections and Archives, University of Denver; the Center for Southwest Research in Zimmerman Library at the University of New Mexico, Albuquerque; the New Mexico State Archives and Records Center in Santa Fe; Special Collections in Norlin Library at the University of Colorado Boulder; and the University Archives in Forsyth Library at Fort Hays State University in Kansas. Three institutions not in the business of preserving the past nonetheless provided me with key records: Caxton Press; University of Oklahoma Press; and the SAG-AFTRA Chicago Local Office. Illustrations not provided by the institutions mentioned above came from the Bernice Fowler Blackwelder Papers, which I received from Doris Lance, Bernice's niece; Barbara Osiek, daughter of Quantrille McClung's maternal cousin; the Denver Posse of the Westerners; and the Smoky Hill Museum in Salina, Kansas.

When I was finalizing illustrations for this book, I learned to my surprise and chagrin that the image of Josefa Jaramillo, Kit Carson's third spouse, I planned to reproduce herein was likely not an image of her after all. Two pictures of Josefa emerged in 1969–70, and they have been reproduced in books and museum exhibits for a half century since. I reproduced one of them in my 2012 article "Writing Kit Carson in the Cold War." But it is probable that neither are pictures of Josefa Jaramillo. I first learned this via Nita Murphy from C. J. Law, the director of the Kit Carson Home and Museum in Taos, New Mexico. The news sent me into a frantic two-month search for the originals of the two images and for information about how they came into the Carson Home and Museum's possession. I have not found the originals, though I have found clues about how the images came to light. The mystery remains—and may never be solved fully—but I think it likely that neither picture is actually an image of Josefa Jaramillo. Both have been claimed as such by a generation of historians, archivists, museum professionals, and descendants. Because my work on this issue is ongoing, here I will simply thank those who already have gone down the research rabbit hole with me and warn them that the search is not over: John Michael Carson (great-grandson of Josefa Jaramillo and Kit Carson), Honor Sachs, Nita Murphy, C. J. Law, Elizabeth Halley, Virginia Dodier, Marni Sandweiss, David and Carol Farmer, Susan Barger, Estevan Rael-Gálvez, Juan Ríos, María Montoya, Anne Hyde, Maggie Bukowski, Elizabeth Nelson, Deirdre Clement, Raquél Casas, Jenni Tifft-Ochoa, Maribel Estrada Calderón, Coi Drummond-Gehrig, Dennis Daily, Jori Johnson, Kevin Smith, Daisy Allen, Tomas Jaehn, Cindy Abel Morris, Jillian Hartke, Gene Lamm, María Martínez, Thayla Wright, Hannah Abelbeck, and Lee Burke. It was fitting that my final work on this problem took me back to something Quantrille McClung had preserved and given to DPL: a near-complete run of *Las Noticias Alegres de la Casa Kit Carson*, the newsletter of the Carson Home and Museum, copies of which no New Mexico repository can currently find, save a few scattered issues in Santa Fe and Albuquerque. The newsletter announced accession of the two supposed images of Josefa Jaramillo in 1970.

I am grateful to be publishing this book with the University of North Carolina Press. For more years than I wish to count, Executive Editor Chuck Grench kindly asked after the project whenever we met at conferences. I told him that I was not seeking an advance contract because I wanted to write the book I envisioned first and then figure out who might best bring it into the world. But I never forgot Chuck's kindness and engagement with my work. Then, too, as I started to draft my bibliography, I noticed how many of the fine works I cited, especially in the fields of western, borderlands, and gender/women's history, had been published by North Carolina. So when the time came, I submitted a proposal to the press. Chuck liked it, solicited the full manuscript, and then saw it through the review process, even reading it closely himself and offering me a third set of comments. (Who else would have caught my misuse of the word "limned"? And chastised me for twice using the word "valorization"? I think I retained one instance just to be contrary, even though he is probably right about the word.) More recently, Chuck announced his retirement after working for forty-five years in scholarly publishing. He told me that mine was the last book he put into production. I told him that if I had heard it once, I had heard it a thousand times: "Chuck Grench is the best in the business." It has been an honor to work with him. I am also grateful to Assistant Editor Dylan White and to everyone else at North Carolina who has shepherded this book along its way: Editorial Director Mark Simpson-Vos, Executive Editor Debbie Gershenowitz, Acquisitions Manager Cate Hodorowicz, Managing Editor Mary Caviness, Marketing Director Dino Battista, and Director of Design and Production Kim Bryant.

People outside of the press also helped to create key parts of this book. I thank the University of Wisconsin Cartography Lab, especially Creative Director Tanya Buckingham, for designing helpful maps. And I am more grateful than I can say to my friend Robin Moore, the artist who created the book's front cover. Robin and I have known each other since 1977 when we both worked at Yellowstone

National Park. We reconnected in recent years after she relocated from California to New Mexico. Robin read my book manuscript and consulted with me about potential cover art until she came up with an ingenious design that overlays a nineteenth-century lithograph of Santa Fe with a twentieth-century photograph of Quantrille McClung and a friend. What Robin did not know when she created the cover art is that she designed it so that Quantrille points toward what is now a Santa Fe hilltop park but was once the site of Fort Marcy, a military base during the U.S.-Mexico War. Before my late spouse Camille Guérin-Gonzales died, she asked her family to scatter her ashes on that hilltop, the highest point in Santa Fe. We did so in July of 2015.

After I finished writing this book but before it went into production, I had the great fortune of joining the faculty in the history department at the University of Nevada, Las Vegas, as the inaugural Harry Reid Endowed Chair for the History of the Intermountain West. I love my new home and new job, and I am more grateful than I can say to all of my new colleagues for making it possible, but especially Willy Bauer, Raquél Casas, Mike Green, David Tanenhaus, and Michelle Tusan, who formed the search committee that recruited me, as well as Department Chair Andy Kirk. Staff members Annette Amdal and Shontai Wilson-Beltran have helped ease my transition to Nevada. Humanities librarian Priscilla Finley introduced me to UNLV library resources. Lisa Weatherman and Wendy Curtis found me a home. And Senator Reid himself has made me feel wonderfully welcome, assisted by his chief of staff, Katie Rozner. It is the greatest honor of my career to hold an endowed chair in the senator's name. I thank him for his six decades of service to Nevada, the West, and the nation.

I do not just have a new job, though; I have a whole new life. That life started three years ago when Honor Sachs walked up behind me at a conference, rested her hand gently on my back, and said, "Can we hang out sometime?" I had known Honor since she was a dissertator at the University of Wisconsin, but I had not seen her except in passing for a decade. She was grown up now, seasoned by the misfortune of entering the academic job market in the dark days of 2008 after a two-year postdoctoral fellowship. She swears she was not flirting with me when she put her hand on my back. I fancied that she was and responded accordingly. A year later, in a conversation about where she should wear a ring I got for her, she asserted that the only thing she would put on her left ring finger was a wedding ring. Confused, but increasingly sanguine, I replied, "Are you even the marrying kind?" She said that she was. So I pushed the matter, asking, "Well, would you marry *me*?" She said yes. A year after that we wed. Now we each wear a ring on our left hand crafted by Navajo silversmith Lyle Secatero. Honor brings a crazy joy to my life, a life I once thought had ended. What is more, she is a remarkably clear-eyed historian (having been trained by my remarkably clear-eyed former colleague, the late Jeanne Boydston), and though I had finished writing this book when we reconnected, Honor read the penultimate draft and saved me from myself in key places. Three years back, Honor Sachs danced into my heart. Now she dances in the car, down the hall, and every last place we hear music. To my wonderment, she has promised to dance me to the end of love.

Notes

PROLOGUE

1. Blackwelder, *Great Westerner*.

2. Quantrille D. McClung, *Carson-Bent-Boggs Genealogy* and *Carson-Bent-Boggs Genealogy Supplement*.

3. I elaborate on this set of ideas below and more fully in part 2. The earliest explication, in 1910, of the notion of a traffic in women was Goldman, "Traffic in Women." Goldman was responding to moral panic over "white slavery"—female prostitution—in the early twentieth-century United States and to how moralists and policy makers attributed the "problem" to new European immigrants generally and Jewish immigrants particularly. She pointed to the economic and social subordination of women as prostitution's root cause; she likened marriage to prostitution; she found the Christian church culpable in maintaining prostitution; and she railed against the association of prostitution with immigrants, especially Jews. Later in the century, anthropologist Gayle Rubin borrowed from Goldman to analyze what she called the "sex/gender system," or that "set of arrangements by which a society transforms biological sexuality into products of human activity, and in which these transformed sexual needs are satisfied." Gayle Rubin, "Traffic in Women," 159.

4. This analysis draws loosely on James C. Scott's *Weapons of the Weak* and *Domination and the Arts of Resistance*. Readers of the manuscript version of this book asked if men can traffic in men. They can and do and have, but the practice involves radically different power relations. Someone should write a book about this—explicitly. Implicitly, a majority of books ever written are located within those power relations. Although it is concerned with the traffic in women—how male homosocial desire is routed through female objects and depends on disavowal of homosexual desire—literary scholar Eve Kosofsky Sedgwick's *Between Men* opened the way toward such analysis decades ago. Historians have not followed suit.

5. I speak here of space and time as if they are separate dimensions for rhetorical purposes, knowing that they are bound up together in what many call space-time; space as produced is always produced in time, and time always *takes place*—that is, time is situated spatially. This means that I never really overlapped with McClung and Blackwelder in space-time, since we occupied the "same" places at different times. For the rendering of space-time relations that informs my thinking, see Massey, "Traveling Thoughts."

6. Jones, *Known World*.

7. In addition to Blackwelder's and McClung's work, also in this genre is work by a female contemporary, M. Morgan Estergreen, whose career as a nonprofessional historian paralleled theirs; see Estergreen, *Kit Carson: A Portrait*. Among professional historians, Harvey Carter did the best work in this vein, but he

notably toiled alongside a female nonprofessional historian, Thelma Guild, in some of what he produced. See Harvey L. Carter, *"Dear Old Kit"*; and Guild and Carter, *Kit Carson*.

8. Simmons, "Kit and the Indians," 73. Simmons is reflecting on work that promoted the Carson-as-villain thesis, such as Trafzer, *Kit Carson Campaign*.

9. The man-of-his-times thesis is advanced in Dunlay, *Kit Carson*; to some extent in Roberts, *Newer World*; in Remley, *Kit Carson*; and in the work of Marc Simmons, perhaps the most prolific living writer on New Mexican history.

10. Sides, *Blood and Thunder*, 7.

11. I could cite scholarship to support the claims made here, but the act of citation would obscure a more important point: the biographical sketches I provide of these figures constitute the sort of information that generations of western historians, both amateur and academic, were expected to have at their fingertips. The field of western history has changed irrevocably over the course of my lifetime in ways I discuss herein, and knowledge of such figures is no longer de rigueur. For better or worse, I have that knowledge, though I always do a fact check when it comes to outlaws and gunmen, who bore me (the best reference work for fact checks, combining as it does both older and newer approaches to the West, is Lamar, *New Encyclopedia*). I display that knowledge here in response to a quick-witted, irreverent reader from outside the field who helpfully critiqued an early draft, reminding me that she did not know "who Kit Carson was or why he was famous." She went on, "His name, like that of Daniel Boone (who I confuse with Pat Boone), Davy Crockett (didn't he wear a raccoon-tail hat?), Buffalo Bill, and Calamity Jane, really is nothing more than a name to me—I have no idea who these people actually were or why they are famous, outside of the evocation in television shows and movies that I don't watch." Beryl Satter, personal communication with author, October 29, 2011. Thank you, Beryl. Thanks, too, for the reference to Calamity Jane, the not-really-an-exception-anyway who proves the rule, not to mention serves as an example of a traffic in things male.

12. All biographical work on Carson covers his association with Frémont and the subsequent reports that introduced Carson to a reading public; e.g., Harvey L. Carter, *"Dear Old Kit,"* esp. 6–9; Guild and Carter, *Kit Carson*, 96–179 passim; Dunlay, *Kit Carson*, esp. 85–147; Roberts, *Newer World*; Sides, *Blood and Thunder*, esp. 59–64; and Remley, *Kit Carson*, esp. 99–110. For the most oft-cited report, see Frémont, *Report*.

13. Herr and Spence, *Letters*, esp. xix–xx, 7–8, 105n3, 352–53, 402–4, 478–79; Herr, *Jessie Benton Fremont*, esp. 2, 79–82, 113, 155–57, 386–87, 392–93; Denton, *Passion and Principle*, esp. 81–82, 85–86. For what Benton Frémont wrote about Carson, see *Union* (Washington, D.C.), June 15, 1847, and discussion of this article in Herr and Spence, *Letters*, xx, 105n3; *New-York Ledger*, February 20, 1875; Benton Frémont, "Kit Carson," *Wide Awake*; and Benton Frémont, "Kit Carson," *Land of Sunshine*.

14. Herr and Spence, *Letters*, 402–4; Gerald Thompson, "'Kit Carson's Ride,'" 145. Thompson reprints both the poem and Beale's response. Herr and Spence state that Miller was "dubbed 'Joaquin' by his cronies after the colorful Mexi-

an bandit Joaquin Murietta [*sic*]." On Murrieta, see Susan Lee Johnson, *Roaring Camp*, 25–53.

15. Herr and Spence, *Letters*, 402–4; Gerald Thompson, "'Kit Carson's Ride.'" Thompson echoes uncritically Beale's assessment of the poem as "indecent" rather than exploring its gender, racial, and sexual politics. For the revised poem, see Joaquin Miller, *Complete Poetical Works*, 55–57.

16. For summaries of work on Carson, see Harvey L. Carter, *"Dear Old Kit,"* 3–36; Dunlay, *Kit Carson*, 1–23; and essays in Gordon-McCutchan, *Kit Carson*, esp. Darlis A. Miller, "Kit Carson," which is far less recuperationist than the rest. For texts mentioned, see Peters, *Life and Adventures*; Sabin, *Kit Carson Days*; Grant, *Story of His Life as Dictated*; and Grant, *Story of His Life: Facsimile*. A list of relevant manuscript collections appears in Simmons, *Kit Carson*, 177–79. For Carson as manly icon, see DeSpain, "'Superior Dignity.'"

17. On dime novels and western heroes in print, see Henry Nash Smith, *Virgin Land*; Slotkin, *Fatal Environment*; Saxton, *Rise and Fall*; Denning, *Mechanic Accents*; and Streeby, *American Sensations*.

18. For full discussion, see Darlis A. Miller, "Kit Carson," quote on 7.

19. Seitz, *Kit Carson*; English et al., *Adventures of Kit Carson*.

20. My work had been under way for three years when the first book focused on Carson's intimate life appeared, Simmons's *Kit Carson*. Exhaustively researched, the book provides a solid narrative of Carson's marriages. Interpretively, it is of the recuperationist school that sees Carson as a flawed, human, but very good man of his times. A more analytically satisfying and historically wide-ranging treatment of intermarriage and its relationship to western trade is Anne F. Hyde, *Empires, Nations, and Families*. See also the work of my cherished colleagues from the 2009–10 Clements Center Symposium, "On the Borders of Love and Power: Families and Kinship in the Intercultural American West," collected in Adams and DeLuzio, *On the Borders*.

21. That older milieu has been the subject of an excellent historiography over recent decades that includes DeBuys, *Enchantment and Exploitation*; Sarah Deutsch, *No Separate Refuge*; Thomas D. Hall, *Social Change*; Ramón A. Gutiérrez, *When Jesus Came*; Nostrand, *Hispano Homeland*; West, *Contested Plains*; González, *Refusing the Favor*; Jacobs, *Engendered Encounters*; Frank, *From Settler to Citizen*; Montoya, *Translating Property*; Rael-Gálvez, "Identifying Captivity and Capturing Identity"; Montgomery, *Spanish Redemption*; James Brooks, *Captives and Cousins*; Nieto-Phillips, *Language of Blood*; Reséndez, *Changing National Identities*; Mitchell, *Coyote Nation*; Blackhawk, *Violence over the Land*; Rivaya-Martínez, "Captivity and Adoption"; Gómez, *Manifest Destinies*; Hämäläinen, *Comanche Empire*; DeLay, *War of a Thousand Deserts*; Mora, *Border Dilemmas*; Anne F. Hyde, *Empires, Nations, and Families*; and Reséndez, *Other Slavery*. This recent scholarship builds on a rich older literature that includes Spicer, *Cycles of Conquest*; Lamar, *Far Southwest*; John, *Storms Brewed*; David J. Weber, *Taos Trappers* and *Mexican Frontier*. Weber's work spans the earlier and later generations; see also his *Spanish Frontier* and *Bárbaros*.

22. Blackwelder to McClung, May 25, 1967, McClung Papers, Western His-

tory Collection, Western History/Genealogy Department, Denver Public Library (hereafter cited as McClung Papers).

23. I qualify my parenthetical remark racially because nonchalance about sexual reputation can be a matter of racial privilege, given that white racism historically has been enacted across a sexual terrain, creating the idea that people of color—especially women of color—are hypersexual and available for white sexual wish fulfillment. In such contexts, protecting sexual reputation has a different, oppositional valence.

24. Appleby, Hunt, and Jacob, *Telling the Truth*, 259–61.

25. Here I am guided by Gayle Rubin's own rethinking of her "Traffic in Women" essay, "The Trouble with Trafficking." See also Vance, "Thinking Trafficking, Thinking Sex." For the definition, see "Human Trafficking," United Nations Office on Drugs and Crime, accessed August 5, 2016, https://www.unodc.org/unodc/en/human-trafficking/what-is-human-trafficking.html. My position on prostitution and a range of other sexual matters is informed by the feminist sexuality debates of the 1980s, in which Rubin was a key voice. I take up my relationship to these so-called sex wars in the epilogue.

26. Goldman, "Traffic in Women"; Gayle Rubin, "Traffic in Women." Rubin is in dialogue with anthropologist Claude Lévi-Strauss (*Elementary Structures of Kinship*) as well as with Marx, Engels, Freud, and Lacan. Rubin's work can be refracted through that of Judith Butler, especially *Gender Trouble*. Thankfully, the two have talked; see Butler and Rubin, "Sexual Traffic." An insightful discussion of the traffic in women appears in a book that has helped to shape this one: Steedman, *Landscape*, 68–70. For another provocative discussion that explores the idea in a western literary context—showing how white women writers likened the marriage market to cattle roundups, thereby enacting a eugenic feminism that critiqued white patriarchy but also distanced white women from the origins of feminism in abolitionism and from the political struggles of African American women—see Lamont, "Cattle Branding."

27. I first used this formulation in my own scholarly traffic in men; see Susan Lee Johnson, *Roaring Camp*, 118.

28. Examples include Bederman, *Manliness and Civilization*; Chauncey, *Gay New York*; McCurry, *Masters of Small Worlds*; Kathleen M. Brown, *Good Wives, Nasty Wenches*; Mary Murphy, *Mining Cultures*; Jameson, *All That Glitters*; Kantrowitz, *Ben Tillman*; Hoganson, *Fighting for American Manhood*; Peck, *Reinventing Free Labor*; Renda, *Taking Haiti*; Perry, *Edge of Empire*; Mercier, *Anaconda*; Norwood, *Strikebreaking and Intimidation*; Summers, *Manliness and Its Discontents*; Estes, *I Am a Man!*; Greenberg, *Manifest Manhood*; España-Maram, *Creating Masculinity*; Barr, *Peace Came*; Kevin Murphy, *Political Manhood*; Syrett, *Company He Keeps*; Perales, *Smeltertown*; Deborah Cohen, *Braceros*; Basso, *Meet Joe Copper*; Perry, *Colonial Relations*; and Sachs, *Home Rule*.

29. McClung Papers.

30. See, e.g., McClung to Blackwelder, June 24, July 6, November 24, 1967; and Blackwelder to McClung, June 15, August 16, 1972, McClung Papers.

31. See esp. Novick, *That Noble Dream*.

32. The WHA places its founding in 1961, but as I show in part 1 of this book, 1962 is probably more accurate. See Western History Association website, accessed November 17, 2017, https://www.westernhistory.org. Issues of race, ethnicity, indigeneity, and gender continued to burn in the WHA in the early twenty-first century. See "The Next Fifty Years Report," Western History Association, accessed August 6, 2016, https://westernhistoryassociation.wildapricot.org/fifty yearsreport; and Peter Iverson [WHA president, 2004–5] to members of WHA, July 25, 2005, *Western History Association Newsletter*, Fall 2005, insert. I first read Iverson's letter online, but it is no longer searchable electronically. David Rich Lewis kindly provided me with a copy of it.

33. Bonnie G. Smith, *Gender of History*; Des Jardins, *Women and the Historical Enterprise*. See also Leckie and Parezo, *Their Own Frontier*.

34. The first chapter of the Westerners was organized in 1944 and Westerners International in 1959. See Westerners International website, accessed August 6, 2016, http://www.westerners-international.org. In part 1, I use the Westerners-Chicago Corral Papers, Newberry Library, Chicago, to reconstruct the group's gender-exclusive history.

35. See Burton, *Postcolonial Careers*, 25 and passim. I am deeply grateful to Burton for sharing her work with me before it appeared in print.

36. Excellent examples are Fitzpatrick, *History's Memory*; and Tyrell, *Historians in Public*.

37. Bonnie G. Smith, *Gender of History*; Des Jardins, *Women and the Historical Enterprise*; Baym, *American Women Writers*; Joan Wallach Scott, "American Women Historians." For a counterexample, see Cott, *Woman Making History*.

38. See works cited in n21 above as well as key conceptual essays: Adelman and Aron, "From Borderlands to Borders"; Truett and Young, "Making Transnational History"; Johnson and Graybill, "Introduction"; Gutiérrez and Young, "Transnationalizing Borderlands History"; and Truett and Hämäläinen, "On Borderlands."

39. On women and "the family," see May, *Homeward Bound*; Spigel, *Make Room for TV*; Meyerowitz, *Not June Cleaver*; and Weiss, *To Have and to Hold*. For Cold War culture generally, see Boyer, *By the Bomb's Early Light*; Whitfield, *Culture of the Cold War*; Nadel, *Containment Culture*; Kuznick and Gilbert, *Rethinking Cold War Culture*; and Robin, *Making of the Cold War Enemy*. On the meanings of the frontier in this era, see Slotkin, *Gunfighter Nation*; and, contextualized differently, Engelhardt, *End of Victory Culture*.

40. I will cite the social movement literature where relevant, especially work on movements as they unfolded in the West generally and places where McClung and Blackwelder lived specifically. Overviews appear in Chafe, *Unfinished Journey*, 8th ed.; Chalmers, *Crooked Places Made Straight*; relevant essays in Cott, *No Small Courage*; Rosen, *World Split Open*; Branch, *Parting the Waters, Pillar of Fire*, and *At Canaan's Edge*; Sugrue, *Sweet Land of Liberty*; and MacLean, *Freedom Is Not Enough*.

41. See, e.g., Dan Carter, *From George Wallace*; McGirr, *Suburban Warriors*; Self, *American Babylon*; Avila, *Popular Culture in the Age of White Flight*; Kruse,

White Flight; Webb, *Massive Resistance*; Lassiter, *Silent Majority*; Dochuck, *Bible Belt to Sunbelt*; and Nickerson, *Mothers of Conservatism*.

42. In thinking through how to deploy this method and integrate myself into the text, I have benefited from the brave work of scholars who have made visible their relationship to the histories they write: Steedman, *Landscape*; White, *Remembering Ahanagran*; Tyson, *Blood Done Sign My Name*; Hartman, *Lose Your Mother*; Satter, *Family Properties*; Echols, *Shortfall*; and Chávez-García, *Migrant Longing*.

43. While I, like you, have read many novels that play with time in this way, the two that most influenced my decision to do the same as a historian are Waters, *Night Watch*; and Doig, *Whistling Season*.

44. For a provocative exception to the rule, see Fox, *Trials of Intimacy*.

45. Scrapbooks and photo albums, McClung Collection, Hart Research Center, History Colorado, Denver.

46. Bernice Blackwelder Diary, 1937–41, Blackwelder Papers, in author's possession. I received these materials from the late Doris Lance of Alpena, Michigan. Lance was Blackwelder's favorite niece, and she was wonderfully generous to me as I worked on this book.

47. Fisher, *Sudden Country*, 90.

48. Quantrille D. McClung, *Memoirs of My Childhood*.

49. Moraga and Anzaldúa, *Bridge Called My Back*; cf. Barbara Smith, *Home Girls*; Beck, *Nice Jewish Girls*. For the sex wars, see Vance, *Pleasure and Danger*; and Snitow, Stansell, and Thompson, *Powers of Desire*.

PART ONE

1. On *The Adventures of Kit Carson*, see "The Adventures of Kit Carson," TV.com, accessed January 30, 2007, http://www.tv.com/the-adventures-of-kit-carson/sh ow/6301/summary.html; Slatta, *Mythical West*, 79; and Yoggy, "Prime Time Bonanza!," esp. 163. About a hundred episodes aired between 1951 and 1955. Shows from the 1950s with similar titles included *The Adventures of Jim Bowie*, *The Adventures of Judge Roy Bean*, and *The Adventures of Wild Bill Hickok*. Two others—*The Adventures of Champion* and *The Adventures of Rin Tin Tin*—featured, respectively, a boy and his horse, Champion, and a boy and his dog, Rin Tin Tin. See Buscombe, *BFI Companion*, 399. Thanks to Lynne Johnson, Scott Johnson, and Camille Guérin-Gonzales for conversation about *The Adventures of Kit Carson*.

2. The federal government first targeted Navajos (and Hopis) for off-reservation employment in the postwar era and then developed comprehensive urban relocation programs for reservation-dwelling Indian people. See, e.g., Rosenthal, *Reimagining Indian Country*, 52–74. For those who did not relocate, the Navajo reservation had few paved roads when *The Adventures of Kit Carson* first aired, and battery-powered radios connected people there to one another and the outside world. The 1950s saw an influx of federal funds that subsidized roads and telephone networks. Television came later. For example, KOAT 7, Albuquerque's ABC affiliate, did not reach viewers throughout New Mexico and parts of Arizona and Colorado until the late 1960s. See KOAT website, accessed February 20, 2007,

ttp://www.koat.com/station/267538/detail.html (this information no longer appears on the website). Thanks to David Salmanson for information about television in the Four Corners area. See also Iverson, *Diné*, esp. 188–90; Robert W. Young, *Navajo Yearbook*, no. 6, 52–57, 98–99; *Navajo Yearbook*, no. 7, 64–67, 125; and *Navajo Yearbook*, no. 8, 5, 133–38, 305; and Underhill, *Navajos*, 245.

3. The pairing of an Anglo Kit Carson and a Mexican El Toro was reminiscent of the longer-running radio and then television series *The Lone Ranger*, which featured the white Lone Ranger and his American Indian sidekick, Tonto. See Slatta, *Mythical West*, 213–15. Toni Morrison describes the role of all such Tonto figures: "To do everything possible to serve the Lone Ranger without disturbing his indulgent delusion that he is indeed alone." Morrison, *Playing in the Dark*, 82. Thanks to Ned Blackhawk for reminding me of this. See also Engelhardt, *End of Victory Culture*, esp. 41.

4. McClung to Estergreen, June 11, 1964, McClung Papers, Western History Collection, Western History/Genealogy Department, Denver Public Library (hereafter cited as McClung Papers). Their conversation continues in Estergreen to McClung, June 14, 1964; and McClung to Estergreen, June 20, 1964, McClung Papers.

5. Blackwelder, *Great Westerner*.

6. Quantrille D. McClung, *Carson-Bent-Boggs Genealogy*.

7. Estergreen, *Kit Carson: A Portrait*.

8. For overview and statistics, see Buscombe, *BFI Companion*, 15–54 and appendix 1, 425–28. In a broader sense, Engelhardt (*End of Victory Culture*) sees 1962 as a turning point, identifying the 1945–62 era of Cold War popular culture as one of "containments" and 1962–75 as an "era of reversals." For the development of the field of western history, see below.

9. For the historiography that supports these claims, see below. While feminism's so-called second wave is generally seen as starting a bit later than civil rights movements on behalf of racial and sexual minorities (and those on behalf of sexual minorities were fledgling when compared to those on behalf of racial minorities), the women's movement's origins were clearly visible in the President's Commission on the Status of Women, 1961–63. See Rosen, *World Split Open*, 65–70.

10. Quantrille D. McClung, *Carson-Bent-Boggs Genealogy*, 3–9, 11.

11. Schaefer, *Hidden Half*; see also Carmack, *Genealogist's Guide*. While genealogical research has been revolutionized in the twenty-first century by internet companies such as ancestry.com, genealogy guidebooks in the first decade of this century still did not highlight such issues, though some did a better job of helping those interested in specific racial and ethnic populations. See, e.g., Szucs and Luebking, *Source*, which includes chapters on African American, Latino, Jewish, and American Indian family histories. Cf. Greenwood, *Researcher's Guide*, which says nothing about particular racial and ethnic populations but does include limited material on one aspect of women's genealogy: how changing women's property rights affect available records.

12. It has been claimed that U.S. genealogists have been more interested in tracing female lineages than those in the United Kingdom. But some U.S. gene-

alogists have actively discouraged practitioners from following female lines of
descent. In the absence of a critical history of the practice of genealogy that ad
dresses this issue, I surveyed published guides to see how genealogists themselves explained their work starting in the late nineteenth century, paying special attention to books McClung likely encountered. Foundational texts include
Phillimore, *How to Write*; and Phillimore, *Supplement*. Phillimore, who was
British, attributed the enthusiasm for genealogy to the "instinctive feeling" of
"all races of men" to find for themselves an "honorable ancestry." ("Even the Red
Indian preserves some traditions of his ancestors," Phillimore wrote.) He found
the origins of modern genealogy in "the rise of heraldry and the general adoption of surnames" but noted that the practice of producing family histories was
most common in the United States, especially in New England (*How to Write*,
1st ed., 1–6). Phillimore contended that, compared to their English counterparts,
American genealogists devoted more "labor to tracing out the female branches"
of family trees. He said this was because the English could trace family lines further back and so sacrificed breadth for historical depth. Americans (he meant
white Americans), with a shorter history in their adopted homeland, could
not go far back in time and so spent more energy tracing "the descendants of
the daughters of a house" (*Supplement*, 2nd ed., 404). He anticipated that U.S.
interest in genealogy would ignite a more general desire among residents of the
former and then current British colonies "to connect their lineage to the old
country" and to knit themselves "more firmly together in one common union
with Anglo-Saxon settlements throughout the world" (*How to Write*, 2nd ed.,
194–95). In 1930, New England genealogist Donald Lines Jacobus argued similarly that interest in genealogy was "inherent in human nature." But he claimed
that in the United States, the practice had become "truly democratic." His *Genealogy as Pastime and Profession* was as much cautionary tale as it was how-to
guide (quotes on p. 1). But like his English counterpart decades before and despite his approval of American democratic impulse, Jacobus displayed racial
assumptions by opening with a story about a Puritan who, for a joke, sent "his
negro" to occupy the pew of a wealthy merchant, disrupting Sunday church
services. Jacobus took for granted that his (white) readers would get the joke
(thereby learning that Puritans, too, had a sense of humor) and that none would
identify with the black man who was bribed to set sail in a sea of worshiping
whites (3–4). And Jacobus was more prescriptive about female lines than Phillimore was: "Never attempt to trace descendants in female lines beyond the children of daughters." Tracing them, he argued, presented insurmountable problems because wives took their husbands' names (106, 119–20). McClung must
have been dismayed by Jacobus's pessimism about doing genealogical work in
the West. He argued that source materials were concentrated in the East: "If you
live in a western town, my inclination is to say: go east, young man or young
woman, or else await your next incarnation to become a genealogist" (50). All
of which is to say that the literature was rife with gender, racial, class, regional,
national, and colonial assumptions that would have shaped McClung's understanding of genealogy. Work by Francesca Morgan, who is completing a book

entatively titled "Nation of Descendants," explores all of this. Meanwhile, see her articles "Lineage as Capital" and "A Noble Pursuit?" Thanks to Morgan for tutoring me before her work reached publication.

13. On genealogy's weak professionalization and its association with women, local history, and antiquarianism, see Weil, *Family Trees*, 52–54, 133, 159–61, 166–69, 175–76; and Tyrell, *Historians in Public*, esp. 212, 215, 224, 228. Both analyses are preliminary; there are worlds of work yet to be done on the feminization of genealogy.

14. Quantrille D. McClung, "Genealogy"; McClung to Blackwelder, February 25, 1956, McClung Papers. The Denver Public Library's Genealogy Division is now part of the Western History/Genealogy Department, the western history and genealogy collections having merged in 1995. See "Department History," Denver Public Library, accessed April 23, 2020, https://history.denverlibrary.org/western-history-collection.

15. As McClung put it, "The Bent and Boggs material grows also and I am wondering if it will not be a good idea just to include it in the Carson book since the families were so closely connected." McClung to Blackwelder, June 30, 1957, McClung Papers. Of McClung's decision to include the Bent and Boggs families, Carson scholar Harvey Carter writes, "It was her happy inspiration to include the Bent and Boggs families as well, certain members of which were so closely connected with Kit Carson that the useful quality of the compilation is greatly enhanced." Harvey L. Carter, *"Dear Old Kit,"* 31.

16. On such families, see Anne F. Hyde, *Empires, Nations, and Families*. In other geographies, see Graybill, *Red and the White*; and Erika Pérez, *Colonial Intimacies*.

17. Blackwelder to McClung, October 30, 1956, McClung Papers.

18. Bernice Blackwelder, "Kit Carson and Family," in Quantrille D. McClung, *Carson-Bent-Boggs Genealogy*, 66–67.

19. This attempt to craft a narrative from McClung's genealogical charts gives me pause, particularly given her own narrative reticence. But it is the case that McClung's genealogy follows Carson's intimacies with Singing Grass (Northern Arapaho), Making Out Road (Southern Cheyenne), and especially Josefa Jaramillo; she traces the children of Carson and Jaramillo through their own often interethnic marriages; and she ends with mostly non-Spanish-surnamed descendants. She also carefully traces those Carsons who did not intermarry with either Indians or *hispanos*. Over half of the genealogy (111 of 181 pages) is devoted to tracing "the line of William Carson" (Kit's grandfather) and "the line of Samuel Carson" (who may or may not have been William's brother and thus may or may not have been Kit's great-uncle). By contrast, one page is devoted to tracing the ancestry of Josefa Jaramillo among the Vigil and Jaramillo families of New Mexico (cf. the four pages devoted to intermarriages between Kit Carson's and Daniel Boone's kin). Quantrille D. McClung, *Carson-Bent-Boggs Genealogy*.

20. Bent had another mixed-ancestry child, Charles, not mentioned here because he was likely the son of Bent's second wife, Yellow Woman. Yellow Woman was Owl Woman's sister, whom Bent married after Owl Woman died. Here, too,

I am trying to find a story in McClung's genealogical charts when she herself es
chewed explicit storytelling. But it is clear that Bent's intimate life and the fate
of his children interested McClung and that she relied on historical as well as
genealogical sources to tell the tale. Bent's lineage fills only four pages, but those
pages are more densely annotated with historical detail than most. McClung,
98–101.

21. Blackwelder to McClung, April 12, 1969, McClung Papers. I discuss Blackwelder's decision in part 2.

22. McClung did not comment on how this relatively inclusive historical impulse reflected her own understanding of human difference. But such an impulse
was not incompatible with the goals of early civil rights movements that called
for equality under the law, universal human rights, and disaffirmation of those
presumed differences that informed hierarchies of race, gender, and sexuality—
even if some later came to critique the unintended normative and assimilation-
ist outcomes such goals could produce. Thanks to Crista DeLuzio for reminding
me of this. The literature that tracks changes over time and across space in civil
rights movement strategies and goals is too vast to cite fully, but relevant titles
include Gerstle, *American Crucible*; Sugrue, *Sweet Land of Liberty*; Self, *American Babylon*; Dudziak, *Cold War Civil Rights*; Branch, *Parting the Waters*; Sitkoff,
Struggle for Black Equality; David Gutiérrez, *Walls and Mirrors*; D'Emilio, *Sexual
Politics, Sexual Communities*; Boyd, *Wide Open Town*; Hurewitz, *Bohemian Los
Angeles*; and Stewart-Winter, *Queer Clout*. I suspect that the influence of second-
wave feminism remained inchoate this early on for McClung, given its slightly
later origins. But see Chafe, "Road to Equality." MacLean, *Freedom Is Not Enough*,
helpfully shows the roots of women's rights claims in the black freedom struggle's
earlier push for jobs and justice, creating a longer trajectory for the women's
movement. But my point here is about how visible various social justice claims
in the late 1950s and early 1960s were to McClung.

23. This grossly simplifies a broader, more complicated range of North American slaveries. On black chattel slavery in the East, see Berlin, *Many Thousands
Gone* and *Generations of Captivity*. Indian slavery was once continental in
scope; only in the nineteenth century was it becoming a mostly western form.
See Gallay, *Indian Slave Trade*; Christina Snyder, *Slavery in Indian Country*; and
Rushforth, *Bonds of Alliance*. For slavery among the southeastern Five Nations,
see Perdue, *Slavery and the Evolution*; Miles, *Ties That Bind* and *House on Diamond Hill*; Saunt, *New Order of Things* and *Black, White, and Indian*; and Krauthamer, *Black Slaves, Indian Masters*. Work on western slavery is cited below, but
see esp. Reséndez, *Other Slavery*.

24. Quantrille D. McClung, *Carson-Bent-Boggs Genealogy*, 13, 168–71. She also
notes that Andrew Carson's son Robert, Kit's cousin, was "said to have been a
Negro trader" in North Carolina (42).

25. On the Carsons' slaveholding, see Carson Family Papers, State Historical
Society of Missouri, St. Louis.

26. See Reséndez, *Other Slavery*; Blackhawk, *Violence over the Land*; James
Brooks, *Captives and Cousins*; Rael-Gálvez, "Identifying Captivity and Capturing

dentity"; and Ramón A. Gutiérrez, *When Jesus Came*. I focus on Native servitude among *hispanos* because the Carson/Jaramillo family engaged in it, but American Indians themselves engaged in a slave trade involving other Indian peoples as well as Mexicans, Anglos, European immigrants, and African Americans, a trade well documented by Blackhawk, *Violence over the Land*; Hämäläinen, *Comanche Empire*; and Rivaya-Martínez, "Captivity and Adoption." Covering different geographies but conceptually key in understanding gendered coercions including but not limited to enslavement are Stacey L. Smith, *Freedom's Frontier*; Erika Pérez, *Colonial Intimacies*; Jagodinsky, *Legal Codes*; and Jacobs, *White Mother*.

27. On the Carson *criados*, see Simmons, *Kit Carson*, 100–102, though analysis provided in the works cited above by Blackhawk, James Brooks, Rael-Gálvez, and Ramón A. Gutiérrez make better sense of such households. For an intimate portrait of one Ute family's journey through this system of slavery, see Skott Brandon Vigil, "'That's All We Knew.'" Anne Hyde alerted me to Carson's earlier participation in the western slave trade when he served as guide and hunter for John C. Frémont's second expedition in 1843–44. German-born cartographer Charles Preuss, who also accompanied Frémont, recorded in his diary that, in what is now Utah, Carson "bought an Indian boy of twelve to fourteen years for forty dollars," noting that the boy "belongs to the Paiute Nation." Record of what became of this boy apparently has not survived. Preuss, *Exploring with Frémont*, 134. This incident is covered in Dunlay, *Kit Carson*, 105–6; and mentioned in Blackhawk, *Violence over the Land*, 182.

28. Quantrille D. McClung, *Carson-Bent-Boggs Genealogy*.

29. McClung, 95, 104–10. Juliana Bent's first name is sometimes given as Juliannah or Julia Ann.

30. McClung, 69–70. I learned of Owl Woman and Making Out Road's kinship from the work of Elliott West: *Way to the West*, 123, and *Contested Plains*, 210. The women may not have been sisters in the way white people understood family relationships but rather in a Cheyenne manner of reckoning kinship. An account of the relationship appears in Rath, *Rath Trail*, 10–14, based on a number of sources, including the recollections of Cheyenne relatives and descendants. Charles Rath married Making Out Road years after she divorced Carson (in between her relationships with Carson and Rath, she married and divorced two Cheyenne men). Making Out Road's name was sometimes translated as Roadmaker. Some said her name referred to "laying out roads," while others insisted it meant "laying down the law." See Rath, *Rath Trail*, 12–13.

31. Quantrille D. McClung, *Carson-Bent-Boggs Genealogy*, 71–83, 88–95, 101–3, 106–8.

32. Blackwelder, *Great Westerner*, 365.

33. In this, McClung and Blackwelder anticipate Conzen, who argues that the nineteenth-century West was a family frontier, "an arena in which culturally variant constructs of the family, carried by individuals pursuing varying family strategies, met, intermingled, and clashed." Conzen, "Saga of Families," 319, see also 323.

34. Blackwelder, *Great Westerner*, 13.

35. Blackwelder, 48, 77, 209–10, 221. The question of Carson's height, especially in relation to that of his third wife, Josefa Jaramillo, has produced on the part of some Carson enthusiasts a spirited defense of Carson's manhood, which for these enthusiasts has to do with his size. See Simmons (*Kit Carson*, 55, 57), who refutes the notion that Josefa was taller than Kit, based in part on a footnote in Estergreen, *Kit Carson: A Portrait*, 125n2, which claims Kit was taller than Josefa based on sources that cannot be found (see n43 below). Simmons's other source, a biography of Josefa's relative Donaciano Vigil, suggests the opposite and more common contention that Josefa was taller than Kit; see Stanley, *Giant in Lilliput*, 129. In a verbal exchange, when I repeated what I thought was an uncontroversial statement about Carson's small stature, a Carson enthusiast in Taos insisted, "He was *big enough*" (the verbal emphasis was his). This incident took place in the first decade of the twenty-first century.

36. Blackwelder, *Great Westerner*, 48, 269. Blackwelder likely based these claims on Brewerton (*Overland with Kit Carson*, 38), who, in remarks first published in *Harper's New Monthly Magazine* in 1853, said that Carson's voice was "as soft and gentle as a woman's"; and on Rusling (*Across America*, 136), who said Carson's voice was "as soft and sympathetic as a woman's." Elias Brevoort also said that Carson had a "rather effeminate voice." See Elias Brevoort, "The Santa Fe Trail," 1884, Bancroft Library, University of California, Berkeley, quoted in Harvey L. Carter, *"Dear Old Kit,"* 185.

37. Blackwelder, *Great Westerner*, 26, 75.

38. Blackwelder to McClung, July 14, 1969, McClung Papers.

39. Blackwelder, *Great Westerner*, 61–65, 85–90, quotes on 64, 90. On Shunar, or Chouinard, see, e.g., Harvey L. Carter, *"Dear Old Kit,"* 63–65; and Simmons, *Kit Carson*, 8–10.

40. Blackwelder, *Great Westerner*, 88, 90; cf. Simmons, *Kit Carson*, 33. On Charlotte Green, see William W. Gwaltney, "Beyond the Pale: African-Americans in the Fur Trade West," accessed March 19, 2007, http://www.coax.net/people/lwf/FURTRADE.HTM (this article has since disappeared from the internet); and Moore, *Sweet Freedom Plains*, 127–28. On women at the fort generally, see Grinnell, "Bent's Old Fort," esp. 52, 56, 60, 61, as well as his ubiquitous references to the Native wives of trappers and traders.

41. Blackwelder, *Great Westerner*, 100n4. The earlier biography was Vestal, *Kit Carson*. Stanley Vestal was the pen name of Walter S. Campbell, who taught English at the University of Oklahoma and interviewed Cheyenne and Arapaho people in his home state as part of his research for the book. These interviews notwithstanding, the biography takes literary license with Carson's life and vexes historians with its lack of documentation. For a typical historian's rant against Campbell's work, see Harvey L. Carter, *"Dear Old Kit,"* 24–27. For an assessment of Campbell's career, see Sherry L. Smith, "Stanley Vestal."

42. Blackwelder, *Great Westerner*, 98–99.

43. Blackwelder does not quote Teresina Bent, who apparently once wrote in a letter, "Uncle Kit was very angry when [a man who had interviewed him] said that he was married to a Cheyenne woman named Making Out Road. He said

here was no truth in that story." Blackwelder cites as the source for this letter the booklet *The Real Kit Carson* by Marion Estergreen. Estergreen, in turn, vaguely cites "a letter from Teresina Bent Scheurich" and, in her bibliography, a "Letter by Teresina Bent Scheurich to her cousin"; see Estergreen, *Real Kit Carson*, iv–v and bibliography, unnumbered page. Estergreen repeats this quotation in *Kit Carson: A Portrait* without clear attribution but refers in her bibliography to the "collected letters" of Teresina Bent Scheurich that were then "owned by Blanche C. Grant" (77, 305). Blanche Chloe Grant was the Vassar-educated, Taos-based artist and writer who edited the first published version of Kit Carson's dictated autobiography, *Kit Carson's Own Story of His Life*. I have not located Teresina Bent's letters. Estergreen says she obtained Grant's research notes a year before Grant died, but it is not clear whether those notes included the letters in question or merely quotations from the letters. See Estergreen, *Kit Carson: A Portrait*, vi.

44. Harvey L. Carter, *"Dear Old Kit,"* 82, and "Kit Carson," esp. 26n116; Simmons, *Kit Carson*, 38–39. The male relative was Jesse Nelson, the husband of Kit's niece, whose statement appears in notebook 8, p. 83, Cragin Papers, Colorado Springs Pioneers Museum, Colorado Springs, Colorado.

45. Grinnell, "Bent's Old Fort," esp. 37. Blackwelder uses this source and cites it in both her footnotes and bibliography. Grinnell was author of *Fighting Cheyennes* and the two-volume *Cheyenne Indians*. Blackwelder also cites Lavender (*Bent's Fort*, 219–21), who affirms the marriage to Making Out Road.

46. Blackwelder, *Great Westerner*, 62.

47. Blackwelder, 97–98.

48. Chávez, *New Mexico Families*, 198–200 (Jaramillo), 311–12 (Vigil); Martínez et al., *María Josefa Jaramillo*, iii, xii–xiii.

49. See, e.g., Ramón A Gutiérrez, *When Jesus Came*, esp. 190–206, 285–92; Frank, *From Settler to Citizen*, esp. 178–81; and Taylor, *In Search of the Racial Frontier*, 29–32, 35–37. On Christian, Muslim, and Jewish interaction in Spain, see Lowney, *Vanished World*; Menocal, *Ornament of the World*; and Dodds, Menocal, and Balbale, *Arts of Intimacy*.

50. González, *Refusing the Favor*, ix–x, 123–24; Nieto-Phillips, *Language of Blood*; Montgomery, *Spanish Redemption*; Mitchell, *Coyote Nation*; Sarah Deutsch, *No Separate Refuge*, vii, 136–37.

51. Blackwelder, *Great Westerner*, 115–117, quote on 117.

52. Blackwelder, 117–24, quote on 124. It was Jessie Benton Frémont, through her writings about her husband's treks, who introduced Carson to a reading public in the East.

53. Blackwelder, 123–46, quote on 145. Blackwelder had no evidence of Carson's thoughts. It also is not clear that Josefa was waiting for him at Bent's Fort in July 1844, though she seems to have been there in July 1843. See Harvey L. Carter, *"Dear Old Kit,"* 95–96, esp. n170.

54. Blackwelder, *Great Westerner*, 147–204, quote on 147. Blackwelder says that Carson made the decision to accompany Frémont again because of a promise he had made "to join any future expedition" the explorer undertook. Carson says the same in his autobiography; Harvey L. Carter, *"Dear Old Kit,"* 95–96.

55. Blackwelder, *Great Westerner*, 204–9. For an account of the rebellion, see Gómez, *Manifest Destinies*.

56. Blackwelder, *Great Westerner*, 210–314, esp. 235, 243–44, 260, 303, 305 quotes on 243, 260, 303. Blackwelder takes the story of Carson's fatherly behavior from what Maj. Rafael Chacón wrote for Edwin Sabin. Sabin, *Kit Carson Days*, 2:681–82.

57. Certainly criticism of Carson circulated in Navajo and other Indigenous circles, but Blackwelder had few Native connections. She probably knew little even of early non-Indian critics such as Taos art patron Mabel Dodge, a transplant from New York to New Mexico who married Tony Lujan of Taos Pueblo. According to Sherry Smith, in the 1950s when Mabel Dodge Luhan was offered a burial plot in Taos's Kit Carson Cemetery, she "decided not to reveal her animosity toward Carson whom she … deemed 'one of the great indian killers.'" Dodge Luhan is buried in that cemetery, though far from the graves of Kit Carson and Josefa Jaramillo. See Sherry L. Smith, *Reimagining Indians*, 211–12. Thanks to Sherry Smith for reminding me of this.

58. Blackwelder, *Great Westerner*, 313 (quote), 317–21. On Navajo-*hispano*-Pueblo relations, see James Brooks, *Captives and Cousins*, 80–116, 208–16, 234–57; Iverson, *Diné*, 21–34; McNitt, *Navajo Wars*; and Brugge, *Navajos*. For the same from the perspective of Utes, see Blackhawk, *Violence over the Land*, esp. 200–225, which also includes insightful analysis of Carson's role in these conflicts. For the perspective from Arizona, see Victoria Smith, *Captive Arizona*.

59. Blackwelder, *Great Westerner*, 317–46, quotes on 318, 321, 325, 339.

60. Blackwelder, 327–55, quotes on 328, 350. In characterizing the Carson children as little savages, she may have been drawing on remarks by William Tecumseh Sherman, who visited Fort Garland and found the children "half-clad and boisterous, as wild and untrained as a brood of Mexican mustangs" (353). See discussion below.

61. Blackwelder, 243, 269, 293.

62. Blackwelder, 269, 355.

63. Blackwelder, 352.

64. Blackwelder, 353; the quote comes from Sherman to Edward S. Ellis, June 25, 1884, reproduced in Ellis, *Life of Kit Carson*, 249.

65. On recapitulation theory, see Bederman, *Manliness and Civilization*, 92–94. My understanding of how the idea of recapitulation continued to circulate well past the time when it was advanced by educational theorists has been enhanced by Paul Schwinn, "Class, Character, and Cultural Epochs: Manliness, Adolescence, and the Boy Scouts of America" (University of Wisconsin–Madison, 2003), which won the history department's William F. Allen Writing Prize for the best undergraduate term paper. Even among developmental psychologists, recapitulation theory retained influence; see Morss, *Biologising of Childhood*. Thanks to Crista DeLuzio for this reference.

66. Blackwelder, *Great Westerner*, 355–65, quotes on 356, 362, 364. Blackwelder misstates the Spanish name of the Purgatoire as El Rio de las Perdida en Purgatorio. English speakers called it the Picketwire. On the Vigil and St. Vrain and

other grants, see LeRoy Hafen, "Mexican Land Grants"; Van Hook, "Mexican Land Grants"; Lamar, "Land Policy" and *Far Southwest*; and Montoya, *Translating Property*. Josefa died of a postpartum infection. Kit likely died of an aneurysm; he had often attributed his failing health to a fall from a horse in 1860, which caused internal injuries. Other biographers count the number of days between Kit's arrival, Josefita's delivery, Josefa's death, and Kit's death differently, but everyone agrees that it all happened very quickly. See, e.g., Estergreen, *Kit Carson: A Portrait*, 273–78; Guild and Carter, *Kit Carson*, 281–83; and Simmons, *Kit Carson*, 141–44.

67. Blackwelder, *Great Westerner*, title page. Eugene Fitch Ware wrote poetry under the pen name Ironquill. See, e.g., Ware, *Rhymes of Ironquill*. For a biography, see "Eugene Fitch Ware Papers," Kansas Historical Society, accessed March 28, 2007, http://www.kshs.org/research/collections/documents/personalpapers/findingaids/ware_eugene_fitch.htm.

68. Most biographers say that Carson's last supper included buffalo steak and coffee, followed by a smoke. See, e.g., Harvey L. Carter, *"Dear Old Kit,"* 177–78; and Estergreen, *Kit Carson: A Portrait*, 278. The meal was prepared by Aloys Scheurich, husband of Kit and Josefa's niece Teresina Bent. The chile may be Blackwelder's invention. The two sources she cites for the death scene do not mention the chile: Albert Thompson, "Death"; and Tilton, *Last Days*. It is, of course, plausible that Scheurich, married to a *nuevomexicana*, prepared the steak New Mexican style, with chile. The chile reappears, entirely undocumented (and now as "red chili"), in Sides, *Blood and Thunder*, 395.

69. On those ideals, see Weiss, *To Have and to Hold*. Thanks to Margaret Jacobs and Crista DeLuzio for posing questions that helped me clarify this argument.

70. Lamar, "Much to Celebrate," esp. 397. For other historical perspectives on the status of western history in the profession over time, see Billington, "Santa Fe Conference" and "New Western Social Order."

71. On Sandoz and Beasley, see Des Jardins, *Women and the Historical Enterprise*, 28, 114–17. In addition to *Crazy Horse*, Sandoz is known for novels like *Slogum House* as well as nonfiction like *Old Jules* and *Cheyenne Autumn*. Against enormous odds, Beasley published *Negro Trail Blazers of California*. Other women working early in western history included Grace Hebard, Angie Debo, and Juanita Brooks. Hebard and Debo both had PhDs, while Brooks had an MA. Of these scholars, only Hebard enjoyed an ongoing faculty position at a university (even though Debo won a prize from the American Historical Association for her first book, *Rise and Fall of the Choctaw Republic*). Brooks, a devout Mormon, was ostracized in the Church of Jesus Christ of Latter-Day Saints for her book *Mountain Meadows Massacre*, which exposed the church's role in the infamous 1857 massacre. See Des Jardins, *Women and the Historical Enterprise*, 96, 101–17. On Hebard, see Scharff, *Twenty Thousand Roads*, 94–114. See also Leckie and Parezo, *Their Own Frontier*, esp. the introduction, as well as Leckie, "Angie Debo," and Wunder, "Mari Sandoz."

72. Cronon, *Nature's Metropolis*.

73. Case quotation from Case to Edwin A. Bemis [secretary, Founders Society of

America], March 17, 1949, box 4, folder 4, Westerners–Chicago Corral Papers, New berry Library, Chicago (hereafter cited as Chicago Corral Papers). Privately, some early Westerners disputed Case's penchant for casting himself as *the* founder rather than *a* founder, of the Westerners. See Don Russell to "Colonel [William Gardner] Bell," March 15, 1965, box 10, folder 8, Chicago Corral Papers; cf. Russell's own brief account of the Chicago Corral's history in Chicago Corral roster, 1964–65, 6–7, box 16, folder 1, Chicago Corral Papers. For histories of the Westerners, see Reynolds, *History of the Westerners*; *Westerners: A Mini-bibliography*; and Case, "Westerners." For published versions of talks delivered at the first two years of Chicago Corral meetings, see *Westerners Brand Book* (1944, 1945–46). For the founding of the Denver Posse, see Bemis, "Conception and Birth." The Chicago Corral grew out of an earlier organization called the Friends of the Middle Border, which was devoted to the study of the Missouri River country. See Case to Bemis, March 17, 1949; and to Jack Reynolds, March 26, 1954, box 4, folder 4, Chicago Corral Papers; Reynolds, *History of the Westerners*; Case, "Westerners"; and Irene Steyskal, "Friends of the Middle Border to Hold Party," *Chicago Tribune*, July 7, 1946. Steyskal notes that the Chicago Corral was an all-male group; see discussion below. On the Inter-Posse Rendezvous, see LeRoy Hafen, *Joyous Journey*, 274, 275, 285–86, 299; Case, "Westerners," 71; and LeRoy Hafen to Russell, April 27, 1954, box 4, folder 4, Chicago Corral Papers. Chicago was also the birthplace of the Civil War Round Table, a similar organization that spread across the United States in the 1940s and '50s. Unlike the Westerners, Civil War Round Tables did not sustain a coordinating council or hold an annual gathering. See Borowick, *Civil War Round Table*. Thanks to Sherry Smith for reminding me of this parallel.

74. Reynolds, *History of the Westerners*, unnumbered 10.

75. See printed membership materials from the Tucson Corral, the Los Angeles Corral, the Kansas City Posse, the Denver Posse, and El Corral de Santa Fe (1950s and '60s), box 14, folder 2; and Chicago Corral roster, 1964–65, box 16, folder 1, all in Chicago Corral Papers. The Chicago Corral clarified its membership rules for women in 1953, noting that it was following Denver's model rather than New York's: "Women are eligible to corresponding membership, without privilege of attending other than open meeting." *Westerners Brand Book* 10, no. 2 (April 1953): 1.

76. Case, "Westerners," 63.

77. Reynolds, *History of the Westerners*, unnumbered 10. Many but not all chapters used these officer titles. El Corral de Santa Fe (established in 1962), by contrast, used the following titles for *los officiales*: *el alguacil, el diputado alguacil, el registrador de marcas y tizónes, el ladrón official*, and *el caporal*. See Westerners Club, El Corral de Santa Fe, Reglas de Gobierno, December 13, 1962, box 14, folder 2, Chicago Corral Papers.

78. William Mathiesen to Don Russell, May 8, 1958, box 6, folder 4, and March 24, 1960, box 7, folder 1; and Bruce McKinstry to Harry Anderson et al., January 22, 1969, box 10, folder 1, both in Chicago Corral Papers.

79. Charles Collins, "Bookman's Holiday," *Chicago Tribune*, April 30, 1946. It was not only outsiders who characterized the Westerners in this manner. An-

ouncing the first ever Ladies Night event in 1945, the Chicago Corral's monthly publication noted that all earlier meetings had been "strictly stag." *Westerners Brand Book* 1, no. 10 (January 1945): 13.

80. Frederick Babcock, "Among the Authors," *Chicago Tribune*, October 1, 1946; Lloyd Wendt, "Way Out West in Modern Chicago," *Chicago Tribune*, October 26, 1947. An undated Chicago Corral roster (ca. 1960s) likewise lists the occupations of some eighty members in fields such as journalism and publishing, retail and real estate, engineering and manufacturing, academia and the professions (law, medicine, dentistry), as well as various business and management positions, in box 1, Chicago Corral Papers. A 1957 roster of the Denver Posse lists fifty members with similar occupations, in box 14, folder 2, Chicago Corral Papers. Some chapters of the Westerners drew on a slightly different membership base, depending on location, but the class status of members seems to have been quite uniform. The Washington, D.C., chapter, for example, called the Potomac Corral, included members employed by the National Park Service and other government agencies. Even Senator Barry Goldwater sometimes attended meetings. See Utley, *Custer and Me*, 57, 113; and Lawson, "Mr. Case."

81. John Randolph, "Chicago Posse Sees Styles of Old West," *Chicago Tribune*, November 25, 1952; "America's First Fashions."

82. Emphasis in originals. Wyoming Westerners Roundup announcement, July 1, 1954, box 5, folder 3; and Chicago Corral barbecue announcement, [July 1962?], box 7, folder 7, both in Chicago Corral Papers. Invitations to Ladies Nights not only from the Chicago Corral but from Westerners nationwide are spread throughout the Chicago Corral Papers; see, e.g., box 10, folder 4. For the Denver Posse, see also LeRoy Hafen, *Joyous Journey*, 248, 259–60. At the Denver group's 1949 Ladies Night, Ann Hafen, a published poet married to LeRoy Hafen who co-authored most of his publications, presented a drama she had written, "The Son of Bird Woman," featuring Baptiste Charbonneau, son of Sacagawea, the Shoshone woman who accompanied the Lewis and Clark expedition. For the Potomac Corral, see Lawson, "Mr. Case," 16–17. Through the 1970s, the Potomac Corral held meetings at the male-only Cosmos Club in Washington, D.C. One meeting a year was held in the club's unrestricted auditorium; this gathering was known first as Squaw Night and later as Ladies Night.

83. I do not mean to suggest that Indigenous names are or were as readily identified as Spanish surnames or even that Spanish surnames are or were a proxy for Latino identity or subjectivity. Colonialism does violence to naming practices of all kinds, so that a Westerners member called John Smith might be Anglo American or American Indian or African American or of mixed ancestry, for example. But given the opacity of available records, and given that I am not writing a history of the Westerners (a history that needs to be written), searching for Spanish surnames and translated Indigenous names that survived forced assimilative processes (or were reclaimed in defiance of them) is one way to find, or not to find, Latino and Indigenous Westerners participants. I combined this method with a survey of Westerners publications and archives, and I made inquiries with older Westerners.

84. Rodríguez was at first a corresponding member of the Chicago Corral until he inquired about why he did not receive notices of regular meetings. A letter from an unnamed officer to "Mr. Rod Roderiguez" [sic] dated October 3, 1960, tells him to attend meetings, introduce himself to the corral's officers, and explain to them his interests, adding, "We like to have new members who hope to contribute something to our meetings and do not come just to be entertained" (box 2, folder 4, Chicago Corral Papers). Thereafter, Rodríguez's name appears frequently on membership lists and meeting sign-in sheets in the Chicago Corral Papers, and he also appears in a group photograph ca. 1974 (scrapbook, box 2, Chicago Corral Papers). By the late 1960s, Rodríguez appears in the Chicago Corral's *Westerners Brand Book*, often alongside Fred B. Hackett, a Plains Indian specialist. The two men traveled frequently to the Pine Ridge Reservation, home of the Oglala Lakotas, and both claimed close relationships with Lakota people. See *Westerners Brand Book* 23, no. 8 (October 1966): 57–59, 64; 30, no. 8 (October 1973): 64; 31, no. 1 (March 1974): 4; 31, no. 10 (December 1974): 77; 31, no. 11/12 (January/February 1975): 85; 32, no. 3 (May/June 1975): 17–19; 33, no. 6 (October 1975): 45; and 33, no. 8 (December 1975): 59. See also esp. Rod Rodríguez, "This and That." This last piece suggests that Rodríguez came to Chicago from New York State. I have badgered Chicago Corral sheriff Jim Schiffer for information about Rodríguez; I am grateful to Schiffer for surveying members about their memories and answering my queries. Older Chicago Corral members remember Rodríguez but not anything about his background. Schiffer finally put me in touch with Father Peter J. Powell, who graciously replied to my inquiry with the following: "Rod Rodriguez and Fred Hackett were close friends, held in affection by us younger men. Rod frequently gave me a lift home after meetings. … Alas, however, he revealed little concerning himself other than his interest in the West, especially Buffalo Bill. In spite of his name we never thought of him as Spanish, so he was not considered a Hispanic presence in our predominately Anglo corral—merely another good man interested in the West." Peter J. Powell, personal communication with author, May 10, 2011. For more on Powell, see n86 below.

85. For Echohawk's corresponding membership (and, more elusively, that of Cheyenne tribal historian John Stands-in-Timber), see materials in box 1, Chicago Corral Papers; and *Westerners Brand Book* 10, no. 2 (April 1953): 1. For Echohawk's correspondence, see *Westerners Brand Book* 10, no. 9 (November 1953); 11, no. 11 (January 1955); 16, no. 7 (September 1959); 17, no. 4 (June 1960); and 30, no. 2 (April 1973). For his Ladies Night presentation, see "Brummett Echohawk." Father Peter J. Powell writes that Echohawk, "although an early associate of the Chicago Westerners, remained our sole Native American member during my active years [1955–75]." Peter J. Powell, personal communication with author, May 10, 2011.

86. The debate over termination was prompted by criticism in a talk Father Peter J. Powell delivered in 1956, "The New Raid on Reservations." (Powell, a Chicago Corral member, had established a Native assistance center at his Episcopal parish and would go on in 1961 to found St. Augustine's Center for American

ndians. He would also publish on Northern Cheyenne history and culture. See Powell, *Sweet Medicine* and *People of the Sacred Mountain*.) Soon, O. K. Armstrong (journalist and former Missouri legislator) delivered a rebuttal in favor of termination, "Set the Indians Free." Later still, John Collier (former commissioner of Indian affairs and central author of the Indian New Deal, which the termination policy repudiated) weighed in with a written response, "Another View of the Indians," in which he indicted Armstrong for his "ignorance," "blindness toward human values," and "overworked prejudice against our American Indians." For Powell's and Armstrong's talks and for Collier's essay, see *Westerners Brand Book* 13, no. 10 (December 1956); 14, no. 2 (April 1957); and 14, no. 6 (August 1957). It may not have been happenstance that Brummett Echohawk was invited to deliver his Ladies Night talk during the period when this controversy unfolded; see "Brummett Echohawk."

87. There may have been other exceptions to this rule, but the research involved in identifying them is beyond the scope of this project. A likely exception is the Santa Fe chapter of the Westerners, El Corral de Santa Fe, located as it was in a place where local *hispanos* had long been involved in commemorations of the regional past (see Nieto-Phillips, *Language of Blood*; Montgomery, *Spanish Redemption*; Mitchell, *Coyote Nation*; and Chris Wilson, *Myth of Santa Fe*). In 1964, e.g., Manuel B. Gonzales served as *el ladrón oficial*, or treasurer, of the chapter; *Westerners Brand Book* 21, no. 2 (April 1964): 12. Meanwhile, Oklahoma corrals and posses may have included American Indian members. Some of those chapters still exist, while others are, in Westerners parlance, "dry camps"—in other words now defunct. One such dry camp is the Tahlequah–Indian Nation Posse, organized in 1969. For a list of active chapters and dry camps, see "Westerners International Active Corrals," Westerners International, accessed January 1, 2017, http://www.westerners-international.org/corrals.shtml.

88. I am grateful to Beryl Satter for this formulation.

89. Utley, *Custer and Me*, 87–89, quote on 88. Utley referred, respectively, to the Southern Historical Association, founded in 1934, and the Mississippi Valley Historical Association, founded in 1907. The latter group increasingly eschewed an exclusive focus on the Mississippi Valley in favor of broader emphasis on the United States, reorganizing officially in 1965 as the Organization of American Historians.

90. Utley, 87.

91. Utley, 89.

92. Utley, 89–90. The program is reproduced following p. 216 in Toole et al., *Probing the American West*; the cover features *Prairie Schooner Lady* by western artist Don Louis Perceval. Ewers's paper appears on pp. 62–70. The "marginal man" theory was developed by sociologists Robert Park and Everett Stonequist to make sense of people situated between cultures, societies, or races. See esp. Park, "Human Migration" and *Race and Culture*; and Stonequist, *Marginal Man*. See also Wright and Wright, "Plea for Further Refinement." To compare, female participation at the annual meeting of the Southern Historical Association in 1960 was 3 percent (it had been 10 percent in 1940 and did not return to double

digits until 1975, when 15 percent of participants were women). "Statistical Report," esp. 283.

93. Utley, *Custer and Me*, 89–90. Utley vividly recalls Hafen's remonstrance but Hafen's own account of the Santa Fe conference, which he attended with his wife, Ann, states only that it was "a delightful affair, with all who attended, including many history 'buffs,' having interests similar to our own"; see LeRoy Hafen, *Joyous Journey*, 302. Billington is best known for *Westward Expansion*, which appeared in new editions a half dozen times over the next half century. See also Billington, "Frontier and I."

94. Following his account of the WHA's founding in *Custer and Me*, Utley presented a shorter version of the same to an appreciative audience at the 2010 WHA annual meeting (October 13–16, 2010, Incline Village, Nevada). Utley's remarks were later published; see Utley, "Remarks." The WHA erroneously billed this 2010 meeting as the "50th Annual" WHA conference—erroneously because although there were western history conferences held in 1961 and 1962, the WHA was not actually founded until 1962. John Porter Bloom explained this error in remarks he delivered in the same forum, and Bloom's remarks were also later published (alongside Utley's); see Bloom, "Reminiscence."

95. Papers from the 1962 conference appear in Ferris, *American West*. The founding of the WHA as well as plans for the magazine *American West* are noted on pp. 252–53. See also Utley, *Custer and Me*, 90–91, 110; Lamar, "Much to Celebrate"; and Billington, "New Western Social Order."

96. Our belief is based on stories that circulate about our bolo-tied forebears, including one about a WHA conference where, as an older male publisher put it to two younger men in the field, "part of the festivities was a 'busload of chippies' unloading at the convention hotel." Since the old days at the WHA may not be entirely over yet, I will follow the practice of journalists here and protect my sources. The two "younger men" are now senior scholars. The "older male publisher" has gone to his final reward.

97. It took twenty years for the WHA to elect its first female president, Mary Lee Spence; she served 1981–82. One woman was privy to conversations among the WHA founders in her role as a graduate student of Donald Cutter, University of Southern California, a member of the organizing committee for the Santa Fe conference; this was Iris Engstrand, who—much later, in 2003–4—would also become WHA president. See Utley, "Remarks," 3.

98. Janet Lecompte, personal communication with author, November 3, 2001. Lecompte wrote *Pueblo, Hardscrabble, Greenhorn* and *Rebellion in Río Arriba*. She expressly excluded historian LeRoy Hafen from her indictment. Her assessment of his kindness toward and encouragement of women is consistent with his own self-presentation in *Joyous Journey*.

99. Blackwelder to McClung, November 18, 1976, McClung Papers. Speaking of the WHA, Blackwelder wrote, "Difficult to believe it was 16 yrs ago that Dr. John Porter Bloom came to our house in Virginia and told me I owed him $5.00 as he had signed me as a charter member!" As Blackwelder wrote this in 1976, the visit she recalled probably took place fourteen or fifteen years earlier, in 1961 or

1962. Most of her reflections on the WHA date from the late 1960s and the 1970s and hence are discussed in part 2 of this book. Bloom, who was the first WHA secretary-treasurer and a member of the Westerners' Potomac Corral (see Lawson, "Mr. Case," 6), has only vague memories of Blackwelder. John Porter Bloom, personal communication with author, November 27, 2001.

100. McClung's work in the Colorado Genealogical Society is evident in the *Colorado Genealogist*, from vol. 1, no. 1 (October 1939), where she is listed as vice president and executive board chair, to vol. 46, no. 3 (August 1985), where a memorial appears. Society member Adelaide French also kept track of McClung's participation; see diaries, esp. 1946–71, boxes 4 and 5, French Papers, Western History Collection, Western History/Genealogy Department, Denver Public Library.

101. See discussion of "minor historians" in the prologue.

102. Billington, review of *Great Westerner*; Sunder, review of *Great Westerner*; *Missouri Historical Review*, unsigned review of *Great Westerner*; Welcome, review of *Great Westerner*; Hutchinson, review of *Great Westerner*; Glen M. Rodgers, review of *Great Westerner*; Tallant, review of *Great Westerner*.

103. Harvey L. Carter, *"Dear Old Kit,"* 30–32. Because McClung's and Blackwelder's interactions with other historians, both amateur and academic, increased after their books were published in 1962, I discuss those interactions more fully in part 2.

104. Blackwelder to McClung, October 18, 1958, McClung Papers.

105. Blackwelder to McClung, January 3, 1959; September 24, 1960, McClung Papers. Blackwelder's publisher, Caxton Press, provided me with copies of materials from her author file, for which I am most grateful. Special thanks to Scott Gipson, great-grandson of James Herrick Gipson Sr., press president when *Great Westerner* was published. Of Caxton Press the publishers say: "The publishing division of The Caxton Printers Ltd., Caxton Press is one of the oldest independent publishing houses west of the Mississippi. Specializing in regional non-fiction, Caxton Press provides a wide array of fine titles by fine authors about the people, culture, history and geography of the American West." See Caxton Press website, accessed April 26, 2007, www.caxtonpress.com; Caxton website, accessed April 21, 2011, www.caxtonprinters.com; and *Idaho Press-Tribune* (Nampa), March 30, 2010. Gipson Sr. was a corresponding member of the Chicago Corral of the Westerners, and he wrote to officers about matters both historical and contemporary. For example, he was an Idaho delegate to the 1952 Republican National Convention, where he supported conservative Robert A. Taft's candidacy over that of the more moderate Dwight D. Eisenhower, who secured his party's nomination and won the presidency. Gipson reported all of this to the Chicago Corral; see "A Statement by J. H. Gipson, Sr., of Caldwell, Idaho, on the Republican National Convention," July 14, 1952, box 3, folder 3, Chicago Corral Papers.

106. Blackwelder to McClung, October 18, 1958, McClung Papers.

107. Blackwelder to McClung, September 24, 1960; May 19, 1962; February 20, July 14, 1969, McClung Papers.

108. Blackwelder to McClung, [January 1, 1961?], McClung Papers.

109. Estergreen, *Kit Carson: A Portrait*.

110. Although until recently more male than female children have been named Morgan, the name remained ambiguous even in the mid-twentieth century because of its association with the female character Morgan le Fay in Arthurian legend. The University of Oklahoma Press generously provided me with materials from Estergreen's author file, which show that it was the publisher's idea for Estergreen to use the name "Morgan" (her surname before she married). A 1961 interoffice memo written by editor Herbert Hyde informs coworkers of the title chosen for the book and adds, "The author is in no way to be identified as a woman"; see Hyde to G. Bradley and D. Palmer, November 15, 1961, Estergreen Author File, University of Oklahoma Press, Norman (hereafter cited as Estergreen Author File). It was the publisher's idea, but Estergreen acquiesced, as indicated by a 1960 letter: "I am still in favor of your suggestion that the book will carry more weight if my name is 'M. Morgan Estergreen'" (Estergreen to Savoie Lottinville, April 12, 1960, Estergreen Author File). In 1963, when working on a new edition, Estergreen reversed herself: "Is there any way you can give me my full by-line ... in the second edition? If this cannot be done, can I be identified as a woman in the back cover by saying 'she lives in Taos'[?] You mentioned years ago that more men will buy the book if they think a man wrote it. I don't agree!" (Estergreen to Lottinville, March 23, 1963, Estergreen Author File). The publisher replied, "Only women change their minds! I don't think you should make the change in the character of your authorship.... It would only create confusion. If you want to do it, however, and feel strongly about it, I see no reason why not" (Lottinville to Estergreen, April 10, 1963, Estergreen Author File). The author's name was not changed.

111. Blackwelder to McClung, April 1, 1962, McClung Papers. Estergreen's earlier short piece was published as the booklet *The Real Kit Carson* (see n43 above).

112. Blackwelder to McClung, June 8, [1962], McClung Papers. The group was established in the 1950s, with Estergreen at the helm, though there were also earlier attempts to create such an organization. See mention in *Desert Magazine*, April 1949, 35, drawn from an article in *El Crepúsculo*.

113. I base the generalizations in this paragraph on my readings of Blackwelder, *Great Westerner*, and Estergreen, *Kit Carson: A Portrait*. Harvey L. Carter echoes some of this in *"Dear Old Kit,"* 30–32. He sums up, "These biographies represent a great advance over previous lives of Carson in their literary qualities, and some advance in scholarship as well" (32).

114. Most vexing is her citation of Blanche Grant's "Notes and Documents on the Life of Christopher Carson," which Estergreen owned (Estergreen, *Kit Carson: A Portrait*, vi, 304). See related discussion in n43 above. Estergreen's use of Grant's notes created problems at the editing stage for the University of Oklahoma Press. Editor Herbert H. Hyde surmised that Grant herself had taken down material from various Carson sources verbatim without indicating that she had done so and that Estergreen, in turn, had reproduced such extracts in her manuscript. As Hyde put it, "I assume that you have used Miss Grant's notes almost exclusively in preparing this book and that she did not make a clear distinction

etween her own notes and those she extracted verbatim from Carson material. f this be the case, then the entire manuscript will have to be checked very carefully ... for we must be absolutely certain that no quoted material is used therein without proper citation." Estergreen responded by checking Grant's notes against her own manuscript to eliminate instances of what amounted to inadvertent plagiarism (twice over), but Hyde reported that Estergreen had not caught them all. Hyde checked many published Carson sources himself but also implored Estergreen to redouble her efforts. He told her that the problem caused by "Blanche Grant's wholesale use of uncited verbatim extracts and parallel passages from various well-known sources" was "not yet solved," even after Estergreen's "careful check of the manuscript." Quotes from Hyde to Estergreen, October 18, 1961; February 15, 1962, Estergreen Author File. See also Hyde to Estergreen, November 1, 1961, March 5, 1962; Estergreen to Hyde, February 20, 1962; and Hyde to J. Cecil Alter, March 5, 1962, all in Estergreen Author File. The last two letters show that the press hired J. Cecil Alter, biographer of Jim Bridger and editor of the *Utah Historical Quarterly*, to sort out the remaining problems at Estergreen's expense (she was charged $200 for Alter's services). Estergreen later donated her own bound research notes to her alma mater, and those volumes include typed copies of passages from primary sources. But it is unclear whether these are materials that Estergreen collected herself or that Grant gathered or perhaps some combination of the two. See Estergreen, "Southwest History," in Center for Southwest Research, Zimmerman Library, University of New Mexico, Albuquerque.

115. On the journal and the WHA, see Hinton, "Short History," esp. 76; and Utley, *Custer and Me*, 91.

116. Blackwelder, review of *Kit Carson*.

117. See, e.g., Estergreen, *Kit Carson: A Portrait*, 21, 79–80, 84, 88, 97, 98, 105–6, 115, 126, 135, 138, 164–66, 239. Blackwelder makes fewer such references and is less apt to use the names of such figures; see, e.g., Blackwelder, *Great Westerner*, 105, 114, 124, 245, 284, 319.

118. Although Estergreen herself did not publish a review of Blackwelder's book, a friend of Estergreen's did try to settle the score. McClung reported to Jack Boyer, director of the Kit Carson Home and Museum in Taos, that she had learned of a review of *Great Westerner* submitted to the *Colorado Magazine* "'so scandalously unfavorable' it cannot be used." McClung told Boyer that the author's name was "Nora Shally-Beck." A few months earlier, Laura Shalley-Beck had written to Estergreen's University of Oklahoma Press editor, Herbert Hyde, reporting on her friend's poor health, as Estergreen was struggling to finish her own book manuscript. Shalley-Beck was distressed on Estergreen's behalf about the publication of *Great Westerner*, which Shalley-Beck thought an awful book. "Knowing something about Carson's life," Shalley-Beck wrote, "I know where [Blackwelder's] poor history leaves off and her poorer fiction takes up." McClung to Boyer, June 1, 1962, McClung Papers; Shalley-Beck to Hyde, February 24, 1962, Estergreen Author File.

119. See *Contemporary Authors Online*, s.v. "Marion Morgan Estergreen," accessed April 21, 2011, https://www.gale.com/c/literature-contemporary-authors.

Other reviews of Estergreen's *Kit Carson: A Portrait* include Sonne, review of *Kit Carson*; King, review of *Kit Carson*; Hurd, review of *Kit Carson*; *Missouri Historical Review*, unsigned review of *Kit Carson*; Furniss, review of *Kit Carson*; Sunder, review of *Kit Carson*; Mortensen, review of *Kit Carson*; Hinton, review of *Kit Carson*; and Davidson, review of *Kit Carson*. Among these, Sonne, King, Hurd, Furniss, Hinton, and the anonymous reviewer in the *Missouri Historical Review* all assume that Estergreen is male. Estergreen's other publications include magazine articles as well as *Taos Guide Book, 1951–52; Taos Guide and Art Directory;* and an auto tour book to northern New Mexican *hispano* villages and Indian pueblos, *Chapels on the Trail*. Estergreen's writing, her local history work, and her activities were often covered in local newspapers. In the *Santa Fe New Mexican*, see, e.g., April 30, June 25, 1952; June 26, 1957; March 19, June 12, 1958; January 7, February 25, 1959; March 18, 1960; March 24, 1968; June 28, 1970; October 7, 1979; March 15, 1981; and May 25, 1984 (obituary). In the *Albuquerque Journal*, see, e.g., January 24, May 1, 1954; September 30, 1956; and November 4, 1962. In the *Taos News*, see, e.g., September 22, 1960; January 19, February 9, April 20, December 14, 1961; November 1, 1962; January 9, 1964; April 15, 1965; August 18, 1966; February 23, 1967; January 11, October 3, 1968; April 21, 1971; March 25, 1982; and June 7, 1984 (obituary). A source connecting Estergreen to the Taos arts community is Estergreen to Mae Reed Porter, November 5, 1956, Dorothy Brett Collection, Center for Southwest Research, Zimmerman Library, University of New Mexico, Albuquerque. In this letter, Estergreen reveals that Angelo Ravagli, third husband of Frieda von Richthofen Lawrence (who was married to D. H. Lawrence at his death), propositioned her after a Taos party in the 1940s. Estergreen reports that she turned "Angie" down but also that Frieda, based on her free-love beliefs, later "very sweetly tried to make a date with me for Angie." Estergreen says she was not interested in dating a married man.

120. Blackwelder to McClung, June 8, [1962]. Elsewhere Blackwelder wrote, "We are supposed to be working for Carson's memory and I wonder what he would think of this hen fight"; Blackwelder to McClung, August 24, 1962. All in McClung Papers.

121. One disagreement was over Carson's birthplace; Blackwelder to McClung, April 1, May 1, 1962, McClung Papers. Blackwelder also complained about Estergreen's earlier booklet *The Real Kit Carson*, whose cover sports Carson in black tie: "When she put a tuxedo on Kit Carson I just could not refrain from mentioning it." Blackwelder to McClung, August 24, 1962, McClung Papers. Blackwelder preferred Carson in the more modest suiting or military garb that he generally wore.

122. Blackwelder to McClung, June 8, [1962], McClung Papers.

123. On Estergreen's origins, see *Santa Fe New Mexican*, March 24, 1968; *Taos News*, November 6, 1986; and U.S. Bureau of the Census, *Fourteenth Census*. I am not sure what happened to Marion Estergreen's husband, Paul Estergreen. The 1968 *Santa Fe New Mexican* story describes him as her "late husband," but I have found neither death record nor obituary. Newspaper coverage of the couple is frequent until 1943 but then stops. Paul seems to have been transferred from Santa Fe to Tucson that year, and newspaper coverage says that Marion moved

here, too. But coverage drops off until 1950, when Marion is back in New Mexico and seems to be single. Blackwelder's reproof notwithstanding, Estergreen lived a life of hardship as well as recognition. Estergreen suffered from tuberculosis when she was young and from debilitating accidents as an adult. In addition to coverage cited above, see *Albuquerque (N.M.) Journal*, January 9, 1938; November 11, 1943; and *Santa Fe New Mexican*, March 23, 1940; May 28, 1941; November 17, 1942; November 10, 1943; December 11, 1950; June 12, 1951. For a lawsuit Estergreen filed in the late 1950s against the property owner of her Taos residence (whom Estergreen held liable for injuries she sustained in a fall), see Marion Estergreen v. Mrs. Paul Martínez, 1958, box 9, case no. 29535, Manuel A. Sánchez Papers, New Mexico Records Center and Archives, Santa Fe (the case was dismissed with prejudice, meaning that Estergreen could not file another lawsuit based on the same grounds).

124. I borrow the phrase "root of bitterness" from the collection of primary sources in Cott et al., *Root of Bitterness* (and see also the first edition edited by Cott).

125. I rely on my own memory for advertising of the book in press catalogs and its display at western historical sites. A 2005 letter returned to the University of Oklahoma Press as undeliverable informed Estergreen's relative that *Kit Carson* had been declared out of print. Dale Bennie to Sheryl Marian Estergreen-Groce, July 25, 2005, Estergreen Author File. Marion Estergreen died in 1984 (U.S. Social Security Administration, *Social Security Death Index*; *Santa Fe New Mexican*, May 25, 1984). Readily available sources range from confusing to opaque on the subject of her offspring. At any rate, reconstructing her intimate life is beyond the scope of this project. For more information, see newspaper coverage cited in n119 and n123 above; correspondence in the Estergreen Author File; and letters from Estergreen to Jack Boyer, Carson Files, Southwest Research Center, University of New Mexico–Taos (in addition to letters from the 1970s, the same files include a 1974 will drafted by Estergreen that disinherits one child in favor of another).

126. Blackwelder reported in 1970 that Caxton was closing out her book; Blackwelder to McClung, January 22, 1970, McClung Papers.

127. Apologies to Herriot's *All Creatures Great and Small* and to the feature film and television series that followed from it.

128. Westerns were called oaters because horses, the key animal in the genre, like oats. The first use of the term in the popular press appears to have been in "The Oaters" in *Time* magazine on December 9, 1946, though it was already in use in the film industry.

129. Here I simplify a longer, more complex process, ably narrated and analyzed by many, e.g., Billington, "Santa Fe Conference," "New Western Social Order," and "Frontier and I"; Cronon, "Revisiting the Vanishing Frontier"; and Cronon, Miles, and Gitlin, "Becoming West."

130. Buscombe (*BFI Companion*, 427) says that 34 percent of films made in 1950 were Westerns. Slotkin, citing Phil Hardy, puts the 1950 figure at 38 percent (and says that in 1956, 46 percent were Westerns). Slotkin, *Gunfighter Nation*, 347, citing Phil Hardy, *The Western: The Film Encyclopedia* (New York: William and

Morrow, 1983). The literature on Westerns is voluminous; an overview is Lenihan, "Westbound."

131. Five years earlier, 17 Westerns ran, and five years later there were only 1 such shows. At no time between 1952 and 1970, however, did the number of TV Westerns on the air dip below 10 per year. See Buscombe, *BFI Companion*, 428 Yoggy, "Prime Time Bonanza!," states that 47 Western series ran in 1959. See also Slotkin, *Gunfighter Nation*, 348.

132. Yoggy, "Prime Time Bonanza!," 160.

133. *High Noon* also featured a resourceful *mexicana* business owner played by Katy Jurado. Synopses of films mentioned in this paragraph appear in Buscombe (*BFI Companion*, 263–64, 269, 277), but of course, nothing substitutes for viewing. See also Lenihan, "Westbound."

134. Until *The Simpsons* outlasted it, *Gunsmoke* (1955–75) was the longest-running series in U.S. television history. *Bonanza* ran 1959–73. See Buscombe, *BFI Companion*, 399, 401, 407, 413; and Yoggy, "Prime Time Bonanza!" David Dotort, *Bonanza*'s creator, later made another family Western, *High Chaparral* (1967–71), with notable female, Mexican, and Indigenous roles, including an Apache character played by my late spouse's first cousin James Almanzar.

135. This analysis draws on Slotkin, *Gunfighter Nation*, esp. 347–486; and Engelhardt, *End of Victory Culture*, esp. 3–154, quote on 7.

136. For an intelligent and fair-minded analysis of how such oppositional thinking continued among a later generation of western historians, see Tatum, "Problem of the 'Popular.'" For a Cold War critique of the relationship between professional historians and producers of popular culture, delivered at a 1958 meeting of the Chicago Corral of the Westerners, see Howard, "Peril." Howard argued that professional historians' ignorance of the methods of modern mass communications left the West to purveyors of popular culture, who in turn produced sensationalized, violent western fictions that became "tools of anti-American propaganda" for communists abroad. He suggested that the Westerners, by contrast, "visualize . . . revitalization of The Freedom Message of the American West" and urged members to find and communicate that message through such diverse historical subjects as meat-packers, steelmakers, bankers, engineers, automakers, pilots, educators, preachers, "the negro cowboy," and "the pioneer Jews."

137. Billington, "Frontier and I," 18. I do not mean to suggest that Billington was a killjoy. According to Lamar, Billington "openly asserted what few of us dared to believe: he said that being a western historian was great fun." Lamar, "Much to Celebrate," 398.

138. Case, "Westerners," 69. William S. Hart was the best-known cowboy star from an earlier generation of Westerns; see Slotkin, *Gunfighter Nation*, 242–53. The 1930s saw a decline of Western feature films, or A Westerns, and the rise of cheap, formulaic B Westerns until the end of the decade, when A Westerns witnessed a brief revival emblematized by John Ford's *Stagecoach* (1939). But World War II saw another steep drop in the production of Western features. See Slotkin, *Gunfighter Nation*, 254–342. While the men who organized the Westerners in the 1940s in some ways partook of the Wild West zeitgeist embodied in Western film,

hey set themselves apart as purveyors of history and not story, fact and not fiction, truth and not myth.

139. Summary drawn from Blackwelder's letters to McClung, 1957–60 passim, McClung Papers, esp. Blackwelder to McClung, October 3, November 5, 1957. The business is listed in *Hill's Arlington County Directory* (1955, 1957). It is not clear whether the eatery was a sit-down restaurant or a takeout business. The residence is listed in *Lusk's Fairfax County* (1959) and *Lusk's Fairfax County* (1963). The house description comes from a 1962 real estate listing in a set of photographs, scrapbook pages, and other documents given to me by Blackwelder's niece Doris Lance of Alpena, Michigan; see Blackwelder Papers, in author's possession (hereafter referred to as Blackwelder Papers). The real estate listing says the house was financed with a GI loan, but this may be in error. I have searched for but not found evidence that either Harold or Bernice Blackwelder were in the military. GI loans derived from the mortgage program for veterans associated with the GI Bill of Rights, or the Servicemen's Readjustment Act of 1944. Bernice did work for the federal government in the 1950s; she was employed by the CIA. But I have found no indication that CIA employees benefited from the GI Bill or similar legislation. It seems possible, then, that the financing designated on the real estate listing was wrong and that the mortgage derived from a Federal Housing Administration (FHA) loan. On housing loans administered by both the Veterans Administration and the FHA and their many exclusions, see, e.g., Freund, "Marketing the Free Market"; Self, *American Babylon*, esp. 42, 97–99, 104, 117; Sugrue, *Origins of the Urban Crisis*, esp. 43–47, 59–72, 182; Nicolaides, *My Blue Heaven*, esp. 179–81, 188–93, 226, 230; Lizabeth Cohen, *Consumers' Republic*, esp. 122, 123, 137–41, 147, 170, 199, 204–5, 214; and Canady, "Building a Straight State" and *Straight State*, 137–73. Thanks to Jennifer Holland and Camille Guérin-Gonzales for conversation about GI loans.

140. Blackwelder to McClung, March 6, 1958, McClung Papers; Vidal, *Small Planet*.

141. Summary drawn from McClung's letters to Blackwelder, 1957–60 passim, McClung Papers; for quote, see McClung to Blackwelder, March 10, 1958. For McClung's meeting attendance, see also diaries, 1957–60, box 5, French Papers, Western History Collection, Western History/Genealogy Department, Denver Public Library. My frequent use of first names in this section, where I am concerned with the women's daily lives as much as their historical practice, is intentional. Where I focus on their work as historians, I follow the disciplinary convention of using their last names.

142. For analysis of this process, see Slotkin, *Gunfighter Nation*. Racial and geopolitical matters were hardly separate domains, even if Blackwelder and McClung might have seen them that way. See, e.g., Cheng, *Citizens of Asian America*; Plummer, *In Search of Power* and *Rising Wind*; Rosier, *Serving Their Country*; Cobb, *Native Activism*; Borstelmann, *Cold War*; Dudziak, *Cold War Civil Rights*; and Von Eschen, *Satchmo* and *Race against Empire*.

143. Blackwelder mentions Eisenhower's note in Blackwelder to McClung, May 19, August 24, 1962; and singing for an inauguration party in Blackwelder

to McClung, December 11, 1970, all in McClung Papers. The note itself has not survived either in the Blackwelder Papers or at the Eisenhower Presidential Library (Thomas W. Branigar, archivist, personal communication with author, May 21, 2007). Eisenhower took great pride in his western upbringing and was a voracious consumer of western fiction. See Slotkin, *Gunfighter Nation*, 2; and more generally, the Dwight D. Eisenhower Presidential Library, Museum, and Boyhood Home website, accessed June 2, 2011, and again April 25, 2020, https:// www.eisenhowerlibrary.gov. See esp. the web pages there titled "Ike and Mamie's Favorites" and "Quotes." Despite his own appropriation of western metaphors to express policy goals, then president John F. Kennedy, who had announced a "New Frontier" when he accepted his party's nomination at the 1960 Democratic National Convention, did not congratulate Blackwelder. Cold Warriors of all stripes loved the West, but they loved party lines more. See Slotkin, *Gunfighter Nation*, esp. 1–3, 489–533; and, more generally, Chafe, *Unfinished Journey*, 4th ed., 177–220. I take up Blackwelder's political leanings more fully in parts 2 and 3.

144. McClung to Blackwelder, May 28, 1958, McClung Papers.

145. For the former, see *New York Times*, May 3, August 3, 1958. For the latter, see McPherson, *Yankee No!*

146. See overview in Chafe, *Unfinished Journey*, 4th ed., 201–5.

147. McClung to Blackwelder, August 17, September 11, 1957; and Blackwelder to McClung, August 24, 1957, McClung Papers. On Cristobal Carson and María Guadalupe Richards Carson, see Quantrille D. McClung, *Carson-Bent-Boggs Genealogy*, 79–81. She does not mention the alleged double murder or possible illegitimacy.

148. Blackwelder to McClung, September 18, [1957]; and McClung to Blackwelder, October 9, 1957, McClung Papers. For information on Julián Carson and Pasqualita Tobin Carson, including a newspaper account that Julián was "shot by his horse" in 1889, see Quantrille D. McClung, *Carson-Bent-Boggs Genealogy*, 75–76, which does not mention the alleged murder. Blackwelder had told McClung that "William [Julián] was accidentally shot *from* his horse rather than *by* it" in the letter dated September 18, [1957], but McClung, who had a sense of humor, reproduced the newspaper quote uncorrected in her book.

149. By contrast, genealogist María C. Martínez investigates both incidents, concluding that Julián, also known as Billy, did indeed shoot Pasqualita's father, frontiersman Tom Tobin, but did not kill him. And she offers newspaper evidence that Cristobal fatally shot both his mother- and father-in-law, Mañuelita Lujan and William Richards (though she does not address Kit Carson III's alleged illegitimacy). Martínez et al., *María Josefa Jaramillo*, 7–8, 13–18.

150. For the first quotation, see Blackwelder to McClung, August 24, 1957; for the second, see McClung to Blackwelder, October 9, 1957, both in McClung Papers.

151. There were several grandsons who claimed the name Kit Carson in the third generation; see Quantrille D. McClung, *Carson-Bent-Boggs Genealogy*, 78, 80, 81.

152. McClung to Blackwelder, May 11, 1958, McClung Papers.

153. For genealogical information on both Rumaldas, see Quantrille D. McClung, *Carson-Bent-Boggs Genealogy*, 84, 89, 91–92, 102, 107, 176.

154. McClung to Blackwelder, May 11, 1958, McClung Papers. McClung also wrote to historian David Lavender (author of *Bent's Fort*) about the Rumaldas; McClung to Lavender, September 10, 1957; and Lavender to McClung, September 30, 1957, McClung Papers. He was no help.

155. Quantrille D. McClung, *Carson-Bent-Boggs Genealogy*, 91.

156. McClung, 177–78, italics in the original.

157. Blackwelder to McClung, July 14, 1969, McClung Papers. I conclude McClung and Blackwelder's encounter with nineteenth-century nonmarital intimacies in part 2.

158. For the dominant discourse, see, e.g., May, *Homeward Bound*. For what that discourse obscured, see, e.g., Weiss, *To Have and to Hold*; and Meyerowitz, *Not June Cleaver*.

159. This was a deeply contested prescription in this era, linked as it was to even larger issues of national identity. See Reumann, *American Sexual Character*; and David Johnson, *Lavender Scare*.

160. Doris Lance, personal communication with author, June 5, 2003, emphasis mine.

161. Phrase and analysis from May, *Barren*, esp. 127–49.

162. McClung to Stephanie Tally, October 29, 1972; for the difficult marriage and subsequent divorce, see Tally to McClung, n.d. [Christmas 1973], both in McClung Papers.

163. On those prescriptions, see May, *Homeward Bound*; and Weiss, *To Have to Hold*, who do not fully agree on their content. May sees stress on containment of women in the home, while Weiss sees a push toward gender egalitarianism in marriage. No doubt the two emphases coexisted—this was a time of change—but both also buttressed heteronormativity.

164. See Karen Manners Smith, "New Paths to Power"; Sarah Deutsch, "From Ballots to Breadlines"; Cott, *Grounding of Modern Feminism*; Rosalind Rosenberg, *Beyond Separate Spheres*; and Stansell, *American Moderns*. It gives me pause to suggest here that McClung and Blackwelder were middle class. They both came from arguably middle-class backgrounds, though not particularly secure ones. As adults, they aspired to maintain such a status and often benefited from seeming to occupy it. But the material conditions of their lives mostly did not match their aspirations.

165. See Freund, "Marketing the Free Market"; Self, *American Babylon*; Sugrue, *Origins of the Urban Crisis*; Nicolaides, *My Blue Heaven*; Lizabeth Cohen, *Consumers' Republic*; Kruse, *White Flight*; and Avila, *Popular Culture in the Age of White Flight*.

166. According to a history compiled by the Arlington County Civic Federation, projects boomed there from the 1930s through the 1950s to house federal employees; they were "among the first FHA ... insured developments," which, given the racially discriminatory practices of lenders countenanced by the FHA, means that a subdivision such as Columbia Heights was racially exclusive. "Social

History of Columbia Heights," Histories of Arlington Neighborhoods and Civic Organizations, Arlington County Civic Federation archived website, accessed May 20, 2017, www.civfed.org/histchca.pdf.

167. *Lusk's Northern Virginia* (1955) shows that the Blackwelders purchased their home in 1952 for $11,800; *Lusk's Northern Virginia* (1962) shows that they sold the home in 1958 for $10,250 and that the purchasers assumed the balance of their mortgage. The description of the duplex and neighborhood comes from these sources; site visit, November 2010; and *Plat Book*, Virginia Room, Arlington Public Library, Arlington, Virginia.

168. Blackwelder to McClung, October 3, November 5, 1957, McClung Papers. The allusion, of course, is to Woolf, *Room of One's Own*; and see the discussion in Walker, *In Search of Our Mothers' Gardens*, 231–43. What is called Alexandria includes both the independent City of Alexandria as well as an area under the jurisdiction of Fairfax County. Bernice and Harold moved to the Fairfax portion. The description of the Alexandria house and neighborhood that follows comes from *Lusk's Fairfax County* (1959, 1963); 1962 real estate listing, Blackwelder Papers; site visit, November 2010; and *Fairfax County Real Property Identification Maps*, Virginia Room, City of Fairfax Regional Library, Fairfax County Public Library, Virginia. Thanks to librarian Suzanne Levy for helping me locate the Blackwelders' Fairfax County home, which was made difficult because Parklawn street addresses were changed in 1965. She helped me find the plat map at Fairfax County, Virginia, website, accessed June 7, 2011, http://icare.fairfaxcounty.gov/Forms/MapDatalet.aspx?taxyear=2012&ownseq=1&roll=REAL&jur=&sIndex=0&idx=1&LMparent=138 (web page no longer available).

169. In the summer of 1962, Bernice wrote to Quantrille, "It is good to hear that you may be visiting in the East and come in this direction. Remember we have an extra room that is 'yours' for as long as you would like to stay. . . . It would be our pleasure to have this opportunity to get better acquainted. We have anything but a routine way of living so you would not be company and could come and go as you like." Bernice also recalled Quantrille's visit in a letter she wrote eight years later. Blackwelder to McClung, August 24, 1962; n.d. [ca. January 5], 1970, McClung Papers.

170. Bernice Blackwelder, letters to the editor, *Washington Post*, March 15, 1957; December 24, 1959. Blackwelder sent the 1957 letter to correct what she saw as a misstatement in an earlier *Post* article, which held that Lt. Edward F. Beale first brought news of the 1848 California gold discovery to the East. Blackwelder maintained that Beale deserved credit only for delivering official news to the federal government, because Carson, as a cross-country courier, carried a California newspaper report of the discovery earlier. In fact, Carson may or may not have been the first to bring the news to the East. See Harvey L. Carter, *"Dear Old Kit,"* 120. Blackwelder's 1959 letter marked the sesquicentennial of Carson's birth.

171. On white, working-class suburbs, see, e.g., Nicolaides, *My Blue Heaven*.

172. This much-simplified summary of city-suburb relationships is derived from Kruse and Sugrue, *New Suburban History*; Freund, "Marketing the Free Market"; Sugrue, *Origins of the Urban Crisis*; Self, *American Babylon*; Lizabeth

Cohen, *Consumers' Republic*; Hirsch, *Making the Second Ghetto*; and Satter, *Family Properties*. No single book covers this process in the Washington, D.C., metropolitan area, but see Krugler, *This is Only a Test*, esp. 145–47; Siskind, "Suburban Growth"; and Friedman, *Covert Capital*.

173. Blackwelder to McClung, May 19, 1962, McClung Papers. The transience of the suburbs was a focus of William Whyte's 1950s classic *The Organization Man* (267–80).

174. Blackwelder to McClung, September 24, 1960, McClung Papers. Two months later, Bernice told Quantrille that she was researching recipes so that they could serve "a traditional Old Dominion" Thanksgiving meal at the restaurant (Blackwelder to McClung, November 19, 1960, McClung Papers). The business was on Franconia Road in Fairfax County, and according to directory listings, it featured barbecue, chicken, prime rib, and steak. *Washington Yellow Pages, April 1960*, 872; *Washington Yellow Pages, May 1961*, 896.

175. Blackwelder to McClung, April 1, May 1, June 8, 1962, McClung Papers. Blackwelder's Barbeque Carry-Out is listed in *Hill's Arlington County Directory* (1963). The shopping center, at a busy intersection on Columbia Pike in Arlington, can be seen in *Plat Book*, Virginia Room, Arlington Public Library, Arlington, Virginia. In November 2010, it was a strip mall called Barcroft Shopping Center (site visit).

176. Blackwelder to McClung, August 24, 1962, McClung Papers. After this letter, there is a three-year gap in the correspondence between McClung and Blackwelder.

177. Real estate listing for property at 7300 Yellowstone Drive, Alexandria, Virginia, Blackwelder Papers. The house was described as a "nice clean Parklawn Rambler, 2 blocks from pool," with a "Fantastic View," and priced at $18,500. The existing loan was $14,200. The house sold in January 1963, and the new mortgage was for $17,500, which suggests that if the new owners made a down payment, the Blackwelders may have received their asking price and walked away with a few thousand dollars; see *Lusk's Fairfax County* (1963).

178. McClung to Blackwelder, January 18, 1975, McClung Papers. McClung had retired on disability in 1948; see part 3.

179. McClung lived at 975 Washington Street until 1962, when she moved to 1285 Clarkson Street. I tracked McClung's addresses through her letters in the McClung Papers; through the *Colorado Genealogist*, which lists addresses for officers and members of the Colorado Genealogical Society; and through Denver city directories (e.g., *Polk's Denver City Directory*, 1960 and 1963). Building descriptions are based on site visits between 2000 and 2010.

180. Leonard and Noel, *Denver: Mining Camp*, 374–75, 389–93.

181. Ono, "Crossroads of Indian Country," 112–13, 117–21. Ono adds that Navajos, unlike members of other tribes, tended to congregate in a single area (southeast of downtown Denver), though most returned to the reservation within a year. See also George, "Mile High Metropole." Despite an influx of American Indians, Capitol Hill in 1960 was 98 percent white; see U.S. Bureau of the Census, *Census Tracts*.

182. Leonard and Noel, *Denver: Mining Camp*, 394; Ono, "Crossroads of India[n] Country," 56–68.

183. Work on black civil rights (a movement that long predated World War II and white response is voluminous. On the response, see esp. Webb, *Massive Resis[tance]*. On the movement and its historiography, see, e.g., Chafe, *Unfinished Jour[ney]*, 4th ed., 146–76; Jacquelyn Dowd Hall, "Long Civil Rights Movement"; an[d] Gaines, "Historiography of the Struggle." On the West, where African American[s] more often lived alongside other racialized peoples, see Taylor, *In Search of th[e] Racial Frontier*, 278–310; and Brilliant, *Color of America*.

184. These two meetings are recalled in Blackwelder to McClung, [January 5], 1970, McClung Papers.

185. Although the context differs, Tyson, *Blood Done Sign My Name*, provides crucial insights into related aspects of white racial etiquette in this period.

186. Pascoe, *What Comes Naturally*.

187. While McClung's lack of concern about Carson's intermarriages and Black-welder's interest in them might be explained by the genre differences between McClung's genealogy and Blackwelder's biography, McClung's letters evince no concern either. Then, too, McClung made conscious decisions to include in her genealogy evidence of nonmarital intimacy in the Carson family tree and to ex-clude evidence of murder, decisions that suggest moral and ideological judg-ments.

188. Although it is about another time and place, Michael Salman's *Embar-rassment of Slavery* informs my thinking. Salman draws from a remark in Patter-son, *Slavery and Social Death*, ix. The embarrassment of slavery also shaped the U.S. Civil War centennial (1961–65), which coincided with the publication of McClung's and Blackwelder's books. A group of amateur and a few profes-sional historians urged the federal government to commemorate the war, and they got their wish in 1957 when the Eisenhower administration established the U.S. Civil War Centennial Commission. The commemoration foundered in large part because the civil rights movement kept the Civil War's relationship to slavery visible in ways that precluded a nationalistic, Cold War casting of the conflict as a sectional dispute that gave rise to a peerlessly powerful United States. Cook, *Troubled Commemoration*.

189. On this issue, see Lamar's classic "From Bondage to Contract" as well as work that builds on his analysis; e.g., Peck, *Reinventing Free Labor*; and Stacey L. Smith, *Freedom's Frontier*.

190. Buscombe, *BFI Companion*, 417. Yoggy ("Prime Time Bonanza!," 176–78) places *The Rifleman* in the context of other domestic Westerns.

191. This sentence and the title of the section owe a debt to Borstelmann, *Cold War*.

PART TWO

1. Quantrille D. McClung, *Carson-Bent-Boggs Genealogy Supplement*.

2. I established the timing of this trip, which my memory placed vaguely in the early 1970s, in part through my own teenage scrapbooks as well as an eight-

ear (1969–77) correspondence I maintained with Lauren Vincent (now Cross) of Kenosha (now Eagle River), Wisconsin; scrapbooks and letters from Lauren Vincent in author's possession. I also consulted with my late mother, Janet Stecker Johnson of Madison, Wisconsin.

3. See discussion of *The Rifleman* in part 1. A memorable episode that reflects the themes developed here is "The Boarding House" (1959), featuring Sarah Selby as Agnes Hamilton, a killjoy eastern woman, and Katy Jurado as the true westerner, Julia Andueza, an alluring Basque boardinghouse keeper.

4. This area is now part of the Beaverhead-Deerlodge National Forest, though in the 1970s Beaverhead National Forest was a separate entity. Jack Creek Canyon was located within it. Beaverhead was created by President Theodore Roosevelt in 1908 from previously established forest reserves. It was merged with Deerlodge into a single administrative unit in 1996. See "Beaverhead-Deerlodge National Forest," U.S. Forest Service, accessed November 25, 2018, https://www.fs.usda .gov/detail/bdnf/home/?cid=stelprdb5050011.

5. See Engelhardt, *End of Victory Culture*; and Slotkin, *Gunfighter Nation*.

6. For varied views of Vietnam, see Bradley, *Vietnam at War*; Lind, *Vietnam*; and Marilyn B. Young, *Vietnam Wars*. On domestic politics and foreign policy, see Suri, *Power and Protest*.

7. Schulman, *Seventies*; Carroll, *It Seemed Like Nothing Happened*; Chafe, *Unfinished Journey*, 4th ed., 381–469.

8. These events are chronicled fully below.

9. Blackwelder to McClung, April 12, 1969, McClung Papers, Western History Collection, Western History/Genealogy Department, Denver Public Library (hereafter cited as McClung Papers). *Dictionary of American Biography* was published in twenty volumes by Charles Scribner's Sons for the American Council of Learned Societies in the 1920s and '30s, with many supplements following. It is superseded by *American National Biography Online*; see American National Biography, accessed June 1, 2017, https://www.anb.org/. *The Biographical Directory of the United States Congress* is now an online resource; see "Biographical Directory of the United States Congress," United States Senate, accessed June 1, 2017, https://www.senate.gov/reference/reference_item/Biographical_Directory .htm. But it was available in print through the 1990s. A bicentennial edition appeared in 1989. Some early editions are entitled *Biographical Directory of the American Congress*.

10. For "my men," see, e.g., Blackwelder to McClung, June 19, 1973; and for "underfoot," see, e.g., Blackwelder to McClung, December 30, 1975, both in McClung Papers. The historical context and gendered mechanisms differ, but Steve Stern's notion of the "pluralization of patriarchs" informs my language and analysis here; Stern, *Secret History of Gender*, esp. 99–103, 105–6.

11. See initial discussion in the prologue.

12. My use of the terms "actual women" and "actual men" may seem to reify binary conceptions of sex and gender—that is, the idea that people can be separated into two opposite biological sexes or social genders. This is not my intent. Leaving aside the problem of "biological sex"—which, of course, cannot be left

aside for long, since rigid notions of "two sexes" underpin binary gender conventions—I use the terms "actual women" and "actual men" to refer to people who routinely experience themselves as "women" or "men," respectively, and who are routinely regarded as occupying that same gender category within a social milieu. I also use the term "actual" to distinguish gender traffic with a stronger material base from gender traffic with a stronger symbolic base. Ultimately, biological sex itself can be understood as a complex interaction between material bodies and both scientific and popular discourses about bodily differences. The literature on this question is voluminous, but foundational works by historians include Laqueur, *Making Sex*; and Meyerowitz, *How Sex Changed*.

13. These practices bear some resemblance to what Jack, then writing as Judith, Halberstam helpfully called "female masculinity," though many women who have engaged in such behaviors have done so selectively, rejecting a broader masculine identification. See Judith Halberstam, *Female Masculinity*; and cf. Jack Halberstam, *In a Queer Time and Place*.

14. My understanding of the disempowerment of actual men and the impact of that disempowerment on gender relations broadly conceived derives from literature on men of color, enslaved men, gay men, trans men, working-class men, colonized men, and the like. That literature is too vast to cite here, but one insightful account of how male disempowerment has affected the set of practices called a traffic in women is Steedman, *Landscape*, esp. 68–70.

15. I examine this overidentification in Susan Lee Johnson, "'Memory Sweet to Soldiers.'"

16. On the nineteenth century, see Cronon, *Nature's Metropolis*. On the twentieth, see Stewart-Winter, *Queer Clout*; Fernández, *Brown*; Satter, *Family Properties*; Heap, *Slumming*; Arredondo, *Mexican Chicago*; Baldwin, *Chicago's New Negroes*; Green, *Selling the Race*; Seligman, *Block by Block*; Gina M. Pérez, *Near Northwest Side Story*; Guglielmo, *White on Arrival*; LaGrand, *Indian Metropolis*; Mumford, *Interzones*; Halpern, *Down on the Killing Floor*; Lemann, *Promised Land*; Grossman, *Land of Hope*; Padilla, *Latino Ethnic Consciousness*; and Hirsch, *Making the Second Ghetto*.

17. Work on Denver is more limited. For overviews, see Leonard and Noel, *Denver: Mining Camp*; and Leonard and Noel, *Short History of Denver*. On the nineteenth century, see West, *Contested Plains*; Brundage, *Making of Western Labor Radicalism*; and Barth, *Instant Cities*. On the twentieth, see Philpott, *Vacationland*; Gutfreund, *Twentieth-Century Sprawl*; Ernesto P. Vigil, *Crusade for Justice*; and Worrall, "Labor." Key dissertations and related articles include George, "Mile High Metropole"; Olden, "Whiteness in the Middle"; Ono, "Crossroads of Indian Country"; Bret A. Weber, "Denver Model Cities Program"; Romero, "Of Race and Rights"; Rebecca Ann Hunt, "Urban Pioneers"; Gilmartin, "'Very House of Difference'"; Watson, "Removing the Barricades"; Olden, "Becoming Minority"; and Romero, "Our Selma Is Here," and "¿La Raza Latina?"

18. This paragraph derives from years of conversation with my late life partner, Camille Guérin-Gonzales, whose work on space, time, difference, and power influenced my own in more ways than I can count. The ideas she was developing

volved from her commitment to working-class history and her reading of scholars such as Raymond Williams, Doreen Massey, Henri Lefebvre, David Harvey, and Edward Soja. I could cite those scholars here, since I am at least minimally conversant with their work, but my understanding of their ideas was from the outset refracted through my more immediate encounter with Camille's work in progress, "Mapping Working-Class Struggle in Appalachia, South Wales, and the American Southwest, 1890–1947" (unfinished book manuscript, once under contract with University of Illinois Press, now—in the form of incomplete chapters, outlines, notes, papers presented, and research materials—collected in Guérin-Gonzales Papers, University Archives, University of Wisconsin–Madison). An early foray into part of this material appears in Guérin-Gonzales, "Ludlow to Camp Solidarity."

19. McClung to Blackwelder, June 2, 1969, McClung Papers.

20. Quantrille D. McClung, *Carson-Bent-Boggs Genealogy*, 95, 178. As part 1 indicates, Ignacia Jaramillo had two daughters named Rumalda, one by her first husband, Rafael Luna, and another whose father was long assumed to be Charles Bent but was probably another man. Alfredo Bent's given name is sometimes rendered as Elfego and Bento Long's as Benito. See Quantrille D. McClung, *Carson-Bent-Boggs Genealogy Supplement*, 252.

21. Quantrille D. McClung, *Carson-Bent-Boggs Genealogy Supplement*, 213–35.

22. McClung to Blackwelder, June 2, 1969, McClung Papers; Quantrille D. McClung, *Carson-Bent-Boggs Genealogy Supplement*, 216.

23. McClung also used the word "electrifying" to describe her discovery of genealogical details relating to Kit Carson's half sister Sarah Carson and her marriages to men named Johnson and Payton (or Peyton). See McClung to Blackwelder, July 20, 1975, McClung Papers.

24. McClung to Blackwelder, June 2, 1969, McClung Papers. The character Trollope thus described in *Barchester Towers* is the older sister of Wilfred Thorne, an unmarried woman enamored with England's history before the Norman conquest (that of both the Saxons and the more ancient Britons). McClung might also have identified with Trollope's physical description of Miss Thorne, who, in addition to being "small" and "elegantly made," boasted "a face from which the glow of … youth had not departed without leaving some streaks of a roseate hue." Trollope, *Barchester Towers*.

25. Evidence of McClung's research fills the *Carson-Bent-Boggs Genealogy Supplement* and is summarized in abbreviated form in her acknowledgments, pp. iii–iv, and bibliography, pp. 543–49. Her 1964 trip to Santa Fe is referenced on p. 204, and her trip to Trinidad is described in McClung to Blackwelder, July 20, 1966, McClung Papers.

26. McClung's correspondence with Jack Boyer, then director of the Kit Carson Home and Museum in Taos, New Mexico, supplements her correspondence with Blackwelder in detailing her research for both the *Carson-Bent-Boggs Genealogy* and the *Supplement*. This correspondence spans from 1957 to at least 1974 (some items lack dates). In a letter dated May 29, 1964, McClung tells Boyer of her research trip to Santa Fe, where she consulted the Prince Papers in the

state archives, a collection that includes documents related to Vigil land grant and claims. McClung explains that the archivist helped her with the Spanish language documents, while she read the English-language sources herself. This is the same trip referenced in the *Carson-Bent-Boggs Genealogy Supplement* (204). In a letter dated June 19, 1957, McClung complained to Boyer about the expense entailed in a research trip to California ("I have not found enough material to have justified the expenditure … the trip has cost me"), though she was consoled that the journey also allowed her to visit friends and relatives. Letters exchanged with Boyer are in the McClung Papers.

27. McClung may not have used this work because it does not trace full family lineages but simply identifies the origins of common surnames in New Mexico. See Chávez, *New Mexico Families*. This 1954 work listed the family names of the Spanish Mexicans who participated in both the original colonization of New Mexico, starting in 1598, and the reconquest that followed a dozen years after the Pueblo Revolt of 1680. As noted in part 1, the Vigils and Jaramillos both arrived after 1692. The 1992 revised edition of *Origins of New Mexico Families* adds new information about these older families as well as a section entitled "New Names in New Mexico, 1820–1850" (403–38), which includes the surnames Carson and Boggs. Curiously, the name Bent appears only in reference to the baptized daughter of a Native woman, Guadalupe Bent—not to be confused with Guadalupe Long, who later married Alfredo Bent. This Guadalupe Bent was an Indigenous servant in the household of "Carlos Bent"—presumably the Charles Bent who became the first U.S. governor of New Mexico and was murdered in the 1847 Taos uprising. The baptized Native child was christened María Soledad Bent, and her mother is described as a woman "ransomed from the 'Indians of the North'"—likely Utes. For the Bent entry, see Chávez, *New Mexico Families*, 407. These Indian members of the Bent household do not appear in either the *Carson-Bent-Boggs Genealogy* or the *Supplement*.

28. Quantrille D. McClung, *Carson-Bent-Boggs Genealogy*, 75–83, for Carson and Jaramillo's descendants. John Michael Carson appears on p. 81. For his activities up to 1990, see Graebner, "Carson Returns to Taos," 3–4. For his more recent activities, I rely on my own memory and conversations with him. In 2017, he was employed at Bent's Old Fort National Historic Site in La Junta, Colorado. In 2008, he appeared as a reenactor in the television documentary *Kit Carson*. A gracious and unassuming person, John Carson has been most helpful to me in this project.

29. See, e.g., Quantrille D. McClung, *Carson-Bent-Boggs Genealogy Supplement*, 5–23, 25–41, 44–55.

30. See, e.g., McClung's elaboration on the descendants of Kit and Josefa's son Julián/William, some of whom were named Martínez, in McClung, 201–2. In fact, there is another line of Carson descendants surnamed Martínez. I learned of this line from the descendants themselves when they attended a lecture I delivered at the Colorado Historical Society on March 18, 2008. Darlene Martínez Chávez and Delfino Carson, who are siblings, along with Doran Chávez, Darlene's son and Delfino's nephew, approached me after my talk, explaining that they descend from Kit and Josefa's son Julián/William, who, in addition to raising chil-

ren with his wife, Pasqualita Tobin, also fathered a child with a woman named Mequelita Martínez (there are various spellings of this woman's given name, including Miquelita). The child, Carlos, took his mother's surname. Carlos was the grandfather of both Darlene and Delfino and great-grandfather of Doran. One of Carlos's two sons and several of his grandsons reclaimed the surname Carson, while the daughters and granddaughters kept the surname Martínez, at least until they married. Doran Chávez reiterated all of this to me in a personal communication on April 8, 2008, and Delfino Carson sent me lovely early twentieth-century photographs of the Martínez/Carson clan in a personal communication on March 20, 2008. I am grateful for their generosity and their insistence that the Carson/Jaramillo family story is even more complicated than McClung represented it to be. This line of Carson/Jaramillo descendants is also charted fully in Martínez et al., *María Josefa Jaramillo*, 8–12. In fact, McClung must have encountered this line in her work, because she recorded an address for Carlos G. Martínez of San Luis, Colorado, in a Carson family mailing list she kept. She prefaced his address with the words "any connection[?]," as if to indicate that she had not figured out Carlos's relation to Kit. Later, she added "Great Grandson" next to the name, suggesting that she had determined the relationship. Her listing for Carlos Martínez probably referred to Kit and Josefa's grandson, the one whose mother was named Mequelita, or else to their great-great-grandson, who was also named Carlos Martínez but later changed his surname to Carson. It is unclear whether McClung did not include these descendants in the *Carson-Bent-Boggs Genealogy Supplement* because she was uncertain about their kin ties or because she realized that they were the offspring of a nonmarital relationship between Julián/William and Mequelita. For the ambiguous reference to Carlos G. Martínez, see undated mailing list, McClung Papers.

31. Quantrille D. McClung, *Carson-Bent-Boggs Genealogy*, 7, 69–70, 171–74, 178–79.

32. McClung, 70. Elsewhere in the same volume she writes that Carson's "second marriage" was "to a Cheyenne maiden who lived with him at Bents [*sic*] Fort, Colorado. Not liking the atmosphere, she left and went with her tribe and died about 1890" (7).

33. Quantrille D. McClung, *Carson-Bent-Boggs Genealogy Supplement*, 196–97. Walter Nathaniel Bate of Corpus Christi, Texas, was author of the pamphlet *Frontier Legend*; he later published *General Sidney Sherman*. McClung reproduces part of a letter from Bate that spells out evidence for Carson's marriage to Making Out Road. Bate's conclusions mirror those of Harvey L. Carter in *"Dear Old Kit,"* 82n126. Carter's own papers include copies of correspondence he collected about Making Out Road, with one letter addressed to Bate from Kit Carson's grandson Charles Wood. Along with his letter to Bate, which seems to confirm the marriage, Wood enclosed one he had received from Ralph Moody, who grew up in Carson country in southeastern Colorado, knew Carson contemporaries, and published the popular biography *Kit Carson and the Wild Frontier*. Moody's letter to Wood also echoes Carter's conclusions about the marriage but relies in part on stories Moody heard as a boy from Carson associates. See Wood to Bate,

August 1, 1963, and Moody to [Wood], n.d., Harvey L. Carter Papers, Special Collections, Tutt Library, Colorado College, Colorado Springs (hereafter cited as Carter Papers). For Blackwelder's denial, see Blackwelder, *Great Westerner*, 100n4. See also discussion in part 1.

34. Quantrille D. McClung, *Carson-Bent-Boggs Genealogy*, 98–101.

35. Quantrille D. McClung, *Carson-Bent-Boggs Genealogy Supplement*, 242–54. See George E. Hyde, *Life of George Bent*; the original letters are in the George Bent Papers, Beinecke Library, Yale University, New Haven, Connecticut. McClung got information on William Henry Bent from letters in what she called the Cress Taylor Collection at Norlin Library, University of Colorado Boulder. The collection was, in fact, donated in 1965 by Cress Taylor to what is now Special Collections, Archives, and Preservation there, but it is called the Bent and St. Vrain Collection. Taylor's full name was Caroline Creswell Heald Taylor; she married James Bent Taylor, a descendant of William Bent's brother John. See Quantrille D. McClung, *Carson-Bent-Boggs Genealogy*, 95–96, and *Carson-Bent-Boggs Genealogy Supplement*, 241. Thanks to archivist David Hays for helping me identify the elusive Cress Taylor Collection, which does indeed include letters and photos from Cheyenne and Lakota descendants of William Bent and Owl Woman.

36. McClung to Blackwelder, April 26, 1968, McClung Papers.

37. Quantrille D. McClung, *Carson-Bent-Boggs Genealogy*, 84, 89, 91–92, 102, 107, 176.

38. Quantrille D. McClung, *Carson-Bent-Boggs Genealogy Supplement*, 219.

39. This information came to light through Samuel P. Arnold, proprietor of The Fort, a Denver-area restaurant. The descendants first approached Arnold with their story and he put them in touch with McClung. For discussion of this unfolding story, see Blackwelder to McClung, September 5, 1965; May 16, 25, September 15, 1967; and McClung to Blackwelder, January 24, February 24, March 16, May 4, 1966; May 20, June 7, September 22, 1967. For McClung's correspondence with Arnold, see McClung to "Mr. and Mrs. Sam Arnold," July 7, 1964; and to Arnold, July 25, 1964; January 24, March 28, 1966. See also McClung to Jack Boyer, March 21, 1966; August 14, 1968. All letters in McClung Papers. Sam Arnold graciously explained these matters to me by telephone on June 13 and 14, 2000. He noted as well that family members called the younger Rumalda "Rumaldita," which helped distinguish her from the older Rumalda. For the relationships of Mary Neugent and María Celia Martínez to Rumalda the younger, see Quantrille D. McClung, *Carson-Bent-Boggs Genealogy Supplement*, 221–33.

40. Blackwelder to McClung, May 16, 1967, McClung Papers.

41. Blackwelder to McClung, May 25, 1967, McClung Papers.

42. McClung to Blackwelder, June 7, 1967, McClung Papers.

43. See Quantrille D. McClung, *Carson-Bent-Boggs Genealogy Supplement*, 219–21.

44. Blackwelder to McClung, September 15, 1967; and McClung to Blackwelder, September 22, 1967, McClung Papers. McClung was likely worried about offending descendants who claimed Charles Bent, and not Céran St. Vrain, as forebear.

45. For quotation, see Blackwelder to McClung, February 20, 1969; see also

Blackwelder to McClung, October 22, 1968, both in McClung Papers. Much of his information they gleaned from LeRoy Hafen, *Mountain Men*. Similarly, they learned that Ignacia Jaramillo herself, after Charles Bent's death, lived for a time with Jesse Turley. Turley came to New Mexico to settle the affairs of his late brother Simeon Turley, distiller of the famous beverage Taos Lightning, a favorite among fur trappers. Simeon Turley was killed in a separate incident of the 1847 Taos rebellion at nearby Arroyo Hondo. Jesse Turley later became the agent for Carson's memoirs. Blackwelder and McClung gleaned this information from Harvey L. Carter, *"Dear Old Kit,"* esp. 148–49. See Blackwelder to McClung, February 15, 1970; January 13, 1978, McClung Papers.

46. McClung and Blackwelder learned of this relationship from Harvey L. Carter, *"Dear Old Kit,"* 82 (who takes it from Jesse Nelson, Carson's niece's husband, in notebook 8, p. 83, Cragin Papers, Colorado Springs Pioneers Museum, Colorado Springs, Colorado). For quotes, see McClung to Blackwelder, June 2, July 2, 1969; and Blackwelder to McClung, July 14, 1969, all in McClung Papers. Other male historians repeat the story, astoundingly referring to Luna as a "loose" woman (they do not call Carson "loose," even as they recount his many loves); see Simmons, *Kit Carson*, 40; and Sides, *Blood and Thunder*, 34 (Sides calls Luna "a woman with a loose reputation" to distance himself from the slur). Lecompte is also judgmental, but she indicts men as well as women for nonmarital sexual relationships and criticizes Anglo men for pinning responsibility for such ties on *nuevomexicanas*: "Like good Anglo-Saxons from the land of the moral double standard, Americans blamed this 'immorality' on the women." Lecompte, *Pueblo, Hardscrabble, Greenhorn*, 72–73.

47. On the sexual revolution in the United States, see, e.g., May, *America and the Pill*; Escoffier, *Sexual Revolution*; Gerhard, *Desiring Revolution*; Allyn, *Make Love, Not War*; and Beth Bailey, *Sex in the Heartland*.

48. Blackwelder to McClung, May 16, 1967, McClung Papers.

49. Quantrille D. McClung, *Carson-Bent-Boggs Genealogy*, 82.

50. Quantrille D. McClung, *Carson-Bent-Boggs Genealogy Supplement*, 203. See also *Weekly New Mexican Review and Livestock Journal*, April 16, 1885; and [Anderson], *History of New Mexico*, 1:140–41.

51. Quantrille D. McClung, *Carson-Bent-Boggs Genealogy Supplement*, 204. Genealogist María C. Martínez has collected evidence that Josefita lived until 1902 and thus died in the asylum at the age of thirty-four. See Martínez et al., *María Josefa Jaramillo*, 1–2. For Josefita Carson's commitment to the territorial insane asylum in 1898, see civil case no. 2054 (1898), box 13290, Colfax County Court Records, New Mexico State Records Center and Archives, Santa Fe, which includes testimony in both English and Spanish as to her "lunacy" and "mania." Because her father was a Mason, Josefita was buried at a Masonic cemetery in Las Vegas. In 1991, her body was disinterred and reburied alongside those of her parents at Kit Carson Memorial State Park in Taos. See *Rocky Mountain News* (Denver), October 9, 1902; *Albuquerque (N.M.) Journal North*, April 26, 1991; and *Santa Fe New Mexican*, July 21, 1991. Special thanks to Jennifer Holland for locating record of Josefita's commitment.

52. The exception is genealogist María C. Martínez, who, as noted above, offer information about Josefita's death in the asylum but not about Rebecca's suicide

53. Blackwelder to McClung, July 21, 1966 (on Young); April 12, 1969 (on Head) March 17, 1972 (on Prowers), McClung Papers. On the marriage and ascent o John Prowers, see West, *Contested Plains*, 246–50, 253, 302, 327; and Hurd, *Boggs ville*.

54. Blackwelder to McClung, January 19, 1972, McClung Papers.

55. Blackwelder to McClung, May 16, 25 (on Chouteau and Gratiot families), June 8, 1967, September 5, 1969 (on Mormons); June 15, 28, 1972 (on her father); May 14, June 17, 1974 (on soldiers and doctors), McClung Papers.

56. Blackwelder to McClung, May 16, October 15, 1967, McClung Papers.

57. DPL's western history and genealogy units merged in 1995, after McClung's death, to form the Western History/Genealogy Department.

58. A good introduction to collections of western Americana appears under the heading "Collectors and collections of Western American books and manuscripts" in Lamar, *New Encyclopedia*, 230–33.

59. Blackwelder to McClung, November 3, December 14, 1966, McClung Papers. David Myrick was then the author of the two-volume *Railroads of Nevada and Eastern California*. Thereafter he published widely on western railroads, including a third volume of the Nevada-California work (now available as the three-volume *Railroads of Nevada and Eastern California*) as well as *New Mexico's Railroads*. In 1967, Blackwelder put out another feeler to freelance magazine writer John Young, but that association did not work out either. Blackwelder to McClung, March 20, 1967, McClung Papers.

60. Blackwelder to McClung, June 15, 1972; and McClung to Blackwelder, June 24, 1972, McClung Papers. Arnold was author of *Eating Up the Santa Fe Trail* and *The Fort Cookbook*. He also starred in a PBS cooking show from 1968 to 1973; see *Sam Arnold's Frying Pans West*. Blackwelder never asked Arnold to collaborate, though she revisited the possibility later; see Blackwelder to McClung, January 12, 1974, McClung Papers. On the Bowl of the Wife of Kit Carson, see Fort Storyteller, "Bowl of the Wife of Kit Carson," *Fort Stories* (blog), The Fort Restaurant, March 17, 2016, http://thefort.com/bowl-wife-kit-carson. I follow Huntley Dent's recipe in *Feast of Santa Fe* (186–88), which is based on the *sopa* he ate at The Fort.

61. Quotes from Blackwelder to McClung, February 23, August 6, 1968; March 24, 1969; October 25, 1971; [June?], October 16, 1972, McClung Papers.

62. Blackwelder to McClung, February 20, April 12, 1969; August 17, 1973; September 17, 1974; April 24, 1975, McClung Papers.

63. For quote, see Blackwelder to McClung, July 20, 1970; see also Blackwelder to McClung, April 12, 1969, both in McClung Papers. It is hard to quantify how hard Blackwelder worked on the two projects, but her letters suggest no drop-off in labor or productivity as she started on the second book.

64. The emphases on the word "men" are Blackwelder's. For quotes, see Blackwelder to McClung, March 25, 1969; October 30, 1972; January 29, June 19, 1973; and May 14, 1974 (which also includes mention of Stobie), McClung Papers. The

eference work Blackwelder consulted was likely *Biographical Directory of the American Congress, 1774–1971*.

65. See Blackwelder to McClung, May 14, 1974, McClung Papers. Because neither Blackwelder's manuscript nor her notes have survived, it is impossible to know if she planned to include other non-Anglo Americans, but she did not mention other men of color in her letters. On Beckwourth, see Beckwourth, *James P. Beckwourth*; and Elinor Wilson, *Jim Beckwourth*. I base my assessment of Beckwourth's looks on the most oft-reproduced daguerreotype image of him, which appears on the cover of the paperback version of Wilson's biography.

66. McClung to Blackwelder, January 31, 1969; and Blackwelder to McClung, April 12, 1969, McClung Papers. The letter where McClung mentioned the article on Washakie has not survived, but McClung kept notes on what she told Blackwelder in her March 27 letter, and those notes include "Washakie" among the subjects she addressed (the notes are interfiled with letters Blackwelder and McClung exchanged in spring 1969). The reference work McClung cites is U.S. Department of the Interior, *Biographical and Historical Index*.

67. Blackwelder to McClung, April 19, 1972; and McClung to Blackwelder, April 25, 1972, McClung Papers. When Blackwelder wrote about "the families of the persons who were k[illed] or captured by Cheyennes," she added "1874" in parentheses, but she probably meant 1864. By 1874, Cheyennes and Arapahos had been removed to Indian Territory. Accounts of Sand Creek and the conflicts that preceded and followed it are legion; a good one appears in West, *Contested Plains*, 271–316. For ongoing strife over memory of Sand Creek, see Kelman, *Misplaced Massacre*.

68. See Denetdale, *Reclaiming Diné History*; Hämäläinen, *Comanche Empire*, esp. 336–39; James Brooks, *Captives and Cousins*, esp. 331–40; Sides, *Blood and Thunder*, esp. 306–88; Iverson, *Diné*, 48–65; and Guild and Carter, *Kit Carson*, 231–60. The New Mexican troops rode with the First New Mexico Volunteer Cavalry Regiment.

69. See Denetdale, "Discontinuities." As Denetdale shows, Diné/Navajo memory shifted again in the late twentieth and early twenty-first centuries to reemphasize the violence and privations of the past, especially those imposed during the Navajo campaign, Long Walk, and Bosque Redondo period. This shift culminated in the 2005 dedication of the Bosque Redondo Memorial at Fort Sumner, New Mexico. On the late 1960s, see also Iverson, *Diné*, esp. 244–45.

70. Denetdale, "Discontinuities"; Iverson, *Diné*, 227–73; Wilkinson, *Blood Struggle*. Wilkinson's narrative of Indian revival in the second half of the twentieth century demonstrates how widespread, and yet tribally specific, struggles for sovereignty were. See also Cobb and Fowler, *Beyond Red Power*.

71. "Biography," in inventory, Witt Papers, Center for Southwest Research, Zimmerman Library, University of New Mexico, Albuquerque; Shreve, *Red Power Rising*, and see Witt's foreword to the book, xi–xiii; Smith and Warrior, *Like a Hurricane*, esp. 42–46; LaGrand, *Indian Metropolis*, 184–93; and Harvey L. Carter, "Curious Case," esp. 95–97, and introduction, 1–3.

72. Harvey L. Carter, introduction, 1.

73. *Catalyst*, September 28, 1972. Thanks to archivist Jessy Randall, Special Col lections, Tutt Library, Colorado College, Colorado Springs, for supplying me with this article.

74. Harvey L. Carter, *"Dear Old Kit."*

75. Harvey L. Carter, "Curious Case."

76. Although "racist" had been in use since the 1920s, it (and "racism") first appeared in *A Supplement to the Oxford English Dictionary* in 1982. See Oxford English Dictionary, s.v. "racist," accessed June 17, 2011, https://www.oed.com.

77. Harvey L. Carter, "Curious Case," 98–105. He also notes that Carson did not oversee the Long Walk.

78. By using the word "debatable," I do not mean to imply that I disagree with Carter's arguments in every particular. I do mean to suggest that most of the actions Carter cites as evidence of Carson's forbearance toward and friendship with Indigenous people can be analyzed and interpreted to different ends. Carson *was* quite unlike contemporaries George Armstrong Custer and James M. Chivington, but he also was, both wittingly and unwittingly, an agent of U.S. empire. For more subtle assessments of Carson's relations with Indigenous peoples, see Dunlay, *Kit Carson*; and Blackhawk, *Violence over the Land*, 201–22 passim.

79. Harvey L. Carter, "Curious Case," passim, quotes on 97, 98, 108.

80. For the early years of the Westerners, including the Denver Posse, see part 1.

81. *Taos (N.M.) News*, July 11, 1973. The group called for Nixon's resignation because of the Watergate scandal; *Taos (N.M.) News*, June 6, 1973. The GI Forum already had chapters elsewhere in New Mexico. On the national organization, see Allsup, *American G.I. Forum*; Ramos, *American G.I. Forum*; and helpful contextualization in David Gutiérrez, *Walls and Mirrors*. On Chicana/o activism broadly in New Mexico, see Maciel and Peña, "La Reconquista."

82. On New Mexicans in the Battle of Bataan and the Bataan Death March, and on the 200th Coast Artillery, see Rogers and Bartlit, *Silent Voices*, 36–82; and Cave, *Beyond Courage*.

83. *Taos (N.M.) News*, July 4, 1973; *Albuquerque Tribune*, July 25, 1973.

84. *Taos (N.M.) News*, July 11, 1973.

85. The UPI story seems to have been based on a press release dated before the Taos GI Forum meeting took place. See *Clovis (N.M.) News Journal*, July 3, 1973; *Albuquerque (N.M.) Journal*, July 6, 1973; *Albuquerque (N.M.) Tribune*, July 6, 1973; *Las Cruces (N.M.) Sun-News*, July 6, 1973; and *Santa Fe New Mexican*, July 8, 1973.

86. *New York Times*, July 8, 1973.

87. *Taos (N.M.) News*, July 11, 1973.

88. This summary of tricultural rhetoric and the emergence of the "Spanish American" in New Mexico relies on Mitchell, *Coyote Nation*; Montgomery, *Spanish Redemption*; Nieto-Phillips, *Language of Blood*; and Chris Wilson, *Myth of Santa Fe*. As Camille Guérin-Gonzales reminded me, New Mexico was part of Mexico for less than three decades (from the 1820s to the 1840s) but a part of the Spanish Empire for over two centuries (from the late sixteenth to the early nine-

eenth century), so it is not simply capitulation to anti-Mexican racism that explains the "Spanish American" moniker.

89. See also Chris Wilson's discussion of the relationship between Mexican and New Mexican versions of triculturalism and the relationship of both to Chicano identity (*Myth of Santa Fe*, esp. 159).

90. *Taos (N.M.) News*, July 10, August 1 (quote), 1973.

91. *Taos (N.M.) News*, July 10, 1973.

92. *Taos (N.M.) News*, July 11, 1973.

93. On equestrian raiding of (and trading with) *hispano* and Pueblo Indian villagers in northern New Mexico and on the 1847 Taos rebellion, see, e.g., James Brooks, *Captives and Cousins*, 80–116, 281–92; Blackhawk, *Violence over the Land*, 36–38, 49, 55–56; Iverson, *Diné*, 21–34; McNitt, *Navajo Wars*; and Reséndez, *Changing National Identities*, 253–63. Pueblo people also engaged in the 1837 Chimayó rebellion, in which *hispano* and Indian villagers of the upper Rio Grande revolted against aspects of Mexican rule; see Reséndez, *Changing National Identities*, 171–96; and James Brooks, *Captives and Cousins*, 273–80. I do not mean to overstate alliances between *hispanos* and Pueblo Indians. Given the history of Spanish colonialism, they were at odds with each other as often, if not more often, than they were allied. I only mean to note the history of intermittent alliance.

94. Dunlay, *Kit Carson*, 157–58, 164–68, 192–93; Blackhawk, *Violence over the Land*, esp. 42–45, 55–58, 213; Hämäläinen, *Comanche Empire*, esp. 81–83; Spicer, *Cycles of Conquest*, esp. 152–71; Ramón A. Gutiérrez, *When Jesus Came*, esp. 158–59.

95. Wilkinson, *Blood Struggle*, 206–20; Gordon-McCutchan, *Taos Indians*; Ebright, Hendricks, and Hughes, *Four Square Leagues*, 293–319.

96. On pan-Indianism, see, e.g., Smith and Warrior, *Like a Hurricane*; and Troy Johnson, Nagel, and Champagne, *American Indian Activism*. For a critique of overemphasis on the Red Power era, with its pan-Indian protests, see Cobb and Fowler, *Beyond Red Power*, esp. introduction; and, both more obliquely and comprehensively, Wilkinson, *Blood Struggle*.

97. *Taos (N.M.) News*, May 30, July 25, 1973, December 5, 1974. The Taos Pueblo People's Committee did not disband until summer 1976, after a major upheaval that unseated elected tribal officials and closed the pueblo to outsiders for two days at the height of tourist season. See *Taos (N.M.) News*, July 29, 1976. Shirley Hill Witt saved documentation of the conflict between the Taos Pueblo People's Committee and the tribal government; see Witt Papers, Center for Southwest Studies, Zimmerman Library, University of New Mexico, Albuquerque, esp. box 5, folder 16. None of the documents Witt collected reflect the People's Committee's endorsement of the GI Forum's drive to change the park name.

98. For a brief period in the early 1970s, the royal court for the Fiestas featured three *reinas*, one Spanish, one Anglo, and one Native American. See "Past Royalty, *Las Reinas de Taos*, 1961–1970," Fiestas de Taos website, accessed June 7, 2017, http://fiestasdetaos.com/past-royalty-1961-1970; and "Past Royalty, *Las Reinas de Taos*, 1971–1980," Fiestas de Taos, accessed June 7, 2017, http://fiestasdetaos.com/past-royalty-1971-1980.

99. For the plans, see *Taos (N.M.) News*, July 16, 1973; UPI, *Clovis (N.M.) News*

Journal, July 13, 1973; and UPI, *Albuquerque (N.M.) Journal,* July 13, 1973. For post rally coverage, see *Taos (N.M.) News,* August 1, 1973; *Albuquerque (N.M.) Journal* July 26, 1973; and *New York Times,* July 29, 1973.

100. Jack Boyer, director of the Kit Carson Memorial Foundation in Taos, remained silent at the height of this controversy but several months later wrote a letter to the editor of the local paper explaining that he had been "a comrade-in-arms with Big Jim Lujan [on the Bataan Death March] and also a family friend for many long years." Boyer broke his silence by stating that the Lujan family had been "grossly and unfairly used" by local activists, and he urged those who still opposed the park name change to contact their state legislators. *Taos (N.M.) News,* January 30, 1974. The park name was not changed, though a movement to do so arose again in 2014; see, e.g., *Albuquerque (N.M.) Journal,* June 20, 2014; *Santa Fe New Mexican,* August 8, 2014; and *Indian Country Today* (Washington, D.C.), June 17, 19, July 12, 16, 2014.

101. Arnold to "Scalpers," March 28, 1974, Carter Papers. See also Corinne Joy Brown, "Fort."

102. *Santa Fe New Mexican,* April 7, 1974.

103. *Santa Fe New Mexican,* April 9, 1974.

104. Arnold interview.

105. Blackwelder to McClung, April 30, 1974, McClung Papers.

106. McClung to Blackwelder, April 15, 1974, McClung Papers; Arnold interview. Estella Carson was also known as Stella and Estafanita. Her husband's full name was Spear Erasmus Wood. Quantrille D. McClung, *Carson-Bent-Boggs Genealogy,* 82, 83, 85. McClung may have written more about the Carson controversies than has survived in her papers. She typed and made carbon copies of her own letters and saved these along with the letters Blackwelder sent to her. McClung did not make, or at least did not save, copies of every letter she wrote. But on the copies she saved, she sometimes jotted notes to herself about matters she had related to Blackwelder in handwriting. No notes about the Carson controversies survive.

107. Blackwelder to McClung, April 30, 1974, McClung Papers; Dee Brown, *Bury My Heart.* This was not the first time the two women corresponded about Brown and his work. When *Bury My Heart at Wounded Knee* was first published, McClung received a copy as a gift from distant relatives of the nineteenth-century Bent family. She described the book to Blackwelder as "a history, by an Indian, of the white conquest of the West from the Indian point of view." Blackwelder replied that she had seen the book at the Chicago department store Marshall Field's and read installments in the newspaper, noting, "I have read other books by him and respect his ability." McClung to Blackwelder, November 22, 1971; and Blackwelder to McClung, December 10, 1971, McClung Papers.

108. Blackwelder to McClung, April 30, 1974, McClung Papers. Blackwelder also reminisced about her role in a 1950s controversy involving the park, when there was a proposal to build a highway through it. Living in suburban Washington, D.C., at the time, she telephoned a National Park Service official at the Department of the Interior, who in turn called a colleague based in the Southwest, which she claimed "did the trick and the park was saved." Various earlier chal-

enges to the park, including proposed highway construction, are covered in the *Santa Fe New Mexican*, February 14, 1965, in an article occasioned by the most recent challenge—a move by the Taos town council to transfer the park from state to city jurisdiction (that move failed).

109. Blackwelder to McClung, May 14, 1974, McClung Papers. Blackwelder also mentioned the Carson controversy in letters dated June 17 and July 30, 1974, mostly reiterating her earlier observations.

110. Blackwelder to McClung, April 16, 1970, McClung Papers. On the "hippie invasion," see Sherry L. Smith, *Hippies, Indians*, 113–44. In 1969, the annual Fiestas de Taos were canceled because of "Hippie Problems." "Past Royalty, *Las Reinas de Taos*, 1961–1970," Fiestas de Taos website, accessed June 7, 2017, http://fiestasdetaos.com/past-royalty-1961-1970.

111. McClung to Jack Boyer, March 19, 1971, McClung Papers. In this letter, McClung describes her collection of clippings, which she thought she might donate to the Kit Carson Home and Museum in Taos. Boyer was the museum's director. In the end, McClung decided to give at least some of these materials to the Colorado Historical Society. A letter from a staff member documents the donation: Alstine F. Salter to McClung, May 30, 1972, McClung Papers. See also the attached deed of gift, dated May 30, 1972, and signed by McClung June 2, 1972.

112. See Lamar, "Much to Celebrate," esp. 400. As Lamar notes, before the *American West* and the *Western Historical Quarterly* were launched, the WHA relied on edited volumes of conference papers, such as Toole et al., *Probing the American West*; and Ferris, *American West*.

113. On Blackwelder's WHA membership, see Blackwelder to McClung, November 18, 1976, McClung Papers.

114. Blackwelder to McClung, September 9, cf. November 18, 1976; for an earlier conference, see Blackwelder to McClung, September 5, 1965, all in McClung Papers. For the material conditions under which Blackwelder and McClung labored, see below.

115. Blackwelder to McClung, March 24, 1969; June 9, 1970; November 18, 1976; September 29, 1978, McClung Papers.

116. Blackwelder to McClung, March 24, 1969, McClung Papers.

117. McClung to Blackwelder, June 24, 1972, McClung Papers.

118. Blackwelder underlined her commitment to facticity when commenting on a fanciful television program featuring Kit Carson and John C. Frémont that McClung had described to her. Blackwelder wrote, "Glad I missed the TV show on Carson and Fremont. Sounds like rubbish. I guess it is too much to ask for historical fact." McClung to Blackwelder, September 20, 1966; and Blackwelder to McClung, September 23, 1966, McClung Papers.

119. Here I rely on Novick, *That Noble Dream*. I do not mean to imply that the ideal of objectivity is the same as the valorization of facts or the eschewal of interpretation. But those most committed to objectivism have believed in and valued facts and trusted only those interpretations that appear to be based on dispassionate reckoning with them. This generalization does not incorporate changes over time in historians' romance with the ideal of objectivity, ably analyzed by

Novick. For his subtle interpretation of the incomplete changes in historians' understandings of objectivity and facts in the postwar era, see Novick, 408–9.

120. The call for an analytical and interpretive western history in this era can be heard in Billington, "Frontier and I." For contextualization of Billington's essay, see Lamar, "Much to Celebrate." For elaboration, see below.

121. Utley describes the decision to launch a scholarly journal, rather than relying on the magazine *American West* as the official publication of the WHA, as the most divisive issue that faced western historians in this period. See Utley, *Custer and Me*, 110–12.

122. Billington, "Frontier and I," 18–19. The first issue of the *Western Historical Quarterly* also included an article on the history of the Westerners, but the author's rollicking tone contrasts with Billington's seriousness of purpose (though Billington's article is hardly without humor), unwittingly lending ammunition to Billington's arguments. See Case, "Westerners."

123. Schoenberger, "Interpretation of Western History." His books are *The Gunfighters* and *End of Custer*. But see also Schoenberger, "Black Man."

124. Schoenberger, "Interpretation of Western History," 232.

125. At the 1976 WHA meeting, 400 people attended the Westerners breakfast. See Ray Allen Billington to Stig [Thornsohn], October 18, 1976, box 12, folder 4, Westerners–Chicago Corral Papers, Newberry Library, Chicago (hereafter cited as Chicago Corral Papers). Billington was writing to Thornsohn about Westerners chapters in Denmark and Norway. Indeed, Billington referred to Thornsohn as "the Johnny Appleseed of the Scandinavian corrals." In 2017, Thornsohn was still sheriff of the Denmark Corral. See "Westerners International Active Corrals," Westerners International, accessed June 8, 2017, http://www.westerners-interna tional.org/corrals.shtml. Thornsohn has published in Danish on U.S. western and American Indian topics. See Thornsohn, *100 Plakater* and *Dineh*. He is co-editor, with Jens Damm and Annette Damm, of *Dream of America*, on Danish immigrants to North America. Thanks to Pernille Ipsen for consultation. On the Westerners breakfast, see also Leland Case to George LeRoy, October 14, 1969, box 10, folder 1; and W. Turrentine Jackson to Alvin Krieg, November 3, 1972, box 11, folder 1, both in Chicago Corral Papers. By 2016, the annual breakfast had become the Westerners International Reception. See conference program, "Expanding Western Horizons," 56th Western History Association Conference, Saint Paul, Minnesota, October 20–23, 2016, Western History Association, accessed April 25, 2020, https://www.dropbox.com/s/gcerqozipgnbaqv/SEPT%2022%20 FINAL%20VERSION%20OF%20ST%20PAUL%20PROGRAM.pdf?dl=0.

126. Utley, *Custer and Me*, esp. 110–11; "Past WHA Presidents and Executive Directors," accessed April 25, 2020, https://westernhistoryassociation.wildapricot .org/pastpresidents.

127. On the early membership policies of both the WHA and the Westerners, see part 1. I do not know precisely when and how each of the various Westerners chapters revised its practices to allow women to join as regular members (rather than merely corresponding members, who were not welcome at regular meetings). But the Chicago Corral Papers are full of references to that chapter's tran-

ition, which seems to have taken place between 1973 and 1975. See Alvin Krieg o "Messrs. Virgines, Russell, Scott, Henn, Kubicek, Cummings, McKinstry, and Krueger," October 18, 1973, box 17, folder 3; [Krieg] to "Messrs. Virgines, Russell, Henn, and Scott," January 7, 1974, box 17, folder 4 ("I've no idea what the current policy line is—whether we're trying to discourage women as active members, or telling 'em our rolls are filled, or whatever"); and cf. Bruce McKinstry to JoAnn Harris, May 2, 1975, box 17, folder 5 ("The Chicago Westerners Club was organized in 1944 for the purpose of bringing together Chicago area men who are interested in western history. . . . Beginning about two years ago women were admitted to resident membership."), all in Chicago Corral Papers. Nonetheless, the Chicago Corral still sponsored Ladies Nights; see Ladies Night announcement, May 19, 1975, box 17, folder 5, Chicago Corral Papers. The Chicago Corral's transition followed a drop in membership that created a crisis in 1972; see Krieg to "Posseman," August 1, 1972 (a general letter to resident members); [Krieg] to "Messrs. Krueger, McKinstry, Russell, and Scott," August 1, 1972; and McKinstry to [Krieg], August 7, 1972, all in box 11, folder 1, Chicago Corral Papers. According to Mike Lawson, the Potomac Corral voted in 1977 to open membership to all "regardless of creed, color, sex, or national origin" but did not fully "lift its restrictions on women until 1988." See Lawson, "Mr. Case," 16–17. As late as 1985, the Omaha Corral still excluded women. In response, Omaha women organized the Rachel Snowden Corral (named after a white pioneer woman), which allowed men to attend meetings but limited membership to women. In 1996, the Snowden Corral reversed policy and permitted men to join. Later, the Snowden Corral merged into the Omaha Corral. See Rachel Snowden Corral website, accessed June 19, 2011, http://www.nonprofitpages.com/rachelsnowdencorral/index.html; and "Current Inactive Corrals—'Dry Camps,'" Westerners International, accessed December 28, 2018, http://www.westerners-international.org/corrals-drycamp.shtml. On the WHA's gender and racial imbalance, which plagued the organization into the early twenty-first century, see "2005 Membership Survey," Western History Association, accessed April 25, 2020, https://westernhistoryassociation.wildapricot.org/2005Survey; and "The Next Fifty Years Report," 2010, Western History Association, accessed April 25, 2020, https://westernhistoryassociation.wildapricot.org/fiftyyearsreport.

128. Kelly to Carter, April 10, 1974, Carter Papers. At this time, Kelly was the author of *Navajo Indians and Federal Indian Policy, 1900–1935* and *Navajo Roundup*. Later he published *Assault on Assimilation* and *Federal Indian Policy*, a book for young readers.

129. [Wickman] to Harvey and Ruth Carter, April 9, 1974, Carter Papers.

130. Billington to Carter, April 1, 1974, Carter Papers. In addition to the letters quoted, Carter also received letters of support from Donald Jackson (editor, *Papers of George Washington*), Eugene Miller (professor, Ursinus College), Harwood Hinton (editor, *Arizona and the West*), Eleanor Adams (editor, *New Mexico Historical Review*), George Ellsworth (editor, *Western Historical Quarterly*), Merle Wells (director, Idaho State Historical Society), Janet Lecompte (independent historian), Charlotte Trego (former Colorado College student), and

Mary Alice Bohling (no identifiers provided in letter). Notably, four of these letters were from white women, one of them (Adams) a scholarly journal editor and another (Lecompte) a nonprofessional historian who would soon publish two books about Kit Carson's stomping grounds in northern New Mexico and southern Colorado (*Pueblo, Hardscrabble, Greenhorn* and *Rebellion in Río Arriba*). All four of the letters from women were as supportive as those from men, though none employed violent imagery.

131. Ottoson to Carter, April 12, 1974, Carter Papers. Ottoson was incarcerated at the state penitentiary in Sioux Falls, South Dakota. He corresponded with Carter about mountain man William S. "Old Bill" Williams. In addition to Ottoson's letter quoted, there are others in the Carter Papers, mostly discussing fur trade history.

132. For a cogent analysis of this process as the discipline of history professionalized, see Bonnie G. Smith, *Gender of History*. The trajectory in the subfield of U.S. western history was somewhat different, in part because professionalization happened later, well after the professionalization of the discipline. The process within western history was one by which the field became increasingly committed to the norms of the discipline as a whole while at the same time defining itself as a distinct area of inquiry. The active presence in western history of nonprofessionals, most of whom were men, created a set of contests both similar to and different from those Smith analyzes.

133. For a good example of this style war, see the contrast between Billington, "Frontier and I," and Case, "Westerners," in the first issue of the *Western Historical Quarterly*, cited above.

134. My comments here should not be read as derisive, or at least not entirely so, since I am heir to all that I chronicle herein. Description and narration mark my own work as much as analysis and interpretation. As for sartorial style, I, too, have sometimes worn boots and bolos at WHA meetings. On the other hand, I have not spoken the mountain man toast, perhaps in part because I could not afford to attend the annual banquet at the WHA conference until the toast (along with other aspects of the banquet) was falling into disrepute among some scholars on the left, many of them women, people of color, and youngish progressives unfamiliar with the history of the WHA. While complaints about the toast (and the banquet more generally) arose from time to time over the years, they reached a fever pitch in 2004 after a particularly controversial banquet in Las Vegas, Nevada. In response, President-Elect Peter Iverson proposed changes that were instituted at the next year's meeting, in Scottsdale, Arizona. I rely on my own memory for these generalizations, but see also "2005 Membership Survey" (cited n127 above), and esp. the individual comments recorded there. As one WHA member put it, "The banquet toast is a divisive ritual and should be dropped. The banquet speakers have been underwhelming as long as I have been a part of the association, and the individuals who speak often seem to have been invited to antagonize another faction of this membership. The cost of the banquet and luncheon also discriminate against poorer members, students, and faculty from institutions with few resources for travel."

135. See earlier discussion of Blackwelder's and McClung's ties to Arnold. For another reference, see McClung to Blackwelder, July 23, 1972, McClung Papers; here, McClung describes a visit to The Fort during which she was "received like the Queen." See also McClung to Arnold, July 19, 1972; and Arnold to McClung, July 27, 1972, McClung Papers. Arnold remembered both women—but especially McClung—fondly. He recalled assisting McClung in her declining years by bringing groceries to her Denver apartment. Arnold interview.

136. For an overview of Rosenstock's life, see Bower, *Fred Rosenstock*. Rosenstock ran the Bargain Book Store and later Fred Rosenstock, Books, in Denver; published widely distributed catalogs of his stock; and collected western art. For an overview of Mumey's life, see Norma L. Mumey, *Nolie Mumey, M.D.* Nolie Mumey published over thirty limited-edition western books, including *History of the Early Settlements of Denver* and *Old Forts and Trading Posts*.

137. For the exchange between McClung and López, see López to McClung, June 26, 1969; and McClung to López, July 10, 1969, McClung Papers. McClung received no reply from López, and a newspaper credited the tombstone's return to a letter of protest received by New Mexico's state archivist, who in turn contacted the governor (*Santa Fe New Mexican*, October 1, 1970). Eventually, Arnold commissioned a replica of the St. Vrain headstone, which was placed on St. Vrain's grave in Mora County, while the original was put on display in the state capitol building (*Santa Fe New Mexican*, September 24, 1971). For McClung's and Blackwelder's responses to the controversy, see Blackwelder to McClung, August 11, September 5, 1969; and McClung to Blackwelder, October 16, 1970, McClung Papers.

138. Blackwelder to McClung, September 5, [?], 1965, McClung Papers. The letter in which McClung criticized Rosenstock has not survived, but the story she told appears to have been about Rosenstock and a charter member of the Denver Posse, Herbert O. Brayer (Colorado state archivist and a writer who published on the cattle industry). In the second letter cited here, Blackwelder wrote, "Looks like that Rosenstock may hang himself on some of the strings he is pulling. I had him sized up about right the first experience with him."

139. McClung to Jack Boyer, January 29, 1959; to Mumey, January 29, 1959; and to Blackwelder, December 24, 1970, all in McClung Papers.

140. LeRoy Hafen, *Mountain Men*. For Hafen's own account of his life and career, see LeRoy Hafen, *Joyous Journey*.

141. Harvey L. Carter, *"Dear Old Kit"* and "Kit Carson."

142. Blackwelder to McClung, March 9, July 14, 1969, McClung Papers.

143. McClung to Blackwelder, March 15, 1973, McClung Papers. I base my suggestion that Blackwelder cared more about scholarly recognition on the fact that she, more often than McClung, discussed such matters in her letters. See, e.g., Blackwelder to McClung, May 19, 1969; January 22, April 16, 1970, McClung Papers. Sam Arnold thought that Blackwelder wished her work had received more attention from historians. Arnold interview. McClung, for her part, could recognize and accept a scholar's gentle criticism. When she first read Carter's *"Dear Old Kit,"* McClung noted, "[Carter] speaks in a complimentary manner of my work and in one place mentions 'a few slips.' Well, I not only know there were

many slips but some actual 'messes' which I believe I have succeeded in clearing up." She also assured Blackwelder, "He takes your book seriously and evaluates it in relation to others." McClung to Blackwelder, July 2, 1969, McClung Papers. For a similar comment on their status vis-à-vis professional historians, see Mc Clung to Jack Boyer, February 15, 1966, McClung Papers; in this letter, McClung proudly notes that Blackwelder, in identifying a number of Carson's ancestors had "scored off some of the professional historians."

144. On the membership policies of the Denver Posse, see part 1. Materials (mostly meeting announcements) that Carter saved from the Pikes Peak Posse show that women not only were admitted as members but also served on committees. Most of the materials are undated, but they appear to be from the mid-to-late 1970s; Carter Papers.

145. Hafen and Hafen, *Handcarts to Zion*. The Hafens' joint publications are too numerous to cite here, but see, e.g., Hafen and Hafen, *Utah Expedition, Fremont's Fourth Expedition*, and *Colorado Story* (for young readers). In addition, when LeRoy published a memoir, it was of his life and work with Ann; see LeRoy Hafen, *Joyous Journey*. As noted elsewhere, Ann Woodbury Hafen was also a writer of fiction and poetry; see, e.g., Ann Woodbury Hafen, *Quenched Fire*.

146. Janet Lecompte, personal communication with author, November 3, 2001. Lecompte explained that Hafen helped her get an article published in the *Colorado Magazine*, which Hafen edited.

147. For correspondence on these honorary degrees, see Lloyd B. Worner to Peterson, March 14, 1978; and to Mrs. Oliver P. Lecompte, March 21, 1979, Carter Papers. Peterson was a political historian who, at that time, was author of *Freedom and Franchise*.

148. The book that resulted from their collaboration is Guild and Carter, *Kit Carson*. Carter saved Guild's letters from the period of their collaboration, 1980–84; see Carter Papers.

149. McClung to Carter, May 20, 1966; and Carter to McClung, May 23, 1966, McClung Papers.

150. McClung to Carter, May 31, June 13, 1966; January 21, 1967; January 31, July 7, 24, 1969; May 8, 1973; and Carter to McClung, January 19, 27, February 15, 1967; July 8, 1969; May 10, 1973, all in McClung Papers. Carter saved just two of these letters: McClung to Carter, January 31 and July 7, 1969, Carter Papers.

151. No copies of Blackwelder and Carter's correspondence survive, but Blackwelder told McClung about exchanging letters with Carter: Blackwelder to McClung, [ca. January 5], January 8, 22, February 15, 1970; February 26, 1971, McClung Papers.

152. See McClung to Blackwelder, January 27, 1969; and Blackwelder to McClung, [ca. January 5], February 15, 1970; February 26, 1971. For other mentions of Carter, see McClung to Blackwelder, May 31, June 13, 1966; January 31, 1969; July 20, 1975; and Blackwelder to McClung, June 6, 1966; February 20, 1969. All letters in McClung Papers.

153. Many thanks to Elizabeth Jameson and Susan Armitage for helping me identify the first degreed women involved in the WHA.

154. Lecompte, *Pueblo, Hardscrabble, Greenhorn*; Lecompte, *Rebellion in Río Arriba*. I am grateful to the late Lecompte for corresponding with me about her knowledge of McClung and Blackwelder, which Lecompte remembered as limited to brief correspondence with McClung. As Lecompte put it, "I don't remember meeting either of your ladies—although of course I knew who they were." Janet Lecompte, personal communication with author, November 3, 2001.

155. I am grateful to Spence for corresponding with me about these matters. Mary Lee Spence, personal communication with author, November 6, 2001.

156. McClung to Lecompte, November 17, 1957, McClung Papers. This was an inquiry about Boggs family genealogy. Lecompte returned the letter to McClung with a brief response penned on the back. There is also an undated letter from Lecompte to McClung in the McClung Papers that appears to have been written in spring 1972. In it, Lecompte anticipates the publication of the *Carson-Bent-Boggs Genealogy Supplement*: "I hope your work on the genealogy is coming along nicely, and that you haven't forgotten that I want a copy as soon as it is published."

157. Blackwelder to McClung, June 25, 1967, McClung Papers.

158. McClung to Blackwelder, July 6, 1967, McClung Papers.

159. Blackwelder to McClung, August 4, 1962; September 5, 1965, McClung Papers. Bernice's niece and nephew did not recall her movements during these years. Lance and Fowler interview; Doris Lance, personal communication with author, June 5, 2003. Lance remembered visiting her aunt in Alexandria in 1962 but then nothing until after 1965, when the Blackwelders moved to Chicago.

160. Bernice Blackwelder to "Director of the Denver Public Library," January 2, 1963, McClung Papers (this letter was postmarked Omaha, Nebraska, and it explained that Bernice had just moved there from Virginia). Blackwelder recalled her Omaha apartment in Blackwelder to McClung, May 30, 1975, McClung Papers.

161. Blackwelder to McClung, August 10, 1976, McClung Papers (this letter recalls the restaurant the Blackwelders considered buying in Loveland in 1963).

162. *Golden City Directory*; *Denver Telephone Directory*. The Dixie Pit Bar-B-Q had two different addresses in 1964. The Golden address was in an apartment building, so Harold may have used this residential address for business correspondence until the eatery opened in North Denver. Thanks to Jennifer Holland for tracking down these references and to librarians at the Golden Library (Jefferson County Public Library) and Denver Public Library for helping to clarify them.

163. *Bresser's Cross-Index Directory*; Margaret Pead to Bernice Blackwelder, February 1, 1965, Blackwelder Author File, Caxton Press, Caldwell, Idaho (the city directory and the author correspondence place Blackwelder at the same Arvada address). Whatever the Blackwelders rented in Arvada, it must have been small, because after they moved to Chicago and family was due for a visit, Bernice noted, "We are much better off here to have company." Blackwelder to McClung, September 5, 1965, McClung Papers.

164. McClung reported these meetings in letters to Jack Boyer, director of the Kit Carson Home and Museum in Taos: McClung to Boyer, January 2, April 23,

May 8, 29, July 15, 1964. Blackwelder recalled the Estes Park outing in Blackwelder to McClung, July 30, 1974; and she lamented Colorado research she did not finish in Blackwelder to McClung, March 9, 1966. All letters in McClung Papers.

165. Blackwelder to McClung, September [8?], 1965; June 28, 1972, McClung Papers.

166. Blackwelder to McClung, October 14, 1965, McClung Papers. The Blackwelders did not stay long enough in Wrigleyville for Bernice to explain what she meant about not living in a "prime neighborhood." But the population of Lake View (the larger area that encompassed Wrigleyville) had started to shrink in 1950 and the aging residential housing stock (primarily rentals) was deteriorating. The Asian-origin and Asian-descent population (primarily Filipino and Japanese) was increasing, and Asian-owned businesses dotted the area of North Clark Street where the Blackwelders lived. Given Bernice's later reflections on changes in Logan Square, where the Blackwelders moved in 1966, it seems likely that some combination of the proximity of the ballpark; the high-density, older housing; white flight to the suburbs; and the growing presence of a nonwhite population contributed to her opinion of Wrigleyville. See Fadragas, "Lake View."

167. Blackwelder to McClung, September 5, [8?], 1965; March [?], May 6, July 14, August 21, 1966, McClung Papers. For the Blackwelders' union membership (and the 1966 merger of segregated Chicago AFM locals), see below and part 3.

168. Blackwelder to McClung, September 5, [8?], 20, October 14, November 3, 22, December 14, 1965; May 6, 11, June 6, 10, 28, 1966, McClung Papers.

169. Blackwelder to McClung, July 14, 1966, McClung Papers.

170. Description based on site visits, May 2007 and September 2014. Years later, Bernice acknowledged that the expressway was across from the apartment building, not in the next block. Blackwelder to McClung, June 19, 1973, McClung Papers.

171. Cynthia R. Field, "Burnham Plan"; Abbott, "Planning Chicago."

172. Blackwelder to McClung, August 21, 1966, McClung Papers. The headline of a *Chicago Daily News* article (February 23, 1963) noted that blight was undermining the "once plush Logan Square" and observed that "worn mansions stare at 'boulevards of millionaires.'" Housing description based on site visits; and photographs of residences taken by Joseph Domin, 1969 and 1970, in Photograph Files on Chicago Neighborhoods, Chicago History Museum Research Center.

173. "Community Survey Report: Logan Square and Avondale," n.d. [1960s], Logan Square file, in Clippings Files on Chicago Neighborhoods, Chicago History Museum Research Center; Hogan, "Logan Square." According to the priest of a parish a block from the Blackwelders' apartment, the building of the expressway also took a toll on Logan Square's Belgian-descent population; in 1977, only a dozen of over 700 Belgian families remained. "The Friendly Little Corner of Logan Square," *Chicago Tribune Magazine*, November 20, 1977. On Logan Square's growing elderly population, see also *Chicago Tribune*, January 3, 1974.

174. *Chicago Daily News*, February 23, 1963. According to an article published a year later, this 1963 piece prompted the formation of both the Logan Square

Neighborhood Association and The Organization of Palmer Square (Palmer Square was located within the Logan Square neighborhood), which began to promote revitalization. *Chicago Daily News*, April 18, 1964. For more on these organizations, see below.

175. McClung to Blackwelder, July 20, 1966, McClung Papers.

176. Blackwelder to McClung, August 21, September 23, October 18, December 14, 1966; March 20, September 5, 1967; January 22, 1970, McClung Papers. Blackwelder often insisted that management duties did not cramp her style, but she rejoiced when all apartments were full, leaving her "quite free" (September 5, 1967).

177. Blackwelder to McClung, April 16, 1970, McClung Papers.

178. Blackwelder to McClung, June 9, 1970, McClung Papers.

179. Lance and Fowler interview; Doris Lance, personal communication with author, June 5, 2003.

180. Blackwelder to McClung, August 21 (cf. September 23), 1966, McClung Papers.

181. Blackwelder to McClung, March 17, September 15, 1972; January 29, 1973, McClung Papers.

182. Blackwelder to McClung, November 7, 1968, McClung Papers.

183. One of the Blackwelders' neighbors was unmarried and had a cat; she was likely young, too, since Bernice referred to her as a "single girl." Blackwelder to McClung, January 29, 1973, McClung Papers.

184. Blackwelder to McClung, March 11, 1968, McClung Papers.

185. Logan Square's black population represented less than 1 percent of residents in 1960 and 1970 and increased to only 2.7 percent in 1980. But the Latino population grew rapidly from about 600 residents in 1960 to 16,000 in 1970 and 44,000 in 1980. By 1980, Latinos represented as much as half of Logan Square's population; 55 percent of those Latinos were Puerto Rican, 34 percent were ethnic Mexican, and 4 percent were Cuban. Hogan, "Logan Square." See also *Chicago Tribune*, January 3, July 21, November 15, 1974; July 17, 1975; January 18, 1981. Hogan recorded a 1980 "Spanish Origin" population of over 50 percent in Logan Square, while the *Chicago Tribune* (January 18, 1981) set the Latino proportion at 40 percent.

186. Blackwelder to McClung, October 4, 1968, McClung Papers.

187. Blackwelder to McClung, July 25, 1973; and see Blackwelder to McClung, June 9, 1970; October 25, November 16, 1971, all in McClung Papers.

188. Blackwelder to McClung, September 16, 1973; February 3, March 4, June 17, 1974, McClung Papers. There were indeed Latino gangs and street violence in Logan Square and the adjacent Humboldt Park neighborhood; Blackwelder was not making this up. What she did not recognize is that gangs—including white ethnic gangs that policed the boundaries of white ethnic enclaves—reflected as much as they shaped the changing demographics and impoverishment of urban neighborhoods. That Blackwelder did not recognize this reflects institutional, structural, and cultural forces. For example, Gina M. Pérez shows how the 1966 Division Street riots in Humboldt Park, in which Puerto Ricans protested police brutality, helped give rise to characterizations of Puerto Rican communities as

plagued by "gangs, drugs, welfare dependency, and violence." Gina M. Pérez, *Near Northwest Side Story*, 83–91, quote on 85. See also Fernández, *Brown*; and Diamond, *Mean Streets*.

189. I take up Bernice (and Harold) Blackwelder's continuing response to Logan Square's increasing Latino population in part 3.

190. Satter, *Family Properties*; Seligman, *Block by Block*. See also Hirsch, *Making the Second Ghetto*.

191. In the 1940s, the Blackwelders lived in the Austin neighborhood; see part 3. For the transformation of Austin in the 1960s and '70s, see Seligman, *Block by Block*.

192. The best accounts of Chicago's Latino population are Fernández, *Brown*; and Gina M. Pérez, *Near Northwest Side Story*. Neither focuses on Logan Square but rather on adjacent neighborhoods such as Humboldt Park and West Towne.

193. Ribufo, "1974–1988," esp. 101, 104–5; Schulman, *Seventies*, esp. 5–6; Porter, "Affirming and Disaffirming Actions," esp. 59; Cowie, "'Vigorously Left, Right, and Center,'" esp. 84; Cowie, *Stayin' Alive*. (In "'Vigorously Left, Right, and Center,'" Cowie marks the 1974–75 recession as a turning point in labor's fortunes, which had appeared brighter in the early '70s.)

194. Blackwelder to McClung, April 30, 1974, McClung Papers. This selective overview of racial politics in the 1970s is based on secondary sources too numerous to cite in full, but see, e.g., Porter, "Affirming and Disaffirming Actions"; Chafe, *Unfinished Journey*, 4th ed., 302–80; Smith and Warrior, *Like a Hurricane*; Wilkinson, *Blood Struggle*; Self, *American Babylon*, esp. 217–55; Sánchez, *Boricua Power*; David Gutiérrez, *Columbia History of Latinos*, "Demography," and *Walls and Mirrors*. On Chicago, see Padilla, *Latino Ethnic Consciousness*; Gina M. Pérez, *Near Northwest Side Story*; and Fernández, *Brown*.

195. For the small number of black residents in Logan Square, see n185 above. The *Chicago Tribune* (January 3, 1974) noted, "Logan Square has had a three-block triangular pocket of black residents just southeast of Milwaukee and Western Avenues for decades but there has been no substantial black movement into the neighborhood." James LaGrand shows that Chicago's American Indian population increased twentyfold between 1940 and 1970, one-third to one-half drawn there by U.S. government efforts to relocate Indian people to cities in the 1950s. Most of Chicago's Native people lived not in Logan Square but in Uptown and other North Side neighborhoods (Indians also lived on the South Side in Hyde Park, though some were displaced by urban renewal in the 1950s and '60s). LaGrand, *Indian Metropolis*, esp. 112–21.

196. *Chicago Daily News*, April 18, 1964. LSNA records are held by the Chicago History Museum Research Center but were unprocessed when I did work there in 2007.

197. On white neighborhood defense, see, e.g., Seligman, *Block by Block*, 5, 163–65, 213–14; and Sugrue, *Origins of the Urban Crisis*, 236–45.

198. *Chicago Tribune*, January 1, 1974 (quote); July 17, 1975; *Chicago Sun-Times*, July 21, 1974; *Chicago Daily News*, November 15, 1974. On gentrification in Chicago, see Bennett, "Gentrification." For evidence of longer-term gentrification

Logan Square, see "Logan Square's Time Comes Round in Chicago," *New York Times*, January 30, 2011.

199. *Chicago Daily News*, November 15, 1974. On the South Side's Citizens Action Program, see D. Bradford Hunt, "Redlining."

200. *Chicago Sun-Times*, August 7, 1977. The quote is from Shakespeare District commander William Hanhardt, who had spent eight years in Logan Square. The article stated that thirty youth gangs claimed turf in Logan Square and detailed tensions between LSNA, which wanted a crackdown on gangs, and Hanhardt, who favored communication with gang members and saw signs of improved relations between older working-class whites and Spanish-speaking newcomers starting to buy homes in the area.

201. For Lincoln Park, see Seligman, "Lincoln Park." For later gentrification in Logan Square, see *New York Times*, January 30, 2011.

202. *Chicago Tribune Magazine*, November 20, 1977. This article, cited n173 above, was committed to portraying the area as one where folks got along, but the interviews conducted with a variety of residents—white ethnics and Latinos, old-timers and newcomers, young people and the elderly, clergy and police—suggest that Hoff's "live and let live" philosophy was not uncommon. As for white flight, Hoff opined, "I live good. I mean, what am I gonna do, sell the house for maybe seventeen-eighteen thousand and buy another one for sixty-five thousand in the suburbs? What for? To work like a fool to pay the mortgage for the rest of my life? No sir! That's what my brothers and sisters are doin', and to tell you the truth I think they might be just a little jealous of me." My analysis here is influenced by Reiff, "Contested Spaces."

203. The following summary of Harold's work comes from Blackwelder to McClung, September 5, October 14, November 3, 22, December 14, 1965; May 6, August 21, December 14, 1966; July 17, 1967, McClung Papers. I discuss both Harold's and Bernice's union connections, especially their membership in the American Federation of Radio Artists, in part 3. The American Federation of Television and Radio Artists superseded the American Federation of Radio Artists in 1952 (only to be superseded by SAG-AFTRA in 2012). As for Harold's affiliation with AFM, I could not locate a union card for him either in the files still held at the Chicago Federation of Musicians Local 10-208 headquarters or in the historical Chicago chapter files of the AFM, Music Information Center, Visual and Performing Arts Department, Harold Washington Library Center, Chicago Public Library. But Secretary-Treasurer Leo Murphy, Local 10-208, found Harold in a 1950 membership directory; Leo Murphy, personal communication with author, May 6, 2014. In letters, Bernice mentioned that Harold had helped an old friend get reelected to the local's highest office. This would have been Local 10's president Bernard "Barney" F. Richards, who unseated the legendary James Petrillo in 1962. Petrillo had ruled the national AFM with an iron hand in the 1940s and '50s, but even after he declined to run again nationally in 1958, he continued as president of Chicago's Local 10 until Richards defeated him. Harold likely knew Richards in the late 1930s and early '40s, when both performed at the Ivanhoe, a Chicago nightclub and restaurant. In addition to letters cited above, see Bernice Black-

welder Diary, 1937–41, October 13, 1941, Blackwelder Papers, in author's posses-sion; and Sengstock, *That Toddlin' Town*, 164–65. The Chicago AFM had segre-gated white and black locals until 1966. Then, under pressure from the AFL-CIO and embarrassed by continuing Jim Crow unionism in light of the civil rights movement, the locals merged. The merger took place under Richards's presi-dency but only after he tried and failed to prevent it—this even though Richards had campaigned for Local 10's presidency under a banner of a more "democratic" union. His notion of union democracy was geared toward white musicians; it was extended to black musicians only reluctantly. Harold renewed his associa-tion with the Chicago Federation of Musicians and campaigned for Richards's re-election at precisely the moment of this struggle. Halker, "History of Local 208"; Seltzer, *Music Matters*.

204. Blackwelder to McClung, June 6, 1966; May 16, 1967, McClung Papers.

205. Blackwelder to McClung, June 10, 28, 1966, McClung Papers.

206. Blackwelder to McClung, September 5, 1967, McClung Papers.

207. Blackwelder to McClung, September 5, October 15, 1967, McClung Papers.

208. Blackwelder to McClung, November 24, 1967, McClung Papers.

209. Most of the letters Blackwelder wrote in the late 1960s and early '70s in-clude discussion of these matters, but this summary is derived especially from Blackwelder to McClung, May 16, November 13, 1967; June 16, 1969; July 20, November 12, 1970; April 14, October 25, 1971; January 19, February 29, May 24, 31, 1972; March 4, 1974, McClung Papers.

210. Quote from Blackwelder to McClung, March 4, 1974; see also June 17, July 30, 1974. On Harold's new position in 1972, see Blackwelder to McClung, July 23, 1972. All in McClung Papers.

211. Blackwelder to McClung, June 15, 1972. Later in the summer, Bernice wrote, "I have stayed close to home—regular housewife, shopping, cooking & a minimum of cleaning ☹." Blackwelder to McClung, August 16, 1972. All in Mc-Clung Papers.

212. McClung to Blackwelder, June 13–14, 1966. For McClung's sewing, see, e.g., McClung to Blackwelder, September 25, 1971 (McClung had been borrowing a neighbor's sewing machine, but the neighbor moved, so here she describes mak-ing both a housedress and a nightgown—with sleeves—by hand!). All in Mc-Clung Papers.

213. See Quantrille D. McClung, *Carson-Bent-Boggs Genealogy*, 4, 7, 12, 16, 17, 23–25, 61, and *Carson-Bent-Boggs Genealogy Supplement*, 22–23, 167–71.

214. McClung to Blackwelder, June 7, 1967, McClung Papers.

215. It was about eight blocks from her apartment at 1285 Clarkson Street to DPL and another couple of blocks to the Colorado Historical Society, which was then housed in the Colorado State Museum building. McClung sometimes took a city bus to the library, which, in 1975 when she was eighty-five, cost senior citizens fifteen cents. McClung to Blackwelder, July 20, 1975, McClung Papers.

216. Smith interview; Garramone and Kroll interview (in this interview, Garra-mone, a Colorado Genealogical Society member, also related information she had gathered from other members who visited McClung's apartment, including

ay Merrill and Shirley Sheets); McClung to Blackwelder, November 18, 1969, Mc-
Clung Papers.

217. McClung to Blackwelder, September 25, 1968; January 31, November 18, 969; October 16, 1970; and McClung to Henry G. Shearouse, September 11, 1970, all in McClung Papers.

218. E.g., McClung to Blackwelder, May 20, December 24, 1970; June 24, 1972, McClung Papers (in the latter, McClung wrote, "I live on the very edge of consciousness all the time. The Library could tell you how often they have to send me home in a cab & at times I lose the power of speech & they order the cab to the back door ... & put me in the care of the guard there until the cab comes."). Intralibrary correspondence also documents McClung's health problems. See Esther Stokes to [John T.] Eastlick, June 1, 1966; and [Betty Jo] Rule to [Henry G.] Shearouse, June 19, 1970; July 8, 1971, all in Denver Public Library Archives, Western History Collection, Western History/Genealogy Department, Denver Public Library (hereafter cited as DPL Archives). Stokes quotes McClung herself as having said, "I have been very ill—do not know just when I will 'shuffle off this mortal coil.'"

219. McClung to Blackwelder, August 31, 1972 ("life-long disability"); to Harvey Carter, January 21, 1967 ("cerebro-vascular-insufficiency"); to Nolie Mumey, April 11, 1980 ("Dr. Mieries Disease"); and to Stephanie [Tally], October 29, 1972 (meningitis and early retirement), all in McClung Papers. See also Quantrille D. McClung, *Memoirs of My Childhood*, 25 (meningitis).

220. McClung to Blackwelder, September 25, 1968; July 23, 1972 (for visits to the same doctor, see also August 14, 27, 1972), McClung Papers.

221. In addition to McClung's reports of falling ill at the library, cited above, see McClung to Blackwelder, November 27, 1965; January 26, May 4, September 20, 1966; June 7, 16, September 22, 1967; January 1, April 17, 1968; June 6, 1972, McClung Papers. McClung described other health problems after 1972, but not blackouts and crippling headaches; see McClung to Blackwelder, April 15, 1974; January 18, 1975, McClung Papers. She did, however, report a relapse in 1980, when she was ninety years old. McClung to Henry Shearouse, May 2, 1980, DPL Archives.

222. The DPL Archives contain materials that document McClung's relationship to the library after her retirement, and some of these materials are duplicated in the McClung Papers. See, e.g., Eastlick to McClung, December 28, 1956; December 30, 1963; February 14, 1964; April 26, 1965; McClung to Eastlick, August 30, 1962; April 22, 1965; July 8, 1969; Eastlick to "Whom it May Concern," September 18, 1962; June 30, 1966; cabinet meeting minutes, February 6, 1962; and "Estimated Cost of McClung Publication," May 28, 1962, all in DPL Archives. For materials generated during Shearouse's librarianship, see n228 below. On free stuff from DPL, see, e.g., McClung to Blackwelder, April 13, 1973, McClung Papers.

223. Eastlick to McClung, November 10, 1967, DPL Archives. When I interviewed James Kroll, manager of DPL's Western History/Genealogy Department, and Bonnie Garramone, member of the Colorado Genealogical Society, both reflected on the old tensions between the Genealogy Division and the Western His-

tory Department, which did not merge until 1995. Garramone remembered the Western History Department as "high-class," and Kroll likewise recalled "a class distinction between the Western History Department and the Genealogy [Division]," noting that western history was "where the doctors came" and "Genealogy was where the common people came." Garramone and Kroll interview.

224. McClung to Blackwelder, November 24, 1967. McClung also refers to Eastlick's "spiteful letter" in a letter to Blackwelder on July 2, 1969. Both in McClung Papers.

225. McClung to Blackwelder, January 27, July 2, 1969, McClung Papers. She wrote in January, "I do wonder what is the matter with me that I continually receive such treatment from librarians since when I am with others I seem to be considered interesting & ... I can keep them in stitches with my stories." McClung published on Colorado governors' genealogies in the *Colorado Genealogist* from 1947 to 1960. See part 3.

226. McClung first met Shearouse at a reception when he was hired, and the change in atmosphere was immediately apparent. Shearouse was cordial to her, insisting that they should "have a talk," while others also greeted her warmly. McClung to Blackwelder, November 18, 1969, McClung Papers. The elderly McClung's tense relationship with Eastlick and her relief when Shearouse assumed the position of head librarian contrasts with the experience of a younger woman who had a crucial role at DPL in the late 1960s and the 1970s—Kay Collins, who served as librarian for the Conservation Library Collection, an exceptional collection of environmental materials that Eastlick had come to champion along with its environmentalist politics. The more conservative Shearouse disapproved of the Conservation Library Collection's and Collins's activist bent, and under his leadership, as the Reagan revolution took its toll, the conservation library became a shadow of its former self. The story is well told in Kirk, *Collecting Nature*, which also includes a fine primer on the history of women and librarianship.

227. McClung to Blackwelder, July 2, 1970, McClung Papers; Betty Jo Rule to Shearouse, November 27, 1970, DPL Archives.

228. Shearouse to "Mr. Tooley," June 5, 1970; to "Mr. Keech," July 23, 1970 (quote); to Lamar Willis, December 8, 1972; to "Mr. Ivy," July 11, 1973 (this memo directs Ivy to pay McClung a royalty of $1,000 for her work as compiler of the *Supplement*); to Betty Jo Rule, August 20, 1970; and to McClung, August 21, 1970; January 21, 1972; "Mr. Ivy" to Shearouse, May 15, 1973 (this memo shows that DPL invested $4,400 in publishing the *Carson-Bent-Boggs Genealogy Supplement*, with a print run of 500 copies); Rule to Shearouse, June 19, 25, August 18, November 27, 1970; July 8, 20, December 21, 1971; July 6, 1972 (Betty Jo Rule was DPL's public information officer, and she reported to Shearouse about progress on the supplement as well as McClung's health problems); and McClung to Shearouse, September 11, 1970, all in DPL Archives. As with materials reflecting McClung's relationship to DPL under Eastlick, some materials cited from Shearouse's tenure are duplicated in the McClung Papers. See also McClung to Shearouse, June 9, 1970; and Shearouse to McClung, August 20, 1970, McClung Papers (letters not saved in the DPL Archives).

229. McClung to Blackwelder, July 2, 1970, McClung Papers.

230. On the proposed but never published second supplement, see Shearouse ⌐ McClung, February 14, April 9, 1980; and McClung to Shearouse, February 20, ⌐lay 2, 1980, DPL Archives.

231. Smith interview.

232. Blackwelder to McClung, February 21, 1967, McClung Papers.

233. McClung to Blackwelder, December 24, 1970, McClung Papers.

234. McClung to Blackwelder, January 25, 1971, McClung Papers.

235. May McClung to Quantrille McClung, December 26, 1970; May 5, 1971 ⌐quotes); see also Denzel McClung to Quantrille McClung, March [8], n.d. [spring], 1971; Quantrille McClung to May McClung, December 26, 1970; and Quantrille McClung to Denzel McClung, December 29, 1970; January 4, February 14, 1971, all in McClung Papers. McClung also exchanged letters with an old family friend named Ruth, originally from Denver, who lived in Kremmling and was critical of May McClung, calling her "the queerest person" and also noting her religiosity; "Ruth" to Quantrille McClung, February 18 (quote), June 24, 1971, McClung Papers.

236. McClung to Blackwelder, September 25 (and see November 22), 1971, McClung Papers. McClung must have told Blackwelder about the disinvitation to the burial in a letter that has not survived, because on August 18, 1971, Blackwelder wrote to McClung that the "last chapter" of McClung's recent letter, which Blackwelder titled "The Grave," "reads like an excerpt from some horror mystery. To think someone like you, so considerate of others, had to be subjected to such treatment!" Denzel McClung died June 12, 1971. See Denzel Horace McClung memorial card, McClung Papers.

237. Blackwelder to McClung, March 17, June 28, 1972. Bernice and Quantrille had a rare long-distance telephone conversation after Denzel's death; see Blackwelder to McClung, June 26, 1971. All in McClung Papers.

238. McClung to Blackwelder, June 24, 1972. On June 28, 1972, Blackwelder responded, "Do hope 'May McC' got the message and will not bother you anymore. … [She is] absolutely without feeling or compassion. How can she sleep nights? She probably came to knock you over with her rejuvenation. Have wondered what her sons would think of such cruelty or don't they care?" See also McClung to Blackwelder, April 4, 1972, in which McClung reported, "I did not receive an Easter card from my Brother's widow, thank Goodness!" All in McClung Papers.

239. McClung to Blackwelder, July 23, 1972; January 18, 1975; Blackwelder to McClung, July 25, August 15, October 17, 1973; February 3, 1974; January 19, 1975. (On October 17, 1973, Blackwelder wrote, "Do hope your peace of mind will not be disturbed further by relatives of relatives wishing to save you.") For threatened visits from nephew Denzel McClung Jr., see Denny and Darlene McClung to Quantrille McClung, January 2, December 16, 1975. All in McClung Papers.

240. In addition, McClung could not have known that she would live so long that what little she had would be all but depleted when she died (in 1985). See epilogue.

241. McClung to Blackwelder, August 27, 1972, McClung Papers. Not only had most of the McClungs died decades before, but the one who survived the longest

was married to a woman who, as McClung puts it, "took offense at us over some thing, we never knew what[;] she was the sort of woman who never forgave or forgot." In other words, there were multiple feuds on all sides of the family.

242. McClung to Blackwelder, July 20, September 20, 1966. McClung later wrote of a California cousin who had "married a wife with money," noting that this couple had been generous toward her; McClung to Blackwelder, March 28, August 27, 1972. All letters in McClung Papers. On these cousins, see part 3 and epilogue.

243. McClung to Blackwelder, June 16, July 6, 1967. For another visit from California cousins, see McClung to Blackwelder, June 6, 1972. All in McClung Papers.

244. On McClung's family relationships in the last years of her life, see epilogue.

245. Denver has not inspired anywhere near as much scholarship as Chicago has. But the Mile High City's history has been neatly chronicled in Leonard and Noel, *Denver: Mining Camp*. I borrow shamelessly from that volume here; see esp. chaps. 5, 6, 21, 22–25 (on Arapahoe, Jefferson, Boulder, and Adams counties, respectively), 28, 29, and appendix 2. See also George, "Mile High Metropole"; and Leonard and Noel, *Short History of Denver*.

246. In addition to Leonard and Noel, *Denver: Mining Camp*, see Simmons and Simmons, "Denver Neighborhood Project," Western History Collection, Western History/Genealogy Department, Denver Public Library. Thanks to Jim Kroll, Western History/Genealogy Department manager, for alerting me to this and other Capitol Hill studies at DPL, cited below.

247. McClung to Blackwelder, January 27, 1969, McClung Papers.

248. McClung to Blackwelder, October 28, 1971, McClung Papers. Echoing McClung's concern about parking lots, a 1973 neighborhood plan approved by the Denver Planning Board noted "land taken up by commercial parking lots serving other than [Capitol Hill] residents," especially to the west toward downtown. "Capitol Hill Neighborhood Plan," Western History Collection, Western History/ Genealogy Department, Denver Public Library.

249. Along with works cited on city-suburb relationships, the following on twentieth-century consumerism, generally, and the rise of supermarkets, specifically, provide context for McClung's street-level view: Lizabeth Cohen, *Consumers' Republic*; Tracey Deutsch, *Building a Housewife's Paradise*; Belasco and Horowitz, *Food Chains*; and Longstreth, *Drive-In*.

250. McClung recognized that the "onslaught of the 'hippies'" was not a city phenomenon alone. When a friend drove her to the mountain town of Ward in 1972, for example, she noted that it had been "taken over by the Hippies." McClung to Blackwelder, August 27, 1972, McClung Papers.

251. McClung to Blackwelder, July 6, 1967, McClung Papers. On urban renewal, the redesign of the civic center, and the new Denver Art Museum, see Leonard and Noel, *Denver: Mining Camp*, esp. 411, 449–50, 461–64.

252. The most comprehensive account of the organization is participant Ernesto P. Vigil's encyclopedic *Crusade for Justice*. My account is derived largely from Vigil, who, in addition to his own recollections, uses FBI records obtained

hrough the Freedom of Information Act (which reveal government surveillance
of the Crusade, a common practice in the civil rights era). For the DPL protest, see
Vigil, *Crusade for Justice*, 293. See also Leonard and Noel, *Denver: Mining Camp*,
386–87, 394–97, which is less sympathetic to the Crusade.

253. Again, my account is based on Ernesto P. Vigil, *Crusade for Justice*, esp.
209–56; and Leonard and Noel, *Denver: Mining Camp*, 386–87. Both cite extensive coverage in mainstream and ethnic press alike.

254. The 1960 statistics are derived from U.S. Bureau of the Census, *Census
Tracts*. The 1980 statistics are from U.S. Bureau of the Census, *Narrative Profiles of
Neighborhoods*. And see Orr, *Profiles of Denver Residents*, Western History Collection, Western History/Genealogy Department, Denver Public Library. The latter
gives similar statistics for Capitol Hill's racial demographics, apparently from
1977; see Orr, *Profiles of Denver Residents*, 48, fig. 9.

255. McClung to Blackwelder, June 2, 1969, McClung Papers.

256. "Capitol Hill Neighborhood Plan" and "Capitol Hill/Cheesman Park,"
both in Western History Collection, Western History/Genealogy Department,
Denver Public Library. As these documents show, Capitol Hill's population was
also disproportionately unmarried. This reflected its appeal to countercultural
youths, who eschewed the institution of marriage, but also reflected a steady
influx of gay men and lesbians. For context, see Noel, "Gay Bars"; and, for how
zoning ordinances fostered LGBT community in Capitol Hill, see Cole, "R-o," esp.
139–78. McClung's apartment was situated in the path of a route that linked the
civic center and Cheesman Park, two gay male cruising areas, and in close proximity to numerous gay bars. When Denver's queer residents staged their first informal gay pride parade in 1975, followed by the first formal parade (with a city
permit) in 1976, the parade routes followed a similar path. See Noel, "Gay Bars";
and Marcus, "PrideFest." By the end of the twentieth century, Capitol Hill was
well established as a queer-friendly neighborhood, home to LGBT commercial
establishments as well as the Metropolitan Community Church of the Rockies,
an LGBT faith community founded in 1973. Metropolitan Community Church of
the Rockies met in several locations, some of them in Capitol Hill, until it eventually purchased a former Congregational church building three blocks from Mc-
Clung's apartment on Clarkson Street. I base these assertions on my own meanderings through Capitol Hill in the first two decades of the twenty-first century,
as well as on "MCC of the Rockies" website, accessed April 26, 2020, https://www
.mccrockies.org/.

257. McClung to Blackwelder, January 1, 1968, McClung Papers.

258. McClung to Blackwelder, April 17, 1968, McClung Papers. Leonard and
Noel (*Denver: Mining Camp*, 383) confirm that Denver newspapers "minimized
the unrest of April 1968," noting, "Years later, the *Rocky Mountain News* summarized the police log for the three days following Doctor King's death: 52 fires; 100
vehicles damaged; 19 stores looted."

259. McClung to Blackwelder, April 17, 1968, McClung Papers. The Shriners'
El Jebel Temple was then at 1700 Sherman Avenue, two blocks from McClung's
Trinity United Methodist Church. In the early twenty-first century, the build-

ing housed the Sherman Street Event Center, and a newer El Jebel Temple wa
located several miles away, closer to Denver's northwest suburbs.

260. McClung to Blackwelder, April 17, 1968, McClung Papers. Beryl Satter sug
gested to me that McClung may have been obliquely lecturing her friend Black
welder in this letter; I agree.

261. Blackwelder reported on campaign activities in 1974 and 1977. She was in
volved in Chicago's special mayoral race that followed the 1976 death of Mayo
Richard M. Daley. Blackwelder to McClung, March 25, 1974; March 5, Good Fri
day [April 8], 1977, McClung Papers. Although Bernice supported Nixon's presidential run in 1968 and held views more common among Republicans, she must
have campaigned for Democrats in Chicago municipal elections. Her niece
Doris Lance remembered that husband Harold, who worked at the City Hall and
County Building, had to support the city's Democratic machine in order to get
and keep his job: "He had to change from being a Republican to a Democrat
because of Daley.... You didn't get a job if you weren't a Democrat." Lance and
Fowler interview. Indeed, the Blackwelders' earlier work managing apartments
in Logan Square may have reflected ward- and precinct-level patronage politics
in Daley's Chicago. For job distribution under Daley, see Rakove, *Don't Make No
Waves*, esp. 112–17.

262. Blackwelder to McClung, September 17, 1968; see also August 22, 1968,
both in McClung Papers.

263. Blackwelder to McClung, March 30, 1968, McClung Papers.

264. Blackwelder to McClung, November 7, 1968; May 28, 1973; see also Novem-
ber 16, 1972; July 25, 1973, all in McClung Papers. On the move to the right that
Nixon signaled, see, e.g., Chafe, *Unfinished Journey*, 4th ed., 373–429; Schulman,
Seventies, 23–52; Farber, *Rise and Fall of Modern American Conservatism*; and
Schulman and Zelizer, *Rightward Bound*.

265. McClung to Blackwelder, November 9, 1972, McClung Papers.

266. For examples of earlier greetings, see McClung to Blackwelder, February
25, 1956; and Blackwelder to McClung, July 7, 1956; for later greetings, see Blackwelder to McClung, April 19, 1972; and McClung to Blackwelder, June 6, 1972, all
in McClung Papers.

267. Blackwelder to McClung, December 11, 1970; and McClung to Blackwelder, October 28, 1971, McClung Papers.

268. See, e.g., Blackwelder to McClung, March 9, May 6, October 18, 1966. In
over 300 letters the two women exchanged, I found reference to only four phone
conversations. See Blackwelder to McClung, June 26, 1971; July 23, October 16,
1972; and October 3, 1974. All letters in McClung Papers.

269. Blackwelder to McClung, May 11, 1966, McClung Papers.

270. Arnold interview; Lance and Fowler interview.

271. McClung to Blackwelder, May 17, 1966, McClung Papers.

272. Blackwelder to McClung, December 14, 1965; September 29, 1978, Mc-
Clung Papers.

273. McClung to Blackwelder, June 2, 1969; March 28, 1972, McClung Papers.

274. McClung to Blackwelder, November 22, 1971; and Blackwelder to Mc-Clung, May 24, 1972, McClung Papers.

275. See, e.g., Blackwelder to McClung, July 17, 1967; May 19, 1969; September 8, 1971; April 19, August 16, October 16, 1972, McClung Papers. The exception to the cheeriness came in 1975, when Bernice's sister, Helen, was dying. See part 3.

276. This statement draws on a generation of scholarship on identity and subjectivity. I reference much of the earlier work in Susan Lee Johnson, "'Memory Sweet to Soldiers.'" See also Sidonie Smith's simultaneously published "Who's Talking." For a critique of the emphasis on subjectivity and identity and a call to revisit intersecting structures of domination, see Einspahr, "Structural Domination." For intersectional analysis broadly, see Cho, Crenshaw, and McCall, "Intersectionality."

277. Schulman, *Seventies*, 84–87.

278. Blackwelder to McClung, March 30, 1968; cf. December 6, 1967; April 16, December 11, 1970; April 14, 1971, all in McClung Papers. Likewise, on February 29, 1972, Blackwelder wrote that her brother, who was active in a local senior citizens' committee, promoted seven words for living: live, love, learn, think, give, try, and laugh. She went on to explain: "I use the next to the last … the most. I go to the refrigerator and Try to remember what I came there for. Then I Laugh."

279. McClung to Blackwelder, April 28, September 25, 1968, McClung Papers.

280. McClung to Blackwelder, September 25, 1968, McClung Papers.

281. McClung to Blackwelder, January 1, 1968, McClung Papers.

282. McClung to Blackwelder, April 18, 1973, McClung Papers.

283. For comments about her own as well as her husband's aging, see Blackwelder to McClung, April 16, December 11, 1970; March 24, 1971; December 7, 1972. Both Bernice and Harold suffered age-related digestive disorders, chronicled in Blackwelder to McClung, April 9, 18, 29, May 28, July 25, August 15, 24, September 16, 1973; April 10, 1974. All in McClung Papers.

284. See part 1.

285. In addition to previous references, see also McClung to Blackwelder, November 24, 1967; and Blackwelder to McClung, August 16, 1972, McClung Papers.

286. McClung to Blackwelder, November 24, 1967, McClung Papers.

287. See Rosen, *World Split Open*. For a wider contextualization of the resurgence, see Freedman, *No Turning Back*.

288. Blackwelder to McClung, June 15, 1972; and McClung to Blackwelder, June 24, 1972, McClung Papers.

289. Blackwelder to McClung, February 21, October 15, 1967; February 29, 1972, McClung Papers.

290. Doris Lance, personal communication with author, June 5, 2003; Elliott interview. Men found Harold demanding, too. Bernice's nephew Stephen echoed Doris's evaluation, and Doris remembered that her father, Bernice's brother, grew exasperated with Harold's requests and would say, "Get up and get your own darn coffee." Lance and Fowler interview.

291. Blackwelder to McClung, September 5, 1965; September 5, 1967, McClung Papers.

292. The phrasing here reflects the title and contents of Stoler, *Haunted b Empire*.

293. Here, I write largely from memory, aided by my scrapbooks and letter from Lauren Vincent, 1969–77. I still wonder how wise the family move was. W stopped fighting about the bathroom but started arguing about money, which always seemed in too short supply in this new home. We also fought about politics, as I explain below.

294. On the antiwar movement in Madison, see, e.g., Maraniss, *They Marched into Sunlight*; Bingham, *Witness to the Revolution*; and Silber and Brown, *War at Home*.

295. The Sterling Hall bombing at the University of Wisconsin–Madison took place August 24, 1970. See Bates, *Rads*.

296. On the history of Madison Central High School, which closed in 1969, see *Madison Central High School History* (blog), accessed June 26, 2011, http://madi sonchshistory.blogspot.com. I started at James Madison Memorial High School in 1968, when the building housed both junior and senior high school grades. By the time I began my freshman year in 1970, younger students were attending middle school in a different building.

297. There were other Wisconsin civil rights struggles in this era; here I cite those that I recall noticing at the time. On these struggles, see, e.g., Marc Simon Rodríguez, "Movement" and *Tejano Diaspora*; Ourada, *Menominee Indians*; Peroff, *Menominee DRUMS*; Loew, *Indian Nations of Wisconsin*, 24–39; Tronnes, "'Where is John Wayne?'" and "Contested Place."

298. Our neighborhood, University Hill Farms, was mostly middle class, with a number of upper-middle-class families, some lower-middle-class families, and many middle-middle-class families, such as mine. An adjacent neighborhood was predominantly lower-middle class, with some working-class families. I base these generalizations on memory and University Hill Farms Association, *University Hill Farms Directory, 1972–1973*, which lists parental occupations.

PART THREE

1. John J. McCurdy obituary, *Lincoln (Kans.) Sentinel-Republican*, May 8, 1958. For an image of McCurdy's headstone, see "John C. McCurdy," Find a Grave, accessed September 13, 2011, https://www.findagrave.com/memorial/11226239 /john-j_-mccurdy. Jaramillo and Carson were both buried in Boggsville, Colorado Territory, in 1868 but then disinterred in 1869 and reburied in Taos; see Guild and Carter, *Kit Carson*, 283. The cemetery where they are buried is home to the graves of over 200 others, including Padre Antonio José Martínez (1793–1867), who married Kit and Josefa but later became a critic of the U.S. conquest; soldiers and citizens killed in the 1847 Taos uprising of *hispanos* and Pueblo Indians against U.S. rule; and Mabel Dodge Luhan (1879–1962), patron of the arts and spouse of Taos Pueblo man Tony Lujan. See "People Buried in Kit Carson Cemetery"; and Phillips, "People Buried in Kit Carson Cemetery," both in Carson Files,

outhwest Research Center, University of New Mexico–Taos. For the cemetery's
istory, see *El Crepúsculo*, March 22, 1950.

2. Blackwelder to McClung, February 21, 1956, and McClung to Blackwelder,
February 25, 1956, Quantrille McClung Papers, Western History Collection, West-
ern History/Genealogy Department, Denver Public Library (hereafter cited as
McClung Papers).

3. Blackwelder to McClung, [June ?, 1972]. Blackwelder reports that McCurdy
"prodded" her into her Carson research, adding that he "promised to get it published if I would write a biography of Kit. He sent me a small fund for expenses:
carfare—photostats, postage etc. (not much as he was *very* thrifty)." McCurdy
also encouraged the work of Blackwelder's nemesis, Marion Estergreen (see
part 1); see Blackwelder to McClung, April 1, 1962. For McCurdy's subsidy of Mc-
Clung's work, see McCurdy to McClung, September 14, 1957; McClung to Edith
Markle, October 22, 1958, January 13, 29, 1959; and Markle to McClung, October
28, 1958; January 12, 15, 24, 1959. For correspondence about McCurdy's death, see
Blackwelder to McClung, May 8, 25, 31, August 29, October 18, 1958; and McClung
to Blackwelder, May 11, 28, August 23, December 18, 1958, January 6, 1959. Blackwelder often referred to McCurdy as the source of her friendship with McClung;
see, e.g., Blackwelder to McClung, August 18, 1971. All letters in McClung Papers.

4. Blackwelder describes the 1928 Taos trip and her relationship with McCurdy
in Blackwelder to McClung [June ?, 1972]. See also McClung to Blackwelder, August 31, 1972 (McClung first writes to "My dear Red Wing"); and Blackwelder to
McClung, September 15, 1972 (Blackwelder comments on McClung's use of "Red
Wing"), December 7, 1972 (Blackwelder reports that she "nearly swooned"). All
letters in McClung Papers.

5. These materials constitute the McClung Papers. McClung published her
Colorado governor genealogies in the *Colorado Genealogist* from vol. 8, no. 1
(January 1947), to vol. 24, no. 4 (October 1960), with additions and corrections
printed later.

6. These materials constitute the Quantrille Day McClung Collection at Hart
Research Library, History Colorado, Denver (hereafter cited as McClung Collection). History Colorado is the rebranded name of the Colorado Historical Society.
From 1915 to 1977—for most of McClung's life—the historical society was housed
in the Colorado State Museum building, across the street from the state capitol
and two blocks from the Denver Public Library.

7. Quantrille D. McClung, *Memoirs of My Childhood*.

8. This discussion of the archives that McClung and Blackwelder created is influenced by critical work on archives, which maintains "that the claims to objectivity associated with the traditional archive pose a challenge which must be met
in part by telling stories about its provenance, its histories, its effects on its users,
and above all, its power to shape all narratives which are to be found there." Burton, *Archive Stories*, introduction, quote on 6. See also Marshall, Murphy, and
Tortorici, "Queering Archives: Historical Understandings"; and Marshall, Murphy, and Tortorici, "Queering Archives: Intimate Tracings." Given the capacious
definition of the archive in interdisciplinary scholarship, I appreciate historian

Regina Kunzel's caution in Arondekar et al., "Queering Archives," 229: "I worr
... that the archive referenced by the 'archival turn,' understood as a universa
metaphor for memory structures, information storage, and knowledge produc
tion, might become so expansive as to include nearly everything and that, as a
result, it will lose any relationship to what I'm tempted, with some embarrass
ment, to call the 'real archives.' ... I hope that some strands of the conversation
about archives remain tethered to material archives ... and engaged with the
practices of working with, in, and sometimes against them." I locate my work
within that strand.

9. Doris Lance, personal communication with author, February 8, 2003.

10. I call that collection the Bernice Fowler Blackwelder Papers, which are currently in my possession (hereafter cited as Blackwelder Papers). As I researched
this book, the late Doris Lance of Alpena, Michigan, generously shared her aunt's
papers with me.

11. John McCurdy tapes and transcripts, McClung Papers.

12. I cite the sources that inform this paragraph as I expand below.

13. I likewise cite the sources that inform the generalizations in this paragraph
as I expand on them below. For now, let me address forthwith my use of the term
"queered" to describe McClung's youthful relationships. Most literally, I use the
term "queer" in its transitive verb form to refer to relationships that did not work
out (relationships that ended for reasons the historical record cannot fully explain). I am aware, of course, that linking any form of the word "queer" to the
word "relationship" has the inevitable effect, in the early twenty-first century,
of evoking human intimacies that reflect some sort of alterity (including but not
limited to same-sex attachments). I mean to evoke that kind of queerness. But
this is not the same thing as suggesting that McClung was gay. I do not know,
and doubt I will ever know, how or whether McClung thought about what people
of my generation might call her "sexuality." In using the term "queered," I mean
to insist on both an older, more capacious definition of the term "queer" *and* a
newer, defiant definition that recognizes the cultural violence of heterosexism
and gender normativity even as it battles a social world predictably structured by
sexualities and genders.

14. I cite the sources that inform the generalizations in this paragraph and the
one that follows as I expand on them below.

15. See Culver, *Frontier of Leisure*, esp. 198–238; and, for the political implications, Dochuck, *Bible Belt to Sunbelt*.

16. I have had trouble locating the Fowler house or houses in greater Brookville
(in 2010, a town of about 250, with a post office and a church and no businesses
to speak of). I am certain that Bernice's father, Wilbur Fowler, owned property
just west of town, and it is that property that I describe in this paragraph. The
description is based on a site visit in early September 2010; plat maps of Spring
Creek Township and Brookville in *Plat Book of Saline County* and *Standard Atlas
of Saline County*; and property records provided by the Saline County Treasurer's
Office (Catherine Silhan to Jennifer Holland, August 31, 2010, in author's possession). Kansas Water Office reports show slightly below-normal precipitation and

ightly above-normal temperatures in Saline County in the weeks before I visited he site. See "Kansas Drought Report and Climate Summary: Current Conditions, Drought Impacts and Outlook, August and September 2010," accessed October 2, 011, http://www.kwo.org/reports_publications/Drought/Rpt_2010_DroughtRe orts.pdf. This report is no longer available online. But the Kansas Water Office maintains a webpage, "Climate and Drought Monitor and Outlook," which in-licates that reports more than five years old are available on request; accessed April 26, 2020, https://kwo.ks.gov/reports2/climate-and-drought-monitoring-re sponse. For historical data on Kansas droughts, see U.S. Geological Survey Kan-sas Water Science Center website, accessed October 2, 2011, https://www.usgs .gov/centers/kswsc. The Fowler plot changed hands between Wilbur Fowler and his brother Arthur, and I suspect that Arthur, his wife Lottie, and their children occupied the site much of the time that it was in the family. I also suspect that Wilbur, his first wife, Hattie, his second wife, Mabel, and the children from his two marriages more often lived in town, though they may have occupied the eighty-acre Fowler plot at times (by 1930, Arthur and Lottie had sold the property and moved to town as well). Given ties between the two families, it seems certain that Bernice Fowler spent time on the Fowler plot described here (as a visitor, a resident, or both). For the house or houses in town, see below.

17. Blackwelder to McClung, September 15, 1972, McClung Papers.

18. This description is based on a site visit made in summer 2007; and on Quantrille D. McClung, *Memoirs of My Childhood*, esp. 1-2, 8, 68 (and foreword by Jack Smith, p. iii). When I returned to the neighborhood just before this book went to press, Quantrille's first childhood home had been razed and replaced by a new house.

19. On Indian captivity in New England, see Demos, *Unredeemed Captive*; Namais, *White Captives*; and Axtell, *Natives and Newcomers*, esp. 189-212.

20. "Donelson," "Donalson," and "Donaldson" all derive from the same Scot-tish surname, and spellings varied.

21. Blackwelder to McClung, September 10, November 12, 1970; February 26 (quote), June 28, 1971, McClung Papers. Blackwelder and other family members produced typescript genealogies variously labeled "Donelson-Fowler Geneal-ogy," "Fowler-Cox-Donaldson Genealogy," and "Fowler-Knapp Genealogy," copies of which I hold in my possession as part of the Blackwelder Papers; these also inform my narrative. Israel Donalson tells his own story of captivity in Evans and Stivers, *History of Adams County*, 66-73 (for biographical sketch, see 549-50). I do not know if Blackwelder read this account.

22. Blackwelder's comment reminds me of Richard White's reflections on Buf-falo Bill's Wild West show, in which whites were often depicted as victimized by Indians. White calls this "a strange story of an inverted conquest," a "conquest won without the guilt," in "Geography of Hope." For in-depth analysis of the same, see Warren, *Buffalo Bill's America*. On the enduring relevance of captivity narratives in the Cold War era, see Slotkin, *Gunfighter Nation*; Engelhardt, *End of Victory Culture*; and Carruthers, *Cold War Captives*.

23. Blackwelder to McClung, September 21, 1975, McClung Papers. For Andrew

and Rachel Jackson's Tennessee home, the Hermitage, see Andrew Jackson's Hermitage website, accessed September 28, 2011, http://www.thehermitage.com.

24. Blackwelder probably did not know that some elite Cherokees also held black slaves and lived in imposing houses; see esp. Miles, *House on Diamond Hill*.

25. Blackwelder to McClung, February 26, 1971, McClung Papers.

26. Shortridge, *Cities on the Plains*, esp. 127–37.

27. Except where otherwise noted, the family history details in this paragraph derive from "Fowler-Cox-Donaldson Genealogy" and "Fowler-Knapp Genealogy," Blackwelder Papers; Mabel L. Fowler obituary, *Salina (Kans.) Journal*, December 5, 1930 (Bernice's mother's first name is mistakenly given here as Lydia; family documents give her full name as Mabel Lydia Knapp Fowler); Wilbur E. Fowler obituary, *Salina (Kans.) Journal*, August 14, 1933; "Kansas Physicians and Midwives, 1881–1900," Kansas Historical Society, accessed April 26, 2020, https://www.kshs.org/genealogy/genealogy_physicians/search/surname:Fowler; *Plat Book of Saline County*; *Standard Atlas of Saline County*; U.S. Bureau of the Census, *Twelfth Census*, *Thirteenth Census*, *Fourteenth Census*, and *Fifteenth Census*; *1905 Kansas State Census*; *1915 Kansas State Census*; and *1925 Kansas State Census*.

28. On professionalization and the new middle class, see Wiebe, *Search for Order*; Bledstein, *Culture of Professionalism*; and Blumin, *Emergence of the Middle Class*.

29. For the marriage record of Hattie Knapp and Wilbur Fowler (July 16, 1884, Green Ridge), see Missouri Marriage Records.

30. Miner, *Next Year Country*, esp. 9–24; Baum, *Wizard of Oz*.

31. Walter Fowler, Bernice Fowler's half brother, married a woman from Brookville and moved to Deming, New Mexico, in 1911, where his wife bore two children, one of whom survived. But Walter died the next year. See *Deming Headlight* (New Mexico), July 5, 1912. The year before he married, Walter served as federal census taker in Brookville and the surrounding Spring Creek Township, recording in a neat hand the family residences of his father, Wilbur, and his uncle Arthur. See U.S. Bureau of the Census, *Thirteenth Census*.

32. For Mabel Knapp and Wilbur Fowler's marriage record (August 24, 1897, Green Ridge), see Missouri Marriage Records. For Mabel Fowler's singing, see Mabel L. Fowler obituary, *Salina (Kans.) Journal*, December 30, 1930; and n42 below. Duane's first name was James, but he went by Duane.

33. Shortridge, *Cities on the Plains*, 157.

34. U.S. Bureau of the Census, *Twelfth Census*; U.S. Bureau of the Census, *Twelfth Census of the United States, 1900, Census Reports*, 172.

35. There is a photograph of Bernice, her siblings, and her mother in this automobile in the Blackwelder Papers. On the reverse, Bernice has written, "Dr. Fowler's family in the Red Cadillac c. 1910." Bernice, her sister, and her mother are all adorned in elaborate headgear, and even her little brother wears a broad-brimmed straw hat (as Bernice writes, "Look at those hats!!"; she adds that this was the "first car in Brookville, Kansas"). For the rest, see *1905 Kansas State Census*; U.S. Bureau of the Census, *Thirteenth Census* and *Fifteenth Census*.

36. Blackwelder to McClung, January 13, 1978, McClung Papers. By this time,

ernice's family was likely living in the town of Brookville. All of the state and federal censuses cited in n27 above show the Fowler family in Brookville, but none list residents' addresses. City directories from nearby Salina list Brookville residents, but the listings do not include addresses (*R. L. Polk*, 356; *Polk's Salina City Directory, 1923*, 423). A local resident who published two volumes of Brookville memories in the 1970s says that the Fowlers lived in town at the northwest corner of Second Street and Perry Street (Lovisa Malone, *Memories*), while longtime local Ward Watkins remembers the Fowler house in the 100 block of Third Street (Ward Watkins, personal communication with author, September 30, 2011). In 2011 there was no longer a house at Second and Perry, and the Third Street house was in poor repair. Brookville city clerk Kay Vanderbilt generously assisted me with this information (Kay Vanderbilt, personal communication with author, September 30, 2011). Meanwhile, it seems likely that the eighty-acre Fowler plot west of town was occupied by the family of Arthur and Lottie Fowler, Bernice's uncle and aunt, much of the time into the 1920s. See U.S. Bureau of the Census, *Thirteenth Census, Fourteenth Census*, and *Fifteenth Census; 1905 Kansas State Census*; and *1925 Kansas State Census*. Arthur and Wilbur Fowler both held an interest in the plot west of Brookville, but the exact nature of that interest for each is likely unrecoverable. I suspect that Wilbur and Mabel Fowler's family may have lived on this land at some point, because Arthur and Lottie Fowler's family relocated to San Bernardino County, California, around the turn of the century and tried their hand at farming there, leaving the Kansas plot to Wilbur and Mabel. See U.S. Bureau of the Census, *Twelfth Census*.

37. Roenigk, *Pioneer History of Kansas*, esp. 164–211; Blackwelder to McClung, May 20, 31, June 15, 1972, McClung Papers.

38. Blackwelder to McClung, May 20, 1972, McClung Papers.

39. Blackwelder to McClung, June 28, 1972, McClung Papers.

40. Blackwelder to McClung, September 28, [1971], McClung Papers. Bernice wrote a similar letter to her niece about this trip; Blackwelder to Doris Lance, September 30, 1971, Blackwelder Papers.

41. Blackwelder to McClung, June 28, 1972, McClung Papers.

42. Based on my reading of Bernice's letters, I asked her niece Doris Lance if she thought Bernice identified more with her father than with her mother. Doris said she could not be sure, because she did not remember her grandparents. But, she added, "I think 'Doc' was pretty prominent in town, and maybe the mother was a homebody." Doris sympathized with Bernice, because Doris herself was "bored" by the possibilities the twentieth century offered to women ("That's why I went back to school," she added). Doris concluded, "I think Bernice identified with men. I identify with men." Lance and Fowler interview. The "Fowler-Knapp Genealogy" (in the Blackwelder Papers), which a family member notes was "compiled by Bernice Blackwelder but edited by many," declares that Mabel Knapp Fowler had "a vivacious personality, [was] a leader in community affairs and possessed a pleasing singing voice." These may or may not be Bernice's words, but they are as close as I can come to an enthusiastically positive assessment of Mabel Fowler by her otherwise loquacious daughter.

43. Family history details derive from Quantrille D. McClung, *Memoirs of My Childhood*, 1 and passim (McClung says that her mother grew up in Atchison County, Kansas, but census records place the Gutzman family in adjacent Doniphan County; McClung must have discovered this, because she later produced *Kiehnhoff Family in America, With Bauer & Gutzman Connections, First Settled in Doniphan County, Kansas*); *1875 Kansas State Census*; U.S. Bureau of the Census, *Tenth Census, Twelfth Census, Thirteenth Census, Fourteenth Census*, and *Fifteenth Census*. There are also genealogical materials in box 7, McClung Papers. On German settlement in Kansas, see Turk, "Germans of Atchison," "Selling the Heartland," and "Germans in Kansas."

44. Quantrille D. McClung, *Memoirs of My Childhood*, 6, 31, 34, 44, 50, 58 (quote), 66. For Quantrille's relationship with an older German couple, see McClung, 70.

45. McClung to Stephanie Tally, January 2, 1965, McClung Papers. McClung writes, "No, I was not named for William Quantrill but for a lady, Quantrille Salle[e] of St. Joseph, Missouri who was greatly admired by an aunt of mine who was with my mother when I was born. I never met the lady but found her family record in a History of Buchanan Co., Mo." The book she consulted would have been *History of Buchanan County, Missouri* (880). For Quantrille Sallee, see also U.S. Bureau of the Census, *1870 U.S. Census* and *Tenth Census*.

46. Quantrille McClung obituary, *Rocky Mountain News* (Denver), July 9, 1985. The obituary claims that this story comes from McClung's "76-page article, 'Memories of My Childhood and Youth in North Denver,'" which I assume is the same thing as her *Memoirs of My Childhood* (a 76-page booklet), but I cannot find the story in the published volume. McClung did tell the tale when a columnist interviewed her following the memoir's publication. See *Denver Post*, January 11, 1981.

47. Quantrille D. McClung, *Memoirs of My Childhood*, 15 (quote), 30.

48. McClung, 18, 22–23, 54–55. Benjamin McClung's natal family is not as easy to track as Hattie Gutzman's kin, perhaps because the McClungs moved so often. But 1885 Iowa census records appear to place twenty-one-year-old Frank McClung (as Benjamin seems to have been known when he was young) in Muscatine County as a farm laborer, and his mother and father (eponymously named Mary and Joseph McClung) farming farther west in Shelby County; *Iowa State Census, 1885*. Quantrille McClung also saved her father's (very good) Iowa school reports in a scrapbook; see "My Memoirs," vol. 1, item 16, McClung Collection.

49. U.S. Bureau of the Census, *Compendium of the Eleventh Census* and *Twelfth Census of the United States, 1900, Census Reports*. The figure for Denver is from 1890, the year Quantrille was born, and the figure for Brookville is from 1900, two years before Bernice was born. The Brookville figure for 1900—729 souls—also includes rural Spring Creek Township, and while rural residents did business in Brookville, they did not live there. Brookville's population was 243.

50. Quantrille D. McClung, *Memoirs of My Childhood*, 11–17, 66–67, quotes on 11, 16. Quantrille did not see this "group of persons from the Middle East" herself. Her father encountered them as he took parcels from Struby-Estabrook Mer-

antile to the Union Station post office. But Quantrille includes the story in the course of describing what her family might see when walking "over town."

51. McClung, 6, 8, 31, 33–35. For North Denver's Italian community, see Rebecca Ann Hunt, "Urban Pioneers"; and Worrall, "Labor, Gender."

52. For varying views of this process, see Jacobson, *Whiteness*; Selig, *Americans All*; Guglielmo, *White on Arrival*; Gerstle, *American Crucible*; and Ngai, *Impossible Subjects*.

53. Quantrille D. McClung, *Memoirs of My Childhood*, 16, 17, 61. Even more literally, she recalled visiting a souvenir store where "they had a lot of relics from the Indian Southwest including a petrified Indian in a glass case," a sight she found "gruesome" but "fascinating" (17). She also attended Buffalo Bill's Wild West show, but she did not remark about Indigenous performers in her memoirs (65).

54. For trenchant analysis of this phenomenon, see Thrush, *Native Seattle*. See also Deloria, *Indians in Unexpected Places*.

55. Quantrille D. McClung, *Memoirs of My Childhood*, 15.

56. See, e.g., Leonard and Noel, *Denver: Mining Camp*, 148, 192–94.

57. Quantrille D. McClung, *Memoirs of My Childhood*, 9–10, 16, 17, 60–61.

58. McClung, 43, 46 (quote), 68–74.

59. McClung, 1–2, 43–44, 68; for context, see Rebecca Ann Hunt, "Urban Pioneers."

60. Quantrille D. McClung, *Memoirs of My Childhood*, 40, 69. Jack Smith wrote the foreword to the memoir; see unnumbered page in front matter. He also spoke with me about the McClungs; Smith interview.

61. Quantrille D. McClung, *Memoirs of My Childhood*, 68.

62. McClung, 70–72.

63. McClung, 1, 25.

64. The description is based on two black-and-white photos in an album (item 26, McClung Collection), so reference to her "golden" hair comes from a self-description she provided six decades later: "I am 82 yrs. old, young for my age, 5 ft 3 in. short, weight 106 lbs., blond (my hair was once a beautiful golden shade, now dirt colored) never bobbed my hair (have a 'thing' about it due to a shocking experience in my early childhood)." McClung to Stephanie [Tally], October 29, 1972, McClung Papers.

65. The framed picture of Rabbi Hillkowitz in the background is now part of the Beck Archives, Special Collections and Archives, University Libraries, University of Denver; it can be viewed at "Rabbi Elias Hillkowitz," accessed April 27, 2020, https://specialcollections.du.edu/object/codu:37776#?c=&m=&s=&cv=&xywh= -1662%2C-1%2C5406%2C3000. Elias Hillkowitz, his wife, Rebecca Hindelson Hillkowitz, and their children emigrated to the United States from Lithuania in 1881, settling first in Cincinnati and then in Denver. The family was instrumental in establishing the Jewish Consumptives' Relief Society, one of two Jewish sanatoria established in Denver for tuberculosis sufferers. The first, National Jewish Hospital, was founded by Reform German Jews, and although it treated patients free of charge, it had strict criteria for admission that favored the affluent. Members of

the Orthodox Russian Jewish community, some of them socialists, deplored such exclusiveness, as well as the hospital's failure to observe Jewish dietary laws. In response, Eastern European Jews in Denver founded the Jewish Consumptive. Relief Society, which ran a sanatorium on West Colfax Street, the only one in Colorado to admit, as historian Jeanne Abrams puts it, "all consumptives, regardless of race or creed, at all stages of the disease—and at no charge." In 1906 (the year her father died), Anna Hillkowitz took a leave of absence from librarianship and served as a field secretary for the organization, traveling the country to solicit support. Abrams, "Chasing the Cure," quote on 99; *Jewish Women Pioneering* esp. 75-78; "*Unsere Leit.*" See also entry for William Hillkowitz in *History of Cincinnati*, 702-3. Thanks to Thyria Wilson of the Rocky Mountain Jewish Historical Society and the Beck Archives for helping me find Rabbi Hillkowitz's death date (January 25, 1906). See "JewishGen Online Worldwide Burial Registry," accessed April 27, 2020, https://www.jewishgen.org/databases/cemetery/jowbr.php?rec =J_CO_0006034.

66. I base this on the presence of the framed picture of Rabbi Hillkowitz in the background of McClung's photos and on an undated entry, likely written in late 1913 or early 1914, in a scrapbook McClung titled "My Memoirs," vol. 2, item 17, McClung Collection. The entry reads, "The 'Depositories' have a Bohemian Party at Miss Hillkowitz['s]," and goes on to list "Miss Anna Hillkowitz" as "Boulevardier," which might be roughly translated as "man-about-town." I am not certain where Anna Hillkowitz lived in 1913–14, but in 1910, a census taker found her on Franklin Street with her brother and sister, and in 1915, a city directory found her on Madison Street with her brother (and probably her sister as well; the sister may not have been listed because she was not gainfully employed). U.S. Bureau of the Census, *Thirteenth Census*; *Ballenger and Richards Forty-Third*.

67. I base the following descriptions on photographs in an album Bernice Fowler saved, now part of the Blackwelder Papers.

68. For the history of Fort Hays Kansas Normal College, now Fort Hays State University, see Miner, *Next Year Country*, 52–54, 158–59; and Shortridge, *Cities on the Plains*, 205–6.

69. Ingersoll, *I Remember*, esp. 2, 5, 9–11, 20, 28–29, 32; see also Leonard and Noel, *Denver: Mining Camp*, 82–83. Ingersoll's father invested in mining, irrigation, and real estate, and the family owned two different homes (serially, not at the same time) in the early streetcar suburb of Montclair, which was later annexed by Denver. They were of the middle class, but the Panic of 1893 compromised their resources, at least for a time. In addition to census records, see newspaper clipping titled "Pioneer Couple Who Celebrated 50th Wedding Anniversary" (1920) in "My Memoirs," vol. 1, item 16, McClung Collection. On the impact of the Panic of 1893 on Denver, see Leonard and Noel, *Denver: Mining Camp*, 102–13. According to the federal census, Helen Ingersoll, who did not marry, continued to live with her parents in Montclair into her fifties. See U.S. Bureau of the Census, *Twelfth Census*, *Thirteenth Census*, *Fourteenth Census*, and *Fifteenth Census*.

70. Quantrille D. McClung, *Memoirs of My Childhood*, 25; items pasted into

crapbook titled "My Memoirs," vol. 1, item 16, McClung Collection, including Denver Public Library. Examination for Entrance to Apprentice Class, April 3rd, 911." On Dana and Dudley and their philosophies, practices, and influences, see ngersoll, *I Remember*, esp. 3–12, 15–17, 18–19, 22–28, 30. Dana continued to be a najor figure in library reform after leaving Denver in 1897 for public libraries in Springfield, Massachusetts, and Newark, New Jersey. He also served as president of the American Library Association. See Garrison, *Apostles of Culture*, esp. 37–38, 93–96, 146, 243.

71. Items pasted and written into scrapbook titled "My Memoirs," vol. 2, item 17, McClung Collection, including undated newspaper clipping entitled "New Class Will Make Librarians" and a photo of the ten chosen as apprentices, whom McClung identifies by name. For McClung's relationship with her fellow librarians, see nine volumes of "My Memoirs" (items 16–24); and photo album, item 26, all in McClung Collection. References to these women are too numerous to cite individually. On Reese, see also Ingersoll, *I Remember*, 29.

72. Kessler-Harris, *Out to Work*, esp. 116–17; Barbara Miller Solomon, *Company of Educated Women*, esp. 126–28; Karen Manners Smith, "New Paths to Power." For statistics on women employed in so-called women's professions from 1910 to 1920, see Hill, *Women in Gainful Occupations*, 56, table 41. On librarians, see Garrison, *Apostles of Culture*, esp. foreword by Christine Pawley, xvii–xxxiv, which reviews relevant literature on the history of women librarians, with tremendous insight, mediating between the concerns of historians affiliated with history departments and historians in the field of library and information science. See also Passett, *Cultural Crusaders*; and Van Slyck, *Free to All*.

73. For cogent analysis of that workscape as it evolved in Carnegie libraries, see Van Slyck (*Free to All*), who does not address the DPL building completed in 1910, perhaps because it was only partly funded by Carnegie. On DPL's card catalog, see Ingersoll, *I Remember*, 21 (and on other physical aspects of DPL in all of its locations, passim).

74. Ingersoll, *I Remember*, 27.

75. The Civic Center was among Mayor Robert Speer's City Beautiful initiatives spearheaded especially during his third term, which began in 1916, but most of the plans were not realized until after his death in 1918. The DPL building was an early public structure on the plaza. See Leonard and Noel, *Denver: Mining Camp*, 140–49.

76. Ingersoll, *I Remember*, esp. 9–10, 16–29, quote on 26.

77. Ingersoll, 26–27.

78. Leonard and Noel, *Denver: Mining Camp*, 85, 142, 160.

79. Ingersoll, *I Remember*, 27–28, 30–34.

80. McClung to William I. Smith, July [?], 1967, McClung Papers. Here, McClung answered a questionnaire sent by a student in a University of Denver library science master's program. The student sought responses from older librarians in order "to upgrade library education and to attract more able personel [*sic*] to the field." McClung complied, informing him that she was doing so "to show what can be accomplished as a result of the kind of training that was given in the

Library in the early days." It was a quiet rebuke to the young man's presumption, but a rebuke nonetheless.

81. McClung to William I. Smith, July [?], 1967; for McClung's recollection of Pearl Look, see McClung to "Mrs. [C. J.] Trimble," August 24, 1976, both in Mc Clung Papers. McClung also notes here that she and her coworkers went to the municipal bathhouse on their days off to "play at swimming." Ingersoll listed the library stations of the 1910s: "One at University Park in connection with the University [of Denver], one at Globeville [another annexed smelter town], one in the Day Nursery at Elyria [where Quantrille encountered the dancers]; one in the North Side Neighborhood house [in Little Italy, near Quantrille's childhood home] and the Municipal Bath house [established 1908]; also one in the Lindquist Cracker Factory, the Denver Dry Goods Company and Daniels and Fisher Stores Company." There were also library stations in public schools. Of the stations, Ingersoll (*I Remember*, 33) recalls, "Trunks were packed with good, wholesome, readable books for children and adult readers, and two assistants from the main library were in charge." McClung saved a DPL pamphlet from 1912 which noted that three library stations had reading rooms, while the rest were depots "for distribution only": these included stations in Globeville and Elyria, as well as those at the municipal bathhouse, the Jewish Settlement House, and the Neighborhood House (which may have referred to either the North Side Neighborhood House, established in 1907 in the Italian district, or the West Side Neighborhood House, established in 1902 in a German, Irish, and Scandinavian area). For the Jewish Settlement House on West Colfax (also called Colfax Settlement, established in 1906 by the Council of Jewish Women) and the neighborhood houses in North Denver and West Denver, see Woods and Kennedy, *Handbook of Settlements*, 25–26. For the pamphlet McClung saved, see "My Memoirs," vol. 1, item 16, McClung Collection. It noted that DPL had acquired books in Yiddish, German, and Swedish and was distributing free reading material in Italian, Polish, and Hungarian about the U.S. Constitution and naturalization procedures.

82. For an overview of the relevant scholarship on Progressive Era reform, see Leach, "1900–1914"; for a transnational view, see Daniel T. Rodgers, "Age of Social Politics"; and on Americanization, see Barrett, "Americanization."

83. I base these generalizations on a survey of census records for the eight women who completed DPL's apprentice class with McClung in 1911. For Hillkowitz, see references cited in nn65–66 above. For Martha Levy, see U.S. Bureau of the Census, *Fourteenth Census* and *Fifteenth Census*. For Gladys Charles and Lucile Jaeger, see U.S. Bureau of the Census, *Twelfth Census* and *Thirteenth Census*.

84. The municipal bathhouse, built in 1908, was at Curtis and Twentieth Streets, about five blocks from the heart of Denver's Chinatown in Hop Alley (in the vicinity of Wazee, Blake, and Market streets). Description based on photographs in DPL's Western History/Genealogy Digital Collections (s.vv. "municipal bathhouse" and "Chinatown").

85. McClung to William I. Smith, July [?], 1967, McClung Papers; *Staff Lookout*

, no. 1 (Winter 1948): 6–7, Western History Collection, Western History/Genealogy Department, Denver Public Library (this is a DPL staff newsletter; the article notes McClung's retirement and describes her career); Ingersoll, *I Remember*, 2–33; Leonard and Noel, *Denver: Mining Camp*, 161. See photographs of the branches in DPL's Western History/Genealogy Digital Collections (s.vv. "Warren Branch Library" and "Park Hill Branch Library"). On the development of public library branches, see Van Slyck, *Free to All*, 101–24. On Park Hill's early affluence as well as its later struggles over racial integration, see "Story of Park Hill," Creating Communities, accessed November 21, 2011, http://creatingcommunities denverlibrary.org/content/park-hill-story. DPL's Creating Communities Project has been discontinued.

86. "Colorado Library Association 35th," 159.

87. The following derives from Cott, *Grounding of Modern Feminism*, esp. 3, 6–7; Levine, *Highbrow/Lowbrow*; and Joan Shelley Rubin, *Making of Middlebrow Culture*.

88. Newspaper clipping [ca. 1924] in "My Memoirs," vol. 6, item 21, McClung Collection. The article credited the library club to "our inspiring and accommodating Park Hill librarian, Miss Quentrill [*sic*] McClung."

89. Quantrille D. McClung, "Denver Neighborhood Library Meetings" (quotes); McClung to William I. Smith, July [?], 1967, McClung Papers; *Staff Lookout* 15, no. 1 (Winter 1948): 6–7, Western History Collection, Western History/Genealogy Department, Denver Public Library. I call these activities middlebrow based on Joan Shelley Rubin, *Making of Middlebrow Culture*; and Levine, *Highbrow/Lowbrow*; but also on James Gilbert's review of Rubin's book, which argues, "Had Rubin wished to explore the impact of these ideas of culture, she might have found more evidence among librarians or public school teachers, who often acted as the instruments in upholding middlebrow standards" (Gilbert, "Midcult, Middlebrow, Middle Class," 546–47). For McClung's radio engagements, listed among her activities in March 1925, see also "My Memoirs," vol. 7, item 22, McClung Collection.

90. Quantrille D. McClung, "Denver Neighborhood Library Meetings," 962. Of this work McClung noted, "The humanizing of library service involves many demands that do not strictly belong to library work and causes considerable intrusion upon one's free time, but every contact, sympathetically treated, may be built into a fine structure of interest which in times of difficulty can prove a strong support." Cf. Novotny, "'Bricks without Straw.'" For Wyer's work establishing the Denver Council of Adult Education, see Ingersoll, *I Remember*, 38; and Wyer, *Books and People*, 37–39.

91. Quantrille D. McClung, "Denver Neighborhood Library Meetings," 962–63.

92. McClung to William I. Smith, July [?], 1967, McClung Papers. *Staff Lookout* 2, no. 5 (March 1935), notes, "The staff regrets that Quantrille McClung is unable to return to work"; vol. 2, no. 6 (April 1935), notes, "Quantrille McClung is improving nicely from her illness, and is able to be out for short intervals"; vol. 2, no. 7 (May 1935), notes, "Quantrille McClung left for Long Beach, California. . . . The staff extends its best wishes for a speedy recovery," all in Western History

Collection, Western History/Genealogy Department, Denver Public Library. Mc-Clung had relatives in Southern California.

93. McClung to William I. Smith, July [?], 1967, McClung Papers; Quantrille D. McClung, "Genealogy," 92; McClung diploma, University of Denver, June 10, 1936, McClung Papers; *Staff Lookout* 3, no. 6 (October 1936), Western History Collection, Western History/Genealogy Department, Denver Public Library. Ingersoll (*I Remember*, 38) recalled that the library school "was housed in a building not far from the Public Library; so many of our staff members were able to receive . . . training there."

94. McClung to William I. Smith, July [?], 1967, McClung Papers.

95. McClung, "Genealogy," 92–93, quote on 93; *Staff Lookout* 3, no. 6 (October 1936), Western History Collection, Western History/Genealogy Department, Denver Public Library.

96. The Western History Department gained prestige with the professionalization of history as a discipline and the later professionalization of the western history subfield, while the Genealogy Department was demoted to the lower status of a "division" (see part 2). Not until 1995, almost forty years after McClung's retirement and ten years after her death, would Western History and Genealogy be combined into the single department they now constitute. Leonard and Noel, *Denver: Mining Camp*, 161–62.

97. Quantrille D. McClung, "Genealogy," 962; *Staff Lookout* 3, no. 6 (October 1936), and 15, no. 1 (Winter 1948), Western History Collection, Western History/Genealogy Department, Denver Public Library.

98. McClung's offices in CGS can be traced in *Colorado Genealogist* 1, no. 1 (October 1939), through 3, no. 1 (October 1941).

99. Quantrille D. McClung, "Genealogy," 962.

100. There is no scholarly overview of Housewives Leagues nationally, let alone of the Denver Housewives League, but secondary work provides insight and context: see Lizabeth Cohen, *Consumers' Republic*, 18–61; Orleck, "'We Are That Mythical Thing'" and *Common Sense*; and Glickman, "Strike." African American Housewives Leagues engaged in a "Buy Where You Can Work" campaign that withheld consumption from businesses that would not employ black people. See Hine, "Housewives' League of Detroit"; and Wolcott, *Remaking Respectability*. Primary sources that provide insight and context include Heath, "Work of the Housewives League"; and Sorenson, *Consumer Movement*, esp. 6–8; and, on the consumer movement generally, "Business Week Reports"; and Dameron, "Consumer Movement." The Denver Housewives League formed in 1910 to secure enforcement "of laws providing for the proper and sanitary production of food supplies," promote "the health and . . . welfare of the community," and cooperate "with any civic effort striving for just and equitable home maintenance." Denver Housewives League, Inc., *Year Book 1936–37*, 1 (this and the 1938–39 yearbook are held by DPL).

101. Weil, *Family Trees*, esp. 143–79.

102. This highbrow/lowbrow delineation appears in typescript in one of McClung's scrapbooks (among items saved from October 1921); see "My Memoirs,"

vol. 5, item 20, McClung Collection. The text seems to be adapted from a 1911 tongue-in-cheek editorial, "High Brows and Low Brows," in *Out West Magazine*, which itself may be adapted from a 1910 tongue-in-cheek article, "Why Only High-Brows and Low-Brows?," *Washington Times*, August 28, 1910. A shorthand categorization in each version of this text involves one's relationship to chewing gum: for the highbrow, "no chewing gum"; for the low highbrow, "chewing gum in private"; for the high lowbrow, "chewing gum with friends"; and for the low-brow, "chewing gum on the street cars." On New Thought, see Satter, *Each Mind a Kingdom*. On workingwomen's consumption of fiction, see Enstad, *Ladies of Labor*.

103. Showing an interest in popular fiction and popular culture, social commentary, frontier themes, and the work of naturalists and conservationists, McClung used the following nine volumes for her scrapbooks: vol. 1, Joseph Louis Vance, *Nobody* (1914); vol. 2, Robert Herrick, *The Healer* (1911); vol. 3, John Muir, *Letters to a Friend: Written to Mrs. Ezra S. Carr, 1866–1879* (1915); vol. 4, James W. Gerard, *My Four Years in Germany* (1917); vol. 5, Harold Bell Wright, *Helen of the Old House* (1921); vol. 6, Margaret L. Talmadge, *The Talmadge Sisters: Norma, Constance, Natalie—an Intimate Story of the World's Most Famous Screen Family* (1924); vol. 7, Ralph Connor, *The Gaspards of Pine Croft, a Romance of the Windemere* (1923); vol. 8, James Oliver Curwood, *The Alaskan, a Novel of the North* (1923); and vol. 9, Martin Johnson, *Safari, a Saga of the African Blue* (1928).

104. Together, these materials constitute the bulk of the McClung Collection.

105. In saying that the scrapbooks "document" McClung's relationships, I do not mean to say that they do so in a straightforward way, as my analysis below demonstrates. I appreciate scholars' contentions that "scrapbooks are not transparently autobiographical"; that "makers incorporate contradictions that cannot be expressed otherwise, substitutes for expressions of the self not allowed elsewhere"; and ultimately that scrapbooks are "a material manifestation of memory—the memory of the compiler and the memory of the cultural moment in which they were made," representing "individual and group identity in cultures increasingly dependent on reading, visual literacy, and consumption of mass-produced goods." Katherine Ott, Susan Tucker, and Patricia Buckler, "An Introduction to the History of Scrapbooks," in Ott, Tucker, and Buckler, *Scrapbook in American Life*, quotes on 2 and 3. See also Garvey, *Writing with Scissors*.

106. This paragraph is based on perusal of 1900, 1910, 1920, and 1930 census records via ancestry.com for Anna Hillkowitz (later Bresler), Helen Ingersoll, Rena Reese, Louise Wells, Lucile Jaeger (later Crary), Helen Black, Martha Levy, Alma Menig, Virginia Strasser, Gladys Charles, Florence Briber, Ina Aulls, and Ella Horan. These are the names found most frequently in McClung's scrapbooks and photo albums that can be traced in the census. Bertha Webb, a member of the 1911 DPL training class, cannot be traced in this manner, though her name appears in McClung's materials. Webb may have married and taken her husband's last name. I suspect she may have wed, because when her friends in the 1911 class came up with mock degree categories for themselves, they listed Webb's as YMCA, "Young Men's Cheerful Assistant," while the others claimed such book-

ish degrees as CSR, "Champion Shelf Reader"; CCD, "Chief Culture Disseminator"; and DDB, "Doctor of Disabled Books." I also suspect Webb married, because when one of her classmates, Lucile Jaeger (who would soon wed), composed a humorous poem about buying cookies for gatherings that each member of the library "family" would most enjoy, Jaeger characterized Webb as one who "lived on love," preferring "kisses" to other sweets. McClung Collection (degrees and poem appear in "My Memoirs," vol. 2, item 17).

107. Ingersoll's records are cited in n69 above. In 1900, Rena Reese was thirty-two and living with her parents in Galion, Ohio. In 1910, she was forty-two and living with another librarian, Luella Magill, in Utica, New York (the census taker listed Reese as Magill's "companion," a designation he used for several households maintained by two women). In 1920, Reese was living alone in Denver (this census taker listed her age as forty-one, but she would have been fifty-one or fifty-two). In 1930, she was sixty-two, still working as a librarian, and living with a woman named Henrietta Pfeffer in Cincinnati, Ohio (this census taker listed Reese as Pfeffer's "lodger"). See U.S. Bureau of the Census, *Twelfth Census, Thirteenth Census, Fourteenth Census,* and *Fifteenth Census.* On Reese's move to Denver to teach the 1911 training course, see Ingersoll, *I Remember,* 29.

108. The widow was Virginia Strasser.

109. The woman who definitely married was Lucile Jaeger (later Crary).

110. Martha Levy's census records are cited in n83 above.

111. For Ina Aulls, see U.S. Bureau of the Census, *Fourteenth Census*; for Florence Briber, see U.S. Bureau of the Census, *Fifteenth Census.*

112. On urban women living apart from family and the upward class diffusion of female independence over time, see Meyerowitz, *Women Adrift.*

113. In the case of Anna Hillkowitz and her siblings, living on their own was not a choice, since their mother died in 1901 and their father in 1906. But other librarian friends of Quantrille's also lived apart from their natal families. For Elias Hillkowitz, see n65 above; for Rebecca Hillkowitz, see "JewishGen Online Worldwide Burial Registry," accessed April 27, 2020, https://www.jewishgen.org/data bases/cemetery/jowbr.php?rec=J_CO_0006037.

114. Photograph album, item 26, McClung Collection.

115. Mephisto and the Witch, from German folklore, also appear in a photograph. The name Saint Valentine generally refers to a Christian martyr in ancient Rome, while Helen and Paris derive from Greek myth; Ivanhoe and Rowena from English fiction; Cinderella and Prince Charming from folktale; Madame Butterfly and Lieutenant Pinkerton from opera; and Valentine and Sylvia from Shakespeare. (Years later, another famous couple named Valentine and Sylvia burst onto the English literary scene: poet Valentine Ackland, born Mary Kathleen, and novelist Sylvia Townsend Warner, who lived together from 1930 to 1969.) See photograph album.

116. See photograph album.

117. Party photograph, June 4, 1913; and guest list, both in "My Memoirs," vol. 2, item 17, McClung Collection. I determined the partygoers' ages by consulting census records on ancestry.com. The average age of the men was just under eigh-

en, while that of the women was twenty-one. Quantrille, at twenty-three, was the second-oldest woman there, after Alma Menig, who was twenty-five and came with her twenty-year-old brother Albert. Lucile Jaeger and John Crary, who later married, were both twenty. For ages at first marriage among U.S. women and men, see U.S. Bureau of the Census, Table MS-2, Estimated Median Age at First Marriage, by Sex: 1890 to Present, www.census.gov/population/socdemo /hh-fam/tabMS-2.pdf. In 1910, men's median age was 25.1; women's was 21.6. In 1920, men's median age was 24.6; women's was 21.2.

118. Handwritten and typed copies of "The Lay of the Last Spree" appear in both the McClung Papers at DPL and the McClung Collection at History Colorado. The typed copies attribute the "epic" poem to "epicureans" Backyard Kindling, Shernard Baw, and Maurice Missinglink, characters who also appear in photographs of the librarians' costume parties (although in the photos, the Rudyard Kipling character is called Barnyard, rather than Backyard, Kindling). On one typed copy, McClung, in her own hand, later identified the writers as "Miss Hillkowitz, Miss Thompson, and Q[uantrille] D[ay] McClung." I have been unable to identify Miss Thompson, though McClung also mentions a woman by that name in September 1913 ("My Memoirs," vol. 2, item 17, McClung Collection). The women mentioned in the poem include librarians Alma Menig, Lucile Jaeger, Cornelia Barnes, Virginia Strasser, Janet Jerome, Frances Sims, Helen Black, Ina Aulls, Helen Ingersoll, Agnes Hall, Anna Hillkowitz, Martha Levy, Rena Reese, and Quantrille herself. The men include Dexter Keezer and Wendell Stocks, who probably worked briefly for the library, as well as the library's chief engineer, Robert Stanley, and head librarian, Chalmers Hadley. I have been unable to identify all the individuals mentioned; the unidentified included Mr. Cree, Kenneth Colley, Miss Crippen, Miss McIntyre, and Miss Greene, as well as those named only as Jean, Dolly, and "Steevie" (spelled "Stevie" in typed copies of the poem).

119. I base this on a tabulation of references in McClung's scrapbooks, "My Memoirs," vols. 1–9, items 16–24; and on photographs in her albums, esp. item 27, all in McClung Collection. Another librarian who appears frequently is Janet Jerome, a children's literature expert who was educated at the University of California, Berkeley, and whose father was one of the founders of Colorado Fuel and Iron, the company later controlled by John D. Rockefeller's financial interests. But Jerome died in 1925, when she was in her thirties, breaking the hearts of her fellow librarians, including McClung. On her death, see materials collected in "My Memoirs," vols. 7–9, items 22–24, McClung Collection. On John L. Jerome, who apparently committed suicide in the wake of Colorado Fuel and Iron's takeover, see Scamehorn, *Pioneer Steelmaker*, 81–83, 91, 93, 98–100, 156, 159, 160–67.

120. See activities noted for July, December 1916; July, December 1919; April 1920, all in "My Memoirs," vols. 3 and 4, items 18 and 19, McClung Collection. The gap between outings from 1916 to 1919 is explained by Eldridge's military service. For the two World War I photographs and the two World War II clippings, see miscellaneous photographs, box 1, folder 12, McClung Collection. The clippings, from Denver newspapers in 1945, document Eldridge's imprisonment by German forces in Poland, first at Schubin and then at Lukenwalde. Before Lukenwalde

was liberated by Allied troops, Eldridge directed a "College of Captivity" at th
camp. The 1930 federal census found Eldridge, a husband and father, working i
the Greeley, Colorado, public schools; see U.S. Bureau of the Census, *Fifteent*
Census. For his prisoner-of-war record, see World War II Prisoners of War Dat
File.

121. See activities noted for August and September 1917 in "My Memoirs,
vol. 3, item 18; and photos in photograph album, item 25, all in McClung Collec
tion. For Silbert's naturalization record, see *Soundex Index*; for his draft registra
tion, see U.S. Selective Service System, *World War I*. For his membership in the
Chicago Palette and Chisel Academy of Fine Art and the exhibition of his work a
the Art Institute of Chicago, see Chris Miller, "Art Institute Exhibit of 1916," *This*
Old Palette (blog), November 16, 2016, http://thisoldpalette.blogspot.com/2006
/11/art-institute-exhibit-of-1916.html; and Chris Miller, "Ben Silbert," *This Old Pal-*
ette (blog), December 18, 2010, http://thisoldpalette.blogspot.com/2010_12_01_ar
chive.html.

122. McClung saved the note from Iris, dated March 17, 1926, in "My Memoirs,"
vol. 8, item 23, McClung Collection. This is the only reference to a person named
Iris in McClung's materials.

123. References to George Prendergast appear frequently in "My Memoirs,"
vols. 5–9, items 20–24, McClung Collection. For the specific references mentioned above, see activities McClung noted for June, July 1922; December, May,
October 1924; April, November, December 1924; January, February 1925; February, October 1926; and January, October 1927, vols. 5–8, items 20–23, McClung
Collection.

124. The Prendergasts lived in Iowa, so when George drove there, he was likely
visiting his family. His letters appear with activities Quantrille noted for June 1926
in "My Memoirs," vol. 8, item 23, McClung Collection. For the kin tie between
George and Quantrille, see William McClung, *McClung Genealogy*, 234.

125. Photos of Quantrille and George in hiking gear appear with activities she
noted for September 1923 and in street clothes with activities she noted for May
1924, both in "My Memoirs," vol. 6, item 21, McClung Collection. McClung often
sewed her own clothing; the dress she wore in the 1924 photograph was perhaps
inspired by the patterns of Austrian designer Emilie Flöge, who was closely associated with the painter Gustav Klimt (Klimt wore Flöge's designs and painted her
as well).

126. Quantrille noted the night of moon gazing in activities she recorded for
August 1927 in "My Memoirs," vol. 9, item 24, McClung Collection.

127. McClung first noted her attendance at a YWHMS meeting on October 12,
1920; see "My Memoirs," vol. 4, item 19, McClung Collection.

128. Given the proximity of the Northrup home and the Park Hill Branch
Library, it is also possible that Quantrille met Donna through the library and
then introduced her to the YWHMS. But none of Quantrille's references to Donna
connect their relationship to Quantrille's library work. The 1920 federal census
places Donna Northrup, who was then nineteen, in the Park Hill neighborhood,
living with her parents and maternal grandmother. Her father is listed as a dis-

ict court clerk, but no occupation is given for the women. See U.S. Bureau of the
Census, *Fourteenth Census*.

129. By 1925, Donna Northrup had moved with her parents to a home near
Denver's City Park, closer to downtown. See *Ballenger and Richards Denver Directory*.

130. References to Donna Northrup appear in "My Memoirs," vols. 5–8, items
20–23, McClung Collection. For references mentioned, see activities McClung
noted for February, May 1922; January, February, June, September, October,
November, December 1923; January, February, March, June 1924; January, April,
October 1925; February, March 1926; and January, October 1927, vols. 5–8, items
20–23, McClung Collection. For references to overnight visits at the Northrup
residence, see February 1922, November 1923, January 1924, April 1925, and October 1925, vols. 5–8, items 20–23, McClung Collection.

131. McClung recorded this July 1924 stay at Rocky Mountain National Park in
"My Memoirs," vol. 7, item 22, McClung Collection.

132. Photograph album, item 25, McClung Collection. Some of the photos bear
captions such as "Big Thompson Canon [*sic*]," "Steads Hotel," and "Estes Park,"
while others are unlabeled. People in the photos are not identified, though Mc-
Clung is recognizable in several. None of the photos are dated.

133. Donna's letters to Quantrille are among items Quantrille saved in her
scrapbook from July 1924; they are dated July 18, 21, 28, and 31 ("My Memoirs,"
vol. 7, item 22, McClung Collection). Donna's Easter card appears among Quantrille's scrapbook entries for April 1924 ("My Memoirs," vol. 7, item 22, McClung
Collection). In the card, Donna quotes from two 1841 Emerson essays: "Friendship," which implores the reader to put aside "false relations" in favor of ties with
"those rare pilgrims whereof only one or two wander in nature at once"; and
"Man the Reformer," which argues that men acquire possessions "only for want of
thought." Emerson, *Friendship* and *Man the Reformer*. A month after the mountain vacation, Quantrille referred to Donna as "Donna Dushka" in a scrapbook
entry; see "My Memoirs," vol. 7, item 22, McClung Collection. Thanks to David
McDonald for assuring me that *dushka* is indeed a Russian endearment (much
like "dear" or "sweetie" in English) and suggesting that English speakers might
have picked it up from reading Leo Tolstoy, Anton Chekhov, or Ivan Turgenev in
translation.

134. In addition, it is worth noting that Quantrille twice spent Valentine's Day
with Donna, something she never did with George. See scrapbook entries for
February 14, 1925 (vol. 7, item 22), and February 14, 1926 (vol. 8, item 23), both
in "My Memoirs," McClung Collection. Although Quantrille's relationships with
George and with Donna developed simultaneously, the two never seemed to be
with Quantrille at the same time (even though other people accompanied Quantrille on her outings with both). The closest Donna and George came to intersecting in time and space, at least as recorded in Quantrille's scrapbooks, is through
the person of Harold Vincent Skene, a Denver painter and also the friend who
played the piano while George and Quantrille hung their Christmas stockings in
1924. Quantrille also knew Harold through a Trinity Methodist Church dramatic

troupe, the Trinity Players; both acted in a play by a local woman, Mrs. Gurn sey Walker, called *Commander-in-Chief*, performed in 1925 in Denver and Fo Collins, including once for the local Women's Christian Temperance Union (se activities noted for October and November 1925; and playbill for Women's Chris tian Temperance Union performance, both in "My Memoirs," vol. 8, item 23, Mc Clung Collection). By 1926, scrapbook entries hint at a triangular relationship among Quantrille, Donna, and Harold (perhaps a quadrangular relationship since George was also friends with Harold). Or they may suggest nothing at all. Ir July 1926, Quantrille had dinner at the Northrups' and noted that she "had a long talk with Donna." Thereafter, Quantrille continued to spend time with Donna, but she never again noted spending the night with her. In August 1926, Quan trille noted that Harold visited her at the house she shared with her parents and that the two had "some good talk." A few months later, Quantrille noted that she and Donna went together to visit "Harold Skene's studio." These references appear among activities McClung noted for July, August, and December 1926 in "My Memoirs," vol. 8, item 23, McClung Collection. Skene seems not to have married; he died in 1978. DPL owns several of his paintings, which include mountain landscapes, urban and industrial subjects, and one called *Taos at Night*. Skene also gave the library a one-page, handwritten autobiography listing his training (Harvard University, Denver Art Academy, Broadmoor Art Academy) and the subjects of his work; see Skene, "Autobiography," Western History Collection, Western History/Genealogy Department, Denver Public Library. In the 1930 census, Skene is listed as a commercial artist living alone in North Denver, a mile from the McClung house; U.S. Bureau of the Census, *Fifteenth Census*.

135. Scrapbook entry, July 12, 1924, "My Memoirs," vol. 7, item 22, McClung Collection. By 1927, Quantrille stopped mentioning Donna in her scrapbooks, and it is not clear what became of her or the bond the two women shared. Apparently, Donna's father died in the late 1920s; then her mother remarried. In 1940, a census taker found Donna, now forty, living with her mother and stepfather in West Palm Beach, Florida. By 1945, Donna lived alone in the same city, working as a housekeeper. There is no evidence that she ever married. She died in West Palm Beach in 1968. See family tree created by a distant relative, which states that Donna's father, Clarence Northrup, died in 1927: Krasulski Bostock and Related Family Tree, consulted June 5, 2012, at ancestry.com. In 1940, Donna and her mother, May, or Mary, were living with her mother's new husband, William Thacher, a realtor; see U.S. Bureau of the Census, *Sixteenth Census*. For the 1945 census, see *Eleventh Census of the State of Florida*; and for the death notice, see U.S. Social Security Administration, *Social Security Death Index*.

136. Quantrille McClung, "Moon Madness," [ca. 1920s], McClung Collection. Drinkwater's "Moonlit Apples" speaks of autumn fruit on orchard boughs keeping "tryst with the moon"; see Drinkwater, *Poems, 1908–1919*, 156.

137. Quantrille McClung, "Moon Madness," [ca. 1920s], McClung Collection.

138. Quantrille D. McClung, *Memoirs of My Childhood*, 75.

139. For Donna's disappearance, see n135 above. George did not vanish from Quantrille's life. He was a schoolteacher in Iowa and Arizona for a time but went

n to become an Episcopalian priest, working first in Flagstaff and then, for the est of his career, in San Diego. In 1940, he married the former Jane Tucker, now Varren (this was her second marriage), who came from a prominent California family. Her maternal grandfather, Edward M. House, had been an advisor to President Woodrow Wilson. Marrying Jane Tucker Warren gave George access to wealth, status, and Hollywood connections. For example, Elizabeth Montgomery, who in the 1960s would star as Samantha in the television series *Bewitched*, served as flower girl for George and Jane's 1940 wedding, when she was seven years old. The Prendergasts sometimes sent Quantrille money as she aged (see McClung to Blackwelder, March 28, 1972, in which Quantrille notes that she received a check for twenty-five dollars from her "dear cousins in California," and August 27, 1972, in which she writes that her "cousin married a wife with money," adding, "They have been very generous to me," both in McClung Papers). For George's marriage and career, see "Prendergast-Warren Nuptials in California," undated newspaper clipping [May 1940], reprinted from *Coconino Sun* (Flagstaff, Ariz.) [May 1940], consulted at ancestry.com; "Intention to Marry," *Los Angeles Times*, May 17, 1940; and Hedda Hopper, Looking at Hollywood, *Los Angeles Times*, May 16, 1947. See also U.S. Bureau of the Census, *Twelfth Census, Thirteenth Census, Fifteenth Census*, and *Sixteenth Census*.

140. For Denzel McClung's 1924 marriage to May Shore, see Marriage Record Report; and U.S. Bureau of the Census, *Fifteenth Census*. For Quantrille McClung's household in 1940, see U.S. Bureau of the Census, *Sixteenth Census*.

141. What follows is based on a generation of work in the history of sexuality helpfully synthesized in Rupp, *Desired Past*, esp. 73–129. Relevant earlier texts include Smith-Rosenberg, "Female World"; Chauncey, "From Sexual Inversion"; Chauncey, "Christian Brotherhood"; Chauncey, *Gay New York*; D'Emilio and Freedman, *Intimate Matters*; Terry, "Theorizing Deviant Historiography"; and esp. Freedman, "'Burning of Letters Continues.'" On the West, see esp. Boag, *Redressing America's Frontier Past*. More recent scholarship has stressed the contingency and limited reach of so-called modern sexuality (that is, the notion that all people have a sexual identity situated within a homo/hetero binary, which is sometimes complicated by a third term, bisexuality, that nonetheless depends for its meaning on the homo/hetero divide). See esp. Kunzel, *Criminal Intimacy*; and Shah, *Stranger Intimacy*.

142. Rupp, *Desired Past* and *Sapphistries*, 127–40; Smith-Rosenberg, "Female World"; Chauncey, "Sexual Inversion to Homosexuality"; Freedman, "'Burning of Letters Continues'"; Sahli, "Smashing." For nuanced analysis of such relationships and their representation, see Love, *Feeling Backward*, chap. 3. The argument that white women were presumed passionless in the nineteenth century has been helpfully complicated by April Haynes in *Riotous Flesh*, but the greater acknowledgement of women's sexual selfhood that characterized the earlier era gave way by midcentury to pronouncements of white women's passionlessness and purity.

143. The evidence I have provided of such happy inversions comes mostly from the 1910s. But evidence from McClung's scrapbooks does not cease in the 1920s,

and it sometimes combines with material that suggests same-sex entanglement. It especially collects around a woman named Sudie Mai Hodnette, a bookkeeper who never married. There is a December 1925 thank-you note from Hodnette to McClung and a fellow librarian, Lucile Beggs, addressed to "Examples of the Flower of Womanhood" (followed by a tiny line drawing of a shapely female form); it thanks McClung and Beggs for a get-well booklet they apparently made for Hodnette when she was ill. A couple of months later, facing scrapbook pages include the following: an invitation from two unmarried librarians, Rena Reese and Mary Weaver, to a luncheon (both worked at DPL and Reese later lived with female companions; see n107 above); a notation that McClung went on Valentine's Day to the symphony with Donna Northrup; a snapshot of a cross-dressed woman captioned "Sudie Mai Hodnette in costume"; and a valentine captioned "Sherma" (I do not know who Sherma was, but Sherma, while a rare given name, is virtually always given to babies born female). Finally, there is a comic letter to McClung in the same handwriting as the 1925 note, dated January 19, 1927, purporting to be from a "Hen Pecked Harry" (but apparently from Hodnette), who lists himself as a resident of the "Violent Ward." It uses mock legal language and pretended bad diction to deny Hen Pecked Harry's responsibility for ninety-six cents' worth of lunch foods "consumed or destroyed" by Lucile Beggs: "May I remind you of that ancient and truthful adage—to wit—'It aint what you used to was; its what you may now is,' which, translated into Modern English, is as follows[:] I used to was guarantor for Miss Lucile Beggs, but since she has attained the age of manhood, 'I may now is *not*.'" All in "My Memoirs," vol. 8, item 23, McClung Collection. Together, these scrapbook entries suggest that McClung and her female friends did not abandon their flirtations with one another or with gender play in the 1920s, even as their engagement with the same may have diminished in frequency or visibility or both. In the 1930s, Hodnette left Denver for Omaha and then San Francisco, where she worked as a bookkeeper and was involved in Bay Area hiking clubs. She died there in 1989. Her residence in Denver, Omaha, and San Francisco is traceable through city directories, e.g., *Polk's Crocker-Langley San Francisco*; for her death, see U.S. Social Security Administration, *Social Security Death Index*. For Hodnette's hiking club ties, see *Oakland (Calif.) Tribune*, February 17, 1949; February 5, June 25, 1953; November 29, 1956; May 30, 1957. For correspondence with McClung when both were older, see epilogue.

144. Stansell, *American Moderns*, 3.

145. Stansell, esp. 225–308; Cott, *Grounding of Modern Feminism*, 13–50 and passim.

146. Burke, *From Greenwich Village to Taos*, esp. 13–43.

147. For Eastern European Jews and bohemian Greenwich Village, I rely on Stansell, *American Moderns*, 6–7, 21–25, 62–66, 126–28, 279–81; and Michels, *Fire in Their Hearts*. For Hillkowitz and the JCRS, I rely on Abrams, "*Unsere Leit.*"

148. In hosting costume parties when she returned to Denver, Hillkowitz might have drawn on masquerade balls sponsored from 1898 to 1917 by New York's largest Yiddish-language socialist newspaper, *Forverts*. Michels, *Fire in Their Hearts*, 105–9.

149. I use "playing bohemian" in the manner that Deloria uses "playing Indian" in *Playing Indian*. There was also a performative aspect to bohemian Greenwich Village that made the distinction between "authentic" bohemians and bohemian "poseurs" a fine (and productive) one, at least before World War I. See Stansell, *American Moderns*; and broadly, Levin, *Bohemia in America*; and also Heap, *Slumming*, 154–88.

150. See activities noted for May 1924, "My Memoirs," vol. 6, item 21, McClung Collection. On women's evolving relationship with the motorcar, see Scharff, *Taking the Wheel*.

151. On this process, see Katz, *Invention of Heterosexuality*.

152. Stansell, *American Moderns*, 89–90, 197–208, 251; Schwarz, *Radical Feminists of Heterodoxy*; Schwarz, Peiss, and Simmons, "'We Were a Little Band.'" "Unorthodox women" was Mabel Dodge's phrase, quoted in Schwarz, *Radical Feminists of Heterodoxy*, 1.

153. See Burke, "Spud Johnson." Most of the evidence Burke presents is from the 1930s, but Spud Johnson, lover of poet Witter Bynner, first went to New Mexico in 1922. On Bynner in Taos, see Burke, *Greenwich Village to Taos*, esp. 159–62.

154. For the photos, see item 26, McClung Collection. For meanings of "gay," see Chauncey, *Gay New York*, 14–23. For West Coast bohemian milieux that fostered complicated ties between politics and same-sex relations, see Hurewitz, *Bohemian Los Angeles*; and Sueyoshi, *Queer Compulsions*.

155. For Denzel McClung's service, see *U.S. Marine Corps Muster Rolls*; for Ralph Munn's draft registration, see U.S. Selective Service System, *World War I*. For letters from Munn, see materials in McClung's scrapbook from late 1918, including an undated note Munn addressed to "Everybody," begun en route to France and continued while stationed there, in "My Memoirs," vol. 4, item 19, McClung Collection.

156. See photographs in album, item 27, McClung Collection.

157. Burke, *From Greenwich Village to Taos*, 26.

158. Stansell, *American Moderns*, 311–38.

159. The next two paragraphs draw on Karen Manners Smith, "New Paths to Power"; Sarah Deutsch, "From Ballots to Breadlines"; Cott, *Grounding of Modern Feminism*; Leonard and Noel, *Denver: Mining Camp*, 158–60; and Abbott, Leonard, and Noel, *Colorado*, 176–81. For a western locale where Prohibition gave women new opportunities to imbibe, produce alcohol, and socialize with men over bootleg drinks, see Mary Murphy, *Mining Cultures*, 42–70.

160. Quantrille D. McClung, *Memoirs of My Childhood*, 26–31, quotes on 26, 30. Photo of McClung with Asbury Methodist Sunday school class in photograph album, item 25; see also record of Standard Bearer activities: e.g., February, April 1918; March, June 1920, "My Memoirs," vol. 4, item 19, all in McClung Collection. By 1925, McClung was a speaker for an Asbury Methodist Standard Bearer meeting; see activities for May 1925 in "My Memoirs," vol. 7, item 22, McClung Collection.

161. See activities listed for October 1920; February, April, September, October, December 1921; May, October 1922; February, April, November 1923; November

1925; and January 1931, all in "My Memoirs," vols. 4–6, 8, 9, items 19–21, 23, 24, Mc
Clung Collection. I assume YWHMS was a branch of the Woman's Home Missio[...]
Society; see Tomkinson, *Twenty Years' History*.

162. See activities listed for July, August 1923; June (includes print material o[...]
San Grael), October 1924; April 1925; and June 1926, all in "My Memoirs," vols. 6–8[...]
items 21–23, McClung Collection.

163. Most of the plays were written by a prominent local woman, Lily Walker
who signed herself Mrs. Gurnsey Walker. See activities listed for November 1923[...]
October 1924; March, October (notes WCTU performance), November (notes[...]
performance at Fitzsimmons Army Hospital in Aurora, where "wet speeches"[...]
met with applause), December 1925; October 1927; and January 1931, all in "My[...]
Memoirs," vols. 6–9, items 21–24, McClung Collection.

164. On Shi Meiyu, also known as Dr. Mary Stone, see activities noted for
November 1915 (when McClung heard Shi Meiyu speak); on "Miss Hopkins of
Korea" and "Mrs. Mei of China," see activities noted for June, July 1920; on "Miss
Shannon of Burma," see activities noted for February 1923; for photos of missionaries Ellen Suffern and Pauline Westcott in China and of unnamed Chinese
people, see first pages of vol. 5 [1920?] and of vol. 6 [1923?]; for a Denver visit by
Pauline Westcott, see activities noted for June 1927; and for photos of unnamed
white missionaries and African people (captioned "[I] think Augusta B. Morton
sent these from Africa"), see vol. 9, all in "My Memoirs," vols. 3–6 and 9, items
18–21 and 24, McClung Collection. On Shi Meiyu, see also Shemo, *Chinese Medical Ministries*; and Hunter, *Gospel of Gentility*, 24, 74–75.

165. These generalizations are based on the essays in Reeves-Ellington, Sklar,
and Shemo, *Competing Kingdoms*, esp. Hunter, "Women's Mission." A key contemporary articulation of Christian internationalism was Merrill's 1919 *Christian
Internationalism*.

166. These generalizations are also based on essays in Reeves-Ellington, Sklar,
and Shemo, *Competing Kingdoms*, but esp. Renda, "Doing Everything."

167. See Renda, "Doing Everything," 384–85; Emily S. Rosenberg, "Rescuing
Women and Children"; and Pascoe, *Relations of Rescue*.

168. See, e.g., Pascoe, *Relations of Rescue*, 34–40; Hunter, *Gospel of Gentility*,
esp. 52–89, 191–97; and Jacobs, "Breaking and Remaking Families."

169. Quantrille D. McClung, *Memoirs of My Childhood*, 1, 20. That her father
abdicated what the family saw as his manly responsibility is further suggested
by an allusive passage in *Memoirs of My Childhood* where McClung notes that
the principal of the school she and her brother attended from the first through
the eighth grade played a key role in her brother's upbringing: "In later life my
brother confided to me that, at a time when it was well for him to be given certain
instruction for his own protection, [the principal] took him aside and told him
what he should know in such a kindly manner and with such real interest in the
welfare of the boy, my brother was eternally grateful to him" (20). According to
1920 and 1930 census takers, Benjamin McClung worked as a "helper" at the U.S.
Mint; the 1940 census shows that he had retired with a pension. The 1920 census

nows that even though Benjamin had a job, the McClungs still had a boarder wing with them. See census records cited in n43 and n140 above.

170. For scrapbook references to Quantrille and Denzel's youthful relationship, see activities noted for November 1913; October, November 1916; August, November, December 1917; and February ("gadding"), April, May, July, August, November 1919, all in "My Memoirs," vols. 2–4, items 17–19, McClung Collection. For her description of his adult life, see Quantrille D. McClung, *Memoirs of My Childhood*, 1.

171. For Quantrille's trip to the Shore ranch and for the birth of Hattie Ellen McClung, see activities noted for July, August, September 1925, "My Memoirs," vol. 8, item 23, McClung Collection. For Denzel and May Shore McClung's family census records, see U.S. Bureau of the Census, *Fifteenth Census* and *Sixteenth Census*. See also Wargo, *Marriages of Grand County*. I found Hattie Ellen McClung (1925–48) buried with her aunt Quantrille and grandparents Benjamin and Henrietta on a 2010 site visit to Crown Hill Cemetery in Wheat Ridge, a Denver suburb. A family friend confirmed the McClung siblings' rift, though he did not know Quantrille well until she was older and did not know the source of the tension. He did recall that when her brother died, Quantrille made sure that Denzel's family "hadn't usurped her place in the cemetery." Smith interview.

172. "Ruth" to Quantrille McClung, February 18, 1971, McClung Papers; see also letters dated June 24, July 21, 1971, which confirm the dispute over family grave plots noted above.

173. Smith interview; McClung to Bernice Blackwelder, July 23, August 27, 1972, McClung Papers. For Quantrille's brief residence in a home on South Williams Street in Denver, see *Colorado Genealogist* 5, no. 1 (January 1944). On Mullen, see Convery, *Pride of the Rockies*.

174. McClung to "Mr. and Mrs. B. F. McClung," July 24, 25, 28, 1935; photos and memorabilia in Wyoming scrapbook, item 13, all in McClung Collection.

175. *Staff Lookout* 15, no. 1 (Winter 1948): 6–7; diary, September 3, 1947, French Papers, both in Western History Collection, Western History/Genealogy Department, Denver Public Library. Adelaide French also recorded McClung's health challenges in diary entries from September 13, 1947; February 20, March 5, April 2, 10, May 4, June 3, 12, September 3, 25, 1959; and August 27, 31, September 5, 7, 1964. For McClung's move to a Capitol Hill apartment at 975 Washington Street, see *Colorado Genealogist* 5, no. 2 (April 1944). See also Library Commission meeting minutes, April 20, 1943, copy in Accession File for McClung Papers.

176. *Staff Lookout* 13, no. 3/4 (Summer/Fall 1946): 1–2, and 14, no. 1 (Winter 1947): 1–2, Western History Collection, Western History/Genealogy Department, Denver Public Library.

177. As noted, McClung served as an officer in CGS in the 1930s and 40s; thereafter, she researched the families of Colorado governors, the results of which the society published from 1947 to 1964. In the 1960s, McClung again served as an officer. *Colorado Genealogist* 1, no. 1 (October 1939), to 26, no. 3 (January 1965).

178. Activities noted for August 1925 (quote about Pearl Look Pang); materials

saved from summer months 1927 (undated newspaper clipping about Frank Loc
and souvenir from Golden Bough shop captioned "Pearl Pang"), all in "My Mem
oirs," vols. 8 and 9, items 23 and 24, McClung Collection.

179. Activities noted for October 1927 and March 1931, "My Memoirs," vol.
item 24, McClung Collection.

180. These sources together constitute the Blackwelder Papers (see n10 above

181. Shortridge, *Cities on the Plains*, 205–6; Miner, *Next Year Country*, 52–54.

182. Melanie Bailey, Fort Hays State University Alumni Association, Hays, Kan
sas, personal communication with author, February 9, 16, 2007.

183. This information comes from yearbooks, some of which have been digi
tized in *Reveille* Yearbook Collection, University Archives, Forsyth Library, Fort
Hays State University, Hays, Kansas. For assistance with yearbooks not yet digi-
tized, I am grateful to librarian Patty Nicholas, Special Collections/University Archives. See *Reveille 1921*, 79, 120, 135, 136; *Reveille 1922*, 58, 59, 152, 153, 154, 164, 168,
174, 190; *Reveille 1923*, 38, 48, 98, 101, 115, 121, 122; and *Reveille 1924*, 38, 116, 124, 128.

184. *Reveille 1921*, 72, 120, 133, 135, 136; and *Reveille 1922*, 54, 62, 70, 151, 152,
153, both in *Reveille* Yearbook Collection; Lance and Fowler interview. Karl Pratt
of the Fort Hays State University Alumni Association (personal communication
with author, April 12, 2014) indicates that Jessie Granger earned a bachelor of
music degree in 1922 but that neither Helen nor Duane Fowler graduated from
Fort Hays.

185. Photograph album, Blackwelder Papers; photograph album, item 26, Mc-
Clung Collection.

186. Photograph album, Blackwelder Papers; photograph album, item 26, Mc-
Clung Collection. For the geographic origins of Bernice's college classmates, I
rely on the *Reveille* Yearbook Collection.

187. Photograph album, Blackwelder Papers; photograph album, item 26, Mc-
Clung Collection. While in college, Bernice Fowler lived in the home of Ed, Ruth,
and James Davis. Bernice must have adored little James, given all the photos she
took of him (he would have been a year old when she started school). Ed Davis
taught at Fort Hays. Melanie Bailey, Fort Hays State University Alumni Association, Hays, Kansas, personal communication with author, February 16, 2007; *1925
Kansas State Census*. On white, middle-class college students, see Fass, *Damned
and the Beautiful*.

188. Thomas Snyder, *120 Years*, 65; Barbara Miller Solomon, *Company of Educated Women*, 62–77.

189. Thomas Snyder, *120 Years*, 65; Barbara Miller Solomon, *Company of Educated Women*, 62–77. Interpretively, this paragraph is influenced by Fass, *Damned
and the Beautiful*.

190. Photograph album, Blackwelder Papers. Victory Highway was part of an
auto trails system that predated numbered highways. Private associations often
organized and maintained them. This highway roughly followed the route that
would become U.S. 40.

191. Blackwelder Author File, Caxton Press, Caldwell, Idaho.

192. On Clare Osborne Reed and the founding of the Columbia School of Music, see *Chicago Tribune*, June 30, 1920 (the article notes an event marking the school's twentieth year); and *Woman's Who's Who*, 665. The latter source notes that Osborne Reed was a member of the Chicago Political Equality League and other women's groups. For the municipal suffrage struggle in Chicago, see Flanagan, *Seeing with Their Hearts*, esp. 74–84.

193. Photograph album, Blackwelder Papers.

194. Like Bernice Fowler, N. Louise Wright had also attended the Columbia School of Music in Chicago. This and all background information on Central College (now Central Methodist University) comes from Samson, "Swinney Conservatory of Music," esp. 19–62.

195. On Missouri's Little Dixie, see Hurt, *Agriculture and Slavery* and "Planters and Slavery"; and Frizzell, "Southern Identity."

196. Bernice would not again work full-time for just one employer until the early 1950s, when she took a job with the CIA in Washington, D.C.

197. Loose scrapbook pages, Blackwelder Papers (these pages include photos taken by Bernice and her acquaintances, portraits of students, images of faculty members cut from college publications, and a group photo of the Central College women's glee club clipped from a pictorial supplement to the *St. Louis Post-Dispatch*, March 31, [1928 or '29]). See also Samson, "Swinney Conservatory of Music," esp. 84, 88, 89, 90, 95, 193, 196.

198. Blackwelder, *Great Westerner*.

199. Blackwelder to McClung, March 4, 1974, McClung Papers. Blackwelder also told McClung that the teacherage where she lived at Central College was the former home of Kit Carson's nephew George Carson, son of Kit's brother William. Blackwelder to McClung, July 20, 1970, McClung Papers.

200. Blackwelder to McClung, December 11, 1970, McClung Papers.

201. All quotes from John McCurdy tapes, McClung Papers. The taped exchange took place on September 21, 1953, at the home of Bess and Fred Heine in Lucas, Kansas. The Heines were a prominent ranching family in Russell County, where, by the 1950s, they owned a thousand head of cattle. They claimed a moment of minor fame during World War II when they purchased the first U.S. Army jeep to be converted to civilian use. *Life* magazine covered the story; see "U.S. Civilians Buy Their First Jeeps." According to a Kansas newspaper article from the early 1950s, the Heines later purchased the first commercial jeep produced for civilians after the war, and they also "pioneered the use of machines instead of horses to ride the range." "Jeep Brings Fame to Its Owners on Farm Near Lucas," undated clipping, [1951, probably a western Kansas paper]; see also a 1944 snapshot of the Heines in their first jeep, both in Blackwelder Papers. Fred Heine was a trustee of the board of directors for the Cowboy Hall of Fame (now the National Cowboy and Western Heritage Museum) in Oklahoma City. According to Blackwelder, he nominated Kit Carson for induction into what is now the museum's Great Westerners Hall of Fame. See "Awards and Halls of Fame," National Cowboy and Western Heritage Museum, accessed July 31, 2013, http://

www.nationalcowboymuseum.org/info/awards-hof/Great-Westerners.asp.
and Blackwelder to McClung, September 24, 1960, McClung Papers. Gerriann
Schaad of the National Cowboy and Western Heritage Museum's Dickinson Re
search Center confirms Heine's trusteeship, which ran from 1955 to 1964, but no
that it was Heine who nominated Carson for inclusion in the Hall of Fame. Gerri
anne Schaad, personal communication with author, August 1, 2013.

202. John McCurdy tapes, McClung Papers.

203. Blackwelder to McClung, June [?], 1972, McClung Papers.

204. Blackwelder to McClung, June [?], 1972, McClung Papers.

205. John McCurdy tapes, McClung Papers.

206. Albert Looking Elk Martínez, later a governor of Taos Pueblo, was one
of the Taos Pueblo Painters. See Witt, *Three Taos Pueblo Painters*, a catalogue of
a 2003 exhibition held at the Harwood Museum of Art of the University of New
Mexico in Taos and the Panhandle-Plains Historical Museum of West Texas A&M
University in Canyon.

207. Blackwelder to McClung, March 12, 1973, McClung Papers.

208. Blackwelder to McClung, June [?], 1972, McClung Papers.

209. U.S. Bureau of the Census, *Fifteenth Census*.

210. Blackwelder to McClung, September 5, 1967, McClung Papers. Architect
Louis Sullivan and engineer Danmark Adler designed the Auditorium. Carey,
"Auditorium Building."

211. *Chicago Tribune*, April 13, 1930. Columnist Edward Moore wrote, "All of the
choristers are Chicago singers.... They are all music students in various Chicago
musical schools or studios, and all have ambitions for operatic careers."

212. Bernice told Quantrille, "When I first met Harold, we were auditioning
for a month of Light Opera. We both were chosen, but he decided to join a radio
quartet." Blackwelder to McClung, July 12, 1978, McClung Papers. Photos and
other materials in Bernice's scrapbook (Blackwelder Papers) identify Harold's
first major singing ensemble in Chicago as the Wanderers.

213. "Light Opera Season to Open April 21," *Voice of Opera* (Chicago Civic
Opera Company), March 22, 1930, in scrapbook, Blackwelder Papers.

214. The scrapbook in the Blackwelder Papers contains playbills for and reviews of these performances, as well as signed photographs from many of the
players. For quote, see Blackwelder to McClung, August 6, 1968, McClung Papers.
This was one of several times Blackwelder reminisced about the 1930 season; see
also Blackwelder to McClung, February 26, 1971, November 26, 1972, McClung
Papers.

215. *Chicago Tribune*, April 22, 1930. Moore wrote enthusiastically about the
season of light opera; see also *Chicago Tribune*, May 6, 11, June 8, 1930. Blackwelder saved these and other reviews, including those published in the *Chicagoan* and other periodicals, in her scrapbook (Blackwelder Papers), where she
underlined each statement about the chorus and every listing of her own name.

216. *Chicago Tribune*, February 8, March 22, 1931.

217. Two clippings in Bernice's scrapbook (Blackwelder Papers), apparently

om Missouri newspapers, note Fowler and Thompson earning places in Chicago's season of light opera. For the Wanderers, see clippings in scrapbook, Blackwelder Papers; and *Chicago Tribune*, February 8, 1931 (quote). Thompson had performed on WGN earlier; see *Chicago Tribune*, November 13, 1927 (describes the on-air vocal contest in which he participated); and November 7, 1928 where he is named as a staff vocalist).

218. Inscribed photo and undated newspaper clipping of wedding notice, Blackwelder Papers; John McCurdy tapes, McClung Papers (on which, in a 1953 conversation, Bernice states, "I never took a wedding trip"); Bernice Blackwelder Diary, November 1, 1938, Blackwelder Papers (hereafter referred to as Blackwelder Diary); she writes, "Moved back to Deming ... across the street from our Honeymoon House"). Although Bernice and Harold married at St. James Cathedral, they do not appear to have been members of the church.

219. Evidence of Bernice Fowler in Chicago Theatre shows appears in photos of mostly unidentified stage productions (Blackwelder Papers). Those photos also show that Harold Blackwelder performed there. Bernice labeled one picture "*Show Boat*, Chicago Theater, 1930," though *Show Boat* seems to have been produced there in 1933 after an earlier run at the Auditorium Theatre. See *Chicago Tribune*, January 30, 1933. On the Chicago Theatre, flagship of the Balaban and Katz theater chain, and on movie palaces and combination theaters generally, see "History of the Chicago Theatre," Chicago Theatre, accessed March 18, 2014, http://www.thechicagotheatre.com/about/history.html; Lizabeth Cohen, *Making a New Deal*, 124–30 passim; and Nasaw, *Going Out*, 221–40.

220. Undated newspaper clippings (reviews of Reinhardt's 1934 production of *A Midsummer Night's Dream*), Blackwelder Papers. See also Charles Collins, review of *A Midsummer Night's Dream*, produced by Max Reinhardt, Auditorium Theatre, Chicago, *Chicago Tribune*, November 25, 1934. In 1971, Bernice recalled her role in the play when she saw another production of it at the same theater (though she misremembered the year as 1935 or 1936); see Blackwelder to McClung, March 24, April 14, 1971, McClung Papers. On the Auditorium, an older venue than the Chicago Theatre, see n210 above; and Edwards and Edwards, *Chicago Entertainment*, 79.

221. On the Duncan Sisters, see Buckner, "Angel and the Imp"; and Wallace, "Uncle Tom's Cabin," esp. 151. From "Uncle Tom's Cabin & American Culture" website, accessed April 27, 2020 (http://utc.iath.virginia.edu/index2 f.html), see W. R., "The Duncan Sisters in 'Topsy and Eva,'" *New York World*, December 24, 1924, http://utc.iath.virginia.edu/onstage/revus/osre13af.html; and John Sullivan, "Topsy and Eva Play Vaudeville," http://utc.iath.virginia.edu/interpret/exhibits/sullivan/sullivan.html. For the Chicago performances, see "The Playbill of Chicago Theaters, Shubert Apollo, Beginning Monday Evening Dec. 25, 1933 ... The Duncan Sisters in *Topsy and Eva*"; and undated newspaper clippings (reviews of 1933 *Topsy and Eva* production at Apollo Theater), all in Blackwelder Papers. One of the clippings is Charles Collins, review of *Topsy and Eva*, Apollo Theater, Chicago, *Chicago Tribune*, December 27, 1933.

222. *Chicago Tribune*, December 27, 1933.

223. Lott, *Love and Theft*; Roediger, *Wages of Whiteness*, 115–31; Nasaw, *Going Out*, 53–60.

224. Glenn, *Female Spectacle*, 49–56; Kibler, *Rank Ladies*, 111–42; Wallace, "Uncle Tom's Cabin"; Buckner, "Angel and the Imp."

225. Quote from Lloyd Lewis, review of *Topsy and Eva*, Apollo Theater, Chicago, [*Chicago Daily News*, 1933?], Blackwelder Papers. On Rosetta Duncan, see Slide, *Encyclopedia of Vaudeville*, 144–46; and Slide, *Eccentrics of Comedy*, 47–56, esp. 56. On the homosexual/heterosexual binary, see n141 above. On the intertwined hardening of sexual and racial categories, see Sommerville, *Queering the Color Line*.

226. Blackwelder Diary, January 1, 1937–January 1, 1941, and passim; for Grace Dunn's divorce, see Blackwelder Diary, June 24, 1938. It is not clear when or where Helen Fowler married Elmer Rollins Dunn, the presumed father of Robert "Bob" Dunn, or when or how the couple separated. Obituaries for Mabel and Wilbur Fowler in 1930 and 1933, respectively, indicate that Helen was married to Mr. Dunn and that the couple lived in Mount Vernon, New York, but the 1930 census finds Mr. Dunn living with his father, his sister Grace, and a female roomer in Brooklyn and working as a clerk in a brokerage house; U.S. Bureau of the Census, *Fifteenth Census*. The 1940 census finds Helen Fowler Dunn, who is a music teacher, and her son living in a rooming house in Oak Park; U.S. Bureau of the Census, *Sixteenth Census*.

227. I rely here on Gregory, *Southern Diaspora*. Harold's time with the Weaver Brothers and Elviry is documented in Blackwelder Diary, January–April 1937 passim, as well as mostly undated newspaper clippings that include ads for and reviews of Weaver Brothers shows from Oklahoma City to San Francisco and from Vancouver to Chicago, Blackwelder Papers. The only dated review is from a Portland paper on January 29, 1937. See also *Big Spring Daily Herald* (Big Springs, Tex.), March 14, 1937. A script for a typical Weavers show, supplied by the Ralph Foster Museum at the College of the Ozarks (Point Lookout, Missouri), appears in Joshua Heston, "The Weaver Brothers and Elviry," State of the Ozarks, accessed April 29, 2014, http://stateoftheozarks.net/culture/music/weaverbros.php; it mentions Harold Blackwelder's performance. See also "Weaver Brothers and Elviry," Ozarkswatch Video Magazine, broadcast January 1, 2010, accessed April 29, 2014, http://video.optv.org/video/1392965657.

228. Quote from clipping of *Oklahoma News* review, ca. March 1937, Blackwelder Papers. Songs Harold performed appear there and within the script in Heston, "The Weaver Brothers and Elviry."

229. Quote from review of a later western tour as Neil Fortune, in undated clipping, *News-Telegram* (Portland, Ore.), ca. July 1939, Blackwelder Papers. The act got similar reviews during his 1938 midwestern and western tours; see undated clippings, ca. 1938–39, Blackwelder Papers. One Portland review claimed that Neil Fortune, even though "reared in North Carolina," had been "born in Wyoming" (undated newspaper clipping, ca. July 1939, Blackwelder Papers). Harold was born and raised in North Carolina.

230. Bill C. Malone, *Country Music, U.S.A.*, 1–175. For thoughtful analysis of the racial and class politics of country music's western turns (in both the 1930s and the postwar era), see LaChapelle, *Proud*, 132–58.

231. Quote in Blackwelder Diary, May 20, 1938; tours and preparation covered in Blackwelder Diary, January–June 1938 passim. Harold's association with Marvin Welt and Benny Meroff appears across the same period of entries. Ads for and reviews of Meroff's *Swing Sing Revue*, in which Neil Fortune performed, appear in undated newspaper clippings, ca. 1938, Blackwelder Papers.

232. Blackwelder Diary, January 14, April 19, July 9, 1938.

233. Quotes from Blackwelder Diary, February 18, 19, 1937. Bernice apparently began her work at WGN in August 1935; see Blackwelder Diary, August 19, 1937, where she wrote that it had been two years since she started. She noted her performances in both the *Pageant of Melody* and *Midday Service* programs in Blackwelder Diary, February 22, 1937 (after several days with *Midday Service*, on Sunday, February 28, she reflected, "Didn't feel guilty about not going to church as I had been there every day this week"). The *Chicago Tribune* (February 22, 1937) announced that *Midday Service* would thereafter be broadcast from a 600-seat auditorium that was open to the public. The same day's radio listings note that *Pageant of Melody*, which aired at 9:45 P.M., would feature tenor Attilio Baggiore, a mixed quartet, and a concert orchestra; Henry Weber conducted.

234. See, e.g., Blackwelder Diary, February 27, March 27, April 7, 1937.

235. Blackwelder Diary, September 17, October 4, 5, 1937.

236. Blackwelder Diary, May–September 1937 passim.

237. Blackwelder Diary, September 25, October 17, 18, 19, 20, 21, 23, 1937. Bernice's and Harold's memberships are also recorded in AFRA Membership Records, SAG-AFTRA Chicago Local Office. The memberships were recorded November 19, 1937, and both paid dues for a year until they were excused November 1, 1938, when they went "to Coast"—that is, to the East Coast. Both were reinstated in 1945, but their records drop off thereafter.

238. For Sam Thompson's and Phil Culkin's AFRA executive board activity, see *Chicago Tribune*, September 28, 29, 1937. Thompson later became vice president of the local; see *Chicago Tribune*, August 24, 1939. On the Wanderers, see n217 above.

239. In 1952, AFRA expanded to include television performers and became the American Federation of Television and Radio Artists. In 2012, the American Federation of Television and Radio Artists merged with the Screen Actors Guild to become SAG-AFTRA. On AFRA's organization and radio workers' grievances, see Harvey, *Those Wonderful, Terrible Years*, esp. 1–36. On broadcast radio, see Hilmes, *Radio Voices*, esp. 34–74. On the consolidation of independent radio stations and their affiliation with national networks in Chicago, see Lizabeth Cohen, *Making a New Deal*, esp. 327. WGN, where Bernice worked, was a founding affiliate of the Mutual Broadcasting System. The other national outfits were CBS, and NBC's Red and Blue networks.

240. The summary in this paragraph and the next draws on a wide literature, but especially on Lichtenstein, *State of the Union*, 20–53; and Lizabeth Cohen,

Making a New Deal; and, for the growth of American Federation of Labor union Tomlins, "AFL Unions" and *State and the Unions*. The CIO was initially called th Committee for Industrial Organization.

241. For Harold Blackwelder's revived union connections in the 1960s, se part 2.

242. Blackwelder Diary, June 27, 28, July 17, October 18, 22, November 4, 5, 6 1940. The 1940 Democratic National Convention was held in Chicago, and while it was going on, Bernice noted, "This town is lousy with Democrats" (Blackwelder Diary, July 15, 1940). Bernice's niece Doris Lance noted that in the 1960s, when Harold gave up on performance and sought a government job in Chicago, he "had to change from being a Republican to a Democrat.... You didn't get a job i you weren't a Democrat." It seems likely that awareness of Republicans' unpopularity in Chicago was not new to the Blackwelders in the 1960s. Lance and Fowler interview. On party politics, the New Deal order, and the labor movement, I follow the early essays in Fraser and Gerstle, *Rise and Fall of the New Deal Order*; Smemo, "'New Dealized'"; and Lizabeth Cohen, *Making a New Deal*. A brief account of the ill-fated Willkie campaign appears in Bowen, *Roots of Modern Conservatism*, 18–19.

243. Blackwelder Diary, December 23, 24, 1937 (for the new car); July 8–17, 1938 (for Harold's and then Bernice's trip to New York).

244. Blackwelder Diary, July 20, 25–27, August 3, 4, 5, 10, 11, 13, 1938. On the Roxy Theatre, see Nasaw, *Going Out*, 226–27.

245. Blackwelder Diary, July, August 8, 9, 12–17, 20, 22–26, 1938. The musician friends were Gus (later called Jimmy) and Mildred Mulcay, a harmonica team. Kim Field, *Harmonicas*, 66–68. Bernice first mentioned them as an act represented by Marvin Welt in Blackwelder Diary, February 27, 1938.

246. For Clarence Blackwelder's ownership of the High Point Café in Spencer, near Salisbury, see *Baldwin's and Post's*, 68; and U.S. Bureau of the Census, *Fifteenth Census*.

247. Blackwelder Diary, August 27, 1938–January 6, 1939 (quotes on October 28, November 1, January 2, 5, 1939). The booking agent was Tom Burchill. See Blackwelder Diary, November 16, 22, 25, 26, 1938; January 9, 1939; and Lloyd, *Vaudeville Trails*, 19.

248. Blackwelder Diary, January 7–27, 1939. Bernice's parents, Mabel and Wilbur Fowler, died in 1930 and 1933, respectively. *Salina (Kans.) Journal*, December 5, 1930, July 7, 1933.

249. Blackwelder Diary, February 6–13, 1939 (quote on February 11); undated clippings, [February 1939, Seattle], Blackwelder Papers (there are two reviews of the Palomar show; the other notes, "Neil Fortune is a resounding cowboy basso who sings 'Down the Oregon Trail' and 'Old Man River' right tunefully").

250. Blackwelder Diary, February 14–28, 1939 (quote on February 28); undated clippings [February 1939, Vancouver], Blackwelder Papers (both advertisements and reviews). For the 1939 license plate, see "Appendix 1E, California License Plate Data (1914–1980)," State of California Department of Motor Vehicles, accessed April 27, 2020, https://www.dmv.ca.gov/portal/wcm/connect/cd01ee3b

...114-49d5-a177-1add4bbd3858/appie_ca_license_plate_data.pdf?MOD=AJPE
...ES&CONVERT_TO=url&CACHEID=ROOTWORKSPACE-cd01ee3b
...114-49d5-a177-1add4bbd3858-mIJn6l8.

251. Blackwelder Diary, February 29–March 19, 1939; undated clippings, [February and March 1939, San Francisco, San Jose, and Oakland], Blackwelder papers.

252. Blackwelder Diary, March 20–April 10, 24, 25, May 3, 15, 1939.

253. Blackwelder Diary, April 10–July 6, 1939 (quotes on April 10, 11, 12, 15, 22, and June 26).

254. Blackwelder Diary, April 10–July 6, 1939 (quotes on May 26, June 26, 29). Harold's trip to Paramount Pictures with Aaron Fox is also documented in a studio pass for "Foxx & Fortune" (that is, Aaron Fox and Neil Fortune) dated June 15, 19[39], and signed by E[ugene] Zukor, son of Adolph Zukor, Paramount's founder, in Blackwelder Papers. William Fox's fall from grace is chronicled in Aubrey Solomon, *Fox Film Corporation*, which also notes Aaron's troubled relationship with his brother and Fox Film, for which Aaron had served as film lab head (18, 133, 137). A 1932 report alleged that William had Aaron put in a Connecticut sanatorium to prevent him from capitalizing on the family name; "Deals and Developments." As for Maude Hilton's husband, in an entry dated March 22, Bernice notes that she saw "Maude and her hus. at the Ritz," and two others, dated March 29 and April 7, mention "Maude and Joe." These are the only three of over forty entries mentioning Maude that also mention Joe. That Maude's marriage to Joe was tenuous at best is suggested by an entry dated July 12, when Maude, Bernice, and Harold reunited in Portland: "Maude has a new love and at her age!" Meeting Maude and one of her female comedy partners a couple of weeks later in Seattle, on July 27, Bernice noted, "Visited Maude and Markie. Things not so kosher there." For Henry Sanders, see U.S. Bureau of the Census, *Thirteenth Census* and *Sixteenth Census*; and *Los Angeles City Directory*, 1827.

255. Blackwelder Diary, March 28, 29, April 5, 6, 7, 17, 21, June 3, 1939. Harold's Orpheum appearance alongside Maude Hilton is also documented in an undated clipping, [March 1939, Los Angeles], Blackwelder Papers. Bernice mentions her work at Goodman's Studio in Blackwelder Diary, March 23–July 1, 1939, passim (quote on May 4). I have been unable to determine how Bernice knew the woman she calls "Mrs. Goodman," who ran the studio. Bernice was not initially convinced that the connection would be fruitful, noting on March 23, "Found Mrs. Goodman. Same old bat." Two days later, on March 25, she changed her mind: "Out to Goodman's Studio to hear her kids and got the surprise of our lives. They can really sing. Maybe it's a good tie up." Thereafter, Bernice spent much time at the studio. The only other mention of a "Goodman" occurs in a diary entry on February 12, 1937, when the Blackwelders were living in Chicago: "Saw 'O Say Can You Sing.' Goodman wasn't bad!" *O, Say Can You Sing?* was a production of the Works Progress Administration's Federal Theater Project. See *Chicago Tribune*, November 29, December 12, 1936; March 21, 1937. It is not clear if this was the same "Goodman" that Bernice later encountered in Hollywood.

256. Blackwelder Diary, May 15–June 16, 1939 (quotes on June 2, 16).

257. Blackwelder Diary, July 3–September 2, 1939 (quotes on July 11, 12, 18, Au gust 8, 19). Harold's top billing appears in an undated clipping, [July 1939, Por land], Blackwelder Papers.

258. See, e.g., Lizabeth Cohen, *Making a New Deal*, 246–49; and Scharf, ? *Work*. Still, public concern about unemployment focused disproportionately o men, and women, especially married women, often lost their jobs to men. Like wise, New Deal policy focused on men as breadwinners. As Nancy Cott puts i "The vast majority of New Deal–instigated benefits went to men as individual who were or would be husbands, fathers, and providers for families." Cott, *Publi Vows*, 172–79, quote on 174.

259. Here I am indebted to the arguments of Glenn, *Female Spectacle*, who ex pands the political interpretations of Cott, *Grounding of Modern Feminism*.

260. Blackwelder Diary, August 21–December 21, 1939 (quotes on October 2, 7, 20, 26, 27, November 18, 22). By 1939, Harold's parents had separated and perhaps divorced, and during the visit, Bernice and Harold shuttled back and forth be tween his mother's home in Spencer and his father's in High Point. The visit made Harold restless to leave; "too much tension," Bernice noted (Blackwelder Diary, December 13–21, 1939, quote on December 15). Clarence Blackwelder's barbecue proprietorship is noted in his obituary in *High (N.C.) Point Enterprise*, May 1, 1961.

261. Blackwelder Diary, December 25, 1939–September 22, 1940 (quotes on January 2, February 9, 28, April 24). For the Blackwelders' Montrose Beach resi dence, see U.S. Bureau of the Census, *Sixteenth Census*. For the nationwide Red Cross drive as it played out in Chicago, see *Chicago Tribune*, May 12, 24, 1940. Ber nice saved ads for and one notice of the Four Royalists' engagement at the Old Hickory on Diversey; see undated newspaper clippings [1940, Chicago], Black welder Papers. The Royalists accompanied their singing with bass, guitar, clari net, and accordion. As for her own performances, Bernice clipped a quarter-page ad for the Northern Wisconsin District Fair from a Chippewa Falls newspaper on August 4, 1940, and pasted it in a scrapbook (Blackwelder Papers); it featured a photograph of a younger "Miss Fowler" and text announcing, "Bernice Fowler, young, magnetic in charm, and beautiful, possesses one of the most thrilling con tralto voices of the present day." It continued, "Music critics have been eloquent in praising the natural beauty of her voice." Bernice was thirty-seven and had performed mostly in groups; she received few reviews of solo performances. Ber nice did not record in her diary where she and Harold lived after they returned from their tours, noting only, "Harold has moved us in at Pete's." A later entry, when they were moving again, mentions that they retrieved a rug in Rogers Park, so they may have been living there (Blackwelder Diary, September 22, Decem ber 1, 1940).

262. Blackwelder Diary, September 24, 25, 30, October 3, 7, 1940.

263. *Chicago Tribune*, October 20, 27, 1940; program for *Non-Stop America*, by Edward Beck, clipped from *Program, 41st Annual Chicago Automobile Show, 1941*, Blackwelder Papers. See also "Looking Back at 1941," Chicago Auto Show, ac cessed June 10, 2014, https://www.chicagoautoshow.com/history/#1941; the pro gram cover is reproduced here, as is a sample fifty-five-cent ticket.

264. Blackwelder Diary, October 7–November 3, 1940 (quote October 27).

265. Blackwelder Diary, October 2, 5, 12, 18 (quote), 20, 24, November 1, 1940.

266. Description of building and neighborhood comes from a site visit in May 007; Martin, "Austin"; and "La Follette (Robert) Park," Chicago Park District, accessed June 23, 2014, http://www.chicagoparkdistrict.com/parks/La-Follette Park/#.U6iVbxYyBvU. La Follette Park is across the street from the apartment.

267. Blackwelder Diary, November 1, 1940–February 29, 1941 (quotes on December 1, 30). The cartoon appears in a clipping from *Chicago Daily News*, January 1941], Blackwelder Papers. According to a newspaper review, the Four Bards performed "old favorites, musical comedy hits, Western songs, college numbers, and a wide smattering of character, language numbers" (unidentified newspaper clipping, Blackwelder Papers). Duke's breed is apparent from the cited diary entries and from family photographs (Blackwelder Papers). I base the estimate that Harold's weekly earnings were almost three times greater than those of manufacturing workers on U.S. Bureau of the Census, *Statistical Abstract*, 385, table 406, which puts the 1941 average weekly earnings in all manufacturing industries at $31.08. See also U.S. Bureau of the Census, *Statistical Abstract*, 397, table 420, which indicates that, in 1939, only executives and salaried corporation officers enjoyed weekly earnings as high or higher than Harold's in 1941. The rub, of course, was that Harold's employment was temporary and episodic.

268. Blackwelder Diary, December 6, 1940–May 6, 1941 (quotes on December 6, 1940, and February 15, 1941).

269. Blackwelder Diary, May 7–December 25, 1941 (quotes on August 4, December 7, 25, 1941). During this period, Harold also considered managing a place in Joliet that Bernice referred to as "the farm." It is not clear what sort of establishment this might have been. After the Japanese attack on Pearl Harbor, the owner "wired that the war changed his plan," and nothing more came of it (Blackwelder Diary, November 29, 30, December 3, 10, 1941, quote on December 10).

270. Blackwelder Diary, December 12, 1937. The bombing that day of the U.S. gunboat *Panay* and Standard Oil tankers, known as the *Panay* incident, is chronicled from a U.S. perspective in a remarkable Universal Newsreel film, Norman Alley's *Bombing of U.S.S. Panay*. See also Herring, *From Colony to Superpower*, 512.

271. Blackwelder Diary, May 30, 1938–December 7, 1941 (the incidents highlighted here are first mentioned on May 30, September 16, 20, 1938; March 15, September 2, 3, December 3, 1939; March 13, April 9, May 8, June 4, 5, 10, 11, July 12, October 1, 1940; and February 13, 29, March 27, April 7, June 21, July 10 [quote], 1941).

272. On U.S. public awareness of European conflict over that in Asia, see Casey, *Cautious Crusade*, esp. 29–30, 39. Casey's larger project is to challenge scholarly and popular misperceptions of the U.S. public's early and united recognition of the Nazi threat by examining the dynamic interplay between public opinion and presidential foreign policy before and after the United States declared war, but his account of the pre–Pearl Harbor era confirms that "America's gaze" was "directed firmly toward Europe" before December 7, 1941 (30). On the trajectory

from isolationism to interventionism (which was hardly universal), see Herring, *From Colony to Superpower*, 484–537 passim. Harold was of an age that would have required him to register for the draft (he was thirty-four when Bernice worried that war would take him from her and thirty-six when Japan attacked Pearl Harbor), but I have not found record of his registration.

273. Blackwelder Diary, February 1, 2, 6, 1939. Adamic's *My America*, some of which had been published earlier (including the influential "Thirty Million New Americans"), is a 600-page compendium of essays on Depression-era people, places, institutions, and ideas, from an all-but-nameless "girl on the road" to the United Mine Workers of America's John L. Lewis, from Cleveland to the San Joaquin Valley, from the CIO to Black Mountain College, and from communism to the Wisconsin Idea. It also includes self-reflection and diary entries. On Adamic as a key participant in the Popular Front of the 1930s, see Denning, *Cultural Front*, esp. 447–49. On Adamic as cultural pluralist, see Selig, *Americans All*, esp. 186–87; Hoelscher, "Conversing Diversity," esp. 383–93; and Shiffman, *Rooting Multiculturalism*, esp. 67–96. Though published before *My America*, see fellow Californian Carey McWilliams's tribute, *Louis Adamic and Shadow-America*.

274. Blackwelder Diary, February 8, 1939; *Seattle Times*, January 23, 1939. This article made light of Laski's presence at the university, quoting one "pretty co-ed" who found him interesting for less-than-intellectual reasons: "I don't always understand him ... but I could sit all day and listen to that cute accent. It's darling!" A later article mocked Laski as a favorite of "university students, downtown Communists, and fellow travelers," noting that he accepted payment for his lectures "from a fund accrued through the hateful capitalistic system." *Seattle Times*, February 15, 1939. In the immediate postwar period, Laski chaired the British Labour Party.

275. Bernice mentions European tensions five times in September 1939 but then not again until after reading Adamic and hearing Laski; fifty mentions of war in Europe follow from March 1939 to December 1941. For the quote about Hitler, see Blackwelder Diary, September 26, 1938, in which she wonders how "such a man" can have followers but also says of U.S. involvement, "Hope we mind our business."

276. These insights build especially on the interplay among Jacobson, *Whiteness*; Selig, *Americans All*; and Denning, *Cultural Front*.

277. For Sanders, see discussion above. For Harold's connection with Bobby Kuhn in the 1930s and 40s, see mention above and Blackwelder Diary, April 3, 1939; May 30, 1940.

278. The German surname Kuhn is common among both Jews and non-Jews. Robert "Bobby" Kuhn was the child of peripatetic German immigrants (his father and mother emigrated from Hesse-Darmstadt and Prussia, respectively) who lived in Saint Joseph, Missouri, when Robert was born. For Robert and his brothers Charles and Paul (who together performed as the Three White Kuhns), see U.S. Bureau of the Census, *Tenth Census* and *Fourteenth Census*. The Three White Kuhns performed widely; see their picture in sheet music for Arthur Lang and Jeff Branen's "To Lou," 1915, in "Historic Sheet Music Collection, 1800–1922,"

brary of Congress, accessed April 27, 2020, https://www.loc.gov/resource/ihas
00006927.0/?sp=1; *New York Times*, November 4, 1917; *Chicago Tribune*, June
5, 1920; and, after Paul died, *Vaudeville News* (New York), November 6, 1925. See
also a feature article on Robert Kuhn ("He Literally 'Beats' Music out of a Fiddle,"
Chicago Tribune, May 20, 1956), which provides a brief biography as well as a mi-
sogynist account of his unconventional bass fiddle playing ("If you've ever seen
a 300 pound man whacking the daylights out of his 90 pound wife you'll have a
slight idea of what it's like when Bob Kuhn performs on his bass fiddle. It's exhausting!"). Most records show that Sylvia Clark Kuhn was born in Palestine,
though a census taker in 1930 listed her birthplace as New York and both parents'
birthplaces as Russia. See U.S. Bureau of the Census, *Fifteenth Census*; cf. U.S.
Bureau of the Census, *Sixteenth Census*; and U.S. Immigration and Naturalization Service, *Passenger Lists*. For Sylvia Clark Kuhn's performances, see, e.g. *Evening News*, January 12, 1927, which notes, "Petite Sylvia Clark, 'vaudeville's little
buffoon,' holds the spotlight.... Sylvia is chic and dainty and withal one of the
cleverest little comediennes that San Jose has lately had the good fortune to witness.... She is given excellent moral and musical support by her husband, Bobby
Kuhn ... himself a vaudeville veteran, formerly [of] the 'Three White Kuhns.'" See
also *Vaudeville News and New York Star*, July 23, 1927; and *Chicago Tribune*, September 19, 1930. And see two photographs in J. Willis Sayre Collection of Theatrical Photographs, Special Collections, University of Washington Libraries, Seattle:
[?] Floyd, *Vaudeville Actress Sylvia Clark*, 1915, http://digitalcollections.lib.washing
ton.edu/cdm/ref/collection/sayre/id/21223; and Maurice Seymour, *Stage, Vaudeville, and Radio Singer and Actress Sylvia Clark*, 1935, http://digitalcollections.lib
.washington.edu/cdm/ref/collection/sayre/id/21542. For the Kuhns' Christian
Science testimonials, see "Testimony," *Christian Science Sentinel*, where Sylvia
attests to healing from constipation, eczema, sore throat, influenza, hoarseness,
colds, headaches, impatience, and (almost) a bad temper, while Robert attests to
healing from habitual use of tobacco, drink, and profanity, as well as from headaches, sleeplessness, colds, and ill temper.

279. For the Blackwelders' ongoing friendship with the Kuhns, see Blackwelder to McClung, September 5 and undated, 1965; December 14, 1966; November 24, December 30, 1967, McClung Papers (quote appears in undated letter
written September 1965). In the 1960s, the Blackwelders and Kuhns spent holidays together.

280. Blackwelder Diary, January 23, 24, 1937. Tony Koplos may have been
born Antonios Kostopoulos; his obituary notes that his brother, who remained
in Greece, was named "Constantine Kotstoppoulos," perhaps a variant or erro-
neous spelling of Kostopoulos; see *Chicago Tribune*, July 16, 1986. An Antonios
Kostopoulos, age seventeen, emigrated to the United States in 1914 aboard the
ship *Carpathia*, and he would have been of age to have married Gertrude Winkler in the 1930s, but it is not clear if this is the Tony Koplos she wed, since the Antonios Kostopoulos who arrived in 1914 told immigration authorities that he was
destined for Wyoming. U.S. Customs Service, *Passenger Lists*.

281. Clogg, *Concise History of Greece*, 100–144; Saloutos, *Greeks*, esp. 326–43;

Kitroeff, "Greek-American Ethnicity," esp. 364–69; on the Greek left, see Geo gakas, "Greek-American Radicalism." The Greek community of the Kople family stood in contrast to the radical communities Georgakas describes an the transient ones analyzed so perceptively by Peck in *Reinventing Free Labo* For "Chicagopolis," see Saloutos, *Greeks*, 327; and *Chicago Herald and Examine* May 2, 1938.

282. Royalist sentiments were hardly the rule in Chicago's Greek America community. For antiroyalist pronouncements in Chicago's Greek press, see, e.g. "Restoration of Monarchy Invites Dictatorship," *Saloniki-Greek Press*, May 30 1935, http://flps.newberry.org/article/5422062_5_1650; and "Are There Greek Roy alists in America?," *Greek News*, September 11, 1935, https://flps.newberry.org /article/5422062_5_1625, both in Chicago Foreign Language Press Survey, New berry Library, Chicago.

283. Blackwelder Diary, January 21, 22, 25, 1938. The Koplos family seems not to have used the name Vasiliki for long, perhaps replacing it in time with "Antonia" after the child's father; by the time she married in 1962, a wedding announcement listed Gert and Tony's daughter as Barbara Antonia Koplos. Barbara married in her mother's Episcopal parish, not her father's Greek Orthodox church. See *Chicago Tribune*, June 3, 1962.

284. In 1937, a directory listed Anthony Koplos as the manager of the Standard Café in La Crosse, and in 1939, another listed him as a waiter at the Eau Claire Café. Both Anthony and Gertrude Koplos applied for Social Security numbers in Wisconsin, suggesting that Gertrude also worked in one or both of these restaurants. *Wright's La Crosse City Directory; Wright's Eau Claire City Directory*; U.S. Social Security Administration, *Social Security Death Index*; Blackwelder Diary, August 7, 8, 1940. On Greek Americans in the restaurant business, see Saloutos, *Greeks*, 265–69.

285. Blackwelder Diary, May 7, June 13, September 13, 14, 21, October 2, 24, 1937; September 4, 1938; undated newspaper clippings, Blackwelder Papers (seven clippings, ca. 1932–33, one of which is from *Chicago Tribune*, January 18, 1933; quote is from undated clipping).

286. Blackwelder to McClung, October 31, 1967, McClung Papers.

287. Blackwelder Diary, May 26, September 30, 1937; January 29 (quote), February 15, April 21 (quote), June 3, 1938; October 4, 1940; March 8, 1941.

288. On Chinatown's insularity (and its shifting physical location), see McKeown, *Chinese Migrant Networks*, 178–223. On Chicago's Italian neighborhoods, see Vecoli, "Formation of Chicago's 'Little Italies'"; and Guglielmo, *White on Arrival*, 16–21.

289. Rudolph Vecoli and Thomas Guglielmo both note that a majority of Chicago Italian Americans supported Mussolini. Vecoli, "Italians"; Guglielmo, *White on Arrival*, esp. 113–28 (Guglielmo also explores the racial implications of this profascism, given Mussolini's imperial aims and actions in Africa).

290. On anti-Japanese activism, see Ling, *Chinese Chicago*, 167–69; and on Chinese restaurants in this era, including Nankin and Hoe Sai Gai, see Ling, *Chi-*

ese Chicago, 74–75. On Americanized Chinese food, see also Gabaccia, *We Are What We Eat*, 102–4; and esp. Chen, *Chop Suey, USA*.

291. This simplifies a complex process by which racial thinkers turned away from an earlier understanding that equated "race" and "nation," and hence saw as many races as there were nations, and toward a later understanding of large, inclusive racial groups—Caucasian, Negroid, and Mongoloid, for example—that cut across national lines and, in effect, left only non-Caucasians as racialized. The process also involved the self-identities of those who clambered for inclusion in the privileged category of whiteness and those who, refused inclusion or uninterested in it, forged oppositional racial categories that refigured or rejected hierarchy. For a nuanced explanation of how this process worked among Chicago Italians, see Guglielmo, *White on Arrival*. See also Jacobson, *Whiteness*; Gerstle, *American Crucible*; and, for earlier stages of the process, Ngai, *Impossible Subjects*.

292. U.S. Bureau of the Census, *Twelfth Census*; *1905 Kansas State Census*.

293. DuVal, *Native Ground*; Thorne, *Many Hands*; Aron, *American Confluence*.

294. The population of Howard County, where Fayette and Central College were located, was over 15 percent African American in 1920. U.S. Bureau of the Census, *Fourteenth Census of the United States, 1920: State Compendium-Missouri*, 39.

295. Blackwelder Diary, November 19, 1937.

296. Blackwelder Diary, May 22, November 19, 1937. On the sexual dimensions of white slumming in black Chicago, see Heap, *Slumming*, 189–230 (though Heap argues that white slumming in black Chicago declined by the early 1930s); and Mumford, *Interzones*.

297. This admittedly elliptical analysis draws on Baldwin, *Chicago's New Negroes*; and also Green, *Selling the Race*.

298. Blackwelder Diary, February 7, 1937; October 6, 1938; and June 9, 1940.

299. Blackwelder Diary, January 3, 4, 11, 1937 (on El Paso, New Mexico and Arizona, and Los Angeles); February 16, July 26, 27, November 25, 26, 1939 (on Vancouver, Seattle, and San Antonio). For the development of Olvera Street in Los Angeles, see Kropp, *California Vieja*, 207–60, 333n23. On Seattle Potlatch festivals, see Thrush, *Native Seattle*, 130–36, quote on 130. On the history of racial formation in Vancouver, and many other parts of the North American West, including the labor migrations and intimate lives of South Asian and Chinese men, see Shah, *Stranger Intimacy*. On the process by which the West's racial past became quaint, see Limerick, *Legacy of Conquest*, esp. 25.

300. Quote appears in Blackwelder Diary, January 29, 1938.

301. The analysis here draws on Jacobson, *Whiteness*; Gerstle, *American Crucible*, esp. 128–86; and, for critical insight into the organizational and textual versions of pluralism from which personal pluralisms like Bernice's no doubt drew, Selig, *Americans All*. I am particularly persuaded by Selig's nuanced elaboration on what Jacobson calls the "consolidation of whiteness"—that is, the ways in which the cultural gifts movement could cut against the grain—and by her argument that cultural pluralism (or a particular expression of it, at least) "failed to

analyze accurately the position of African Americans and other racial minoritie It tended to minimize the harsh realities of the time—the Jim Crow laws, lyncl ings, disenfranchisement, segregation, maldistribution of resources, and violer racism deeply embedded in America's legal and political system—as well as th history of slavery, and instead presumed a universe of cultural equality in whicl all groups operated on the same level, giving and receiving without subordina tion or exploitation" (89).

302. Blackwelder Diary, January 1–20, 1937, quotes on January 7.

303. Blackwelder Diary, January 20, 1937–February 26, 1938, passim, quotes on August 8, 1937; February 19, 26, 1938. Bernice did not mention the address where Grace moved in 1938, but the 1940 census found Grace living on Drexel Boulevard near East Forty-First Street, in a white neighborhood adjacent to a mostly black area. See U.S. Bureau of the Census, *Sixteenth Census*. Maps of the South Side abound in the literature; see Baldwin, *Chicago's New Negroes*, 24. For Grace's musical career, see U.S. Bureau of the Census, *Fourteenth Census*, which lists her as a twenty-two-year-old music teacher living with her parents in Fort Wayne, Indiana; and *Chicago Tribune*, September 30, 1945; December 19, 1948, which show her performing for women's clubs.

304. Blackwelder Diary, October 7–December 9, 1939, passim. The household Bernice shared with her husband and Grace Prince resembled a similar household in Southern California, where Bernice lived with Harold and comedian Maude Hilton. See discussion above.

305. Blackwelder Diary, January 31, 1937.

306. Blackwelder Diary, February 24, March 6, July 23, 25, October 13 (quote), 1937; January 2, 28, March 12, 13, 19, 20, May 6, 24 (quote), September 6, October 11, 30, November 8, December 5, 1938; April 25, September 8, 20, 1939; February 16, 29, March 1, 2, 5, June 19, 28, November 15, 22, 1940; January 30, 31, February 10, 11, March 4, May 21, June 19, 20, July 20, September 10, 11 (quote), November 15, 22, December 28, 1941, and passim.

307. Blackwelder Diary, March 22, April 26, May 6, 8, July 26, November 28, 1937; January 3, March 28, June 27, August 30, September 27, October 15, December 23, 1938; March 31, August 18, 20, 21, 28, September 1, 11, December 29, 1939; February 22, 29, March 22, 29, April 8, 15, 16, 17, May 19, 26, June 5, 17, October 13, December 2, 24, 27, 28, 1940; January 3 (quote), 22, February 9, June 25, September 4, 24, October 20, November 19, December 10, 1941.

308. See references in n226.

309. Blackwelder Diary, January 22, 24, February 27, March 5, 1937; April 12, 13, 16, 17, 18, May 19 (quote), 27, 28, 29, June 3, 5, 19, July 16, October 5, December 15, 21, 31, 1938; September 10, December 25, 1939; January 10 (quote), February 10, 25, April 30, May 24, July 13 (quote), October 13 (quote), 1940; April 3 (quote), September 8, 1941. For Grace Dunn's career on radio, see daily radio broadcast schedules, *Chicago Tribune*, October 1, 1934–May 22, 1935, passim. For her office job, see U.S. Bureau of the Census, *Sixteenth Census*.

310. Blackwelder Diary, February 16, 24 (quote), March 17 (quote), June 26, December 14 (quote), 23, 1937; March 9 (quote), 23, April 17, May 1 (quote), 4, 8,

, 25, June 1, 8, 9, 17, 20, July 8, 10, October 16, November 24, December 13, 1938; June 12 (quote), 25, July 12, 13, August 9, 10, 19, 22, September 6, 30, October 14, 3, December 4, 25, 30, 31, 1939; January 8, February 9 (quote), 14, March 9, 11, 15, 1940.

311. Blackwelder Diary, March 22, 28, June 4, 10, 26, July 2, 4, 5, 18, September 5, 27, 30, October 11, 19, November 4, 23, December 11, 18, 25, 1940; January 17, 29, February 5 (quote), 7, 12, March 5, 9, April 12, May 3, 17, 23, December 6 (quote), 24, 25, 1941. For Helen Fowler Dunn Tron's illness and death, see Blackwelder to McClung, March 20 (quote), April 24, June 25, September 3, 1975, McClung Papers. In the September 3 letter, reporting Helen's death, Bernice said that she and Helen had "straightened out" their differences, but all evidence suggests a distant relationship.

312. Blackwelder Diary, 1937–41 passim, quotes on November 1, 17, 1937; January 26, 1938; May 9, November 4, 1939; April 21, 1940; October 28, 30, 1941.

313. Blackwelder Diary, March 8 (quote), July 17, September 12 (quote), 1937; March 17, June 25 (quote), 30, 1938; March 3, June 25, 1940; July 19 (quote), September 2, 21, 22, 29, October 22 (quote), 1941.

314. Blackwelder Diary, January 29 (quote), March 25, June 16, 23, 27 (quote), August 11 (quote), 21, September 1, 18, December 5, 10 (quote), 15, 1937; February 12, March 23, April 12, 13, 14, May 27, 28, 29, August 31, October 11, December 25, 1938; January 18, May 11, December 6, 7, 18, 25, 1940; January 17, 18, March 29, September 20, 21, October 26 (quote), 1941.

315. *Chicago Telephone Directory*, 1941–47. The listing disappears in 1948.

316. For the Vocaliers, see *Daily Times* (Davenport, Iowa), March 26, 1946; and Bernice Blackwelder to Jessie and Duane [Fowler], n.d. [ca. 1947]; and photos, both in Blackwelder Papers. In the letter to her brother and sister-in-law, Bernice notes that her trio sang at Chicago's Lake Shore Athletic Club, adding, "If that's my swan song it was a perfect one because it was a beautiful party and they really listened to us." For the Gentlemen of Note, see "A Daily Listener" [from New Orleans] to Harold Blackwell [*sic*], December 11, 1942; Dick Stevens, Music Corporation of America, to Harold Blackwelder, Gentlemen of Note, June 4, 1943; undated clippings [194?, Youngstown, Ohio; Miami, Florida; St. Louis, Missouri; and others]; and photos, all in Blackwelder Papers. For Tony Carsello and his Commodores, see Discus Lake Shore Club Casino-in-the-Air flyer, July 1944, Blackwelder Papers; and *Chicago Tribune*, July 2, 1944.

317. For the 1940s performance and the relationship with the USO, see photo labeled "Camp Shenango, Transfer, Pennsylvania"; and USO pin, both in Blackwelder Papers. For Harold's earlier blackface performances, see playbill from Alamo Theatre, April 30, [1933], which advertises the World's Fair Minstrels, including Harold; and what is likely a photograph of this troupe, undated, both in Blackwelder Papers. On Camp Shenango and its racial violence, see "Camp History," Camp Reynolds Shenango Personnel Replacement Depot, 1942–46, accessed August 4, 2015, http://www.campreynolds.com/history_page.htm.

318. Hilmes, *Hollywood and Broadcasting*; Boddy, *Fifties Television*; Spigel, *Make Room for TV*; Baughman, *Republic of Mass Culture*.

319. For the contemplated move to North Carolina, see Bernice Blackwelder to Jessie and Duane [Fowler], n.d. [ca. 1947], Blackwelder Papers. For residence and employment in Greensboro, see *Hill's High Point City Directory*. For the Pickwick, see "Meet You at the Pickwick." For mentions of the Blackwelders' time in North Carolina, see Bernice Blackwelder to McClung, July 16, September 3, 1975, McClung Papers.

320. For Bernice's sister's Alexandria residence, see Bernice Blackwelder to Jessie and Duane [Fowler], n.d. [ca. 1947], Blackwelder Papers. For the Blackwelders' residences in Arlington and Alexandria, see part 1.

321. Scott Koch, CIA information and privacy coordinator, to author, April 19, 2007 (this letter denies my Freedom of Information Act request); Blackwelder, *Great Westerner*, book jacket; Blackwelder to McClung, June 25, 1967; February 29, 1972; May 28, 1973; February 16, 1975, McClung Papers; Lance and Fowler interview.

322. Elliott interview.

323. This paragraph and the next follow Friedman, *Covert Capital*, 1–122. *Covert Capital* focuses on the 1960s and beyond, after Blackwelder quit the CIA and left Virginia, but it also reviews the early growth of the agency and the suburbs where employees lived. Its arguments, while compelling, do not fully allow for the dynamics that unfolded among low-level (but not maintenance) workers like Blackwelder, her friend Nancy Elliott, and the black women who worked alongside them. For broad historical context, I rely on Freeman, *American Empire*.

324. Blackwelder to McClung, May 28, 1973, McClung Papers; Elliott interview; Friedman, *Covert Capital*, 30–31.

325. Elliott interview.

326. The following paragraphs are based mostly on family stories, but I have checked those stories against the federal census from 1900 to 1940 and a Wisconsin census for 1895. I have also compared my memory of family stories with that of my sister, Lynne Johnson. In addition, because, in 2011, I prepared papers left behind by my maternal grandfather, Bernard Joachim Stecker, for donation to the Wisconsin Historical Society Library and Archives, my perusal of those papers and conversations about them with his daughter (my late mother), Janet Stecker Johnson, informs my memory. Those papers have been organized into two separate collections: Reverend Bernard J. Stecker Papers, 1919–71, and Harold Stecker Papers, 1915–19, both at the Wisconsin Historical Society Library and Archives, Madison. It is of little relevance here but still curious that my great-uncle Harold Stecker, who died of appendicitis at Camp MacArthur in Texas during World War I, was at the same base when he passed away as was Benjamin Silbert, possibly one of Quantrille McClung's suitors and definitely one of her friends. See discussion above.

327. There is one family story that places my paternal great-grandfather, Nels Johnson, briefly in New York City before his arrival in Wisconsin. In that story, he emigrated with a male friend from Denmark and the two men worked together in New York. The friend sent money to his Danish girlfriend to join him, but he had to work the day she arrived. So, according to the story, my great-grandfather

et her at the dock and then ran off with her and married her. If that is a true story, then my paternal great-grandmother, Catherine Johnson, became my fore-ear by romantic happenstance enabled by industrial work discipline. Thanks to ynne Johnson for reminding me of this story.

328. In thinking about Neenah and the larger Fox River Valley and Lake Winne-ago area, I have benefited from Tronnes, "Corn Moon Migrations"; and Jacklin, Paper Dreams."

329. According to Lynne Johnson, our grandmother wanted to become a doc-or herself but had to give up schooling when her mother became ill. She talked about attending the "Aggie college"—no doubt the College of Agriculture that developed within the University of Minnesota under the provisions of the Mor-rill Act. Apparently she did not attend long. On the college, see Folwell, *History of Minnesota*, 4:77–97.

330. Ernest R. Ball, "Let the Rest of the World Go By," with lyrics by J. Keirn Brennan, 1919. See sheet music, "Let the Rest of the World Go By," Historical American Sheet Music, Duke University Libraries Digital Collection, Durham, North Carolina, http://library.duke.edu/digitalcollections/hasm_a2962. My mother took small liberties with the lyrics. When she was eighty, I had her write them out as she remembered them; they are very close to the lyrics quoted here (though her sky is "western" rather than "kindly"). "Let the Rest of the World Go By," lyrics handwritten by Janet Stecker Johnson, 2005, in author's possession.

331. *Bismarck Daily Tribune*, September 16, 1900. Soon-to-be president Roose-velt is quoted here in conversation with acquaintances from the time he spent in the North Dakota Badlands, where he retreated in the 1880s following the death of his wife and mother: "Theodore Roosevelt, sitting upon a broncho, born and 'busted' in the valley of the Little Missouri, looking down upon the tiny town of Medora and surrounded by a few old friends of his cow-punching days, today said, 'Here the romance of my life began.'" Thanks to Brendon George for track-ing down this reference. For Roosevelt's western influences, see, e.g., Canfield, *Theodore Roosevelt*; DiSilvestro, *Theodore Roosevelt*; and Brinkley, *Wilderness Warrior*.

EPILOGUE

1. Cale, *Brief History*. Serra House is the home of the Clayman Institute for Gender Research, a later iteration of the Center for Research on Women. The building has been moved twice, in 1983 and 2006. I worked there from 1981 to 1985, with a year spent decamped in another building while Serra House was re-located.

2. Historians have adopted the notion of a Spanish "fantasy heritage" from California writer Carey McWilliams; see McWilliams, *North from Mexico*, esp. 35–47. The argument between the Roman Catholic Church and Indigenous Cali-fornians has gone on for decades. It came to a head in 2015, when Serra was finally canonized; see, e.g., "Sainthood of Junípero Serra Reopens Wounds of Colonialism in California," *New York Times*, September 29, 2015.

3. Starr, *California*, 174.

4. For an intelligent overview of this process, see Daniel T. Rodgers, *Age Fracture*, 144–79.

5. Camille Guérin-Gonzales, personal conversation with author, February 2▮ 2015. The phrasing here is from memory; it is approximate. She was explainin▮ her understanding of the multiverse and its relationship to her impending deatł Of the multiverse, she wrote in 2002, "Quantum theory describes physical realit▮ as a multiplicity of universes—a multiverse rather than a single universe. Withi▮ this multiverse, any occurrence physically possible has taken place in a multi tude of space-times, and everything that exists in one universe has its counter part in the others. Differences among universes are a consequence of difference▮ in action, behavior, and events taking place in each universe. The present of one universe is the future of another. Everything possible according to the laws o▮ physics exists in the multiverse." Unfinished manuscript, in author's possession and in Guérin-Gonzales Papers, University Archives, University of Wisconsin-Madison. That collection includes research materials from her unfinished book project, "Mapping Working-Class Struggle in Appalachia, South Wales, and the American Southwest, 1890–1947," as well as from her book *Mexican Workers and American Dreams*.

6. Blackwelder to McClung, January 29, 1973, Quantrille McClung Papers, Western History Collection, Western History/Genealogy Department, Denver Public Library (hereafter cited as McClung Papers). The reference work she consulted was likely the *Biographical Directory of the American Congress, 1774–1971*. In her next letter, Blackwelder spoke of wanting to return to the Newberry: "Such a wonderful feeling just to be there in the quiet luxury with freedom to browse among the publications." Almost all later references to major libraries expressed her wish (and her inability) to visit them (see Blackwelder to McClung, [mid-February 1973]; November 19, 1975; February 24, 1979). For an exception, see Blackwelder to McClung, March 25, 1974. Blackwelder did use a local branch of the Chicago Public Library, which she could reach by a single bus without a transfer; see, e.g., Blackwelder to McClung, September 11, 1980. All letters in McClung Papers.

7. Blackwelder to McClung, June 19, 1973, McClung Papers (see also Blackwelder to McClung, March 4, 1974).

8. Blackwelder to McClung, December 30, 1975; January 14, 1976, McClung Papers.

9. Blackwelder often referenced this typist as well as her own typing labor. See Blackwelder to McClung, February 3, March 4, December 8, 1974; January 19, March 20, 1975; February 10, August 10, September 9, November 18, 1976; March 7, [April 8], May 23, 28, June 14, July 8, August 12, 1977; January 3, 13, March 6, April 13, June 5, September 29, November 30, December 14, 1978; January 22, February 24, March 28, 1979; January 22, 1981, McClung Papers.

10. Blackwelder to McClung, September 11, 1980, McClung Papers.

11. Blackwelder to McClung, August 15, 1973; see also Blackwelder to McClung, April 24, 1975; February 10, April 14, 1976, all in McClung Papers.

12. Blackwelder to McClung, September 4, [1977], McClung Papers. Elsewhere

the letter, she wrote, "How much I have learned from you!!! How much you mean to me every day!"

13. This trip is covered in part 3.

14. Blackwelder to McClung, May 28, 1977, January 13, 1978, McClung Papers. In the latter, Bernice also complained that Harold would be off work for the upcoming Martin Luther King Jr. holiday even after taking compensatory time off the week before: "Nice to have him home but I cannot accomplish much on my project." (The federal King holiday was not passed into law until 1983, but Illinois approved a state holiday in 1973.)

15. Blackwelder to McClung, September 21, November 19, 1975; February 10, April 14 (quote), June 14, August 10, September 9, 1976; March 5, [April 8], May 28, 1977; January 3, March 6 (quote), June 5, 1978, McClung Papers.

16. Blackwelder to McClung, September 29, 1978; February 24 and March 28 (quote), 1979, McClung Papers.

17. Blackwelder to McClung, May 9, 1979, McClung Papers.

18. Blackwelder to McClung, June 2, 1979, McClung Papers.

19. These dynamics are explained and analyzed in part 2.

20. Hogan, "Logan Square." As noted in part 2, while Hogan reported a 1980 "Spanish Origin" population of over 50 percent in the neighborhood, the *Chicago Tribune* (January 18, 1981) put the Latino proportion at 40 percent. In 1977, Bernice estimated that her neighborhood was "half Puerto Rican"; Blackwelder to McClung, March 5, [1977], McClung Papers.

21. Blackwelder to McClung, November 19, 1975; June 14, August 10, 1976; May 23, 1977, McClung Papers.

22. *Chicago Tribune*, June 5, 6, 1977.

23. *Chicago Tribune*, June 5, 6 (quote), 7, 10, 11, 12, 15, 1977. Scholars of Puerto Rican Chicago have focused not on this event but rather on an earlier uprising in 1966, also in Humboldt Park and also connected to the Puerto Rican parade (the inaugural parade was in 1966, organized by community members after Mayor Richard Daley announced that early June would see the first ever Puerto Rican Week in Chicago). The contours of the so-called Division Street riots of 1966 are strikingly similar to those of the 1977 uprising: police intervention in an alleged dispute between community members that ended with an officer shooting a young Puerto Rican man, followed by community protest that spiraled into violence. Scholars credit the Division Street riots with prompting political activism and community organizing among Chicago Puerto Ricans in the following decade, including, for instance, the evolution of the Young Lords Organization from a street gang into a revolutionary civil rights and Puerto Rican nationalist group. That a similar conflict emerged eleven years later demonstrates the limited headway such organizing had made in addressing the inequities and injustices that plagued the Puerto Rican community, including poverty and unemployment, job and housing discrimination, and police harassment, as well as the ongoing struggle over Puerto Rico's colonial relationship with the United States. For accounts and analysis of the 1966 uprising, see Fernández, *Brown*, 134–35, 163–70; and De Genova and Ramos-Zayas, *Latino Crossings*, 45–48. Some comparison of

the 1966 and 1977 events appears in Gina M. Pérez, *Near Northwest Side Stor*
83–88.

24. Blackwelder to McClung, June 14, 1977, McClung Papers.

25. See discussion in part 3; quote from Blackwelder to McClung, February 2 1971, McClung Papers.

26. There was, in fact, a high rate of fire in Chicago's Puerto Rican and Africa American neighborhoods from the 1950s to the 1980s. As Fernández explains, "I a community of declining property values, buildings in disrepair or with sever code violations mysteriously burned down at high rates. . . . Whether these fire were caused by the faulty conditions of aged buildings, by negligent tenants, o by premeditated arson, a surprisingly high number of property owners dispose of real estate by collecting insurance claims." Fernández, *Brown*, 172. There is no evidence that people of color set fires to drive whites away.

27. A good summary of this colonialism appears in De Genova and Zayas-Ramos, *Latino Crossings*, 7–11.

28. Blackwelder to McClung, July 12, 1978, McClung Papers (cf. Blackwelder to McClung, March 5, September 4, 1977; January 3, June 5, 1978).

29. U.S. Bureau of the Census, *Census of Population*, 86, table 27.

30. Cunningham, *Klansville, U.S.A.* In North Carolina, nothing symbolized the shift so clearly as the 1973 election of Jesse Helms, a conservative and former Democrat, as the state's first Republican senator since 1903.

31. Blackwelder to McClung, September 11, 1980, McClung Papers. I see this as an oblique reference to Latino neighbors because Bernice had attributed street disorder for so long to Puerto Ricans that "crime" itself had become racialized in her letters, whether or not she explicitly identified those she saw as the "criminals."

32. Blackwelder to McClung, April 4, 18, 29, May 28, June 19, July 25, August 15, 24, September 16, 1973; March 25, 1974, McClung Papers.

33. Blackwelder to McClung, July 8, August 12, 1977; April 13, 1978, McClung Papers. In her August 12, 1977, letter, Bernice told Quantrille of an earlier Field Museum visit to see a King Tut exhibit, made possible because she had temporary relief from sciatica. Ironically, Bernice returned home and picked Harold up at the L station after this "perfect day," only to call an ambulance for him hours later because of a nosebleed that would not stop.

34. Blackwelder to McClung, November 30, December 14, 1978, McClung Papers; Lance and Fowler interview.

35. See, e.g., the letter Bernice wrote two months after being hospitalized, where she reports that she is organizing her own notes as well as her typist's work, adding, "She has kept on typing all the time since I went to the hospital. . . . Hope we will have a manuscript . . . to submit to a publisher before we leave for North Carolina." Blackwelder to McClung, January 22, 1979, McClung Papers.

36. Blackwelder to McClung, January 2 (quote), September 11, December 8, 1980; January 22, 1981 (quote), n.d. [December 1981] (quote), McClung Papers.

37. Doris Lance, personal communication with author, June 5, 2003; Lance and Fowler interview.

38. Blackwelder to McClung, January 29, December 20, 1973; July 30, October 2, December 8, 31, 1974; November 19, December 30, 1975; November 18, 1976; January 8, June 14, August 12, 1977; January 313, 1978; January 2, 1980, McClung Papers. These letters include references to shared holiday celebrations and concert outings. Bernice's illness and the 1978–79 North Carolina move interrupted the get-togethers.

39. Blackwelder to McClung, December 20, 1973; December 30, 1975; January 3, 1978 (quote), McClung Papers. Both the 1975 and 1978 letters note Harold's high earnings, which Bernice attributes to the union scale on which musicians were then working, in contrast to the low wages of the 1930s. On the Blackwelders' union ties, see parts 2 and 3. Another letter from 1978 notes that Harold will be "caroling at the bank for the 11th year" (Blackwelder to McClung, December 14, 1978, McClung Papers).

40. Blackwelder to McClung, September 1, 1982, McClung Papers. All quotes in this paragraph are from this letter.

41. Doris Lance, personal communication with author, February 8, 2003.

42. Harold Blackwelder was seventy-eight when he died in 1983; U.S. Social Security Administration, *Social Security Death Index*. Bernice's niece Doris recalled that Harold "used to stutter when you talked to him, but he never stuttered when he sang. He had a *beautiful*, very deep bass voice … a richer bass voice than most men have." Lance and Fowler interview.

43. Bernice Blackwelder had just turned eighty-four when she died in 1986. U.S. Social Security Administration, *Social Security Death Index*; Lance and Fowler interview; site visit to Maple Hill Cemetery, Cadillac, Michigan, June 13, 2004; 4 × 7-inch black notebook, n.d., Blackwelder Papers, in author's possession.

44. Doris Lance, personal communication with author, June 5, 2003; Lance and Fowler interview.

45. Blackwelder, *Great Westerner*, 365. The verse is borrowed loosely from Sir Walter Scott's "Coronach" (part of the narrative poem *The Lady of the Lake*), which ends the line "How sound is thy slumber" with an exclamation point rather than a question mark. It is Blackwelder's added question mark that seems to invoke, in this historical context, the misgivings of empire. Scott, by contrast, is certain that the man with the bloody hand sleeps peacefully: "Fleet foot on the correi, / Sage counsel in cumber, / Red hand in the foray, / How sound is thy slumber!" Benton Frémont used neither question mark nor exclamation point: "Fleet foot in the forest, / Sage head in the cumber / —Red hand in the foray! / How sound is thy slumber." See Benton Frémont, "Kit Carson," *Will and the Way*, 23–50, quote on 50. Carson himself was familiar with this verse, having heard *The Lady of the Lake* read to him repeatedly by a U.S. Army officer, who reported that Carson "regarded it as the finest expression of outdoor life that he had ever heard." Walter Scott, *Lady of the Lake*; Sabin, *Kit Carson Days*, 2:817.

46. Esther Stokes to [John T.] Eastlick, June 1, 1966, Denver Public Library Archives, Western History Collection, Western History/Genealogy Department, Denver Public Library (hereafter cited as DPL Archives). In this intralibrary memo, Stokes quotes McClung quoting Shakespeare with regard to her health.

47. Rule to Shearouse, November 27, 1970, DPL Archives.

48. Shearouse to McClung, January 21, 1972; and McClung to Shearouse, February 14, 1972; see also Rule to Shearouse, July 8, 20, December 21, 1971, all in DPL Archives.

49. Shearouse to McClung, February 14, April 9, 1980; and McClung to Shearouse, February 20, May 2, 1980, DPL Archives. See also McClung to Nolie Mumey, April 11, 1980, McClung Papers. The materials McClung collected toward a second supplement are now part of the McClung Papers. James Kroll, manager of DPL's Western History/Genealogy Department, says that "members of the genealogy community" have looked through the papers hoping to find "volume three," but "all they found were scattered notes." Kroll thinks that McClung had enough for another supplement, but much of it was "in her head." Garramone and Kroll interview. I agree with Kroll's assessment. In box 4 of the McClung Papers, there are nine file folders of genealogical charts and notes, but turning them into a book would indeed likely require the knowledge that McClung stored "in her head."

50. Office memo, "Monna" to "Mr. S[hearouse]," June 24, 1983, DPL Archives.

51. Shearouse to McClung, July 19, 1972, DPL Archives. McClung saved this letter in her papers, too, and also her response, in which she says that a full transcription might not be necessary. She volunteers to listen to the tapes and take notes on them first. See McClung to Shearouse, August 5, 1972, McClung Papers. Ultimately, the tapes were transcribed, though not entirely accurately. The tapes themselves, McClung's notes on them, and the rough transcription are all part of the McClung Papers. I discuss the tapes in part 3.

52. McClung to Shearouse, August 22, September 2, 1974; and Shearouse to McClung, August 28, 1974, DPL Archives; John Ward to McClung, March 20, 1980, McClung Papers (on this letter, McClung wrote, "I phoned him to say I intended my book to be placed in Western History" and noted his response); Quantrille D. McClung, *Memoirs of My Childhood*.

53. Garramone and Kroll interview. Kay Merrill gave some of this information to Garramone, who relayed it to me.

54. Smith interview.

55. Arnold interview.

56. Smith interview.

57. Smith interview; McClung to Henry Shearouse, September 2, 1974, DPL Archives.

58. Garramone and Kroll interview, quote from Garramone.

59. Smith interview; Garramone and Kroll interview, quote from Kroll. Former DPL librarian Philip Panum agrees with Kroll, remembering that he "had a great deal of respect" for McClung and that other staff members did, too. Philip J. Panum, personal communication with author, August 16, 2006. I am sure that my interest in McClung has influenced the way that DPL staff members have talked to me about her. Those staff members, now retired, were quite young when they knew McClung, which also shapes how they remember her.

60. Philip J. Panum, personal communication with author, August 16, 2006.

61. McClung to Blackwelder, July 20, 1975, McClung Papers.

62. Arnold interview. On the Bowl of the Wife of Kit Carson, see part 2.

63. Smith interview.

64. Smith interview.

65. Meals-on-wheels menu, January 1984, McClung Papers. The program was sponsored by the nonprofit Volunteers of America.

66. Order of service, Trinity United Methodist Church, September 2, 1979, McClung Papers.

67. McClung to Blackwelder, August 14, 1972, McClung Papers. Later letters from Blackwelder, in which she commiserated with her friend, suggest the health issues and financial burdens that McClung faced in the last decade of her life. See Blackwelder to McClung, February 10 ("It is simply impossible to believe that you can survive some of your experiences"), August 10, 1976; January 8, July 8 (she is pleased that McClung's recent letter for once contained "not one word of sickness or ill health"), 1977; May 23, 1978, McClung Papers.

68. Several of Blackwelder's letters to McClung comment on the up-and-down relationship McClung had with her late brother's family. See Blackwelder to McClung, July 25 ("Wonder if your nephews came to visit you as expected. Why don't they leave you alone or be more considerate?"), August 5 ("I was glad to hear that you enjoyed the visit with your nephew's family. It must have been heartening after so many rebuffs from your sister-in-law."), 1973; February 2, 1974; January 19, 1975. See also Denzel Jr. and Darlene McClung to Quantrille McClung, January 2, 1975, in which Denzel Jr. writes, "I was told before that you said you never wanted to see any of us McClungs but I'm coming anyway—if you don't want to see us then, you can tell me! OK?" After receiving this letter, McClung wrote to Blackwelder, "Believe I told you of the threatened visit of the wife of my elder nephew. So far no one has appeared." McClung to Blackwelder, January 18, 1975. All letters in McClung Papers.

69. For references, see part 3, n139. In 1972, McClung told Blackwelder, "The relatives who are closest to me in affection all live in Calif., & in no position to help me altho one cousin married a wife with money & they have been very generous to me. These two are invalids." (McClung to Blackwelder, August 27, 1972, McClung Papers).

70. McClung to Blackwelder, November 9, 1972; and Blackwelder to McClung, May 23, June 14, 1977; January 3, 13 ("It was gratifying ... to read about your enjoyable visit to Memphis [which] reads like a novel of Southern hospitality, reminding me of some of the old Virginia mansions"), December 14, 1978; January 22, 1979; December 8, 1980; January 22, 1981, all in McClung Papers.

71. McClung's relationship with Morgans is documented in McClung to Blackwelder, January 18, July 20, 1975; and Blackwelder to McClung, May 30 (quote), June 25, July 16, 1975, McClung Papers; and Smith interview.

72. This is based on DPL's Accession File for the McClung Papers; and on [Quantrille McClung], "Materials to be given to Denver Public Library Genealogical Division or Western History [Department]," n.d. [ca. 1970s]; McClung to John T. Eastlick, September 27, 1961; Eastlick to McClung, June 20, 1969; Henry

Shearouse to McClung, August 20, 1970; and McClung to Shearouse, September 11, 1970; August 5, 1972, all in McClung Papers. Thanks to James Kroll for providing me with the Accession File. The McClung Papers consist of eleven linear feet (eleven archival boxes) of paper files plus the reel-to-reel tapes of John McCurdy, Bernice Blackwelder, and Fred and Bess Heine. Besides the Carson, Bent, and Boggs and Colorado governors genealogy papers, other contents include newspaper clippings, maps and travel ephemera, genealogy and history publications, family genealogical records, limited family correspondence, correspondence with former colleagues, record of charitable contributions, and items from local institutions such as Trinity United Methodist Church and the Denver Art Museum.

73. Gene Rock and Byron E. Rogers Jr., Committee to Re-elect Rogers to Congress, to "Friend," n.d. [1970], McClung Papers. Jack Smith does not recall McClung expressing political views, though he says that of the Colorado governors' families she knew, she particularly liked John and Ann Love, who were Republicans, and disdained Democrats Stephen and Marjory McNichols because, as she told Smith, "they don't know who their own grandfather was." Smith interview. In addition to roughly equal numbers of Republican and Democratic governors, there was also one chief executive in the 1890s, Davis Waite, from the People's Party. On Rogers, see Leonard and Noel, *Denver: Mining Camp*, 249, 380, 517n43; Byron Rogers obituary, *New York Times*, January 2, 1984; and *Biographical Dictionary of the United States Congress, 1774–Present*, s.v. "Byron Giles Rogers," accessed June 23, 2017, http://bioguide.congress.gov/scripts/biodisplay.pl?index= R000389.

74. Virginia Culver, "Church Asks for Bishop's Resignation," *Denver Post*, January 18, 1983, clipping in McClung Papers; Wheatley and Wheatley, "Oral History Interview."

75. See part 3. More evidence of McClung's exposure to eclectic late nineteenth- and early twentieth-century sexual meanings and practices can be found in the personal library she built over the course of her life. Perhaps because she had access to DPL and the Colorado Historical Society, most of her books were not in western history and genealogy. Most focused on European (especially British) history, art, and culture. A much smaller number covered other parts of the world. Notably, several volumes were literary works by (or commentary on) writers such as H.D. and Oscar Wilde, who were known for their sexual alterity, as well as participants in London's sexually adventurous Bloomsbury group, including Vita Sackville-West and E. M. Forster. See the rough list entitled "Quantrille McClung Books," compiled by DPL staff after her death, in the Accession File for the McClung Papers. Cousin Sharon Morgans gave the books (over 400 of them) to DPL.

76. For the handmade greetings that McClung's friends exchanged in the 1910s and '20s, see, e.g., the Halloween party invitation entitled "The Ghost Walk," October 1921, "My Memoirs," vol. 5, item 20, McClung Collection, Hart Research Library, History Colorado, Denver.

77. "Jim [Judd]" to [McClung], valentine, n.d. [ca. 1970s/'80s], McClung Papers.

78. Judelowitz/Judd details come from collection description, Judd Family
Papers, Special Collections and Archives, University Libraries, University of Denver, accessed April 28, 2020, https://duarchives.coalliance.org/repositories/2/re
sources/502#. For the Hillkowitz family and JCRS, see part 3. For a JCRS board
listing, see "Report of the Work."

79. Blackwelder to McClung, September 16, 1973 (quote); June 17, July 30, September 17, 1974; March 5, [1977], McClung Papers.

80. "Special Recognition." At first, McClung did not tell Blackwelder about this
honor, perhaps worrying that it would underscore her friend's malaise. McClung
jotted on a letter Blackwelder sent, "Wrote to her 5-23-76. Did not tell about Cer-
tif[icate] of Appre[ciation]"; Blackwelder to McClung, April 14, 1976, McClung
Papers. But a few months later, perhaps when the *Colorado Genealogist* notice
was published, McClung relented, earning this response from Blackwelder:
"I was glad to hear about your ... Certificate of Appreciation from the Colo[rado]
Gen[ealogical] Soc[iety]. About time you were getting some recognition." Blackwelder to McClung, August 10, 1976, McClung Papers.

81. *Denver Post*, January 11, 1981. Thanks to Jim Kroll for finding this article by
staff writer Kit Miniclier, prepared for the *Post*'s Western Profiles column. Quantrille may have taken two other international trips in the 1950s, one to Mexico
and one to Brazil. For her travel in the 1950s, see record of a four-month trip
to England in 1953 in New York, Passenger and Crew Lists, 1820–1957, https://
www.ancestry.com/search/collections/7488; U.S., Departing Passenger and Crew
Lists, 1914–1966, https://www.ancestry.com/search/collections/60882; and U.K.,
Incoming Passenger Lists, 1878–1960, https://www.ancestry.com/search/collec
tions/1518; and record of a six-month trip to England in 1955 in New York, Passenger and Crew Lists, 1820–1957, https://www.ancestry.com/search/collections
/7488; U.S., Departing Passenger and Crew Lists, 1914–1966, https://www.ances
try.com/search/collections/60882; U.K., Incoming Passenger Lists, 1878–1960,
https://www.ancestry.com/search/collections/1518; U.K., Outward Passenger
Lists, 1890–1960, https://www.ancestry.com/search/collections/2997; a travel
document from Brazil signed at the Brazilian consulate in New Orleans on April
16, 1951, in Rio de Janeiro, Brazil, Immigration Cards, 1900–1965, https://www
.ancestry.com/search/collections/9800; and a passenger list for a flight from
Mexico City to Houston, July 13, 1951, in Texas, Passenger Lists, 1893–1963, https://
www.ancestry.com/search/collections/8722. Quantrille also went to England in
1930; see New York, Passenger and Crew Lists, 1820–1957, https://www.ancestry
.com/search/collections/7488 (ancestry.com erroneously says she went to Bremen, Germany, but she traveled to England on a ship named the *Bremen*). The
1930 trip would have been before she met the little Englishman.

82. Jack E. Smith, "Honor." The article reproduces the governor's proclamation, a copy of which is in the DPL Archives.

83. "A History Unto Herself," *Denver Post*, March 3, 1983. Jim Kroll attended the
event and recalls the head scarf; Garramone and Kroll interview.

84. Smith interview.

85. McClung to Shearouse, March 7, 1983, DPL Archives.

86. Hodnette to McClung, February 19, 1982, McClung Papers; Quantrille McClung, *Memoirs of My Childhood*, 2; Beatty, *Reds* (Beatty also plays John Reed; Keaton's singing as Louise Bryant transfixes Eugene O'Neill, played by Jack Nicholson. See also film review, *New York Times*, December 4, 1981.

87. "Julia" to McClung, February 18, 1983, McClung Papers. I have been unable to determine who Julia was. There were Ingersoll sisters named Jean, Julia, and Sarah (from a different Ingersoll family than that of McClung's friend and mentor Helen Ingersoll) who worked with McClung in the early twentieth century, but it is unclear if the Julia who wrote in 1983 was Julia Ingersoll (whose last name likely would not have been Ingersoll anymore, since she refers in the letter to a Marvin who was likely her husband).

88. "Julia" to McClung, March 15, 1985, McClung Papers. For Barrett, see U.S. Bureau of the Census, *Sixteenth Census*.

89. Smith interview; Garramone and Kroll interview; Quantrille McClung obituary, *Denver Post*, July 9, 1985; Quantrille McClung obituary, *Rocky Mountain News* (Denver), July 9, 1985; U.S. Social Security Administration, *Social Security Death Index*.

90. Smith interview; Garramone and Kroll interview; Quantrille McClung obituary, *Denver Post*, July 9, 1985; Quantrille McClung obituary, *Rocky Mountain News* (Denver), July 9, 1985; "In Memoriam." This summary also reflects a site visit I made to Crown Hill Cemetery, now Olinger Crown Hill Mortuary and Cemetery, Wheat Ridge, Colorado, on May 23, 2010, and a personal communication from Linda Leochner (Olinger Crown Hill employee) on July 13, 2016. There was a family dispute about the McClung gravesites that I have been unable to untangle. The dispute is referenced by others in Blackwelder to McClung, August 18, 1971, and "Ruth" to McClung, July 21, 1971, McClung Papers. See related discussion in parts 2 and 3.

91. *Manita* and *manito* are terms of self-identification New Mexican *hispanos* use; they derive from *hermanita* and *hermanito*, "little sister" and "little brother." See, e.g., Chris Wilson, *Myth of Santa Fe*, 155.

92. I base what follows on the stories Camille told me over twenty-three years of life together, on our journeys through her homeplace, and on perusal of census and other materials on ancestry.com.

93. See "James Almanzar," IMDb, accessed June 23, 2017, http://www.imdb.com/name/nm0021754.

94. Except where noted, this and what follows is written from memory.

95. Stevie Wonder, "Black Man," *Songs in the Key of Life*, Tamla/Motown Records, 1976.

96. See the articles collected in Neuenschwander, *Kenosha County*, esp. Buenker, "Immigration and Ethnic Groups"; Zophy, "Invisible People"; Keehn, "Industry and Business"; and Bailey, "Labor's Fight." John Neuenschwander, Jonathan Zophy, and John "Ben" Bailey were my college professors, along with Thomas Noer, author of "Popular Culture and Leisure Time." Ben Bailey introduced me to American Indian history and the history of the American West.

97. The instructors were Jonathan Zophy and Angela Howard.

98. Susan Lee Johnson, "Women's Households and Relationships."

99. Moraga and Anzaldúa, *Bridge Called My Back*. Kitchen Table: Women of ~olor Press, Third Woman Press, and the State University of New York Press pub-~shed later editions. My first copy was the 1983 second edition, published by ~itchen Table. Barbara Smith, *Home Girls*; Beck, *Nice Jewish Girls*. Anzaldúa, *~orderlands/La Frontera*, came later.

100. Writings from the sex wars era are legion. For the publication that emerged ~rom the Barnard conference, see Vance, *Pleasure and Danger*. I have bene-~ited from a recent retrospective: Echols, "Tangled Up." My thanks to Echols for ~haring it with me before publication. During the sex wars, *Signs* solicited pieces ~or a forum on the issues, which was published as Ferguson et al., "Forum."

101. This is a two-part essay. The first was published as Arguelles and Rich, "Homosexuality, Homophobia, and Revolution," part 1. This and the other essays ~rom the *Signs* special issue "The Lesbian Issue" were reprinted in a book ver-~ion, which also included essays published elsewhere in *Signs*. See Freedman ~et al., *Lesbian Issue*. The second part of the essay appeared as Rich and Arguelles, "Homosexuality, Homophobia, and Revolution," part 2.

102. Newton, "Mythic, Mannish Lesbian," quote on 557. This essay has been reprinted several times, starting in the book version of the special *Signs* issue (Freedman et al., *Lesbian Issue*) but also in Duberman, Vicinus, and Chauncey, *Hidden from History*; and Newton, *Margaret Mead*.

103. Newton, "Mythic, Mannish Lesbian," 560.

104. Although editing Newton's "Mythic, Mannish Lesbian" was utterly trans-formative, it was not long after I had done so that I found myself equally moved, and more aroused, by an oft-reprinted conversation between two feminist activ-ists—poet, playwright, and essayist Cherríe Moraga and writer, filmmaker, and public intellectual Amber Hollibaugh; see Moraga and Hollibaugh, "What We're Rollin Around in Bed With." This conversation was first published in "Sex Issue," *Heresies #12* 3, no. 4 (1981), and later in Snitow, Stansell, and Thompson, *Powers of Desire*; and Nestle, *Persistent Desire*.

105. Susan Lee Johnson, "'The gold she gathered'" and the longer book version, *Roaring Camp*. I owe my understanding of the decolonial imaginary to Emma Pérez, *Decolonial Imaginary*. I distinguish the study of "men" from the study of "men as men" because, until recently, most histories of men have not seen men as gendered beings but rather as normative humans. The phrase "women as women" is less useful, since historians have almost always seen women as cir-cumscribed by gender, but I use it here for parallelism and analytical emphasis.

106. In the early twenty-first century, this sort of sentence invites another question: Do I identify as transgender? I could not begin to phrase an answer to this question better than has my pal and confidant Reg, who put it thusly in a pri-vate conversation I have permission to reference: "I am not not transgender." Reg publishes as Regina Kunzel; see *Criminal Intimacy* and *Fallen Women, Problem Girls*. For the record, I do not often identify as lesbian, though I do so in solidarity when configurations of homophobic and sexist power demand it and in solidarity with many of my dearest friends. I will also identify more robustly as transgender

when configurations of transphobic power demand it and when strongly identified transgender people need staunch allies and fellow travelers in the trenches which is where most transgender people currently live. You can call me queer or gender nonconforming or masculine of center. You can call me gay or butch for old time's sake, because I am an old-timer. Whatever name you call me, just make sure that you smile when you say it.

Bibliography

In a work of this nature, it is difficult to distinguish between primary and secondary sources, especially since I use works by historians as both primary and secondary sources. Accordingly, I include in a single category published books, articles, and reviews; periodicals cited generally; unpublished PhD dissertations and MA theses; and a few other sources. I do not cite dates when I accessed census, marriage, naturalization, passenger list, military, and Social Security records on ancestry.com or U.S. government sites because these are stable government records that can be accessed in physical form. In the course of my research, I also consulted many online sources, including websites and blogs. These sources are cited fully in my endnotes and not repeated here.

ARCHIVAL AND MANUSCRIPT SOURCES

Author's possession
> Bernice Fowler Blackwelder Papers. Courtesy of the Late Doris Lance, Alpena, Michigan

Caxton Press, Caldwell, Idaho
> Bernice Blackwelder Author File

Center for Southwest Research, Zimmerman Library, University of New Mexico, Albuquerque
> Dorothy Brett Collection
> Marion M. Estergreen. "Southwest History: The Unpublished Research Notes," 2 vols.
> Shirley Hill Witt Papers, 1610–1991

Chicago History Museum Research Center
> Clippings Files on Chicago Neighborhoods
> Photograph Files on Chicago Neighborhoods

Colorado Springs Pioneers Museum, Colorado Springs
> Francis W. Cragin Papers

Duke University Libraries Digital Collection, Durham, North Carolina
> Historical American Sheet Music

Hart Research Library, History Colorado, Denver
> Quantrille Day McClung Collection

Newberry Library, Chicago
> Chicago Foreign Language Press Survey
> The Westerners–Chicago Corral Papers

New Mexico State Records Center and Archives, Santa Fe
> Colfax County Court Records
> Manuel A. Sánchez Papers

SAG-AFTRA Chicago Local Office
> AFRA Membership Records. Microfiche.

Southwest Research Center, University of New Mexico-Taos
Kit Carson Files
Special Collections and Archives, University Libraries, University of Denver
Beck Archives
Judd Family Papers
Special Collections, Archives, and Preservation, Norlin Library, University of
Colorado Boulder
Bent and St. Vrain Collection
Special Collections, Tutt Library, Colorado College, Colorado Springs
Harvey L. Carter Papers
Special Collections, University of Washington Libraries, Seattle
J. Willis Sayre Collection of Theatrical Photographs. Digital Collections.
State Historical Society of Missouri, St. Louis
Carson Family Papers
University Archives, Forsyth Library, Fort Hays State University, Hays, Kansas
Reveille Yearbook Collection, 1921–24, some in Forsyth Library Digital
Collections.
University Archives, University of Wisconsin–Madison
Camille Guérin-Gonzales Papers
University of Oklahoma Press, Norman
M. Morgan Estergreen Author File
Virginia Room, Arlington Public Library, Arlington, Virginia
Plat Book of Arlington County, Virginia. Philadelphia: Franklin Survey Co.,
1952. With revisions entered for 1953, 1955, 1957, 1959, and 1962.
Virginia Room, City of Fairfax Regional Library, Fairfax County Public Library,
Fairfax, Virginia
Fairfax County Real Property Identification Maps. Department of
Assessments, Fairfax County, Virginia, 2010.
Western History Collection, Western History/Genealogy Department, Denver
Public Library
Adelaide A. French Papers
"Capitol Hill/Cheesman Park: Update and Analysis, June 1976." Denver
Planning Office, 1976.
"Capitol Hill Neighborhood Plan." Denver Planning Office, 1973.
Denver Public Library Archives
Las Noticias Alegres de la Casa Kit Carson, 1969–78, 1979, 1983
Quantrille McClung Papers
Orr, Elizabeth A. *Profiles of Denver Residents.* Denver: Office of Policy
Analysis, 1979.
Simmons, R. Laurie, and Thomas H. Simmons. "Denver Neighborhood
Project, 1993–94: Capitol Hill Neighborhood." Prepared for City and
County of Denver, Denver Landmark Preservation Commission, and
the Office of Planning and Community Development, by Front Range
Research Associates, January 1995.

Skene, Harold Vincent. "Autobiography."
   Staff Lookout, 1935–36, 1946–48
Wisconsin Historical Society Library and Archives, Madison
   Reverend Bernard J. Stecker Papers, 1919–71
   Harold Stecker Papers, 1915–19

INTERVIEWS BY THE AUTHOR
Transcripts of all interviews are in the author's possession.
Samuel P. Arnold, by telephone, June 13 and 14, 2000.
Nancy Elliott, Hanover, New Hampshire, May 21, 2009.
Bonnie Garramone and James Kroll, Denver, Colorado, August 16, 2008.
Doris Lance and Stephen Fowler, Alpena and Cadillac, Michigan, June 13, 2004.
Jack Smith, Denver, Colorado, August 16, 2008.

NEWSPAPERS
Albuquerque (N.M.) Journal, 1938–62, 1973, 1991, 2014
Albuquerque (N.M.) Tribune, 1973
Big Spring (Tex.) Daily Herald, 1937
Bismarck (N.D.) Daily Tribune, 1900
Catalyst (Colorado College, Colorado Springs, Colo.), 1972
Chicago Daily News, 1933, 1941, 1963, 1964, 1974
Chicago Herald and Examiner, 1938
Chicago Sun-Times, 1974, 1977
Chicago Tribune, 1920–86
Clovis (N.M.) News Journal, 1973
Coconino Sun (Flagstaff, Ariz.), 1940
El Crepúsculo (Taos, N.M.), 1950
Daily Times (Davenport, Iowa), 1946
Deming (N.M.) Headlight, 1912
Denver Post, 1981, 1983, 1985
Evening News (San Jose, Calif.), 1927
High Point (N.C.) Enterprise, 1961
Idaho Press-Tribune (Nampa), 2010
Indian Country Today (Washington, D.C.), 2014
Las Cruces (N.M.) Sun-News, 1973
Lincoln (Kans.) Sentinel-Republican, 1958
Los Angeles Times, 1940, 1947
New-York Ledger, 1875
New York Times, 1917, 1958, 1973, 1981, 1984, 2011, 2015
Oakland (Calif.) Tribune, 1949, 1953, 1956, 1957
Rocky Mountain News (Denver), 1902, 1985
Salina (Kans.) Journal, 1930, 1933
Santa Fe New Mexican, 1940–68, 1970–74, 1979, 1981, 1984, 1991, 2014
Seattle Times, 1939

Taos (N.M.) News, 1960–86

Union (Washington, D.C.), 1847

Vaudeville News (New York), 1925

Vaudeville News and New York Star, 1927

Washington Post, 1957, 1959

Washington Times, 1910

Weekly New Mexican Review and Livestock Journal (Santa Fe), 1885

GOVERNMENT DOCUMENTS

U.S. DECENNIAL CENSUS SCHEDULES, ORGANIZED BY YEAR

U.S. Bureau of the Census. *1870 U.S. Census, Population Schedules.* Washington, D.C.: National Archives and Records Administration, n.d. Consulted at ancestry.com.

——. *Tenth Census of the United States, 1880.* Record Group 29. National Archives, Washington, D.C. Consulted at ancestry.com.

——. *Twelfth Census of the United States, 1900.* Washington, D.C.: National Archives and Records Administration, 1900. Consulted at ancestry.com.

——. *Thirteenth Census of the United States, 1910.* Record Group 29. National Archives, Washington, D.C. Consulted at ancestry.com.

——. *Fourteenth Census of the United States, 1920.* Record Group 29. Washington, D.C.: National Archives and Records Administration, n.d. Consulted at ancestry.com.

——. *Fifteenth Census of the United States, 1930.* Washington, D.C.: National Archives and Records Administration, 1930. Consulted at ancestry.com.

——. *Sixteenth Census of the United States, 1940.* Washington, D.C.: National Archives and Records Administration, 1940. Consulted at ancestry.com.

U.S. CENSUS BUREAU REPORTS, SUPPLEMENTS, AND COMPENDIA

U.S. Bureau of the Census. *Census of Population: 1970.* Vol. 1, *Characteristics of the Population.* Part 35, *North Carolina.* Washington, D.C.: Government Printing Office, 1973.

——. *Census Tracts: Denver, Colo. Standard Metropolitan Statistical Area.* U.S. Censuses of Population and Housing: 1960. Final Report PHC(1)-38. Washington, D.C.: Government Printing Office, 1961.

——. *Compendium of the Eleventh Census: 1890, Part I—Population.* Washington, D.C.: Government Printing Office, 1892. Consulted at www.census.gov/library/publications/1895/dec/volume-1.html.

——. *Fourteenth Census of the United States, 1920: State Compendium—Missouri.* Washington, D.C.: Government Printing Office, 1924. Consulted at www2.census.gov/prod2/decennial/documents/06229686v20-25_TOC.pdf.

——. *Narrative Profiles of Neighborhoods in Denver, Colo.* Neighborhood Statistics Program. Washington, D.C.: Government Printing Office, [1983].

——. *Statistical Abstract of the United States, 1942.* Washington, D.C.: Government Printing Office, 1943.

——. *Table MS-2, Estimated Median Age at First Marriage, by Sex: 1890 to*

Present. 2004. Consulted at www.census.gov/population/socdemo/hh-fam
/tabMS-2.pdf.

U.S. GOVERNMENT NON-CENSUS RECORDS

*Soundex Index to Naturalization Petitions for the United States District
and Circuit Courts. Northern District of Illinois and Immigration and
Naturalization Service District 9, 1840–1950.* Washington, D.C.: National
Archives and Records Administration, [1917]. Consulted at ancestry.com.

U.S. Customs Service. *Passenger Lists of Vessels Arriving at New York, New York,
1820–1897.* Record Group 36. Washington, D.C.: National Archives, n.d.
Consulted at ancestry.com.

U.S. Immigration and Naturalization Service. *Passenger Lists of Vessels Arriving
at Honolulu, Hawaii, Compiled 02/13/1900–12/30/1953.* Record Group
85. Records of the Immigration and Naturalization Service, 1787–2004.
Washington, D.C.: National Archives, n.d. Consulted at ancestry.com.

U.S. Marine Corps Muster Rolls, 1893–1958. Washington, D.C. National Archives,
n.d. Consulted at ancestry.com.

U.S. Selective Service System. *World War I Selective Service System Draft
Registration Cards, 1917–1918.* Washington, D.C.: National Archives and
Records Administration, [1917]. Consulted at ancestry.com.

U.S. Social Security Administration. *Social Security Death Index.* Consulted at
ancestry.com.

World War II Prisoners of War Data File. Records of World War II Prisoners of
War, 1942–1947. Records of the Office of the Provost Marshal General. Record
Group 389. College Park, Md.: National Archives, n.d. Consulted at ancestry
.com.

STATE GOVERNMENT RECORDS, ORGANIZED BY STATE

Colorado

Marriage Record Report. Division of Vital Statistics, State of Colorado.
Consulted at ancestry.com.

Florida

Eleventh Census of the State of Florida, 1945. Tallahassee: State Library and
Archives of Florida, 1945. Consulted at ancestry.com.

Iowa

Iowa State Census, 1885. Iowa City: Iowa State Historical Society, 1885. Consulted
at ancestry.com.

Kansas

1875 Kansas State Census. Topeka: Kansas State Historical Society, n.d.
Consulted at ancestry.com.

1905 Kansas State Census. Topeka: Kansas State Historical Society, n.d.
Consulted at ancestry.com.

1915 Kansas State Census. Topeka: Kansas State Historical Society, n.d.
Consulted at ancestry.com.

1925 Kansas State Census. Topeka: Kansas State Historical Society, n.d.
Consulted at ancestry.com.

Missouri

Missouri Marriage Records. Jefferson City: Missouri State Archives, n.d. Consulted at ancestry.com.

DIRECTORIES

Baldwin's and Post's Salisbury, North Carolina, City Directory, 1935. Charleston, S.C.: Baldwin Directory Company and the Salisbury Post, 1935.

Ballenger and Richards Denver Directory and Classified Buyers Guide 1925. Denver: Gazetteer, 1925.

Ballenger and Richards Forty-Third Annual Denver Directory 1915. Denver: Will H. Richards, 1915.

Bresser's Cross-Index Directory of Greater Denver, 1965–66. Denver: Walter Bresser and Sons, 1965.

Chicago Telephone Directory. Chicago: Illinois Bell Telephone Company, 1941–47.

Denver Telephone Directory. Denver: Mountain Bell, 1964.

Golden City Directory. Englewood, Colo.: XL Directory Service, 1964.

Hill's Arlington County Directory. Richmond, Va.: Hill Directory, 1955, 1957, 1963.

Hill's High Point City Directory. Richmond, Va.: Hill Directory, 1949.

Los Angeles City Directory, 1939. Los Angeles: Los Angeles Directory, 1939.

Lusk's Fairfax County, Virginia, Real Estate Directory Service. Transfers from September 8, 1953, through June 9, 1959. Washington, D.C.: Rufus S. Lusk and Son, 1959.

Lusk's Fairfax County, Virginia, Real Estate Directory Service. Transfers from January 30, 1961, through February 7, 1963. Washington, D.C.: Rufus S. Lusk and Son, 1963.

Lusk's Northern Virginia Real Estate Directory Service. Washington, D.C.: Rufus S. Lusk and Son, 1955, 1962.

Polk's Crocker-Langley San Francisco City Directory 1944. San Francisco: R. L. Polk, 1944.

Polk's Denver City Directory, 1960. Denver: R. L. Polk, 1960.

Polk's Denver City Directory, 1963. Denver: R. L. Polk, 1963.

Polk's Salina City Directory, 1923. Salina, Kans.: R. L. Polk, 1923.

R. L. Polk and Company's Salina City Directory, 1921. Salina, Kans.: R. L. Polk, 1921.

University Hill Farms Association, *University Hill Farms Directory, 1972–1973.* [Madison, Wisc., n.d.] Copy in author's possession.

Washington Yellow Pages, April 1960. Washington, D.C.: Chesapeake and Potomac Telephone Company, 1960.

Washington Yellow Pages, May 1961. Washington, D.C.: Chesapeake and Potomac Telephone Company, 1961.

Wright's Eau Claire City Directory, 1939. Milwaukee: Wright Directory, 1939.

Wright's La Crosse City Directory, 1937. Milwaukee: Wright Directory, 1937.

FILM AND TELEVISION

Bailey, Norman. *Bombing of U.S.S. Panay*. Newsreel. Universal City, Calif.: Universal Pictures, 1937. www.youtube.com/watch?v=WujTPNkjSeM. Accessed July 30, 2014.

Beatty, Warren, dir. *Reds*. Los Angeles: Paramount Pictures, 1981.

English, John, et al., dirs. *The Adventures of Kit Carson*. Universal City, Calif.: MCA Television Revue Studios, 1951–55.

Ives, Stephen, dir. *Kit Carson*. Insignia Film for American Experience. Boston: WGBH Educational Foundation, 2008.

Ives, Stephen, dir. *The West*. Part 7, "The Geography of Hope." DVD. Alexandria, Va.: PBS; Washington, D.C., WETA-TV, 1996.

Lewis, Joseph H., et al., dirs. *The Rifleman*. Los Angeles: Four Star Productions, 1958–63.

Sam Arnold's Frying Pans West: The National TV Series (1968–1973). DVDs and companion cookbook. N.p.: Fur Trade, 2011.

Seitz, George B., dir. *Kit Carson*. Los Angeles: Edward Small Productions, 1940.

Silber, Glenn, and Barry Alexander Brown, dirs. *The War at Home*. DVD. 1979; New York: First Run Features, 2003.

BOOKS, ARTICLES, REVIEWS, PERIODICALS, DISSERTATIONS, AND THESES

Abbott, Carl. "Planning Chicago." In Grossman, Keating, and Reiff, *Encyclopedia of Chicago*, 613–17.

Abbott, Carl, Stephen J. Leonard, and Thomas J. Noel. *Colorado: A History of the Centennial State*. 4th ed. Boulder: University Press of Colorado, 2005.

Abrams, Jeanne. "Chasing the Cure in Colorado: The Jewish Consumptives' Relief Society." In *Jews of the American West*, edited by Moses Rischin and John Livingston, 95–115. Detroit: Wayne State University Press, 1991.

———. *Jewish Women Pioneering the Frontier Trail: A History in the American West*. New York: New York University Press, 2006.

———. "*Unsere Leit* ('Our People'): Anna Hillkowitz and the Development of the East European Jewish Woman Professional in America." *American Jewish Archives* 37, no. 2 (November 1985): 275–89.

Adamic, Louis. *My America, 1928–1938*. New York: Harper, 1938.

———. "Thirty Million New Americans." *Harper's*, November 1934.

Adams, David Wallace, and Crista DeLuzio, eds. *On the Borders of Love and Power: Families and Kinship in the Intercultural American Southwest*. Berkeley: University of California Press, 2012.

Adelman, Jeremy, and Stephen Aron. "From Borderlands to Borders: Empires, Nation-States, and the Peoples in Between in North American History." *American Historical Review* 104, no. 3 (1999): 814–41.

Allsup, Carl. *The American G.I. Forum: Origins and Evolution*. Center for Mexican American Studies, University of Texas, Austin, Monograph 6. Austin: University of Texas Press, 1982.

Allyn, David. *Make Love, Not War: The Sexual Revolution, An Unfettered History*. Boston: Little, Brown, 2000.

"America's First Fashions: Frederic H. Douglas of Denver Art Museum Gives Indian Style Show with Models for Westerners Ladies Night Program." *Westerners Brand Book* 9, no. 10 (December 1952): 73–75.

[Anderson, George B.] *History of New Mexico: Its Resources and People.* 2 vols. Los Angeles: Pacific States, 1907.

Anzaldúa, Gloria. *Borderlands/La Frontera: The New Mestiza.* 1987. 2nd ed. San Francisco: Aunt Lute Books, 1999.

Appleby, Joyce, Lynn Hunt, and Margaret Jacob. *Telling the Truth about History.* New York: Norton, 1994.

Aquila, Richard, ed. *Wanted Dead or Alive: The American West in Popular Culture.* Urbana: University of Illinois Press, 1996.

Arguelles, Lourdes, and B. Ruby Rich. "Homosexuality, Homophobia, and Revolution: Notes toward an Understanding of the Cuban Lesbian and Gay Experience." Pt. 1. In "The Lesbian Issue," edited by Estelle B. Freedman, Barbara Charlesworth Gelpi, Susan L. Johnson, and Kathleen M. Weston. Special issue, *Signs* 9, no. 4 (Summer 1984): 683–99.

Armitage, Susan, and Elizabeth Jameson, eds. *The Women's West.* Norman: University of Oklahoma Press, 1987.

Arnold, Samuel P. *Eating Up the Santa Fe Trail.* Niwot: University Press of Colorado, 1990.

———. *The Fort Cookbook: New Foods of the Old West from the Denver Restaurant.* New York: HarperCollins, 1997.

Aron, Stephen. *American Confluence: The Missouri Frontier from Borderland to Border State.* Bloomington: Indiana University Press, 2005.

Arondekar, Anjali, Ann Cvetkovich, Christina B. Hanhardt, Regina Kunzel, Tavia Nyong'o, Juana María Rodríguez, Susan Stryker, Daniel Marshall, Kevin P. Murphy, and Zeb Tortorici. "Queering Archives: A Roundtable Discussion." *Radical History Review* 2015, no. 122 (May 2015): 211–31.

Arredondo, Gabriela. *Mexican Chicago: Race, Identity, and Nation, 1916–39.* Urbana: University of Illinois Press, 2008.

Avila, Eric. *Popular Culture in the Age of White Flight: Fear and Fantasy in Suburban Los Angeles.* Berkeley: University of California Press, 2004.

Axtell, James. *Natives and Newcomers: The Cultural Origins of North America.* New York: Oxford University Press, 2001.

Bailey, Beth. *Sex in the Heartland.* Cambridge, Mass.: Harvard University Press, 1999.

Bailey, John W. "Labor's Fight for Security and Dignity." In Neuenschwander, *Kenosha County,* 223–74.

Baldwin, Davarian L. *Chicago's New Negroes: Modernity, the Great Migration, and Black Urban Life.* Chapel Hill: University of North Carolina Press, 2007.

Barr, Juliana. *Peace Came in the Form of a Woman: Indians and Spaniards in the Texas Borderlands.* Chapel Hill: University of North Carolina Press, 2007.

Barrett, James. "Americanization from the Bottom Up: Immigration and the Remaking of the Working Class in the United States, 1880–1930." *Journal of American History* 79, no. 3 (December 1992): 996–1020.

arth, Gunther. *Instant Cities: Urbanization and the Rise of San Francisco and Denver*. New York: Oxford University Press, 1975.

asso, Matthew L. *Meet Joe Copper: Masculinity and Race on Montana's World War II Homefront*. Chicago: University of Chicago Press, 2013.

ate, Walter Nathaniel. *Frontier Legend: Texas Finale of Capt. William F. Drannan, Pseudo Frontier Comrade of Kit Carson*. New Bern, N.C.: O. G. Dunn, 1954.

———. *General Sidney Sherman: Texas Soldier, Statesman, and Builder*. Waco, Tex.: Texian Press, 1974.

Bates, Tom. *Rads: The 1970 Bombing of the Army Math Research Center at the University of Wisconsin and Its Aftermath*. New York: HarperCollins, 1992.

Baughman, James. *The Republic of Mass Culture: Journalism, Filmmaking, and Broadcasting in America since 1941*. 1992. 3rd ed. Baltimore: Johns Hopkins University Press, 2005.

Baum, L. Frank. *The Wonderful Wizard of Oz*. Chicago: George M. Hill, 1900.

Baym, Nina. *American Women Writers and the Work of History, 1790–1860*. New Brunswick, N.J.: Rutgers University Press, 1995.

Beasley, Delilah. *The Negro Trail Blazers of California: A Compilation of Records from the California Archives in the Bancroft Library at the University of California, in Berkeley; And from the Diaries, Old Papers and Conversations of Old Pioneers in the State of California*. Los Angeles: Times Mirror, 1919.

Beck, Evelyn Torton, ed. *Nice Jewish Girls: A Lesbian Anthology*. Watertown, Mass.: Persephone, 1982.

Beckwourth, James P. *The Life and Adventures of James P. Beckwourth: Written from His Own Dictation by T. D. Bonner*. 1856. Reprint, Lincoln: University of Nebraska Press, 1981.

Bederman, Gail. *Manliness and Civilization: A Cultural History of Gender and Race in the United States, 1880–1917*. Chicago: University of Chicago Press, 1995.

Belasco, Warren, and Roger Horowitz, eds. *Food Chains: From Farmyard to Shopping Cart*. Philadelphia: University of Pennsylvania Press, 2009.

Bemis, Edwin A., comp. "Conception and Birth of the Denver Westerners." In *The 1962 Brand Book of the Denver Posse of the Westerners*, 367–74. Boulder, Colo.: Johnson, 1963.

Bennett, Larry. "Gentrification." In Grossman, Keating, and Reiff, *Encyclopedia of Chicago*, 333.

Benton Frémont, Jessie. "Kit Carson." *Land of Sunshine* 6, no. 3 (February 1897). Reprinted in *Historical Society of Southern California Quarterly* 42, no. 4 (December 1960): 331–34.

———. "Kit Carson." *Wide Awake*, March 1889. Reprinted in *The Will and the Way Stories*, edited by Jessie Benton Frémont. Boston: D. Lothrop, 1891.

Berlin, Ira. *Generations of Captivity: A History of African-American Slaves*. Cambridge, Mass.: Harvard University Press, 2003.

———. *Many Thousands Gone: The First Two Centuries of Slavery in North America*. Cambridge, Mass.: Harvard University Press, 1998.

Billington, Ray Allen. "The Frontier and I." *Western Historical Quarterly* 1, no. 1 (January 1970): 4-20.

———. "The New Western Social Order and the Synthesis of Western Scholarship." In *The American West: An Appraisal*, edited by Robert G. Ferris 3-12. Santa Fe: Museum of New Mexico Press, 1963.

———. Review of *Great Westerner: The Story of Kit Carson*, by Bernice Blackwelder. *Chicago Tribune*, March 11, 1962.

———. "The Santa Fe Conference and the Writing of Western History." In Toole et al., *Probing the American West*, 1-16.

———. *Westward Expansion: A History of the American Frontier*. New York: Macmillan, 1949.

Bingham, Clara. *Witness to the Revolution: Radicals, Resisters, Vets, Hippies, and the Year America Lost Its Mind and Found Its Soul*. New York: Random House, 2016.

Biographical Directory of the American Congress, 1774-1971. Washington, D.C.: U.S. Government Printing Office, 1971.

Blackhawk, Ned. *Violence over the Land: Indians and Empires in the Early American West*. Cambridge, Mass: Harvard University Press, 2006.

Blackwelder, Bernice. *Great Westerner: The Story of Kit Carson*. Caldwell, Idaho: Caxton, 1962.

———. Review of *Kit Carson: A Portrait in Courage*, by M. Morgan Estergreen. *Arizona and the West* 6, no. 2 (Summer 1964): 158-60.

Bledstein, Burton J. *The Culture of Professionalism: The Middle Class and the Development of Higher Education in America*. New York: W. W. Norton, 1976.

Bloom, John Porter. "Reminiscence—WHA 50th Annual Conference." *Western History Association Newsletter*, Fall 2010, 1-3.

Blumin, Stuart M. *The Emergence of the Middle Class: Social Experience in the American City, 1760-1900*. New York: Cambridge University Press, 1989.

Boag, Peter. *Re-dressing America's Frontier Past*. Berkeley: University of California Press, 2011.

Boddy, William. *Fifties Television: The Industry and Its Critics*. Urbana: University of Illinois Press, 1990.

Borowick, Matthew. *The Civil War Round Table Handbook*. Self-published, Amazon Digital Services, 2013. Kindle.

Borstelmann, Thomas. *The Cold War and the Color Line: American Race Relations in the Global Arena*. Cambridge, Mass.: Harvard University Press, 2001.

Bowen, Michael. *Roots of Modern Conservatism: Dewey, Taft, and the Battle for the Soul of the Republican Party*. Chapel Hill: University of North Carolina Press, 2011.

Bower, Donald E. *Fred Rosenstock, a Legend in Books and Art*. Flagstaff, Ariz.: Northland, 1976.

Boyd, Nan Alamilla. *Wide Open Town: A History of Queer San Francisco*. Berkeley: University of California Press, 2003.

Boyer, Paul S. *By the Bomb's Early Light: American Thought and Culture at the Dawn of the Atomic Age*. New York: Pantheon, 1985.

Bradley, Mark Philip. *Vietnam at War*. New York: Oxford University Press, 2009.

Branch, Taylor. *At Canaan's Edge: America in the King Years, 1965-68*. New York: Simon and Schuster, 2006.

———. *Parting the Waters: America in the King Years, 1954-1963*. New York: Simon and Schuster, 1988.

———. *Pillar of Fire: America in the King Years, 1963-65*. New York: Simon and Schuster, 1998.

Brewerton, George D. *Overland with Kit Carson: A Narrative of the Old Spanish Trail in '48*. 1930. Reprint, Lincoln: University of Nebraska Press, 1993.

Brilliant, Mark. *The Color of America Has Changed: How Racial Diversity Shaped Civil Rights Reform in California, 1941-1978*. New York: Oxford University Press, 2010.

Brinkley, Douglas. *Wilderness Warrior: Theodore Roosevelt and the Crusade for America*. New York: HarperCollins, 2009.

Brooks, James. *Captives and Cousins: Slavery, Kinship, and Community in the Southwest Borderlands*. Chapel Hill: University of North Carolina Press, 2002.

Brooks, Juanita. *Mountain Meadows Massacre*. Stanford, Calif.: Stanford University Press, 1950.

Brown, Corinne Joy. "The Fort." *Persimmon Hill*, Winter 2000, 25-29.

Brown, Dee. *Bury My Heart at Wounded Knee: An Indian History of the American West*. New York: Holt, Rinehart, and Winston, 1970.

Brown, Kathleen M. *Good Wives, Nasty Wenches, and Anxious Patriarchs: Gender, Race, and Power in Colonial Virginia*. Chapel Hill: University of North Carolina Press, 1996.

Brugge, David. *Navajos in the Catholic Church Records of New Mexico, 1694-1875*. 1969. 2nd ed. Tsaile, Ariz.: Navajo Community College Press, 1986.

"Brummett Echohawk Tells Pawnee Story: Indian Artist Recounts Tribal History from the Time of Earth Lodges to That of Boarding Schools and Itchy Uniforms." *Westerners Brand Book* 14, no. 3 (May 1957): 17-19, 22.

Brundage, David. *The Making of Western Labor Radicalism: Denver's Organized Workers, 1878-1905*. Urbana: University of Illinois Press, 1994.

Buckner, Jocelyn L. "The Angel and the Imp: The Duncan Sisters' Performances of Race and Gender." *Popular Entertainment Studies* 2, no. 2 (2011): 55-72.

Buenker, John D. "Immigration and Ethnic Groups." In Neuenschwander, *Kenosha County*, 1-49.

Burke, Flannery. *From Greenwich Village to Taos: Primitivism and Place at Mabel Dodge Luhan's*. Lawrence: University Press of Kansas, 2008.

———. "Spud Johnson and a Gay Man's Place in the Taos Creative Arts Community." *Pacific Historical Review* 79, no. 1 (February 2010): 86-113.

Burton, Antoinette, ed. *Archive Stories: Facts, Fictions, and the Writing of History*. Durham, N.C.: Duke University Press, 2005.

———. *The Postcolonial Careers of Santha Rama Rau*. Durham, N.C.: Duke University Press, 2007.

Buscombe, Edward, ed. *The BFI Companion to the Western.* London: Atheneum 1988; New York: Da Capo, 1991.

"Business Week Reports to Executives on the Consumer Movement." *Business Week*, April 22, 1939.

Butler, Judith. *Gender Trouble: Feminism and the Subversion of Identity.* 1990. 2nd ed. New York: Routledge, 1999.

Butler, Judith, and Gayle Rubin. "Sexual Traffic: An Interview with Gayle Rubin by Judith Butler." In *Deviations: A Gayle Rubin Reader*, edited by Gayle Rubin, 276–309. Durham, N.C.: Duke University Press, 2011.

Canady, Margot. "Building a Straight State: Sexuality and Social Citizenship under the 1944 GI Bill." *Journal of American History* 90, no. 3 (December 2003): 935–57.

———. *The Straight State: Sexuality and Citizenship in Twentieth-Century America.* Princeton, N.J.: Princeton University Press, 2009.

Canfield, Michael R. *Theodore Roosevelt in the Field.* Chicago: University of Chicago Press, 2015.

Carey, Heidi Pawlowski. "Auditorium Building." In Grossman, Keating, and Reiff, *Encyclopedia of Chicago*, 52–53.

Carmack, Sharon DeBartolo. *A Genealogist's Guide to Discovering Your Female Ancestors: Special Strategies for Uncovering Hard-to-Find Information about Your Female Lineage.* Cincinnati: Betterway Books, 1998.

Carroll, Peter. *It Seemed Like Nothing Happened: America in the 1970s.* 1982; New Brunswick, N.J.: Rutgers University Press, 2000.

Carruthers, Susan L. *Cold War Captives: Imprisonment, Escape, and Brainwashing.* Berkeley: University of California Press, 2009.

Carter, Dan. *From George Wallace to Newt Gingrich: Race in the Conservative Counterrevolution, 1963–1994.* Baton Rouge: Louisiana State University Press, 1999.

Carter, Harvey L. "The Curious Case of the Slandered Scout, the Aggressive Anthropologist, the Delinquent Dean and the Acquiescent Army." *Denver Westerners Brand Book*, no. 28 (1973): 93–112.

———. *"Dear Old Kit": The Historical Christopher Carson.* Norman: University of Oklahoma Press, 1968.

———. Introduction to Simmons and Gordon-McCutchan, *Short Truth*, 1–3.

———. "Kit Carson." In LeRoy Hafen, *Mountain Men*, 6:105–31.

Case, Leland D. "The Westerners: Twenty-Five Years of Riding the Range." *Western Historical Quarterly* 1, no. 1 (January 1970): 63–76.

Casey, Steven. *Cautious Crusade: Franklin D. Roosevelt, American Public Opinion, and the War against Nazi Germany.* New York: Oxford University Press, 2001.

Cather, Willa. *One of Ours.* 1922. Reprint, New York: Vintage Books/Random House, 1991.

Cave, Dorothy. *Beyond Courage: One Regiment against Japan, 1941–1945.* Las Cruces, N.M.: Yucca Tree, 1992.

hafe, William H. "The Road to Equality, 1962–Today." In Cott, *No Small Courage*, 529–86.

———. *The Unfinished Journey: America since World War II*. 1986. 4th and 8th eds. New York: Oxford University Press, 1999, 2015.

Chalmers, David. *And the Crooked Places Made Straight: The Struggle for Social Change in the 1960s*. 1991. 2nd ed. Baltimore: Johns Hopkins University Press, 1996.

Chauncey, George, Jr. "Christian Brotherhood or Sexual Perversion? Homosexual Identities and the Construction of Sexual Boundaries in the World War I Era." In Duberman, Vicinus, and Chauncey, *Hidden from History*, 294–317.

———. "From Sexual Inversion to Homosexuality: Medicine and the Changing Conceptualization of Female Deviance." *Salmagundi*, no. 58/59 (Fall–Winter 1982–83): 114–46.

———. *Gay New York: Gender, Urban Culture, and the Making of the Gay Male World, 1890–1940*. New York: Basic Books, 1994.

Chávez, Fray Angélico. *Origins of New Mexico Families: A Genealogy of the Spanish Colonial Period*. 1954. Rev. ed. Santa Fe: Museum of New Mexico Press, 1992.

Chávez-García, Miroslava. *Migrant Longing: Letter Writing across the U.S.-Mexico Borderlands*. Chapel Hill: University of North Carolina Press, 2018.

Chen, Yong. *Chop Suey, USA: The Story of Chinese Food in America*. New York: Columbia University Press, 2014.

Cheng, Cindy I-Fen. *Citizens of Asian America: Democracy and Race during the Cold War*. New York: New York University Press, 2013.

Cho, Sumi, Kimberlé Williams Crenshaw, and Leslie McCall, eds. "Intersectionality: Theorizing Power, Empowering Theory." Special issue, *Signs* 38, no. 4 (Summer 2013).

Clogg, Richard. *A Concise History of Greece*. Cambridge: Cambridge University Press, 1992.

Cobb, Daniel M. *Native Activism in Cold War America: The Struggle for Sovereignty*. Lawrence: University Press of Kansas, 2008.

Cobb, Daniel M., and Loretta Fowler, eds. *Beyond Red Power: American Indian Politics and Activism since 1900*. Santa Fe, N.M.: School for Advanced Research Press, 2007.

Cohen, Deborah. *Braceros: Migrant Citizens and Transnational Subjects in the Postwar United States and Mexico*. Chapel Hill: University of North Carolina Press, 2011.

Cohen, Lizabeth. *A Consumers' Republic: The Politics of Mass Consumption in Postwar America*. New York: Knopf, 2003.

———. *Making a New Deal: Industrial Workers in Chicago*. 1990. 2nd ed. New York: Cambridge University Press, 2008.

Cole, B. Erin. "R-0: Race, Sexuality and Single-Family Zoning in Denver's Park Hill and Capitol Hill Neighborhoods, 1956–1989." PhD diss., University of New Mexico, 2014.

Colorado Genealogist. 1939–85.

"Colorado Library Association 35th Annual Meeting, Boulder, Colorado, September 11–13, 1924." *Colorado Libraries* 3, no. 10 (September 1924): 158–6❲

Convery, William Joseph. *Pride of the Rockies: The Life of Colorado's Premier Iris Patron, John Kernan Mullen.* Boulder: University Press of Colorado, 2000.

Conzen, Kathleen Neils. "A Saga of Families." In *The Oxford History of the American West,* edited by Clyde Milner, Carol O'Connor, and Martha Sandweiss, 315–57. New York: Oxford University Press, 1994.

Cook, Robert J. *Troubled Commemoration: The American Civil War Centennial, 1961–1965.* Baton Rouge: Louisiana State University Press, 2007.

Cott, Nancy F. *The Grounding of Modern Feminism.* New Haven, Conn.: Yale University Press, 1987.

———, ed. *No Small Courage: A History of Women in the United States.* New York: Oxford University Press, 2000.

———. *Public Vows: A History of Marriage and the Nation.* Cambridge, Mass.: Harvard University Press, 2000.

———, ed. *A Woman Making History: Mary Ritter Beard through Her Letters.* New Haven, Conn.: Yale University Press, 1991.

Cott, Nancy F., Jeanne Boydston, Ann Braude, Lori Ginzburg, and Molly Ladd-Taylor, eds. *Root of Bitterness: Documents of the Social History of American Women.* 1972. 2nd ed. Boston: Northeastern University Press, 1996.

Cowie, Jefferson. *Stayin' Alive: The 1970s and the Last Days of the Working Class.* New York: New Press, 2010.

———. "'Vigorously Left, Right, and Center': The Cross-Currents of Working-Class America in the 1970s." In *America in the 70s,* edited by Beth Bailey and David Farber, 75–106. Lawrence: University Press of Kansas, 2004.

Cronon, William. *Nature's Metropolis: Chicago and the Great West.* New York: W. W. Norton, 1991.

———. "Revisiting the Vanishing Frontier: The Legacy of Frederick Jackson Turner." *Western Historical Quarterly* 18, no. 2 (April 1987): 157–76.

Cronon, William, George Miles, and Jay Gitlin. "Becoming West: Toward a New Meaning for Western History." In *Under an Open Sky: Rethinking America's Western Past,* edited by William Cronon, Jay Gitlin, and George Miles, 3–27. New York: W. W. Norton, 1992.

Culver, Lawrence. *Frontier of Leisure: Southern California and the Shaping of America.* New York: Oxford University Press, 2016.

Cunningham, David. *Klansville, U.S.A.: The Rise and Fall of the Civil Rights–Era Ku Klux Klan.* New York: Oxford University Press, 2013.

Dameron, Kenneth. "The Consumer Movement." *Harvard Business Review* 17, no. 3 (Spring 1939): 271–89.

Davidson, Gordon W. Review of *Kit Carson: A Portrait in Courage,* by M. Marion Estergreen. *Western Folklore* 23, no. 1 (January 1964): 64–65.

"Deals and Developments." *Time,* July 11, 1932.

Debo, Angie. *The Rise and Fall of the Choctaw Republic.* Norman: University of Oklahoma Press, 1934.

eBuys, William. *Enchantment and Exploitation: The Life and Hard Times of a New Mexico Mountain Range*. Albuquerque: University of New Mexico Press, 1985.

e Genova, Nicholas, and Ana Y. Ramos-Zayas. *Latino Crossings: Mexicans, Puerto Ricans, and the Politics of Race and Citizenship*. New York: Routledge, 2003.

eLay, Brian. *War of a Thousand Deserts: Indian Raids and the U.S. Mexican War*. New Haven, Conn.: Yale University Press, 2008.

eloria, Philip J. *Indians in Unexpected Places*. Lawrence: University Press of Kansas, 2004.

———. *Playing Indian*. New Haven, Conn.: Yale University Press, 1999.

'Emilio, John. *Sexual Politics, Sexual Communities: The Making of a Homosexual Minority in the United States, 1940–1970*. Chicago: University of Chicago Press, 1983.

D'Emilio, John, and Estelle B. Freedman. *Intimate Matters: A History of Sexuality in America*. New York: Harper and Row, 1988.

Demos, John. *The Unredeemed Captive: A Family Story from Early America*. New York: Knopf, 1994.

Denetdale, Jennifer Nez. "Discontinuities, Remembrances, and Cultural Survival: History, Diné/Navajo Memory, and the Bosque Redondo Memorial." *New Mexico Historical Review* 82, no. 3 (Summer 2007): 295–316.

———. *Reclaiming Diné History: The Legacies of Navajo Chief Manuelito and Juanita*. Tucson: University of Arizona Press, 2009.

Denning, Michael. *The Cultural Front: The Laboring of American Culture in the Twentieth Century*. New York: Verso, 1997.

———. *Mechanic Accents: Dime Novels and Working-Class Culture in America*. New York: Verso, 1987.

Dent, Huntley. *The Feast of Santa Fe: Cooking of the American Southwest*. New York: Simon and Schuster, 1985.

Denton, Sally. *Passion and Principle: John and Jessie Fremont, the Couple Whose Power, Politics, and Love Shaped Nineteenth-Century America*. New York: Bloomsbury, 2007.

Denver Housewives League, Inc. *Year Book 1936–37*. Denver: n.p., [1937].

Des Jardins, Julie. *Women and the Historical Enterprise in America: Gender, Race, and the Politics of Memory, 1880–1945*. Chapel Hill: University of North Carolina Press, 2003.

DeSpain, S. Matthew. "'The Superior Dignity of Such a Character': Nineteenth-Century American Manhood and the Image of Kit Carson." *Rocky Mountain Fur Trade Journal* 1 (2007): 47–73.

Deutsch, Sarah. "From Ballots to Breadlines: 1920–1940." In Cott, *No Small Courage*, 413–72.

———. *No Separate Refuge: Culture, Class, and Gender on an Anglo-Hispanic Frontier in the American Southwest, 1880–1940*. New York: Oxford University Press, 1987.

Deutsch, Tracey. *Building a Housewife's Paradise: Gender, Politics, and American*

Grocery Stores in the Twentieth Century. Chapel Hill: University of North Carolina Press, 2010.

Diamond, Andrew. *Mean Streets: Chicago Youths and the Everyday Struggle for Empowerment in the Multiracial City, 1908–1969.* Berkeley: University of California Press, 2009.

DiSilvestro, Roger L. *Theodore Roosevelt in the Badlands: A Young Politician's Quest for Recovery in the American West.* New York: Walker, 2011.

Dochuck, Darren. *From Bible Belt to Sunbelt: Plain-Folk Religion, Grass Roots Politics, and the Rise of Evangelical Conservatism.* New York: W. W. Norton, 2011.

Dodds, Jerrilynn, María Rosa Menocal, and Abigail Krasner Balbale. *The Arts of Intimacy: Christians, Jews, and Muslims in the Making of Castilian Culture.* New Haven, Conn.: Yale University Press, 2009.

Doig, Ivan. *The Whistling Season.* New York: Houghton Mifflin Harcourt, 2006.

Drinkwater, John. *Poems, 1908–1919.* Boston: Houghton Mifflin/Riverside, 1919.

Duberman, Martin, Martha Vicinus, and George Chauncey Jr., eds. *Hidden from History: Reclaiming the Gay and Lesbian Past.* New York: New American Library, 1989.

Dudziak, Mary. *Cold War Civil Rights: Race and the Image of American Democracy.* Princeton, N.J.: Princeton University Press, 2000.

Dunlay, Thomas. *Kit Carson and the Indians.* Lincoln: University of Nebraska Press, 2000.

DuVal, Kathleen. *The Native Ground: Indians and Colonists in the Heart of the Continent.* Philadelphia: University of Pennsylvania Press, 2006.

Ebright, Malcolm, Rick Hendricks, and Richard W. Hughes. *Four Square Leagues: Pueblo Land in New Mexico.* Albuquerque: University of New Mexico Press, 2011.

Echols, Alice. *Shortfall: Family Secrets, Financial Collapse, and the Hidden History of American Banking.* New York: New Press, 2017.

———. "Tangled Up in Pleasure and Danger." *Signs* 42, no. 1 (Autumn 2016): 1–12.

Edwards, Jim, and Wynette Edwards. *Chicago Entertainment between the Wars, 1919–1939.* Chicago: Arcadia, 2003.

Einspahr, Jennifer. "Structural Domination and Structural Freedom: A Feminist Perspective." *Feminist Review* 94, no. 1 (2010): 1–19.

Ellis, Edward S. *The Life of Kit Carson, Hunter, Trapper, Guide, Indian Agent and Colonel U.S.A.* Chicago: M. A. Donohue, 1889.

Emerson, Ralph Waldo. *Friendship: An Essay.* 1841. BiblioBytes, eBook Collection, EBSCOhost. June 6, 2012.

———. *Man the Reformer.* 1841. BiblioBytes, eBook Collection, EBSCOhost. June 6, 2012.

Engelhardt, Tom. *The End of Victory Culture: Cold War America and the Disillusioning of a Generation.* New York: Basic Books, 1995.

Enstad, Nan. *Ladies of Labor, Girls of Adventure: Working Women, Popular*

Culture, and Labor Politics at the Turn of the Twentieth Century. New York: Columbia University Press, 1999.

scoffier, Jeffery, ed. *Sexual Revolution*. New York: Thunder's Mouth, 2003.

spaña-Maram, Linda. *Creating Masculinity in Los Angeles's Little Manila: Working-Class Filipinos and Popular Culture, 1920s–1950s*. New York: Columbia University Press, 2006.

stergreen, M. Morgan. *Chapels on the Trail*. [Taos?], N.M.: n.p., [1960?].

———. *Kit Carson: A Portrait in Courage*. Norman: University of Oklahoma Press, 1962.

———. *The Real Kit Carson*. Taos, N.M.: El Crepúsculo, 1955.

———. *Taos Guide and Art Directory*. Santa Fe, N.M.: n.p., 1959.

———. *Taos Guide Book, 1951–52*. Taos, N.M.: n.p., 1950.

Estes, Steve. *I Am a Man! Race, Manhood, and the Civil Rights Movement*. Chapel Hill: University of North Carolina Press, 2005.

Evans, Nelson W., and Emmons B. Stivers. *A History of Adams County, Ohio, from Its Earliest Settlement to the Present Time*. West Union, Ohio: E. B. Stivers, 1900.

Fadragas, Angela M. "Lake View." In *Local Community Fact Book, Chicago Metropolitan Area, Based on the 1970 and 1980 Censuses*, edited by Chicago Fact Book Consortium, 14–17. Chicago: Chicago Review Press, 1984.

Farber, David. *The Rise and Fall of Modern American Conservatism*. Princeton, N.J.: Princeton University Press, 2010.

Fass, Paula S. *The Damned and the Beautiful: American Youth in the 1920s*. New York: Oxford University Press, 1977.

Ferguson, Ann, Ilene Philipson, Irene Diamond, Lee Quinby, Carole S. Vance, and Ann Barr Snitow. "Forum: The Feminist Sexuality Debates." With introduction by Estelle B. Freedman and Barrie Thorne. *Signs* 10, no. 1 (Autumn 1984): 102–35.

Fernández, Lilia. *Brown in the Windy City: Mexicans and Puerto Ricans in Postwar Chicago*. Chicago: University of Chicago Press, 2012.

Ferris, Robert G., ed. *The American West: An Appraisal*. Santa Fe: Museum of New Mexico Press, 1963.

Field, Cynthia R. "Burnham Plan." In Grossman, Keating, and Reiff, *Encyclopedia of Chicago*, 108–9.

Field, Kim. *Harmonicas, Harps, and Heavy Breathers: The Evolution of the People's Instrument*. 1993. Reprint, New York: Cooper Square/Rowman and Littlefield, 2000.

Fisher, Karen. *A Sudden Country*. New York: Random House, 2005.

Fitzpatrick, Ellen. *History's Memory: Writing America's Past, 1880–1980*. Cambridge, Mass.: Harvard University Press, 2002.

Flanagan, Maureen A. *Seeing with Their Hearts: Chicago Women and the Vision of the Good City, 1871–1933*. Princeton, N.J.: Princeton University Press, 2002.

Folwell, William Watts. *History of Minnesota*. 4 vols. 1921–30. Rev. ed. St. Paul: Minnesota Historical Society Press, 1956–69.

BIBLIOGRAPHY

Fox, Richard Wightman. *Trials of Intimacy: Love and Loss in the Beecher-Tilton Scandal*. Chicago: University of Chicago Press, 1999.

Frank, Ross. *From Settler to Citizen: New Mexican Economic Development and the Creation of Vecino Society, 1750–1820*. Berkeley: University of California Press, 2000.

Fraser, Steve, and Gary Gerstle, eds. *The Rise and Fall of the New Deal Order, 1930–1980*. Princeton, N.J.: Princeton University Press, 1989.

Freedman, Estelle B. "'The Burning of Letters Continues': Elusive Identities and the Historical Construction of Sexuality." *Journal of Women's History* 9, no. 4 (1998): 181–200.

——. *No Turning Back: The History of Feminism and the Future of Women*. New York: Ballantine Books, 2002.

Freedman, Estelle B., Barbara Charlesworth Gelpi, Susan L. Johnson, and Kathleen M. Weston, eds. *The Lesbian Issue: Essays from SIGNS*. Chicago: University of Chicago Press, 1985.

Freeman, Joshua B. *American Empire: The Rise of a Global Power, the Democratic Revolution at Home, 1945–2000*. New York: Viking Penguin, 2012.

Frémont, John Charles. *Report of the Exploring Expedition to the Rocky Mountains in the Year 1842, and to Oregon and North California in the Years 1843–44*. S. Doc. No. 28-174 (1845).

Freund, David. "Marketing the Free Market: State Intervention and the Politics of Prosperity in Metropolitan America." In Kruse and Sugrue, *New Suburban History*, 11–32.

Friedman, Andrew. *Covert Capital: Landscapes of Denial and the Making of U.S. Empire in the Suburbs of Northern Virginia*. Berkeley: University of California Press, 2013.

Frizzell, Robert W. "Southern Identity in Nineteenth-Century Missouri: Little Dixie's Slave-Majority Areas and the Transition to Midwestern Farming." *Missouri Historical Review* 99, no. 3 (April 2005): 238–60.

Furniss, Norman. Review of *Kit Carson: A Portrait in Courage*, by M. Marion Estergreen. *Montana: The Magazine of Western History* 13, no. 3 (Summer 1963): 73–74.

Gabaccia, Donna. *We Are What We Eat: Ethnic Food and the Making of America*. Cambridge, Mass.: Harvard University Press, 1998.

Gaines, Kevin. "The Historiography of the Struggle for Black Equality since 1945." In *A Companion to Post-1945 America*, edited by Jean-Christophe Agnew and Roy Rosenzweig, 211–34. Malden, Mass.: Blackwell, 2002.

Gallay, Alan. *The Indian Slave Trade: The Rise of the English Empire in the American South, 1670–1717*. New Haven, Conn.: Yale University Press, 2002.

Garrard, Lewis H. *Wah-to-yah and the Taos Trail*. 1850. Reprint, Norman: University of Oklahoma Press, 1955.

Garrison, Dee. *Apostles of Culture: The Public Librarian and American Society, 1876–1920*. 1979. Reprint, Madison: University of Wisconsin Press, 2003.

Garvey, Ellen Gruber. *Writing with Scissors: American Scrapbooks from the Civil War to the Harlem Renaissance*. New York: Oxford University Press, 2013.

eorgakas, Dan. "Greek-American Radicalism: The Twentieth Century." In *The Immigrant Left in the United States*, edited by Paul Buhle and Dan Georgakas, 207–30. Albany: State University of New York Press, 1996.

eorge, Brendon. "Mile High Metropole: Denver and the Making of U.S. Empire." PhD diss., University of Wisconsin–Madison, 2019.

erhard, Jane. *Desiring Revolution: Second-Wave Feminism and the Rewriting of American Sexual Thought, 1920 to 1982*. New York: Columbia University Press, 2001.

Gerstle, Gary. *American Crucible: Race and Nation in the Twentieth Century*. Princeton, N.J.: Princeton University Press, 2001.

Gilbert, James. "Midcult, Middlebrow, Middle Class." *Reviews in American History* 20, no. 4 (December 1992): 543–48.

Gilmartin, Katie. "'The Very House of Difference': Intersection of Identities in the Life Histories of Colorado Lesbians, 1940–1965." PhD diss., Yale University, 1995.

Glenn, Susan A. *Female Spectacle: The Theatrical Roots of Modern Feminism*. Cambridge, Mass.: Harvard University Press, 2000.

Glickman, Lawrence B. "The Strike in the Temple of Consumption: Consumer Activism and Twentieth-Century American Political Culture." *Journal of American History* 88, no. 1 (2001): 99–128.

Goldman, Emma. "The Traffic in Women." In *Anarchism and Other Essays*, 183–200. New York: Mother Earth, 1910. Reprinted in *The Traffic in Women and Other Essays on Feminism*, edited by Alix Kates Shulman, 19–32. Ojai, Calif.: Times Change, 1970.

Gómez, Laura E. *Manifest Destinies: The Making of the Mexican American Race*. New York: New York University Press, 2007.

González, Deena. *Refusing the Favor: The Spanish-Mexican Women of Santa Fe, 1820–1880*. New York: Oxford University Press, 1999.

Gordon-McCutchan, R. C. *The Taos Indians and the Battle for Blue Lake*. Santa Fe, N.M.: Red Crane Books, 1991.

———, ed. *Kit Carson: Indian Fighter or Indian Killer?* Niwot: University Press of Colorado, 1996.

Graebner, Char Boie. "Carson Returns to Taos." *Ayer y Hoy en Taos: Yesterday and Today in Taos County and Northern New Mexico*, Winter 1991.

Grant, Blanche C., ed. *Kit Carson's Own Story of His Life: Facsimile of Original 1926 Edition*. Santa Fe, N.M.: Sunstone, 2007.

———, ed. *Kit Carson's Own Story of His Life as Dictated to Col. and Mrs. D. C. Peters about 1856–57, and Never Before Published*. 1926. Reprint, Taos, N.M.: Kit Carson Memorial Foundation, 1955.

Graybill, Andrew. *The Red and the White: A Family Saga of the American West*. New York: W. W. Norton, 2013.

Green, Adam. *Selling the Race: Culture, Community, and Black Chicago, 1940–1955*. Chicago: University of Chicago Press, 2007.

Greenberg, Amy. *Manifest Manhood and the Antebellum American Empire*. Cambridge: Cambridge University Press, 2005.

Greenwood, Val D. *The Researcher's Guide to American Genealogy*. 3rd ed. Baltimore: Genealogical, 2000.

Gregory, James N. *The Southern Diaspora: How the Great Migrations of Black and White Southerners Transformed America*. Chapel Hill: University of North Carolina Press, 2005.

Grinnell, George Bird. "Bent's Old Fort and Its Builders." In *Collections of the Kansas State Historical Society, 1919–1922*, vol. 15, edited by William E. Connelly, 28–91. Topeka: Kansas State Printing Plant, 1923.

———. *The Cheyenne Indians: Their History and Ways of Life*. 2 vols. New Haven, Conn.: Yale University Press, 1923.

———. *The Fighting Cheyennes*. New York: Charles Scribner's Sons, 1915.

Grossman, James R. *Land of Hope: Chicago, Black Southerners, and the Great Migration*. Chicago: University of Chicago Press, 1989.

Grossman, James R., Ann Durkin Keating, and Janice L. Reiff, eds. *The Encyclopedia of Chicago*. Chicago: University of Chicago Press, 2004.

Guérin-Gonzales, Camille. "From Ludlow to Camp Solidarity: Women, Men, and Cultures of Solidarity in U.S. Coal Communities, 1912–1990." In *Mining Women: Gender in the Development of a Global Industry, 1670 to 2005*, edited by Jaclyn Gier and Laurie Mercier, 296–324. New York: Palgrave Macmillan, 2006.

———. *Mexican Workers and American Dreams: Immigration, Repatriation, and California Farm Labor, 1900–1939*. New Brunswick, N.J.: Rutgers University Press, 1994.

Guglielmo, Thomas A. *White on Arrival: Italians, Race, Color, and Power in Chicago, 1890–1945*. New York: Oxford University Press, 2003.

Guild, Thelma S., and Harvey L. Carter. *Kit Carson: A Pattern for Heroes*. Lincoln: University of Nebraska Press, 1984.

Gutfreund, Owen. *Twentieth-Century Sprawl: Highways and the Reshaping of the American Landscape*. New York: Oxford University Press, 2004.

Gutiérrez, David. "Demography and the Shifting Boundaries of 'Community': Reflections on 'U.S. Latinos' and the Evolution of Latino Studies." In David Gutiérrez, *Columbia History of Latinos*, 1–42.

———. *Walls and Mirrors: Mexican Americans, Mexican Immigrants, and the Politics of Ethnicity*. Berkeley: University of California Press, 1995.

———, ed. *The Columbia History of Latinos in the United States Since 1960*. New York: Columbia University Press, 2004.

Gutiérrez, Ramón A. *When Jesus Came, the Corn Mothers Went Away: Marriage, Sexuality, and Power in New Mexico, 1500–1846*. Stanford, Calif.: Stanford University Press, 1991.

Gutiérrez, Ramón A., and Elliott Young. "Transnationalizing Borderlands History." *Western Historical Quarterly* 41, no. 1 (Spring 2010): 27–53.

Hafen, Ann Woodbury. *Quenched Fire and Other Poems*. Denver: World Press, 1937.

Hafen, LeRoy. *The Joyous Journey of LeRoy R. and Ann W. Hafen: An Autobiography*. Glendale, Calif.: Arthur H. Clark; Denver: Old West, 1973.

———. "Mexican Land Grants in Colorado." *Colorado Magazine* 4, no. 3 (May 1927): 81–93.

———, ed. *The Mountain Men and the Fur Trade of the Far West*. 10 vols. Glendale, Calif.: Arthur H. Clark, 1965–72.

Hafen, LeRoy, and Ann W. Hafen. *The Colorado Story: A History of Your State and Mine*. Denver: Old West, 1953.

———. *Handcarts to Zion: The Story of a Unique Western Migration, 1856–1860; With Contemporary Journals, Accounts, Reports, and Rosters of Members of the Ten Handcart Companies*. Glendale, Calif.: Arthur H. Clark, 1960.

———, eds. *Fremont's Fourth Expedition: A Documentary Account of the Disaster of 1848–1849, with Diaries, Letters, and Reports by Participants in the Tragedy*. Glendale, Calif.: Arthur H. Clark, 1960.

———. *The Utah Expedition, 1857–1858: A Documentary Account of the United States Military Movement under Colonel Albert Sidney Johnston, and the Resistance by Brigham Young and the Mormon Nauvoo Legion*. Glendale, Calif.: Arthur H. Clark, 1958.

Halberstam, Jack. *In a Queer Time and Place: Transgender Bodies, Subcultural Lives*. New York: New York University Press, 2005.

Halberstam, Judith. *Female Masculinity*. Durham, N.C.: Duke University Press, 1998.

Halker, Clark. "A History of Local 208 and the Struggle for Racial Equality in the American Federation of Musicians." *Black Music Research Journal* 8, no. 2 (Autumn 1988): 207–22.

Hall, Jacquelyn Dowd. "The Long Civil Rights Movement and the Political Uses of the Past." *Journal of American History* 91, no. 4 (2005): 1233–63.

Hall, Thomas D. *Social Change in the Southwest, 1350–1880*. Lawrence: University Press of Kansas, 1989.

Halpern, Rick. *Down on the Killing Floor: Black and White Workers in Chicago's Packinghouses, 1904–54*. Urbana: University of Illinois Press, 1997.

Hämäläinen, Pekka. *Comanche Empire*. New Haven, Conn.: Yale University Press, 2008.

Harjo, Joy. "She Had Some Horses." In *She Had Some Horses: Poems by Joy Harjo*, 59–68. 1983. Reprint, New York: W. W. Norton, 2008.

Hartman, Saidiya. *Lose Your Mother: A Journey along the Atlantic Slave Route*. New York: Farrar, Straus and Giroux, 2007.

Harvey, Rita Morley. *Those Wonderful, Terrible Years: George Heller and the American Federation of Television and Radio Artists*. Carbondale: Southern Illinois University Press, 1996.

Haynes, April R. *Riotous Flesh: Women, Physiology, and the Solitary Vice in Nineteenth-Century America*. Chicago: University of Chicago Press, 2015.

Heap, Chad. *Slumming: Sexual and Racial Encounters in American Nightlife, 1885–1940*. Chicago: University of Chicago Press, 2009.

Heath, Mrs. Julian. "Work of the Housewives League." *Annals of the American Academy of Political and Social Science* 48 (July 1913): 121–26.

Herr, Pamela. *Jessie Benton Fremont: A Biography*. New York: Franklin Watts, 1987.

Herr, Pamela, and Mary Lee Spence, eds. *The Letters of Jessie Benton Frémont*. Urbana: University of Illinois Press, 1993.

Herring, George C. *From Colony to Superpower: U.S. Foreign Relations since 1776*. New York: Oxford University Press, 2008.

Herriot, James. *All Creatures Great and Small*. New York: St. Martin's, 1972.

"High Brows and Low Brows." *Out West*, n.s., 1, no. 4 (March 1911): 221–22.

Hill, Joseph A. *Women in Gainful Occupations, 1870–1920*. Census Monographs 9. Washington, D.C.: Government Printing Office, 1929.

Hilmes, Michele. *Hollywood and Broadcasting: From Radio to Cable*. Urbana: University of Illinois Press, 1990.

———. *Radio Voices: American Broadcasting, 1922–1952*. Minneapolis: University of Minnesota Press, 1997.

Hine, Darlene Clark. "The Housewives' League of Detroit: Black Women and Economic Nationalism." In *Visible Women: New Essays on American Activism*, edited by Nancy Hewitt and Suzanne Lebsock, 223–41. Urbana: University of Illinois Press, 1993.

Hinton, Harwood P. Review of *Kit Carson: A Profile in Courage*, by M. Marion Estergreen. *Pacific Historical Review* 32, no. 4 (November 1963): 428–30.

———. "A Short History of *Arizona and the West: A Quarterly Journal of History*." *Arizona and the West* 27, no. 1 (Spring 1985): 73–78.

Hirsch, Arnold. *Making the Second Ghetto: Race and Housing in Chicago, 1940–1960*. 1983. Reprint, Chicago: University of Chicago Press, 1998.

The History of Buchanan County, Missouri, Containing a History of the County, Its Cities, Towns, Etc. St. Joseph, Mo.: Union Historical, 1881.

History of Cincinnati and Hamilton County, Ohio: Their Past and Present. Cincinnati: S. B. Nelson, 1894.

Hoelscher, Steven. "Conversing Diversity: Provincial Cosmopolitanism and America's Multicultural Heritage." In *Textures of Place: Exploring Humanist Geographies*, edited by Paul C. Adams, Steven Hoelscher, and Karen E. Till, 375–402. Minneapolis: University of Minnesota Press, 2001.

Hogan, Will. "Logan Square." In *Local Community Fact Book, Chicago Metropolitan Area, Based on the 1970 and 1980 Censuses*, edited by Chicago Fact Book Consortium, 55–58. Chicago: Chicago Review Press, 1984.

Hoganson, Kristin. *Fighting for American Manhood: How Gender Politics Provoked the Spanish-American and Philippine-American Wars*. New Haven, Conn.: Yale University Press, 2000.

Hollibaugh, Amber L. *My Dangerous Desires: A Queer Girl Dreaming Her Way Home*. Durham, N.C.: Duke University Press, 2000.

Howard, Robert West. "The Peril of the American West." *Westerners Brand Book* 15, no. 1 (March 1958): 1–3, 7–8.

Hunt, D. Bradford. "Redlining." In Grossman, Keating, and Reiff, *Encyclopedia of Chicago*, 683.

Hunt, Rebecca Ann. "Urban Pioneers: Continuity and Change in the Ethnic

Communities in Two Denver, Colorado Neighborhoods: 1875–1998." PhD
diss., University of Colorado Boulder, 1999.

Hunter, Jane. *The Gospel of Gentility: American Women Missionaries in Turn-of-the-Century China*. New Haven, Conn.: Yale University Press, 1989.

———. "Women's Mission in Historical Perspective: American Identity
and Christian Internationalism." In Reeves-Ellington, Sklar, and Shemo,
Competing Kingdoms, 19–42.

Hurd, Charles W. *Boggsville: Cradle of the Colorado Cattle Industry*. Boggsville,
Colo.: Boggsville Committee, [1957?].

———. Review of *Kit Carson: A Profile in Courage*, by M. Marion Estergreen.
Colorado Magazine 40, no. 2 (April 1963): 146–48.

Hurewitz, Daniel. *Bohemian Los Angeles and the Making of Modern Politics*.
Berkeley: University of California Press, 2007.

Hurt, R. Douglas. *Agriculture and Slavery in Missouri's Little Dixie*. Columbia:
University of Missouri Press, 1992.

———. "Planters and Slavery in Little Dixie." *Missouri Historical Review* 88,
no. 4 (July 1994): 397–415.

Hutchinson, W. H. Review of *Great Westerner: The Story of Kit Carson*, by
Bernice Blackwelder. *Southern California Quarterly* 45, no. 2 (June 1963):
188.

Hyde, Anne F. *Empires, Nations, and Families: A History of the North American
West, 1800–1860*. Lincoln: University of Nebraska Press, 2011.

Hyde, George E. *Life of George Bent: Written from His Letters*. Norman:
University of Oklahoma Press, 1967.

Ingersoll, Helen Frances. *I Remember: The Reminiscences of My Years in the
Denver Public Library*. Denver: n.p., 1947.

"In Memoriam." *Colorado Genealogist* 46, no. 3 (August 1985): 121.

Iverson, Peter. *Diné: A History of the Navajos*. Albuquerque: University of New
Mexico Press, 2002.

Jacklin, Jillian Marie. "Paper Dreams: Working-Class Cultures and Political Drift
in the Fox River Valley, 1850s–1950s." PhD diss., University of Wisconsin-
Madison, 2020.

Jacobs, Margaret D. "Breaking and Remaking Families: The Fostering and
Adoption of Native American Children in Non-native Families in the
American West, 1880–1940." In Adams and DeLuzio, *On the Borders*, 19–46.

———. *Engendered Encounters: Feminism and Pueblo Cultures, 1879–1934*.
Lincoln: University of Nebraska Press, 1999.

———. *White Mother to a Dark Race: Settler Colonialism, Maternalism, and the
Removal of Indigenous Children in the American West and Australia, 1880–
1940*. Lincoln: University of Nebraska Press, 2009.

Jacobson, Matthew Frye. *Whiteness of a Different Color: European Immigrants
and the Alchemy of Race*. Cambridge, Mass.: Harvard University Press, 1998.

Jacobus, Donald Lines. *Genealogy as Pastime and Profession*. New Haven,
Conn.: Tuttle, Morehouse, and Taylor, 1930.

Jagodinsky, Katrina. *Legal Codes and Talking Trees: Indigenous Women's*

Sovereignty in the Sonoran and Puget Sound Borderlands, 1854–1946. New Haven, Conn.: Yale University Press, 2016.

Jameson, Elizabeth. *All That Glitters: Class, Culture, and Community in Cripple Creek*. Urbana: University of Illinois Press, 1998.

John, Elizabeth A. H. *Storms Brewed in Other Men's Worlds: The Confrontation of Indians, Spanish, and French in the Southwest, 1540–1795*. College Station: Texas A&M University Press, 1975.

Johnson, Benjamin H., and Andrew R. Graybill. "Introduction: Borders and their Historians in North America." In *Bridging National Borders in North America: Transnational and Comparative Perspectives*, edited by Benjamin H. Johnson and Andrew R. Graybill, 1–29. Durham, N.C.: Duke University Press, 2010.

Johnson, David. *The Lavender Scare: The Cold War Persecution of Gays and Lesbians in the Federal Government*. Chicago: University of Chicago Press, 2004.

Johnson, Susan Lee. "'The gold she gathered': Difference, Domination, and California's Southern Mines." PhD diss., Yale University, 1993.

———. "'A memory sweet to soldiers': The Significance of Gender in the History of the 'American West.'" *Western Historical Quarterly* 24, no. 4 (1993): 495–517. Reprinted in *A New Significance: Re-envisioning the History of the American West*, edited by Clyde Milner, 255–78. New York: Oxford University Press, 1996. Also reprinted in *Women and Gender in the American West: Jensen-Miller Prize Essays from the Coalition for Western Women's History*, edited by Mary Ann Irwin and James Brooks, 89–109. Albuquerque: University of New Mexico Press, 2004.

———. *Roaring Camp: The Social World of the California Gold Rush*. New York: W. W. Norton, 2000.

———. "Sharing Bed and Board: Cohabitation and Cultural Difference in Central Arizona Mining Towns, 1863–1873." *Frontiers* 7, no. 3 (1984): 36–42. Reprinted in Armitage and Jameson, *Women's West*, 77–91.

———. "Women's Households and Relationships in the Mining West: Arizona, 1863–1873." MA thesis, Arizona State University, 1984.

———. "Writing Kit Carson in the Cold War: 'The Family,' 'the West,' and Their Chroniclers." In Adams and DeLuzio, *On the Borders*, 278–318.

Johnson, Troy, Joane Nagel, and Duane Champagne, eds. *American Indian Activism: Alcatraz to the Longest Walk*. Urbana: University of Illinois Press, 1997.

Jones, Edward P. *The Known World*. New York: HarperCollins, 2003.

Kantrowitz, Stephen. *Ben Tillman and the Reconstruction of White Supremacy*. Chapel Hill: University of North Carolina Press, 2000.

Katz, Jonathan Ned. *The Invention of Heterosexuality*. New York: Dutton, 1995.

Keehn, Richard H. "Industry and Business." In Neuenschwander, *Kenosha County*, 175–221.

Kelly, Lawrence C. *The Assault on Assimilation: John Collier and the Origins of Indian Policy Reform*. Albuquerque: University of New Mexico Press, 1983.

———. *Federal Indian Policy*. New York: Chelsea House, 1990.

———. *The Navajo Indians and Federal Indian Policy, 1900–1935*. Tucson: University of Arizona Press, 1968.

———. *Navajo Round-up: Selected Correspondence of Kit Carson's Expedition against the Navajo, 1863–1865*. Boulder, Colo.: Pruett, 1970.

Kelman, Ari. *A Misplaced Massacre: Struggling over the Memory of Sand Creek*. Cambridge, Mass.: Harvard University Press, 2013.

Kessler-Harris, Alice. *Out to Work: A History of Wage-Earning in the United States*. New York: Oxford University Press, 1982.

Kibler, M. Alison. *Rank Ladies: Gender and Cultural Hierarchy in American Vaudeville*. Chapel Hill: University of North Carolina Press, 1999.

King, Robert W. Review of *Kit Carson: A Profile in Courage*, by M. Marion Estergreen. *Journal of the West* 2, no. 1 (January 1963): 106–7.

Kirk, Andrew Glenn. *Collecting Nature: The Environmental Movement and the Conservation Library*. Lawrence: University Press of Kansas, 2001.

Kitroeff, Alexander. "Greek-American Ethnicity, 1919–1939." In *To Hellenikon, Studies in Honor of Speros Vryonis, Jr.* Vol. 2, *Byzantinoslavica, Armeniaca, Islamica, the Balkans and Modern Greece*, edited by Jelisaveta Stanojevich Allen et al., 353–71. New Rochelle, N.Y.: Aristide D. Caratzas, 1995.

Krauthamer, Barbara. *Black Slaves, Indian Masters: Slavery, Emancipation, and Citizenship in the Native American South*. Chapel Hill: University of North Carolina Press, 2013.

Kropp, Phoebe S. *California Vieja: Culture and Memory in a Modern American Place*. Berkeley: University of California Press, 2006.

Krugler, David F. *This Is Only a Test: How Washington, D.C., Prepared for Nuclear War*. New York: Palgrave Macmillan, 2006.

Kruse, Kevin M. *White Flight: Atlanta and the Making of Modern Conservatism*. Princeton, N.J.: Princeton University Press, 2005.

Kruse, Kevin M., and Thomas Sugrue, eds. *The New Suburban History*. Chicago: University of Chicago Press, 2006.

Kunzel, Regina. *Criminal Intimacy: Prison and the Uneven History of Modern Sexuality*. Chicago: University of Chicago Press, 2008.

———. *Fallen Women, Problem Girls: Unmarried Mothers and the Professionalization of Social Work, 1890–1945*. New Haven, Conn.: Yale University Press, 1993.

Kuznick, Peter, and James Gilbert, eds. *Rethinking Cold War Culture*. Washington, D.C.: Smithsonian Institution Press, 2001.

LaChapelle, Peter. *Proud to Be an Okie: Cultural Politics, Country Music, and Migration to Southern California*. Berkeley: University of California Press, 2007.

LaGrand, James. *Indian Metropolis: Native Americans in Chicago, 1945–75*. Urbana: University of Illinois Press, 2002.

Lamar, Howard Roberts. *The Far Southwest, 1846–1912: A Territorial History*. 1966. Rev. ed. Albuquerque: University of New Mexico Press, 2000.

———. "From Bondage to Contract: Ethnic Labor in the American West, 1600–

1890." In *The Countryside in the Age of Capitalist Transformation*, edited by Steven Hahn and Jonathan Prude, 293–324. Chapel Hill: University of North Carolina Press, 1985.

———. "Land Policy in the Spanish Southwest, 1846–1891: A Study in Contrasts." *Journal of Economic History* 22, no. 4 (December 1962): 498–515.

———. "Much to Celebrate: The Western History Association's Twenty-Fifth Birthday." *Western Historical Quarterly* 17, no. 4 (October 1986): 397–416.

———, ed. *The New Encyclopedia of the American West*. New Haven, Conn.: Yale University Press, 1998.

Lamont, Victoria. "Cattle Branding and the Traffic in Women in Early Twentieth-Century Westerns." *Legacy: A Journal of American Women Writers* 22, no. 1 (2005): 30–46.

Laqueur, Thomas. *Making Sex: Body and Gender from the Greeks to Freud*. Cambridge, Mass.: Harvard University Press, 1990.

Lassiter, Matthew D. *The Silent Majority: Suburban Politics in the Sunbelt South*. Princeton, N.J.: Princeton University Press, 2006.

Lavender, David. *Bent's Fort*. 1954. Reprint, Lincoln: University of Nebraska Press, 1972.

Lawson, Mike. "Mr. Case Comes to Washington: A Retrospective on the Founding of the Potomac Corral." http://www.potomac-corral.org/pdfs /Potomac_Corral_Retrospective.pdf. (PDF no longer available; copy in author's possession.)

Leach, Eugene E. "1900–1914." In *A Companion to 20th-Century America*, edited by Stephen J. Whitfield, 3–18. Malden, Mass.: Blackwell, 2004.

Leckie, Shirley A. "Angie Debo: From the Old to the New Western History." In Leckie and Parezo, *Their Own Frontier*, 65–96.

Leckie, Shirley A., and Nancy J. Parezo, eds. *Their Own Frontier: Women Intellectuals Re-envisioning the American West*. Lincoln: University of Nebraska Press, 2008.

Lecompte, Janet. *Pueblo, Hardscrabble, Greenhorn: The Upper Arkansas, 1832–1856*. Norman: University of Oklahoma Press, 1978.

———. *Rebellion in Río Arriba, 1837*. Albuquerque: University of New Mexico Press, 1985.

Lemann, Nicholas. *The Promised Land: The Great Migration and How It Changed America*. New York: Knopf, 1991.

Lenihan, John H. "Westbound: Feature Films and the American West." In Aquila, *Wanted Dead or Alive*, 109–34.

Leonard, Stephen, and Thomas Noel. *Denver: Mining Camp to Metropolis*. Niwot: University Press of Colorado, 1990.

———. *A Short History of Denver*. Reno: University of Nevada Press, 2016.

Le Sueur, Meridel. "The Ancient People and the Newly Come." In *Ripening: Selected Work, 1927–1980*, edited by Elaine Hedges. Old Westbury, N.Y.: Feminist Press, 1982.

Levin, Joanna. *Bohemia in America, 1858–1920*. Stanford, Calif.: Stanford University Press, 2010.

evine, Lawrence W. *Highbrow/Lowbrow: The Emergence of Cultural Hierarchy in America*. Cambridge, Mass.: Harvard University Press, 1988.

évi-Strauss, Claude. *The Elementary Structures of Kinship*. Boston: Beacon Press, 1969.

ichtenstein, Nelson. *State of the Union: A Century of American Labor*. Princeton, N.J.: Princeton University Press, 2002.

imerick, Patricia Nelson. *The Legacy of Conquest: The Unbroken Past of the American West*. New York: W. W. Norton, 1987.

ind, Michael. *Vietnam: The Necessary War; A Reinterpretation of America's Most Disastrous Military Conflict*. New York: Free Press, 1999.

ing, Huping. *Chinese Chicago: Race, Transnational Migration, and Community since 1870*. Stanford, Calif.: Stanford University Press, 2012.

lloyd, Herbert. *Vaudeville Trails thru the West, Chicago to the Coast—to the Gulf, "By One Who Knows."* Philadelphia: Herbert Lloyd, 1919.

Loew, Patty. *Indian Nations of Wisconsin: Histories of Endurance and Survival*. Madison: Wisconsin Historical Society Press, 2001.

Longstreth, Richard. *The Drive-In, the Supermarket, and the Transformation of Commercial Space in Los Angeles, 1914–1941*. Cambridge, Mass.: MIT Press, 1999.

Lott, Eric. *Love and Theft: Blackface Minstrelsy and the American Working Class*. 1993. 2nd ed. New York: Oxford University Press, 2013.

Love, Heather. *Feeling Backward: Loss and the Politics of Queer History*. Cambridge, Mass.: Harvard University Press, 2007.

Lowney, Chris. *A Vanished World: Muslims, Christians, and Jews in Medieval Spain*. 2005. Reprint, New York: Oxford University Press, 2006.

Maciel, David, and Juan José Peña. "La Reconquista: The Chicano Movement in New Mexico." In *The Contested Homeland: A Chicano History of New Mexico*, edited by Erlinda Gonzales-Berry and David Maciel, 269–301. Albuquerque: University of New Mexico Press, 2000.

MacLean, Nancy. *Freedom Is Not Enough: The Opening of the American Workplace*. Cambridge, Mass.: Harvard University Press, 2008.

Malone, Bill C. *Country Music, U.S.A.* 1968. 2nd rev. ed. Austin: University of Texas Press, 2002.

Malone, Lovisa. *Memories*. 2 vols. N.p., [1975].

Maraniss, David. *They Marched into Sunlight: War and Peace in Vietnam and America, October 1967*. New York: Simon and Schuster, 2003.

Marcus, Aaron B. "PrideFest: A History of Denver's Gay Pride Celebration." *Colorado Heritage*, May/June 2011, 26–35.

Marshall, Daniel, Kevin Murphy, and Zeb Tortorici, eds. "Queering Archives: Historical Understandings." Special issue, *Radical History Review*, no. 120 (Fall 2014).

———, eds. "Queering Archives: Intimate Tracings." Special issue, *Radical History Review*, no. 122 (May 2015).

Martin, Judith. "Austin." In Grossman, Keating, and Reiff, *Encyclopedia of Chicago*, 53–54.

Martínez, María C., et al. *María Josefa Jaramillo, Wife of Kit Carson: Her Descendants, Ancestors and Primos*. N.p., 2003.

Massey, Doreen. "Traveling Thoughts." In *Without Guarantees: In Honor of Stuart Hall*, edited by Paul Gilroy, Lawrence Grossberg, and Angela McRobbie, 225–32. London: Verso, 2000.

May, Elaine Tyler. *America and the Pill: A History of Promise, Peril, and Liberation*. New York: Basic Books, 2010.

———. *Barren in the Promised Land: Childless Americans and the Pursuit of Happiness*. New York: Basic Books, 1995.

———. *Homeward Bound: American Families in the Cold War Era*. 1988. Rev. ed. New York: Basic Books, 1999.

McClung, Quantrille D. "The Denver Neighborhood Library Meetings." *Library Journal* 55 (1935): 961–63.

———. "Genealogy in the Denver Public Library." *Colorado Genealogist* 29, no. 4 (December 1968): 89–94.

———. *Memoirs of My Childhood and Youth in North Denver*. Denver: Colorado Genealogical Society, 1979.

———, comp. *Carson-Bent-Boggs Genealogy: Line of William Carson, Ancestor of "Kit" Carson, Famous Scout and Pioneer of the Rocky Mountain Area, with the Western Branches of the Bent and Boggs Families, with Whom "Kit" Was Associated, and the Line of Samuel Carson, Supposed to be a Brother of William Carson*. Denver: Denver Public Library, 1962.

———. *Carson-Bent-Boggs Genealogy Supplement: Additions and Corrections for Line of William Carson, Ancestor of "Kit" Carson, Famous Scout and Pioneer of the Rocky Mountain Area, with the Western Branches of the Bent and Boggs Families, with Whom "Kit" was Associated, and the Line of Samuel Carson, Supposed to be a Brother of William Carson, with Some Attention to the Boone Family*. Denver: Denver Public Library, 1973.

———. *The Kiehnhoff Family in America, with Bauer and Gutzman Connections, First Settled in Doniphan County, Kansas*. Denver: n.p., [1981].

McClung, William. *The McClung Genealogy: A Genealogical and Biographical Record of the McClung Family from the Time of their Emigration to the Year 1904*. Pittsburgh: McClung, 1904.

McCurry, Stephanie. *Masters of Small Worlds: Yeoman Households, Gender Relations, and the Political Culture of the Antebellum South Carolina Low Country*. New York: Oxford University Press, 1995.

McGirr, Lisa. *Suburban Warriors: The Origins of the New American Right*. Princeton, N.J.: Princeton University Press, 2001.

McKeown, Adam. *Chinese Migrant Networks and Cultural Change: Peru, Chicago, Hawaii, 1900–1936*. Chicago: University of Chicago Press, 2001.

McNitt, Frank. *Navajo Wars: Military Campaigns, Slave Raids, and Reprisals*. Albuquerque: University of New Mexico Press, 1972.

McPherson, Alan. *Yankee No! Anti-Americanism in U.S.–Latin American Relations*. Cambridge, Mass.: Harvard University Press, 2005.

cWilliams, Carey. *Louis Adamic and Shadow-America*. Los Angeles: Arthur Whipple, 1935.

———. *North from Mexico: The Spanish-Speaking People of the United States*. Philadelphia: J. B. Lippincott, 1949.

"Meet You at the Pickwick." *UNCG Alumni Magazine*, Summer 2012. http://ure.uncg.edu/magazine/2012_summer/feature_robertwatson_rel.htm.

Menocal, María Rosa. *Ornament of the World: How Muslims, Jews, and Christians Created a Culture of Tolerance in Medieval Spain*. New York: Little, Brown, 2002.

Mercier, Laurie. *Anaconda: Labor, Community, and Culture in Montana's Smelter City*. Urbana: University of Illinois Press, 2001.

Merrill, William Pierson. *Christian Internationalism*. New York: Macmillan, 1919.

Meyerowitz, Joanne. *How Sex Changed: A History of Transsexuality in the United States*. Cambridge, Mass: Harvard University Press, 2002.

———. *Women Adrift: Independent Wage Earners in Chicago, 1880–1930*. Chicago: University of Chicago Press, 1988.

———, ed. *Not June Cleaver: Women and Gender in Postwar America, 1945–1960*. Philadelphia: Temple University Press, 1994.

Michels, Tony. *A Fire in Their Hearts: Yiddish Socialists in New York*. Cambridge, Mass.: Harvard University Press, 2005.

Miles, Tiya. *The House on Diamond Hill: A Cherokee Plantation Story*. Chapel Hill: University of North Carolina Press, 2010.

———. *Ties That Bind: The Story of an Afro-Cherokee Family in Slavery and Freedom*. Berkeley: University of California, 2005.

Miller, Darlis A. "Kit Carson and Dime Novels: The Making of a Legend." In Gordon-McCutchan, *Kit Carson*, 1–19.

Miller, Joaquin. *The Complete Poetical Works of Joaquin Miller*. 1897. Reprint, San Francisco: Whitaker and Ray, 1904.

Miner, Craig. *Next Year Country: Dust to Dust in Western Kansas, 1890–1940*. Lawrence: University Press of Kansas, 2006.

Missouri Historical Review. Unsigned review of *Great Westerner: The Story of Kit Carson*, by Bernice Blackwelder. Vol. 57, no. 1 (October 1962): 119.

Missouri Historical Review. Unsigned review of *Kit Carson: A Profile in Courage*, by M. Marion Estergreen. Vol. 57, no. 3 (April 1963): 321–23.

Mitchell, Pablo. *Coyote Nation: Sexuality, Race, and Conquest in Modernizing New Mexico, 1880–1920*. Chicago: University of Chicago Press, 2005.

Montgomery, Charles. *The Spanish Redemption: Heritage, Power, and Loss on New Mexico's Upper Rio Grande*. Berkeley: University of California Press, 2002.

Montoya, María. *Translating Property: The Maxwell Land Grant and the Conflict over Land in the American West, 1840–1900*. Berkeley: University of California Press, 2002.

Moody, Ralph. *Kit Carson and the Wild Frontier*. 1955. Reprint, Lincoln: University of Nebraska Press, 2005.

Moore, Shirley Ann Wilson. *Sweet Freedom Plains: African Americans on the Overland Trails, 1841-1869*. Norman: University of Oklahoma Press, 2016.

Mora, Anthony. *Border Dilemmas: Racial and National Uncertainties in New Mexico, 1848-1912*. Durham, N.C.: Duke University Press, 2011.

Moraga, Cherríe, and Gloria Anzaldúa, eds. *This Bridge Called My Back: Writings by Radical Women of Color*. Watertown, Mass.: Persephone Press, 1981.

Moraga, Cherríe, and Amber Hollibaugh. "What We're Rollin Around in Bed With—Sexual Silences in Feminism: A Conversation toward Ending Them." "Sex Issue," *Heresies #12* 3, no. 4 (1981). Reprinted in Hollibaugh, *My Dangerous Desires*, 62-84.

Morgan, Francesca. "Lineage as Capital: Genealogy in Antebellum New England." *New England Quarterly* 83, no. 2 (June 2010): 250-62.

———. "A Noble Pursuit? Bourgeois America's Use of Lineage." In *The American Bourgeoisie: Distinction and Identity in the Nineteenth Century*, edited by Sven Beckert and Julia B. Rosenbaum, 135-51. New York: Palgrave Macmillan, 2010.

Morrison, Toni. *Playing in the Dark: Whiteness and the Literary Imagination*. 1992. Reprint, New York: Vintage, 1993.

Morss, John. *The Biologising of Childhood: Developmental Psychology and the Darwinian Myth*. Hove, U.K.: Lawrence Erlbaum, 1990.

Mortensen, A. R. Review of *Kit Carson: A Profile in Courage*, by M. Marion Estergreen. *New Mexico Historical Review* 38, no. 4 (October 1963): 352-53.

Mumey, Nolie. *History of the Early Settlements of Denver, 1599-1860*. Glendale, Calif.: Arthur H. Clark, 1942.

———. *Old Forts and Trading Posts of the West: Bent's Old Fort and Bent's New Fort*. Denver: Artcraft Press, 1956.

Mumey, Norma L. *Nolie Mumey, M.D.* Boulder, Colo.: Johnson, 1987.

Mumford, Kevin J. *Interzones: Black/White Sex Districts in Chicago and New York in the Early Twentieth Century*. New York: Columbia University Press, 1997.

Murphy, Kevin. *Political Manhood: Red Bloods, Mollycoddles, and the Politics of Progressive Era Reform*. New York: Columbia University Press, 2008.

Murphy, Mary. *Mining Cultures: Men, Women, and Leisure in Butte, 1914-41*. Urbana: University of Illinois Press, 1997.

Myrick, David. *New Mexico's Railroads: An Historical Survey*. 1970. Reprint, Albuquerque: University of New Mexico Press, 1990.

———. *Railroads of Nevada and Eastern California*. 2 vols. Berkeley, Calif.: Howell-North Books, 1962-63.

———. *Railroads of Nevada and Eastern California*. 3 vols. Reno: University of Nevada Press, 1992-2007.

Nadel, Alan. *Containment Culture: American Narratives, Postmodernism, and the Atomic Age*. Durham, N.C.: Duke University Press, 1995.

Namais, June. *White Captives: Gender and Ethnicity on the American Frontier*. Chapel Hill: University of North Carolina Press, 1993.

asaw, David. *Going Out: The Rise and Fall of Public Amusements*. 1993. Reprint, Cambridge, Mass.: Harvard University Press, 1999.

estle, Joan. "The Fem Question." In Vance, *Pleasure and Danger*, 232–41.

———, ed. *The Persistent Desire: A Femme-Butch Reader*. Boston: Alyson, 1992.

euenschwander, John A., ed. *Kenosha County in the 20th Century*. Kenosha, Wisc.: Kenosha County Bicentennial Commission, 1976.

Iewton, Esther. *Margaret Mead Made Me Gay: Personal Essays, Public Ideas*. Durham, N.C.: Duke University Press, 2000.

———. "The Mythic, Mannish Lesbian: Radclyffe Hall and the New Woman." In "The Lesbian Issue," edited by Estelle B. Freedman, Barbara Charlesworth Gelpi, Susan L. Johnson, and Kathleen M. Weston. Special issue, *Signs* 9, no. 4 (Summer 1984): 557–75.

Ngai, Mae M. *Impossible Subjects: Illegal Aliens and the Making of Modern America*. Princeton, N.J.: Princeton University Press, 2004.

Nickerson, Michelle. *Mothers of Conservatism: Women and the Postwar Right*. Princeton, N.J.: Princeton University Press, 2012.

Nicolaides, Becky. *My Blue Heaven: Life and Politics in the Working-Class Suburbs of Los Angeles, 1920–1965*. Chicago: University of Chicago Press, 2002.

Nieto-Phillips, John. *The Language of Blood: The Making of Spanish-American Identity in New Mexico, 1880s–1930s*. Albuquerque: University of New Mexico Press, 2004.

Noel, Thomas. "Gay Bars and the Emergence of the Denver Homosexual Community." *Social Science Journal* 15, no. 2 (April 1978): 59–74.

Noer, Thomas J. "Popular Culture and Leisure Time." In Neuenschwander, *Kenosha County*, 83–123.

Norwood, Stephen. *Strikebreaking and Intimidation: Mercenaries and Masculinity in Twentieth-Century America*. Chapel Hill: University of North Carolina Press, 2002.

Nostrand, Richard. *The Hispano Homeland*. Norman: University of Oklahoma Press, 1992.

Novick, Peter. *That Noble Dream: The "Objectivity Question" and the American Historical Profession*. Cambridge: Cambridge University Press, 1988.

Novotny, Eric. "'Bricks without Straw': Economic Hardship and Innovation in the Chicago Public Library during the Great Depression." *Libraries and the Cultural Record* 46, no. 3 (2011): 258–75.

"The Oaters." *Time*, December 9, 1946.

Olden, Danielle R. "Becoming Minority: Mexican Americans, Race, and the Legal Structure for Educational Equity in Denver, Colorado." *Western Historical Quarterly* 48, no. 1 (Spring 2017): 43–66.

———. "Whiteness in the Middle: Mexican Americans, School Desegregation and the Making of Race in Modern America." PhD diss., Ohio State University, 2013.

Ono, Azusa. "Crossroads of Indian Country: Native American Community in Denver, 1950–2005." PhD diss., Arizona State University, 2008.

Orleck, Annelise. *Common Sense and a Little Fire: Women and Working-Class Politics in the United States, 1900–1965.* Chapel Hill: University of North Carolina Press, 1995.

———. "'We Are That Mythical Thing Called the Public': Militant Housewives during the Great Depression." *Feminist Studies* 19, no. 1 (Spring 1993): 147–72.

Ott, Katherine, Susan Tucker, and Patricia Buckler, eds. *The Scrapbook in American Life.* Philadelphia: Temple University Press, 2006.

Ourada, Patricia. *The Menominee Indians: A History.* Norman: University of Oklahoma Press, 1979.

Padilla, Felix. *Latino Ethnic Consciousness: The Case of Mexican Americans and Puerto Ricans in Chicago.* Notre Dame, Ind.: University of Notre Dame Press, 1985.

Park, Robert. "Human Migration and the Marginal Man." *American Journal of Sociology* 33, no. 6 (May 1928): 881–93.

———. *Race and Culture.* Glencoe, Ill.: Free Press, 1950.

Pascoe, Peggy. *Relations of Rescue: The Search for Female Moral Authority in the American West, 1874–1939.* New York: Oxford University Press, 1991.

———. *What Comes Naturally: Miscegenation Law and the Making of Race in America.* New York: Oxford University Press, 2009.

Passett, Joanne E. *Cultural Crusaders: Women Librarians in the American West, 1900–1917.* Albuquerque: University of New Mexico Press, 1994.

Patterson, Orlando. *Slavery and Social Death: A Comparative Study.* Cambridge, Mass.: Harvard University Press, 1982.

Peck, Gunther. *Reinventing Free Labor: Padrones and Immigrant Workers in the North American West, 1880–1930.* Cambridge: Cambridge University Press, 2000.

Perales, Monica. *Smeltertown: Making and Remembering a Southwest Border Community.* Chapel Hill: University of North Carolina Press, 2010.

Perdue, Theda. *Slavery and the Evolution of Cherokee Society.* Knoxville: University of Tennessee Press, 1979.

Pérez, Emma. *The Decolonial Imaginary: Writing Chicanas into History.* Bloomington: Indiana University Press, 1999.

Pérez, Erika. *Colonial Intimacies: Interethnic Kinship, Marriage, and Sexuality in Southern California, 1769–1885.* Norman: University of Oklahoma Press, 2017.

Pérez, Gina M. *The Near Northwest Side Story: Migration, Displacement, and Puerto Rican Families.* Berkeley: University of California Press, 2004.

Peroff, Nicholas. *Menominee DRUMS: Tribal Termination and Restoration, 1954–1974.* Norman: University of Oklahoma Press, 1982.

Perry, Adele. *Colonial Relations: The Douglas-Connolly Family and the Nineteenth-Century Imperial World.* Cambridge: Cambridge University Press, 2015.

———. *On the Edge of Empire: Gender, Race, and the Making of British Columbia, 1849–1871.* Toronto: University of Toronto Press, 2001.

Peters, DeWitt Clinton. *The Life and Adventures of Kit Carson, the Nestor of the*

Rocky Mountains, from Facts Narrated by Himself. New York: W. R. C. Clark, 1858.

eterson, Norma L. *Freedom and Franchise: The Political Career of B. Gratz Brown*. Columbia: University of Missouri Press, 1965.

hillimore, W. P. W. *How to Write the History of a Family: A Guide for the Genealogist*. 1887. 2nd ed. London: Elliot Stock, 1888.

———. *A Supplement to How to Write the History of a Family: A Guide for the Genealogist*. 1896. 2nd ed. London: n.p., 1900.

hilpott, William. *Vacationland: Tourism and Environment in the Colorado High Country*. Seattle: University of Washington Press, 2013.

lat Book of Saline County, Kansas. Minneapolis: Northwest, 1903.

lummer, Brenda Gayle. *In Search of Power: African Americans in the Era of Decolonization*. New York: Cambridge University Press, 2012.

———. *Rising Wind: Black Americans and U.S. Foreign Affairs, 1935–1960*. Chapel Hill: University of North Carolina Press, 1996.

Porter, Eric. "Affirming and Disaffirming Actions: Remaking Race in the 1970s." In *America in the 70s*, edited by Beth Bailey and David Farber, 50–74. Lawrence: University Press of Kansas, 2004.

Powell, Peter J. *People of the Sacred Mountain: A History of the Northern Cheyenne Chiefs and Warrior Societies, 1830–1879*. 2 vols. New York: Harper and Row, 1979.

———. *Sweet Medicine: The Continuing Role of the Sacred Arrows, the Sun Dance, and the Sacred Buffalo Hat in Northern Cheyenne History*. 2 vols. Norman: University of Oklahoma Press, 1969.

Preuss, Charles. *Exploring with Frémont: The Private Diaries of Charles Preuss, Cartographer for John C. Frémont on His First, Second, and Fourth Expeditions to the Far West*. Edited and translated by Erwin Gudde and Elisabeth Gudde. Norman: University of Oklahoma Press, 1958.

Quade, Kirstin Valdez. *Night at the Fiestas: Stories*. New York: W. W. Norton, 2015.

Rael-Gálvez, Estevan. "Identifying Captivity and Capturing Identity: Narratives of American Indian Slavery, Colorado and New Mexico, 1776–1934." PhD diss., University of Michigan, 2002.

Rakove, Milton. *Don't Make No Waves . . . Don't Back No Losers: An Insider's Analysis of the Daley Machine*. Bloomington: Indiana University Press, 1975.

Ramos, Henry A. J. *The American G.I. Forum: In Pursuit of a Dream, 1948–1983*. Houston: Arte Público, 1998.

Rath, Ida Ellen. *The Rath Trail*. Wichita, Kans.: McCormick-Armstrong, 1961.

Reeves-Ellington, Barbara, Kathryn Kish Sklar, and Connie A. Shemo, eds. *Competing Kingdoms: Women, Mission, Nation, and the American Protestant Empire, 1812–1960*. Durham, N.C.: Duke University Press, 2010.

Reiff, Janice L. "Contested Spaces." In Grossman, Keating, and Reiff, *Encyclopedia of Chicago*, 203–7.

Remley, David. *Kit Carson: The Life of an American Border Man*. Norman: University of Oklahoma Press, 2011.

Renda, Mary A. "Doing Everything: Religion, Race, and Empire in the U.S. Protestant Women's Missionary Enterprise, 1812–1960." In Reeves-Ellington, Sklar, and Shemo, *Competing Kingdoms*, 367–89.

———. *Taking Haiti: Military Occupation and the Culture of U.S. Imperialism, 1915–1940*. Chapel Hill: University of North Carolina Press, 2001.

"Report of the Work of the Jewish Consumptives' Relief Society for the Year 1906." *Denver Medical Times* 25, no. 10 (April 1907): 389–91.

Reséndez, Andrés. *Changing National Identities at the Frontier: Texas and New Mexico, 1800–1850*. New York: Cambridge University Press, 2005.

———. *The Other Slavery: The Uncovered Story of Indian Enslavement in America*. New York: Houghton Mifflin Harcourt, 2016.

Reumann, Miriam. *American Sexual Character: Sex, Gender, and National Identity in the Kinsey Reports*. Berkeley: University of California Press, 2005.

Reynolds, J. E. *History of the Westerners: A Monograph History of all the Corrals and Posses*. Glendale, Calif.: Los Angeles Corral, 1957. Reprinted from *Westerners Brand Book*, no. 7.

Ribufo, Leo P. "1974–1988." In *A Companion to 20th-Century America*, edited by Stephen J. Whitfield, 101–22. Malden, Mass.: Blackwell, 2004.

Rich, B. Ruby, and Lourdes Arguelles. "Homosexuality, Homophobia, and Revolution: Notes toward an Understanding of the Cuban Lesbian and Gay Experience." Pt. 2. *Signs* 11, no. 1 (Autumn 1985): 120–36.

Rivaya-Martínez, Joaquín. "Captivity and Adoption among the Comanche Indians, 1790–1875." PhD diss., University of California, Los Angeles, 2006.

Roberts, David. *A Newer World: Kit Carson, John C. Frémont, and the Claiming of the American West*. New York: Touchstone, 2000.

Robin, Ron. *The Making of the Cold War Enemy: Culture and Politics in the Military-Intellectual Complex*. Princeton, N.J.: Princeton University Press, 2001.

Rodgers, Daniel T. *Age of Fracture*. Cambridge, Mass.: Belknap Press of Harvard University Press, 2011.

———. "An Age of Social Politics." In *Rethinking American History in a Global Age*, edited by Thomas Bender, 250–73. Berkeley: University of California Press, 2002.

Rodgers, Glen M. Review of *Great Westerner: The Story of Kit Carson*, by Bernice Blackwelder. *Southwest Review* 48, no. 3 (Summer 1963): 300–301.

Rodríguez, Marc Simon. "A Movement Made of 'Young Mexican Americans Seeking Change': Critical Citizenship, Migration, and the Chicano Movement in Texas and Wisconsin, 1960–1975." *Western Historical Quarterly* 34, no. 3 (Autumn 2003): 274–99.

———. *Tejano Diaspora: Mexican Americanism and Ethnic Politics in Texas and Wisconsin*. Chapel Hill: University of North Carolina Press, 2011.

Rodríguez, Rod. "This and That about Indians." *Westerners Brand Book* 33, no. 7 (November 1976): 55–56.

Roediger, David R. *The Wages of Whiteness: Race and the Making of the American Working Class*. 1991. 2nd ed. New York: Verso, 2007.

oenigk, Adolph. *Pioneer History of Kansas*. Lincoln, Kans.: A. Roenigk, [1933].

ogers, Everett M., and Nancy R. Bartlit. *Silent Voices of World War II: When Sons of the Land of Enchantment Met Sons of the Land of the Rising Son*. Santa Fe, N.M.: Sunstone Press, 2005.

omero, Tom I. "¿La Raza Latina? Multiracial Ambivalence, Color Denial, and the Emergence of a Tri-ethnic Jurisprudence at the End of the Twentieth Century." *New Mexico Law Review* 37, no. 2 (Spring 2007): 245–306.

———. "Of Race and Rights: Legal Culture, Social Change, and the Making of a Multiracial Metropolis, 1940–1975." PhD diss., University of Michigan, 2004.

———. "Our Selma is Here: The Political and Legal Struggle for Educational Equality in Denver, Colorado, and Multiracial Conundrums in American Jurisprudence." *Seattle Journal of Social Justice* 3, no. 73 (2004): 73–142.

Rosen, Ruth. *The World Split Open: How the Modern Women's Movement Changed America*. New York: Penguin, 2000.

Rosenberg, Emily S. "Rescuing Women and Children." *Journal of American History* 89, no. 2 (2002): 456–65.

Rosenberg, Rosalind. *Beyond Separate Spheres: The Intellectual Roots of Modern Feminism*. New Haven, Conn.: Yale University Press, 1982.

Rosenthal, Nicolas G. *Reimagining Indian Country: Native American Migration and Identity in Twentieth-Century Los Angeles*. Chapel Hill: University of North Carolina Press, 2012.

Rosier, Paul C. *Serving Their Country: American Indian Politics in the Twentieth Century*. Cambridge, Mass.: Harvard University Press, 2009.

Rubin, Gayle. "The Traffic in Women: Notes on the 'Political Economy' of Sex." In *Toward an Anthropology of Women*, edited by Rayna R. Reiter, 157–210. New York: Monthly Review Press, 1975.

———. "The Trouble with Trafficking: Afterthoughts on 'The Traffic in Women.'" In *Deviations: A Gayle Rubin Reader*, edited by Gayle Rubin, 66–86. Durham, N.C.: Duke University Press, 2011.

Rubin, Joan Shelley. *The Making of Middlebrow Culture*. Chapel Hill: University of North Carolina Press, 1992.

Rupp, Leila J. *A Desired Past: A Short History of Same-Sex Love in America*. Chicago: University of Chicago Press, 1999.

———. *Sapphistries: A Global History of Love between Women*. New York: New York University Press, 2009.

Rushforth, Brett. *Bonds of Alliance: Indigenous and Atlantic Slavery in New France*. Chapel Hill: University of North Carolina Press, 2012.

Rusling, James F. *Across America, or The Great West and the Pacific Coast*. New York: Sheldon, 1874.

Russell, Marian. *Land of Enchantment: Memoirs of Marian Russell along the Santa Fe Trail as Dictated to Mrs. Hal Russell*. 1954. Reprint, Albuquerque: University of New Mexico Press, 1981.

Sabin, Edwin L. *Kit Carson Days, 1809–1868*. 2 vols. 1914. Reprint, Lincoln: University of Nebraska Press, 1935, 1995.

Sachs, Honor. *Home Rule: Households, Manhood, and National Expansion on the Eighteenth-Century Kentucky Frontier.* New Haven, Conn.: Yale University Press, 2015.

Sahli, Nancy. "Smashing: Women's Relationships before the Fall." *Chrysalis* 8 (Summer 1979): 17–27.

Salman, Michael. *The Embarrassment of Slavery: Controversies over Bondage and Nationalism in the American Colonial Philippines.* Berkeley: University of California Press, 2001.

Saloutos, Theodore. *The Greeks in the United States.* Cambridge, Mass.: Harvard University Press, 1964.

Samson, David W. "The Swinney Conservatory of Music at Central Methodist University: An Historical Study." PhD diss., University of Mississippi, 2011.

Sánchez, José Ramón. *Boricua Power: A Political History of Puerto Ricans in the United States.* New York: New York University Press, 2007.

Sandoz, Mari. *Cheyenne Autumn.* New York: McGraw Hill, 1953.

———. *Crazy Horse: The Strange Man of the Oglalas.* New York: Knopf, 1942.

———. *Old Jules.* Boston: Little, Brown, 1935.

———. *Slogum House.* Boston: Little, Brown, 1937.

Satter, Beryl. *Each Mind a Kingdom: American Women, Sexual Purity, and the New Thought Movement, 1875–1920.* Berkeley: University of California Press, 1999.

———. *Family Properties: Race, Real Estate, and the Exploitation of Black Urban America.* New York: Henry Holt, 2009.

Saunt, Claudio. *Black, White, and Indian: Race and the Unmaking of an American Family.* New York: Oxford University Press, 2005.

———. *A New Order of Things: Property, Power, and the Transformation of the Creek Indians, 1733–1816.* New York: Cambridge University Press, 1999.

Saxton, Alexander. *The Rise and Fall of the White Republic: Class Politics and Mass Culture in Nineteenth-Century America.* New York: Verso, 1990.

Scamehorn, H. Lee. *Pioneer Steelmaker in the West: The Colorado Fuel and Iron Company, 1872–1903.* Boulder, Colo.: Pruett, 1976.

Schaefer, Christina K. *The Hidden Half of the Family: A Sourcebook for Women's Genealogy.* Baltimore: Genealogical, 1999.

Scharf, Lois. *To Work and to Wed: Female Employment, Feminism, and the Great Depression.* Westport, Conn.: Greenwood Press, 1980.

Scharff, Virginia. *Taking the Wheel: Women and the Coming of the Motor Age.* 1991. Reprint, Albuquerque: University of New Mexico Press, 1992.

———. *Twenty Thousand Roads: Women, Movement, and the West.* Berkeley: University of California Press, 2003.

Schoenberger, Dale T. "The Black Man in the American West." *Negro History Bulletin* 32, no. 3 (March 1969): 7–11.

———. *End of Custer: The Death of an American Military Legend.* Surrey, B.C., and Blaine, Wash.: Hancock House, 1995.

———. *The Gunfighters.* Caldwell, Idaho: Caxton, 1971.

———. "Interpretation of Western History: Academics versus Buffs." *Western Historical Quarterly* 2, no. 2 (April 1971): 232–33.

Shulman, Bruce. *The Seventies: The Great Shift in American Culture, Society, and Politics*. 2001. Reprint, Cambridge, Mass.: Da Capo, 2002.

Shulman, Bruce, and Julian Zelizer, eds. *Rightward Bound: Making America Conservative in the 1970s*. Cambridge, Mass.: Harvard University Press, 2008.

Schwarz, Judith. *Radical Feminists of Heterodoxy: Greenwich Village, 1912–1940*. 1982. Rev. ed. Norwich, Vt.: New Victoria, 1986.

Schwarz, Judith, Kathy Peiss, and Christina Simmons. "'We Were a Little Band of Willful Women': The Heterodoxy Club of Greenwich Village." In *Passion and Power: Sexuality in History*, edited by Kathy Peiss and Christina Simmons, 118–37. Philadelphia: Temple University Press, 1989.

Scott, James C. *Domination and the Arts of Resistance: Hidden Transcripts*. New Haven, Conn.: Yale University Press, 1990.

———. *Weapons of the Weak: Everyday Forms of Peasant Resistance*. New Haven, Conn.: Yale University Press, 1985.

Scott, Joan Wallach. "American Women Historians, 1884–1984." In *Gender and the Politics of History*. 1988. Rev. ed. New York: Columbia University Press, 1999.

Scott, Walter. *The Lady of the Lake*. Edinburgh, Scotland: James Ballantyne, 1810.

Sedgwick, Eve Kosofsky. *Between Men: English Literature and Male Homosocial Desire*. 1985. 30th anniversary ed. New York: Columbia University Press, 2015.

Self, Robert. *American Babylon: Race and the Struggle for Postwar Oakland*. Princeton, N.J.: Princeton University Press, 2003.

Selig, Diana. *Americans All: The Cultural Gifts Movement*. Cambridge, Mass.: Harvard University Press, 2008.

Seligman, Amanda. *Block by Block: Neighborhoods and Public Policy on Chicago's West Side*. Chicago: University of Chicago Press, 2005.

———. "Lincoln Park." In Grossman, Keating, and Reiff, *Encyclopedia of Chicago*, 477–78.

Seltzer, George. *Music Matters: The Performer and the American Federation of Musicians*. Metuchen, N.J.: Scarecrow, 1989.

Sengstock, Charles A., Jr. *That Toddlin' Town: Chicago's White Dance Bands and Orchestras, 1900–1950*. Urbana: University of Illinois Press, 2004.

Shah, Nayan. *Stranger Intimacy: Contesting Race, Sexuality, and the Law in the North American West*. Berkeley: University of California Press, 2011.

Shemo, Connie A. *The Chinese Medical Ministries of Kang Cheng and Shi Meiyu, 1872–1937: On a Cross-Cultural Frontier of Gender, Race, and Nation*. Bethlehem, Pa.: Lehigh University Press, 2011.

Shiffman, Dan. *Rooting Multiculturalism: The Work of Louis Adamic*. Madison and Teaneck, N.J.: Fairleigh Dickinson University Press, 2003.

Shortridge, James R. *Cities on the Plains: The Evolution of Urban Kansas*. Lawrence: University Press of Kansas, 2004.

Shreve, Bradley G. *Red Power Rising: The National Indian Youth Council*. Norman: University of Oklahoma Press, 2011.

Sides, Hampton. *Blood and Thunder: An Epic of the American West*. New York: Doubleday, 2006.

Simmons, Marc S. "Kit and the Indians." In Gordon-McCutchan, *Kit Carson*, 73–90.

———. *Kit Carson and His Three Wives: A Family History*. Albuquerque: University of New Mexico Press, 2003.

Simmons, Marc S., and R. C. Gordon-McCutchan, eds. *The Short Truth about Kit Carson and the Indians*. Taos, N.M.: Kit Carson Historic Museums, 1993.

Siskind, Peter. "Suburban Growth and its Discontents: The Logic and Limits of Reform in the Postwar Northeast Corridor." In Kruse and Sugrue, *New Suburban History*, 161–82.

Sitkoff, Howard. *The Struggle for Black Equality*. 1981, 1993. Rev. ed. New York: Hill and Wang, 2008.

Slatta, Richard W., ed. *The Mythical West: An Encyclopedia of Legend, Lore, and Popular Culture*. Santa Barbara, Calif.: ABC-CLIO, 2001.

Slide, Anthony. *Eccentrics of Comedy*. Lanham, Md.: Scarecrow, 1998.

———. *Encyclopedia of Vaudeville*. 1994. Reprint, Jackson: University Press of Mississippi, 2012.

Slotkin, Richard. *The Fatal Environment: The Myth of the Frontier in the Age of Industrialization*. Middletown, Conn.: Wesleyan University Press, 1985.

———. *Gunfighter Nation: The Myth of the Frontier in Twentieth-Century America*. New York: Atheneum, 1992.

Smemo, Kristoffer. "A 'New Dealized' Grand Old Party: Labor and the Emergence of Liberal Republicanism in Minneapolis, 1937–1939." *Labor: Studies in Working-Class History of the Americas* 11, no. 2 (Summer 2014): 35–59.

Smith, Barbara, ed., *Home Girls: A Black Feminist Anthology*. New York: Kitchen Table: Women of Color Press, 1983.

Smith, Bonnie G. *The Gender of History: Men, Women, and Historical Practice*. Cambridge, Mass.: Harvard University Press, 1998.

Smith, Henry Nash. *Virgin Land: The American West as Symbol and Myth*. New York: Vintage, 1950.

Smith, Jack E. "An Honor for One of Ours." *Colorado Genealogist* 44, no. 2 (May 1983): 79–81.

Smith, Karen Manners. "New Paths to Power: 1890–1920." In Cott, *No Small Courage*, 353–412.

Smith, Paul Chatt, and Robert Allen Warrior. *Like a Hurricane: The Indian Movement from Alcatraz to Wounded Knee*. New York: Free Press, 1996.

Smith, Sherry L. *Hippies, Indians, and the Fight for Red Power*. New York: Oxford University Press, 2012.

———. *Reimagining Indians: Native Americans through Anglo Eyes, 1880–1940*. New York: Oxford University Press, 2000.

———. "Stanley Vestal." In *Historians of the American Frontier: A Bio-bibliographic Sourcebook*, edited by John R. Wunder, 697–712. Westport, Conn.: Greenwood, 1988.

Smith, Sidonie. "Who's Talking/Who's Talking Back? The Subject of Personal Narrative." *Signs* 18, no. 2 (Winter 1993): 392–407.

nith, Stacey L. *Freedom's Frontier: California and the Struggle over Unfree Labor, Emancipation, and Reconstruction.* Chapel Hill: University of North Carolina Press, 2013.

mith, Victoria. *Captive Arizona, 1851–1900.* Lincoln: University of Nebraska Press, 2009.

mith-Rosenberg, Carroll. "The Female World of Love and Ritual: Relations between Women in Nineteenth-Century America." *Signs* 1, no. 1 (1975): 1–29.

nitow, Ann, Christine Stansell, and Sharon Thompson, eds. *Powers of Desire: The Politics of Sexuality.* New York: Monthly Review Press, 1983.

nyder, Christina. *Slavery in Indian Country: The Changing Face of Captivity in Early America.* Cambridge, Mass.: Harvard University Press, 2010.

nyder, Thomas, ed. *120 Years of American Education: A Statistical Portrait.* Washington, D.C.: National Center for Education Statistics, 1993.

olomon, Aubrey. *The Fox Film Corporation, 1915–1935: A History and Filmography.* Jefferson, N.C.: McFarland, 2011.

olomon, Barbara Miller. *In the Company of Educated Women: A History of Women and Higher Education in America.* New Haven, Conn.: Yale University Press, 1985.

Sommerville, Siobhan. *Queering the Color Line: Race and the Invention of Homosexuality in American Culture.* Durham, N.C.: Duke University Press, 2000.

Sonne, Conway B. Review of *Kit Carson: A Profile in Courage,* by M. Marion Estergreen. *Utah Historical Quarterly* 31, no. 1 (Winter 1963): 81.

Sorenson, Helen. *The Consumer Movement: What It Is and What It Means.* New York: Harper and Bros., 1941.

"Special Recognition." *Colorado Genealogist* 37, no. 2 (Summer 1976): 45–46.

Spicer, Edward H. *Cycles of Conquest: The Impact of Spain, Mexico, and the United States on the Indians of the Southwest, 1533–1960.* Tucson: University of Arizona Press, 1962.

Spigel, Lynn. *Make Room for TV: Television and the Family Ideal in Postwar America.* Chicago: University of Chicago Press, 1992.

Standard Atlas of Saline County, Kansas, Including a Plat Book of the Villages, Cities and Townships of the County. Chicago: Geo. A. Ogle, 1920.

Stanley, F. *Giant in Lilliput: The Story of Donaciano Vigil.* Pampa, Tex.: Pampa Print Shop, 1963.

Stansell, Christine. *American Moderns: Bohemian New York and the Creation of a New Century.* New York: Henry Holt, 2000.

Starr, Kevin. *California: A History.* New York: Modern Library, 2005.

"A Statistical Report on the Participation of Women in the Southern Historical Association, 1935–1985." *Journal of Southern History* 70, no. 2 (May 1986): 282–88.

Steedman, Carolyn Kay. *Landscape for a Good Woman: A Story of Two Lives.* New Brunswick, N.J.: Rutgers University Press, 1986.

Stern, Steve. *The Secret History of Gender: Women, Men, and Power in Late Colonial Mexico.* Chapel Hill: University of North Carolina Press, 1995.

Stewart-Winter, Timothy. *Queer Clout: Chicago and the Rise of Gay Politics*. Philadelphia: University of Pennsylvania Press, 2016.

Stoler, Ann Laura, ed. *Haunted by Empire: Geographies of Intimacy in North American History*. Durham, N.C.: Durham University Press, 2006.

Stonequist, Everett. *The Marginal Man: A Study in Personality and Culture Conflict*. New York: Charles Scribner's Sons, 1937.

Streeby, Shelly. *American Sensations: Class, Empire, and the Production of Popular Culture*. Berkeley: University of California Press, 2002.

Sueyoshi, Amy. *Queer Compulsions: Race, Nation, and Sexuality in the Affairs of Yone Noguchi*. Honolulu: University of Hawai'i Press, 2012.

Sugrue, Thomas. *The Origins of the Urban Crisis: Race and Inequality in Postwar Detroit*. 1996. Reprint, Princeton, N.J.: Princeton University Press, 2005.

———. *Sweet Land of Liberty: The Forgotten Struggle for Civil Rights in the North*. New York: Random House, 2008.

Summers, Martin. *Manliness and Its Discontents: The Black Middle Class and the Transformation of Masculinity, 1900–1930*. Chapel Hill: University of North Carolina Press, 2004.

Sunder, John E. Review of *Kit Carson: A Profile in Courage*, by M. Marion Estergreen. *Journal of Southern History* 29, no. 3 (1963): 397–98.

———. Review of *Great Westerner: The Story of Kit Carson*, by Bernice Blackwelder. *Arizona and the West* 4, no. 2 (Summer 1962): 185–87.

Suri, Jeremi. *Power and Protest: Global Revolution and the Rise of Détente*. Cambridge, Mass.: Harvard University Press, 2003.

Syrett, Nicholas. *The Company He Keeps: A History of White College Fraternities*. Chapel Hill: University of North Carolina Press, 2009.

Szucs, Loretto Dennis, and Sandra Hargreaves Luebking, eds. *The Source: A Guidebook to American Genealogy*. 3rd ed. Provo, Utah: Ancestry, 2006.

Tallant, Jay. Review of *Great Westerner: The Story of Kit Carson*, by Bernice Blackwelder. *Denver Westerners' Roundup* 18, no. 7 (July 1962): 27–28.

Tatum, Stephen. "The Problem of the 'Popular' in the New Western History." In *The New Western History: The Territory Ahead*, edited by Forrest Robinson, 153–90. Tucson: University of Arizona Press, 1997.

Taylor, Quintard. *In Search of the Racial Frontier: African Americans in the American West, 1528–1990*. New York: W. W. Norton, 1998.

Terry, Jennifer. "Theorizing Deviant Historiography." *Differences* 3, no. 2 (1991): 32–61.

"Testimony." *Christian Science Sentinel* 36, no. 10 (November 4, 1933): 144.

Thompson, Albert. "The Death and the Last Will of Kit Carson." *Colorado Magazine* 5, no. 5 (October 1928): 183–91.

Thompson, Gerald. "'Kit Carson's Ride': E. F. Beale Assails Joaquin Miller's Indecent Poem." *Arizona and the West* 26, no. 2 (Summer 1984): 135–52.

Thorne, Tanis. *The Many Hands of My Relations: French and Indians on the Lower Missouri*. Columbia: University of Missouri Press, 1996.

Thornsohn, Stig. *Dineh*. Aarhus, Denmark: Lobo Agency, 1981.

———. *100 Plakater og Forestillinger om Buffalo Bills Wild West*. Kongerslev, Denmark: GMT, 1977.

Thornsohn, Stig, Jens Damm, and Annette Damm, eds. *The Dream of America*. Translated by Hanne Ejsing Jørgensen and Daniel McCarthy. Højbjerg, Denmark: Moesgaard, 1986.

Thrush, Coll. *Native Seattle: Histories from the Crossing-Over Place*. Seattle: University of Washington Press, 2007.

Tilton, H. R. *The Last Days of Kit Carson*. Grand Forks, N.D.: Holt, 1939.

Tomkinson, Laura E. *Twenty Years' History of the Woman's Home Missionary Society of the Methodist Episcopal Church, 1880–1900*. Cincinnati: Woman's Home Missionary Society of the Methodist Episcopal Church, 1903.

Tomlins, Christopher L. "AFL Unions in the 1930s: Their Performance in Historical Perspective." *Journal of American History* 65, no. 4 (March 1979): 1021–42.

———. *The State and the Unions: Labor Relations, Law, and the Organized Labor Movement, 1880–1960*. New York: Cambridge University Press, 1985.

Toole, K. Ross, John Alexander Carroll, Robert M. Utley, and A. R. Mortensen, eds. *Probing the American West: Papers from the Santa Fe Conference*. Santa Fe: Museum of New Mexico Press, 1962.

Trafzer, Clifford. *The Kit Carson Campaign: The Last Navajo War*. Norman: University of Oklahoma Press, 1982.

Trollope, Anthony. *Barchester Towers*. 1857. Project Gutenberg, 2002. http://www.gutenberg.org/files/3409/3409-h/3409-h.htm.

Tronnes, Libby. "Contested Place: The Menominee Warriors Society, Native and Non-Native Placemaking, and Identity Construction in Rural Wisconsin, 1975." MA thesis, University of Wisconsin–Madison, 2007.

———. "Corn Moon Migrations: Ho-Chunk Belonging, Removal, and Return in the Early Nineteenth-Century Western Great Lakes." PhD diss., University of Wisconsin–Madison, 2017.

———. "'Where is John Wayne?': The Menominee Warriors Society, Indian Militancy, and Social Unrest during the Alexian Brothers Novitiate Takeover." *American Indian Quarterly* 26, no. 4 (Autumn 2002): 526–58.

Truett, Samuel, and Pekka Hämäläinen. "On Borderlands." *Journal of American History* 98, no. 2 (September 2011): 338–61.

Truett, Samuel, and Elliott Young. "Making Transnational History: Nations, Regions, and Borderlands." In *Continental Crossroads: Remapping U.S.-Mexico Borderlands History*, edited by Samuel Truett and Elliott Young, 1–32. Durham, N.C.: Duke University Press, 2004.

Turk, Eleanor L. "Germans in Kansas." *Kansas History* 28, no. 1 (Spring 2005): 44–71.

———. "The Germans of Atchison, 1854–1859: Development of an Ethnic Community." *Kansas History* 2, no. 3 (Autumn 1979): 146–56.

———. "Selling the Heartland: Agents, Agencies, Press, and Policies Promoting German Immigration to Kansas in the Nineteenth Century." *Kansas History* 12, no. 3 (Autumn 1989): 150–59.

Tyrell, Ian. *Historians in Public: The Practice of American History, 1890–1970*. Chicago: University of Chicago Press, 2005.

Tyson, Timothy. *Blood Done Sign My Name: A True Story*. New York: Crown, 2004.

Underhill, Ruth M. *The Navajos*. Norman: University of Oklahoma Press, 1956.

"U.S. Civilians Buy Their First Jeeps: Heines of Lucas, Kan. Take a Ride." *Life*, January 3, 1944.

U.S. Department of the Interior. *Biographical and Historical Index of American Indians and Persons Involved in Indian Affairs*. 8 vols. Boston: G. K. Hall, 1966.

Utley, Robert. *Custer and Me: A Historian's Memoir*. Norman: University of Oklahoma Press, 2004.

———. "Remarks of Robert M. Utley at WHA Awards Banquet, Lake Tahoe, Nevada." *Western History Association Newsletter*, Fall 2010, 3–4.

Vance, Carole S., ed. *Pleasure and Danger: Exploring Female Sexuality*. Boston: Routledge and Kegan Paul, 1984.

———. "Thinking Trafficking, Thinking Sex." *GLQ* 17, no. 1 (2010): 135–43.

Van Hook, Joseph. "Mexican Land Grants in the Arkansas Valley." *Southwestern Historical Quarterly* 40, no. 1 (July 1936): 58–76.

Van Slyck, Abigail A. *Free to All: Carnegie Libraries and American Culture, 1890–1920*. Chicago: University of Chicago Press, 1995.

Vecoli, Rudolph J. "The Formation of Chicago's 'Little Italies.'" *Journal of American Ethnic History* 2, no. 2 (Spring 1983): 5–20.

———. "Italians." In Grossman, Keating, and Reiff, *Encyclopedia of Chicago*, 439–40.

Vestal, Stanley. *Kit Carson: The Happy Warrior of the Old West, a Biography*. Boston: Houghton Mifflin, 1928.

Vidal, Gore. *Visit to a Small Planet: A Comedy Akin to Vaudeville*. Boston: Little, Brown, 1957.

Vigil, Ernesto P. *The Crusade for Justice: Chicano Militancy and the Government's War of Dissent*. Madison: University of Wisconsin Press, 1999.

Vigil, Skott Brandon. "'That's All We Knew': The Vigil Family History of the Southwest, 1807–1970." MA thesis, University of Wyoming, 2006.

Von Eschen, Penny. *Race against Empire: Black Americans and Anticolonialism, 1937–1957*. Ithaca, N.Y.: Cornell University Press, 1997.

———. *Satchmo Blows Up the World: Jazz Ambassadors Play the Cold War*. Cambridge, Mass.: Harvard University Press, 2004.

Walker, Alice. *In Search of Our Mothers' Gardens*. San Diego: Harcourt Brace Jovanovich, 1983.

Wallace, Michele. "Uncle Tom's Cabin before and after the Jim Crow Era." *Drama Review* 44, no. 1 (2000): 137–56.

Ware, Eugene Fitch [Ironquill, pseud.]. *Rhymes of Ironquill*. Topeka, Kans.: T. J. Kellam, 1885.

Wargo, Philip A. *Marriages of Grand County, Colorado: The First Hundred Years*.

Hot Sulphur Springs, Colo.: published by the author, 1991. http://www.wargo
.org/grandcobridesmz.htm.

Warren, Louis. *Buffalo Bill's America: William Cody and the Wild West Show.*
New York: Knopf, 2005.

Waters, Sarah. *The Night Watch.* New York: Riverhead Books, 2006.

Watson, Frederick Douglas. "Removing the Barricades from the Northern
Schoolhouse Door: School Desegregation in Denver." PhD diss., University
of Colorado Boulder, 1993.

Webb, Clive, ed. *Massive Resistance: Southern Opposition to the Second
Reconstruction.* New York: Oxford University Press, 2005.

Weber, Bret A. "Denver Model Cities Program." PhD diss., University of Utah,
2007.

Weber, David J. *Bárbaros: Spaniards and Their Savages in the Age of
Enlightenment.* New Haven, Conn.: Yale University Press, 2005.

———. *The Mexican Frontier, 1821–1846: The American Southwest under Mexico.*
Albuquerque: University of New Mexico Press, 1982.

———. *Spanish Frontier in North America.* New Haven, Conn.: Yale University
Press, 1992.

———. *The Taos Trappers: The Fur Trade in the Far Southwest, 1540–1846.*
Norman: University of Oklahoma Press, 1971.

Weil, François. *Family Trees: A History of Genealogy in America.* Cambridge,
Mass.: Harvard University Press, 2013.

Weiss, Jessica. *To Have and to Hold: Marriage, the Baby Boom, and Social
Change.* Chicago: University of Chicago Press, 2000.

Welcome, Henry G. Review of *Great Westerner: The Story of Kit Carson,* by
Bernice Blackwelder. *Journal of the West* 2, no. 1 (January 1963): 107–8.

West, Elliott. *The Contested Plains: Indians, Goldseekers, and the Rush to
Colorado.* Lawrence: University Press of Kansas, 1998.

———. *The Way to the West: Essays on the Central Plains.* Albuquerque:
University of New Mexico Press, 1995.

The Westerners: A Mini-bibliography and a Cataloging of Publications, 1944–1974.
Vol 1. Glendale, Calif.: Arthur H. Clark, 1974.

Westerners Brand Book (Chicago). 1944–77.

Wheatley, Melvin, and Lucile Wheatley. "Oral History Interview: Mel Wheatley."
By Mark Bowman. LGBTQ Religious Archives Network. October 10, 1994.
https://lgbtqreligiousarchives.org/media/oral-history/melvin-e-wheatley
/MWheatley.pdf.

White, Richard. *Remembering Ahanagran: Storytelling in a Family's Past.* New
York: Hill and Wang, 1998.

Whitfield, Stephen. *The Culture of the Cold War.* 1991. 2nd ed. Baltimore: Johns
Hopkins University Press, 1996.

Whyte, William H. *The Organization Man.* 1956. Reprint, Philadelphia:
University of Pennsylvania Press, 2002.

Wiebe, Robert H. *The Search for Order, 1877–1920.* New York: Hill and Wang,
1967.

Wilkinson, Charles. *Blood Struggle: The Rise of Modern Indian Nations.* New York: W. W. Norton, 2005.

Wilson, Chris. *The Myth of Santa Fe: Creating a Modern Regional Tradition.* Albuquerque: University of New Mexico Press, 1997.

Wilson, Elinor. *Jim Beckwourth: Black Mountain Man and War Chief of the Crows.* Norman: University of Oklahoma Press, 1972.

Witt, David L. *Three Taos Pueblo Painters: Albert Looking Elk Martínez, Albert Lujan, and Juan Mirabal.* Taos, N.M.: Harwood Museum, 2002.

Wolcott, Victoria. *Remaking Respectability: African American Women in Interwar Detroit.* Chapel Hill: University of North Carolina Press, 2001.

Woman's Who's Who of America, 1914–15: A Biographical Dictionary of Contemporary Women of the United States and Canada. New York: American Commonwealth, 1914.

Woods, Robert A., and Albert J. Kennedy, eds. *Handbook of Settlements.* New York: Charities Publication Committee, Russell Sage Foundation, 1911.

Woolf, Virginia. *A Room of One's Own.* London: Hogarth, 1929.

Worrall, Janet E. "Labor, Gender, and Generational Change in a Western City." *Western Historical Quarterly* 32, no. 4 (2001): 437–67.

Wright, Roy Dean, and Susan N. Wright. "A Plea for Further Refinement of the Marginal Man Theory." *Phylon* 33, no. 4 (1972): 361–68.

Wunder, John. "Mari Sandoz: Historian of the Great Plains." In Leckie and Parezo, *Their Own Frontier,* 97–136.

Wyer, Malcolm Glenn. *Books and People.* Denver: Old West, 1964.

Yoggy, Gary A. "Prime Time Bonanza! The Western on Television." In Aquila, *Wanted Dead or Alive,* 160–95.

Young, Marilyn B. *Vietnam Wars, 1945–1990.* New York: HarperCollins, 1991.

Young, Robert W., comp. *The Navajo Yearbook,* no. 6, *Fiscal Year 1957.* Window Rock, Ariz.: Navajo Agency, 1957.

———. *The Navajo Yearbook,* no. 7, *Fiscal Year 1958.* Window Rock, Ariz.: Navajo Agency, 1958.

———. *The Navajo Yearbook,* no. 8, *1951–1961, a Decade of Progress.* Window Rock, Ariz.: Navajo Agency, 1961.

Zophy, Jonathan W. "Invisible People: Blacks and Mexican-Americans." In Neuenschwander, *Kenosha County,* 51–81.

Index

45, 300, 421n201, 442n51, 443–44n72; typist for, 288–89, 295; urban change, experience of, 69–71, 119–26, 290–94; in Western History Association, 57, 109–10, 352–53n99; at WGN radio station, *182*, *183*, 251, 252, 425n233; and whiteness, 55, 65, 72–73, 141, 195, 208, 269–70; youth, 196, 199, 206–7. *See also* biographical dictionary project; correspondence between McClung and Blackwelder; *Great Westerner: The Story of Kit Carson*

Blackwelder, Clarence "Dad Black" (Harold Blackwelder's father), 254, 257, 259, 276, 428n260

Blackwelder, Harold, 4, 23, 28, 68, *155*; "blue moods," 273–74; changing residence of, 69–71, 118–20, *153*, *155*, *181*, 247–61, 275–76, 290, 293–95 ; as Cook County worker, 4, 128, 289–91, 294; death of, 297, 441n42; health problems, 294, 440n33; later years, 289–97; musical career, 85–86, 127, *179*, *183*, *184*, *186*, *187*, 194, 195–96, 246–47, 249–61, 265, 273–76, 296, 422n412; as Neil Fortune, Gentleman from the West, 4, 85, *183*, 250–51, 254–55, 257, 258, 273, 274, 424n229; North Carolina origins of, 29, *178*, *179*, 194, 246–47, 276, 289, 293, 424n229; as object of exchange, 28, 85–86, 144–45, 439n14; relationship with Bernice Blackwelder, 127–28, 140, 144–45, 272–74, 288–90, 294–95; restaurant business and, 4, 64, 70–71, 118–19, *153*, 261–62, 363n174; stutter, 297, 441n42

Blackwelder's Barbeque (Arlington, Virginia), 64, 70–71, 196, 363n175

Blackwelder's Country House (Franconia, Virginia), 71, *153*, 363n174

Bloom, John Porter, 94, 352n94, 352–53n99

Blue Lake (Taos Pueblo), 105

Blumenschein, Ernest, 243

Boggs, Lilburn W., 41

Boggs, Rumalda Luna (daughter of Ignacia Jaramillo and Rafael Luna) 41, 50, 67, 90, 367n20, 370n39. *See also* Jaramillo, Rumalda; Rumaldas, mystery of

Boggs, Thomas (Tom), 27, 37, 41–42, 50 67, 90, 93

Boggsville, Colorado, 51, 93

The Bohemian Girl (Balfe), 246

bohemianism, 23, *162*, *188*, 223, 227, 229–31, 237, 239, 306–7, 311, 417n149

"Bohemian Party" (McClung and friends), *162*, *163*, 207, 217–18, 230–31, 307, 404n66

Bonanza (television series), 62, 75, 358n134

Boone, Albert Gallatin, 95–96

Boone, Daniel, 10, 41, 95, 145, 334n11

Boone, Panthea, 41, 96

borderlands, 16, 22, 37, 49, 56, 59, 64, 68, 92; racial, 269

Bosque Redondo, 7, 49, 99, 373n69

Boston marriage, 228

Boyer, Jack, 107, 367–68n26, 376n100

Brave Woman (granddaughter of William Henry Bent), 90

Briber, Florence "Flossie," 217, 221, 409n106

This Bridge Called My Back: Writings by Radical Women of Color (ed. Moraga and Anzaldúa), 30, 320, 447n99

Bridger, Jim, 43

Brookville, Kansas, 29, *159*, *174*, 194, 195, 196–200, 202, 206–7, 238, 255, 257, 266, 398–99n16, 400–401n36, 402n49

Brown, Dee, 107–8, 376n107

Brown v. Board of Education, 72

Bryant, Louise, 311, 446n86

Buffalo Bill, 10, 334n11, 399n22, 403n53

Burnham, Daniel, 120

Bury My Heart at Wounded Knee: An Indian History of the American West (Brown), 107, 376n107

butch/femme, 320–21

Printed in the USA
CPSIA information can be obtained
at www.ICGtesting.com
LVHW080007151123
763951LV00009B/46